TREASURY

TREASURY

THE NEW ZEALAND TREASURY, 1840–2000

Malcolm McKinnon

AUCKLAND UNIVERSITY PRESS
in association with the
MINISTRY FOR CULTURE AND HERITAGE

First published 2003
Auckland University Press
University of Auckland
Private Bag 92019
Auckland, New Zealand
http://www.auckland.ac.nz/aup

© Crown Copyright 2003

This book is copyright. Apart from fair dealing for the purpose of private study, research, criticism, or review, as permitted under the Copyright Act, no part may be reproduced by any process without the prior permission of the publisher.

ISBN 1 86940 296 0

Designed/typeset by Chris O'Brien
Printed by Publishing Press, Auckland

Contents

Preface *7*
Introduction *11*

Part One: **Clerks**

1 The colonial Treasury, 1840–1910 *24*

Part Two: **Accountants**

2 Counting for something? The Treasury, 1910–1930 *74*
3 Treasury during the Great Depression, 1930–1935 *112*
4 A new world? Treasury and the first Labour government, 1935–1949 *151*
5 Backwards or forwards? The Treasury, 1949–1961 *188*

Part Three: **Economists**

6 Mandarins or lemons? The Treasury, 1961–1978 *226*
7 Advice and dissent, 1978–1984 *274*
8 Managing the economy, 1984–1993 *313*
9 Managing government, 1984–1993 *359*

Afterword

10 Consolidation: The Treasury, 1993–2000 *404*

Appendix: Governments, Ministers, Treasury Secretaries and major events, 1890–2000 *428*
Notes *432*
Select bibliography *483*
Index *517*

Preface

This history of the New Zealand Treasury, a department of government founded in 1840, was commissioned by the Treasury and researched and written under the auspices of the Ministry for Culture and Heritage's History Group.

The task of writing the first-ever history of such an important department was an exciting and stimulating one. I hope some of that excitement comes through in the text.

The archives disclosed a story of Treasury activity in the 1920s that has largely been forgotten since. And for the post-war decades, the interviews I conducted with officials and politicians put 'flesh and blood' on what could too readily have become a dry-as-dust narrative.

But the task was also daunting. The massive documentation generated by the department's activities over 160 years could only be sampled. I followed two principal themes: those of 'Treasury control' — of the government's finances — and of economic management. Many other areas of Treasury activity — day-to-day payroll tasks, aspects of its internal life, its role in external economic policy — await further study.

Closer to the present there were other challenges. Treasuries have long enjoyed an almost inbuilt unpopularity, but in the 1980s and 1990s controversy over the department's ideas, preferred policies and influence reached unprecedented levels. Many formidable individuals who had devoted much thought, energy and penmanship to the controversy were not only still living, but mostly still living in Wellington. Complementary to their recollections, though rarely invoked by them, there was a documentary record even more massive than that for earlier decades, but no more able to be other than selectively explored in the time available.

If I nonetheless got to 'the end' it was not without accumulating a weighty set of debts which it is a pleasure to acknowledge. That acknowledgement must go in the first instance to Alan Bollard, Secretary to the Treasury from 1998 to 2002, for commissioning this history, for supporting the project once it was under way, and for engaging in many discussions with the author about it. His successor, John Whitehead, maintained that commitment. Treasury's deputy secretaries, all very busy individuals, read and commented on drafts of the later chapters. Both they and the Secretary did so in a spirit of full respect for the writer's intellectual independence.

Many other individuals at Treasury gave a great deal of assistance to the writer. Roger Hurnard read a large part of the manuscript, and both he and Bob Buckle answered, patiently and with good humour, a great many questions of the kind that non-officials put to officials and non-economists to economists. Jean Fraser tracked down a number of photographs for me. Information services staff, notably Helen Vaughan-Dawkes, Brad Cook, Jo Harris, Sanjay Pasupuleti and Raewyn Peters, dealt with my many requests very helpfully. Communications staff Sian Robyns, Rowan Macrae, and Elisa Eckford and the current team, looked after me in the fashion for which they are renowned.

Successive Chief Historians Claudia Orange, Jock Phillips and Bronwyn Dalley oversaw the project at the Ministry for Culture and Heritage. Jock in particular, whose tenure of the office accounted for most of the duration of the project, offered valuable advice on the draft chapters, all of which he read. Martin Matthews, CEO of the Ministry, and with past experience at the Audit Office, also frequently discussed the project with the writer, and made many acute observations. Gavin McLean, the supervising historian for the project, kept a friendly and watchful eye on it and the author from across the corridor, and also brought his lengthy publishing experience very helpfully to bear. David Green carried out a characteristic, but no less remarkable for that, scrupulous and intelligent editing of the text. Pam Ward and Fran McGowan went beyond the call of duty in dealing with many interloan requests. Sherryl Allen did a great deal of the photograph research, including the often tedious task of securing permissions, whilst Emma Dewson checked many references. Kathryn Hastings, Pauline Hoy and Gwen Calnon were all successively indispensable. I could have done without neither Megan Hutching's expertise in oral history and common sense in life, nor Ian McGibbon's collegiality. Fellow contract historians — Neill Atkinson, Susan Butterworth, Alan Henderson, Margaret McClure, John E. Martin and David Young — writing about other government departments made many helpful suggestions. Simon Cauchi prepared the index.

Four individuals — Brian Easton, Harvey Franklin, Gary Hawke, and John Martin — read drafts of the entire manuscript. Their often vigorous comments, queries and suggestions immensely improved the text. The many one-on-one discussions I had with them were one of the real bonuses of the project for me. It is difficult to exaggerate how crucial these exchanges were, and the four of them are for that reason all the more exempt from any responsibility for the remaining faults in the book. As are a number of other individuals — Harry Broad, Peter Coleman, Peter Hall and Stevan Eldred-Grigg — unlucky enough to be (perhaps 'have been') the writer's friends, who 'volunteered' to read all or parts of the manuscript — and, not content with that effort, took time to make helpful comments and suggestions.

Those whom I interviewed deserve special thanks for the unfailing courtesy and kindness which they (and in some instances their spouses) displayed to the writer, and, especially if met with in the first days of the project, their tactful seeming obliviousness to the naivety of many of his questions. A large number of other individuals contributed information and comment, amongst them Robin Andrew, Geoff Bertram, Jonathan Boston, Ralph Chapman, Margaret Clark, Philip Colquhoun, Peter Fraser, Don Gray, Hauraki Greenland, Bob Gregory, Terence Hayden, Anthony Hubbard, Paul Jones, David King, Tony Nightingale, Roger Procter, Grant Scobie, Anne Scoular, David Skilling, Brian Smith, David Smyth, Geoff Swier, Fred Watson, David White and Charlotte Williams.

Some of those comments were made in response to papers I presented on aspects of the Treasury's history to the New Zealand Historical Association's 2001 conference, to the School of History, Philosophy and Politics at Massey University, to the staff of the Alexander Turnbull Library, in the History Group's public seminar series, in a series of in-house Treasury seminars, and to Victoria University of Wellington's Stout Research Centre and its interdisciplinary seminar convened by Bob Tristram. I wish in particular to acknowledge Bob, whose record of promoting the exchange of ideas in a scholarly environment is second to none.

The list of important sources which I have overlooked is undoubtedly lengthy, but was shortened by the steers provided me by a number of individuals — James Belich, Mary Boyd, Ashley Gould, Gwenda Jensen, Julie Keenan, Ted Lundy and Phil Parkinson — to specific records, theses, articles, books or journals.

Staff at Archives New Zealand, the Alexander Turnbull Library, the National Library, the Hocken Library, the Parliamentary Library, and Rosemary Collier at the Bank of New Zealand Archive, all provided helpful and intelligent guidance to the records and sources within their domain. Like so many other writers it is a particular pleasure to acknowledge the indispensable assistance of Joan McCracken and the staff at Turnbull Library Pictures. Linda Evans and Jocelyn

Chalmers at the Turnbull's Oral History Centre regularly bailed me out of many a tape recorder near-debacle.

I am indebted to Barry Ashwin for permission to see and cite from material in his possession; to the Chief Librarian, Alexander Turnbull Library, for permission to consult the Marshall Papers; to both the Chief Librarian, Alexander Turnbull Library and Frank Corner for permission to cite from material in the McIntosh Papers; to the Chief Archivist, Archives New Zealand and the leader of the National Party for permission to consult the Muldoon Papers.

A variety of individuals generously lent written records, photographs, cartoons and other memorabilia: John Anderson, Carl Bakker, Bob Buckle, John Chetwin, Brian Easton, Averall Gibson, Donald Hay, Roger Hurnard, Irene Lake, Jas McKenzie, John Martin, Mark Prebble, Roger Procter and Bill Robinson.

At Auckland University Press Elizabeth Caffin and the staff were as always a pleasure to work with.

Last but most, I am indebted to friends and family who lived with this Treasury history for two and a half years, an experience as startling and demanding for them as it was rewarding for me — the more rewarding because of their understanding, support and affection. I deeply regret that one bracingly sardonic, very loyal friend, Jonathan Dennis (1953–2002), who encouraged me to take on this project, is not here to see it finished.

Malcolm McKinnon
March 2003

Introduction

Treasury. The word is laden with sober, serious, sometimes affectionate, often angry meanings. But in its origins, it is a magic word, conjuring 'riches beyond measure', troves of wealth, chests of gold coins, hoards of precious stones, jewel-encrusted reliquaries, crowns and crucifixes, sovereigns and states, pirates and plunder. The word arrived on the shores of the islands of New Zealand in 1840 with centuries of English history behind it and millennia of Mediterranean history behind that. By then, of course, it was its second meaning — 'a government department in charge of finances and especially the collection, management and expenditure of public revenues', that had become pertinent. But is it fanciful to think that the earlier meaning informed the life of an institution which at the end of the twentieth century was, if not a storehouse of wealth, then certainly one of power?

Despite its importance in government — and in the country generally — there is no history of the Treasury. Until 1984 relatively little was written about it. Indeed, in contrast to all other departments of government, the Treasury did not table an annual report to Parliament until 1989. A 1935 doctoral thesis, a scattering of journal articles from the 1940s to the 1970s, the hard-to-trace references in more ephemeral organs such as daily newspapers, weekly and monthly journals — that was about it. There is no biography of a Secretary to the Treasury, although Brian Easton's work on Bernard Ashwin and Henry Lang, most recently in *The Nationbuilders*, is path-breaking. Only two Secretaries to the Treasury made it into the *Dictionary of New Zealand Biography* (though more undoubtedly will become eligible in due course). There are no published memoirs, although some manuscript material survives. There is one privately published novel.[1]

The contrast with another government department with which the writer has had acquaintance could not be greater. While there is no departmental history as such, the student of the Ministry of Foreign Affairs can turn to memoirs and explorations of historical episodes by retired diplomats, collections of letters and other correspondence by serving diplomatic officers, and numerous scholarly studies of aspects of policy and of the institution itself.

This dearth may seem surprising to New Zealanders who have lived through the political and economic changes of the last two decades, in which the Treasury has been accorded such a prominent role — saviour or sinner, depending on one's point of view, but prominent irrespective. And certainly those changes, and Treasury's role in them, have generated a substantial literature, much of which will be reviewed in the latter chapters of this study. But relatively little of that literature is informed by more than a cursory exploration or even description of the pre-1980 Treasury, other than to explain that it was either far worse (or again, better) than what came after. In fairness to many of those studies, such historical perspective was not their aim; further, a number do mention the pressing need for a history of the Treasury.

How then to approach the task of writing a history of the New Zealand Treasury? For some assistance in answering this question, we can turn to histories written in Australia and Britain. Australia only gained a single Treasury department in 1901, the year of federation, and the main history of the twentieth-century Treasury, by Greg Whitwell, *The Treasury Line*, covers 'only' the period from 1945 to 1985. 'The book', he writes,

> sets out to provide a guide to the nature of Treasury thought over the past 40 years ... to set Treasury's outlook in context by outlining the changing economic conditions and policy problems which have prevailed since the war; and it uses the Treasury as a vehicle for making some broad comparisons with the dominant ideas and interests of the Australian economics profession ... [It] also aims to explain the adoption of Keynesianism in Australia and to show that the department's outlook has slowly changed since the war from a predominantly Keynesian model to a predominantly neoclassical one.[2]

The approach of the two principal histories of the British Treasury is rather different. Henry Roseveare's *The Treasury: The Evolution of a British Institution* was published in 1969. Despite the long history of the institution, this was the first attempt at a general history. Far from starting in 1945, the post-war years (nearly two decades fewer than Whitwell had to play with, of course) are covered in just one chapter, preceded by eight others tracing the Treasury from its medieval origins. Roseveare's explanation of what he is about is more individual than Whitwell's, but his focus *is* on the institution (as suggested by the title) more than the ideas, and in particular on the mid-nineteenth century:

Introduction

> The measures which transformed this institution into the relatively formidable instrument of Gladstonian economy are, therefore, the most important in its history and they have a correspondingly large place in this narrative. They reformed a rather dreary luncheon club for superannuated gentlemen into the hard-working Victorian elite of first-class minds.[3]

The impact on the Treasury of the mid-twentieth-century Keynesian revolution in economic policy (of which more later) is understandably not the focus of Roseveare's work, but it is central to writing about the post-war British Treasury in the 1960s and early 1970s by Samuel Beer and Sam Brittan,[4] whilst the first volume of a projected two-volume history of the twentieth-century Treasury, *The Treasury and British Public Policy, 1906–1959*, by George Peden, has now appeared. Peden has written extensively on aspects of Treasury policy and the institution itself over the last 30 years, and this first volume is — as expected — authoritative. Like Roseveare he follows a narrative approach, his main thesis being

> that the Treasury sought at all times to maintain rules that would ensure that the nation's financial system would remain sound, that government business was conducted in an orderly way, and that policy commitments did not outrun the prospective resources available.[5]

Whitwell, Roseveare and Peden all tell a story — their accounts proceed chronologically, as does this one. Narrative has its weaknesses, but in venturing into a sphere of enquiry where little 'history' has been written, it exercises a powerful and useful control on too ready generalisation. But what should that narrative focus on?

In New Zealand, the Treasurer was one of the offices established in 1840, along with the Colonial Secretary and the Surveyor-General. In the 163 years since then the Treasury has not even undergone a name change, and its task of looking after the government's finances, if no longer its only task, remains a task. But to dwell on such continuity in a history of the institution would be misleading. It is the changes in the Treasury, and in particular the changes which have seen its influence and power grow, that give its history interest. For the first part of the colonial era the department was only a few officials — just four in 1860 — making a not very good fist of handling the government's day-to-day financial affairs, including, most recurrently, paying its officials and its bills. The numbers expanded with the expansion of the colony in the 1860s and 1870s, but the growth levelled off after that. The department had a staff of 69 in 1912 compared with 40 in 1879, a period of time during which the population more than doubled. At no stage in the colonial era did the department exercise, or attempt to exercise, a supervision — 'Treasury control' — of other departments' spending.

It took on some of that responsibility in the 1920s, and with it the oversight of government borrowing. From then until the 1960s, this financial activity *was* the Treasury. Most of its staff still dealt with payroll matters — a department of 78 in 1922 had become one of 229 by 1971, an expansion proportionate to that of the public service. But the important staff worked as 'investigating officers' on either financial matters or departmental spending. The latter interrogated departments on their spending proposals and reported thereon to the Cabinet, in so doing performing a professional rather than a clerical function.

By 1971 Treasury had also acquired a role in the provision of *economic* advice: advice about the economy as a whole, not just the government's finances, which was provided by economic rather than financial experts, economists rather than accountants. This role has continued to the present day. The nature of this 'economic management', as it was called, changed markedly over time, in parallel with changes in circumstances and economic thinking, change being most evident to the public in 1984. During and after that year, not only did economic management acquire a visibly neoliberal cast, but financial management was also comprehensively overhauled.

We thus have two major developments: the advent of financial management in the 1920s, and of economic management in the 1960s. We can explain both beginnings and their subsequent course by exploring the structure and evolution of both bureaucracies and economies. Some readers may have expected the focus to be entirely on the latter, but this book is analysing not economic policy per se, but the department of government that was, amongst other things, involved in it.

We can take as a starting point for the bureaucratic approach the story of how the influence and the professionalism of the department's officials changed — and mostly increased — through successive decades. It is part of a more general story first analysed by the German scholar Max Weber, who studied the ways governments had become more systematic and orderly, and how this was mirrored in a rise in the status and expertise of officials.[6] This rise can be seen instrumentally — as a necessary accompaniment to the greater technical and administrative complexity of the tasks of government in the nineteenth and twentieth centuries. But other dimensions can also be discerned. Gordon Tullock

> challenged the dominant orthodoxy of modern political science and public administration, exemplified in the works of Max Weber and Woodrow Wilson, by asking the simple question: what are the rewards and penalties facing a bureaucrat located in a hierarchy and what sorts of behaviour would describe his efforts to maximise his own utility? The analysis of bureaucracy fell readily into place once this question was raised. The mythology of the faceless bureaucrat ... motivated only to forward the 'public interest' was not able to survive the logical onslaught ... and the modern theory of bureaucracy was born.[7]

James Buchanan, one of the early contemporary exponents of the 'economics of politics' or, 'as we prefer to call it, public choice', explained this as 'the application and extension of economic theory to the realm of political and governmental choices.' Just as a market could be seen to operate as the outcome of a whole series of individual decisions and choices, so could the public or political sphere be similarly analysed. Buchanan makes explicit the contrast between this approach and the view which sees the 'public good' as something over and above the sum of preferences — as 'the romantic notion that government seeks only to do good ... and that government could ... accomplish most of what it set out to do.'[8]

Other scholars are more reluctant to analyse bureaucratic decisions as the sum of individual preferences, not so much because such preferences might not exist as because the explanatory tool is too crude to apply to 'real life' situations: 'firms and agencies are complex entities with an internal life far more subtle and changeable than anything which could be described as maximised utility'.[9] One oft-cited work in this vein is a 1974 study by Hugh Heclo and Aaron Wildavsky, aptly titled *The Private Government of Public Money: Community and Government Inside British Politics*.[10] This book engaged in a sociological analysis of the management of public expenditure by Whitehall, and looked in particular at the ways in which public servants in both the Treasury and 'spending' departments interacted with each other, understood each other, and achieved their goals vis-à-vis each other. In a subsequent monograph, Heclo argued that institutions learned as well as acted, something captured in his phrase that governments 'not only power, they puzzle'.[11]

We can use these different approaches to analysing bureaucracies to help us understand the Treasury. The history of the department can be seen as the story of the relationship between its officials and their superiors — Governors, Colonial Treasurers, Ministers of Finance. British officialdom evolved out of the royal household, and the hierarchy of lord or master on the one hand, and servants — however able or literate — on the other, long survived the completion of that separation. Indeed, far from obliterating the pattern, the advent of parliamentary government rejuvenated it by providing a new set of masters. Ministers of the Crown, in the first flush of taking office, would see officials compromised by association with the 'ancien regime', rather as an inheritor to an estate might wonder about the fidelity of the existing staff. But then, settled in office, ministers would get used to — indeed reliant on — the 'servants' around them. To these patterns of conduct and outlook are counterposed the drives of the officials themselves, for security of tenure, freedom from arbitrary treatment, opportunities for advancement, and — or therefore — recognition of professional standing. And in a shadowy zone, the notion that officials (and indeed the country) can do without ministers much more readily than ministers (or the country) can do without officials. A promise of 'bureaucracy', in other words.

For this book, the idea of a profession is a crucial part of the larger story. In eighteenth-century Britain there were only three recognised 'liberal' or 'learned' professions — 'divinity, physic and law' — which could legitimately be pursued by gentlemen, especially younger sons for whom the family estate could not provide a sufficient 'competence' or independence. So a large part of the story of the nineteenth-century middle class was that of the striving for professional status by individuals in other occupations, such as architecture, surveying, engineering, accountancy and the civil service.[12]

Such campaigning may seem remote from the rough and tumble of colonial life, but while that rough and tumble gave the story a different cast, it did not do away with it. The first Treasury officials, including the Colonial Treasurer, were little more than the 'official' servants of the Governor, able to 'figure' maybe but regarded by most colonists as venal or incompetent or both. That colonial attitude mirrored the drive of the British middle class, articulated through Parliament, to wrest control of government and officialdom from a corrupt and inefficient Crown and its ministers. By 1840 Parliament in Britain had long since accomplished that goal, and the same was achieved in New Zealand with the advent of responsible government.

Britain matched this change with a civil service reform in the 1860s that instituted entry by examination to the upper levels of the service, but New Zealand did not follow suit, for reasons that will be explored in Chapter 1, and officials remained little more than 'retainers'. However, towards the end of the nineteenth century accountancy followed other occupations in acquiring professional status. This was more of a challenge for accountancy than for some of the other incipient professions, because it was an adjunct of commerce rather than government. Indeed the profession developed first in Scotland, where accountants, thanks to their important role in the legal system, were closer to the state. In the early twentieth century this latest professionalisation reached New Zealand, where it was catapulted into the world of the public servant with the election of the Reform government in 1912.

Thus a first turning point saw a drive to equip Treasury and other government officials dealing with financial matters with accountancy qualifications. It was at this time that the image of the Treasury inspector — the 'abominable no man' — came into focus. Cabinet's requirement that all spending proposals be accompanied by a Treasury report was Treasury's powerful lever over the rest of the bureaucracy, the means by which it waged war on waste and inefficiency — these were *fiscal* bureaucrats. But they were still public *servants*, a fact of which they were firmly reminded by the election in 1935 of a Labour government more determined than any administration since 1912 to impose its authority over officialdom — a determination, moreover, that worked against rather than in favour of the fiscal bureaucrats.

Meanwhile, a second turning point had come with the advent of a new sphere of professional expertise — that of the economist. Political economy was an intellectual pursuit rather than a profession in nineteenth-century Britain. The *profession* developed first in the universities, from which economists sallied forth during the 1930s Depression to 'doctor' the 'body economic'. Thereafter, in many parts of the world, young economists filtered into government.

In New Zealand, Labour politicians held the process at bay — if they talked to economists, they were as likely to communicate with professors as with public servants. The significant exception was B. C. Ashwin, an Assistant Secretary at the Treasury and its Secretary from 1939, whose combination of economic and financial expertise with consummate political skill gave him a central position in what would later be called 'economic management'. But Treasury remained in

Ashwin's shadow rather than being advanced with him. With the end of the Labour government, would the Treasury economist flourish? Hardly, because they were so few. Only in the 1960s did economists advance to a central place both within the Treasury and in giving advice to the government.

As with accountancy, so the approaches of professional economists bore on the pattern of relations between ministers and officials. The sharp shift in 1984 saw not just ministers paying more attention to economic advice from the Treasury, but also the reinvigoration of a role for Treasury in financial advice and practice on a scale not seen since the Depression. The creation of an economic and financial analyst class in the public service in 1986 was a direct demonstration that this phase of professionalisation had reached a new benchmark. Further, in shedding most of its original book-keeping and payroll functions, the Treasury as a whole became more 'professional' than at any time in its history.

So this book is a tale of professionalism. The professional advancement of certain officials — first accountants, then economists — is central to explaining how the department changed and how its place in government evolved. A glance at the table of contents will show that this approach shapes the structure of the book as a whole.

But it is not the whole story nor the whole book, not least because on its own it does not explain all change. To grasp that, we need to examine the political economy — that terrain where power, financial and economic activity and economic theory meet and jostle. For mid-nineteenth-century Britain — and to a fair degree therefore its colonies, including New Zealand — the 'laws of political economy' told the informed that prosperity lay in lifting all restrictions on trade. This 'laissez-faire' doctrine looked back to the work of the eighteenth-century Scottish political economist Adam Smith, which was elaborated on by a number of nineteenth-century English scholars, notably David Ricardo, Nassau Senior, and James and John Stuart Mill. In the monetary sphere it was matched by the gold standard — the practice of the Bank of England being prepared to meet all claims on the currency in gold, and its readiness to alter its discount rate (the rate at which it would lend) to ensure that such claims could be met.[13]

With Britain at the height of its commercial supremacy in the mid-nineteenth century, the doctrine found favour amongst crucial middle-class elements in British public life, and was entrenched by their victory in the anti-Corn Law campaign in the 1840s. Thenceforth, the tripod of free trade, the gold standard and a balanced Budget shaped the political economy and informed politics. Behind or above it lay the notion of the importance — the sanctity, even — of contract, without which commerce could neither be secure nor prosper. The Treasury in Britain played a central role in just one of the three parts of the tripod — the balanced Budget — but its officials were aware of the other two. In the colonies, belief in the tripod held good in theory but there were a number of departures in practice, heresies that were acceptable to British financial interests on the grounds that the colonies were a species of developing estates.

The New Zealand economy changed in the early twentieth century: many more individuals and families had capital, its population became predominantly urban and their expectations of government more complex. Business interests sought 'efficiency' in government, and who better to police that than the Treasury, which at this time adopted the role that British Treasury officials had first assumed in the 1860s. As with the latter, it was only this one leg of the tripod that occupied the Treasury. Treasury did not get involved in tariff-setting, nor in the regulation of labour and living conditions that had developed since the 1890s; and trading banks were expected to handle currency matters. In response to a query in May 1920 from J. F. Ward of Wanganui, Treasury explained that it was 'not in a position to inform you of the exact rate of exchange between New Zealand and the United States of America but your bankers should be able to supply the information required.'[14]

But the international political economy had changed irrevocably with the First World War, as even the fact of Ward's enquiry suggests. Treasury officials might imagine that they could look after the public accounts whilst money and trade looked after themselves, but it was not to be. New Zealanders had treated their pound as identical to the English pound, with the banks charging a premium for or against it depending on circumstances, but during the 1920s the variations became more noticeable and less predictable. The Bank of England fostered the establishment of central banks throughout the British world as a way of providing the stability that the gold standard (to which Britain had returned in 1925, having suspended the link at the outbreak of war in 1914) seemingly could not. But before this process of adjustment was completed, catastrophe interposed — the Great Depression saw Britain come irrevocably off the gold standard in 1931, and also abandon its 90-year-old free trade policy. New Zealand Treasury officials found themselves fighting a rearguard action to preserve what we can in shorthand fashion call the 'economic constitution'.

The Depression also changed economics. Alongside neoclassical economics, which had been distilled most thoroughly in Alfred Marshall's 1890 *Principles of Economics*, came new thinking associated particularly with John Maynard Keynes, who challenged the notion of the self-equilibrating character of an open economic system. It was a theory — developed most fully in his 1936 *General Theory of Employment, Interest and Money* — which explored the regulation of the demand for, as well as the supply of, goods and services, and suggested that governments had a role in such regulation, or 'management' — a role they had not played before the Depression. This was a way to rehabilitate capitalism. Thus while the professional story provides a turning point in the 1910s and 1920s, the political economy story gives us a turning point in the 1930s. The second turn took place everywhere, but made more headlines in New Zealand than in many countries — Australia and Britain, for instance — where conservative governments held office throughout the 1930s. In New Zealand the election of a Labour government in 1935 drew a bold line between the past and the future. 'The people' took charge, the central bank survived but was 'nationalised', and the regulated economy of the 1890s was markedly expanded — compulsory unionism for workers on awards, the licensing of imports and exchange controls were some of the most salient examples. During and after the Second World War, however, Labour's economic policy lost its socialist tone, and (mainly under National) through the 1950s and 1960s 'economic management' along the Keynesian lines adopted elsewhere in the world became familiar in New Zealand.

A second shift in the political economy, comparable in significance with that during the Depression, took place in the 1970s as stagflation — a combination of unemployment and inflation — pulled the rug out from under the post-war Keynesian consensus. The ascendancy of macroeconomics passed; microeconomics — the economics of the individual and the firm, of supply rather than demand — was in the ascendant, and with it, growth theories that argued for the importance of influencing production rather than consumption.

Treasury, frustrated by the failures of macro-management, took to the new/old economic thinking and the political implications — deregulation, not regulation; balanced Budgets, not deficits; an independent central bank, not a government-run monetary authority. In other words, the tripod was back in business in modern dress. Unsurprisingly, Treasury's financial management, which had lain in the shadow of economic management for a quarter-century, experienced a rejuvenation.

Laid over the story of professionalisation, the story of the political economy completes our chapter grid. It is no accident that changes of government, or at least elections, demarcate most chapters from each other. At those moments — of hard-fought party contests, of changes in Prime Ministers and ministries — the professional and the ideological parts of the story knot, relations between ministers and officials, politicians and public servants, come to white heat, and we see the structure more clearly.

Yet such drama should not lead us to assume that the history of the New Zealand Treasury is unique. A perusal of the Australian *Centenary of Treasury, 1901–2001: 100 Years of Public Service* provides an almost eerie sense of the parallelism between the stories of the two Treasuries (the vagaries of state–Commonwealth relations in Australia aside). This is partly because both institutions responded to the global trends in professional and intellectual life and economic activity. But it even extends to individuals; words such as 'he is a straight shooter who gives advice fearlessly and forcefully', used to characterise an Australian Treasury Secretary, could have been applied to officials in the New Zealand Treasury at the same time.[15]

This is *a*, not *the*, history of the Treasury. There should be many more. And any completed at a different date would have a different feel from this one. A history written in 1980 would have completely missed the change that was about to take place (despite its antecedents), and very likely focused on Keynesian economic management as a culmination. A history written in 1990 would have been too close to the 1980s to have perspective. What of histories written in 2010, or 2020? As we cannot read the future, we turn now to the past, which we can.

Part One
CLERKS

Chapter 1

The colonial Treasury, 1840–1910

The first Treasurer

'He says', wrote the diarist of his travelling companion, that 'it is the tide in our affairs, which is sure to lead to fortune, and has embraced his present situation with precisely the same feeling as myself — namely, to hold no faith with the scoundrel government which has used us so vilely, but to make use of them for our own purposes and to throw them off as soon as it suits our convenience.'[1]

The speaker was neither Cassius nor Brutus, nor even Mark Antony, but George Cooper, New Zealand's first Treasurer, as quoted by fellow official Felton Mathew at the time of their shipping from Port Jackson to the Bay of Islands in northern New Zealand to set up an administration for the new colony under Captain (soon to be Lieutenant-Governor) Hobson. Colonies were organised on the cheap in 1840, and they sometimes got officials to match. Hobson was not allowed to recruit in England, where 'high emoluments' would be demanded, so he hired in Sydney, presumably with Governor George Gipps helping by pointing out — or hiding from view — the able amongst his own officials. Cooper was an Irishman, 'a middle aged man of reputable and serious countenance and deportment', according to at least one informant. In that respect at least, Treasury officials have not changed. He had spent his working life in the United Kingdom's Customs, apart from three years in the same employ in New South Wales, although at the time of his appointment to New Zealand his official position was given as 'Superintendent of Distilleries'.[2] Being appointed to the offices of both Treasurer, who looked after the money, and Collector of Customs, who collected it, made sense, not least to Cooper himself. At £600 per annum for the two jobs, he wasn't badly off, earning more than any other officer of the government aside from the Chief Commissioner of Land Claims — and, of course, the Lieutenant-Governor himself.[3]

'Absolute frugality' was the watchword. The Treasury and the Colonial Office

The Colonial Treasury, 1840–1910

Gold ingots awaiting shipment to Australia. In the early 1840s, however, gold and coins were in very short supply. Alexander Turnbull Library, F-28120-½

in London insisted on 'the absolute necessity of … revenue being raised to defray the expenses of the government' — that is, there would be no grants.[4] But as customs or land revenue could hardly be expected to flow in from day one — there was the small matter of a treaty to be signed with the New Zealanders themselves, then the establishment of the apparatus of revenue collecting — Cooper's first task was to bring money into New Zealand. The British government lent £5000, of which £3000 was deposited to the credit of the New Zealand Treasury with the Bank of Australasia in Sydney and the balance was to be provided in gold coins. One of the first documents germane to the history of the New Zealand Treasury was a memorandum from Cooper to Hobson, informing him that 'the money is to be taken out of the Treasury Chest at Six o Clock tomorrow morning and … taken on board immediately after in strong boxes provided for it. Can we take the Iron Chest in the *Herald*?'[5] Did Cooper accompany the strongboxes down to the waterfront, and supervise their loading? How long did Emily — Mrs Cooper — linger after the ship's departure? What did Hobson and his newly appointed officials talk about on the voyage over to New Zealand? How did they get on with Captain Nias? Did they converse, or ignore each other? Perhaps it is just as satisfactory to let our imaginations take over at this point than to be trammelled by a surfeit of probably mundane facts.

Cooper did not stay long in the job. In March he went back to Sydney on 'personal business', and it was only Gipps' inability to find a competent replacement for New Zealand that led to him returning there in the middle of the year,

Captain William Hobson, RN, the first Governor of New Zealand, 1840–42.
Alexander Turnbull Library, G-826-1

with the desire to assure himself of a pension probably an incentive.[6] He stayed another two years, long enough to participate in the move to Auckland and the establishment of the government offices on the high ground above the waterfront, where Emily Place to this day memorialises his wife. He was accused of embezzlement but became insolvent — presumably the latter precluded the former.[7] The government too came close to insolvency in the first few years, and governors and administrators — Hobson, Shortland, FitzRoy — resorted to a variety of stratagems including (in FitzRoy's case) issuing debentures to pay its bills. FitzRoy's successor George Grey owes some of his reputation for effectiveness to the fact that London baled out the colony with grants during his term in office.[8] Cooper's successor, Alexander Shepherd, held the office of Treasurer until 1856, when the government pensioned off the senior officials, whose places were taken by members of the newly-constituted House of Representatives. The day of the politician had arrived, but not the day of the Treasury. Most of the rest of this chapter is devoted to explaining why the Treasury remained unimportant in the colonial period, despite the financial activity entailed by colonisation, war, borrowing and retrenchment. And why does this unimportance need explaining? To answer that question, we turn to the history of the British Treasury.

The colonial Treasury, 1840–1910

Alexander Shepherd, the second Treasurer.
Auckland City Libraries, Neg. A46

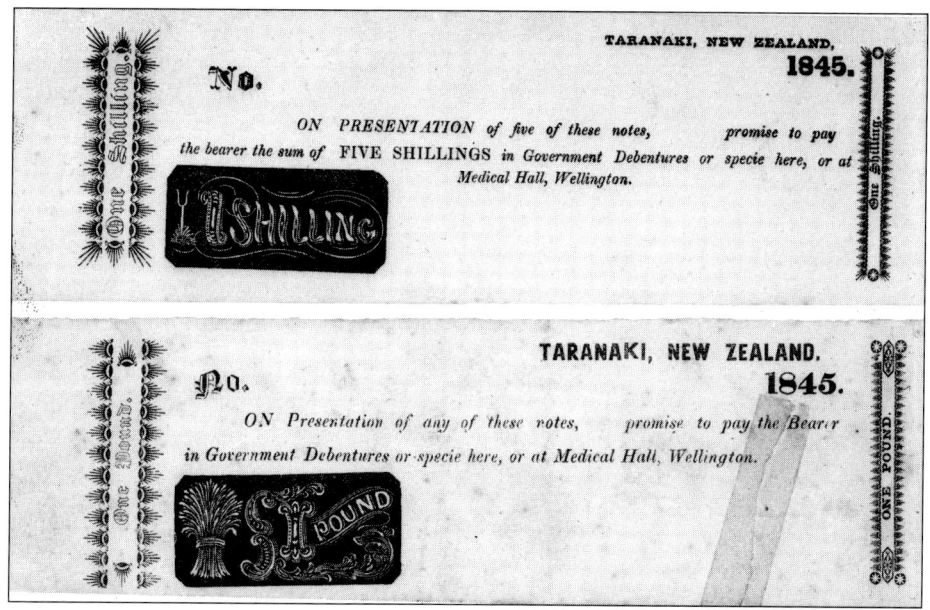

Would they believe the promise? Debentures issued in Taranaki to meet the government's lack of money, 1845. Alexander Turnbull Library, F-17085-½

The British Treasury and the road to fiscal control

While there are a number of ways of approaching the story of the colonial Treasury, the extent to which it did or did not resemble the metropolitan institution is most illuminating. In an inversion of the assumption that aspects of New Zealand life started off by resembling British patterns and then steadily diverged, the story of the colonial Treasury is almost the reverse — in its early history it did not resemble the British Treasury, but it came to do so more at the end of the colonial era, as will be discussed in the next chapter.[9]

From the Middle Ages the British Treasury looked after the monarch's revenues and disbursements, which in due course became those of a government whose activities reached far beyond those of the immediate needs of the royal household. In the course of that evolution the notion that Parliament must approve the Crown's expenditures ('appropriations') and for no more than a year at a time became established. This was to be a hallmark of government accountability to Parliament from that time on (and was a practice brought to New Zealand when a Parliament was established in 1854). But this occurred initially — after the 1688 'Glorious Revolution' — only in respect of military expenditure.[10] In domestic matters the balance of power remained firmly with the Crown, not least because it could use its resources so effectively in the political sphere. And it used them through the Treasury, that 'master-manipulator of the political world, deploying unrivalled resources of patronage in Parliament and the electorate at large'.[11]

The effectiveness of the Treasury in this regard meant that the capacity or inclination of parliamentarians in the House of Commons to demand any kind of accountability of the Crown for its spending was inhibited — 'the Treasury, quite simply, was not called to account'. This was most evident in the scale of the Civil List — what were regarded as the ongoing costs of government — which was voted by Parliament to the monarch at the beginning of his or her reign. The most significant demonstration of a changed parliamentary attitude to the Crown's expenditure came in 1782, when Parliament established its full right to scrutinize and reform any civil expenditure.[12] Thus Treasury, from being an agent of the Crown, was to become the instrument through which the Commons exercised control over the Crown:[13]

> An ethic transmuted into a cult, this ideal of economical and therefore virtuous government passed from the hands of prigs like Pitt into those of high priests

like Gladstone. It became a religion of financial orthodoxy whose Trinity was Free Trade, Balanced Budgets and the gold Standard, whose Original Sin was the National Debt.[14]

This change mirrored a wider social and economic transformation as the bourgeoisie, with its own attitudes to money and finance, slowly acquired greater political power, and landed wealth slowly ceded it. At the time colonial government in New Zealand was established, the transformation was still under way. The first 'authoritative' parliamentary demands in the United Kingdom for joint financial control by a responsible Treasury and a watchful House of Commons were made in the 1820s.[15] And it was only with the Exchequer and Audit Departments Act, in 1866, that the process reached a kind of culmination.[16] These acts tied together the processes of estimate, appropriation, expenditure and audit in 'one coherent system'. The holder of the new office of 'Comptroller and Auditor-General' was paid directly from the Consolidated Fund — that is, free of the annual procedure of a parliamentary vote, with a tenure like that of judges. The Treasury appointed him, but his sole responsibility was to the House of Commons. The first machinery for a retrospective, annual audit of government expenditure put a willing Treasury 'on its mettle' to enforce the strictest standards of financial propriety. In a minute of April 1868, the Treasury Lords recognised that it would be 'beyond the function of this Board to control the ordinary expenditure placed under the charge of several departments … [but they] consider that … sanction should be required for any increase of establishment, of salary, or of cost of a service, or for any additional works or new services which have not been specially provided for in the grants of Parliament.'[17]

Roseveare points out that Cobden, one of the great promoters of free trade, was asked by the Chancellor of the Exchequer, William Gladstone — Roseveare's 'high priest' of fiscal rectitude — to be the first Auditor-General, thus neatly linking financial reform to the wider political economy within which it developed. He goes on to discuss how closely the notion of economy in expenditure was grounded in the need to make free trade work and also in the drive to reduce the national debt. Gladstone's spirit animates this story. His mid-century feat was to reduce the debt from the half of public expenditure which it absorbed in the years before the Crimean War of 1854–56 to a fifth in 1890.[18] In aiming to fully introduce free trade (with all that implied for loss of revenue), Gladstone in his first Budget in 1853 proposed to abolish income tax in seven years, by which time prosperity would provide sufficient revenue from a much narrower base of

The start of it all. William Ewart Gladstone (1809–98) was the British Chancellor of the Exchequer (1852–55, 1859–66) and later Prime Minister on four separate occasions between 1868 and 1894. Alexander Turnbull Library, F-96510-¹/₂

taxable items. Crimea put paid to that goal, but the drive to at least reduce income tax persisted until the late 1870s.[19]

Paralleling this reform was a revolution — the word is not too strong — in the staffing of the Treasury and the other departments of government. From the later 1840s Assistant Treasury Secretary Charles Trevelyan was arguing for the filling of senior vacancies by men of university education (not merely 'gentlemen'), men who might go on to political careers. 'Civil service' reform (the term itself was novel, imported from the East India Company, which had civil and military services), and in particular recruitment through open competition, followed by promotion on merit, lay at the heart of the famous Northcote–Trevelyan Report to Parliament of 1854.[20] While deriving in part from the now longstanding critique of patronage and privilege, this also drew on more recent ideas about social progress.[21] Its recommendations were not implemented until 1870, and then partly in the context of a rationalisation of the organisation of work which allowed a reduction in staff numbers.[22] The establishment of 'Treasury classes', as they came to be called — occupational classes common to the whole civil service, for which open competition was the means of entry — first took shape at this time.[23]

Ministers and officials

The British changes provide a backdrop to the early years of the New Zealand Treasury, and of officialdom in the colony generally. To further set the scene, a snapshot of the colony will be helpful. Or rather, two snapshots, because it is the rapidity of change between 1840 and 1910 that is most striking. 'An observer in 1770 suddenly transported to 1840 would have seen much that was familiar ... But observers of the New Zealand world in 1840 would have been immobilised by what they saw in 1910.'[24] New Zealand became a British colony in 1840. Over the next 70 years, the population increased from around 100,000 to over 1 million. The non-Maori population rose from 2000 to 1 million, whilst the Maori population halved, so that a population 98 per cent Maori became 95 per cent Pakeha. War in the North Island in the 1860s had sealed the ascendancy of the colonists over Maori throughout the colony. The most rapid changes came in that and the following decade — between 1860 and 1880 large-scale immigration saw the Pakeha population increase from 60,000 to half a million. But through the whole 70 years the colonists — often with Maori participation — built roads, railways, ports, telegraph lines, churches, factories, office buildings and schools; burnt tussock and bush, and drained swamps to make pasture; mined gold and coal, and fossicked for every other kind of mineral; introduced a host of new kinds of plants and animals that altered the appearance of many parts of the country.

This was not an even 'upward' progression. Booms were followed by busts, and gold rushes by ghost towns. Thriving sheep flocks were laid low by rabbits or scab, low prices followed high prices, emigration followed immigration. Retrenchment was the dark twin of borrowing for development. Individuals, firms and the government saw revenue vanish as trade fell away — but debts remained. The latter years were the most prosperous and stable — in 1914 the 'Dominion' (as the colony had become in 1907) could look back on two prosperous decades, interrupted only in 1908/09.

Against this backdrop of rapid change, while colonists sought to emulate British practice, circumstances often made for a different outcome. From 1840 to 1856 the colony was governed by an appointed Governor who in turn appointed officials — a system much disliked by many colonists. In 1854 an elected Parliament assembled for the first time, and in 1856 a government was formed from members of that Parliament and enjoying its confidence — an adoption of the British practice that has lasted since that time. Indeed, the first session of the Assembly immediately resolved to adopt the British practice of voting funds for one financial year only, thus assuming 'the greatest of all the privileges which we as Englishmen possessed — namely, the right of Parliament to control the finances of the country.'[25]

However, precedent did not operate in all respects, and this is where the colonial story departs from the British one. This section will analyse relations between ministers and officials in the colony, and the next will consider why the Auditor-General was more important than the Treasury. The following section will examine the crucial role played by the City of London and the British Treasury in New Zealand's financial dealings.

The pair to parliamentary control over finance, the use of the Treasury as a tool of the parliamentarians, did not follow in the colony. For the politicians, representative government provided an opportunity for *them* to control the operations of government, not rely on officials, however competent. Through the first parliamentary session and up to the eve of the second, in 1856, the appointed officials held on to their jobs. The drive to remove them and replace

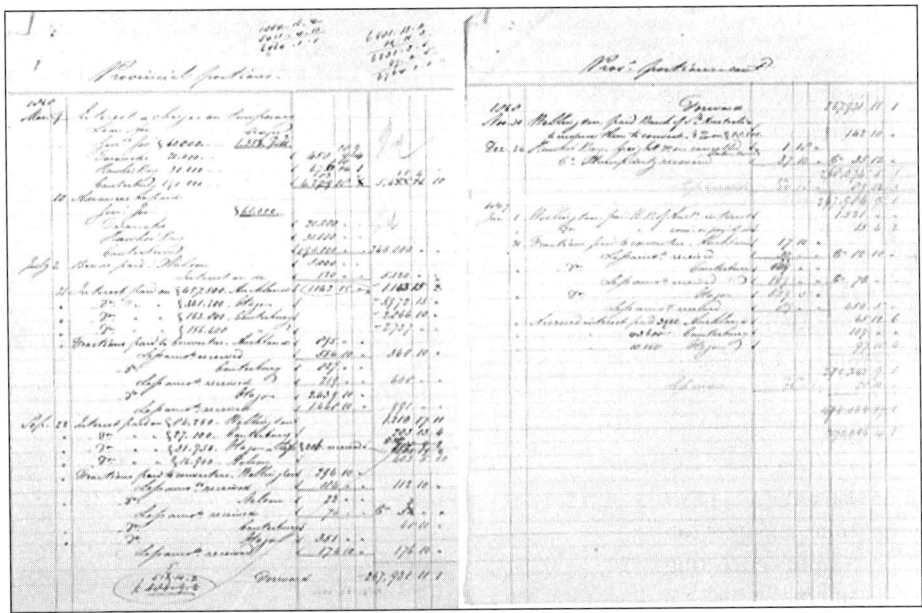

The Colonial Treasurer does the calculations for the public accounts. William Fitzherbert working papers on provincial/central government finances, 1867/8. T 20/3, Archives New Zealand

them with 'one of their own' — with parliamentarians — informed the calls for 'responsible government'.

The fact that the officials were not just appointed but incompetent reinforced the drive. The reports of the select committees in 1854, 1855 and 1856 suggested that it was futile to attempt to patch up the existing accounts.[26] When Alexander Shepherd had taken over from Cooper as Treasurer in 1842 it had seemed there might be some improvement. But when Shepherd still held office more than a decade later, Henry Sewell, one of the Canterbury settlement politicians, saw him, along with Sinclair, the Colonial Secretary, as one of the 'incapables', a mere 'stuffed figure' with whom Governor George Grey did what he pleased ('and whom he is said to have kicked and cuffed now and then').[27]

So the goal was not to have one agency of government controlling others, but to have ministers doing what the principal officials had done, with other officials carrying out 'clerical' tasks. Vogel himself said, in an aside a few years later, when the Public Revenues Act was amended to close a loophole, that 'it imposed a very large amount of check on the Treasury'.[28] The 1856 'revolution' was not a change from the Governor appointing officials to the parliamentarians appointing them. The 'revolution' was that the parliamentarians took on an official role, that the Governor had to appoint from the Assembly, not from outside it. Shepherd's successor in office did not therefore become what we now call the Secretary to the Treasury but the Colonial Treasurer, as Shepherd had been — what is now known as the Minister of Finance.

This notion that ministers were officials as well as politicians, offering advice *and* acting on it, whilst those who we think of as officials performed clerical tasks, is reinforced when the work habits and activities of ministers are recorded. Frederick Weld was overwhelmed, both at the suddenness of his elevation and the range of his tasks:

> you and Mary will alike open your eyes when I tell you that at this present writing I am a Minister of New Zealand! [I] have it in my power if I wish and have abilities to wield the Assembly to be prime minister!! in 2 or 3 months time, and have for the last day or two been closeted from ten o'clock am till 12 pm concocting a line of policy & manufacturing draft bills … dealing summarily (with my two colleagues of the cabinet) in measures of revenue — estimates — . . . etc etc etc.[29]

Edward Stafford (centre top), Frederick Aloysius Weld (left top), and Christopher Richmond (Colonial Treasurer, 1856–61, right top), were ministerial colleagues in the first Stafford ministry, but at other times rivals. Alexander Turnbull Library, F-12439-½

Each minister had responsibility for drafting bills for his own department, and an energetic minister like Edward Stafford was always busy: 'alone in his office from 11 until 7 dealing with every aspect of public business — even drawing up new tax forms.'[30]

Regrettably, evidence about Budget preparation is very sparse, a reflection in part of the confidentiality that surrounded the writing of the financial statements. It does seem clear that it was primarily the ministers who wrote these, assisted but not guided by the permanent officials — clerks. Christopher Richmond, who was Colonial Treasurer in 1857 and 1858, told the House in the latter year that he was unable to present a financial statement:

> The mechanical difficulties were very considerable, and, when honourable members desired to have everything at once, they forgot the amount of work to be accomplished … He therefore hoped that honourable members would have a little mercy, and not ride the willing horse to death…[31]

William Fitzherbert, the newly appointed Colonial Treasurer, spoke to the House on 7 December 1864 in very personal terms:

The Colonial Treasury, 1840–1910

Left: *William Fitzherbert, physician, politician and Colonial Treasurer (1864–65 and 1866–69).* Alexander Turnbull Library, F-25518-1/2 Right: *All the provinces borrowed money in London in the early 1860s. This 1865* Punch in Canterbury *cartoon shows Canterbury looking happier than its rival, Otago. Some provinces got into difficulties and William Fitzherbert, the Colonial Treasurer, ended the practice.* Alexander Turnbull Library, PUBL-0078-35

> The scheme I have to propose, for enabling the colony to extricate itself from its financial difficulties and maintain its credit, is contained in the following propositions, viz:
> To raise one million sterling by Treasury Bills at short date and increased rate of interest
> To raise the rate of interest to 6% on the unsold bonds of the permanent loan of Three Million
> To increase the taxation of the country by raising the tariff.[32]

Three years later the detailed work of consolidating all the provincial loans was also carried out by Fitzherbert, who had held the job for all but ten months in the interim. Pages and pages of calculations survive, and he appears to have done these himself manually — there was not even a clerk in this instance, let alone a calculator.[33]

From this perspective, ministers were expected to know 'their' departments well, better even than in Whitehall perhaps. As the Premier, William Fox, said on one occasion:

> It did necessarily happen sometimes that a member of a Government was compelled to discuss a subject with which he could not profess to be very familiar; but for his own part he had always endeavoured, as far as possible, to leave to his honorable colleagues who were the *heads of departments* all matters relating to their respective departments.[34]

When the Briton James Froude travelled through the Australasian colonies in the mid-1880s he was not sure that this was a good system, but in commenting on it he also provided implicit evidence that politicians were not unlike the permanent departmental heads of a later time when he wrote that it 'would be far better if *heads of department* could be selected with reference simply to ability and character, and were relieved, as they are in the United States, from responsibility to the legislature.'[35]

The biographies of Vogel, Atkinson and Ballance, all of whom served as Colonial Treasurer, are silent on the contribution of officials to Budget making and convey a sense that this was a responsibility of the Treasurer.[36] Treasury records from the period do not tell us much more — tacit demonstration, perhaps, that the Budget was very much the minister's, but also a comment on the need for secrecy in preparing a statement in which tax changes might be announced.

Financial statements focused in fact not on 'the Budget' for the forthcoming year, but on the accounts of the year just past. Indeed one 'improvement' made in 1879 was to shift the terminating date of the financial year from 30 June to 31 March, 'to enable the Financial Statement and the Estimates for the year to be prepared and placed before Parliament as soon after its meeting as the convenience of members would permit.'[37] The estimates for the current year were presented in large categories, which could have fairly readily been gathered by the Treasurer from his ministerial colleagues. In 1883 Atkinson discussed those estimates in little more than a page of a sixteen-page financial statement, explaining some of the increases and decreases but deciding not to 'weary the Committee by going into a lengthy comparison of the two years' estimates.' The task of compilation was also simplified because of the great weight of debt in the estimates: annual appropriations for departments were nearly equalled by debt servicing expenses — for 1883/84, £2 million compared with £1,567,430. On the revenue side, the process also seemed fairly rudimentary and in the hands of the minister: 'I anticipate that we shall receive a total ordinary revenue of £3,573,800 for the current year, exclusive of land sales, if our taxation remains unaltered. I have thought it prudent not to increase the estimated receipts from Customs duties more than £20,000 above the estimate of last year; but I hope [for] £1,520,00 from these duties.'[38]

When criticism was voiced of a stock operation, a politician like Vogel took the financiers to task himself and deployed his own informed opinion about recent operations in a lengthy comment for the attention of the Cabinet. It was the kind of discussion that in the twentieth century would more likely have been made by an appointed official in a memorandum to the minister:

> I consider the past conversion operations have been very ill advised. The conversions of the 5-30s bearing $4^1/_2$ per cent interest has placed a large mass of stock on the market blocking more profitable operations. I have used the words 'conversion operations' above; but I must say the operations were not strictly of a conversion nature, or at any rate only partially so. The placing of short-dated debentures in the category of a conversion operation only was, as Sir F D Bell has not denied, deceptive, since the object was also to sell part of them. In my opinion what we should have done … was to have scheduled only the 5-30s bearing 5 per cent interest… [39]

Further, while the 1866 commission of inquiry was composed of officials (though of high status, such as Charles Knight, the Auditor-General, and William Gisborne, who was soon to enter political life) it was the ministers who wanted to see economies (the principal reason for the inquiry). This was equally true in the 1880s, when 'retrenchment' was frequently called for. The 1880 commissioners — four individuals from secondary centres — were asked to 'consider by what means the cost of [the Civil] Service … may be reduced without impairing or lessening' its efficiency, and whether it might be reorganised or reconstituted.[40] Indeed the Treasury — and the Audit Department itself — was on this occasion seen as a source of inefficiency — 'serious inconvenience and loss of time is caused to surveyors, engineers, and others, who are imprest officers, by the amount of account-keeping thrust upon them … In some cases … officers who have small payments to make are not made imprestees; consequently these payments have to be made by cheques from the Treasury, to which, on receipt, a countersignature, involving a long journey to obtain, is required before payment.'[41]

Similarly, when legislation on hospital and charitable aid boards was debated in 1885, one speaker referred to the fact that the bill made the local bodies 'dependent on the goodwill of the Treasurer'[42] — not the Treasury. Or take tariffs. The devising of the tariff, which in the twentieth century would elicit papers from officials setting out the pros and cons of particular courses of action, lay firmly in the hands of ministers in the nineteenth century. It was they who fielded the enquiries and representations.[43] If we consider the tariff revision which was announced by Vogel in his 1885 Budget, we see that the correspondence is essentially between interested individuals and associations on the one hand, and the politicians — both Vogel, the Treasurer, and Stout, the Premier — on the other.[44] There was nothing subtle about these submissions. The Manufacturers Association supplied a table with the precise tariff levels (all increases) which it favoured on a variety of items, ranging from jewellery, opera glasses, safes and stationery to steam vessels, hydraulic rams, engine fittings and service cocks. Thomas Harbutt replied to a telegram from Vogel after the tariff revision had been announced that he was 'quite satisfied with old tariff on brooms but we cannot get broom corn here nor wont for years and as we pay highest colonial wages and more than is paid in America if you tax raw materials it will swamp us'.[45] For his part, J. Hodge congratulated the government on 'this action ... in revising the tariff so as to encourage colonial industries and production ... a step in the right direction [which] has the full support of the working men of [Christchurch].'[46]

Equally, when the government considered (quietly) taking a greater shareholding in the Wellington–Manawatu railway, this also did not entail any consultation with officials. The lines of discussion were between Dillon Bell, the Agent-General in London (where the operation would have to be conducted) and the ministers in Wellington.[47] A draft of the Mortgage Debentures Amendment Act in 1886 was prepared in the Crown Law Office without any apparent consultation with other officials. In comparison, private individuals, presumably with legal or commercial experience, from Christchurch and Wellington, do appear to have been consulted.[48]

We can take this discussion about the respective roles of ministers and departmental officials further. The years 1866 and 1867 saw a surge of administrative reform, provoked in part by the financial strains produced by the wars of the early 1860s. The civil service was reported on, and a Public Revenues Act established both new forms of public accounts and the office of Comptroller of Public Accounts. All provincial loans were consolidated, further borrowing by the provinces was stopped, and the funding of the provinces was put on a capitation basis. However, plans to introduce an income tax did not succeed.[49] This was a massive effort to put the colony's official apparatus on a more systematic basis than had previously been the case. The investigation of the civil service in particular was influenced by events elsewhere — by efforts in Victoria to reform its civil service and, it seems likely, by the reform of the British civil service.[50]

The reform effort *might* have fostered the development of a more professional civil service, with entrance examinations to the substantial positions, as was becoming the case in Britain, but this did not eventuate. The New Zealand Civil Service Commissioners recognised in 1866 that a system of parliamentary government must 'frequently place in office gentlemen unacquainted with the administration of public affairs, and who must rely to a very great extent upon the officer of the Civil Service they find in charge of any department under their Ministerial control'.[51] This suggested an awareness of the value of appointing able individuals — the new British model — but such an aspiration bumped against the reality of a very small number of public servants and the wish of the newly incumbent 'heads' of departments, that is, the politicians, to retain influence. As a result the entrance examination provided for 'soon fell into disuse and appointments were practically made at the pleasure of the Ministry.'[52]

Treasury and the Auditor-General

The Civil Service Commissioners looked at the colony's finances and the systems for scrutinising them, invoking precedents from Canada and Victoria (which had investigated its civil service the year before, and whence one of the commissioners came), as well as the United Kingdom. In talking of the need to look at examples from other colonies, the 1866 commission of inquiry referred to the value of examining 'what has been done by Legislatures in other Colonies to check abuses in the expenditure of … public moneys … where it has been thought necessary to establish effectual safeguards against the misappropriation of public revenues.'[53] The Public Accounts committee of Parliament established in 1870 was modelled on the British committee of the same name.[54]

But it was the Auditor-General, the officer of Parliament, rather than the Treasury per se, that was the focus of most attention. Indeed the commission was headed by Charles Knight, a 'graduate in medicine and botanist of sorts', who had worked with George Grey in South Australia and been brought with him to New Zealand in 1845 to serve as Auditor-General. In that role he was also de facto Treasurer because of Shepherd's incompetence.[55] Knight remained Auditor-General until the position was disestablished with the change to responsible government in 1856, and was reappointed when the office was re-established two years later as one answerable to Parliament, not the Governor. In staying on until 1865, he was unique in length of service under the old and new orders, and he held similar appointments until 1878.[56]

There is a parallel in the Canadian experience. The Minister of Finance in the newly formed Dominion in 1867, John Rose,

> could not have prepared a detailed financial statement, the Estimates, and a new set of excise duties, without substantial help from officials. He received it chiefly from the auditor, John Langton ... who served not only as the auditor but as the minister's chief adviser ... he became deputy minister of finance and secretary of the Treasury Board as well as auditor general in 1870. This arrangement was at odds with the doctrine of the independence of the auditor general, but it had the great advantage of centralizing influence and administration in the hands of a very capable man.[57]

New Zealand's Civil Service Commissioners noted in respect of British practice that 'it was not until about a year since that an Act was passed placing the Commissioners of Audit in a somewhat more independent position, by making the Comptroller of the Exchequer, who is one of the high functionaries of State, the Chairman of the Board of Audit; so that now in England the same officer who controls the issue of public moneys sees that they are appropriated in strict accordance with the Votes of Supply.'[58] At the end of the 1865 session an act was passed establishing the office of Comptroller of the Public Accounts; an appointment was to be made as soon as convenient.[59] The Comptroller's primary task was to be to countersign the transfer of funds from the Public Account to the account of the Colonial Treasurer, from which disbursements would duly be made. At the beginning of 1867 a Comptroller was appointed — James Edward FitzGerald, a Canterbury politician and a rival of the then Premier (and fellow Irishman) Edward Stafford.[60]

At this point the positions of Comptroller and Auditor-General were quite separate, both in function and in person. But this was soon to change. In 1872 the Comptroller and the Auditor-General were associated into one joint 'Com-

James Edward FitzGerald (1818–96), politician but also long-serving Comptroller and (from 1878) Auditor-General. H. J. Schmidt Collection, Alexander Turnbull Library, F-1317-¹/₁

missioners of Audit' able to do jointly what either office had previously been able to do individually. Knight and FitzGerald were the two individuals concerned. FitzGerald was made both Comptroller and Commissioner of Audit — for life. The Public Revenues Act 1878 made him Auditor-General at the time of Knight's retirement.[61]

FitzGerald was therefore to be a far more enduring figure in financial control than any Assistant Treasurer — or Secretary to the Treasury, as the office was retitled some time in the 1870s. His class position and status in colonial politics ensured that he was the equal of ministers, not of civil servants. Equally, Treasury officials went in effect 'on promotion' to the Audit Department — men like Charles Batkin, who was Secretary to the Treasury from 1873 to 1878 and then, aged 55, became Assistant Controller and Auditor, offices he held until his retirement in 1890.[62] J. C. Gavin became Assistant Controller and Auditor on his retirement from the Treasury in 1890.

In 1884 the Audit Department was still the same size as Treasury.[63] And in 1888 it was the Audit Department, not the Treasury, which presented to Parliament an analysis of New Zealand's public accounts since 1832.[64] The same pattern obtained in other colonies — indeed, Victoria's *Votes and Proceedings* reported

A Treasury voucher from which payments were authorised, 1868.
Audit Queries 1868–74, T 20/3, Archives New Zealand

the Treasurer's financial statement within the framework of the Commisioner of Audit's report on it.[65] So despite the fact that the organisation of the public finances in 1867 had made a clearer demarcation between the tasks of Treasury and of the Audit Department than had been the case before, the most important task of scrutiny remained that carried out by the Comptroller, not the Treasury.

Colonisation, war and borrowing; London and New Zealand[66]

It is reasonable to assume that the tasks of colonisation and the embroilment of the colony in war in the 1860s would have enhanced the role of the colonial Treasury. Colonisation involved the related activities of bringing in immigrants, buying land from Maori, public works to open up that land, and the selling of it to settlers. It was a massive transformation. Between 1840 and 1892, 13.6 million acres was freeholded — a 'privatisation' far overshadowing those of the late twentieth century — and while that comprised only about 20 per cent of the total land area, it was 'the great bulk of the best lands of New Zealand'.[67]

At every stage colonisation raised financial issues, and so did the war. Money had to be found to pay for local militias and volunteers, and for war-related infrastructure such as the Great South Road from Auckland. But while short-term accommodation might be made by banks in New Zealand, longer-term and more substantial borrowing had to be in London. So what both these enterprises — colonisation and war — demonstrated was that the colonial state was self-reliant politically but not financially. In the latter respect, the capital of the colony was clearly neither Auckland nor Wellington (to which the seat of government was shifted in 1865), but London. And it was in that capital that both the money and 'Treasury control' were found.

One of the first things the colonists did on gaining control of the government in 1856 was to arrange for one of their number — Henry Sewell — to travel to England to arrange a half-million pound loan.[68] When Reader Wood, the Colonial Treasurer, left for England on a similar mission in January 1864, his colleague Frederick Whitaker explained that the government did not 'desire to fetter you with specific and minute instructions, a strict adherence to which might be the means of causing the miscarriage of your mission … but rather it desires to indicate generally its view of the manner in which your mission should be performed.'[69]

The principal trigger for Wood's journey was the war. Imperial forces had invaded the Waikato in July 1863. The Commissariat, the branch of the British Treasury responsible for financing them, was authorised to make temporary advances on the Governor's requisition 'in order to meet a colony's military expenses in times of emergency', but the Secretary of State for the Colonies became increasingly sceptical of the colony's demands after the Maori defeat at Rangiriri in November 1863.

Wood arrived in London in March and immediately had meetings with the financial authorities. He wanted to secure an Imperial guarantee of the £3 million loan the ministry had announced the year before. This would make the loan much easier (and cheaper) to raise, but the Treasury was cautious. To what extent, officials asked, was the loan required for defence expenses, and to what extent might it have been defrayed out of revenue? What security was envisaged for it? Wood identified one-third of the loan as being required to meet the cost of the local regiments raised; half a million pounds for other military purposes; and £1.5 million for colonisation, including the introduction of armed settlers into rebel districts.[70] Despite casting the whole loan in military or quasi-military garb, Wood was only able to get a guarantee for £1 million. The first million to be offered for tender was *not* guaranteed and attracted only £6100, partly because shortly before the tender opened news was received of the 'sad reversal of our troops at Tauranga'. This was the battle at Pukehinahina/Gate Pa in which there was considerable British loss of life, though the forces kept their hold on the district. Wood had then to arrange with the Crown Agents for the colonies,

It all had to be paid for: British soldiers camped at Waitotara, Taranaki, 1865.
Alexander Turnbull Library, E-047-q-036

Messrs Julyan and Sargeaunt, and Falconer Larkworthy of the Bank of New Zealand, to raise the finance by other means, so that payments into the Bank could be made on the required dates.[71] The City of London was as important as the Treasury — Treasury help might make borrowing easier, but it was in the City that the money had to be found.

The Weld ministry which took office in November 1864 inherited the problem. It found itself dependent on advances from the Bank of New Zealand to pay its daily expenses, and its overdraft was £¼ million. In addition, the Commissary-General was refusing to supply further pay or rations to the colonial forces, and demanding immediate repayment of past advances.[72] This time it was William Fitzherbert, the new Treasurer, who made the three-month voyage to London. His task would not have been helped by FitzGerald, the future Auditor-General and an opponent of the war policy, writing to Gladstone in February that

> I am more than ever convinced that had England absolutely refused to help us at all, there would have been no Maori War, and the Maoris would have got substantial justice at our hands … I hope you and the House of Commons will do the colony justice in refusing to guarantee the loan.[73]

Treasury did refuse to extend any further financial aid, although that in turn 'ensured that the advances already made to the colony through the Commissariat would never be repaid' beyond a first half-million pound instalment.[74]

London remained crucial through later decades when, with conditions in New Zealand becoming settled again, borrowing *was* engaged in for colonisation. With the appointment of an Agent-General in London, visits by the Colonial Treasurer became less compelling and the London focus of the government's finances was if anything strengthened. Featherston, the first Agent-General, was the agent for the loans issued between 1871 and 1875, but he acted with Julyan and Sargeaunt as before. In practice Featherston, preoccupied with immigration issues and with little financial experience, left the work to the Crown Agents.[75] This changed with the next two incumbents of the office, Julius Vogel (1876–1880) and Francis Dillon Bell (1880–1891). It was Vogel who lobbied hard to get New Zealand (and other colonial) loans issued as 'inscribed stock' — a more elevated status than they presently enjoyed, one which meant that the Bank of England, not the Crown Agents, would act for New Zealand. This was eventually accomplished with the passing of the Colonial Stock Act in 1877.[76]

Julius Vogel, Premier and later Agent-General, who became an expert at both spending and raising money.
Alexander Turnbull Library, F-92898-¹/₂

The financial aspects of both Vogel and Dillon Bell's Agent-Generalships are analysed by Raewyn Dalziel in her study of the office, as are Vogel's in her biography of him.[77] Dalziel notes of Vogel that hard times, combined with unfavourable publicity about his business activities, led to a strong attack on the office of Agent-General. When in 1880 the House cut its budget by 25 per cent, the component that was regarded as least dispensable by the mover was the commercial side.[78] But the Premier, John Hall, did contend that the colony's representative in London

> should not be a mere clerk or agent, but a gentleman of position and influence … [and] of sufficient knowledge of the political history, the finances, and general conditions of the colony.[79]

This description fitted both Vogel and his successor, Dillon Bell, who would 'investigate thoroughly every financial proposal and reported with exhaustive detail.' In particular he addressed the issue of converting New Zealand's earlier loans into inscribed stock, making a very thorough study of the subject soon after his arrival in 1881 and reporting that this would be profitable.[80]

By the mid-1880s, Julyan had been acting on behalf of the colony for more than twenty years. He was paid an annual honorarium of £666 from 1882 to 1884; the Agent-General's salary was £1250, that of the Premier in the latter year £1750. In one letter Julyan noted that while he was paid a fee for conducting stock operations, he also acted as an agent for raising new loans, as one of the Sinking Fund trustees, as a commissioner of the public account, and as an agent for dealing with debt guaranteed by the imperial government.[81]

It was London rather than New Zealand opinion that continued to determine the fortunes of borrowing endeavours. City of London opinion inveighed against inefficiency and extravagance, as New Zealand business interests were to do in the next century. The narrowly-averted prospect of a default on interest payments on a London loan by the New Plymouth Harbour Board in 1889 was a sobering experience. Dillon Bell reported to Atkinson that Penrose Julyan was averse to making enquiries in the City — 'the minute they were made, default would be assumed with an evil result on our credit.'[82] Both the harbour board and the borough of Oamaru got into difficulties, and the *Financial Times* spoke

Follow the money. The Royal Exchange, in the City of London, in the 1880s.
Alexander Turnbull Library, F-60008-$^1/_2$

Railway and port construction was expensive. The financial difficulties of both the Oamaru Borough Council and the Oamaru Harbour Board affected the colony's reputation in the City of London in the early 1890s. Alexander Turnbull Library, C-22767-1/2

bitterly of the 'recklessness or worse' of colonial borrowers.[83] The sad situation of Australia in the 1890s, reported the *Economist,* was all that should have been expected in the light of foolish policies, especially protection, the failure to federate, punitive taxes on the upper classes, inadequate controls over the public service and excessive borrowing. The so-called 'Treasury view' — that public expenditure detracted from and discouraged productive investment in the private sector — was repeatedly applied to the colonies, according to one historian of economic thought. The leading economist Alfred Marshall was sceptical on efficiency grounds of such aspects of the Australasian political economy as the eight-hour day and high wage levels.[84]

In the early 1890s Flora Shaw (later Lady Lugard) described colonies as 'more like corporations than nation states'.[85] Adapting a phrase of Miles Fairburn's, it is useful to see the colonial government as a form of 'associational machinery', analogous to the corporations, be they private or municipal, found in all spheres of British life. Particularly was this the case with the colonising project, with its 'managers', operations and operatives in the colony, but its stockholders or owners in London.[86] The colonial state was an 'enterprise' in a way in which neither

France, nor England, nor even the United States (as distinct from, say, individual states west of the Mississippi) was.

From this perspective, colonial New Zealand was not a prelude to what came after, but a rather distinct 'animal', one that was in many ways more distinct from the metropolis, from its European origins, than was twentieth-century New Zealand. We might oppose to the 'ideal society / experiment' view, the 'corporation' view. This would see New Zealand, not as an incipient nation, but as a (British) corporation. Colonial politicians participated in the British political economy like local worthies or entrepreneurs in the United Kingdom itself, building, spending and, hopefully, prospering. From this perspective nation-, or rather state-building, did not so much stop at the end of the colonial era, as start. Belich suggests with his concept of 'recolonisation', as start.[87]

The Treasury officials: the men and their work

When responsible government was introduced in 1856, the new Colonial Treasurer — Francis Dillon Bell — had just one clerk to assist him,[88] although sub-Treasuries (in practice, one part-time official) also existed in all the provincial capitals. Under the circumstances it was not surprising that the office of 'Secretary to the Treasury' took a while to be established — R. F. Porter, the Accountant at the Treasury, and William Gisborne, the Under-Secretary at the Colonial Secretary's office, both spent some time as acting head before C. W. Richmond, the Colonial Treasurer for all but two months between 1856 and 1861, appointed Porter as 'Assistant Treasurer' in August 1858.[89] While Richmond's own appointment was made by the Governor, he could appoint the officials in his department. He was their 'employer' much as the Secretary to the Treasury was to be after 1988. This underlines the extent to which the later offices of Minister of Finance and Secretary to the Treasury were in effect combined in one person in colonial times.

By 1859 there were still only two officials besides Porter — C. T. Batkin, the Cashier, and J. N. Ward, a clerk.[90] What of their professionalism? When Richmond spoke in a supply debate in September 1860, he concluded by paying a tribute to 'my friend the Assistant Treasurer … for his excellent arrangement of the colonial accounts … I should have found it quite impossible to lay before you such a statement of the colonial accounts as I have given this evening if the Treasury books were not kept upon a most lucid and intelligible plan.'[91] We get a different view from J. C. Gavin, the Secretary to the Treasury from 1878 to 1890, who, recalling his first years of employment, told of how one day Porter came to him and said,

> 'Mr Gavin, I cannot balance my books, I wish you would help me.' ... Instead of making random shots at the error, as he had been doing, I set to work systematically to find the mistake ... I persevered for a day or two until his patience becoming exhausted ... he took the book away and in a minute returned saying, 'I have found it on the page next to where you left off.'[92]

Porter retired on his pension when still quite young, intending to go into business. But according to Gavin, he had little success in either business or life:

> I think his unfortunate marriage had a good deal to do with his reserved manner ... [his wife] was what is what is commonly called a 'bad lot'. She had left him and fallen on evil ways. One day someone came to his office and announced that the woman was dead ... That Dicky refused [to pay the funeral expenses] must be taken as evidence of the great wrong she had done him. By-and-by ... he married again ... the match proved however unfortunate. The last time I saw him was in Cummings restaurant. He was so tipsy that he could hardly walk — I avoided him. I was told he had taken to beer. Poor old fellow, the end was sad.[93]

Gavin himself was an emigrant from Scotland who had first come to the colony in 1853, venturing to Queensland after three years, but later returning to Auckland, where

> in February 1860 my uncle interested himself in getting employment in town ... so it came about that after an interview he had with Mr Richmond, then Colonial Treasurer and Commissioner of Customs, I was offered temporary employment in the Treasury at £140 a year....[94]

Gavin thereby became the fourth member of a department whose intimate and ad hoc scale is vividly captured in his memoir. If he wanted to see Richmond, he just 'went upstairs'. But if Richmond was home sick, as was often the case (he suffered from asthmatic attacks), Gavin took papers to his house in Parnell.

Officials in the mid-century colony were only just beginning to shed the circumstances and outlook of the household retainers from whom they traced their

J. C. Gavin, the Secretary to the Treasury from 1878 to 1890, was one of just four employees when he joined the department in 1860.
Treasury

origins. The term 'civil servant' reminds us that long before professionalism, clerks were servants — servants who could write, but still servants. Throughout the history of the Treasury the notion of official as servant has a resonance that never entirely vanishes. In the 1860s it was much more than a resonance. Pay and conditions, for instance, were much more like those of a large household or business than of a modern office. Gavin challenged Richmond about his pay after learning that a clerk in the Audit Office who had joined after him was to receive £20 more per year — 'on what grounds I fail to perceive'. The next day 'he came to my desk and softly said "you are quite right, you shall have £160."'[95] And further, with Gavin practically doing some work which was formally Porter's, the latter twice gave Gavin a cheque for £10 out of his own pocket.[96]

What did Porter, Gavin and his colleagues work at, besides assisting the Treasurer to prepare the annual accounts for submission to the Assembly? The register of inward correspondence that was opened in the last months of 1856 shows that most exchanges were with the Customs Department. That was logical, because customs duties were the main source of revenue. Other correspondence came from the government's bankers (the Union Bank of Australia, at this time), and from other officials handling revenue or expenditure — Resident Magis-

Auckland in 1864, its last year as the capital. Photographer Daniel Manders Beere took the image from Wesley College, Greys Avenue. D. M. Beere Collection, Alexander Turnbull Library, G-96105-½

trates, the Native Secretary, Land Commissioners and the like, and the Auditor-General. There is no sense that the Treasury (all two of it!) was doing more than being a 'mailbox'. Communications from individuals most often concerned customs matters.[97] Other tasks were not necessarily welcome. The department had to license importers of arms and ammunition. Gavin was 'instructed to receive applications, over the counter', which he found 'not a pleasant duty', as he had to 'take stock of all the licensed dealers under the Act, to debit them with all importations and to credit them all sales ... and to inspect [their] stock periodically.'[98]

The offices of the Treasury in the early 1860s were in Graham Buildings, just opposite Government House gate at the corner of Auckland's Princes Street and Eden Crescent.[99] Most of the town's 10,000 inhabitants lived within half a mile of Queen Street, with a more scattered population in 'outlying' areas like Parnell and Dedwood (Ponsonby from 1873). The development of the South Island settlements, none of which had existed when the colony and Auckland were established in 1840/41, gave rise to arguments for moving the capital to the centre of the colony. Major gold discoveries in Otago from 1861, the onset of war in Auckland province in 1863, and the lack of any early prospect of overland

The Colonial Treasury, 1840–1910

The intersection of Lambton Quay and Molesworth Street, Wellington, in 1863, just before the town became the seat of government. Government House, originally Colonel William Wakefield's house, is to the left and Parliament Buildings, built originally for the provincial government, are to the right.
Ferguson Collection, Alexander Turnbull Library, F-3693-1/2

communication through the North Island, tipped the balance. At the conclusion of the 1864 parliamentary session, arrangements were put in train to shift the government's offices to Wellington. Porter did not move, but was appointed sub-Treasurer for Auckland. He was succeeded as Assistant Treasurer by Jonas Woodward, the Treasury Accountant.[100]

Sea travel was erratic, and it must have taken Woodward and the other officials several days to get from Auckland to Wellington, with a wait at New Plymouth. It was, however, an uneventful voyage (unlike that of the *White Swan*, which was shipwrecked carrying officials and records to Wellington in 1862), and the government paid some £9500 compensation for removal expenses.[101]

What did Woodward and his colleagues think of their new home? Auckland, which had grown fat on war spending in 1863–64, was a boom and bust town — the bust coming after the officials and soldiers left. Wellington had not had the boom. Pioneer romanticism glosses over the fact that in 1865 it had only a thousand more people (5000 in total) than had lived there within months of the first settlement in 1840. It lacked good land communication with its hinterland; nor had any gold been found. None of this would change because some 120 officials[102] and half a dozen ministers shifted into the town, and members of the Assembly gathered for a couple of months each year. Perhaps the most congenial thing about the move was that it placed the officials closer to the booming provinces of Canterbury and Otago, and further from the most active war theatres. They were initially housed in the vicinity of the General Assembly building, in the government quarter within the block formed by Molesworth, Sydney, Hill and Museum Streets.[103]

In 1866 the Treasury had a staff of nine in Wellington, and fourteen (a sub-Treasurer in each of the eight provinces, and additional clerks in Auckland, Taranaki and Canterbury) elsewhere.[104] Its internal operations needed improvement, the Civil Service Commissioners thought. They identified major weaknesses in the ways the accounts were currently managed. Revenue was 'paid daily into a bank to the credit of the Colonial Treasurer … not into the "Public Account"'. The Colonial Treasurer thus held

> sole control over the issue of the Public Revenues … The revenue accounts, when received at the Treasury, instead of being blended into one account, are forwarded separately to the Auditor of Public Accounts for examination…. The sub-Treasurers render weekly accounts of their transactions. These, supported by vouchers, are forwarded separately to the Auditor … The Treasury thus throws upon the Auditor the work of collecting into one account these numerous accounts current of his agents.

If this system were rationalised, the Auditor would be 'relieved of the anomalous duty of making up the public accounts from not less than 700 separate weekly accounts'. The system would work much better if

> The several Ministers should for each quarter of a year supply the Treasurer with a statement of funds required by them … The Treasurer should … after such consideration of the state of the finances at the time as the Government may deem necessary, issue authorities for incurring expenditure … This system … secures the control of all expenditure in the hands of the Treasurer.[105]

The Public Revenues Act of 1867 went some way towards remedying such weaknesses, in particular by establishing a public account into which all revenue was to be paid, and which would be divided into four branches, of which the most significant was the Consolidated Fund. The various provisions of this act, and an 1872 amendment, put the handling of the public finances on a much

The Colonial Treasury, 1840–1910

The new Government Buildings, Wellington, housed virtually all the civil service when opened on the new reclamation in 1876. The architect had wanted stone, but the government saved money by building in wood. Tyree Collection, Alexander Turnbull Library, G-11623-1/2

more systematic basis.[106] Julius Vogel, who was Colonial Treasurer from 1869 to 1872, and on subsequent occasions, claimed 'for the officers of the Treasury much credit that the actual results [for 1868/69] assimilated closely to those which their industry and ability enabled me to put before you.'[107]

From the advent of self-government until their abolition in 1876, Treasury's work was complicated by the existence of provincial governments, which did not have distinct sources of revenue. Debtor and creditor accounts were established with each province to determine the proportion of revenue each should receive, and squabbles and adjustments were frequent.[108] While Treasury continued to maintain offices in other towns, these were no longer sub-Treasuries after the provincial era. Along with other departments of government, Treasury moved into the capacious new Government Buildings, which were constructed on reclaimed land below the old offices located on the site where Parliament now stands.[109] The Treasury was to stay on this site for more than 60 years, until its move to the Departmental Building on Stout Street early in the 1940s.

The post-1876 Wellington focus of the department, and the routine nature of its operations, would have limited its contact with Maori — and indeed with most colonists. The most overt contact with Maori was through the payment of pensions. In a tabulation of these made in 1888, one-third of the 300 names were Maori, most of whom were being paid from the Civil List for 'Native Purposes'. Most of the Pakeha were either former civil servants or military personnel.[110]

Misfortune sometimes favours the historian. We can gain a snapshot of the make-up of the 1880s Treasury from a file on salaries that was initially assembled to calculate salary reductions during the fiscal crisis of the early 1880s. In the year 1879/80 £8710 was voted for the Treasury, of which £700 was the salary of the Secretary and nearly another £1000 the combined salaries of the next two senior officials, the Accountant and the Chief Clerk and Cashier. The 37 other officials on the establishment, 22 of whom were known as clerks, included three cadets (trainees).[111]

Another table classified people by work rather than by process. The Accountant, Heywood, had four clerks in his office. The Chief Clerk worked with a cashier and a clerk. 'The cashier's job is one of great responsibility', Gavin reported in support of claims for increased pay. 'Besides making payments to the amount of over £116,000 p a, and acting as a receiver of revenue as well, the cashier is the custodian of the reserve block of stamps amounting in nominal value at present to considerably over a million pounds.'[112]

The record office had three clerks, loan accounts two. There was a supervisor, three keepers of the abstract books, two for requisition purposes, two for bank ledgers, two for cheques, one for vouchers, three despatch clerks, and two others. There were nine provincial auditors, five clerks and a cadet in the Receiver-General's office, and twenty clerks in the Paymaster-General's office.[113] The principal function of the Treasury in 1880, the disbursement of funds, was one that it would not possess at all just over a century later.

The extent of the reductions in salaries paid or numbers employed is not clear from this file, but by 1886 Treasury's spending was £5887 on a staff of 26. The 32 officers had cost £8152 in 1875/76, and numbers and spending had been even greater four years later.[114] In 1885 alone the government 'dispensed with' seven Treasury officers with a combined salary of more than £1500, only one of whom was entitled to a pension (most of the rest got a year on half pay). The cost of the department in 1885/86 represented its yearly cost 'based on the reduced staff recommended by the officers who last year inspected the various departments in the Government Buildings at Wellington.'[115]

> Should it be found practicable to carry on the system of direct payment from Wellington, without recording details of expenditure in the Treasury Books — leaving such details to be kept by the Departments authorizing the payments — further reductions in staff will be made. An experiment is now being made ... confined to Public Works, Railways and Defence expenditure for which accounts in detail must necessarily be kept in the Departments, without regard to what may be done by the Treasury.[116]

In his notes on his subordinates in that year pursuant to a claim for pay increases, Gavin put some colour on the department. Heywood

> really does the work of assistant Secretary. I have always held the view that in a department like the Treasury the officer next in status to the permanent head should be capable of taking charge of the Department in any emergency. Heywood is ... capable, and takes a thorough interest in the working of the office in every branch.[117]

Heywood's capability took him to the office of Secretary to the Treasury in 1890, an appointment which coincided with the beginning of the final phase of the colonial era, that of the Liberal government.

The impact of the Liberals

The arguments given here for the colonial Treasury's unimportance — that ministers themselves, and the Auditor-General, played the role that Treasury officials were to play in the twentieth century, and that the financial dimensions of colonisation, the principal activity of government, were centred in London, not the colony — hold through the era of Liberal government (1891–1912). But this period merits special attention because both contemporary commentators and historians have seen it as a time in which government activity expanded, in which 'state socialism' was the order of the day:

> About the middle of the nineteenth century, in the heyday of the Manchester School, when political economy was a science and free trade a gospel, it was common for writers on political questions to ... assign limits to the sphere of government activity ... to a New Zealander of the present generation these are words from the tomb.[118]

W. H. Oliver has suggested that the 'true Liberal revolution' was an administrative one, with the Secretary of Labour, Edward Tregear as the 'Thomas Cromwell

Railways were seldom far from ambitious politicians' minds. In this 1900 sketch new Minister of Railways Joseph Ward takes credit for cheaper fares. Alexander Turnbull Library, B-094-025

of New Zealand'.[119] A number of studies of aspects of Liberal government have drawn attention to the influence of officials such as Tregear, Duncan MacGregor of the Hospitals and Charitable Aid Department, George Hogben of Education, and S. Percy Smith of Lands and Survey (as it became).[120] We can see too from the Labour Department's publication of a journal that public servants were ready to provide information and provoke discussion on economic and social issues. The *Journal of the Department of Labour* was modelled '"somewhat on the lines" of the British *Board of Trade Journal* and was intended to provide reports "on the condition of labour, alterations in tariffs, customs returns, imports and exports, immigration and emigration, bank returns and general information on economic topics attracting attention during the previous month"'.[121]

But against this evidence of an enlarged — and implicitly more powerful — officialdom other factors can be counterposed. Firstly, numbers of staff. While total numbers did grow, most of this increase was in the Post Office and the Railways, and these were staff 'in the field', not in departmental offices in Wellington.[122] It is also useful to be reminded of J. B. Condliffe's observation about the Liberal era:

> the so-called state socialism of the nineties involved practically no new departure so far as State enterprise is concerned. In particular, the trading ventures in economic fields already taken up by capitalist organisation, which are generally suggested by the phrase 'State Socialism' are conspicuous by their absence ... it is to certain Australian states rather than New Zealand that one must look for experiments in State shipping services, brickworks, butchers' shops, bakeries, fisheries etc.[123]

So the Liberals did not socialise, but they did regulate, particularly in labour matters, with the introduction of compulsory wage arbitration, laws on trading hours and business practices, and also over the tariff. But apart from the fact that the fiscal implications of what we might now call the microeconomic sphere were minor compared with the impact socialist policies would have had, regulatory responsibility fell to departments other than the Treasury, such as Customs, Lands and Survey, Labour and Agriculture. The latter two departments, indeed, were established in the early 1890s. And it was in such spheres that the great officials of the Liberal era were found.[124]

Treasury staff numbers did grow from the retrenched figure of 26 in 1886 to 32 in 1896 and 55 in 1914. In the years from 1896 this increase was roughly proportionate to that of the civil service other than the Railways and Post Office. As Treasury's primary task was to manage the government's receipts and payments, including salaries and wages for those two large departments, the wonder is that the increase was not greater.[125]

The suspicion of the new ministers of the officials they had to deal with echoed that of the 1850s politicians of the officials they had replaced. As with the notion of the official as 'servant', only more visibly, it was also manifest after all the twentieth-century changes of government. Most of the senior officials had served through the 1870s and 1880s, and could be expected to have loyalties to other political figures. At the beginning of the 1890s, far from a desire to expand the civil service, there was widespread support for further retrenchment. This was partly fiscal — hard times meant less revenue — and partly ideological. Ballance's motives in cutting salaries and staff levels were primarily fiscal.[126] But one government supporter saw the alternative to political control over appointments as rule by a civil service elite untouchable by the people's elected representatives.[127] Since the Civil Service Reform Act of 1886, staff were supposed to be recruited by competitive examination, but the Liberals made widespread use of a section that permitted the appointment of 'skilled' persons and 'extra clerks' on a temporary basis.[128]

And certainly the new ministers were determined to stress that they were in charge, not the officials. Thus although Jock McKenzie, the Minister of Lands and Agriculture, took advice from departmental heads and other officials, he made it quite clear that he was 'in control' and that Agriculture was 'his' department:

> it is the duty of the Minister to look personally into papers, especially certain papers of importance, and see what they can do in the interests of the country to save money or devise better things than the Under-Secretary recommends … I do not blame the Secretaries for any neglect of duty, but they have not the practical knowledge in dealing with matters which Ministers have.[129]

Even if we concede that in other spheres of government, such as the administration of labour laws, there was an expansion of government activity, the Treasury did not play a significant role in this. Nor does its Secretary through most of the period, James Heywood, appear to have been comparable in status and influence to individuals like MacGregor and Tregear, despite the status implied by his title.

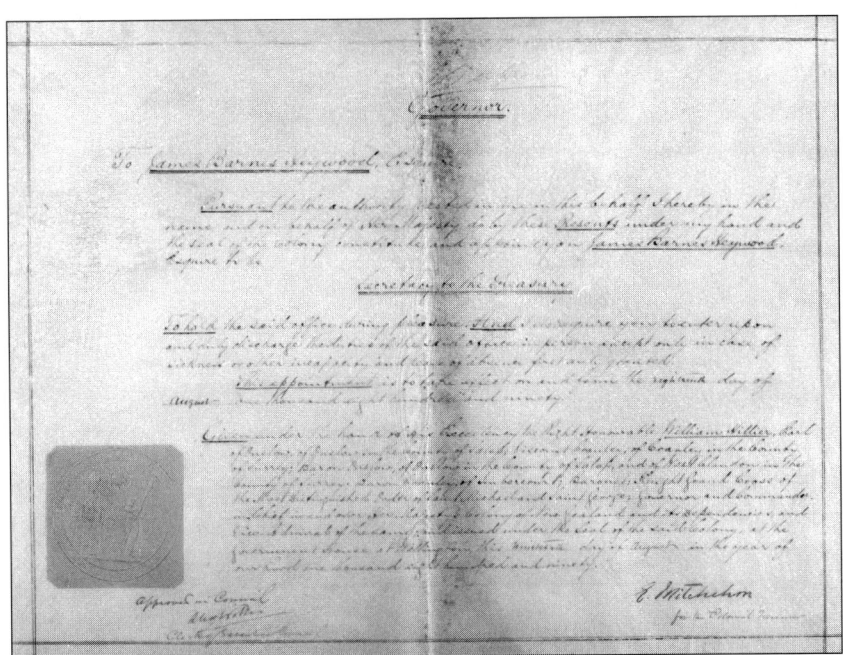

Jas Heywood's commission as Secretary to the Treasury, 1890. Heywood papers, T 20/10, Archives New Zealand

While Tregear worked as a draughtsman until 1891, and MacGregor was a professor at Otago University until 1886, Heywood had been a long-serving official in Wellington since the 1870s — which may have made a difference. Equally, there is little evidence that the process of assembling the public accounts and the estimates for the forthcoming year involved Treasury clerks in more than compiling the figures supplied by other departments; and the work of managing loans remained primarily a matter for the Agent-General's office. The evidence Heywood gave to the Public Accounts Committee in 1892 over the operations of the Consolidated Stock Act displayed considerable technical knowledge, but on this occasion evidence was also taken from J. C. Gavin, Heywood's predecessor as Secretary and now the Assistant Controller and Auditor.[130] Equally, during an 1898 investigation of unauthorised spending by the Post Office, the Secretary to the Treasury explained that 'These accounts are not under my control at all. The Treasury is only connected with them in the matter of finding funds for the Post Office'.[131] Under further questioning, Heywood showed his irritation at being expected to be knowledgeable about the Post Office's spending:

> 'Is it correct that the payments exceeded the imprest advances by £39,000?'
> I have nothing to do with that except to find the funds.
> 'At whose request do you find the funds?'
> At the request of the Post Office.
> 'The imprests are made to the Post Office by the Treasury?'
> Yes.
> 'Would it not be your duty to ascertain whether the amount is covered by the imprest advances asked for by the Post Office?'
> No.
> 'You issue imprest advances without seeing that such imprests cover the amount of payments made?'
> That is so.
> 'Do you think that is right?'
> I do not see how it can be done otherwise.[132]

Nor did this finding seem to disturb the Public Accounts Committee, which reported blandly that 'the time at its disposal not permitting that consideration which the importance of the subject demands, it places the evidence at the disposal of the House.'[133]

Certainly the records suggest that the relationship between Heywood and his successive ministers — Ballance, Ward and Seddon — was one of friendship but

A youthful Joseph Ward (1856–1930).
General Assembly Library Collection.
Alexander Turnbull Library, F-97-35mm-F

deference, with the reins firmly in the hands of the minister. When a letter came from the South Australian Premier calling for lobbying of the British government on the matter of authorising trustee investment in colonial stocks, Seddon minuted, 'the Hon Mr Ward, I think our agent-general should be advised accordingly, what do you think?', to which Ward minuted, 'I think you should reply to Downer that the Agent-General has full instructions concerning this'. Seddon then minuted to Gavin seeking a 'reply in terms of Mr Ward's suggestions.'[134]

Many of the exchanges were of a kind that would now pass between ministers and speechwriters — particularly when Ward was electioneering away from Wellington: 'Please wire me early tomorrow amount of the loan issued by the Atkinson government and in addition to this the annual increase for their term of office in the public debt.'[135] And three weeks later: 'Wire me highest amount of Treasury bills during any period of each year for the last seven years that were current at one time giving each year separately. I want this for tonight. Reply urgent.'[136]

A little of Heywood's personality comes through in his exchanges by telegram with Joseph Ward when the latter is away from Wellington. On one occasion Ward wired:

> I am in receipt of yours of the 13th inst and note that there is nothing to say re Treasury business. This is satisfactory … Certainly, use my room and desk by all means. Your own room will be all the better for doing up in the way you suggest. The extra key was sent to Mr Crow, who has been advised by this mail to give it to you.[137]

It is clear from the tone of these messages that the two had become personally friendly: 'Miss Scully desires me to tell you that that the girls are awfully pleased with the clock and thank you muchly'.[138] Heywood even felt able to approach Ward for assistance over housing, but in a fashion revealing of his self-image as a public *servant*, or retainer, rather than an official of equal standing to his minister, as MacGregor or Tregear might have considered themselves:

> I have not been able to hear of any house … and there seems little probability of one at this end if we cannot secure the Ministerial residence in Molesworth St. Would you kindly say a good word for us to Mr Seddon, the situation would be so handy at session time and as an old Government Servant I may be allowed some claim as against the outside public all other things being

Jas Heywood asks his minister Joseph Ward for help with accommodation. Telegram, Heywood to Ward, 5 December 1894, Heywood papers, T 20/10, Archives New Zealand

> equal. It would be a great relief to know we were settled in some abode not far away from ones official duties.[139]

It appears that Heywood's request was not granted, but when Ward was about to travel overseas in February 1895 he cabled, 'Goodbye old chap and don't forget to send me duplicates of financial figures after 31 March, one copy to Frisco and the other either to Aden or Colombo. I will probably cable you from London upon the matter.'[140] Budgets, about which there remained a great deal of secrecy, seem to have been compiled by the minister himself:

> I will be glad to know how our revenue had come up for December: and also the expenditure of the various departments[.] I trust they are keeping their expenditure down. In fact, I think it would be well to send a memorandum round to each of them from me, requesting that every effort be exercised to keep expenditure down from now to the end of the financial year. This refers particularly to the Lands and Public Works Department. And the Labour Department are also, I think, inclined to be a little easy going, as far as finance is concerned, and are continually pressing for works which there is very little need of being hurried on.[141]

Was this the beginning of a colonial 'Treasury control'? On the other hand, the regular Budget surpluses may have weakened any drive to fiscal surveillance. Ballance was proud of his 1892 surplus, Ward equally so of his in 1893.[142] In presenting the Budget in 1900, Seddon dwelt on the evidence of prosperity as indicated through both the 'phenomenal returns from our Railways and Customs' and increased revenue from land and income taxes.[143] It was left to Sir Robert Stout to place an idiosyncratic spin on Gladstonian finance by arguing in 1897 for the moral and practical merit of deficits.[144] Through these years, so buoyant was the revenue that it became customary to finance development not so much from borrowing as from transfers from the Consolidated Fund to the Works Fund — a strategy that Ballance had engaged in as a way of reducing future borrowing.[145] This was true even in 1899/1900, despite the 'strain of increased expenditure', in particular on old age pensions and defence. And in 1904 it was 'my duty', Seddon told his fellow parliamentarians, 'at the risk of wearying you … to announce the oft-reiterated statement that we found, on closing our books for 1903–4, that we had a very large surplus.' On this occasion, no less than £350,000 was transferred to the Works Fund, still leaving a balance of £650,000 in the Consolidated Fund, on a total revenue of approximately £7 million.[146]

Similarly, in 1907/08 Ward, now Minister of Finance and Prime Minister, transferred £800,000 to the Works Fund, leaving a balance of £768,000 on revenue of some £9 million.[147] One observer was aware of the significance of these surpluses:

> The besetting sin of the social reformer is the deficit. There were, then, strong grounds for fear, from the financial point of view, in a policy of reform at any price, carried out by ministers who had something of the demagogue in them … But … Mr Seddon once more proved that the politicians of the Antipodes are often extremely clever business men. Despite the new and heavy expenditure necessitated by many and costly reforms, despite the very heavy burden of the public debt, despite the sacrifices which the Transvaal War entailed [he produced in 1901/02] a credit balance of £256,924.'[148]

This was a marked contrast to the fiscal situation in the United Kingdom, which was hamstrung by free trade. As 'social and military expenditure advanced … free trade was placed on the defensive',[149] and Treasury's Gladstonian scrutiny of expenditure became ever more assertive, in a manner that would only become recognisable to New Zealand officials dealing with their Treasury counterparts after the Second World War. One official recalled that "'the juniors got first bite at the papers: they could put minutes or drafts on them before passing them up to their superiors, thus getting a chance of showing their quality'", whilst another, who entered the Treasury in 1913, found himself 'being sent on missions to other departments, "invariably to see officials very much senior to myself and to lay down the law to them. No wonder the Treasury was disliked in those days!"'[150]

As the Prime Minister, Lord Salisbury, put it in 1900:

> The Treasury has obtained a position in regard to the rest of the departments of the Government that the House of Commons obtained in the time of the Stuart dynasty. It has the power of the purse, and by exercising the power of the purse it claims a voice in all decisions of administrative authority and policy. I think that much delay and many doubtful resolutions have been the result of the peculiar position which, through many generations, the Treasury has occupied.[151]

However it was fiscal pressure and the reluctance to reduce it by abandoning free trade, not Treasury's overweening ambitions, that underlay this comment, which unleashed a debate in the press. There were frequent references to the immaturity of Treasury officers ('youthful pedants') and the appointment of former

Treasury officials to positions of influence in other departments. While the immediate uproar demonstrated only (as on previous occasions) that Treasury control was working, behind it lay a larger issue: 'the survival of the Gladstonian tradition of rigid economy against the mounting demands of a nearly democratic state ... an issue of minimal, balanced Budgets against large, continuous programmes of social and military expenditure.'[152]

No such issues faced the New Zealand Treasury. And the motor of colonial finance remained on the other side of the world. When the Bank of New Zealand came to the government at the end of June 1894 'like a thunderclap, without the least warning' of its desperate financial situation, it was in London that the colony's guarantee to a 4 per cent issue of new capital had to be acted on, and it was the Agent-General's office, not even that of the Colonial Treasurer, which directed the process, as Ward made clear in a cable to London:

> After very anxious consideration and consultation with Mr Murray [of the BNZ] I decided that you and your financial advisers are in the best position to know what will induce the public to subscribe on the most advantageous terms and I therefore determined to allow you a free hand to make the best possible arrangements for both the Bank and the Government. — only asking you to keep me fully supplied with all possible information.[153]

Ward proved to be not quite as happy as this message implied he expected to be with Perceval's actions:

> I was therefore much concerned and disappointed to receive ... your telegram ... pointing out that the deed of settlement of the bank limited individual holding of shares to two thousand...[154]

But again, it was the Agent-General, not any Treasury officer or financial specialist, who took the decision to proceed with the loan even though the terms were not quite as he had hoped:

> On my pressing upon the Board of Directors the expediency of carrying into effect, so far as possible, the urgent wish of the Government that the Bank should receive par, they represented that virtually that would be the case, at the same time they did not disguise the fact that there would be certain miscellaneous expenditure ... The arrangements for the issue had, however, proceeded so far and there had already been so much unexpected delay that it would have been exceedingly hazardous, particularly at this time of the

year, to have postponed the issue any further. The financial portion of the City were already leaving London, and any further postponement would have necessitated another reference to the underwriters ... these other considerations weighed with me so heavily, that I considered that I should be justified in allowing the stock to be issued at the price which I have named.[155]

Ward was active in seeking finance in London — he had to go there for that purpose, and it was his endeavour, not that of the Treasury clerks in Wellington: 'I have had endless troubles since my arrival in connection with the new issues. If it had been possible I should have put this through our own Bank; we could have had it completed before this'.[156] London continued to dominate the government's loan financing in the early twentieth century: 'London is for New Zealand a great reservoir of capital. Of the total debt £46,430,126 was raised in England; £181,000 in Australia; and £6,274,721 in New Zealand ... England is for them a banker provided by nature.'[157] Even Ballance, who as Premier from 1891 to 1893 was determined to reduce New Zealand's reliance on loan finance and promote its self-reliance and independence, conceded that 'the assertion of our independence is, of course, subject to many qualifications: We are not independent of the London Money Market, and I am not sure whether we shall be for a generation, if so soon.'[158]

In her study of the Agent-General, Dalziel argues that Perceval and Reeves, the holders of the office in the 1890s and early 1900s,

> never had the same degree of responsibility over financial affairs as did Vogel and Bell ... the degree of freedom and influence that Vogel and Bell had enjoyed was curtailed as Premiers and Colonial Treasurers once again began visiting England. The cable, too, was being used more frequently.[159]

But was this the case? A precis of the history of the 1910 £5 million loan shows that most messages about it originated from the High Commission (as the Agent-General's office was called from 1907), not from Wellington. Thus the original proposal comes from there, when the High Commissioner asks for particulars of the loan requirements authorities 'to enable him to take advantage of the best market conditions'. It is the High Commissioner who determines how much money he needs to arrange the loans, and the Minister of Finance duly arranges to send the money. An order in council passed a few days later delegates the power to raise the loan to the High Commissioner. And so on.[160] And it is the High Commissioner's department — not the Treasury — which supplies the

Specimen debenture coupons for the 1910 £5 million loan. 1910, T 17/21, Archives New Zealand

lengthy report of the office on the 'financial work transacted during 1911' — including principally the 1910 loan.[161]

The important shift that *was* to take place was not so much from the Agent-General to the government as from a 'politician' like the High Commissioner to public servants — in the Treasury. That shift was paralleled by the shift from London to Wellington as governments started to borrow in New Zealand as well as in London, but even more so, as financial decisions were made in Wellington rather than London. Treasury also won approval to despatch one of its own to London to handle financial matters.[162]

The one specific area in which more might have been expected of the Treasury was the banking crises of 1894–1896 which saw the Bank of New Zealand and then the Colonial Bank rescued by the government. They were not the only banking crises of the period — the BNZ had faced one in 1889, as had the National Bank in 1885 and 1891, whilst Australian banks got into trouble in the early 1890s. And in the City of London itself, Barings Bank was only saved in 1890 by a Bank of England intervention backed by the government.[163]

The New Zealand government was drawn deeply into the 1894–96 crises.

The fact that Joseph Ward was heavily in debt to the Colonial Bank made a complex story even more complex.[164] In this politically charged environment it does seem that Heywood dealt with individuals in the commercial and financial worlds in a way not visible before 1890. Was this change a comment on his personality or on the change in the political environment brought about by an energetic new government? In 1893 and 1894 Heywood had discussions with Tolhurst and Butt of the Bank of New Zealand, although the former exchanges seem to have been almost a private rather than an official correspondence — Tolhurst's letters (Heywood's have not survived) are labelled private, and the correspondence was lodged with personal papers of Heywood's.[165]

On one recorded occasion, however, Tolhurst provided information on note circulation, citing Canadian and South African precedents. It may be that Heywood, who was close to Ward, was acting as a channel for the latter; Tolhurst asked, 'For the Treasurer to get what he wants, need there be any legislation next year?'[166] Similarly, on one occasion he reported that he had seen 'Butt for a few minutes on Thursday. I told him I thought you would like him to let us know as soon as possible what was his opinion of the real position of Global?'[167]

And Heywood was active while Ward was away:

> Am drafting Regulations for the Controls and this reminds me to ask you if you have made up your mind as to the rate of interest to be allowed. Watson wishes? He said to talk to you about finding further investments and has offered me advances at four per cent. We shall soon be wanting money for Native Land purchase and for Roads but the worst of it is that we shall only require to issue debentures according to the expenditure so as to economize the payment of interest and again these debentures will be payable in the colony and not in London, but it may suit the Bank to take up some of them.[168]

A bit later, when a 'storm' blew up about the appointment of an auditor in London, Heywood told Ward that 'I would like you to hold over action until we can have a chat about it'.[169]

Heywood was also active in 1896 in dealings with Butt and Watson of the BNZ over the extent of balance sheet information that the Bank should supply to the government, which was still its guarantor. Heywood minuted to Ward at the beginning of June 1896 that he did not think 'the form of balance sheet as submitted contains sufficient information', and went on to detail the ways in which it might be improved.[170] Heywood also had an opinion on the kind of auditor the government needed to see appointed to the Bank of New Zealand after Butt resigned:

> I am strongly of the opinion that the next Colonial Auditor need not be a Banking expert. We require someone with a great deal more general and practical business knowledge combined with a knowledge of the value of properties, stocks etc than is to be found amongst most Bankers. We need a great deal more than the assurance that the accounts and books are perfectly kept.[171]

Such requirements were particularly significant given the existence of the Assets Realisation Board, which had been set up after the government took over the BNZ's property investments in 1896. The board was entrusted as a form of statutory manager to liquidate those investments and refund the state for its advance of funds.[172] Heywood believed that the board should be reported on by a

> man who has ... considerable experience in stock and station business; a banking expert is of little good for such requirements. I think we should go outside Bankers and take a man like Mr Harry Kember of this City ... whose ability and experience is undoubted.[173]

Heywood's suggestion would have required a change in the law and was not adopted. Nor do the early annual reports of the ARB suggest that the Treasury had representation on the Board.[174] And it may also be that the replacement of the bankrupted Ward by Seddon as finance minister, and the waning of the banking crisis, saw Heywood's role revert to the more limited one he had played before the crisis broke.

Conclusion

A Treasury was established in the new colony on its inception in 1840. In Britain, the political economy of the age shaped a Treasury whose permanent officials were fiscal guardians against extravagance and waste. The Treasury in the new colony was a different animal. New Zealand's fiscal guardians were found in London, not in the colony itself; and the colonial ministers who replaced nominated officials from 1856 were in practice also officials. 'Treasury control' was exercised by the Treasurer, by the Comptroller and Auditor-General, by London, but not by the officials of the Treasury Department. In the 1910s and

1920s both these distinctive characteristics were to change.

In 1909, far from introducing the Budget by talking of economic buoyancy, Ward left it until late in his statement to refer to the fact that 'The extraordinary drop in the value of some of our principal products brought about an alteration in the commercial condition of the country that told its tale upon the revenue, and more particularly with respect to that derived from the Customs branch.' The government had taken action that was appropriate in its own view, and probably that of most voters: 'the removal of men from their positions, with the trouble it entails upon themselves and families, is a most painful duty for any Government to perform, [but] became a necessity'.

In also setting up 'a Committee, consisting of five of the high officers of the public service of wide financial experience … for the purpose of examining … the whole system of accounts as carried on in the various Departments, with the view to the establishment of a uniform system',[175] Ward was aiming at further economies but also foreshadowing a new phase in the story of the role of Treasury, which over the next two decades was to be energised by the advent of a new government, the fiscal stresses of war and depression, the maturing of the colonial political economy, and a new professionalism which reshaped its staff.

Part Two
ACCOUNTANTS

Chapter 2

Counting for something? The Treasury, 1910–1930

Introduction

In 1934, 65-year-old James Jacob Esson succeeded the outgoing Governor-General, Lord Bledisloe, as Grand Master of the Order of Freemasons in New Zealand. It was a substantial attainment for one of eight sons of a pioneering Marlborough family. He had joined the Post Office as a twelve year old in 1881, worked in it for the next 25 years, then in Treasury for another twenty. Esson saw service in the Great War, and his career with Treasury culminated in his becoming its Secretary in 1922, from which office he retired voluntarily in 1925. The government then retained him as its 'financial adviser', and he sat on and in many cases chaired significant commissions of inquiry and boards over the next six years. Esson died in 1940 leaving an estate of £8400 — perhaps $600,000 in 2003 terms. He had gained a 'substance' of wealth, but even more substantial power and influence. And, surely uniquely among Treasury Secretaries, he left his military effects — staff cap, Sam Browne belt, sword, service revolver — to his daughter.[1]

Esson's journey from boy clerk to the equal of ministers of the Crown and Governors-General distils the transformation of the Treasury in the second and third decades of the twentieth century. In 1910 the Treasury was in all essentials the department of government it had been for many decades, and its officials remained servants or clerks. They managed the government's accounts in the sense that they 'kept count' of its revenue (they did not collect it) and payments. The New Zealand High Commission in London (the renamed Agent-General's office) remained more important for managing financial affairs, and particularly loans, than were Treasury officials in Wellington. The Minister of Finance, as the Colonial Treasurer had been known since 1907, wrote his own Budgets with only clerical assistance from the Treasury, whose officials had neither the right nor the inclination to scrutinise or make recommendations about revenue (taxation) or

John Jacob Esson, Secretary to the Treasury 1922–25 and the 'power behind the throne' for the next half-dozen years, in the robes of the Grand Master of the Order of Freemasons, which office he assumed in 1934. Earle Andrew Collection, Alexander Turnbull Library, G-13869-¹/₁

spending. The head of the Audit Office, the Controller and Auditor-General, was the pre-eminent figure of parliamentary control over the accounts, in tandem with the Public Accounts Committee of the House of Representatives.

Over the next decade and a half the Treasury's place in government was transformed. Financial management, which had rested with ministers, the Auditor-General and Parliament, and with financial interests in London, came to rest with the senior officials of the department. This turning point in the history of the New Zealand Treasury was similar but not identical to the Gladstonian revolution of the 1860s in Great Britain, which, as we have seen, was never fully implemented in the colony. That revolution was grounded in a political economy of strict parliamentary control of public spending, with Treasury as the 'constable on the block'. The 1920s revolution in New Zealand was informed by the practice of that revolution, but took new shape in a new age.[2] In particular, a new generation of officials gained advancement not by having undergone university education in the classics, but by qualifying professionally as accountants.

That new age brought economic uncertainty on a scale not seen for a generation. On 6 August 1914 James Allen, the Minister of Finance in Massey's Reform government, ended his Budget statement to Parliament by saying that 'the general prosperity which we have enjoyed for some years past still continues ... and I can see no unfavourable signs within the Dominion at the present time which are likely to mar the prospects for the immediate future. New markets for our produce have been developed, and our exports have touched a point which has never before been reached in the history of the country. The Dominion is also, I am happy to say, enjoying industrial peace, and there is at the present time no cloud upon the horizon which is likely to disturb the industrial and social conditions in the community. Should this happy state of affairs continue, I fully anticipate that the present year will prove to be one of unexampled prosperity.'[3]

This resounding conclusion resembled that to many other financial statements through the years of steadily rising export prices since 1896. It was in marked contrast to the statement presented by the Minister of Finance and Prime Minister, George Forbes, seventeen years later, on 30 July 1931. This statement was dominated by the 'economic storm' of which the Dominion had had to withstand the 'full force'. Forbes concluded by reminding his fellow parliamentarians — and the public — of 'our heavy loss of national income' and that 'our objective, therefore, must be such a readjustment of the relation between costs and prices as will restore the main industries of the Dominion to a healthy state.'[4]

The contrast could hardly have been more striking, but the heavier irony lies in the fact that the events which laid out the course from the optimism of 1914 to the pessimism of 1931 were unfolding even as Allen spoke. Just two days earlier, Britain — and thus its Empire, including New Zealand — had declared war on Germany. 'The Statement I have just read,' explained Allen, 'was in print before the Empire became involved in war ... every New-Zealander looks forward to the future with anxiety ... but with the calm assurance that everything which it is possible to do is being done'.[5] All of that 'calm assurance' would be needed in economic matters over the next two decades, as the economic stresses of war were followed by those of post-war depression from 1921 to 1923, and then, after a respite in the mid-1920s, by steadily deteriorating economic conditions. Difficult times alone do not explain the 'rise' of the Treasury, but they were an inescapable backdrop, fuelling pressures for the exercise of 'fiscal responsibility' that more prosperous times did not.

Accountants and accountancy

Accountancy is much more important to this part of the Treasury story than economics. In the early twentieth century, commentators looked to commerce for guidance as to how the government should manage its finances, and 'economic management' had not yet been thought of. Account-keeping practice can be identified in many societies. It seems very likely to have originated, paradoxically given its modern reputation as an arm of capital, out of the requirements of the state; 'some kind of organisation must have been necessary to collect and account for the public revenues' — 'a power of holding count and reckoning' which was to be 'copied by corporations and individuals for their own private affairs'.[6] But the next development arose from the requirements of commerce. Book-keeping was 'the outcome of continued efforts to meet the necessities of trade as they gradually developed'. Account books evolved incrementally until 'finally it was realized that the transactions of a business formed a homogenous whole which is capable of being marshalled in the framework of a system' through the system known as 'double-entry'.[7] The first practical treatise on double entry book-keeping, produced by Luca Paciolo in the great merchant republic of Venice in 1494, was soon in use all over Europe.[8]

It was one thing to have book-keeping, another to have a profession of accountants. The latter development was a product of the commercial and industrial 'explosion' of the nineteenth century, and in particular in the size and scale of enterprises. More specific factors also played a part. When accountants first incorporated, in Scotland in the 1850s, the key reason seems to have been the extent of their involvement in legal questions which in England were dealt with by lawyers.

The Edinburgh accountants sought a professional status which would be conferred by membership of the society, admission to which existing members would control. Similar developments can be observed in engineering and dentistry, to take two examples. Royal charters empowered each society to appoint a 'Committee of Examiners' to, among other things, administer 'the course of education to be pursued and the amount of general and professional acquirement to be exacted from entrants'.[9] From the granting of the charter came the name — 'chartered accountant'.

Commerce also drove professionalisation, and England followed only two decades behind Scotland. The Institute of Chartered Accountants in England

and Wales was formed in 1880. Its use of 'chartered' made that the standard designation throughout the English-speaking world.[10] The Institute lobbied unsuccessfully for a greater degree of restriction than its charter granted — for instance, to restrict the practice of public accountancy to chartered accountants.[11] In England, and elsewhere, such lobbying was related to a tendency for rival societies to be established; a Society of Accountants was incorporated in England in 1885.[12]

Professionalisation in the colonies followed that in England. The Incorporated Institute of Accountants of New Zealand was established in 1894 and from 1899 joined with institutes in the Australian colonies to examine candidate accountants. The New Zealand Accountants' and Auditors' Association was incorporated in 1898, and admitted a number of women to its ranks in its first years. By 1903 the Institute had 100 members and 43 associates and the Society 155 members, of whom 40 were in public practice.[13] New Zealand followed England in making the auditing of company accounts compulsory from 1900, and legislative recognition was given to the Society of Accountants in 1908. In 1911 agreement was reached with the University of New Zealand on the latter conducting examinations on behalf of the Society — following Scottish practice, in this instance. The first issue of a journal, *Accountancy and Commerce*, appeared in 1914.[14]

Accountancy in the public service to 1916

What effect did these developments have on the New Zealand public service? The Treasury had had an accountant since the 1850s, but the Controller and Auditor-General was the pre-eminent public accounting figure in the later colonial era. This was partly a tribute to FitzGerald's personal eminence, but also derived from the authority vested in the office at a time when there was no statutory regulation of commercial accounting or auditing. When the registration board for the Society of Accountants was established under the Act, it comprised the Controller and Auditor-General, the Commissioner of Taxes, the Government Insurance Commissioner, the Secretary to the Treasury, and the Solicitor-General. Its secretary, D. G. Clark, was a future Commissioner of Taxes. Thus the state-sponsored quality of professionalisation was clear from the start.

Conversely, it was not surprising that attention began to be paid to the quality of accounting work within the government. This reached into the public domain when in 1910 it was determined to replace a pre-audit with a post-audit of the public accounts. Under the existing system, vouchers were sent first to the Audit Department and, if passed, on to the Treasury for payment. Under post-audit, the voucher would go to the Treasury in the first instance. As Ward explained in introducing the legislation, it was a matter of 'catching up' with practice elsewhere in the world:

> In all the other more important countries the system of post-audit is in force and not the pre-audit system as we have it here ... [It] is the same one that is in operation in the case of all the commercial houses and public companies in this country.[15]

A former Controller and Auditor-General, J. K. Warburton, quoted from observations made by the chairman of the Audit Board in Britain when the system was introduced there in the 1860s: 'the duty of an auditor of public accounts should be to pass in review the acts of an accountant after those acts have been completed.' The effect of the change, he observed, would be that Treasury responsibility would now be 'real responsibility. They will be surchargeable with the loss of any money due to any fault in payment'.[16]

The reform was suggestive of a wider preoccupation with 'efficiency' that characterised the years before the Great War. Editorialising on cutbacks in the public service in 1909, the *New Zealand Times* opined that 'economy in administration is one of the cardinal principles of true liberalism, and Sir Joseph Ward is to be congratulated ... in insisting upon adherence to it'.[17] In their study of 'state socialism in New Zealand', Le Rossignol and Stewart discussed efficiency in the public service, arguing that 'on the side of cost, it appears as though expenditure, per unit of result, were higher than the corresponding expenditure in large private undertakings ... there is a tendency towards stagnation in both public and private service; but the financial measuring rod can more easily be applied to private employees'.[18] They also discussed the decision to charge a more commercial rate of interest on the capital invested in the railways (the rate had long been 3 per cent), and the merits of placing the network under commercial management:

> The commission that had charge of the railways from 1889 to the end of 1894 has frequently been accused of despotism and inefficiency, but in reality its administration compares very favourably with that which preceded it,

and the country gained little or nothing by reverting to direct parliamentary control.[19]

The Reform government which took office in 1912 was determined to apply 'reform' to the public service as well as to other spheres of national life. The impulse was perhaps more negative than positive. Reform politicians had for years inveighed against inefficiencies and favouritism in the public service, implicitly invoking the memory of Parliament securing its ascendancy over a corrupt and incompetent Crown — and every new government in the twentieth century would do the same. But the virtues of 'business methods', whether followed by 'businessmen' — now that 'capitalist' had become unpopular — or the government, were also part of the outlook of the day. As the public service became larger, it was more likely to attract this kind of attention. Alexander Herdman in particular, who was to become Attorney-General and Minister of Justice in the new government, was an enthusiast for reform, sure of the need for business methods, and convinced that 'unnecessary' taxation limited enterprise.[20]

W. D. Hunt, the managing director of the important and rapidly growing stock and station firm, Wright Stephenson Co. Ltd, who later became prominent in the Businessmen's Efficiency League, chaired the Royal Commission set up to investigate the public service in 1912 by the lame-duck Mackenzie ministry. The other members were Peter Barr, who was prominent in Dunedin business, the president of the New Zealand Society of Accountants, and a pioneer of professionalisation, and James Macintosh, also a stock, station and financial agent.[21]

The Public Service Act passed by the new Reform government on 7 November 1912 established an independent, non-political Public Service Commissioner responsible to Parliament.[22] Treasury was seen to be the key department for ensuring that the new 'businesslike methods' were introduced in respect of financial matters. But Treasury needed first to upgrade itself. In his first years the Public Service Commissioner issued substantial annual reports which took swipes at the Treasury and other departments as it sought to bring them up to scratch. Thus in his second report the Commissioner, Donald Robertson, referred to the fact that the Treasury was a department which 'in theory, at all events, holds a commanding position in its relations with other Departments.' And further, 'whatever commanding position the Treasury may have held in the past appears largely to have disappeared' because of its lack of modern methods.[23]

Peter Barr, first president of the New Zealand Society of Accountants, 1909–13. S. P. Andrew Collection, Alexander Turnbull Library, G-13489-¹/₁

The standard-bearer for this chapter, J. J. Esson, then the Assistant Accountant at the Treasury, was a member of a committee of expert accountants established by the Commissioner to report on account-keeping throughout the public service. Many of the recommendations in their report, which was published as an appendix to the first report of the Public Service Commissioner, implied or sought a supervisory role for the Treasury. The committee concluded that 'the present system of accounting for revenue collected is unnecessarily cumbersome, leading to duplication of work as between the Treasury and the Departments'. They recommended that 'the responsibility of keeping the net expenditure against each item should be cast upon Departments. The net votes should be kept in the Treasury, and the totals of items as kept by Departments should be balanced quarterly with the Treasury figures.' A series of forms in triplicate would obviate unnecessary manual recording of expenditure. The top copy would stay with the department and the second and third go to Treasury, with the third in due course being forwarded to the Audit Office. Each would be of a different colour. 'The form which the estimates take should be made more subject to the Treasury than at present', with 'all entries of like nature brought into line in accordance with a form prepared by the Treasury.'[24]

The benefits of using 'office' (presumably calculating) machines were frequently instanced, in contrast to the current situation where, 'although there are one or two machines in the Treasury they seem to be very little used.' A Remington-Wahl machine could be used to prepare debit and credit requisitions in the proposed Accounts Branch. It was 'absolutely necessary' that the proposed Ledger Branch have a 'millionaire' and a 'comptometer'. One of the purposes of bringing in machines was to allow carbon copies to replace 'press-copying', the current practice.[25]

Professionalism was also to shape the Treasury in other ways — 'it would be an advantage', noted the committee, 'if a small and up-to-date library of works on accountancy and finance were established in the Treasury. This would be useful to the senior officers for reference, and to the juniors for study.'[26] Indeed, 'the changes recommended in the work of the Treasury will increase the importance and responsibility of those entrusted with it. We cannot too strongly urge that in selecting the officers who are to carry on the work in future, those chosen should be the best available quite irrespective of present duties or claims which cannot be supported by sterling merit ... From the quality of the work which came under our notice and its general neatness and accuracy, we are of opinion that there will be no need to go outside the present Treasury staff to find the necessary officers.' And in order that Treasury regulations be followed, 'and a proper observance of any new system decided upon may be enforced, it is essential that a fully competent senior officer be appointed Treasury Inspector.'[27]

Esson was duly appointed Inspecting Accountant and provided with an assistant. This is the first recorded use of a title which in its later form of 'investigating officer' captured the key link between the Treasury and the financial activities of other departments. Treasury reported that 'proper co-operation between the account-keeping of other Departments and the Treasury is assured, and more efficient control by the Treasury is established ... Forms and books have been revised ... these reforms, combined with the use of modern machines, are gradually replacing old methods, and the reorganization of staff has already resulted in a reduction of eleven hands without any loss of efficiency.'[28]

But the war supervened. Two years later, the Commissioner found that 'there is so much doubt as to the functions of the Audit and Treasury Departments and the Department particularly concerned that no one of the three appears to regard itself as responsible for the method of account-keeping.'[29] 'There is still a tendency', it had observed in 1915, 'on the part of some officers to introduce obsolete and unwieldy methods of account-keeping. Such officers are, it need scarcely be said, those who have not passed the Accountants' Examination, and it will have to be considered whether the position of Accountant in any Department of the Public Service should not be reserved for officers who have so qualified. The opportunities offered by the University are now so extensive, and the proved value of accountants who have passed the University test is so marked, that it is time Government was receiving the advantages of such special education'.[30]

The impact of war, 1914–1920

If in this way war slowed things down, in other ways it accelerated change. Two years into the war nearly half of Treasury's staff of 55 had enlisted, and many more women were employed than before the war.[31] And war also had an impact on the department's work, because of both increased borrowing and increased taxation and spending. Circumstances in the London money market accelerated the 'repatriation' of the management of New Zealand's borrowing and debt:

> Owing ... to the enormous demand upon the finances of the Old Country, it was at once seen that the London market would be practically closed to New Zealand and it became necessary therefore to adopt the only possible alternative and to raise money within the Dominion for the purpose of the War. It must be remembered that this Country had hitherto been dependent upon the London Market for raising its Loans, consequently the floatation of large sums within New Zealand was in the nature of an experiment and there were those who doubted if the resources of the Country would prove sufficient to stand the strain of providing the large amounts of money that would be required.[32]

From 1916 New Zealand undertook to raise within its own territory all funds for war expenditure, apart from the cost of maintaining troops in the field. The change was dramatic. In 1917 around half a million pounds was raised in New Zealand — in 1918 £9.5 million, and in 1919 over £19 million. Debentures increased from £16 million in 1914 to nearly £58 million in 1919. Up to 30 June 1919 a total of £43,761,655 had been raised within the Dominion, while the amount advanced by the imperial government amounted to £26,340,243. The work of the Treasury markedly increased:

> I may say that the raising of large amounts of loan money in New Zealand has rendered the work of ... a large number of Treasury officers much more arduous. This applies especially to the Cashier's Branch.[33]

Paying for the war and acting like a post office. Patriotic investors could contact Treasury to invest in the 1918 Liberty Loan. Alexander Turnbull Library, Eph-D-WAR-WI-1918-01

As the department's subsequent account of its role put it:

> the conscription of wealth was the necessary complement to the conscription of men, and it may fairly be said that the success of the N.Z. Expeditionary Force was due very largely to these two principles of compulsion, the former of which was controlled by the Treasury...[34]

Percentage of government debt raised in each market and outstanding in 1908/09 and 1918/19:[35]		
Market	1908/09 %	1918/19 %
London	77.01	54.35
New Zealand	17.53	43.72
Australia	5.46	1.93
	100	100

The labour movement would have said that conscription of wealth was exactly what did *not* happen, and this was closer to the reality. Compulsion was only provided for in respect of one loan, and even in this instance was infrequently invoked — 'it may here be stated that it was to the credit of the very great majority of the public of this Country that … there were very few instances where attempts had been made to entirely shirk financial responsibility'.[36] Further, the Treasury's self-congratulatory statement overlooks the extent to which the Dominion persisted, in the first years of the war, in trying to raise public works loans in London, and had to be firmly dissuaded by the British authorities. In June 1915 the Secretary to the Treasury, G. F. C. Campbell, reckoned that money could be raised in New Zealand at 4.5 per cent if it were considered advisable, especially if an appeal were made to the patriotic feelings of the public:

> Such an appeal would of course be most effective if the money could be used for War purposes. On the other hand we can doubtless more easily obtain money in England for War purposes than for Works and it would therefore suit us better to utilize the money raised here for the latter purpose.[37]

The British were not thinking of civil expenditure at all. They wanted the Dominions to raise money at home for war purposes (perhaps with a guarantee from the British government) at the very least to finance the war expenditure of Dominions themselves, and beyond that to on-lend to the imperial government at the same rate.[38]

The New Zealand government having fallen into line with British wishes, there was plenty for the Treasury to do. For it was not just borrowing activity that had increased — so had taxation and spending. The former rose from £12.2 million in the year ended March 1914 to £26 million in the year ended March 1920, whilst expenditure rose from £11.8 million to £23.7 million over the same period. Only half of this increase was accounted for by rising prices, leaving a substantial real increase.[39] Increases in Treasury staff numbers and salaries during the war were explained in one memorandum as also resulting from 'additional duties and responsibilities placed on the Department … in connection with … Imperial pensions, and control of department revenue and expenditure'.[40]

There were tax increases in 1915, 1916 and 1917, and the number of taxpayers trebled from around 14,000 in 1914 to 43,000 in 1919. Receipts from income tax soared from half a million pounds in 1914 (less than from land tax) to £6.2 million in 1919 (four times land tax, which had approximately doubled). And

Dreaming of better times during the 1921–22 recession. The Free Lance *satirises Massey as 'William the Good Fairy'.* New Zealand Free Lance Collection, Alexander Turnbull Library, PUBL-0096-1921-12-21-001

while revenue increased, so did expenditure. In 1916 Treasury started submitting regular statements on the government's revenue and expenditure to the Minister of Finance.[41]

Nor did the war's end see a diminution in Treasury activity. Initially this was because of the post-war boom conditions. 'The cessation of the War', submitted one memorandum, 'has not brought Treasury much relief ... owing to the largely increasing activities of the Public Works Department and other Departments of State'.[42] But the collapse of many prices for primary produce during the 1920/21 season also entailed the Treasury in activity — in this case, expenditure control. At the end of 1920, when the consequential fiscal collapse had become unmistakeable, W. F. Massey circularised ministers calling for them to 'direct Heads of Departments under your control that Departmental expenditure must be reduced as much as possible.' The Prime Minister and Minister of Finance added that 'before committing the State to any abnormal expenditure', departmental heads should 'first be instructed to ascertain from the Treasury that the cash can be provided without undue cost'.[43] Massey carried out the work on the

Massey and Ward at the end of their unlikely political collaboration in the wartime National government, 1915–19.
H. J. Schmidt Collection, Alexander Turnbull Library, G-1542-¹/₁

public accounts at this time with the help of Esson, now returned from the war and Acting Secretary to the Treasury, and D. G. Clark of the Land and Income Tax Department. Both were present at an important meeting between the Prime Minister and a delegation of 'Business Men' in January. 'He did not suppose', said Massey at one point in the discussion about reducing taxation, 'that those present had the faintest idea of the time and attention which his two friends (Mr Clark and Colonel Esson) and himself had given to this subject during the last few months'.[44]

As the Auditor-General explained in reference to a wish not to increase his department's staff numbers, this was a time 'when Treasury is finding it necessary to curtail expenditure as much as possible'.[45] In examining revenue and expenditure trends in mid-1922, Esson explained that 'the Departments whose votes show an increase are in accordance with your wishes, being asked to explain the cause'.[46]

Finally, the war, and the diplomatic and financial activity that it drew New Zealand into, took not just Massey but also Ward, the wartime Minister of

Finance, away from the country for lengthy periods of time, both during and after the conflict. Inevitably, more responsibility devolved on the officials. And certainly an official like Campbell had no difficulty with this. His regular reports on revenue and expenditure have a confident, first-person tone about them. In 1921, Massey, by now Finance Minister, was away at an imperial conference:

> Prior to the Prime Minister's departure a Commission of experts in the Service was set up for the purpose of examining how services could be curtailed, and how savings could be effected. This Commission has been continuously at work, and its Report is in course of preparation and I hope will be ready by the time the Prime Minister returns.[47]

The war and the post-war depression might have led to the 'promotion' of the Treasury, but this didn't quite 'take'. The 1921–22 retrenchment, for instance, resembles the Cabinet-driven austerities of the 1880s and 1909 more than it does the later official-driven ones. The regular statements on revenue and expenditure become steadily more attenuated during the mid-1920s as prosperity returned. Bernard Ashwin's responsibilities as an inspector from 1925 read more like those of an auditor than those of the vote analysts of a later era. He was authorised to:

> Inspect and examine all official cash books of account, vouchers and other official documents, and to require from officers of the Public Service such information and explanation as may be necessary for the performance of his duties.[48]

Areas of government activity such as taxation and the setting up of primary producer boards that might have been expected to promote a larger role for Treasury did not do so. This was partly because Treasury continued to be at arm's length, as it had been in the 1890s, from the economy as distinct from public finance. In the case of taxation, the Minister of Finance took advice from the Land and Income Tax Department.[49] Nor does Budget preparation, usually a key building block of a system of expenditure control, appear to have entailed Treasury reporting on departmental estimates or spending proposals. When Downie Stewart wrote about the 1926 Budget it was in personal terms: 'I have been trying to cut down expenditure, especially in connection with public works … I got Cabinet to insist on a 15% reduction in capital expenditure in all the big departments.'[50] But in fact, the institutional and professional transformation of the Treasury and the government was about to reach the 'critical mass' that allowed the exercise of Treasury control. Before examining this change, it will be useful to explore the developments that enabled it to occur.

'Business methods' in government in the 1920s

As the fact of Massey meeting 'business men' suggests, Reform's preoccupation with business methods in government continued after the war. The National Efficiency Board, a wartime entity charged with ensuring the best possible war effort on the home front, and with improving business leadership, made recommendations on proper account-keeping in government departments.[51] The Board of Trade had two investigating accountants appointed to undertake its work after its powers were expanded in 1919.[52] Treasury thought about such matters too. Campbell recommended that one particular task

> should be undertaken by Accountants who are in the habit of analysing balance sheets of business concerns, and I strongly recommend that the Income Tax inspectors be instructed to undertake the work ... I should have recommended the Assistant Accountant to the Treasury, Mr Morgan, had it been possible for him to have put aside his Treasury duties.[53]

In fact the work was ultimately undertaken, after Massey himself had chased it up, by Barr and Hercus, a Dunedin firm of auditors.[54] In respect of the Treasury's own work, Campbell made a case to the Public Service Commissioner for:

> the appointment of two expert examiners ... promising officers possessed of more than average ability, who are qualifying for the accountancy examination ... the expenditure examiner should have a fair acquaintance with ordinary commercial practices, as well as a good general knowledge of market rates and different sources of supply.[55]

During the 1920s there were recurrent calls from most segments of the business community for a reduction in the direct tax burden, which had become much greater in the latter stages of the war, and for state enterprises — and government departments — to be run on business lines. With the maximum rate of company tax at 44 per cent and 70 per cent of income tax coming from companies, the political agitation of business against 'their own' government was unsurprising.

The 1922 Taxation Committee comprised not public servants or tax experts but business interest groups — chambers of commerce, farmers, sheep-owners, accountants, lawyers and manufacturers. It was chaired by Ernest W. Hunt, the representative of the Society of Accountants.[56] Its first recommendation was that 'to reduce taxation, it is imperative that further substantial economies in administration should take place, and that the public expenditure of the Dominion should be still further reduced.' And it also recommended that 'all Government and public-body trading undertakings should be subject to land and income taxes'.[57] Tax reductions over the following years mollified capital, and slowly customs revenue resumed its traditional prominence as a source of revenue. What John E. Martin has called the 'tax revolt of the better-off' had succeeded.[58]

Changes in the management and financing of state departments and trading agencies were a part of this wider picture. The House of Representatives Public Accounts Committee took a more active approach to its investigation of the estimates of spending for 1925/26:

> The procedure adopted in the consideration of the Estimates was to summon the head of each Department of State, together with the departmental accountant, before your Committee, and to examine such officers on the several items and votes of the classes of their Department or Departments.[59]

The Committee recorded that 'the Secretary to the Treasury (Mr R. E. Hayes) and the Assistant Secretary (Mr A. D. Park) were also requested to attend during the examination of the [departmental] officers and materially assisted the Committee in their investigations.'

When Gordon Coates became Prime Minister after Massey's death in May 1925, he announced that the great need of the country was 'less political activity and greater concentration on business-like management and organisation of the various State Departments.' Sceptical of the Reform Party's efforts nonetheless, disgruntled business and political interests formed the '1928 committee' to challenge the role and activities of state enterprises. But in the 1928 election campaign, Reform Party publicity compared the ministry to a board of directors reporting progress to shareholders.[60]

The economist J. B. Condliffe wrote in 1930 that 'within the last three or four years there has been a definite and sustained attempt to extend this principle of commercial operation to all the public service.'[61] Condliffe's use of the passive voice regrettably obscures the source of the 'attempt', but it seems likely

British Prime Minister David Lloyd George (right) congratulates William Massey (left) on his ten years as Prime Minister of New Zealand in 1922. Alexander Turnbull Library, F-44098-1/2

that Treasury played a role. The reinvigoration of Treasury control over public spending in the United Kingdom in the aftermath of war would have been reported in financial circles in the Dominion.[62] And in New Zealand a special committee of professional accountants had been set up in 1920/21 to assist the Treasury to introduce professional accounting systems.[63] The Public Service Commissioner praised the outcome:

> an effective spur to economy and efficiency will thus be afforded, particularly in the administration of those Departments where undertakings of a commercial or semi-commercial nature are carried on … It is hoped that by the end of the financial year the greater portion, if not the whole of Departments will be able to produce complete sets of commercial accounts for presentation in Parliament.[64]

In 1940 a commentator observed that 'by applying principles of commercial accounting to state activities New Zealand has moved further than most British countries to a rational system of public accounting.'[65] Prompted by the same impulses a Government Stores Board was established in 1922, initially under the chairmanship of the Minister of Public Works, but soon to fall within the Treasury's orbit.[66]

In respect of the Railways, Treasury Secretary J. J. Esson concluded in 1924 that 'in normal years freight and fares are not high enough to meet the working expenses and the fixed interest rate of $3^3/_4$% charged on the capital cost of the open lines.' He went on to comment on ways in which railways were subsidised, noting that

> interest charges on unopened lines, which in a Railway Company would immediately become a capital charge, are in the Government Railways at present borne by the Consolidated Fund until such time as the Railway takes over the line for traffic purposes. The loss in interest under this heading at $3^3/_4$% for the last ten years is estimated at £1.25m. If these charges were borne by the Government Railways as in commercial railways, together with superannuation liability, estimated to be at least £170,000 per annum, the present Railway Revenue, without allowing for any increased expenditure in other directions, would not earn anything like the interest margin required to meet public debt charges.[67]

In an attempt to get a grip on railways finances, railways revenue and expenditure was separated from the ordinary revenue accounts. In place of the revenue, the Consolidated Fund received a transfer from the Working Railway Account to cover interest on railways' capital liability.[68]

The Post and Telegraph Amendment Act 1927 provided for the separation of Post Office accounts from the Treasury as of the 1928/29 financial year:

> Provision has been made for the determination of capital liability at the commencement of the new arrangement, and of the rate of interest payable on the loans represented by the capital liability. The creation of depreciation and other reserves and the investment of surplus funds has been authorized.[69]

It seems likely that the Post Office rather than the Treasury initiated this shift.[70] But there were many other developments which suggest a more influential Treasury at work.[71] A new Public Revenues Act was passed in 1926, and in the same year the government retained Esson as its 'Financial Adviser'. This new position may have owed something to the British government's appointment of an 'economic adviser' to its Treasury immediately after the war. It may also have been a deliberate emulation of practice in the business world, in which accountants were

Public Works Department engines and workmen at a camp on the western side of Whangamomona burden, Taranaki. James McAllister Collection, Alexander Turnbull Library, G-10075-1/1

sometimes called on to report on particular questions of policy, or to investigate the position of affairs in distant parts of the world. In some cases an accountant has been retained, with a handsome salary, not as a member of the Board of Directors, but as a sort of financial adviser.[72]

It seems at least plausible that Esson himself, given the regard in which he was held, may have suggested the appointment. When he relinquished it he was followed by Hayes and then Park, both in their capacity as Secretary to the Treasury. The two roles were thereby amalgamated, and thus was initiated the practice whereby the Secretary or his nominee came to have a seat on the board of trading — and lending — departments such as Government Life Insurance and State Fire. Perhaps this was Esson's aim in the first place: 'A knowledge of what boards contemplate is necessary to prevent conflict with Treasury's own operations and is generally useful in promoting co-ordination in the financial operations of government institutions.'[73]

The new Reform Minister of Finance, William Downie Stewart — the same Stewart who had co-authored the study of 'state socialism' a decade and a half earlier — was sympathetic to a more prominent Treasury role. He wrote to Coates in October 1926 that

> Esson is very keen that Hayes should also go to England, so as to understand finance from that end ... also more particularly in view of the fact that we hope to try out the State Advances bonds on the London market next year ... I am inclined to think it would be advantageous for [Hayes] to study the finance of the High Commissioner's Office, and also the question of finance generally.[74]

In 1925 the Treasury increased its staff of inspectors in order to keep more closely in contact with the activities of government departments.[75] On Native Department issues, to take one example, Treasury expressed an opinion on the compensation settlements proposed by the Sim Commission on confiscated lands and the Native Land Commission of 1920/21, which looked at the South Island land purchases from Maori. It didn't like the idea of permanent appropriations, noting that 'it is true that such an arrangement has been made with the Arawa Trust Board and the Tuwharetoa Trust Board at Taupo, but these had not been reviewed by the Treasury before becoming law'.[76]

Treasury also took an interest in hospital board financing for the first time.[77] Equally, the establishment of a Local Government Loans Board in 1926 enhanced Treasury influence. Probably because local authorities were more likely than national ones to borrow within New Zealand, the existence of the Board allowed for 'expert investigation' of local authority loans. Financial expertise would be drawn from Treasury, and engineering advice from the Public Works Department. This joint representation neatly prefigured the post-Second World War position of Treasury and the Ministry of Works as 'control' departments in respect of capital projects.[78]

Place and people

We can track these changes more vividly as a story of a new place and new people. The shift from London to Wellington has already been discussed in connection with the borrowing activity during the Great War. It suffices here to underline that this shift had been likely to take place anyway. The New Zealand economy was growing and maturing, and both trends led to an increase in the amount of domestic saving — and in the government's access to this.[79]

The growing financial importance of Wellington was less visible. An early indication was the establishment of the head office of the Bank of New Zealand there in 1894 (from Auckland via a four-year sojourn in London). Its first Wellington-based board consisted of four prominent local capitalists: William Booth, W. W. Johnston, Martin Kennedy, and T. G. McCarthy.[80] In the first decades of the twentieth century Wellington boomed. The combination of new rail links, bush clearance and a pastoral economy producing meat, butter and cheese for export meant that its hinterland, which had long languished behind those of its South Island rivals, took off, and so did its port trade. Wellington overtook both Dunedin and Christchurch in population, and for a time grew faster than even Auckland. Moreover, all towns were growing faster than country areas from 1906, and from 1921 a majority of New Zealanders lived in towns and cities. Complementing these developments, Wellington became the financial capital of the Dominion. By 1920 there were more New Zealand head offices of banks and insurance companies in Wellington than in the established financial centres of Dunedin and Auckland combined.

During the 1920s these businesses constructed handsome new headquarters, mostly in the precinct around the intersections of Lambton Quay with Featherston Street and Customhouse Quay. Wellington became a 'capital' in more ways than one. From the point of view of Treasury officials, there was now a critical mass of accounting and financial expertise in Wellington that had not existed in 1910. Without this the institutional advances I have described may still have happened, but later, and in different fashion.

The story is biographical as well as geographical. The 1926 *Public Service List* included five Treasury officials who had passed the revealingly named 'accountancy professionals' examination, one of whom (B. C. Ashwin) also had an MCom. Another six officers had passed the preliminary accountancy examination. By 1932 Treasury had fifteen qualified accountants and another twenty who had passed the preliminary examination. They included G. C. Rodda, who was to be Secretary from 1935 to 1939, but also men like A. B. ('Johnny') Taylor, D. W. Barker, A. McGregor and D. F. Anderson, all in their late twenties, who would reach senior positions after the Second World War.[81] The numbers are significant because after its wartime expansion the Treasury's staffing did not increase much in the 1920s. Its establishment of 55 at the beginning of the war had become 78 in 1921/22 and 87 in both 1926 and 1931/32.

That women did not participate in this professionalisation was a regression from the status they had won before and during the Great War. From 1900 women had been appointed to the public service as clerical cadets after succeeding in the examinations, and by the war there were quite a number in the

Treasury, as in other departments. In 1914/15 there were five at quite senior levels, plus another four typists and 'machinists'.[82] In 1919, with the war over, women appealed against appointments of lower-graded male clerks to superior positions:

> The position is that we have in the Treasury three competent female clerks in the £300 class who have arrived at that stage when the question of their promotion to higher positions should be definitely settled for the reason that the continued agitation over the promotion of male clerks to positions to which the female clerks aspire, but for which they are not considered suitable, is detrimental to the efficiency of the Department. It is not considered advisable to place women in charge of mixed staff, because it is found that male clerks are disinclined to accept such a condition of employment ... As the promotion of the senior female clerks to higher positions in the Treasury is impracticable, I would suggest that those who are dissatisfied should be given the opportunity of transferring to some other Branch of the Service where opportunities of further advancement may exist.[83]

One of the appellants, Miss L. M. McIntosh, was to be informed that 'the selection of an officer to relieve the Cashier, does not hinge upon the question of sex or seniority, but is a matter of suitability and experience. Mr Clapson ... is in my opinion, the most suitable Officer at present available, and will take up the duties.'[84] Miss McIntosh was plainly not one to take such advice lying down. By September she had appealed again, along with Miss Ralston and Miss Schramm, against the appointments of two men as sectional clerks. Miss McIntosh may have been rewarded for her perseverance — her appeal alone was successful.[85]

Ten years later all three women were still employed by the department, albeit on lower salaries thanks to the wage cuts (imposed on all public servants) of 1921/22, 1931 and 1932. But McIntosh had been reduced to the same salary as her colleagues in the first of these cuts. And no new women recruits had joined the clerical class, because in 1921 the Public Service Commissioner had ruled that no female clerical cadets were to be appointed, a ruling that remained in force at the outbreak of the Second World War.[86]

While women lost status and opportunity, the most senior male officials of the department gained it, and none more so than the successive Secretaries to the Treasury. These men — Collins (1907–09), Poynton (1910–12), Campbell (1913–22), Esson (1922–25), Hayes (1925–30), and Park (1930–35) — were far more influential and socially eminent than their predecessors had been. This

Two Treasury clerks: Nell Batham (second from left) and Mona Dumbell (centre), who worked for the department during or immediately after the First World War, with two Khandallah friends.
Malcolm McKinnon

was not because of their origins. Esson's we already know. J. W. Poynton was a lawyer and magistrate before becoming Secretary to the Treasury — with his Invercargill antecedents, it is likely that he was a connection of Joseph Ward's.[87] While Campbell was related to John Logan Campbell, the 'father' of Auckland, he, like his successors, was colonial-born, and had started as a youth in the civil service, in his case in Vogel's time. Campbell engaged in financial work, initially for the Public Works Department and then in a variety of others. Park, from modest circumstances in North Otago, spent twenty years with Works (to 1919), then assisted the Public Service Commissioner for five years before joining Treasury in 1925. Such varied experience gained may well have been valuable as Treasury sought control over other departments' spending.

Both Campbell and Park made their reputations as sportsmen. Between 1875 and 1883 Campbell played in all Wellington's representative rugby matches, captaining the team in most of them. He was later president of both the Wellington and New Zealand rugby football unions, and of the Star Boating Club. Indeed

Public servants in the Government Buildings, c. 1920s. Tourist & Publicity Department Collection, Alexander Turnbull Library, G-21381-¹/₁

the *Dictionary of New Zealand Biography*'s file on him, under the heading, 'Why Important', reads 'Leading early New Zealand rugby player, sports administrator and' — a poor third — 'prominent civil servant'. Park was a provincial representative in both rugby and hockey.[88]

Treasury Secretaries were not recruited from or into an administrative elite, as had become the norm in England since the 1870s. Given their own progress through 'the ranks', it was likely all would have agreed with Robertson, the Public Service Commissioner, who in 1914 concluded that 'any arrangement under which promotion to a higher class would be debarred to officers already in a lower one would be difficult, if not impossible, to apply in a country such as New Zealand, where the Public Service and the education system have had to adapt themselves to altogether different conditions than exist in Great Britain, and where so many public servants do credit to themselves and the Service by university-work done by them after their appointment'.[89]

Campbell was the most formidable of this group. A *Free Lance* article at the time he was appointed Secretary in 1912 described him as 'one of the solid men who give distinction and security to New Zealand's Civil Service.' He was a

> strict disciplinarian of the amiable type. He loathes all muddle and slovenliness, instinctively … He has held all through his life that a man not physically capable and fit is little likely to do the State or any private employer really good service.[90]

With Campbell, the Treasury had a Secretary who was more than ready to 'take charge'. His relationship with Ward as Minister of Finance in the wartime coalition was cordial and businesslike. Campbell seemed 'to have been in and out of the Minister's office almost daily', a habit that would have been the more conspicuous with the shift of ministerial offices from Government Buildings to the new Parliament building on Molesworth Street.[91] Campbell did not pull his punches:

> The total amounts shown in the lists would indicate that instead of economizing during War time as I think the public has been led to expect, we are continuing our loan expenditure on much the same scale as before, and it is necessary for me … to place before you what I conceive to be the difficulties that are ahead of us if we commit ourselves to all this expenditure.[92]

In 1922 Campbell followed R. J. Collins, the only previous Treasury Secretary to become, not *Deputy* Controller and Auditor-General, as in colonial times, but Auditor-General. This was a mark of the increased standing of the office of Secretary. In fact, future Auditors-General would come from the next levels down in the Treasury, and the respective statuses of the two departments and their permanent heads were to be reversed during Campbell's own tenure as Auditor-General. The salaries of permanent heads and some of their senior colleagues were not gazetted between the wars, but whereas in 1926 the second-ranked Audit Department employee was paid considerably more than the number three in Treasury, in 1931 the gap had shrunk, and by 1941 Treasury's number four was paid the same as the number two at Audit.[93]

As we have observed, Esson achieved influence in other ways. He had a less abrasive personality, nor was he precluded, as Campbell was by being Auditor-General, from taking on other responsibilities after his retirement as Secretary. As well as financial adviser, he became chair of the Public Service Appeal Board, was the most active member of a royal commission on rural credits, and chaired

G. F. C. Campbell, Secretary to the Treasury from 1913 to 1922, plagued the department as Comptroller and Auditor-General (1922–37). Treasury

the Rural Intermediate Credit Board established in 1928 as a result of that royal commission to facilitate borrowing by the farming community, only to prove too cautious for farmers' liking.[94] He chaired the Railways Commission established in 1931, and was the most important member of the 1932 National Expenditure Commission which recommended massive cuts in public expenditure and institutional reforms. Dick Campbell, an economist who worked for Coates from 1931 to 1935, said it was commonly thought that the Treasury wouldn't have made the mistakes over short-term borrowing it did in 1931 if Esson had still been around.[95] But Esson and his successor, A. D. Park — whom Dick Campbell disliked — were close. When Esson made his will in November 1932, Park was one of his two executors.[96]

What are we to make of all this? G. F. C. Campbell, Esson and Park (it is difficult to be certain about Collins and Hayes) all attained a prominence in Wellington life, not just public service life, unmatched by their colonial predecessors. What's striking about them all is that, lacking altogether family wealth or wealth of their own, they are so securely at the centre of political and economic life by the time each becomes Secretary to the Treasury. This is evident in

> THIS IS THE LAST WILL AND TESTAMENT of me JAMES JACOB ESSON of the City of Wellington in the Dominion of New Zealand Retired Public Servant I HEREBY REVOKE all wills and testamentary dispositions heretofore made by me and declare this to be my last will and testament
>
> 1. I APPOINT Alexander Dallas Park Public Servant and Charles William Nielsen Solicitor both of the said City to be executors and trustees of and under this my will and I declare that in the interpretation of this my will the term "my trustees" shall where the context permits mean and include the trustees or trustee for the time being hereof whether original or substituted
>
> 2. It is my wish that my mortal remains be buried at Picton Marlborough in New Zealand

'The Last Will and Testament' – Esson's 1932 will names Park as an executor.
AAOM 6030, 1940, no. 888, Archives New Zealand

a host of ways. Both Campbell and Esson were active in the (military) volunteer movement, and both used the most senior rank they had reached — Colonel — in civilian life, as did Collins.[97] Campbell was an honorary ADC to the Governor in 1914, whilst Esson, as we have seen, succeeded Governor-General Bledisloe as Grand Master of the Freemasons in 1934. Park took holidays in Taupo, which was much favoured by well-off North Islanders for its trout fishing. All — including Hayes — were honoured with the CMG (the 'colonial' honour), in the case of at least Campbell and Park while they were Secretary.[98] In sum, their social promotion mirrors their readiness to expand the influence of their department, and it is difficult to distinguish cause and effect.

Controlling expenditure

Treasury's new power and influence became visible during a Budget crisis in 1927/28. Public works spending was the focus of concern because, funded as it was mostly by borrowing, it had the most serious fiscal consequences. That borrowing was still mostly done in London, and the debt-servicing burden could not be cut back, as tax-financed spending within New Zealand could be. In the later 1920s debt servicing accounted for around 40 per cent of all spending, exclusive of public works — as much as all annually voted expenditure.[99] For this story, the important point is not that debt servicing weighed so heavily — it had done so from the 1870s to the 1890s — but that Treasury, not just the ministers, was active in addressing the situation. The two secular changes — the shift in financial management from London to Wellington, and the shift in the balance of expertise and analysis from ministers to officials — had come together to produce this result.

Treasury knew that its minister would be receptive — in November 1927 he had written to Andre Siegfried, of *Democracy in New Zealand* fame, that he was 'trying hard to get borrowing curtailed'.[100] In December Hayes pointed out to Downie Stewart that the total of departmental estimates to be provided for out of loan expenditure for the 1928/29 year involved a far bigger sum than the government was envisaging borrowing. But 'to provide for any such sum from revenue would', Hayes added, 'obviate any possibility of a reduction in taxation' — a big political issue for the Reform Party.[101] He went on to stress that

> it will be seen that the items enumerated above absorb practically £1 m more than this year's London loan, so that this million, as well as other requirements, including State Advances, have to be provided for out of local borrowing. This year £350,000 of the amount for Highways is being provided by a temporary transfer from the Revenue Fund, which will have to be repaid out of loan money later. It is at this point that criticism that our annual borrowing is too heavy is not unwarranted, and tapering off policy should be steadily and firmly pursued until the annual loan requirements are more in keeping with the increase in population and wealth of the country.[102]

Cabinet directed the setting up of a committee including Hayes, representatives of all the works departments — Post and Telegraph, Public Works and Railways — and the indispensable Esson.[103] Was this Esson's idea? The first 'conference' was held at the Treasury on 16 January, and Treasury's interest in co-ordinating the activities of both lending and spending departments was soon in evidence. For instance, Hayes recommended that the Public Trust Office, on which Treasury now had representation, be informed that 'it is the intention of the Minister to require these subsidies to be re-invested during the next financial year in our inscribed stock.'[104]

Equally, Treasury attempted to crack the whip with the major loan spending departments, notably Public Works and Railways. This was no easy task. They had two of the biggest departmental budgets,[105] and were headed by strong personalities, both ministerial and official, none of whom had experience — or the desire to acquire any — of being pushed around by the Treasury. Coates, the Prime Minister, had held the Railways portfolio since 1923, and retained influence over Works even after shedding the ministerial responsibility in 1926. F. W. Furkert (1876–1949), had been Engineer in Chief and Under-Secretary of Public Works since 1920, as well as chair of the State Highway Board, in which capacities he had formed strong alliances with Coates.[106]

Treasury was driven, as it was to be in the 1980s, by what it saw as the inefficiencies of this public spending. As Hayes explained to Downie Stewart in April 1928 in respect of Railways, that department had responded to the possibility of reducing their loan requirement to £1.6 million by submitting a schedule for railway improvement authorisations totalling £2.273 million, £473,000 over their own original proposal.[107] The public servants debated among themselves; Furkert, whose department built the railways, was more visible than Railways itself. He suggested, perhaps tongue in cheek, that motor vehicles be heavily taxed as a way of diverting business to rail, to which Treasury predictably took exception on accounting practice grounds.[108]

The presentation of the Budget put an end to this phase of bargaining, which duly resumed for the following year. By then, however, there was a new government in office, and the environment for financial management was at a stroke made problematic. The Reform Party had been in government since 1912, either on its own, or, as during the war, in a coalition with the Liberals. It was a conservative party, and some — but not all — of its fiscal instincts had accorded with those of financial interests and of the Treasury. By 1928 it had fallen out of favour with many of its business supporters. The United Party, which gained fewer votes than Reform, was able to form a minority government with Labour Party support on crucial votes. It was led by the former Liberal Prime Minister and Finance Minister, Joseph Ward, who was now 72 years old, and its electoral success may have owed much to his seemingly mistaken claim that the party would borrow £70 million to promote public works and development. This was ironic, given that Reform had expected Ward to attack it for excessive borrowing, as he had in 1927.[109] Ward's claim was rapidly clarified as a ten-year programme to borrow approximately £7 million each year, but the larger figure had caught the imagination of the voting public. The files give no indication of official questioning of this programme, but given the work done on loan expenditure through 1927–28 the Treasury can hardly have been acquiescent.

The government was not only committed to what Treasury undoubtedly saw as fiscally unwise expenditure, it was also inexperienced. United was a 'made-up' party that hadn't existed as recently as 1925, when the successor party to the Liberals — the Nationalists — had made little electoral headway. The new party governed on the strength of Ward's reputation. Only two of its other ministers — Wilford and Ngata — had held office before. Four had never sat in Parliament.[110] Ward naturally assumed the finance portfolio as well as the prime ministership. But finance proved to be the area of greatest difficulty. On 16 December, six days after taking office, Ward announced that the outgoing government had sought to borrow in London against the assurance that New Zealand would borrow relatively little in the following year. Even worse, £24 million of loans would have to be refinanced at the end of 1929. Hayes could not believe that Ward could have been so ignorant of the state of the London money market, and it does seem implausible. But certainly he was no longer in ignorance. The £5 million loan envisaged by Downie Stewart was increased to £7 million, but hopes of a large infusion of capital from overseas were dashed.[111]

The rapid negotiation of the loan early in 1929 took some of the pressure off interdepartmental relations at that time, but the long-term outlook remained bleak.[112] As railway patrons continued to buy cars and money was invested in non-revenue-producing improvements such as locomotive workshops and line deviations, it seemed clear that losses would have to be met from taxation — perhaps through Furkert's scheme for a petrol tax.[113] For interest purposes the capital value of the railways had been written down by £8 million in 1929. But even with that — the equivalent of a £345,000 subsidy — more than £1 million of running costs for 1930/31 would have to come from the Consolidated Fund:

> The development of motor transport has in effect destroyed a large part of the capital invested in the railways. The obvious thing would be to write the capital down to its true earning power, but as it now consists wholly of borrowed money this cannot be done without paying off an equivalent amount of Public Debt.[114]

The lending side of the ledger was also unhealthy. State Advances, a department set up in the 1890s to assist farm and later house buyers, had lent so much money during 1928 that a further £5 million might have to be borrowed overseas to assure its financial soundness. Ward took action to reduce its lending.[115]

Ward's ailing government, and advisers 1930. Front row, left to right: Harry Atmore, George Forbes, Ward, Sir Apirana Ngata and William Veitch. Second row, left to right: Arthur Stallworthy, John Cobbe, Philip de la Perrelle, William Taverner and Ethelbert Alfred Ransom. Back row, left to right: Vincent Ward, F. Thompson, and C. A. Jeffrey. Alexander Turnbull Library, F-50300-$^1/_2$

Because of the loans maturing at the end of 1929, Treasury in late 1927 had to cajole 'lending' departments' into making funds available to meet the government's requirements. The Native Trustee duly surrendered £50,000 of London investments.[116]

During 1929 Ward had been unwell, and the government lived 'from day to day, dependent on the flickering state of the Prime Minister's energy'. He suffered a stroke in October, and spent most of the first months of 1930 convalescing at Rotorua, from where he resigned in May. George Forbes' succession as Prime and Finance Minister did not reinvigorate the government, which had also been weakened by other resignations and the loss of seats in by-elections.[117] And the economic outlook continued to worsen, both at home and overseas.

Treasury, the Auditor-General and Otto Niemeyer

The political uncertainty, which was to last into 1931, was both threat and opportunity for the Treasury. Without leadership from the Minister of Finance, Treasury was stymied in its efforts to control expenditure. But the other departments were also weaker than they had been when they had had the weight of the Prime Minister — Coates — behind them. The discussions on the estimates in the first half of 1930 saw Treasury in unprecedented conflict with both Furkert and Lands and Survey. When W. A. Veitch became Minister of Railways in the reconstructed government, quarrels also erupted with that department.[118] The advisability of spending to provide work for the unemployed now became the contested terrain. In June 1930 Forbes accepted Park's argument for restraint, but this did not stop the ministers of Public Works and Railways differing over how what money there was should be allocated, with Treasury almost a 'piggy in the middle'.[119]

Treasury was also less able to influence lending departments. Depressed trading conditions swallowed up domestic savings. The Treasury hoped to obtain £8 million from the Post Office and through issues to the public. But only £2.5 million was obtained from the public during the first four months of the 1930/31 financial year — and nothing from the Post Office Savings Bank, from which massive withdrawals had been made.[120] Treasury did not want to allocate a further £500,000 to unemployment relief because it was not clear where the money could be borrowed from. On the eve of going overseas in August, Forbes decided to allocate this sum from the State Advances loan programme.[121] In September, £120,000 of the half million was allocated to Railways to manufacture rolling stock — a victory for Veitch.[122]

But if political uncertainty created difficulties for Treasury, it did provide opportunities for administrative changes which might not have got through a more effective Cabinet. We can see this particularly in the pressure the department applied to curtail the influence of the Auditor-General, to formalise the principle of Treasury scrutiny of all public spending, and to promote the establishment of a central bank. The first two of these issues are discussed below, the third in chapter 3.

The contest with the Audit Office was a contest between past and future, with former Treasury Secretary Campbell, now Auditor-General, the standard-bearer of the past, his successors the advocates of a new order. In the nineteenth century the Comptroller and Auditor-General had enjoyed higher status than the Secretary to the Treasury because of the personalities involved, the importance placed on parliamentary control of the government's finances, and practices distinct to the New Zealand public accounts, such as the reliance on pre- rather than post-audit. The first two factors remained.

Campbell was irascible, a perfectionist, and jealous of the prerogatives and powers of his office. What had been a vital part of the machinery of financial management became, under his stewardship, a parody of itself. In 1920 the public accounts occupied about 130 pages in the *Appendix to the Journals of the House of Representatives*; in 1925, more than 400. In the latter year the Minister of Finance was moved to allude publicly to the fact that the powers of the Controller and Auditor-General 'call for the exercise of judgement and tact ... In the report this year ... the meaning taken from the various subjects referred to ... appears to be out of due proportion to the actual facts'.[123] Campbell exasperated the Treasury and the Law Drafting Office with a series of detailed criticisms of the methods by which the public accounts were kept, raising problems which only amending legislation could fix. Christie of the Law Drafting Office commented to Hayes that

> legislation of a similar kind is not to my knowledge to be found elsewhere in the English-speaking world, and the briefest and most general directions with respect to the keeping of accounts are to be found everywhere except in New Zealand ... under the present system the Statute-book may well be mistaken for a text-book on the art of book-keeping.[124]

Such strictures were unlikely to drive Campbell — sportsman, military man and disciplinarian — off this bureaucratic playing field. He was more than a match for efforts by Treasury and the Law Drafting Office to amend the Finance Act to put an end to his activities, invoking in particular the sacred phrase, 'parliamentary control'. Even Hayes' argument that 'far greater powers than are contained in these proposals are conferred upon the British Treasury constitutionally without any express legislative provisions', and his citing of the 'standard authority' that 'the primary object of Treasury ... is to complete and secure the control of Parliament over the public expenditure, and to maintain financial order throughout the service', could not outweigh Campbell's greater status and influence, and after the latter talked directly to Downie Stewart the proposed changes were not proceeded with.[125]

With a new government in office in 1929, Treasury had another try. Clauses in that year's Finance Act provided for revoking certain borrowing authorities; making expenditure of certain loan moneys subject to appropriation by Parliament; and making the Financial Adviser a member of boards that invested public money. Above all, clause 14 aimed to 'save the time of the House and all concerned by obviating the present necessity for obtaining year after year legislative authority in detail on matters of accounts and internal financial administration.' This clause got as far as Parliament. Two senior Treasury officers, Park and B. C. Ashwin, appeared before the Legislative Council's Statutes Revision Committee to emphasise the new role of accountancy:

> in Treasury opinion it is neither economical nor practicable to carry on professional accountancy and give effect to the technique of same by having to prescribe for all entries by legislation ... [Further] as Parliament had by statute recognised professional accountancy and had also provided for recognition ... of those qualified to handle the intricacies of the profession, there should be no further need on behalf of parliament itself to require every detailed entry or adjustment in its own accounts to be founded specifically on some section of an Act ... [Further] what would be the position if the whole mercantile and commercial fabric of the community were to have a restriction placed upon it that all its accounting transactions were to first have a basis of specific law before any action could be taken.[126]

But this initiative was shot down by James Allen, the former Minister of Finance, and Robert Stout, the former Premier and Chief Justice, almost certainly at Campbell's instigation — Campbell and Allen having been respectively Secretary and Minister from 1912 to 1915, and again in 1919–20.[127]

A *third* attempt was made a year later, when a senior Bank of England official, Sir Otto Niemeyer, visited Australia to advise the government on financial matters. At Park's instigation, the New Zealand government invited Niemeyer to New Zealand.[128] The primary purpose of the invitation was to seek Niemeyer's advice on the banking system, and in particular on the merits of establishing a central bank on the lines of the Bank of England. Ransom, who was acting Prime Minister and Minister of Finance in Forbes's absence, wrote to Niemeyer to also seek advice on the 'powers of Treasury'. Ransom referred to the failed clause 14, 'which was drafted for the Finance Bill last session, whereby it was proposed to authorise Treasury to determine certain questions that may arise in the method of accounting and internal book-keeping of the public finances ...

the changes involved the introduction of professional accounting systems, but in order to give full effect to them certain difficulties have arisen from the absence in many instances of statute law.'[129]

The rest of the letter was very like the memoranda Treasury had written on the subject the previous year, and also demonstrated the extent to which Treasury's frustration with the spending departments was a factor in its campaign:

> There is nothing definite in our Act giving Treasury such authority as is contained in Section 27 of the Imperial Exchequer and Audit Act, 1866. This enactment means that the authority of the Treasury must be given for all expenditure, and expenditure can only be passed by the Audit Office which has received the sanction of the Treasury. The existence of so many capital accounts funded by loan has enabled Departments to incur heavy expenditure on avowedly capital objects, with Cabinet approval certainly, but without any prior examination or investigation by the Treasury. It is felt that if some such procedure were established in New Zealand departments would be more concerned about the financial prospects of any capital undertaking than they appear to be at present. During the last few years it has been necessary to write off large sums that have been spent on drainage and other land operations, where heavy losses have been experienced. A few years ago legislation was obtained preventing any amounts being written off without Treasury or Audit sanction, but it appears desirable that the sanction of the Treasury should be obtained before the undertakings are entered into, instead of getting Treasury sanction to clearing up the trouble after it has taken place.[130]

Niemeyer found, like others before him, that Campbell was not to be easily persuaded, but he wisely did not get into a fight with him — or at least not one that Campbell could readily detect. After Campbell and Niemeyer met, Campbell produced ten pages of detailed criticisms of the proposed amendment. Niemeyer replied with a polite $1\frac{1}{2}$-page letter, thanking Campbell for sending him 'so full a statement of your views', conceding that the proposed clause was probably unnecessary, but resolute on the 'fundamental fact' that 'within the general principles laid down by Parliament … the responsibility for specific financial direction must rest with the Treasury'.[131]

That Niemeyer, while formally invited by the government, was collaborating with the Treasury is evident from the tone of some of the correspondence. He copied to Park a letter he sent to Ransom with the annotation, 'Here is a copy of a letter which you do not know that I have sent and will be surprised to hear of when your Minister mentions it.'¹³² And when Niemeyer wrote to Downie Stewart, he explained that he hoped 'my letter to Mr Ransom may have done no harm and some good ... the subjects dealt with ... were entirely outside the particular mission on which the New Zealand Government asked me to come and I therefore wrote it as a private letter ... He subsequently asked me if he might publish it.'¹³³

When Ransom tabled Niemeyer's letter in Parliament on 20 October, he explained that a number of small separate accounts would be abolished in accordance with Niemeyer's recommendations, but that his main recommendations would be held over until the following year.¹³⁴ But while this smacked of prevarication, Niemeyer's intervention had shifted the locus of financial 'control' in government from the Audit Office to Treasury and further established the status of accountancy, to which mast Treasury had nailed its colours:

> as Parliament has by Statute recognised the profession of accountancy, there should be no further need on behalf of Parliament itself to require every detailed entry or adjustment of its own accounts to be founded specifically on some section of an Act.¹³⁵

Park was also able to enlist Niemeyer's help in a related area — Treasury's control over expenditure. On two separate occasions during the 1930 Budget round, Treasury had got the Prime Minister to require departments to clear new spending proposals with the Minister or, on the latter occasion, with Treasury itself.¹³⁶ Did Treasury fear this requirement would be forgotten, or regarded as applying only for that year? Niemeyer obligingly wrote that

> At home, after the war, in order to accentuate the financial authority of the Treasury, we [ruled] that the financial resolution which is required before the Committee stage of any Bill imposing an extra charge on public funds should be put on the Parliamentary order paper in the name of the Treasury though actually defended in the House by the Department concerned. The effect of this regulation was to secure that no Bill involving expenditure could proceed in the House without full consultation previously with the Treasury ... the procedure ... was of real use in strengthening the always difficult question of Treasury control over expenditure proposals by Departments.¹³⁷

A Cabinet minute of 13 October 1930 duly reiterated that 'no new proposals are to be submitted for Ministerial or Cabinet consideration without being accompanied by a report thereon by the Treasury.'[138] This requirement has remained at the heart of Treasury's role at the centre of government — even though a later generation of Treasury officials thought it dated to the 1970s.[139]

These developments in 1930 marked the biggest single advance in the status and influence of Treasury in the two decades under review here. But although this advance can be seen in its specifics to reflect the demanding financial circumstances of 1930, it was also grounded in long-term changes, in particular the professionalisation of financial management and the shift in its locus from London to Wellington. Without these changes, the official reaction to the expenditure and fiscal crises would have followed a very different trajectory. Mackay's statement in 1938 that 'finance is the principal co-ordinating factor in a well-regulated system of public administration, and it follows that the Treasury, under the direction of the Minister of Finance, is the Department most qualified to undertake this responsibility',[140] identified a 'this, therefore that' which only made sense given those developments in the 1910s and 1920s.[141]

Chapter 3

Treasury during the Great Depression, 1930–1935

Introduction

Writing some weeks later of the political events in January 1933 which led to his resignation from the United–Reform coalition government formed in September 1931, the Minister of Finance, William Downie Stewart, recalled that on the morning of the 11th,

> we met the Economists. After some vague talk I got irritated and told Forbes and Cabinet we were making no headway and that the worst crime a Govt could be guilty of was vacillation — that we had to meet the House in a fortnight and it would be disastrous if we had no clear plan ready. I suggested we thank the Economists for their report and settle to work. In about an hour they had gone and we sat round the Cabinet Table. Forbes said 'What will we do? What do you suggest Downie?' I was very irritable and said 'Well do something — I am tired of this delay. I have felt for 12 months that I am regarded as the Black Sheep of the Cabinet who is blocking everything the farmers want and it would be simpler for everyone if Cabinet decided on its plan and those who don't agree can get out.' Coates said in a very curt way, 'You are not the black sheep — you are not so important as you think you are' … I said 'Well let us call me a black lamb.' Coates — 'No you are not even that.'[1]

This new low in high politics pitted two exact contemporaries and political allies, but completely contrasting individuals, against each other. Coates, from pioneering and not very well-off Northland farming stock, was tall, handsome, and action-oriented in both his public and private life — rumours about his extra-marital affairs were never put to rest. Stewart, the scion of a Dunedin Presbyterian family which had accumulated both commercial and landed wealth, was a lawyer and a reflective intellectual. He never married, and from the mid-1920s was wheelchair-bound with rheumatism.

The black lamb and the lion? Downie Stewart (seated, left) and Gordon Coates (standing, right), 1932. They are accompanied by Stanley Bruce (seated, right), a former Prime Minister of Australia who led the Australian delegation to the Ottawa Conference, and Henry S. Gullett, the Australian Minister of Customs (standing, left). New Zealand Free Lance Collection, Alexander Turnbull Library, C-20908-¹/₂

That contrast dramatises their conflict over the shape of the political economy. Four days later Cabinet ordered the banks to raise the exchange rate of the New Zealand pound against the British pound, and Stewart did resign. The devaluation, as we would now call it, increased the income in New Zealand pounds of anyone who earned money in England — the exporters of wool, frozen meat and dairy produce, the farmers whose incomes had been hard hit by the catastrophic fall in commodity prices since 1929. But for Stewart it was a short-term response to a long-term problem — the fall in farming profitability — and one, moreover, that would have disastrous side effects. Figures the Treasury supplied Stewart suggested that the deficit in the public accounts, already expected to be £6 million, would probably increase to £9 million.[2] The devaluation might also threaten the establishment of a New Zealand central bank, an institution that would replicate in monetary matters Treasury's fiscal control over the spending of other government departments, and it was a breach of economic orthodoxy that could only open the way to other, even more questionable policies.

Treasury officials shared Stewart's apprehension. Their view of public finance was under siege. Were the Treasury's achievements in the 1920s, recounted in the last chapter, about to be taken from it? That threat dominates the story of the Treasury during the Great Depression. It makes it impracticable for this chapter to focus simply on the further development of financial management and the related story of the establishment of a central bank. These stories are important, but they cannot be separated from the broader story of the Depression, which was at its most intense between 1931 and 1933. And as the reference to 'economists' suggests, Treasury was drawn into a wider sphere of policy — and politics — than arose from its focus on management of the public accounts.

In focusing on the Treasury, those institutions with which it had dealings, and the challenges it faced, it may seem that the terrible aspects of the Depression — the unemployment, the ruined businesses, farms and lives — become invisible. To take just one example, the National Expenditure Commission conducted its investigations from February to May 1932. In April and May there was rioting by unemployed people and others in the streets of Auckland, Wellington and Dunedin. Not even a hint of this appears in the documents, and that is also true for all the other historical moments in which the Treasury was not directly involved. This does not prove that Treasury officials and those who worked with them, such as the businessmen on the National Expenditure Commission, were indifferent to such developments. But they did believe that balancing the Budget was a necessary prelude to national recovery. The Economists' Committee, which met for two weeks in February 1932 and recommended a change in the exchange rate, in that respect had a different view of what kind of adjustment was required — but even it recommended massive expenditure cuts.

In the aftermath of the Depression, and in particular against the backdrop of the recovery that took place under the Labour government, it became natural to call the Coalition government of 1931 to 1935 unimaginative and callous. Looking back with our own longer perspective, it is illuminating to reflect on how, in many circumstances, but particularly in the face of a crisis, individuals can find it enormously difficult to break free of long-held preconceptions — indeed, the very fact of crisis may make this harder. Take one snapshot. In 1929/30, exports had fallen by £10 million compared with 1928/29 — that is, by about 20 per cent. Who would have then judged that in the following twelve months they

New Zealand remained highly dependent on a few agricultural products. These watersiders are loading meat from the Longburn freezing works at a Wellington wharf in the 1930s. Making New Zealand Collection, Alexander Turnbull Library, F-1541-¹/₂-MNZ

would fall by *another* £10 million? In two years, income from exports nearly halved — in a country with a small population and high per capita overseas trade. Imports followed suit as banks, with vanishing external balances, restricted funds — from £48 million in 1928/29 (a boom figure which boosted the government's accounts) down to a more normal £44 million in 1929/30, followed by a collapse to £26.5 million in 1930/31.[3] Servicing debt, particularly overseas debt — so easily accumulated, so hard to reduce — accounted for over 40 per cent of government expenditure. Because interest payments on debt *had* to be met, all other government expenditure was acutely vulnerable.[4]

To such situations individuals react according to their temperament, which may itself be a compound of 'accidental' elements such as age, background, and associations. Some responded by hewing to orthodoxies, while others found 'heresies' more congenial. It is perhaps natural that a generational split is discernible: men (this story is mostly about men) in their fifties, whose formative experiences had taken place before the Great War, found orthodoxy a support, whilst those in their twenties and thirties did not.

We will first examine the further pursuit of 'Treasury control' and the related campaign for a central bank. Then we will investigate the campaign to raise ('inflate', in Treasury language) the exchange rate, which, in the eyes of Treasury and its minister, threatened the 'economic constitution'. We will conclude this chapter by assessing the extent to which Treasury's objectives survived the devaluation.

Controlling spending, 1930 to 1932

Treasury may have attained the authority to exercise fiscal *control* by the end of 1930, but it did so at a time when fiscal *balance* was a receding mirage. In 1929/30 the government's accounts, which had gone into deficit in 1928/29, recorded a £150,000 surplus. Arising partly from increases in revenue, this was arguably a fatal improvement, because it tempted the government to assume that 'the worst was over'. At the end of 1930 it became evident that money was simply 'disappearing'. An initial rise in imports despite falling exports (for instance, wool receipts fell by 32 per cent in 1929/30) led to an unfavourable external balance, adjustment by banks of the selling price of sterling, and then a fall in customs revenue (because of a belated fall in imports) in 1930/31. In the last months of 1930, the losses on the Railways Account, unemployment relief and increased debt charges accumulated to produce a prospective deficit of £3 million.[5] It seems very likely that the 'bad blood' between Treasury and Veitch, the Minister of Railways, inclined the former to emphasise the contribution of railways finances to the fiscal debacle.[6] Niemeyer too had written extensively to Acting Prime Minister Ransom about railways finances, almost certainly at Park's suggestion.[7] Park informed a Cabinet minister that he was 'arranging for a special consultation by a Treasury official with the Chief Accountant of the Railways with a view to ascertaining, if possible, to what extent the amount of interest to be paid by the Working Railways Account to the Consolidated Fund will fall short, if at all, of the Budget figure, viz £1.38m.'[8]

When it became evident that this payment would be less than £1 million, Park asked Ransom to call a crisis meeting of ministers and permanent heads to organise spending cuts. This was probably the first time that the Secretary to the Treasury had 'taken charge' in such a fashion. The railways issue was 'so critical from the point of view of finance', Ransom duly wrote to Veitch, 'that I am cabling today a précis of the position to the Rt Hon the Prime Minister'.[9]

In the aftermath of the conference of ministers and heads of departments, it was Treasury which co-ordinated the departmental submissions on proposed savings and 'recommended' that Cabinet authorise the proposals.[10] This action was preparatory to the summoning of an Economy Committee. Park was again active, pointing out to Ransom that to do its work the committee would need some figures — which Treasury would supply, for the most part.[11] The Committee itself comprised just three ministers (Ngata in the chair, Veitch and Masters), Park, and Verschaffelt, the Public Service Commissioner.[12] When Park took a short holiday over Christmas, he wrote to Ngata explaining — not reporting — just what Treasury had done and had still to do.[13] In 1921, businessmen had played key roles in the expenditure control process. The more purely political character of the 1930/31 exercise may suggest that business opinion did not want to become involved with the United government, preferring that it combine with the Reform Party to form a stronger government. In any case, Treasury's status was enhanced.

The Economy Committee first met on 6 January. Forbes, who had recently returned from a five-month trip to attend the Imperial Conference in London, announced its decisions — 'the Cuts', as they were simply known — in the middle of February, just ten days after an earthquake had devastated Hawke's Bay and killed 256 people.[14] Debt repayments, which accounted for nearly half of all expenditure, could not be cut because this would breach the 'sanctity of contract' — or, more potently, the ability to borrow in the future.[15] The determination of New South Wales' Labor Premier, Jack Lang, to suspend all overseas debt repayment was abhorred. The burden of expenditure cuts thus had to fall on the remaining 60 per cent of expenditure. Public service wages were cut by 10 per cent, the education vote was cut, and increased taxation was canvassed.[16] Another committee was to be set up to look for further cuts in education, which absorbed nearly half of *annually* approved spending.[17] Despite these measures, the problem had become evident so late in the financial year that it was not possible to avoid a deficit of approximately £1.5 million — around 7.5 per cent of total expenditure.[18] On the political front, the cuts caused the Labour Party to withdraw its support from the United government, which became a minority 'lame duck' administration.[19]

Forbes's announcement did not deal with public works, but on 11 March Treasury recommended curtailing loan expenditure by about £4 million. The biggest single saving would come from the cessation of work on rail construction.

Wage reductions would affect the figures across the board, and in respect of roads, 'probably about 1250 men will have to be put off'.[20] The committee also decided that the Railways would come under a non-political board from the middle of the year. This course followed Niemeyer's advice to Ransom the previous September, and was favoured by Treasury. The correspondence in May–June 1931 of a frustrated Forbes (wearing his Minister of Finance hat) with Veitch bears a strong Treasury imprint.[21] And the indispensable J. J. Esson was appointed to chair the new board.[22] Almost certainly, too, it was Treasury which proposed that the Post Office should contribute its profits to the Consolidated Fund.[23]

Probably Park and possibly Esson played a more significant role in these decisions. In these circumstances political weakness enhanced the role of Treasury, but political paralysis would limit it. In Canada, a powerful and able Prime Minister and Minister of Finance, R. B. Bennett, who took office in July 1930, drove through major changes in expenditure control on the advice and with the assistance of senior departmental officials.[24] Forbes also held both portfolios, but he lacked ability[25] and his government was tottering. More economies were announced in the Budget which he presented at the end of July 1931. But less than three weeks later Forbes sent for Downie Stewart, the last Reform Minister of Finance, and told him that the position of the United government was desperate; it would have to call an election unless Reform supported it. Stewart's diary for that winter records a number of meetings with Park and B. C. Ashwin. Fifty years later, such meetings between officials and opposition politicians would be considered inappropriate, unless they were sanctioned by the government (see chapter 8). It is difficult to discern what the situation was in 1931 — whether Forbes knew of the meetings, and if so whether he countenanced them. But in view of his wish to seek a coalition with Reform, it's at least possible he instigated or at least acquiesced in them.[26] Within a week Coates, the Reform leader, moved in Parliament that

> in the opinion of this House, the serious economic and financial position of this Dominion necessitates urgent and immediate action to cope with the fall in national income as revealed by the latest figures and the consequences arising therefrom; that, with this object in view, it be a recommendation to the Government that representatives of the political parties should be called together in order to decide what remedial steps should be taken to adjust the national expenditure and to provide for equality of sacrifice and a proper distribution of the burden; that, in arriving at its conclusions, this Committee should obtain the best expert advice and assistance from financiers and others.[27]

The motion passed, and a committee was duly established consisting of Forbes, Ngata, Ransom (government); Coates, Downie Stewart and Jones (Reform), and Holland, Savage and McCombs (Labour). It met on 24 August and continued sitting until 15 September, when its deliberations were suddenly ended by Forbes announcing that it must agree to the formation of a national government and the postponement of the forthcoming election. There is no evidence that Treasury played a major role in the hearings of the Special Economy Committee — the parliamentary arena had become central, and until the locus of power there had been clarified, Treasury was impotent. Park did give evidence, but it seems that Treasury's only follow-up activity was to ask all 'lending' departments about the state of their investments — presumably anticipating a possible call on them to bail out the government's finances.[28]

British events would have played a part in shaping the political outcome in New Zealand. The May Report on the British public accounts, published on 31 July, foreshadowed a prospective Budget deficit of £120 million. After the Labour government resigned on 24 August, Prime Minister Ramsay Macdonald accepted a commission to form a 'National' — all-party — government.[29] In New Zealand, a United–Reform coalition government was formed on 22 September, and Downie Stewart became Minister of Finance for the second time. Given his association with 'sound finance', his familiarity with the portfolio, and the fact that he had a robust majority in Parliament behind him, Park and the other Treasury officials must have felt that the public finances were now in much more secure hands, even before the new government secured a mandate from the electorate. A note from Park dated 24 September enclosed 'confidential notes setting out various points'. Most of these were proposals to increase taxation and reduce expenditure in the face of falling revenue from the principal sources, notably Customs, which only five months into the financial year was already down £640,000. But for the first time the Treasury also provided economic advice. Under the heading 'other matters', Park suggested that the courts be enabled to adjust mortgage interest rates, and that the arbitration and conciliation wage-fixing system be heavily modified, making it easier to reduce wages.[30]

We will return to this aspect of Treasury advice later. The financial statement delivered by Downie Stewart on 6 October — the *third* that year — is in full typescript on the Treasury file, suggesting that it may at least have been typed there before being printed. Soon afterwards, the Labour MP Peter Fraser accused

Treasury of having 'extraordinary powers of veto', citing particularly what he claimed were the efforts of the Unemployment Board to determine policy. Downie Stewart responded that Treasury was not at all like its British counterpart — in the United Kingdom, a minister 'could hardly move' without Treasury backing. But Fraser's comments, which presumably alluded to constraints on how much the Unemployment Board could spend, were prescient. And even Downie Stewart conceded that there were bound to be 'plenty of vetoes because one of the main functions of the Treasury was to control expenditure'.[31] Not too far back in time such a comment about the department, as distinct from a minister, would have been most unusual.

In December, Park, who had now been Secretary for nearly two very turbulent years, got Ashwin, who had become Assistant Accountant in 1930, promoted again. Park made the case that

> the present difficult economic and financial conditions have greatly increased the responsibility and work of the Treasury. In addition the Secretary to the Treasury is chairman of the Local Government Loans Board, and is also carrying out the functions of the Financial Adviser to the Government, which largely consists in acting as a co-ordinating link between the various investment boards of the Departments of State and between these boards and the Minister of Finance. The executive functions of the Treasury have grown to such an extent that it has been found absolutely necessary to appoint an additional administrative officer.[32]

That stress on financial responsibilities is revealing of how the Treasury saw the expansion of its role in the preceding few years. Much later, Park was to emphasise to one historian the importance of his status as Financial Adviser being mentioned.[33] And the timing — just before the 2 December election — would not have been accidental. Certainly the Treasury would have seemed a more congenial partner for a politician like Downie Stewart than the crowds he and Forbes confronted while electioneering:

> The scene in the huge Town Hall was an unprecedented sight — the whole vast Assembly hooting and shrieking during [the] whole [of Forbes's] speech. I was on the platform, first behind Forbes and could study the whole scene — it was like a group of French Revolution faces in many parts, filled with hate … and shouting till their voices gave out … I have never seen such a disgraceful scene.[34]

Despite this hostility, the election was a resounding success for the new coalition government. Downie Stewart took off to Hawaii over Christmas and New Year, partly for health reasons, partly to negotiate a trade treaty with Canada. After the holiday a National Expenditure Commission, modelled closely on the May Commission, was appointed to report on 'the public expenditure in all its aspects', to consider both policy and administration, and 'generally to make recommendations to the Government for effecting forthwith all possible reductions in public expenditure'. This commission *did* consist principally of businessmen. Its chair, George Shirtcliffe, was chairman of directors of A. S. Paterson, a former president of the Wellington Chamber of Commerce, and had sat on both the 1922 and 1924 taxation committees. J. L. Griffin, a 40-year-old Wellington accountant, had been president of the Society of Accountants in 1929. James Begg, a retired Otago sheepfarmer, had been a member of the wartime Efficiency Board and the 1924 taxation committee. A. Macintosh, the oldest member of the commission, had been involved in banking for many years — the newspaper report failed to mention that he was now 90 years old! And last there was — of course — J. J. Esson.[35]

A flavour of the approach taken by the Commission is given in one letter to Forbes from a business correspondent who identified the Secretary to the Treasury as 'my friend Mr Park', and who argued that the 'Economy Committee' provided 'the supreme opportunity when some at least of the various Government Departments can be brought into line with outside business organisations and their policies developed … along positive business lines.'[36]

The parallels to the 1980s reform of government that we have already seen in Treasury initiatives of the 1920s are thus underlined. The commission may have been one of businessmen but the records, imperfect though they are, make it clear that the Treasury, almost certainly in conjunction with Esson, made the running. All departments were required to submit information on their expenditure to Treasury, which in turn provided a report on each of them.[37] The Treasury seems to have been particularly important in attacking the Public Works Department — and in particular its chief, Fred Furkert — much as it had driven the 'attack' on Railways in 1930/31. The minutes of a meeting of the Commission on 23 February record that it 'considered the question raised by the Treasury regarding the possibility of establishing a National Board of Works, and heard the views of the Engineer-in-Chief, Public Works Department, on the matter.'[38]

Unsurprisingly, the Commission sided with the Treasury on this question, both its interim and its final reports advocating a board along the lines of the Local Government Loans Board.[39] For Furkert, the Commission's recommendations 'were another blow to his efforts to maintain the organisation he had so energetically built up'.[40] More generally, the Commission advocated the

> setting up of controlling Boards in connection with several departments of State. Our investigations have disclosed that sound administrative principles have often been subordinated to pressure exerted under the influence of both local and general politics. We regard it as essential that steps be taken to counteract this influence.[41]

This was the business vision of the political economy of the 1920s, unmodified for harsher times. Coates announced that while during the 1931/32 financial year his Public Works Department had spent just over £6 million of borrowed money, it was proposed in 1932/33 to reduce this to £1.3 million.[42] Organisationally, the Commission's recommendations amounted to the dismemberment of the department as a construction agency:

> We feel so confident that a reversion to the contract system is the only satisfactory basis upon which true economy can be obtained that we have not considered it necessary to inquire into the possibilities of effecting economy, assuming the present policy is to be continued.[43]

Treasury attacked all borrowing. Bassett comments that Coates, having announced the drastic curtailment of the works programme on 1 March, was not able to get money from Cabinet for any compensatory programme that would help men on to the land.[44] Ransom, now Minister of Lands, attempted to hold on to £300,000 for land disposal purposes. Treasury went to war on this proposal, pointing out that the borrowing would produce an additional 'gross interest and redemption burden of £100,000 per annum resulting in the settlement of some 800 new settlers at approximately £2000 each.' Treasury was particularly concerned to avoid 'the creation of any artificial and competitive stimulus to land and stock values which has been a feature under previous land subdivisional schemes of any magnitude.'[45] And Treasury finally got its way, against the wishes of the Auditor-General in this instance, with the abolition of the host of special accounts that had grown up like topsy alongside the Consolidated Fund during the 1920s.[46]

Relief workers repairing second-hand boots, 1932. Alexander Turnbull Library, F-49822-¹/₂

As in 1931, expenditure from taxation as well as from borrowing was scrutinised. In response to a request from Shirtcliffe, Treasury provided an analysis of expenditure on what it called 'social services' from 1914/15 to 1931/32. This was probably the first time that this sphere of government activity had come so definitely under Treasury scrutiny. In these reports, alongside the expenditure cuts per se, we see the outlines of a new approach to government. A new social services department which would take over pensions, health and even education was proposed (unsuccessfully).[47] Substantial proposals were also made for the reorganisation of education, school and hospital boards.[48] As in 1931, it was education that came under most pressure, with two teachers' colleges being closed.[49] It was reckoned that the proposed hospital reorganisation would account for about £300,000 of the total £800,000 in savings.[50] The amalgamation of local government authorities to gain greater efficiencies was also canvassed. Permanent appropriations (other than debt) did not escape either, with Treasury proposing the abolition of the £7000 allocated to 'Native Purposes' on the Civil List.[51] The government, for its part, extended the parliamentary term by a year, to four years.

Not everyone suffered. Racegoers at Trentham in January 1935. Evening Post Collection, Alexander Turnbull Library, G-48767-1/4

The Commissioners had recorded their 'thanks to the Treasury Department for its valuable reports on the administration of the various State Departments'.[52] This was an understatement. Much of the process was driven by Park and his colleagues, such as Ashwin, in conjunction with Esson. Treasury, the Commission, the government and many economists agreed that expenditure cuts were necessary. As would happen in the 1980s, the institutions themselves as well as their expenditure were scrutinised. Treasury thrived in the harsh climate of 1932, playing the role in the political economy that it had forged for itself in the 1920s.

Getting a central bank, 1930 to 1932

As well as pursuing more rigorous control of expenditure, Treasury was also keen to see the establishment of a central bank independent of the government. Recall the tripod of balanced Budgets, the gold standard and free trade. The 'patriation' and 'professionalisation' of financial management which we traced in chapter 2 was paralleled by a similar process with respect to monetary policy in the early 1930s. As in Canada at the same time, Treasury was involved partly because there was no central bank.[53] The ultimate purpose of its endeavours was to insulate monetary or currency policy from politics, and even from its own surveillance.

The Treasury drive arose not from a preoccupation with inflation, as it would in the 1980s, but from long-term trends in currencies that mirrored the changes in finance. During the war, the gold backing of the currency had been suspended. With the war over, the failure to return to the pre-war currency system with gold coin in circulation revealed that New Zealand relied not on gold in the first instance but on balances held in London — in British pounds sterling — to meet its import and overseas debt servicing requirements. As Ashwin explained to ministers, New Zealand therefore operated a 'sterling exchange' system. Ashwin was indebted to work done by A. H. Tocker at the University of Canterbury which in turn was derived from J. M. Keynes's pre-war work on the Indian monetary system.[54] Ashwin presented his findings to the Economic Society in 1930, and they were fully reported in the press in June that year.[55]

Depending on the volume of the sterling balances, the trading banks might place a premium or a discount on the transaction — in other words, more or less than a New Zealand pound might be required to buy a British pound sterling. In setting such 'loadings' the banks usually had regard to the financial circumstances of both Australia and New Zealand, but especially the former. During 1929 and 1930, New Zealand users of exchange — importers and the government — believed they were being charged an unfair premium. Arnold Hore, the audit officer at the New Zealand High Commission in London, pointed out that with a positive trade balance of £19 million, the New Zealand pound should have been at a premium instead of effectively depreciated by 5 per cent. 'Is it not time', he asked in a letter to the London *Times*, 'that New Zealand, which is geographically and politically separated from Australia, should terminate this bondage? Personally, the only remedy I can suggest is the creation of a Central Banking system'.[56]

For their part, the banks denied the charge but also refused to separate out their reserves for New Zealand purposes, preferring the flexibility of being able to utilise them as they saw fit. When the government enquired later of the National Bank about New Zealand's exchange position (as distinct from Australia's), A. T. Grose, its General Manager, asked Forbes patronisingly for 'what useful purpose the information is required, particularly as the returns you have asked for are practically impossible of ascertainment. There are no special assets or funds held for the purpose of New Zealand or indeed of any other exchange.'[57]

The idea of a New Zealand central bank which would manage these matters on the country's own behalf was therefore 'in the air', but there is no doubt that it was the Treasury that instigated Niemeyer's visit to New Zealand to report on such a central bank (on which it duly piggy-backed the powers of Treasury and other public accounts issues discussed in chapter 2) in 1930. Treasury drafted the memorandum that Forbes sent to Niemeyer about the government's concerns — 'I have framed a review of the question of banking and currency from a general Treasury standpoint', Park commented to Forbes.[58]

Bank of England opinion accorded with this New Zealand thinking. In the aftermath of the Great War, and given the improbability of returning to a fully-fledged gold standard, the Bank had been keen to regulate international monetary affairs through arrangements between bankers rather than politicians. 'Autonomy became sacrosanct in [his] mind', writes one recent historian of Montagu Norman, who had become the Bank's Governor in 1920, 'and he subsequently refused either to entertain Ministers of Finance at Threadneedle Street, or to visit countries which lacked a central bank.'[59] Norman was active both in the new countries of central and eastern Europe and in the Empire, the self-governing dominions of which had effectively also become independent monetary entities. Henry Strakosch, a City of London banking and foreign exchange expert, had advised on the establishment of a Reserve Bank in South Africa in 1920. Later but essentially similar developments took place in Australia and India, and from November 1928 the Bank of England sent a fortnightly letter to the new Empire central banks.[60] Niemeyer's visit to New Zealand and subsequent report to the government therefore fitted squarely with international and imperial developments. He finished his report and sent it to New Zealand early in the new year. 'My dear Park', he wrote from London on 23 January 1931,

> I am now going to Brazil ... and may be [away] three or four months. This is merely a hasty note to say that I have not forgotten my obligations to New Zealand. I hope before going to send you (1) a formal report which you can publish; (2) after discussion with Christie [the Crown Law drafting officer in New Zealand] a bank law and statutes of a Reserve Bank; (3) some <u>private</u> comments on confidential points.[61]

The rise in the exchange rates in London to 10 per cent at the end of January made the Treasury even keener to act, but Niemeyer stressed that the establishment of a central bank could not be hurried and suggested instead some short-term

The Aorangi, *on which Coates and Downie Stewart sailed to Canada.*
Gavin McLean

measures to relieve the situation, such as the establishment of a fixed rate of exchange with Australia (coupled with the provision of additional gold in London to meet any likely increase in demand). This task proved impracticable because each trading bank acted independently of the others.[62] For the rest, his report recommended, as was hardly surprising, that a Reserve Bank be established in New Zealand as in the other dominions. He concluded, as Norman would undoubtedly have wished, that 'the establishment of such a bank would provide an instrument for co-operation with the Central Banks of other countries — a co-operation which is becoming of increasing importance and which at present finds no suitable point of contact in New Zealand.'[63]

The government's weakness meant that no further steps were taken in the meantime. After the election Park resubmitted the report, but it was 'stood over'[64] — presumably because of the focus on public expenditure matters — and the issue was only taken up again when Downie Stewart and Park visited London late in 1932, after the Ottawa conference of the empire's prime ministers. Downie Stewart met Strakosch in both Ottawa and London, and Montagu Norman in London. The latter came to Stewart's hotel, where he explained that

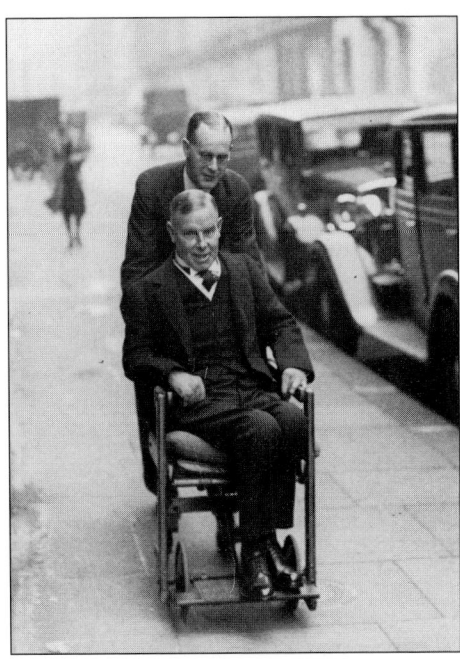

Downie Stewart in London, 1932. Alexander Turnbull Library, F-92656-¹/₂

when this question of a Central Bank was settled it would be quite easy to discuss all other points he had in mind, two of which were the refunding of the £5m 5% bonds 1932/34, hopefully at 4%, which should be held over for now [Downie Stewart agreed], and the issuing of Treasury bills in the early months of the New Zealand financial year ie April to June 1933, to be repaid out of revenue to be collected later in the year.[65]

The last reference was to an episode in the previous year in which the Treasury had issued short-term bills in London in anticipation of a long-term loan which had not been secured by the time many of the bills fell due.[66] Downie Stewart and Park concluded from the meeting that Norman 'was almost determined to make [the creation of a central bank] a sine qua non of helping us.'[67] Neither would have been averse, but both were aware of the opposition to the idea from the trading banks, and in particular the Bank of New Zealand (despite the government having a large shareholding in it), whose chair, Sir Harold Beauchamp, was also in London at the time. 'My dear Park', wrote Norman a month after the hotel meeting,

I have spoken to Mr Lubbock, and he will impress on Beauchamp that the

A. D. Park, Secretary to the Treasury, 1930–35, defended the 'economic constitution'. Treasury

Reserve Bank is certainly coming: that general financial opinion in London regards it as desirable and indeed almost necessary and that it is not wise for the Bank of New Zealand to make enemies and not friends; and that the Regency Buck should be encouraged to conduct himself accordingly.[68]

Not everyone in London agreed that it would be desirable to establish a New Zealand central bank — the *Financial Times*, for instance, commented cautiously after the announcement that the government intended to introduce legislation in the 1932/33 session.[69] Drew of the New Zealand High Commission reported after Park's return to New Zealand that

> I am sorry to say that the atmosphere has been such that I have not been able to achieve very much more than I have already reported upon, in the propaganda line. In referring to 'atmosphere' I mean that other papers that I saw — or rather their Financial Editors — expressed a preference to wait until the Bill is actually referred to in the House of Representatives before making any comment on it. I had … copies of the Niemeyer Report and these I took personally … to the Financial News, Financial Times, and the Financial Editors of The Times, Telegraph and Morning Post. The last three are the ones preferring to wait.[70]

Park's trip to London was nonetheless a pinnacle of his career. The former civil service cadet from Waitaki mixed on 'last-name' terms with distinguished financial figures such as Norman, Niemeyer, Strakosch, and Lord Queensborough, and attended Buckingham Palace to have his CMG awarded by the King himself.[71] His rise had been as impressive as that of his mentor, Esson.

The threat to the economic constitution, 1930 to 1933

Treasury had 'matured' as the government's financial controller during the 1910s and 1920s. The requirement for a central bank took the Treasury into the realm of monetary policy, if only as a temporary expedient pending the bank's establishment. Treasury expected to remain the guardian of only one of the elements of the Gladstonian 'tripod'. But as the Depression deepened it became plain that the tripod entire — laissez-faire capitalism itself — was under siege, and Treasury officials found themselves defending its assumptions and practices. The phrase 'economic constitution' nicely expresses the grounding of this defence in law as well as in the principles of economics. In September 1931, before the formation of the coalition government, Park sent Downie Stewart pages of evidence from the British Colwyn Report on the national debt and taxation. This material had one theme: the 'sanctity of contract', the support for this in the business community, and the effect that compulsory conversions of government debt to a lower rate would have on investment. Treasury advocated increasing the tax on interest, which would bring in revenue without denting the 'sanctity of contract'. However, Downie Stewart agreed — reluctantly — to statutory reductions in interest rates, speaking out against the measures but staying in office.[72]

From the point of view of our story, what's important is not so much what Treasury officials were saying as the fact that they were saying it. In another paper which he sent to Downie Stewart when the latter took up the finance portfolio in September 1931, Park made suggestions about the wage-fixing system, including the suspension of Arbitration Court awards in primary industries, the general suspension of awards with compulsory conciliation and optional arbitration, and the establishment of a closer relationship between wages and the unit costs of producing goods — in sum, the deregulation of the labour market.[73] Treasury was being drawn from guarding one to guarding all elements of the tripod. In the language of a later era, it was moving from financial to economic advice and management. The endeavour did not get far at this time, but it provides a significant context for the economic advice and management role of Treasury in later years.

During 1932 the 'economic constitution' was most powerfully threatened by pressure, from farming interests in particular, to raise the exchange rate — a particular variant, in the eyes of Downie Stewart and the Treasury, of breach of contract. Both could recognise economic arguments for raising the rate — just as there were arguments for keeping it at parity with sterling, or with sterling at no more than a 10 per cent premium, as was currently the case. Both felt the economic arguments for *not* raising the rate were more compelling. As Park told Forbes in February 1931, after the trading banks had raised the rate by 10 per cent, while this benefited exporters, whose earnings were worth 10 per cent more in New Zealand,

> the 10 per cent penalty on the importer has the same effect as a 10 per cent general increase in Customs tariff in accentuating the slump in restricting business, increasing the cost of living and working costs generally, and accentuating the budgetary difficulties of the State.[74]

Beyond such arguments there was the weight of opinion which Park most respected — that of the bankers, financial experts and urban businessmen opposed to experimentation and concerned to protect the value of money — rather than that of the farmers and producer boards who were most avid for the increase, or the economists who supported them. Park and the other Treasury officials had lived through the inflation of farm prices in the 1920s and seen the levels of debt that had accumulated as a result.[75] To devalue on a major scale in 1932 would be to reward farmers for their profligacy. That the Labour Party also opposed devaluation, because of the effect this would have on the cost of living through increased import prices, underlines the complexity of the political alignments on this issue.

Esson, Park's mentor, would almost certainly have had the same view, one shared by both Downie Stewart and Francis Dillon Bell, a former Reform Cabinet minister:

> With all who set the country first I am grateful to you for resisting the assault on the Treasury led by interested bankers from Australia. I think it is the first occasion on which such sordid 'reasons' for debasing this Dominion's currency have been promulgated.[76]

Wellington businessmen like Beauchamp, Buckleton and Grose, and the Governor-General, Lord Bledisloe, were similarly inclined.[77] These were the exponents of 'sound' finance. A famous mystery writer voiced the appropriate sentiments through one of her characters:

> It's Blunt and his group who are standing solid behind the present Government. Good sound Conservative finance … A lot of damned fools would try a lot of very costly experiments. And that would be the end of stability — of common sense, of solvency. In fact, of this England of ours as we know it.[78]

Moreover, exchange rates were set by the banks. For the government to assume this function would be a blow to the proper relationship between government on the one hand and business and finance on the other.[79] Part of the argument for a central bank was the desirability of putting in place a new institutional framework that would avoid just that outcome:

> compulsory enactments by the State in connection with the reductions in interest and rents, and the variation in contracts between one national and another, are unnecessary and will bring evils in their train which will be regretted.[80]

In the government itself, the exchange rate contest was played out between the two Reform politicians, Downie Stewart and Coates, with an unhappy Forbes in the middle. The first round was fought at the turn of 1931/32, precipitated by the Treasury bill debacle referred to above. The emergency creation of an exchange pool, with the government taking a prior claim over all other purchasers of exchange (such as importers) to meet its obligations in London, was a 'bomb exploded' on the business community just before Christmas.[81] But this also worked against the raising of the premium. Coates was alert:

> I have not lost sight of the contention of the Treasury that increased difficulties will be placed on their meeting their obligations in London if the exchange rate moves higher. Yet this immediate disability should not be allowed to have priority over the recovery of the industry on which depends the economic soundness of the country and, consequently, the ultimate stability of our public finance.[82]

The economist Douglas Copland and many others advocated a devaluation that would increase prices in New Zealand currency.
Alexander Turnbull Library, C-26200-¹/₂

Coates was not prepared to challenge fiscal responsibility ('the ultimate stability of our public finance') head on but sought a different route to it, one which embraced rather than precluded a change in the exchange rate. It was particularly disturbing to Coates that the government had still not assumed the right to set this rate:

> The present regulations as gazetted do not correctly convey the conclusion which was arrived at by Cabinet after discussion with the General Manager of the Bank of New Zealand and Treasury officers. I am sure our understanding was that the Minister of Finance, after consultation with the banks, should fix the rate of exchange. Indeed, it will be remembered that the General Manager of the Bank of New Zealand himself concurred in this proposed course. The feeling, as expressed round the table, was that this would allow of time for necessary discussion and decision as to future policy rather than leave the complete control in the hands of the banks. This was felt to be the better course as an emergency measure because Government finance in London demanded immediate action.[83]

But Coates was only one member of a government in which he was neither Prime Minister nor Minister of Finance. He could lobby, but not decide. He was supported in his lobbying by A. C. Davidson of the Bank of New South Wales and the New Zealand-born economist Douglas Copland, professor at the University of Melbourne. That January Davidson was in Wellington urging that New Zealand adopt the reflationary-cum-economising measures known as the 'Premiers Plan' or 'Copland Plan'. The Bank of New South Wales was the only bank trading in New Zealand which supported a depreciation: 'I spent two months in New Zealand', Davidson wrote three years later, 'investigating the position there and I think I can say that it was through my realisation of the position and influence with the Government that the Economic Committee was appointed with Dr James Hight [of Canterbury University College as chairman].'[84] Copland, A. H. Tocker (also from Canterbury), and Horace Belshaw of Auckland University College were the other three economists. Belshaw, Copland and Tocker were all former students of Hight.[85]

This was not the first time economists had played a role in public discussion, although they were now far more prominent. Economics as a specialist form of knowledge had come to prominence in the mid-Victorian era, when the findings of political economy — in particular our familiar trio of free trade, a gold standard and balanced Budgets — were regarded as not far short of laws. In the later nineteenth century, with the Cambridge economist Alfred Marshall in the vanguard, the discipline turned its attention to individual preferences, the beginnings of what would become known as microeconomics. The economists Francis Jolly, Dr James McIlwraith, Professor Hugh Segar, Francis Wilson and Walter Mills all contributed research evidence obtained using the framework of the classical and neoclassical monetary theories of the day to the 1912 Royal Commission on the Cost of Living, which set out to investigate what determined price levels in New Zealand.[86] Hight was one of the members of the Commission. Economists had also been asked to make presentations to the National Industrial Conference in 1928. Prime Minister Coates, introducing them, explained that they would 'give [us] a useful lead on certain questions, and their papers will certainly form the foundations for profitable discussion and for thought.'[87]

The malfunctioning of the economy brought economists into increased prominence. If the economy was 'sick', who better to fix it than economic 'doctors'? As Copland said on one occasion, 'by their training economists were at least partially equipped to consider national interests before any other … It was true that economists differed, so did medical men, but no one suggested that [they] should be spurned in favour of the layman, or the medicine man of a darker civilisation.'[88] During 1931 they became increasingly conspicuous in public debate, especially in the newspapers. Copland published articles on the measures taken in Australia, and visited Downie Stewart and other politicians in Wellington during the winter. A number of economists gave evidence before the parliamentary Economy Committee of August–September 1931.[89] This echoed events in England in 1930, when economists had given evidence to the Macmillan Committee established by the newly formed Labour government to investigate the condition of finance and industry.[90] Similar developments occurred in Australia.[91] When the remedies being considered by businesspeople amounted to no more than applying the orthodoxies of the last 60 years, it was natural to turn to 'expert' advice for illumination. The fact that a number of these experts occupied university chairs gave added weight to the consultation.

What are we to make of Treasury's relationship to this development? Looking back from any time after 1970 we may be puzzled by the seeming lack of connection between economists and the Treasury. Surely the two were almost synonymous? Hardly so in 1930, when the Treasury was dominated by accountants who were close to bankers and businesspeople, and economists were mostly employed in universities.[92] Brian Easton refers to Ashwin as the Treasury's only economist in the 1930s,[93] but even this may be misleading. For Ashwin, as for Esson or Park, his day-to-day focus was on public finance. The closest approach to economics was over currency matters and the banking system, in which Treasury had perforce interested itself in the later 1920s, and about which Ashwin wrote a paper — but that field also brought Treasury officials close to bankers like Niemeyer, who was not an economist. For his part, Harold Beauchamp, the chair of the Bank of New Zealand and an opponent of exchange rate changes, wrote to Forbes passing on a comment by Neville Chamberlain, the British Chancellor of the Exchequer, who had ruled out a particular committee being chaired by any 'distinguished economist. They wanted a man who had practical working knowledge of business'. Beauchamp directed Forbes's attention 'particularly to Mr Chamberlain's opinion of distinguished economists, in reference to business or financial matters.'[94] Thomas Wilford, the High Commissioner in London, recounted the tale that the British government had 'consulted six of the world's greatest economists and received seven opinions — two of which came from Keynes.'[95]

So when economists argued for exchange rate changes, this was not sufficient to make the Treasury change its mind — and there were, after all, economists who did not advocate the change.[96] Indeed, theoretical justifications could be advanced on both sides, and perhaps the more important issue is to explain why it was so likely that Treasury would line up on one rather than the other.

Everything in its stance and experience during the 1920s had led it to be sympathetic to financial and commercial interests and lenders, less sympathetic to farming interests and borrowers, and therefore unlikely to endorse a direction which was supported above all by farmers.

Park may not have been especially sceptical of economists, but he was unhappy about the establishment of the committee. After all, he had been reporting on the financial situation for the current and the new year, including loan finance, capital works and redemptions for the latter. Others were pleased that, if it were to convene, Park was on it:

> I was relieved to see your name quoted amongst those members of the Committee appointed last week to report on the economic and financial position. I imagine you will have a hard time balancing the various interests that may legitimately be considered. That the result must be a balance and not a rigid adherence to theories on either side, I am quite convinced.[97]

The report was completed within two weeks, and signed off with expressions of gratitude to both Park and 'Mr Ashwin of the Treasury who was constantly in attendance'.[98] But this could not disguise the fact that Park had appended a minority report dissenting from the main recommendation of the committee: the raising of the exchange rate. The economists presented the problem as one of adjusting the country's economy to a reduced external price level. In theory this could mean deflating the entire economy until its price structure was congruent with that for exporters, who had suffered the biggest collapse in prices and whose prices and costs were therefore the most misaligned. But rather than embark on such an extreme deflation — far more extreme than that entailed by the Depression to date — the economists recommended raising the New Zealand currency price of British pounds (in which exporters were mostly paid). In other words, rather than lower everyone's costs and incomes to the level of the exporters, the exporters' New Zealand currency income would be raised, whilst that of others — who would have to pay more for imported items — would fall.[99] As one newspaper commented in March 1932 after the release of the report calling for a change in the exchange rate, the proposal was

> little short of revolutionary. If it is adopted it will be in line with the agitation which has been proceeding for some months past for high exchange and compulsory interference with interest … The Government must consider

not only the immediate effect, which would probably be an alleviation of the present troubles, but the ultimate result, which cannot fail to be disturbing to our credit at Home, and confidence in New Zealand.[100]

Such views carried the day — or, as Park put it 'wiser counsels prevailed and it was decided to leave well alone, much to the disappointment of the interested Australian parties who carried out an extensive propaganda campaign throughout New Zealand.'[101] On 11 March, Forbes announced that the exchange rate would not be altered. With the export season by now well past its peak, it was unlikely that the issue would be as intensely fought again until the next season got under way. Further, Coates and Stewart, the two main protagonists, were out of the country throughout the middle of the year.

Renewed campaigning for a change in the rate duly began with the new export season later in the year. Coates returned from Ottawa and started lobbying for it, while Downie Stewart and Park went on to London to discuss financial matters. There they encountered Keynes and one of his opinions:

> He is a peculiar looking man, very tall, with dark hair and black moustache. I told him of our difficulties in New Zealand ... he says Copland is right on the exchange problem and that so far from damaging Australia's credit Copland's policy saved it. He thought it might be wise for New Zealand to approximate the Australian rate of exchange. I told him the two countries were entirely different and that all our advice from London was to keep as close to sterling as possible. He said ... that it would be better to keep as open a mind as possible. I asked him if he would borrow if he was in NZ in order to get through the crisis. He said, 'Yes, certainly if I were you I would borrow if I could, but if you asked me as a lender I doubt whether I would lend to you.'[102]

Farming MPs put pressure on Forbes as Stewart and Park were sailing towards New Zealand, producing vigorous cable traffic from ship to shore: 'learned confidentially from banks proposed arrangement ... for private member to move resolution ... requesting banks to increase rate.'[103] In November Forbes twice publicly denied that such action would be taken, saying that the exchange must remain in the hands of the banks, but the political pressure did not abate. Hight's committee resubmitted its case for a devaluation, and Coates himself, assisted by his aide R. M. Campbell, circulated a memo along the same lines in January.[104] Perhaps most significantly for evaluating the role of Treasury at this time,

Park had fallen ill with an internal haemorrhage soon after his return to New Zealand.[105]

> To my great astonishment I found you had had a pretty bad spin. I am extremely sorry to hear this, particularly at the present time … Take great care of yourself, old man, and do not under any circumstances allow Ministers or anybody else to get you out of bed or about, until you are perfectly satisfied you are absolutely alright.[106]

The illness effectively put Park off work for three months, although he did manage to get to one meeting. His absence would not have strengthened the anti-devaluation cause.[107] The Treasury provided advice on the fiscal implications of the change. Adding exchange costs to the deficit would increase it from around £6 million to over £9 million — an extra £1 million in debt servicing, £1.5 million lost in customs revenue because of the impact on imports, and a £500,000 decline in income tax. £1 million would also be required for a guarantee to the banks.[108] Stewart's sense that the government's first responsibility was to its own accounts — 'the direct effect of our depreciation is to throw some millions of pounds more on to the budget, when we already had an enormous gap to fill'[109] — would have been shared by the Treasury.

The decision to devalue — the outcome of the stand-off recounted at the beginning of this chapter — met with near-universal condemnation from Treasury's allies, established 'city' opinion and those main-centre newspapers which supported it. It was 'playing with dynamite' (*Auckland Star*), 'a disastrous blunder' (*Evening Post*), an 'arbitrary depreciation by the deliberate exercise of political power' (*New Zealand Herald*).[110] It was also noted that with Downie Stewart's resignation the Cabinet would have no urban or financial expertise. 'The commercial community's protest' was the banner headline in the *Evening Post* on 26 January over a report of a packed meeting of Wellington businesspeople. 'When I contemplate the members of the Cabinet — I must confess it is difficult to speak about them in calm language — those 'wise and honourable gentlemen who comprise the Cabinet — (laughter).' More in such vein followed.[111]

When Parliament reassembled early in February, there was a further assault on principles Stewart and the Treasury held dear. Coates pushed through a conversion of the public debt to a lower rate of interest. A voluntary conversion had been carried out in Britain in mid-1932. While the New Zealand measure was voluntary in form, the subsequent Finance Act provided for a 33.3 per cent tax on the interest earned on all securities not converted by 1 April 1933. Almost certainly Park was as opposed to this move in 1933 as he had been in 1931, but his ill-health may have reduced his influence at this crucial time. In any case, a determined Coates would now have got his way.[112]

What happened to the 'economic constitution' after 1933?

Did devaluation mean the end of the 'economic constitution'? Some commentary implies that. Coates's aide, R. M. Campbell, saw the Treasury — ready to take New Zealand 'back to the soup kitchens of the 90s' — defeated by the enlightened Coates. As Campbell commented when Park died in 1971,

> we read that Park has gone to his reward … presumably you'll not wholly omit references to persons Coates had to cope with? … So Park gets a place; and if you assign him bad marks, you would [to] all my prejudices be just right.[113]

In *The Nationbuilders*, Brian Easton stresses Coates's 'remarkable' economic management. Surrounding himself with 'able young advisers', he instigated the 'beginning of the modern Treasury' at a time when the institution itself was unprepared for the task.[114] Michael Bassett argues similarly: 'Coates was ensuring that he had access to wider views than those of the Treasury. A. D. Park was a stolid, self-satisfied conservative who, like Downie Stewart whom he had served loyally, instinctively thought of reasons not to innovate.'[115]

There is something in this. Coates did have young economists working in his office: Dick Campbell from mid-1931 until he left for England in early 1935; W. B. Sutch (born 1907), who had completed his doctoral work at Columbia University from mid-1933; Horace Belshaw (born 1898), on leave from Auckland University College's economics department, from early 1932 until 1935. All three favoured devaluation and the associated measures. And much conservative opinion was exasperated with many of Coates's policies, disenchantment that found a political voice in the Democratic Party which was to contest the 1935 election. Equally, there is no doubt that Park did not want to tamper with exchange or interest rates, and that he was 'moved on' in 1935, when he could reasonably have expected another seven or eight years as Secretary (he was 53), to the newly formed Mortgage Corporation.

But we can also detect continuities between the old and the new orders, especially if we shift our focus from the short-term adjustment measures to longer-term strategies such as the establishment of the central bank, expenditure control, and economic regulation. But this is even true in respect of the adjustment policies. Downie Stewart's deflation and Coates's intervention in exchange and interest rates were two routes to the same end: the realignment of domestic and external costs.

The creation of the central bank has been seen in 'left–right' terms, with the Labour Party supporting it and Coates implementing it with a more generous mandate than Downie Stewart had intended. Farland draws on Campbell and Sutch in emphasising the break with the original scheme. Bassett notes that Stewart drafted the first Reserve Bank bill but places the weight of explanation elsewhere, relating the establishment of the bank to the fact that 'whenever interest rates rose and primary producers felt the squeeze, advocates of a state bank emerged. The [Reserve] bank's primary duty was to act so that "the economic welfare of the Dominion may be promoted and maintained". This was a significant step in the State's paternalism towards its citizens'.[116]

But this emphasis is less convincing if we look at the situation from the viewpoint of Treasury, which was hostile to devaluation but a strong supporter of a central bank. The latter issue crossed left–right lines: Treasury's and Coates's strongest ally in the fight for it against the trading banks was the Bank of England. If the reconstructed government proceeded with the central bank then much would be retrieved — future decisions on the exchange rate would have been 'knave-proofed'. Similarly, if the new Minister of Finance could be reminded of the merits of a balanced Budget, all would not be lost.

It will now be useful to track both these stories — that of the central bank, then that of the balanced Budget — under Coates. The central bank bill had a shaky introduction in December 1932. Park's collapse was an added complication — 'naturally I was relying upon [Park] for a great deal of detail about the central bank bill and matters that arose in London.'[117] That advice would have been all the more desirable because of the New Zealand bankers' hostility to the measure:

> I met all the bankers one day and they showed such hostility to the bill I got angry and said if they were going to organise a bankers' ramp against it I would fight them and expose the position to the House and the country as when I left for Ottawa the only bank actively opposed was the Bank of New Zealand.[118]

Power and presence: the Bank of New Zealand's elaborate banking chamber, Wellington, 1935.
Earle Andrew Collection, Alexander Turnbull Library, F-18514-1/₁

As it transpired, the bill was waylaid by the exchange crisis. Would Coates now follow the same line as Downie Stewart? The visiting London banker J. L. Fisher informed Kershaw that he had been assured by the convalescent Park that 'it will go through … I think Coates feels that Downie Stewart should have pushed the Bill through when he was in office and before any opposition movement could make itself felt. When I saw Downie Stewart I got the impression that his physical disability rather tends to sap his courage. He told me he would have liked a Central Bank expert at his elbow while the Bill was before the House.'[119]

So much for Coates and Downie Stewart being on opposite sides. The cumulative effect of recurrent tussles with the trading banks over financial matters probably underlined the merits of a central bank to all politicians. We have observed the trading banks' fury at the imposition of the exchange pool at the end of 1931. Similarly, before accepting devaluation they had demanded indemnification against any losses they might incur — the law requiring this was the first introduced when Parliament resumed in early February 1933.[120] And later in 1933, the Bank of New Zealand in particular would resist to the utmost the requirement and terms of a transfer of gold holdings to the Reserve Bank. As Coates wrestled with this last problem, the Bank of England recognised that he needed political support:

> Forbes must be persuaded that the establishing of the Reserve Bank would be very much to the advantage of New Zealand; it would be a piece of modern financial machinery which would strengthen and make more liquid the existing bank structure; that it would be of great help to the Government in the management of its loan policy and that it is indispensable if New Zealand is effectively to co-operate financially with the United Kingdom and the Dominions.[121]

It is true that the ultimate form of words defined the 'primary duty' of the bank as being 'to exercise control, within the limits of the powers conferred on it by this Act, over monetary circulation and credit in New Zealand, to the end that the economic welfare of the Dominion may be promoted and maintained.'[122] This seems more likely to have been careful politics than a fundamental shift to a Labour-style bank. Dick Campbell unintentionally revealed this when he recalled, in respect of the issue of private shareholders for the bank,

> the central Treasury, specifically Park faith: they'd give oh such valuable safeguards against possible wild (even JA Lee! type) men of the future. 'Why all this elaborate set-up?' Coates demanded after so many tedious hours. I, RMC, gladly would be bracketed with you in recalling Park's glib 'Bank must be assured of independence. It's all right while you're there, but the future might bring in dangerous, wild men.'[123]

But Campbell also recalled Coates's anger at his 'over-insistence' against shareholders, and the bill's lack of precision on the appointment of Governors.[124] And certainly a brief exchange in February 1934 suggests that Park and Coates were in accord.[125] Moreover, when during debate on the bill in the House Coates referred to a clause on the economic welfare of New Zealand, he had just commented on the fact that only one of the six trading banks had its headquarters in the Dominion. And he was explicit that 'the fundamental basis of the bill is not different from that of the Bill introduced last year', and that in policy it was 'substantially in line' with Niemeyer's proposals.[126] Further, the Bank of England supplied the first Governor; and the Secretary to the Treasury would be a non-voting member of the board. Both measures suggest that the conservative vision of the Bank was the dominant one.[127] And when the Solicitor-General was asked for an opinion about the legal character of the bank — whether or not it was a government department — his opinion was unequivocal: 'The Reserve Bank of New Zealand is a corporate body, distinct from the State which has created it ... it is not in law a department of state. It is not a function of the Crown but a separate legal person.'[128]

What about expenditure control? Would 'Treasury control' survive under Coates, given especially the fiscal cost of altering the exchange rate?[129] It's important to recall that even Coates's allies, the economists who recommended devaluation, wanted to cut spending by over a third.[130] And many of the state initiatives of the Coates years, for instance the Mortgage Corporation and the Executive Commission for Agriculture, continued the 'arms-length' approach that had characterised institutional reform in the 1920s, and were partly designed to protect the Crown against financial risk.

On the other hand, many of the rationalising recommendations of the National Expenditure Commission were never implemented. The Public Works Department, for instance, survived. Partly this was practicality — the government could hardly use private contractors when there were no public works to let by tender. Ironically, the department's function as a relief agency was the most important factor in its survival until economic conditions once more allowed it a more constructive role.[131] And neither hospital boards nor local government were reorganised as envisaged.

Limits to Treasury control of longer standing were evident in another sphere — the investigation conducted by the Native Affairs Commission into the administration of Native Affairs, and in particular the Native Department's land development schemes. Historians have seen the hand of Treasury at the centre of this investigation, and this was certainly true of the scrutiny of the Native — and other — departments by the National Expenditure Commission in 1932.[132] But the record of the 1934 inquiry suggests that Treasury's sins — or sanctions — were those of omission, not commission.[133] This investigation was triggered not by Treasury action but by complaints laid by the Audit Department, and it was the latter and the Native Department itself which were most involved in the investigation. The Commission found that in relation to accounts, the organisation of the department was 'so defective that it reached the verge of a breakdown.'[134]

Treasury, the Public Service Commissioner's office and the Audit Department all had roles to play in overseeing the affairs of departments. But the report found that 'during the present period of depression the Treasury has not had sufficient officers to spare to make independent inspection of the Native Department.' Further, recognising that much of the direction of the land development schemes came from the Minister, Sir Apirana Ngata, the report pointed out that 'the Permanent Head of the Treasury and the Public Service Commissioner cannot be expected by virtue of their own offices alone to control … a Minister. They must all have recourse to other Ministers whom they may approach, but the Controller and Auditor-General, by virtue of his freedom from responsibility for any part of the administration of a Department, holds a key position.'[135]

The most significant tactical move the Treasury made on expenditure control was the decision to 'hypothecate' (borrow against) mortgages issued to those on soldier settlement schemes. Park explained in 1932 that 'fortunately for us … we still have about £10m surplus revenues invested in [such] mortgages … these reserves should prove of considerable value in seeing us through.'[136] Coates must have accepted this stratagem because it was repeated in 1933 and 1934, in both years turning a substantial deficit on the Consolidated Account into a surplus. Coates must also have agreed to Treasury reporting on all new expenditure. A circular letter of June 1933 invoked the memorandum of 13 October 1930 that was discussed at the end of the last chapter. The injunction that 'no new proposals are to be submitted for Ministerial or Cabinet consideration without being accompanied by a report thereon by the Treasury' was underlined.[137] We can see the impact of this in what was to become familiar language from other departments:

> For some time officers of the Treasury have been pressing me for a statement of the amount of money that will be needed to carry on Public Works next financial year … It is quite clearly impossible in the absence of a Government direction as to future construction programme and a definite idea of the number of men, single and married, that we will have on our books, together with the assistance available from the Unemployment Board, to prepare a fixed estimate of requirements, and I have made it plain to the Treasury that the figure of £2.2m is subject to confirmation by the Minister and yourself.[138]

It is possible, for reasons that will be discussed below, that Treasury had little to do with Coates's first Budget, which was not presented until November 1933, even later in the year than the 1932 Budget. With estimated expenditure of £24.2 million and revenue of only £22.306 million, Coates had a deficit to defend:

> Budgeting for a deficit cannot be regarded as satisfactory, and in normal times such a course would be inexcusable. At present, however, we are driven to it by the adversity of circumstances over which we have no control ... to have attempted to achieve a balance this year, either by increasing taxation or by further slashing expenditure, would have involved a far greater strain on the internal structure of the country than would have been advisable in present circumstances.[139]

Campbell contrasted Park's 'narrow orthodoxy in subordinating all else to a Balanced Budget'[140] with Coates's adventurousness, but is it too easy to magnify the difference? Coates gave up the Works portfolio in April 1933 to concentrate on Finance.[141] His stance late that year on the inadvisability of expanding public works would have been consistent with Treasury thinking — certainly it has echoes in Treasury statements in both the 1920s and later in the 1930s:

> The Government is being urged to expand public works as a means of giving a fillip to industry and relieving unemployment. What must be borne in mind, however, is that the counterpart of capital expenditure out of loan moneys is the public debt and interest and debt repayment charges. Furthermore, unless the works undertaken are productive, these charges fall upon the taxpayer. A large and relatively sudden expansion of public works would no doubt act as a stimulant, but, having regard to the other side of the picture in present circumstances, with the relative weight of all existing debt charges greatly increased by the fall in prices, it is obvious that any such expansion could not be maintained for long, and when the effect of the stimulant had worn off the community would be in a worse position than it is now.[142]

And he went on to point out that while

> It is true that the putting in hand of extensive public works has been strongly advocated by prominent economists in Great Britain and elsewhere ... such proposals were intended only for creditor nations, the basic idea being that the expansion thus brought about would help to lift prices in markets ... and thereby ... aid debtor countries such as New Zealand.[143]

Further, memorandums of 9 February and 15 September 1934 stressed, like that of 1933, that without a Treasury report no recommendation would be considered.[144] As these instructions went out under the name of the Minister of Finance, it can fairly be assumed that Coates and Treasury were in accord over them.

Certainly we can see Treasury conducting a similar Budget process in 1934 to that in previous years:

> The Right Hon the Minister of Finance has directed that Heads of Department be requested to put in hand preparations of the estimates of expenditure for the financial year 1934–35, which should be forwarded to the Treasury not later than the 30th instant.[145]

And as in previous years, Treasury paid attention to the loan expenditure programme:

> The Treasury has asked for tentative details of the Department's loan programme for the coming financial year. As there is a tendency for the tentative programme to become the adopted one, the question has been gone into carefully and in considerable detail, and I propose to take up with the Treasury not only the loan programme but the whole financial programme, as the two are related so closely.[146]

It may be that Treasury had also approached a little closer to Coates: 'Having regard to current economic conditions a capital programme of moderate dimensions is probably necessary to maintain the progress now being made towards recovery.'[147] Can the sense of common ground between minister and department be distilled in a phrase such as 'different mountain, different view'? From 1919 to 1928 and from 1931 to 1933 Coates was either actual or de facto Minister of Works (he relinquished the portfolio for most of his term as Prime Minister, but his successor, K. S. Williams, was ranked last in the Cabinet). In this capacity, his differences with Treasury had their roots in long-standing debates about the respective merits of borrowing for development or fiscal responsibility, debates in which he was firmly on the side of development. But once he gave up Works, Finance was his principal portfolio, and his ministerial responsibility was not to build bridges but to balance books.

Regulating the economy

The discussion in this chapter has focused on Treasury's preoccupation with balancing the Budget, the threat it perceived to that goal from the exchange rate change in January 1933, and the subsequent continuation of that endeavour despite the fact that Coates, the great proponent of the change, was now Minister of

Finance. Treasury's preoccupation with the 'regulated' economy — that is, the diverse ways in which state action, be it through taxes, tariffs or regulations, shaped trade, production and employment — remained confined to evaluating the fiscal implications of policies and was not broadened to embrace comment on the merits of the policies themselves. Major departments such as Land and Income Tax, Customs, Agriculture or Labour might accept Treasury scrutiny of their accounts, but were not likely to share or shed either their responsibilities or their advice-giving role.

G. W. Clinkard, who was appointed as Secretary of Industries and Commerce in 1930, 'grappled with industry monitoring and regulatory issues such as the supply and price of flour, the production and distribution of bread, and prices of motor spirits.'[148] In contrast, it is not possible to identify an active Treasury stance on employment policy, apart from its specific fiscal dimensions. In this limited sense Treasury certainly played a role. It was probably therefore responsible for ensuring that the Board set up at the end of 1930 was self-funding after an initial period — relief payments would be financed from the Unemployment Tax. It is harder to explain why no departments, not even Treasury or Labour, were represented on it, but this may have owed something to the determination of the government to kept it at arms' length from the standard processes and finances of government.[149] Treasury did ally itself with the Board to oppose a proposal by Coates to set payment scales which would deplete the Board's funds:

> A combined Treasury and Unemployment Board report came by Stewart's hand to Cabinet. Board's income "x" four weekly. Coates' proposal favoured scale would exceed 'x' by say £180,000. Impossible! Back from Cabinet to show an aide (packing for Ottawa) with shared satisfaction the red-stamped, FD Thomson-signed <u>IN CABINET-APPROVED</u>, the full impossible sum.[150]

G. C. Rodda, the Acting Secretary to the Treasury, was present at a conference on unemployment in November 1932 but raised only financial questions, for example about the state guarantee of debentures which the Board proposed to issue.[151] And Coates retooled the finances of the Board in 1933 in ways of which Treasury must have approved:

> The increasing magnitude of the problem necessitated a complete overhaul of the finances of the Unemployment Fund. The levy was reduced, and the

contribution from the Consolidated Fund was abolished. On the other hand an emergency charge on salaries and wages and on other income was increased to give the Board the necessary revenue to carry out its functions. As a result the finances of the ... Fund were, during 1932–33, entirely divorced from those of the Consolidated Fund and placed upon a self-contained basis.[152]

Similarly with overseas trade. The discussions at the Ottawa conference on tariffs and other trade relationships involved Downie Stewart (as Minister of Customs) and Coates (as Deputy Prime Minister), but not Park.[153] Indeed despite being in Ottawa, Park was unaware that the Canadians had sent material on their sales tax to Dr Craig of the New Zealand Customs.[154] When Coates introduced the tax the following February he wore his Minister of Finance hat, but the tax was to be administered by Customs, since its sales tax inspectors operated throughout the country, not just at ports of entry.[155] Similarly, the tobacco duty introduced at the same time to protect the domestic industry was a Customs Department responsibility.[156]

The most sustained area of activity was the primary produce sector, reflecting Coates's preoccupation with farm costs and activity at 'both ends' — negotiating access to the British market, and the financial circumstances of the many near-bankrupt farms. In these spheres Coates dealt directly with the leaders of the producer boards — Davy Jones, a former Cabinet colleague and close friend, at the Meat Board, and William Goodfellow, the chairman of the New Zealand Co-operative Dairy Company, at the Dairy Board.[157] We need to see Coates's 'brains trust' of bright young economists partly in this context.[158] Their main activities were not in areas in which Treasury was active; equally, they were not so involved in areas — public expenditure, the new central bank — in which Treasury was. The brains trust focused on primary production, the sphere which had made Coates such an active exponent of an exchange rate change, and which only indirectly impinged on the public accounts. Campbell, for instance, played a major role in drafting the Agriculture (Emergency Powers) Act — although he conceded that the title came from the United Kingdom. The members of the Executive Commission for Agriculture set up under the act were two industry representatives and a judge.[159]

In this area, as with unemployment, Treasury only became involved where there were fiscal implications. Bernard Ashwin, reporting before the 1934 Budget, argued for a mortgage corporation that would raise funds from bonds, but also for a corporation that would combine urban and rural lending and eliminate the duplication of state lending departments. Depression was an opportunity as much as it was a cause:

> The necessity for reform along these lines has been expedited by the general difficulties of the mortgage situation. Nevertheless, such a reform is due apart from the depression, and weaknesses in the direction of overlapping in lending operations by Government Departments has been reported by Treasury on several occasions.[160]

An interdepartmental report of 1 October 1934 written in response to a proposal in the Budget made a strong argument against a general state guarantee of the bonds, which

> would largely destroy the whole proposal as a long-range project in which the basic idea is to organise the investment of private capital in mortgages … if however the bonds are to be guaranteed by the State it practically amounts to ousting private capital and the State taking over an ever-increasing amount of mortgages; for, in fact, the borrowing would be on the security of the public revenues and not on the mortgages.[161]

A summing up

An enormous number of developments during these five years have barely been mentioned in this chapter.[162] My aim has been to focus on those aspects of the Depression story which bear most strongly on the character and development of the Treasury. Two key documents confirm the extent to which the 'Treasury view' of public finance and the role of government in the economy survived the Depression. In April 1935 Ashwin addressed the Commerce Society of Victoria University College on 'problems in public finance': 'a rational individual finding his income shrinking looks round and decides that he can no longer afford this or that. With State expenditure the matter is much more complicated but the same principle should apply.'[163]

Equally, Coates's 'farewell' financial statement of 3 December 1935, while defending the raising of the exchange rate in 1933, expressed other sentiments exactly aligned with those of the Treasury. Why did he make such a statement when he was about to leave office? He wished to 'place on record the main aspects of this Government's policy during the past four years, since it is on these that success in balancing the Budget and in promoting business recovery has largely depended.'¹⁶⁴ The conjunction of these two goals was revealing. Treasury would have adopted a similar position, except that it might have stressed the importance of balancing the Budget *to* the promotion of business recovery. Equally, the Reserve Bank was identified as an organ to do no more than 'co-ordinate, consolidate and control the banking system' — the Treasury view.¹⁶⁵

In sum, Coates's statement suggests, Treasury and he might have diverged on means towards ends, but agreed on those ends. If economic recovery continued, it seemed that Treasury and the Reserve Bank could, with co-operative ministers, respectively manage public finances and the monetary system, and through both the economy. And possibly Coates and Downie Stewart could have been those ministers, equably supported by Treasury. Coates wrote to Stewart in the aftermath of the 1935 defeat in a tone quite different from the bitter exchanges of 1933. 'The work has never been quite the same since you left the Cabinet. While I did not agree with many of your arguments, I always felt there was a sound loyal friend to whom I could turn in difficulties.'¹⁶⁶

Chapter 4

A new world? Treasury and the first Labour government, 1935–1949

Introduction

'When the government took office the constitutional practice of Cabinet responsibility was replaced by party responsibility and all major matters had to be submitted to caucus and its decisions accepted,'[1] wrote Treasury Assistant Secretary Bernard Ashwin of the first Labour government elected in November 1935. This was an exaggeration, but it reminds us of the political 'revolution' that followed Labour's election victory in 1935. Labour asserted the primacy of politics and politicians over officials and experts. And it asserted the primacy of government over business, public over private ownership, people over profits, labour over capital, and equity — to use the terminology of a later generation — over efficiency.

Labour's outlook was at odds with the orientation of the Treasury, which favoured expertise over politics, and business over — or in — government. During the 1920s and early 1930s Treasury officials had sought efficiency in government, taken control of the public accounts, and helped inaugurate a parallel control over monetary affairs through the establishment of the Reserve Bank. These building blocks of a laissez-faire economic constitution were lauded by Coates in his farewell address in 1935. But they seemed old-fashioned even then, echoes of a faith in the private organisation of economic life that had been battered by the Depression and replaced by a receptiveness to government intervention — 'the political theory behind much of the activity has been the converse of the political theory of the twenties. Then it was a question of State interference to prevent abuses or undesirable competition.' The public had now learned that 'the ultimate authority and the ultimate economic power in the community rested in Parliament rather than in the captains of industry.'[2] And in

Parliament, not in officialdom: 'each department is one of the Ships of State and the whole fleet is now under the command of the Labour Government. I am Captain of this Ship of State and you are the crew'.³

These political and bureaucratic dimensions to the experience of Treasury (and all other government departments) under the Labour government are easily overlooked. The origins of 'Treasury control' in the 1910s and 1920s are now forgotten, and references to the Treasury's role in particular debates, such as that over the 1938 Social Security Act, give little sense of how recent was such a role — and the seemingly timeless parsimony that accompanied it. Other writers, in focusing on economic management, have also blurred the politics:

> during the twentieth century ... the Treasury's responsibilities and activities have greatly expanded, as have those of its counterparts throughout the Western world ... In part this simply reflects the enormous growth in governmental activities ... yet it also stems from the change in economic philosophy which occurred in the wake of the Great Depression. Under the impact of the Keynesian revolution and the ascendancy of socialist or social democratic thought, modern governments came to accept responsibility not merely for ensuring reasonable price stability and protecting property rights, but also for maintaining an acceptable level of aggregate demand, output and employment.⁴

As a contemporary commentator noted, 'even in the more conservative countries, such as the United Kingdom, there have been important concessions to such a principle, while in the United States, State enterprise and control have made rapid inroads into the preserves that were once regarded as the prerogative of private enterprise.'⁵ But Labour's victory in New Zealand made Treasury involvement in a process which had socialist rather than Keynesian origins less, not more likely. The advent of the new government slowed down rather than accelerated the enlargement of Treasury's capacities — in addition to calling into question Treasury's existing approaches and financial priorities.

The new political economy

This new political economy was evident in every initiative of the Labour government. The most prominent was its 'nationalisation' of the Reserve Bank. The independence of the bank, and Treasury's fiscal control, were the 'twin pillars' of the pre-1935 economic constitution. That Labour would act in this sphere had long been anticipated. In debate over the 1933 Budget, for example, Michael Joseph Savage, Labour's new leader, had stressed that the party had argued 'repeatedly that it is possible for the Government ... to control the monetary system of this country, and by so doing to guarantee prices to the producers in the first place and incomes to those whom they employ in the second.'[6]

On the day of the election, a file note was made in the Bank of England on a *Times* report of the main planks of the Labour platform. This recorded (and underlined) that the Reserve Bank would be state-controlled.[7] Reserve Bank Governor Leslie Lefeaux cabled Norman in mid-January 1936 that

> events appear to be moving towards a crisis ... Main point at issue is the control of credit and currency. My view is that transfer of our responsibility to the Government thus opening up way for unlimited inflation would render the Reserve Bank a menace instead of a useful part of financial machine.[8]

The more politically astute Harvey, the Deputy Governor of the Bank of England, reminded Lefeaux that they had had no news of a crisis, and that it was important to remember that, while 'ultimate authority regarding credit and currency must rest with Governments', any central bank 'had unrivalled opportunities for pressing its views on the Treasury thus gradually provoking recognition of them'.[9] The Bank of England also noted that Savage had said that the government did not intend to 'turn the handle of the printing press' or cause any weakening of New Zealand's credit. However, it believed that 'the course of events is likely to be inflationary sooner or later'.[10] One Bank of England official had talked to the New Zealand economist J. B. Condliffe, who

> told me that he knew well many of the leaders of the Labour Party ... Nash ... explained quite frankly that there was a lot of discontent [with] the monetary system, and that they intended to exploit it ... but ... there was not going to be any tinkering with the monetary system. They would probably nationalise the Reserve Bank, but they did not intend to change its functions ... Nash expected to be Finance Minister and he had no sympathy with extreme or heretical proposals of any kind.[11]

Nash reported his plan to nationalise the bank to the Labour Party caucus on 20 and 21 February 1936, and the Reserve Bank Amendment Act became the government's first piece of legislation — 1936, No. 1. This provided for the buying out of the bank's private shareholders, and required it 'within the limits of its powers, to give effect as far as may be to the monetary policy of the Government, as communicated to it from time to time by the Minister of Finance'.[12] This was a firm assertion of political control over the Bank and monetary policy.

Treasury's records are unforthcoming on the department's role in the drafting of the amendment Act, which appears to have been primarily produced in the law drafting office.[13] One memorandum noted that 'in connection with recent discussions on monetary policy, confidential statements, as per copies attached, have been supplied to you setting out Treasury views on proposals in respect of the Reserve Bank Act amendment, guaranteed prices and the credit appropriation bill.' These statements do not survive, but it is suggestive that the memorandum was 'forwarded in order that Treasury viewpoints may be recorded on the official files.'[14] It seems likely that Treasury's views were not being heeded at this time — yet it is also true that, as Condliffe had predicted, the Reserve Bank's functions were not changed.

What then of public spending and the public accounts, the Treasury's more immediate responsibility? The change in the status of the Reserve Bank was echoed in other areas with implications for Treasury's fiscal role. Labour had repeatedly promised to end the practice of appointing non-representative boards and tribunals to carry out duties which 'rightly belonged to Parliament'.[15] Thus the Government Railways Amendment Act abolished the Government Railways Board and returned its functions to the Minister of Railways and a Railways general manager — the institutional arrangement that Treasury had been so keen to end in 1931. With that change, the Transport Co-ordination Board was also abolished.[16] A month later, the shareholding structure of the Mortgage Corporation was altered. A. D. Park, who had been eased out of the Treasury Secretaryship the year before, retained his status as managing director, but all bar one of the directors of the renamed State Advances Corporation were to be appointed by Cabinet. The other was the Treasury representative — who was expected to act on the instructions of the Minister of Finance.[17] Nash said when he introduced the bill in May:

> in the matter of providing public facilities there is just as much competence and ability for doing the right thing in Government circles as there is in business or commercial acquisitiveness. I suppose our friends on the Opposition benches will say, in connection with this Bill, 'You will have to pay for the alteration you are making in connection with the Mortgage Corporation.' Well, if the price as I see it is the price we have paid in the past

for private control, all I can say is that we are not going to pay that price any longer. We believe that there are just as good brains, and just as sound, able, and competent men in Government circles as there are in what are known as commercial and business circles. But these people who are keen on opposing Government ownership and Government control say, 'Yes, have the public ownership, but let the private people control it'. That only proves that people who talk in that way do not believe in public ownership at all.[18]

These institutional changes were accompanied by others in respect of production and labour, areas in which Treasury's role had been more peripheral. Radio broadcasting was transferred from the board control established in 1932 to ministerial control.[19] The Executive Commission for Agriculture was abolished and its functions handed over to the newly-established Marketing Department, the function of which was to purchase dairy output at guaranteed prices and then sell it. Compulsory unionism was introduced for many occupations. Overall, these measures must have brought home to Treasury that its place at the heart of government was at risk of dilution or even deletion. Would this then be followed by a return to 1920s extravagance in public works or other kinds of spending, or worse? The economist Copland was reassuring:

> At the moment [the new government is] pursuing a moderate financial policy, relying on traditional methods of financing their current needs and their public works policy. As regards the latter they may even be thought to be conservative. They are financing half their loan programme from the proceeds of special taxation — half of what Governments before the depression borrowed in England for. They have decided not to go in for external borrowing, and to this extent they will not increase the real burden of public debt ... [they seem] to have been influenced by [the Reserve Bank's] argument that it would not be desirable to increase unduly the volume of central bank credit at the present time. To this extent also the Government is proceeding on somewhat orthodox lines.[20]

And in one fundamental respect Treasury retained its controlling role. Within days of taking office, the new government had reaffirmed the requirement that all expenditure proposals that came before Cabinet would have to be accompanied by a Treasury report:[21]

> The Government has found it necessary to have an independent expert review of the proposals placed before them and what more suitable Department is

there for such a review than the Treasury, for after all [it] has the initial responsibility for 'balancing the budget'. Treasury control in this connection has in fact increased in recent years and there is a standing instruction by Cabinet that all proposals involving the State in financial commitments must be referred to Treasury for report.[22]

Did Treasury officials move swiftly to have this still-new rule reaffirmed, was there a coincidence of interests, or did the government itself initiate the reconfirmation? If the latter, instead of the Treasury tail wagging the government dog (as in 1930), the Treasury was both the government's 'bark and bite' (to mix the metaphor). But in any event, the requirement *had* been reaffirmed.

Economic advice

The political economy had changed: government, not business, was at the centre, and with this shift came the notion of what would later be called 'economic management'. The nineteenth-century political economy, with its tripod of gold standard, balanced Budgets and free trade, did not need 'managing' — it was meant to be self-regulating. The new political economy, with its commitment to protecting the living standards of the entire population, did. Indeed, as one Treasury official put it in 1938, there might be 'further substantial advances along the lines of a semi-planned economy'.[23]

Was it at all likely that Treasury, alongside its responsibility for financial control, could assume the role of providing economic advice in such an environment? On the face of it, the hurdles were insurmountable.

The first was Labour's suspicion of officials. By December 1938, more than 50 bodies within the Labour Party had forwarded remits to annual conferences asking the government to 'remove the reactionary departmental officials who by deliberate intention or through lack of social background or outlook stood in the way of the efficient operation of the administrative machine'.[24] Was this a matter of class differences? Education was one expression of these differences. Just one minister in the new Cabinet had a university degree, and ten of the thirteen had only completed primary school.[25]

Such suspicion had major implications for the entire public service. The example of the divide between Treasury and the new government that is most often cited is the latter's social security legislation. Ashwin sat on an interdepartmental committee which investigated the government's superannuation and pension proposals, but Treasury's favoured approach of a contributory scheme was disliked by the government. The rift surfaced in Parliament when Savage was provoked to assert, when challenged as to why the head of the Treasury was not to give evidence to the parliamentary committee on the health aspects of the bill, that 'the Head of the Treasury would know about as much about the medical profession as the honourable member for Central Otago — absolutely nothing. In any event, we did not want the head of the Treasury to tell us what our policy was to be.'[26] A strong memorandum by Ashwin to Nash on this subject two weeks earlier may have contributed to the sharpness of Savage's response.[27]

It is also illuminating to look at a memorandum from Ashwin to Nash of 27 April 1937 (when Nash was in England) warning that while the financial year just concluded had turned out well, New Zealand could not afford to borrow too much and should be encouraging the men presently employed on public works (who were paid for from revenue) into other employment. In any case, it would be difficult to borrow anything like the £20 million that was being talked about, unless the money came from the Reserve Bank, which would cause inflation. W. B. Sutch, who was in London with Nash, agreed that public works should be financed as much as possible from taxation, and he also agreed that contract wages should be decreased relative to others to encourage men to shift to unsubsidised employment.[28] In Nash's 1937 Budget, public works spending was to total £17 million. While this was somewhat less than Ashwin had feared, Nash fudged the issue of how it would be financed, explaining only that 'amounts received from the Post Office Savings-bank and other departmental sources, will be sufficient to provide all that is required for this programme.'[29] He avoided any reference to the Reserve Bank.

A second hurdle faced by Treasury in adopting an economic advice role was that Labour politicians were wary not just of officials but of economists. In 1931, Downie Stewart had confided to his diary during the political and financial crisis that

> the Labour men violently opposed the idea of an expert committee and said they would heed the experts but it was an insult to Parliament to suggest that we could not judge matters [until] after hearing experts. They complained bitterly of Copland who had spoken in Timaru and said the politicians could not do the job and had to call in experts.[30]

Labour vigorously opposed raising the exchange rate because this would increase

W. B. Sutch, economic adviser to Coates, then Nash, and later Secretary of Industries and Commerce (1958–65). This photograph was taken in May 1947 when Sutch was a United Nations Relief and Rehabilitation Administration delegate at the first meeting of the UN's Economic Commission for Europe at Geneva. Alexander Turnbull Library, C-22835-1/2

the cost of living (by raising the cost of imported goods) for working people, so the fact that many economists recommended devaluation also did them no good.[31]

For all that, Labour ministers had met and talked with economists. Condliffe had taught classes at the Workers' Educational Association attended by Nash, Fraser and Savage. Belshaw, who had met Keynes at Cambridge, and A. G. B. Fisher, who first taught at Otago, had both had contact with Nash — indeed, Nash was best man at Fisher's wedding in 1929. W. B. Sutch worked as Nash's private secretary in the late 1930s.[32] Fisher and Belshaw were both more attuned to the outlook of Labour politicians than were economists closer to the neoclassical tradition, such as Hight and Copland. Fisher and Belshaw provided a foil to the social credit thinking that was influential in the Labour movement in the 1930s.

Then there was Keynes. Keynesian thinking, with its readiness to conceive of the economy in aggregate categories such as investment, savings and consumption, held out the possibility of a progressive form of economic management that could ensure full employment and a buoyant economy without resort to socialist ownership. Capitalism could be reformed rather than overthrown. Sutch reviewed Keynes's *General Theory*, albeit critically, within months of its publication.[33]

But the movement of young Keynesians into other British Commonwealth treasuries was not replicated in New Zealand. In Canada, for instance, Robert Bryce joined the Finance Department in 1938. A graduate in engineering from the University of Toronto, he had gone on to postgraduate study in economics at Cambridge University under Keynes before studying at Harvard, an early centre of Keynesian thinking in the United States.[34] In Australia, H. C. Coombs, one of the most notable of the Australian Treasury's economists, recalls that when he went to Sydney in the mid-1930s to join the Commonwealth Bank, he came in contact with a group of economists who shared his excitement over Keynes's work. Other economists influenced by Keynes were also recruited to the Australian Treasury and played important roles in the influential Financial and Economic Advisory Committee between 1939 and 1941.[35]

This absence is in turn related to the third hurdle Treasury faced in adopting an economic advice role: the fact that its expertise was financial rather than economic. Treasury was on many occasions 'out of the loop' on economic issues, even where these had a financial dimension. Nash introduced the Primary Products Marketing Act, which with its commitment to guaranteed purchase had major fiscal implications, but he did so wearing his newly-donned hat as Minister of Marketing. Treasury was not represented on the Dairy Industry Advisory Committee which helped prepare the bill. If Treasury did provide advice on the bill, this does not survive. A later file is confined to the financial aspects of purchasing Picot Brothers, a private firm the government acquired to give it the advice it needed to carry out its economic policy.[36]

The very nature of the financial expertise that was required seemed to rule Treasury, if not other arms of government, out of a role in the new economic order. Revealingly, a 1938 article on 'government and economic planning' which advocated a new organisation answering to a minister of trade, commerce and economics, envisaged it embracing the new marketing department, Customs, and Industries and Commerce. The Treasury was not even mentioned.[37]

The development of the Institute of Public Administration and its Diploma of Public Administration course at Victoria University College owed much to the 'new impetus given to State participation in social and economic affairs, by the first of the total wars of the twentieth century and by the economic disruptions which followed.' The two-year diploma course, which got under way in

1939, was devised for 'public servants with some executive experience'. The course was to cover institutions, public finance, economic history, public economics and public administration, plus a number of electives.[38] But no Treasury officers were selected for it before it was suspended because of the war. And discussion about accountancy in the public service stressed the need not for business methods in government, but for accountancy to adapt to the requirements of the public sector:

> The accountancy course has been drawn up with the needs of the commercial and financial community. Hardly a subject in the accountancy course has any relation whatever to the work involved in governmental accounting and yet hundreds of Public Servants are qualifying in this field.[39]

As was described in chapter 3, from 1921/22 the public accounts had been prepared on a commercial (balance sheet) as well as on a cash basis. This was part of a wider scheme of applying business methods which also involved changes to the railways and post office accounts. The need, as described in 1935, was for 'accounts in a form that will show up relative efficiency and costs of services'. Even by the latter years of the coalition government, it was clear that the arrangement hadn't had quite the effect on the public accounts that had been hoped for. The new accounts had 'as it were been grafted on as an extra and much remains to be done to co-ordinate them with the old forms of accounts on a cash basis.'[40] While they continued beyond the term of the first Labour government, from 1941 only a limited number of such balance sheets were published.[41] The Public Accounts Committee itself lost much of the investigative capacity it had gained in the 1920s during the Depression, and did not recover it.[42]

At a banal level, during the interwar years Treasury headed the list of departments in the annual *Public Service List* — but by 1940 these were being listed in alphabetical order. Was Treasury's actual significance to be no higher than its place in the alphabet?

Enter Ashwin[43]

Insofar as this proved not to be the case, much of the credit goes to Bernard Ashwin, who became Secretary to the Treasury on 9 February 1939. Just 42 years old, but long regarded as the department's most able official, Ashwin might have become Secretary when Park was moved to the Mortgage Corporation in

A new world? Treasury and the first Labour government, 1935–1949

B. C. Ashwin, Secretary to the Treasury, 1939–55. Treasury

1935, but for the strong presumption that the next in line, G. C. Rodda, who was 22 years older than Ashwin (and four and half years older than Park), should have his turn.

To appreciate the particular character of Ashwin's achievement, consider his efforts biographically. On the one hand, he is a product of the 1920s transformation in the Treasury, possessing a robust sense of the virtues of fiscal responsibility and the merits of his department in guarding it. As he said in a lecture in 1935, 'as none of [the departments] can do very much without finance, the Treasury, under the Minister of Finance, is the keystone of the whole operation'.[44] Easton accurately describes him as a 'fiscal conservative … Government expenditure policy involves numerous ministers and departments, all anxious to spend the government's money on the public's behalf, and the lone Treasury and its minister have to raise the money'.[45]

But Ashwin became aware in the 1930s that governments had adopted a much more vigorous approach to managing the economy. Was there scope for officials and economists to play a role in that management, and what would it be if there was? Clearly, given the outlook of the first Labour government, it could not be that of recommending a return to the old 'economic constitution'. But if Ashwin was prepared to offer a different kind of advice, does this mean that he had adopted the new economics pioneered by Keynes and others?

If he had, it is a very difficult process to track. Ashwin's writings are not overly reflective. His diary for 1939 is a narrative rather than an analysis of an economic crisis. It is possible that during the Depression he was more receptive to the adjustment measures taken by Coates, including devaluation and statutory reductions in interest rates, than was Park, but we can't be sure. There are more clues later. An effort was made to prepare national income accounts in 1939. Such accounts were a marker of thinking about the economy in Keynesian terms, and Ashwin was probably involved.[46] And at the 1940 Economic Stabilization Conference, he was clearly familiar with concepts such as national income and savings.[47]

But too much focus on intellectual mainsprings misses the practical nature of Ashwin's 'genius'. Ashwin talked with academics, but there was never any sign that he wanted to be one. After retiring from Treasury he was active in business, not in scholarship. It was policy, politics and power that engaged him. It is from this perspective that we can most readily explain his tactics. He would have recognised that in this new age a Treasury that confined itself — or was confined — to financial control would be sidelined, as the Audit Office had been before it, and he was too energetic and too able to let or want that to happen.

But he was also too astute to forgo the influence that financial control gave. That leverage he used in two ways — on other departments, and with the government itself. Throughout his secretaryship Ashwin was alert to the enhancement of Treasury influence in government, and at key moments he ensured that it was Treasury, not other departments, that played a co-ordinating economic role. He was, for instance, ready to take on a much bigger role in areas such as primary product marketing, wages and tariffs than was traditional. But even more striking is the way he used the office of Secretary to the Treasury as a springboard for a much more ambitious but individual and personal role — that of *economic adviser to the government*.

Whether that advice was informed by neoclassical or Keynesian thinking, it was always *usable*. The nature of the Labour government made this approach necessary, but it also suited Ashwin. So a process that in other treasuries involved outsiders or new recruits was in New Zealand driven by the departmental head. Easton rightly sees Ashwin as a pioneer of economic management, but it is the very distinctive nature of such pioneering being carried out by a *head* of the

Treasury whose antecedents and career lay almost entirely *within* that department, and who was not an out-and-out Keynesian, that merits emphasis. In the longer term, this meant that the transformation of the *Treasury* into an economic adviser informed by Keynesian precepts, as occurred in other Commonwealth countries in the 1940s, came about *later* in New Zealand.

We will follow Ashwin the economic adviser through three episodes: the exchange crisis of 1938–39, the implementation of wartime stabilisation, and the nature of post-war economic policy. And we will stop en route to look at what happened to the department that provided Ashwin with his 'power base' but lay very much in his shadow in these years.

Ashwin had already established a reputation for giving frank advice — over social security and borrowing — by 1938, when the exchange crisis developed. Both because it was a crisis, and because it involved classic Treasury concerns, the exchange crisis facilitated the enhancement of the role of the Treasury — or at least of Ashwin (his predecessor, Rodda, who was within weeks of retirement, was not as active). Lefeaux, the Reserve Bank Governor with experience at the Bank of England, was as restrained and formal as Ashwin was adept and agile. The crisis built up in the second half of the year, as a rapidly expanding economy, coupled with capital flight, drained New Zealand's overseas reserves at an increasingly rapid rate. While it had some awareness of this development throughout 1938, the government did nothing to address the situation, mindful perhaps of the forthcoming election (which proved to be its greatest political triumph) on 15 October.[48] A month later, the Bank of England was well aware of the gravity of the situation:

> The affairs of the Reserve Bank [of New Zealand] are fast approaching a critical stage. Thus, while [it] is receiving roughly £400,000 sterling a week from sales of dairy produce, its payments of sterling have recently been at the rate of roughly £1,000,000 a week. There is thus a net outflow of about £600,000 a week, and the Reserve Bank's sterling funds have now fallen below £5,000,000 ... At the current rate of decrease [these] funds can last only another seven or eight weeks. Concurrently, advances to the State in New Zealand ... have been mounting steadily since June. Thus on the 6th June the amount was £NZ300,000 and by the 7th November ... [it] had risen to £8,050,000. Of this amount £NZ5,000,000 has been advanced since early September.[49]

The 1938–39 crisis prefigured a succession of what came to be called 'balance of payments crises' in the post-war era. These were a true marker of the new political economy. In the old order, if purchasing power built up internally, New Zealand prices would rise relative to those of the rest of the world and an adjustment would take place. The mechanism would vary, but for practical purposes it amounted to one of the two strategies followed in the early 1930s — deflation or devaluation. Deflation — a general reduction in purchasing power — was anathema to Labour because it created unemployment. Knowing that deflation was out of the question, one London observer pondered whether the New Zealand currency would be devalued — 'I am very interested in that lovely, odd, exasperating country. Such news as I get is the reverse of reassuring. I cannot see — if they go on as heretofore — how they can avoid an ultimate serious depreciation — 150 or more.'[50] But devaluation of the New Zealand currency — a transfer of resources to those who earned overseas income — was equally unwelcome to Labour, because it would increase the cost of living as imports cost more. Labour's approach was therefore to control — to restrict the movement of currency overseas, to pay for imports or for any other reason — so that the expansion of purchasing power would not spill over into increased imports and threaten the balance of payments. Exchange control and the licensing of imports were introduced on 6 December 1938. In the 1970s, that decision was to be seen as a turning point for the New Zealand political economy, but it was inherent in the approach the government had taken since it was first elected.

The speedy implementation of the measures and the number of agencies involved — Customs, the Reserve Bank, Treasury, the trading banks and industry organisations — created major problems of co-ordination.[51] Who was better equipped to take a leading role than the new Secretary to the Treasury?[52] The Treasury's financial expertise was crucial at this time because loans falling due in London at the beginning of 1940 would have to be renegotiated, and British financial interests were not much more sympathetic to the Labour government in 1939 than they had been in 1935. There was also the broader issue of the economy as a whole, but the finance and the economics could not in practice be separated.

R. M. Kershaw of the Bank of England had congratulated Ashwin on his appointment and expressed the hope of seeing him in London soon, but the latter replied that 'with all the far reaching changes now taking place in New Zealand, it is difficult to forecast when we will get back to stabilised conditions, and until that desirable state of affairs is again reached there will be no opportunity for me to leave the Dominion.'[53] There lay the opportunity, but also the risk. Would the government want to take Ashwin's advice? He and E. D. Good, the Comptroller of Customs, advised the Cabinet that it was impossible to reduce imports to the extent required to balance receipts and payments without endangering employment and living standards. Other measures such as taxation, local borrowing, and a reduction in public works would be needed. A large rise in local costs and prices had also somehow to be avoided.[54] In other words, a deflation of some kind was unavoidable. Privately, Ashwin was even blunter. The government's determination to increase citizens' purchasing power, he wrote in his journal, was 'a very pleasant but poisonous doctrine economically'. Increases in pensions and social services, as well as the 'enormous programme' of public works and subsidised relief work, meant that capital expenditure was now well ahead of savings and the Reserve Bank held nearly £1.6 million of Treasury bills. The lavish expenditure had only been possible because of the reserves built up since devaluation in 1933.[55]

'I don't think', Ashwin confided to his journal in April 1939, 'Savage appreciates the gravity of the situation, whilst the rank and file of people continue to enjoy prosperity without realising that the foundations are crumbling beneath them.' So there was no guarantee that the politicians would listen. Success with the leaders was achieved in the face of what, in Ashwin's eyes, were 'Party' sentiments on economic issues that were directly inimical to the best practice: 'many in the Party object to paying interest at all', and some were lobbying for an elective ministry, partly as a way of getting rid of Nash. Lee, the leader of the 'left wing', in Ashwin's eyes, had not quite enough support in caucus to get rid of Nash.[56]

It was with Savage that Ashwin had his successes. Did it help Ashwin to have his minister out of the way in London and to be able to deal directly with Savage and the rest of the government? 'Nash is definitely not a man of action … his room is referred to as "the cemetery" by other ministers, yet he has the best brains in the ministry. His failings are indecision and a passion for detail.' It was Ashwin who told Nash that he would have to go to London over the loans falling due in January 1940, whilst he attempted to convince Savage of the need for the internal loan. 'Yesterday I had a long discussion with the PM and I think was successful in showing him the economics of the situation.'[57]

Whether or not Ashwin's advice would have been heeded by Nash, weeks later he told his journal that 'aided by Lefeaux was finally successful in getting PM to meet the market for an internal loan.' Savage in turn got it through caucus. Sullivan, another minister, told Ashwin that Savage made a good speech and understood his subject.[58] Later again, with Nash still in London, Ashwin spent 'three hours in Cabinet at the PM's invitation fighting to get the works programmes reduced'. While £5 million was cut, he thought that the total of £20 million was still twice as large as it should have been, given the volume of savings and other calls on them. Ashwin complained to his journal that Paddy Webb, the Minister of Works, 'went ahead building commitments around the country, even though the employment promotion fund had been replaced by a social security fund'. At a more immediate level, the government's own finances were complicated because of the drain of money from the Post Office Savings Bank. Some withdrawals, by women especially, Ashwin thought, were being made in fear of what might happen to savings.[59]

So while Ashwin did not have much good fortune with the Cabinet as a whole, he was making headway with Savage, whom he found easier to work with than Nash. Savage even conceded to Ashwin that, given the choice again, he would set the social security limit at 65, not 60. 'I think', Ashwin confided to his diary, that 'I have achieved a good deal in educating him up to the serious nature of the position economically and financially. He gives me his full confidence and for that reason is much easier to work with than Nash.'[60]

Maybe Ashwin was overstating this. But certainly he saw a lot of the ministers at this time. Ashwin was in daily contact with the full Cabinet during the final weeks of Nash's negotiations with the British authorities. Semple would regularly suggest that the British be told to 'go to hell', a comment, Ashwin noted, that most of the Cabinet were inclined to support. Each time, he had the task of pointing out that New Zealand was not in a position to do that: 'Montagu Norman came in for some abuse. But underwriters could not be arranged and we were facing default when the Bank of England and the big trading banks came to the rescue without commission and agreed to virtually underwrite.'[61] And Ashwin was pleased that New Zealand managed to get an interest rate of 3.5 rather than 4.5 per cent, although Belshaw's view was that the lower rate was no compensation for the draconian repayment conditions.[62]

Back in Wellington, Ashwin continued to be impressed by Savage, whom he was meeting daily: 'He will face facts and has courage.'[63] Officials, of course, always say that when the minister agrees with them. In his only Budget speech, which he delivered as acting Minister of Finance, Nash having not yet returned to New Zealand, Savage explained, in terms that echoed Ashwin's memoranda of two years earlier, that 'the present basis on which we have reached full employment cannot be anything but [a] temporary phase because it is not economically sound to keep so many men engaged permanently on works, however desirable they may be, that do not add to the present flow of consumable commodities.'[64] Ashwin confided to his journal that Savage had 'agreed to my ideas being written into the Budget, but he had to go to hospital the morning after he delivered it.'[65]

The journal, which Ashwin had only started when he became Secretary in February, inconveniently ends at this point, but circumstantial evidence suggest that, with Nash's return, and the waning of the crisis, Ashwin's 'leverage' was reduced. But the possibilities were there. In remarks to the annual conference of the Institute of Public Administration in March 1940, Nash himself referred to difficulties of exchange control being overcome by a co-operative departmental effort' — with 'tremendous credit … due to the Treasury in particular.'[66]

This compliment suggests a more general point. Ashwin used the phrase 'economically and financially' in his diary. This was not loose writing. 'Financial' was the imperatives of public finance — the sphere of action to which the Treasury was dedicated. 'Economic' was the management of the whole economy. Treasury's — or Ashwin's — opportunities to have a voice in the economic sphere arose from issues, such as exchange and import control, which had financial and economic implications that could not readily be separated. For Ashwin, the first sphere was an indispensable point of entry into the second.

War and stabilisation

When Nash paid Treasury his compliment, New Zealand had been at war for six months. What was until 3 September 1939 known as the 'Great War of 1914–18' had propelled the Treasury into the financial role described in chapter 3. The nature of economic policy at the outset of the Second World War meant that financial and economic issues were inextricably linked, but Ashwin's point of entry into the debate was, as always, financial. It was to be more than three long years before Ashwin established for himself the central position in economic management that one suspects he had envisaged from the onset of war.

Ashwin concentrated his energies initially on fiscal issues. He hoped for a flat-rate war tax of 6d in the pound on all wages and income, a 10 per cent supertax on income tax, and a 'system of national savings'. The Labour caucus argued for week over an alternative plan for a supertax of 15 per cent, increases

Paying for the war. Prime Minister Peter Fraser purchases National Savings Certificates at the Chief Post Office in October 1940. Evening Post Collection, Alexander Turnbull Library, C-22752-¹/₂

in death duties and postal charges, and levies on beer and tobacco. The balance of the sum required would come via inflation.[67] Politicians, as well as Ashwin, opposed the latter plan:

> If money is to be borrowed to the extent of £10m or £50m for the purpose of prosecuting this war then let it not be borrowed from the Reserve Bank with resultant inflation, but let it be borrowed, if necessary compulsorily, from the people who have it, whether they have it in large amounts or small amounts.[68]

Nash, too, was determined to pay for the war substantially out of taxation and internal borrowing.[69] With changes to income tax, the amount of direct tax per head of population increased steadily from £8 17s 5d in 1938/39 to £41 2s 3d in 1944/45.[70] In his Budget speeches in 1940 and 1941, and in his speech to the 1940 Economic Stabilization Conference, Nash 'turned his face sternly against inflationary credit issues'. His policy was to tax to the economic limit for war purposes, and borrow for essential productive works and to meet any remaining war requirements. 'It was at this time Nash began to earn his reputation as a rapacious taxer.' While he did so along the lines that Ashwin had canvassed, the taxes on petrol, liquor, tobacco and cigarettes were also raised.[71]

Beyond taxes, internal borrowing provided most of the funds for the war. After 1939 a substantial loan was floated in each year of the war, with two in 1942. This policy saw the proportion of the public debt held in New Zealand rise from 47 per cent in March 1939 to 80 per cent in March 1946.[72] It was seen as particularly important to borrow money directly from the public, as this was more likely to reduce spending power than borrowing from the banks (which might still lend to the public — but at least would not also be lending to the government).[73] Of the increase of £327 million in domestic borrowing between March 1939 and March 1946, only some £42 million was not balanced by the withdrawal of spending power from the private sector and therefore tended to be inflationary.[74]

But though the war strengthened the connections between public finance and the economy as a whole, there was no expectation at its outset that initiatives in these areas would be co-ordinated or led by the Treasury. Reflecting across-the-board Labour concern about profiteering, all prices were immediately brought under control through a Price Tribunal for which legislation had been passed in June 1939. In December the Minister's powers were delegated to the Price Tribunal, an organisation not linked to the Treasury.[75]

Despite the internal loan and the Price Tribunal, prices continued to rise in 1940. The first wartime general order of the Arbitration Court, which took effect in August 1940, granted a 5 per cent increase to all workers subject to the Court's awards, reflecting increases in prices since March 1939. In September the government convened the Economic Stabilization Conference to consider the possibility of stabilising costs, wages and prices; again, Treasury was not prominent in its deliberations.[76] It was a conference of interest groups, with representation from those identified as employer groups, namely manufacturers, the Primary Producers' Council, the Farmers' Union, the sheep-owners, the Dairy Industry Council, the Employers' Federation, the chambers of commerce, the shipowners, the coal-mine owners, and banking representatives. These were matched by employee representatives — the Federation of Labour, but also delegates from a variety of individual trade unions. Public servants were in an advisory position — their role was to make submissions to the conference. Ashwin did so, but he was the only Treasury witness amongst a mass of officials from other departments — there were no less than five witnesses from Industries and

Commerce, and others from Labour, Internal Marketing, Customs, the Standards Institute and the Price Tribunal.[77]

The conference demonstrated that the government still saw the management of the economy as a political rather than an expert or bureaucratic process. 'Political' in this context denoted the significant interest groups in the economy, and the departments of government which 'serviced' them. Prime Minister Peter Fraser reported two years later that it had been 'the most representative conference of economic interests ever held in this country. [It] unanimously urged the Government to stabilize prices, wages and costs so that the cost of the war is not thrown unfairly on one group to the benefit of another. The Government made this proposal its policy and appointed a committee to carry on the work thus begun.'[78]

In fact not enough was done for a year, during which the futility of any attempt at stabilisation which was not fully comprehensive was becoming increasingly obvious. In August 1941 some of the recommendations of the Conference were put into effect, when the prices of 38 essential items were fixed from 1 September. At the same time, recognising that even this was inadequate, an Economic Stabilization Committee was set up to work out the details of a comprehensive plan.[79]

The Committee consisted of the Minister of Finance, the Minister of Industries and Commerce, the acting Chair of the Stabilization Conference, and five employer and employee representatives. By the beginning of 1942 some of the requirements were beginning to emerge, and an Index Committee was set up in January to prepare a new price index suitable for wartime conditions. At the same time, the Arbitration Court took the unusual action of rejecting calls from workers for pay increases. Ultimately, the Court did grant a 5 per cent general wage order with effect from April 1942, because it had become evident that continued price increases had left workers worse off than they had been under the 1940 order. This award had the novel provision that it was not to apply to any portion of pay over £5 a week for adult males and £2 10s for adult females. Awards had tended to be passed on to all wage and salary earners, irrespective of whether they were covered by awards, and did nothing to stop further price and wage rises.[80]

Ashwin's rise to 'prominence' arose out of his dissatisfaction with this Stabilization Committee:

> Meetings could only be arranged for two to three days once a month and in the time available it was impossible for the committee to deal with the mass

A New World? Treasury and the First Labour Government, 1935–1949

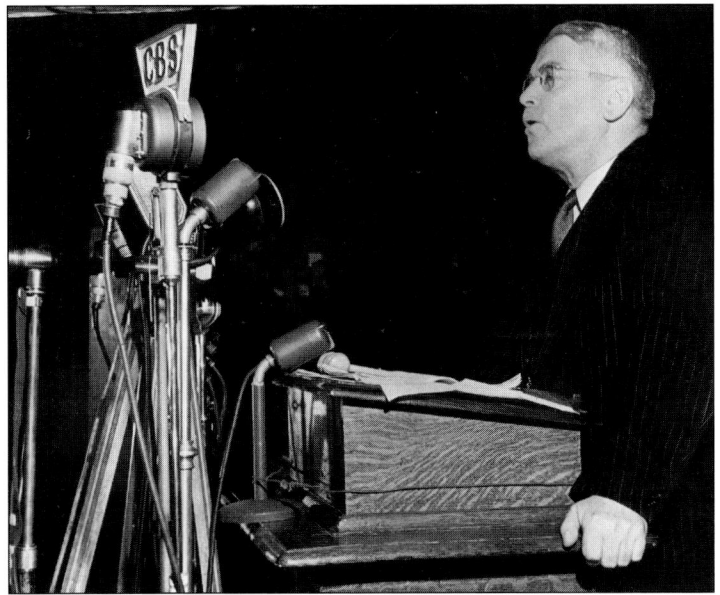

Walter Nash addresses the International Labour Organization conference in Philadelphia over which he presided in 1944. War History Collection, Alexander Turnbull Library, F-36300-¹/₂

of material relating to particular cases. The Committee tended, however, to spend its limited time on such detail, principally because it was dissatisfied with the recommendations of the Price Tribunal. The result was that there was little opportunity to consider the larger questions ... [There was an] issue too with the attitude of the chairman ... [It] seems that Mr Donnelly is not anxious to continue as Chair of the Committee. It may be advisable to appoint a chair resident in Wellington. Wd most probably be desirable for the chair to be a permanent official ... The same official could be director of an economic secretariat. It could be attached to the PMs Dept. It would be valuable not just as an adjunct of the Economic Stabilization Commission, but as an organ of economic co-ordination to assist the Cabinet and the War Cabinet. This would, in fact, be its more important function.[81]

By this time Walter Nash had left for Washington DC to be New Zealand's minister to the United States, and it may be that with Fraser handling the finance portfolio, Ashwin felt more able to take initiatives:

> The fact that Nash refused to resign when he took up his position in Washington did make things a little awkward for me although I had no

difficulty in carrying on without him … Nash could not hope to run Treasury from 12,000 miles away.[82]

Was Ashwin involved in the July 1942 decision of the Economic Stabilization Committee that a 'liaison committee of officers in key economic positions should meet regularly in order to pool information on matters affecting stabilisation'? J. S. Reid from Nash's office was the chair, and the four other members included H. L. Wise of the Price Tribunal and R. G. Hampton of Industries and Commerce. The short-lived bipartisan War Administration welcomed the offer of the Economic Stabilization Committee to act as an advisory committee which would make recommendations to the War Cabinet from time to time on the action which should be taken to protect the country against inflation and stabilise prices. But, wrote Ashwin to the Prime Minister in October, it hadn't worked:

> in my opinion the whole policy is likely to remain ineffective until the scope of the action to be taken to stabilise wages, cost of living and farmers' prices and costs has been defined and authority given to someone to organise and initiate such action. At the appropriate time the approved comprehensive scheme must be published … resolute positive action is essential.[83]

Ashwin had met the members of the committee on 16 October, just before writing this letter, so it can be assumed that he was well-informed and probably that they agreed with his initiative.[84]

Had Ashwin by this time established the rapport and trust with Fraser he had achieved with Savage? It seems that the circumstances were similar — in mid-1939, with Nash away, Savage was acting Minister of Finance and had to present the Budget; in 1942, Nash was away again and Fraser had to present the Budget. By the time Nash came back, their mutual trust had reached the point that if there were a difference between Ashwin and Nash that couldn't be resolved, Ashwin, like other permanent heads, could arrange to see Fraser on a Saturday morning. Fraser was now a final court of appeal between minister and official.[85]

When Fraser introduced the full stabilisation policy in December 1942, it was evident from his announcement that it would embrace every aspect of domestic economic activity:

> When we wish to keep prices fixed we cannot do it without fixing within narrow limits the price of labour, which is wages, and also the level of rents

> ... this is the main part of the decision of the War Cabinet which I am announcing ... all incomes are to be stabilized by one means or another.[86]

It is difficult to separate stabilisation from the overriding claims of the war. The Economic Stabilization Commission, which had replaced the Stabilization Committee, was not another department of state arousing inter-departmental jealousies. A commentator writing shortly after the war highlighted its role of

> dual co-ordination of departmental administration and of group interest [which was] unusual, and could only be achieved by an independent semi-representative body. Economic Stabilization covers prices, wages, rents, transport — in fact every activity of the individual. The Departments dealing with these activities all have problems which are also the concern of the Commission. The Commission is the central intelligence and 'economic general staff' service for the Government. It must maintain contact, through its officers, with the various departments dealing with economic affairs, recommend particular courses of action which it believes to be in harmony with the general policy, and withal keep the Government continually informed of the economic state of the country.[87]

In this account, Jim Moriarty stressed that no other country had anything quite like the Stabilization Commission. In Australia, the United Kingdom and Canada, cabinets and ministers were much more directly involved in interest group negotiations than they were in New Zealand, where, as Leicester Webb, who was to succeed Ashwin as Director of the ESC, put it, the Commission had been 'of great value in easing the pressure on the political executive. It carries out negotiations on prices and payouts with representatives of farming interests, the manufacturing industries and other economic interests.'[88]

Australia had a price stabilisation committee comprising the Prices Commissioner, Treasury representatives, and the War Organization of Industry. This could not stand between the government and economic pressure groups to the same extent as the New Zealand Commission could. Thus negotiations in 1943 and 1944 with the dairy industry about product prices were successfully concluded by the Commission, whereas in Australia they were negotiated with Federal ministers. In the United Kingdom, co-ordination was undertaken at ministerial level.[89] The failure to establish a fully cross-party War Cabinet in New Zealand, or even a successful War Administration — a halfway house to such a Cabinet, set up in mid-1942 but lasting only three months before National pulled out — provides another explanation for the importance of the Commission, and indeed for its establishment just two months after the demise of the War Administration.

As an investigating entity, the Stabilization Commission's activities in many ways echoed, but reached further than, those that had been acquired by the 1920s Treasury in respect of government departments, as this description of one officer's duties in 1948 demonstrated:

> Investigation of applications for price increases and subsidies submitted through the Price Tribunal, Mines Department, Milk Marketing Division, Dept of Industries and Commerce, and also those received direct. Marshalling of information and preparation of reports and recommendations for consideration by the Commission, more particularly those relating to the town milk industry, clothing, woollen milling and footwear industries and the coal-mining industry.[90]

It was the Economic Stabilization Commission, not Treasury, which advertised on occasion for economists.[91] Its files are full of detailed reports on the costs and price structures of various industries, and of correspondence with companies or industry associations about such matters:[92]

> Any industry that wanted to put up a price, for instance the price of tea, which was a subsidy, the price of sugar. The companies concerned would have to put in a return, these are our accounts, these are our costs, these are our profits and so forth, and we would say, 'Well, that's enough profit for you'.
> *How were you expected to confirm their figures?*
> You took them as audited accounts.
> *An element of trust?*
> Yes. You would make a recommendation and it would go to the Commission.
> *You would be questioned by them?*
> Yes.[93]

As in other countries, the existence of such an entity overshadowed the peacetime Treasury.[94] But in New Zealand the moving figure in the new order became the Secretary to the Treasury himself. The 'natural' public servant for this role might have been L. Schmitt, the Secretary of Industries and Commerce — the department, both on its own account and through subsidiary agencies such as the Price Tribunal, that was most involved in the regulated economy. Was it the crucial fact of Treasury's role in public finance that tipped the balance, or was it

Ashwin's personality and his ability to get on with Fraser?[95]

In July 1943 the Commission was reconstituted by reducing its membership to three. The two original members who continued in office were joined by the Secretary of the Treasury, who had been the *Director* of Stabilization, as chair.[96] It is from this time that the Ashwin of later memory comes into focus — the individual who, above all others, was at the centre of the New Zealand political economy of the day:

> In the late 1940s he was often at the Dairy Products Marketing Commission (DPMC), and other primary producer places. He would attend the monthly Reserve Bank board meetings, and frequently be with the Cabinet or elsewhere in Parliament Buildings. He would lunch at the Wellington Club and see Walter Nash in the early evening — or at least start a meeting with him — they would frequently go on late into the night. Overall, he was so rarely at his own desk that discussion with Treasury staff was not that common.[97]

Another Treasury official remembers 'coming back towards office from, say, walk along wharves or something. Ashwin was in front of me. He'd obviously come out of lunch at the Wellesley Club and was going along ... sort of clicking his fingers, like he was really thinking.'[98] Indeed it's hard to get a 'still' picture of Ashwin, who was someone seen most often in motion, as it were. He even 'wound up like a baseball player preceding execution of his "incomparable" signature.'[99] He worked predominantly by conversation and wrote relatively little, sharing a typist — Marjorie Dobell — with others. Once the Stabilization Commission was in being, he spent some hours on most days in its offices, two floors up.[100] His most frequent visitors at this time were, in order of frequency, Webb, his successor as Director of the ESC (and sometimes Jim Moriarty, also from the ESC); E. R. McKillop, who was Commissioner of Works from 1945 to 1955; Judge Tyndall from the Arbitration Court; George Duncan of the Dairy Products Marketing Commission; and Federation of Labour leader F. P. Walsh.[101]

If the relationship with Fraser was crucial, so was that with Walsh. It was a significant endorsement of the Wartime Price Index when the Federation of Labour unanimously approved the stabilisation scheme, and no doubt the presence of Walsh on the Stabilization Commission helped: 'union co-operation was essential and Walsh had to take much of the credit for that. Statistics were juggled to ensure that prices did not increase by more than 5%.'[102] Henry Lang, whose first job was with the Stabilization Commission, recalled a clothier saying, 'Henry, you are too tough. But never mind, we will cut a bit of cloth off all the shirt-tails.' One historian thinks that 'juggling' probably wasn't necessary because subsidies held the prices of a large enough proportion of the components of the Wartime Price Index, but if Ashwin's memory is faulty on that matter, the nexus with Walsh was real enough. The latter established his own office, just two doors down the corridor. 'He'd get in all his colleagues to abuse and tick off'; 'he'd also use the services of his office and the staff of the ESC to write his speeches etc.'[103] Walsh was also chair of the Index Committee.[104]

The nature of New Zealand's economic relations at the time meant that Ashwin's orbit extended globally as well as nationally. From 1943 an intensive phase of international economic diplomacy saw the creation of the World Bank and the International Monetary Fund, and the planning of an International Trade Organisation. Further, the extent of wartime trading by the state required intensive negotiations with both the United Kingdom and United States governments.[105] In all these spheres of activity, Ashwin was closely involved. Many anecdotes were told about his negotiating ability — internationally as well as in Wellington. There is the widely circulated story that on one occasion there was a gap of a farthing a pound in negotiations over the price of butter, which was settled by a snooker game, in which Ashwin represented New Zealand.[106] Schmitt recalls the lend-lease negotiations with the Americans in Washington, at one point in which Ashwin was 'rambling on', seemingly without purpose, about the cabbage planting they'd done on the family farm near Cambridge in Waikato:

> It took the rest of us a while to cotton on, that he was talking about the way that they helped the war effort. Then he called for an adjournment, then re-did sums — $US prices for butter, meat — and cabbages of course — worked out they owed US, $2m. Eugene Black, the American negotiator, was heard to say that 'if ever a New Zealander starts talking about cabbages, you might as well give him what he wants and save your time.'[107]

And in 1951, at the time of an official visit by Ashwin to Canberra, the High Commissioner wrote back to Wellington that 'Mr Ashwin himself is, of course, a tower of strength … his semi-good humoured method of negotiating is something all his own and it is wonderful to see what he can really get away with. His decisions are quick, clear and almost invariably correct.'[108]

A NEW WORLD? TREASURY AND THE FIRST LABOUR GOVERNMENT, 1935–1949

What happened to 'Treasury control'?

Both during the exchange crisis and in wartime, Ashwin's rise to principal economic adviser, while it had foundations in the Treasury, left the department and to some extent its longer-established role of financial watchdog in the shadows. Webb, perhaps not coincidentally an 'outsider' who joined Ashwin at Economic Stabilization, identified two public services:

> One consists of the old-established departments which have carried on through the war with depleted staffs and with some addition of special war functions. The other consists of new agencies which have sprung up to carry out special war tasks and which are staffed in a large measure by men and women without public service training … the [old] public service has been markedly reluctant to prepare itself for the work of regulating or actively directing economic enterprises; in these respects it is still very much the product of the reforms of 1912 — reforms conceived by men whose instinct was to set the narrowest possible limits to State activity.[109]

It seems reasonable to put Treasury into the first category, even though Treasury officials themselves, remembering the 1920s and 1930s, would probably have put it in a more positive light.

Although the records are not illuminating, it seems most unlikely that Ashwin lost sight of this 'core business' of Treasury, and one or two initiatives of which he must at least have approved confirm this. From the late 1930s, the title of 'investigating officer' replaced that of 'inspector', with the 'Chief Inspector' being replaced by the 'Chief Investigating Officer'. This change may seem minor, but it probably reflected the more active role that Treasury officers were taking in financial matters since Treasury reports on spending proposals had been required. The number of investigating officers increased from eight in 1940/41 to 28 in 1951/52. Systematic records of Treasury's dealings with other government departments — the main work of investigating officers — date from this decade.

Whether this increase in numbers and expertise shifted the balance between minister and officials in Budget-making remains difficult to judge, as few Budget files survive. One 1945 comment described the Budget as 'primarily a plan of the public revenues and expenditures prepared by the Treasury in the process of managing the state finances'. This statement suggests, if only by omission, that the Budget was still regarded as an exercise in financial management, not economic policy. The article in which it is found is not illuminating on the respective contributions of ministers and officials.[110]

One initiative in financial management took place during the war. The Ministry of Works was set up to 'establish more appropriate control over the execution of all construction works, including housing construction', in 1943.[111] Given the role that the expansion and financing of the state housing programme had played in creating the boom conditions of 1937/38, this was a significant development. The concept seems to have arisen in discussions between officials of the Defence Construction Council. James Fletcher suggested to Cabinet that a small group be set up to 'study every major proposal that other departments were considering, examine it objectively in relation to other calls on Government finance, and establish its priority'.[112] The involvement of the Treasury was central, as is evident from a memorandum from the Engineer-in-Chief to his senior officers:

> In association with Treasury to ensure that all schemes for construction involving expenditure of Government funds are thoroughly examined independently of the source from which they originate, both from an economic and a technical point of view. In this connection not only will proposals coming through Government departments be examined, but also the proposals of local bodies or private interests where such carry with them Government subsidies.[113]

Ashwin's style can be seen in this instruction. As has been noted above, McKillop, the Commissioner of Public Works, was one of the most frequent visitors to his office. Recalling the experiences of the late 1920s, Ashwin must have been determined that Treasury continue to have an influence on this aspect of government, just as it continued to be represented on the boards of entities such as the Reserve Bank, the State Advances Corporation and the Local Government Loans Board.

What sort of a place was this Treasury that was still primarily a financial control institution — a department of accountants that was also grappling with economic issues? The department, along with many others, occupied in the 1930s a portion of the Government Buildings on Lambton Quay, below Parliament.[114] That accommodation dated back to the erection of the building in the 1870s, but was regarded as superior to the adjacent 'temporary' structure, the 'tomato house' erected on the land between the Government Buildings and the court buildings on what is now Whitmore Street. Bernard Greig contracted

A NEW WORLD? TREASURY AND THE FIRST LABOUR GOVERNMENT, 1935–1949

The 'Tomato House', the temporary accommodation for public servants that stood for decades adjoining Government Buildings. W. H. Raine Collection, Alexander Turnbull Library, G-21608-1/1

tuberculosis, probably while he was working with Pensions, then Inland Revenue, in the 'tomato house'. 'There was no known remedy for TB … I knew that vaguely. I heard [of] all these awful cases in Pensions, in Inland Revenue. You can put that down entirely to working conditions. I looked round Treasury and thought, well this is a bit more airy.'[115] Greig sought and got a transfer.

Noel Lough started as a cadet, aged seventeen, with Treasury itself, in 1937,

> in the Records room. I started part time study for the Accountants' Professional qualification. In those days you studied at a private college for which you had to pay. Accountancy was not included in any university degree course. I was then transferred to accounts, which were all done manually, cheques written by hand. The ledgers were at high desks with stools.[116]

Treasury, along with a number of other departments, moved to the Departmental Building on Stout Street (colloquially known as 'the Kremlin') in the early 1940s.[117] Treasury was on the fifth floor, while the Economic Stabilization Commission was to be on the seventh. Here the Treasury stayed until its move to the National Provident Building, 1 The Terrace, in 1979.

The bulk of the senior officers in the department, Ashwin included, had joined the public service as school-leaver cadets. They had studied part-time for a Bachelor of Commerce, climbing the hill to Victoria University College or going elsewhere in town to one of the several private accountancy colleges:

It was called 'the Kremlin'. Treasury moved into the Departmental Building on Stout Street in the early 1940s and stayed until 1979. Gordon Burt Collection, Alexander Turnbull Library, F-15910-1/1

> The B Comm. had fifteen subjects of which nine constituted the professional accountancy course, taken not at university but at the accountancy colleges. The other six were Economics I (two papers), commercial law (two), economic history, economic geography, public finance, currency and banking. The obstacle was Accountancy III — there were lots of 'all but' B Comms around. It was therefore a tough course; there were no easy options, and those who got through it were no mere 'book keepers' and needed determination to persevere to the end.[118]

By 1936 half of the department (48 of 98 staff) either had or were studying for an accountancy qualification, a proportion that only fell after the war because so many formerly temporary female employees recruited during the war were put on the permanent establishment. Accountancy training changed after the war, when the university colleges, Victoria included, took on all the accountancy teaching. Cadets like Noel Lough experienced both systems:

> When I returned to VUC [after the war], they had taken on accounting. The examinations which I had passed for the Accountants Professional examination were recognised as part of that degree. I had to go there to do Accounting III and Auditing III, and also Economics II and III. I finished [a] B Comm with [a] double major in Accounting and Economics.[119]

Lough was relatively unusual in doing so much economics. If the pre-1933 political climate had continued, the expert requirements for the public service might have been built on this basis, with aspiring officials expected to acquire ever more expertise in accountancy, commercial law and economics. One shift that confirms a continued vitality in Treasury's financial role was the practice in the 1930s 'for Treasury staff to be recruited from officers who have gained experience in other Departments, as such officers are likely to have a more impartial outlook on the various problems which confront the Treasury from day to day.'[120]

What kind of staff did the department have at this time? The number of permanent staff increased from 95 in 1936/37 to 240 in 1951/52, a period during which New Zealand's population grew from 1.5 to 2 million. Most of the increase in staff numbers took place in the latter part of the period as part of the wartime and post-war expansion of government. Much of Treasury's work was still routine; in 1945, the department issued 2000 cheques daily.[121]

In 1948, 60 of the permanent staff were women — an historic departure that became possible only when long-standing restrictions on women in the public service were lifted after the Second World War. The 1912 regulation requiring women to resign on marrying was rescinded, and six months' maternity leave without pay was introduced to encourage married women to remain in the public service. The Public Service Commission also revoked the 1921 restrictions on women public servants holding permanent positions, and started recruiting female clerical cadets. These changes were realistic as well as principled — even with men returning from the armed forces there were labour shortages. While the *Public Service List* does not tabulate temporary employees by department, in the service as a whole their numbers fell from nearly 16,000 in 1946 to 4500 in 1947. In 1936/37 Treasury had three permanent women employees and 92 men — by 1951/52, 73 and 167.[122]

In the latter year, most men and all but six of the women were in the 'general' class. Probably more than half of those in the clerical and administrative divisions had an accountant's professional or better qualification. Attached to the department were six other agencies — the Actuarial Branch, the ESC, the

Superannuation Board, the National Provident Fund, the Stores Control Board, and the War Assets Realisation Board — employing nearly another 200 staff in total. In all these divisions collectively there were perhaps two Maori, if surnames are any guide. Even taking all the ancillary agencies into account, the department was much smaller than 'giants' such as Land and Income Tax (with 489 staff in 1946), and Price Control.[123]

Since Ashwin's senior colleagues of the 1940s were to lead the organisation well into the 1960s, it is worth paying some attention to them. Arguably their effectiveness was enhanced by working with such an able superior: 'I think Ashwin's performance rubbed off on them. Issues such as investigation of projects, control of contracts, and of public finance were dealt with by others highly competent.'[124]

When Ashwin was promoted to Secretary, G. G. Rose and E. L. Greensmith both moved up one notch, Rose becoming the first Assistant Secretary and Greensmith the second Assistant Secretary. R. M. Sunley, who had been in the High Commission office in London, returned to become Assistant Accountant, and C. R. J. Atkin (who was to be Controller and Auditor-General from 1952 to 1960) became Chief Investigating Officer.[125] Athol Mackay took on Ashwin's responsibilities as Treasury Accountant:

> The most senior accounting officer was fourth in line — his concerns were not with book-keeping, but with what the books showed — with control, adherence to voted amounts, flow of revenues, borrowing and conversion of debt, estimates to be put to Parliament, by departments which aggregated an acceptable total, negotiating departments' estimates down where necessary to achieve this, and so on. Apart from this position and possibly one or two of the more senior accounting people every senior position was clearly not a book keeping one.[126]

The 1948 *Public Service List* shows nine senior officials, headed by Ashwin himself; Greensmith, the Assistant Secretary, who had an MCom and a solicitor's qualification; and Mackay, the second Assistant Secretary, who had an MCom and a PhD from the University of London, gained while he was working in the High Commission. The next six included four with the accountancy professional qualification and one with a BCom and a London DPA. These positions included the Finance Officer and Accountant, and the Chief Investigating Officer.

Some are recalled to this day. Rose, who was around 60 in 1940, was remembered by Schmitt for rolling his own pipe-plug tobacco cigarettes. Athol Mackay was a quiet and pleasant fellow whose tobacco tastes ran to special cigarettes, which he smoked using a cigarette holder. Mackay drowned in the late 1940s while trying to rescue a child of his from the sea at Otaki:

> What a loss [it was] when [Mackay] drowned, not very long after I came back into the organisation. He was brilliant. He not only had a brilliant brain but he was a very able, common-sense fellow.[127]

Greensmith's first two decades in the public service were spent with the Public Works Department, and he transferred to Treasury initially on a temporary basis, to help out with investigating work. A. B. ('Johnny') Taylor and Doug Barker were both to become Chief Investigating Officer. According to Schmitt, Taylor was a 'pleasant enough fellow' who gave the impression that he didn't push things. First Greensmith, then Barker would succeed Ashwin as Secretary to the Treasury.[128] Tom Atkin, who had served during the First World War, was, Bill Robinson recalled,

> a nice guy, but he was moody — I think he suffered a lot from that war wound, but no one knew much about it. I remember at a social committee subcommittee meeting, a second one I think it was, we decided [we] wanted to have a mid-year party. Tom said, 'Yes, this will be fine'. We were sitting around that fifth floor oval boardroom table, he's up at the top, and says, 'yes, I think that's quite a good idea. Now I don't want you to think I am a wowser, but there will be no liquor'. There was a shocked silence from the three of us there. Both those other guys are dead now, God bless 'em — Les Mitchell and Clem Kilkelly. 'Mr Atkin', I said, 'when you say liquor, what do you say about a keg of beer? Because some of us don't include that in our vocabulary as being liquor ... I am sure that speaking for myself — I can't speak for these others — I don't think we can have a very successful social with just orange juice and lemonade.'[129]

After the war

Ashwin's influence reached its peak in 1943 and 1944, the heyday of the Stabilization Commission. What would happen after the war? Was economic stability really 'an end to be pursued after the war just as much as during the war ... the basic controls necessary to stabilization arise from the nature of the New Zealand economy ... it would be impossible to abandon controls at an early

The 1940s was a time of micro-management by politicians. Here Prime Minister Peter Fraser (left), the Minister of Supply, Dan Sullivan (right), and civil servants examine bread baked with flour of 80 per cent extraction, a more intensive use of New Zealand wheat that was ordered to help prevent famine overseas. Alexander Turnbull Library, C-4756-1/2

date'.[130] And if so, would Ashwin, or some institution in which he was influential, play a key role?

The impact of British policy, and in particular of Keynes's and Beveridge's schemes for avoiding a return to depression conditions in the post-war world, found echoes in New Zealand. An October 1945 paper, 'Full Employment in New Zealand', rehearsed at length Beveridge's arguments about post-war employment, including by asserting that 'our chief annual budget will not be a Revenue and Expenditure Budget but an Economic Budget, covering National Expenditure of all kinds, public and private.'[131]

Full employment had become a leitmotif for post-war policy in many other parts of the world, as governments throughout the world determined not to return to the unemployment of the pre-war era. One former United Kingdom Secretary to the Treasury argued in respect of that country's employment white paper that it

> might never have been written but for the greater degree of agreement amongst economists and the closer relations established, in the Second World War,

between economists and others charged with handling central problems of government. In it the government accepted as one of its primary aims 'the maintenance of a high and stable level of employment after the war, that fiscal measures are among those which should be rightly used to this end; and that public investment should be carefully planned to offset unavoidable fluctuations in private investment'.[132]

The British Budget of 1941 and full employment proposals of 1944, along with the Australian white paper of 1944 on full employment, are instanced as Keynesian turning points.[133] The 1941 British Budget was the first to talk in terms of the national economy rather than the public accounts — indeed, the first to produce national income accounts, albeit sketchy ones. This was the Keynesian fiscal revolution, in this instance applied to an inflationary situation, the greatest wartime economic enemy. Inflation could best be restrained if the government used the taxation and revenue systems not to balance its own accounts but to ensure that excess purchasing power in the economy as a whole was soaked up — an element of what was to become known as demand management.[134]

For its part, *Full Employment in Australia* argued that expenditure levels across the economy as a whole could be regulated by varying public capital expenditure. Similarly, in 1946 the Australian Treasury commented that it was 'now fully accepted government policy that in framing the Budget, in scrutinising expenditure proposals and preparing revenue measures, the Treasury must be guided not only by narrow financial considerations but also by its assessment of the existing and prospective level of employment and National income'.[135]

The decision to retain government responsibility for the level of economic activity in peacetime raised issues of co-ordination. Developments in the United Kingdom were analysed elegantly by Samuel Beer. In the early post-war years a large ministerial committee, arising out of wartime practice, supervised 'the whole field of home and economic affairs', whilst inter-departmental committees, whose work was supervised by a committee of the permanent heads of the main economic departments, were used to achieve co-ordination. A fuel crisis in February 1947 and the crisis provoked the following August when sterling was made freely convertible into dollars forced a recognition that the division of responsibility for economic affairs was unsatisfactory, and Treasury emerged from the latter crisis as the centre of economic planning and co-ordination.[136]

The equivalent developments in New Zealand will be more fully discussed in chapter 6. Some comments on why they did not occur immediately after the war are pertinent here. Would the politicians take over from the Stabilization Commission? Or would the Commission remain as a permanent economic co-ordinating department, similar to the United States Bureau of the Budget.[137] What would be Treasury's role?

In 1938 Mackay had advocated that, in view of the expansion of government activities during and after the Depression, the Treasury 'should develop a staff of highly-trained officers of wide experience who will be capable of investigating and advising impartially on the various proposals which come up for consideration.' He was opposed to the idea of a 'brains trust' (that is, of expertise operating outside the regular channels of advice to government), but with the establishment of the ESC this co-ordination role was not located in the Treasury.[138] The sensitivity surrounding this issue was evident from a comment made in 1948 by the anonymous reviewer of a recent publication on the British civil service:

> His comments on the necessity for central planning could well apply to New Zealand. The difficulties of any planning theory as he points out are its relationship to the Treasury which has the ultimate responsibility for the finance of the country, and he agrees that Treasury should be closely associated with any attempt at national economic planning because of its position as 'department of departments.'[139]

The outcome was not to be the Organisation for National Development that had been set up in 1944 and intended to convert New Zealand's 'economic policy into a centrally co-ordinated detailed plan. Though the Labour Party has often been accused of being socialistic, it was not ready for this'.[140] The last meeting of the Executive Committee of the OND took place on 4 September 1945. Ashwin, who chaired the Committee, subsequently advised that no more meetings would be held in view of a Cabinet minute of 19 November. Ashwin had been working with Walsh on a post-war stabilisation plan, so cannot have been an enthusiast for the OND.[141] The minute noted, inter alia, that 'special departmental committees under the chairmanship of the Secretary to the Treasury will meet to deal with specific problems' and report to a special Cabinet committee which would handle 'major problems involving rehabilitation and post-war construction. Research functions would be passed to the new National Employment Department and physical planning functions to the Ministry of Works.'[142]

New Zealand therefore did not acquire a powerful rival to the Treasury analogous to the Postwar Reconstruction Department in Australia, whose Director-

General was the economist H. C. Coombs.[143] A more plausible (because low-profile) candidate was an inter-departmental balance of payments committee that was set up at the time of the mid-1947 sterling convertibility crisis. This committee included Alex Ross (chair of the Reserve Bank), Pete Johnsen (Customs), Jack White, an economist at the Department of Agriculture, George Wood (Statistics) and Geoff Schmitt. In one year at least it made detailed decisions on the import licensing schedule. Two businessmen also played a less weighty role — one wanted to tighten up on motorcycle imports and loosen up on rifles.[144] This committee was to prove a precursor to a system for co-ordinating economic advice that was devised after the change of government in 1949.

Another possible direction was flagged with the passing of the Economic Stabilization Act in 1948, when the Commission was constituted as an advisory body to the Minister of Industries and Commerce.[145] But while Labour remained in office, and Nash was still Minister of Finance — as he had been since 1935 — he was dominant. Nash's 'go it alone' decision on the revaluation of the New Zealand pound in 1948 to parity with sterling, which he took against the advice of both the Governor of the Reserve Bank and the Treasury, was only the sharpest instance of this.[146] Officials, including Ashwin, remained subordinate, and so by the end of the decade there was no firmly established *peacetime* pattern of economic advice to the government, be it Keynesian or otherwise, from Treasury or anywhere else.

Out of office

On Nash's last day in office after Labour's election defeat in 1949, Ashwin was told that the Minister wanted to see him. 'The Minister *always* wanted to see him, especially at the end of a long day, and would ask him to come in at 9 p.m. Ashwin would sit in the ante-room listening to Nash turning over papers, sometimes for two or three hours. On this very last day he finally got in to see Nash. Ashwin really wanted to get some of his files back, amongst other things. When he went in Nash said, "There are a few files we ought to go over. I have got here a proposal to build a new lavatory block at the Hutt primary school. This seems a very high figure. I'm not certain whether or not I could possibly agree to this." Ashwin got it all back in one move. He looked at his watch and said, "Well, Minister, you've got exactly three minutes to decide."'[147]

Chapter 5

Backwards or forwards? The Treasury, 1949–1961

National's failed counter-revolution, 1949–1951[1]

Throughout the last term of the Labour government, and in particular during the 1949 election campaign, National had argued vehemently for an end to controls, a restoration of 'freedom' — particularly 'economic freedom' — and a radical reduction of the overwhelming economic power of the state. Sidney Holland underlined the importance of finance by taking the portfolio, which he was the first Prime Minister for nearly two decades to hold.

Holland's agenda was far more radical than any other National government would implement until the 1990s. It was identical in its essentials to the view of the political economy that had been articulated by Coates in 1935, and to the Douglas/Treasury view of 1984. Its key elements were fiscal conservatism, the conduct of monetary policy independent of the state, and a reliance on the market rather than on controls or state ownership. This was a post-war New Zealand version of the nineteenth-century 'tripod' of free trade, gold standard and balanced Budget. The most significant way in which it differed from the prescriptions of the nineteenth century, the 1920s and 1980s was that it was more at odds with the orthodoxy of the day.

'We have given the people their freedom', Holland proclaimed, and 'they know there will be no more socialisation. Farmers can now develop their farms and increase production safe and secure from the fear of the Government. More and more freedoms will be restored as the days go by.'[2] The Prime Minister was riding a political groundswell. One of his supporters wrote from the Northern Club in Auckland that

> your start on the removal of restrictions here in Auckland at any rate has been greatly appreciated … the extra [petrol] ration for launches was a splendid move. There are thousands of launches in Auckland and I hear great praise

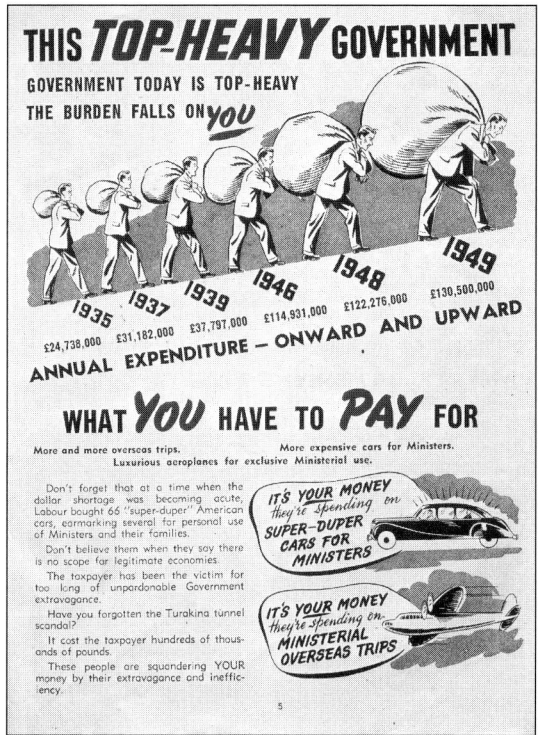

Top-heavy government. National's A Family Affair *1949 election booklet.* Alexander Turnbull Library, F-l06471-¹/₂-CT

on all sides from the owners … every lawyer … is enthusiastic about our promise to ease up … irksome restrictions [on land sales].[3]

The new government accelerated the reductions in wartime controls which Labour had begun. Controls over land sales, both urban and rural, were abolished, along with many building controls, including those over materials. A number of industries were delicensed, and sterling exchange regulations were relaxed. Many items were taken off the import licensing schedule, and many tariffs (43 by May 1954) were reviewed.[4] Price control was abolished on some clothing, footwear, electrical goods, furniture, groceries, haberdashery and office equipment.[5] State houses began to be sold to their tenants.[6]

A direct assault on the government's own spending complemented these liberalisation measures. Holland's primary short-term economic concern on taking office was inflation, which was seen as the outcome of government extravagance.

'The task', he said on 1 February, was to 'study the remedies required to restore stability and sound finance'. For Holland, the major culprits were soaring government expenditure and borrowing. The solution was to cut both.[7] There was a strong traditional flavour to both Holland's rhetoric and the government's actions:

> There is clear indication of the need for arresting the drift to expenditure beyond our means. This applies both to loan money being spent on capital works and to payments from taxation and other revenue receipts … We are introducing into the Government's financial administration business methods and [the] plain commonsense that is so badly needed today.[8]

In notes for his first Budget, Holland recorded that 'forty-nine State departments go to great pains to say what is <u>desirable</u> … social security, houses, land development, tourist, works, education, hospitals and all the rest. They are not required to even think where all the money comes from'.[9]

As promised, the government did increase social security benefits and remove the 33.3 per cent tax on unearned income, but these measures only intensified the need to control expenditure in other spheres. Holland reserved his particular wrath for the 'subsidy system that has grown to huge proportions in recent times', explaining its perniciousness through a simple example:

> If, say a manufacturer finds the cost of producing a certain article is 20/-, which he has to sell for less than 20/-, he will quickly examine his costs of production and then he will set about to improve his methods so as to eliminate his losses and inefficiency. If, however, he can make up his losses by, say, a Government subsidy, then the urge to efficiency and economy largely disappears.[10]

Fiscal conservatism thus overlapped with a wish to put 'state undertakings' (or 'state enterprises' — both terms were used)[11] on a business basis. In respect of the National Airways Corporation (NAC) — the state-owned domestic airline — the new government went even further. Stan Goosman, the Minister for Civil Aviation, convinced Cabinet in July 1950 that it should look at withdrawing from providing commercial air services and 'allow private interests to take over the business upon some agreed-on basis'. The word 'privatisation' had not yet been devised: Goosman announced that the government intended to sell NAC 'lock, stock and barrel', if possible.[12]

In other spheres of state activity, the recovery of costs was the theme — 'it was more equitable', said Holland, that services should be paid for by those who used them rather than by the taxpayer.'[13] Treasury came up with proposals for increased Post Office charges that would turn a 1949/50 loss of £250,000 into a £500,000 profit.

Holland explained, echoing the debate of the 1920s and early 1930s, and foreshadowing those of the 1980s, that the railways had lost £1 million in one year — or if the non-payment of interest on capital was included, £3.8 million. Rail charges were increased, and in 1952 — after a royal commission — the railways were once again removed from political control, being placed under a Rail Commission which was obliged to run 'efficient and economical passenger and goods services'. The Rail Commission restructured services, further increased user charges, and turned a £1.4 million loss in 1952 into a £1.46 million profit in 1955.[14] This was a typical expression of the oscillation on ownership between conservative and Labour politics: 'governments of the left normally prefer to have state services and utilities under their direct control, governments of the right to delegate control to boards of managers.'[15]

Holland's approach to borrowing also echoed the earlier era. It was officially estimated, he claimed, that the 'works programme would cost £250m more than can be raised by borrowing from the public on the basis of present investments by the public in Government loans. Such a programme is ludicrous.'[16] Development should only be financed by funds obtained from the public for the purpose. To that end, the first new loan would be offered on terms that were more attractive than previously:

> The immediate problem then is to raise the £20m balance required to complete the finance for our capital programme. This will be done ... by inviting subscriptions during a fixed period of four weeks ... it is evident that government loans have not met with a ready response from the public as the terms have not been in line with what the public considered reasonable.[17]

When this loan was oversubscribed by £900,000,[18] one commentator argued that its success indicated that the community was behind the government in opposing the use of further 'Reserve Bank credit' for capital development.[19] Holland was relentless in his criticism of the creation of such credit — money which increased the money supply 'without increasing the supply of goods and services available for purchase'.[20] National also moved to repeal the Minister of

Top-down development. A Grumman Avenger trials aerial topdressing after the war. RNZAF Collection, Alexander Turnbull Library, F-23039-1/2

Finance's statutory power to dictate to the Reserve Bank. Currency and credit questions should be determined by economic considerations, not ministerial direction.[21] In debate on the bill, Holland declared that the government was fulfilling its election pledge to divorce 'responsibility for the issue and control of currency and credit and for the maintenance of a stable internal price level … from political control and ministerial dictation'.[22]

In sum, the new government was committed to conservative economic management, to 'sound money' and 'business-like' practices. But despite not just the rhetoric but the range of policy measures cited above, the revolution did not succeed in taking the New Zealand political economy back to 1933, for three reasons. Firstly National remained, as Reform and United had been in the past, a party of developers as well as of fiscal conservatives. Secondly, the outbreak of the Korean War forced the continued use of economic controls. Thirdly, and most importantly, National would neither dismantle social security nor endanger full employment. National was the descendant, not the twin, of the pre-1933 conservative political formation — right-wing politics had changed, and 'managing' the economy was now an acceptable task of government.

The failure to pursue the goal of selling NAC illustrates the first two of these aspects. There was criticism of the plan not just from Labour but from important National Party supporters — from regions with poor land communications

Should NAC be in state or private ownership? Aircraft service the pre-Christmas rush at Wellington's Paraparaumu airport, 23 December 1949. New Zealand Free Lance Collection, Alexander Turnbull Library, G-102234-1/2

such as Northland, and from business interests anxious lest Australians muscle in on the aviation sector. The Korean War, and in particular the waterfront dispute, helped restore the airline to profitability — with 'shipping services delayed or locked up, air transport enjoyed a boom year in 1951'.[23]

Even the conservative press could reconcile the government's enthusiasm for development with the need for fiscal orthodoxy:

> Action to reduce government expenditure, and thereby taxation generally, must necessarily be introduced carefully. Essential services must be maintained, and there are still many requests for State financing of particular projects, including some in or near Dunedin.[24]

The relatively healthy fiscal position made it possible to reconcile fiscal responsibility and development. In 1950/51, for example, taxes were expected to total £13.4 million more than the previous year. Even allowing for extra spending on social security (£5 million) and defence (£7 million), there would be more money in the coffers. And in 1952, Treasury Secretary Ashwin was able to reassure ministers that there would be no difficulty in providing the finance for public works for 1952/53, because there was a £16 million surplus in the War Emergency Account.[25]

The War Emergency Account had been established in May 1951 to prepare for the possible 'catastrophe' of a major war.[26] The outbreak of the Korean War the year before had led to sharp price increases, and while this benefited New Zealand's commodity exporters it also provoked increased inflation. In such a 'wartime' environment, with the memory of the Second World War still vivid, it was natural that the Cabinet should turn to the direct controls which had a proven track record.

Bassett attributes the return of controls to the waterfront dispute, which broke out in February 1951 and stopped normal work at ports for five months, but this wider context was also a factor. Price stabilisation subsidies were significantly increased in the latter half of 1950, when the wool retention scheme, in which half of the proceeds of the astronomical wool returns were 'frozen', was also introduced.[27] There was to have been a further round of price decontrol in February 1951, but after a general wage increase was announced it was decided not to proceed with this. As the Minister of Industries and Commerce, Jack Watts, rationalised it, 'if in the time of present inflation we wish to continue some form of stabilising economic policy then it is necessary to continue with price control.'[28]

With a deteriorating balance of payments and continued inflation, more direct controls were reimposed in 1952. The control of capital issues was tightened, interest rates for building and investment society deposits were raised, and an exchange allocation scheme was introduced under which Reserve Bank approval was required before overseas funds could be obtained for imports in excess of 80 per cent of the level in 1950.[29]

Matching these powerful trends was a shared sense that there had been a fundamental shift in the political landscape — to full employment. While this had been initially supported mainly by the trade unions, explained one commentator, the 'maintenance of a high level of effective demand, which is the means of achieving full employment, has turned out to be a great benefit to all traders and manufacturers who depend for their livelihood on the domestic market.'[30]

And further, 'full' meant 'full': 'when full employment was a proposition in White Papers rather than an operative policy, it was understood to involve a margin of unemployment — perhaps 3 per cent of the work force — sufficient to avert a degree of competition for labour and a level of demand which would have generated inflationary pressures. Electoral opinion has largely eliminated the safety margin.'[31]

The Treasury's tasks

If Holland's 'counter-revolution' had succeeded, we might have seen a reinvigoration of the 1920s Treasury and its vigorous attempts to exercise fiscal control. And there are traces of this, and indeed of the department shaping the new ministers. For example, the Secretary of External Affairs, A. D. McIntosh, wrote to an overseas correspondent in February that 'Treasury have succeeded all too well in scaring the new Government stiff'.[32] But events took a different turn. For one thing, Holland was not that malleable. Secondly, senior Treasury officials were committed not just to fiscal control but to economic stabilisation — in particular, to controlling inflation. We will look at that activity, and its implications for relations between the department and ministers, in later sections of this chapter. But for the Treasury as a *whole*, the new 'gospel' of economic co-ordination and economic management preoccupied individuals but did not transform the institution. The 1962 Royal Commission on the State Services, in looking at Treasury's work, did not even mention its role in advising on economic management.[33] And Treasury's own draft submission to the Royal Commission stated that:

> the primary objective of the Treasury is to secure/ensure the control of/by the Government and/or Parliament over public expenditure and to maintain financial order throughout the State Services.[34]

In this section, I will concentrate on these aspects of Treasury's work. In the 1950s, most of Treasury's staff were employed to look after the government's accounts, investigate spending proposals, handle estimates, and administer borrowing and debt servicing. The primary division within the department was, as it had been since the 1920s, that between those who did the day-to-day work of processing the government's receipts and payments, and those working on investigative and financial tasks. Numbers increased only from around 240 to 280 during the decade, with women making up between a third and a quarter of the total. 'We collected revenue', recalled one junior official,

> that went into the public account, and issued all cheques on behalf of government departments. That was what Treasury was about when I joined in 1951. The people there had School Certificate, and some would have University Entrance. I opened the mail for the first two or three weeks, under guidance of course. I soon learnt who did what and where, in the different sections in this great big accounts room.[35]

Cliff Terry had a similarly humble start. Despite having already worked for seven years in Public Trust and Industries and Commerce, and completed his accountancy professional exams, 'when I got to Treasury I spent six months putting vouchers together with cheques, learning about the accounting system, as if I were a cadet. "Part of the training!" — that's what they said.'[36]

Powers–Samas machines were installed in the 1950s to process all cheques. In 1956 there were 22 machinists — all women, most aged under twenty — and seven 'mechanicians' who oversaw the machines (in effect the forerunners of today's 'IT' people) — all men, most rather older.[37] Don Rangi recollects his first days, aged seventeen, in 1959, when he was newly arrived from the East Coast:

> Arthur [Ashley-Jones] took me up to see Jack Lang on the fifth floor. I was introduced to his assistant [J. O.] Bonifant and to accounts work. 'Bonny' took me down a long narrow corridor. You couldn't see much, just frosted glass windows behind which were the machines. They had punchcard-type things. Someone would check to see that all the payments added up — the girls would hand-write each cheque out. That information would then be punched on to a card, sent over to the Samas machine for sorting and another printing production done. It was just like a factory and reminded me of the wool press back home. There was a room where the girls did the sorting, there was also another area where people were busy writing paper cheques, looked like the old Dickens. There were about 30 of these older women — or that's what they seemed to me, they were probably around 30 or 40 — with one male supervisor — it was Ron Simms at that stage.[38]

Those long corridors and glass windows were in the Departmental Building in Stout Street. When Don Rangi started work, the investigating officers were on the seventh floor, the Superannuation Division on the sixth, and Accounts, the Secretary and his deputies and assistants on 'mahogany row' on the fifth. The Government Stores Board, another entity affiliated to the Treasury since the 1920s, was on yet another floor. In his new job, Don learnt how to print the cheques:

> You had the name of [the] person, but the amount had to be encoded by the machine. It was just like in a factory — 'here's your work, this is what you do, this is what I want, you go to that machine and key it in'. I started off with 1d to see how it worked. When the chap came to check the batch, he couldn't reconcile because there was this extra penny.[39]

Several other cadets started at the same time:

> Phil Morgan from Wales, Phil Wilkinson, and Alec Phillips. Some would have had UE. The last one to retire was Rodney Stubbs — he was a bit older than me … Alec Phillips was Maori. And some of the women in the punching pool — perhaps a couple out of the 30 or so.[40]

Women made the tea, but this was one area that experienced radical change in the 1950s:

> The tea looked like nothing else on God's earth. Some of the girls who were making the tea had not a clue. I say 'girls' — men in the department were not permitted into the room to make the tea because it was adjacent to the ladies' restroom.
> *Were these tea ladies?*
> No, they were not, they were staff. We never had a paid tea lady.
> *A tea room?*
> We didn't get that until 1951. They would bring the tea round on trays — I don't think they even had a trolley.[41]

Bill Robinson was among those who set about organising a social club, which organised a self-supporting tea club as an offshoot. This was highly successful, particularly when it 'got away from the dry biscuits, and managed to get into chocolate biscuits, then scones and things like that.'

'Paying the bills' for all departments — and 'doing the accounts' — was 'what Treasury was about', but it was not *only* what it was about. There was also, as John Anderson recalled, 'the other side'. But those 'others' were not, in the 1950s, economists — though they were there — but the

> investigating officers, the research officers, and the hierarchy. Another term we used was the 'brains trust'. But to 'go round there' you had to have a qualification, a minimum qualification. So in those days, you could cut out the accountancy professional exams in three years … accounting I, II and III, then auditing was a stage III unit, then you had commercial law I, II, etc. They got short of investigating officers, so I was invited round the other side, even though I hadn't qualified.[42]

The more usual route was from elsewhere in the public sector. 'When I was recruited into the Treasury', remembered Cliff Terry, 'most appointments were made from other departments and qualifications were sought in the accounting or BCom fields. Most of the recruits were put into accounting or investigating jobs.'[43]

Gaining a qualification (which entitled the officer to a pay increase) often coincided with marriage in a period when newly married women frequently stopped doing paid work: 'I got married in February 1948, by which time I had completed accountancy and was a qualified public accountant. I still had a couple of units to do for a BCom, which I did in the first year of marriage.'[44]

The department's structure in the 1950s was simple. On this 'other side' there were three 'chiefs' — the Finance Officer, the Chief Research Officer and the Chief Investigating Officer. For much of the 1950s, the latter was 'Jacko' [J. P. G.] Pound.[45] Ken Durrant describes the nature of investigating work when he joined: 'you would report to the minister on whether the Director-General of the Post and Telegraph Department should be allowed his claim for excess travel expenditure.'[46] Ministers frequently convinced Cabinet to support particular expenditure programmes. As a Treasury memorandum to Holland explained:

> the real problem which existed when you took office and has become intensified since, arises in the capital works programme which has grown to such an extent that it is impossible to finance it from borrowings from orthodox sources ... the trouble forecast by Treasury in 1950 intensified in 1952/53 and there has been little administrative effort to correct the position. On the contrary, ministerial statements that more is being spent by the present administration than the last ... not only influence public opinion but also affect the attitude of departments in their continuing demand for additional funds ... after the 1952/53 Consolidated Fund allocations were made, request[s] for additional funds totall[ing] £11m were received.[47]

The experiences of young Treasury investigating officers were not necessarily adversarial: 'if you were negative on something, they would be [hostile], but employment in the public service was interchangeable and you might be working for [someone else] yourself ... the service was a service'.[48]

The investigating officers were the backbone of Treasury in the 1950s. Few important responsibilities were delegated, and most works projects and new programmes needed Cabinet or Cabinet committee approval, and therefore a Treasury report.[49] The 1962 Royal Commission described how expenditure control was exercised: through reports on the financial and economic implications of new proposals, and of particular proposals even where approval had already been given to the vote or programme within which they fell; and through scrutiny of both capital works programmes and annual estimates.[50] A 1955 staff training manual, 'Notes on Investigating', nicely captures the flavour of the time when it attempts to answer the question, 'what qualities are required in an investigating officer?' He (it was always a 'he') should have a 'well developed critical faculty and not be given to accepting statements at face value … a persistent enquirer and a digger into facts.'

Little stress was laid on financial skills as such. The investigating officer was not required to read a balance sheet or analyse a business plan, but to 'deal with problems as objectively as he can, present the pros and cons fairly, not let personal views sway his judgement and be able to come … to a firm, clear and concise recommendation.'[51] Or, as another Treasury document put it, he should pay particular attention to:

> whether the project seems justified
> what degree of priority it should be accorded
> whether funds are available
> whether it is within policy

The only 'financial' comment which followed — 'frequently there is no direct return from expenditure but where there is, an effort is made to see that the 'user pays' principle is adopted to the extent practicable'[52] — suggested how far the conception of Treasury control had shifted from the vision of the 1920s. This zone of activity was now less contentious, perhaps because there was less fiscal pressure than there had been in the 1920s. But the habits of control were still there. John Martin has described 'the typical Treasury "no men" (hearts like cash registers): Sol Greenberg, Ross Carroll, Ron Muir, Ralph Leathwick and Alan Wilson, for instance', of his first years in the Treasury:

> To other departments they were the 'hard face' of the Treasury, with enormous experience, detailed knowledge of what departments did and skilled in crisp reports to the minister of Finance and Cabinet. They were jealous of the tradition that Treasury reported to the minister and departments didn't get to see the treasury report until the Minister of Finance sent it on to the spending minister. They were the inheritors of the talisman that every expenditure proposal (except within delegated ministerial or Permanent Head authority) required a Treasury report. Their Bible was the brown, hard-covered, loose-leaf compendium (regularly updated), the *Treasury Instructions*

Likely lads. The Treasury rugby team, c. 1955. John Anderson

(accompanying the Treasury Regulations). Every investigating officer had a copy in the top right hand drawer. The daily output of the Treasury (apart from the cheques) was the large number of 'Treasury reports', which were overwhelmingly the product of the investigating staff, signed by the Chief Investigating Officer or his assistants.[53]

The most important task of these senior officers may have been to mentor:

> It was all done by on-the-job training — they would give you a file, see what you could make of it, and discuss it with the section head. And you would also go to see senior people in other departments. You would ring them up — 'I have some questions to ask' — then go over there. Education had a bloke who was the chief building man. He was about five feet tall, and a great talker, at great speed. We had great tussles. I remember Doug Barker saying to someone once, 'Oh Christ, you should take a leaf out of Cliff Terry's book — he saved us £7 million' (or some such ... figure).[54]

The dealings were with departments, not with the wider population. Thus Treasury dealt with the Maori Affairs Department (as it had now become), but not with Maori themselves. Investigations of Maori land settlement examined the over- or under-expenditure of the vote, not the rationale for the settlement programme.[55]

One of John Anderson's most demanding early encounters was with the Department of Scientific and Industrial Research (DSIR):

> When you get into the science field, you're dealing with PhDs and you say to yourself, 'Here am I, a young investigating officer …', but you soon learn. You had to have an ability to absorb from talking, whether it be about building schools or nuclear reactors and accelerators.[56]

On the finance side, two deputies supported the Finance Officer. One dealt with loans, and the other with the votes and the public accounts.

> Public finance was an imprecise sort of thing [in] those days. We didn't have a very good system, we never knew exactly where we stood. Incidentally, there was room for a great deal of manipulation to adjust the surplus or deficit. It is much more precise nowadays. You couldn't use those devices now. Computerisation makes a difference — you get instantaneous results.[57]

Sam Parker spent some years in London, where he had responsibility for New Zealand's financial dealings. On one occasion 'we did something that wasn't very well known — we arranged a standby with a bank: we thought we might not have been able to balance the books and we had to be ready to fill the gap. It was initiated by the Treasury, not by politicians. Les Williams was the man in Treasury who did that sort of thing.'[58] With all its imprecision and rough and ready solutions, Finance was certainly one 'way to the top'. Perhaps it was not surprising therefore that it

> was an area you couldn't easily get into, as there were only three senior positions … The assistant investigating officers, the investigating officers and the senior investigating officers were all saying, 'How do you get one of those three jobs in Finance?' They'd say, 'Oh, it's always open'. Henry Lang got into the one that dealt, amongst other things, with the public accounts. He learnt it all very quickly, and that served him a long, long time.[59]

Doug Barker was a 'bricks and mortar man, not an economist. Then you had Cop Davis, N. R. Davis. He was a finance man, not so much … bricks and mortar.'[60] One important task of these 'bricks and mortar' and finance men was to survey the Crown's investments, and it is from this perspective that it makes sense to consider Treasury's involvement in the 'Murupara project'. This was the establishment of a pulp and paper mill by a company established for the purpose

— Tasman Pulp and Paper — at Kawerau in the Bay of Plenty, to process the timber from the Crown's Kaingaroa Forest. The company's story will be discussed briefly here because it provides a useful insight into the Treasury's role in the 1950s.[61]

Bassett's assertion that the National government became involved in the project in 'a burst of entrepreneurial zeal worthy of Vogel or ... Muldoon' is misleading.[62] The project arose in the first place because the government's forests were reaching maturity. The Labour government leant towards a state endeavour, which the New Zealand Forest Service and its Director, Pat Entrican, also favoured. Ashwin's plan, which he outlined to Nash in August 1949, entailed the scheme being operated not by the government but by a company established for the purpose. The government would assist by advancing half of the capital costs as interim funding. Ashwin was concerned about the timing and financial structure of the project, did not want it financed from loan expenditure, and thought it crucial that 'a £25 million project should not be commenced until the finance for completing it in a business-like manner is assured'. These Treasury sentiments would not have been out of place in the 1920s.[63]

When Holland became the new minister, he 'did not want to put any money into the venture if he could help it', which was just what Ashwin wanted to hear. The plan he had presented to Nash was close to what emerged six years later, but the intervening journey was a tortuous one, partly because of the scale of the project and the commitment of major international interests to endeavours elsewhere. The government became involved in four ways: by building the infrastructure to allow its trees to be exploited, by investing (modestly) in the company, by helping to arrange finance, and by providing loans during the construction period. Apart from the infrastructural work which did not involve the company directly, the state's most significant involvement was as banker.[64] A committee report to the Prime Minister in December 1951 indicated that the principal difficulty was that of

> capital finance. The total cost of all the works required, both those directly the concern of the company and the ancillary government works, is approximately £28 million ... an amount of £7 million would be available from the [US] export-import bank and ... the sponsors of the company would put up £1m. This leaves £20m to be obtained by public subscription or from Government sources and the scheme as drawn up is based on the Government underwriting the whole undertaking. The Secretary to the

> Treasury advises that this amount could not be raised in New Zealand in addition to other requirements for finance in the next 2½ years.[65]

A tabulation in October 1953 reveals what happened. The government committed £13.33 million to infrastructural works which included railway lines, housing, and harbour works.[66] The company's capital of £6 million at this time was less than half of what was expected to be needed to set it up. Both the government and Fletcher Holdings invested in the company (Fletchers £700,000; the government £1 million), and the government also lent it money at 4 per cent interest. In due course more capital would be raised from other sources, and the loans would be repaid.[67] At the same time, the search for a large investor would continue. By this time a board had been appointed which included three government directors: Aswhin, Entrican, and E. R. McKillop, the Commissioner of Works, the heads of the three government departments that were most involved in the enterprise.

Treasury's involvement was thus primarily financial, and its advice to its minister and Cabinet reflected that fact:

> From a practical point of view a heavy investment and a substantial voice in the controlling Board is likely to be embarrassing to the Government. To be successful it must be run as a commercial enterprise. But if the Government has a large say in the management there will likely be constant representations to Government on alleged unfair treatment in contracts, in respect of agencies and by personnel ... for the government to take more than a minor share in the capital and management ... is unnecessary and unwise politically and financially.[68]

The government took this advice, although because of the vagaries of private investment in the company it remained more embroiled in its affairs than was intended. So did Ashwin himself, perhaps with more intent: 'there was always a hint of Treasury being too close to Tasman because of the Fletcher–Ashwin connection at Stabilisation and the way Ashwin became Director of Finance at Tasman after he left the Treasury.'[69]

Such closeness to industry was not confined to Ashwin. It reflected the three-decades-old practice of having Treasury representation on any board or company in which the government had a financial interests. 'I remember them all — Atkin, Barker, John Taylor, and so on down', recalled Sam Parker of Ashwin's senior subordinates. They were 'all of a mould, apart from Greensmith. They had moved with industry during the war, they had an outward-looking approach to life, and they were pragmatic.'[70]

Tasman has received a great deal of attention. It is useful to place Treasury's role in that project in context by looking at other areas of government involvement with industry. In his original plan for Tasman, Ashwin had instanced the oil company BP (New Zealand) Ltd, in which the New Zealand government had taken a 51 per cent stake in 1945, as a model.[71] A 1950 memorandum briefing the new government on that decision suggests that tax avoidance may have been Treasury's major preoccupation — it listed five tax compliance episodes involving oil companies between 1933 and 1949, and argued that such difficulties had diminished with the availability of 'inside knowledge.'[72]

Another example of Treasury financial management relates to the gas industry, which by the 1950s was in a sorry state. In 1952 there were 37 gasworks; fourteen were operated by companies, 22 by local authorities, and one by a gas board. Those in the four main centres (three of which were companies) produced about 75 per cent of the gas sold. The number of consumers was declining, whilst production costs had risen well above levels at which they could be recouped. The subsidies which had been provided since 1943 were ended in 1950, but restored in 1951 following strong lobbying from the industry. By September 1953, all gas undertakings were in doubt because of increased costs. A report from Industries and Commerce argued that, since 'the government could not, with equanimity, watch the larger gas works go out', but nor could it increase the subsidy, the best solution would be for the electricity consumer to bear some of the cost. This could best be accomplished by merging the uncompetitive gasworks with electricity supply authorities.[73]

Ashwin reputedly sank this proposal by suggesting to Holland that it would produce headlines about the extension of socialistic controls. Be that as it may, throughout the negotiations Treasury's major role was to consider the financial implications of any strategy for the government. In this activity 'Johnny' Taylor was the active official, and he focused on the fact that, as in so many areas, a subsidy was involved. Writing to the Minister of Finance about the proposal to merge electric power authorities and gas undertakings, Taylor observed that if it were left to the parties concerned he was 'reasonably certain from my six years of experience with this problem that very little, if any, result would follow.'[74] In 1958 (by which time none of the proposals had eventuated and the subsidy was still being paid), Taylor agreed that setting up a gas corporation would be costly and might not lead to a solution. He supported the establishment of a gas council, with advisory powers and control functions, on which Treasury, other official and industry interests should be represented. More substantively, Treasury argued for bringing in an expert, citing a 1956 visit by an English gas engineer who had found, amongst other things, that

> The Wellington Gas Company, generally regarded as a relatively efficient undertaking by New Zealand standards, could save over £50,000 per annum on present costs with more efficient operation and management (at the moment WCC is receiving £80,000, £90,000 per annum by way of subsidy).[75]

In sum, much of Treasury's work during the 1950s was dedicated to tasks that were not inconsistent with the vision of the department that had been articulated in the 1920s, even though the overall drive for fiscal control was more muted. We can round this discussion off by noting some of the legislative changes of the period. Ashwin wanted the Treasury to be identified as a department in its own right because the existing situation was that it was

> defined as the Minister of Finance and therefore legally is no more than the office of the Minister of Finance … it would be more in accord with the facts of the situation and the doubts and difficulties that arise from time to time if the act were amended to provide that Treasury meant 'Secretary to the Treasury' and inserting the word 'Minister' where it was thought desirable to reserve to the Minister any powers at present conferred on Treasury.

He also argued for the creation of an office of Deputy Secretary; such an appointment was not uncommon, and it was

> probably more warranted in the case of the Treasury than any other Department because the head of this department is involved so much in broad economic and financial policy matters that the first assistant has in large degree to undertake the ordinary administration of the Department. In England and Australia also I know that the second officer in the Treasury is recognised as being more or less the counterpart of the normal administrative head.

Although this letter was annotated, 'the Minister does not propose to take any action on this report', that was almost certainly because the government had called and won an early election on its handling of the waterfront dispute. Amending legislation on these lines was passed in 1952.[76] In addition, the Local

Government Loans Board Act, another product of 1920s' thinking about public finance, was amended in 1954 to give the Secretary to the Treasury more power over the Board.[77] With that goal accomplished, it could be said that Ashwin had done as much as was possible both to align government policy with the Treasury, and to ensure that Treasury control over the public accounts, which he had done so much to foster, would survive future turns of the political wheel.

Economic co-ordinators?

We return now to economic matters, and to differences between the Holland government and the Treasury. Initially the new government was distrustful of the entire public service, in which only one permanent head had served in that capacity before the election of the Labour government in 1935. One commentator noted that 'like the [United States] Republicans in 1953, the Nationalists in 1950 were imbued with a suspicion of, almost a hostility towards, the administrators'.[78] At the same time, as for Labour in 1935, the Treasury was a 'tool' that could immediately be put to use by the new government. Treasury could withhold as well as disburse, and the new — like the old — Cabinet adhered to the principle of all new spending proposals being accompanied by a Treasury report.

It might be thought that Treasury itself would have been happy with the broad direction of Holland's policies, which were not unlike those of Downie Stewart seventeen years before. But Ashwin and his colleagues had been tempered both by wartime and post-war experience, especially with inflation, and by the Keynesian ideas of economic management which had become familiar to officials by the end of the 1940s. The former made senior Treasury officials alert to the dangers of an ill-thought-out loosening of controls: 'until inflation with its disruptive pressures can be effectively checked it is in the interests of farmers, wage earners and in fact every section of the community that the general policy of stabilisation be continued.'[79]

The latter fostered a belief in the long-term merits of 'economic management', albeit not the directive variety favoured by the outgoing Labour government but something more subtle, drawing on the insights of Keynes and his followers into the workings of a national economy. Thus a memorandum on investment which Ashwin submitted to Holland in March 1950 contained 'comment on broader issues and assesses the effect of the Government works programme combined with (a) current trends in local authority and private capital programmes and (b) the effect of total investment programmes combined with movements in the general level of savings in the community.'[80] In the memorandum the Treasury was introducing the Prime Minister to the notion of thinking about trends and relationships in the economy as a whole, rather than solely the government's own finances. One implication — that the government ('the public sector') could tolerate an excess of investment over savings provided that business ('the private sector') did the reverse — would not necessarily have occurred to Holland. Ashwin thus provided a 'macroeconomic' argument about inflation rather than a traditional one.

Similarly, in September 1950, in calling for a co-ordinated anti-inflation policy,[81] Ashwin dwelt on the origins and character of the inflation, and argued for a number of measures to combat it. He could see little scope for change on the 'supply' side — increasing imports, for instance, was ruled out by the lack of overseas resources. Wage control would help slow down the increase in local purchasing power, and a Budget surplus and a complete freezing of the anticipated large increases in wool receipts would also help.[82] In this instance, the government took Treasury's advice. In another memorandum in the same month, Ashwin probably hoped to exploit Holland's well-known affection for Britain, citing as he did the precedent of its anti-inflationary policy: 'the policy of surplus budgeting to combat inflation was employed in the United Kingdom during the post-war years.'[83] It was in this fashion that Keynesian ideas came to inform the provision of economic advice in the early 1950s.

Both factors — war and post-war experience, and receptivity to the idea of economic management — encouraged thinking about channels of influence and advice. We have examined this development in the 1920s in respect of financial management. In the 1940s, while Ashwin claimed a role in economic management, its direction remained with Fraser and Nash. Would there now be scope in the post-Labour, post-Nash era for a shift in the minister–official balance towards the officials; to put it in officialese, for new structures that would allow officials to advise more effectively, for advice that was co-ordinated and institutionalised rather than prey to the whim of the minister and Cabinet? Within this intellectual framework, there was thinking about the role that Treasury would play vis-à-vis not just ministers, but also other departments and outside expertise.

The biggest change was engineered by Foss Shanahan, the head of the Prime Minister's Department,

Foss Shanahan, the architect of Cabinet co-ordination. New Zealand Free Lance Collection, Alexander Turnbull Library, C-23682-½

who set up the proper framework of delegations and all the rest of it. It was a very effective and sensible arrangement. Foss Shanahan was a brilliant man. Foss could never have got the change through Nash. There were no Cabinet minutes under Nash — a stamp went on a submission, 'approved by Cabinet, sgd W Nash'. But sometimes a decision hadn't ever gone to Cabinet, and there were no rules to stop that. Foss must have seen rules were needed and he organised it.[84]

When an economic survey was being prepared to accompany the 1951 Budget, the group of officials working on it met frequently with a group of ministers interested in the economy. Out of these meetings developed a permanent Cabinet Economic Committee presided over by the Deputy Prime Minister, Keith Holyoake. Associated with that committee of ministers, and meeting with it fairly frequently, an officials' committee comprising the heads of the departments concerned was established.[85]

This institution-building included consideration of *Treasury*'s role. In the 1940s, Treasury, although not its Secretary, was on the periphery rather than at the centre of economic management. Would this change in the 1950s? The lengthiest discussion of the issue of co-ordination came in a paper by Geoff Schmitt that was first submitted for the Diploma in Public Administration. In it

Schmitt explored the question of the selection of a 'single economic coordinator'. After dismissing the notion that such co-ordination could be satisfactorily carried out at Cabinet level, he canvassed a number of alternatives before concluding that its locus should be the Treasury.[86] Certainly Ashwin was at the centre of economic policy-making and wanted to stay there. As he reported of his visit to Australia in March 1951:

> as well as [the] subjects covered at formal meetings, I had private discussions in the Treasury Department on budget policy, stabilization, wage price and subsidy policy, the economic aspects of defence programmes and the financing of capital development programmes. I also discussed privately with the Department of Commerce and Agriculture the position of the dairy and meat contracts with the United Kingdom and the Wool Conference to be held shortly in Washington.[87]

This was quite some brief, and it reflected that Ashwin continued to play the central role in government that he had taken on in 1942. Thus, early in 1950, he had swiftly attacked the notion that any import licensing body could have other than a narrow mandate: 'a shift of some responsibility for import licensing from the Government to the proposed Board of Trade should not be allowed to weaken the responsibility which the Government has, under existing conditions of internal inflationary pressures, to prevent the country entering into overseas commitments which, because of limited overseas exchange resources, the country cannot afford.'[88]

It may be that because of the need to forge links with a new minister and Cabinet, Ashwin was readier than before to strengthen his department's role. And while Shanahan was active in setting up the committee system, it was Treasury rather than the Cabinet Office which was the principal beneficiary during this phase of the process by which officials' power vis-à-vis ministers was enhanced.[89] Treasury chaired both the officials' committee and the working party which supported it, and provided the secretarial services for both bodies. They dealt more with external than internal economic matters — their nearest precursor was a balance of payments committee which met between 1947 and 1949.[90] The impact of external economic relations on the balance of payments was indisputable, and it was via this route, combined doubtless with Ashwin's surefootedness in such matters, that Treasury acquired the co-ordinating role in this sphere.

Beyond the issue of co-ordination lay that of the co-ordinators. The most far-seeing comments on the implications of change were made by Leicester Webb, the Director of Stabilization from 1945 to 1948, in a paper to the 1953 conference of the Institute of Public Administration:

> The problem which faces administrators as a result of the quest for economic stability is not in essence new; rather it is an intensification of a problem which first became apparent with the decline in laisser faire and the acceptance of Keynesian economics. In its simplest terms, the problem is that of adjusting administration to the idea that the overall management of the economy is both practicable and necessary.

What did this mean for the role of economists in government? 'It is natural', Webb went on, 'to conclude that economists are specially qualified to contribute to the making of national policy, and in deference to this view most departments have in the last ten years recruited economics graduates.' But how had they been used?

> In some departments they have been tucked away in research sections, there to suffer the fate of all those whose function is to write memoranda for others to use and interpret. In other departments economists, once it has become clear that they have no touchstone which provides them with solutions to practical problems, have drifted into ordinary administrative work ... Their influence on policy making is therefore indirect. The hierarchical structure of government departments means that they do not ordinarily take part in those crucial discussions between ministers and permanent heads at which decisions are made, and in any case the language of these discussions is manifestly not the language of economics.[91]

Webb pointed out that because in New Zealand there was none of the interchange between academic economists and public servants that was happening elsewhere in the British Commonwealth, officials were missing out on the fertilisation that such exchanges could bring.[92]

In the light of Webb's comments, how ready were Treasury's officials to guide the government in *economic* policy-making? If Ashwin himself had economic expertise, his decision to increase its level in his department happened fortuitously, according to one of those involved:

> P. B. Marshall transferred to the Ministry of Works after losing out to Clinkard

at Industries and Commerce and advertised there three positions for 'economist types', to be called research officers. The successful candidates were Albert McGregor, Lou Durbin and Geoff Schmitt. When Ashwin heard of this he got on to the Public Service Commission and had the positions relocated to the Treasury, and thus the research division of the Treasury was formed. And Henry Lang joined quite soon after when the Stabilisation Commission was disbanded. So it didn't arise because of any initiative in Treasury but because of a reaction to Marshall.[93]

Another recruit from the Stabilization Commission was Jim Moriarty, who was later to head the Department of Trade and Industry (formerly Industries and Commerce). Schmitt, of course, had been Ashwin's private secretary throughout the 1940s. Lang had worked with J. V. T. Baker, who was to become the Government Statistician, on 'Economic Policy and National Income', a thesis for the Diploma of Public Administration which was published in the *Official Yearbook* in 1950.[94] Its topic fell squarely within the current preoccupation with how to maintain economic stability:

> The central proposition in Part I [of the thesis] is that economic policies designed to alter quantity levels, such as the physical total of employment or production, may clash with policies designed to preserve a better balance in the economy. In other words, a policy of full employment, for example, may clash with a policy of price stability ... We find [in Part II], for example, that the attempt to achieve full employment creates inflationary pressures.[95]

Issues of economic co-ordination and management were addressed in numerous articles in the *New Zealand Journal of Public Administration* in the early 1950s, and in the papers from the Institute of Public Administration's 1953 annual conference which were published as *Economic Stability in New Zealand*. Schmitt, Lang and Moriarty presented papers to the 1953 conference: Moriarty on agriculture, Lang on prices and wages, and Schmitt on the balance of payments. Each paper addressed in a different way the question of how to manage the new political economy of full employment and social security, given that these very goals created instability. All three worked within what might loosely be called a Keynesian framework.[96]

The new research division was responsible for the economic surveys which accompanied each Budget from 1952. The first surveyed the period from 1939 to 1951; 'each year since then it has dealt, apart from general information, with some particular aspects, such as the capital programme or overseas exchange. It is not written by the Minister but by the Economic Research Section of the Treasury and it has always maintained a high standard. It is usually laid on the table of the House about a week before the Budget.'[97]

Noel Lough and Ken Durrant also transferred from the Economic Stabilization Commission into the research division. Noel was involved in writing the first economic survey, which accompanied the 1951 Financial Statement. Bert Brownlie, who was to become Professor of Economics at the University of Canterbury, remembered the work as 'pretty serious economic analysis'.[98] When John Martin joined the Treasury in 1960, the division reported regularly through the Officials' Economic Committee to the Cabinet Economic Committee on the current economic situation and the outlook for overseas exchange transactions (the balance of payments), and also paid attention to taxation and monetary policy and the import licensing schedule — broadly, anything which had macro-economic implications. This reporting was in addition to the regular briefing of the Minister of Finance.[99]

The word 'macroeconomic' only came into common usage during the 1950s (in his paper in *Economic Stability in New Zealand*, Belshaw used 'macroscopic'). Brownlie recollects that his first year of studying economics (1950) was the first year that Samuelson's classic textbook, which embodied both the new Keynesian and the established neoclassical economics, was used at Auckland University College. When he told Samuelson of this years later, the latter smiled and said, 'Ah! A first edition man!'[100] The existence of the division gave the first inkling of the dominance economists and economics were to exercise in the Treasury in the future:

> 'The gravy train' was the term used by people on fifth floor [of the Departmental Building] to describe the research division, the implication being that research people would get faster promotion. I would think that these were the people that were doing much more difficult and serious work as far as it affected the economy as a whole.
> *And a slight degree of resentment?*
> Yes.[101]

Albert McGregor, who had a master's degree in economics, headed the research division initially. McGregor was pulled out of the Treasury in 1955 to help service the Royal Commission on the monetary, banking and credit systems. To

Frank Holmes, 'Albert was a very bright bloke — his cross-examinations were penetrating, and I had a lot of admiration for him.'[102] From the Treasury itself, 'Henry Lang, Noel Lough and I', recalled Bert Brownlie, 'were involved in preparing the department's submission to the Royal Commission. We slaved through one Easter to get it done in time.'[103]

Perhaps the biggest impetus to an enhanced role for economists and economics in policy making came with the findings of the Royal Commission, which recommended the establishment of both an economic research institute and an economic advisory council.[104] The former came into existence as the New Zealand Institute of Economic Research in 1958, while the latter took shape as the Monetary and Economic Council in 1961. Both contributed to economic commentary and analysis with a regularity not previously seen in New Zealand. The first private economic consultancy service — Business and Economic Research Ltd (BERL) — was founded by three economists, Norman Macbeth, Hew Walls and Bryan Philpott, in 1958, and the New Zealand Association of Economists came into being about the same time.[105]

In a comment on the Royal Commission's report, the economist Alan Danks queried the merits of an 'economic advisory council', suggesting that this would raise

> difficult questions arising out of the relative powers and functions in Government of the lay politician and technical expert ... If greater powers to co-ordinate and undertake economic enquiries are needed within the framework of Government ... surely the answer lies in strengthening the appropriate division within the Treasury, which, as the Department already responsible for the co-ordination of our revenues and expenditures, should exercise all broad powers associated with this.[106]

But the Treasury ran out of steam. Ashwin retired in the middle of 1955. On paper his successor, Ted Greensmith, was his equal. Born in 1900, he had transferred to Treasury from the Public Works Department in 1935, qualified as an accountant, gained a Master of Commerce in economics, and been admitted as a solicitor in 1940. But he had a quite different personality to Ashwin, with

> a very pedantic mind and would often quote Greek phrases at parties. He would mark parts of reports he didn't like with a little green pencil. He would memorise reports when chairing officials' committees, saying he thought it very important to have done this.[107]

Ashwin on his retirement day, 30 June 1955, with Jack Watts, the Minister of Finance (centre), and Ted Greensmith, the incoming Secretary to the Treasury. Archives New Zealand: National Publicity Studios Collection, Alexander Turnbull Library, F-27634-1/2

A more dynamic individual than Greensmith might have advanced Treasury's role in economic management. But the research division remained a small entity sitting apart from the department's most important tasks of investigating spending, borrowing and the preparation of the Budget. Because of the initial influx from the ESC, few economics graduates were recruited to the department. Bernie Galvin, who joined in 1955, was an exception.

Ashwin's departure may therefore have enhanced the influence of the Reserve Bank and its Governor, E. C. Fussell, who had held the position since 1948. Fussell's introduction to a memorandum to the Minister of Finance in May 1962 — 'about this time of the year the Bank normally indicates the main lines which it thinks the Budget should follow' — suggests that the Bank saw its ambit reaching well beyond monetary policy. And other departments also had high profiles — Industries and Commerce entered a vigorous phase with the appointment of the economist W. B. Sutch as its permanent head in 1958, whilst in the preparation of the 1961 Budget, advice on tax issues seems to have come from Inland Revenue rather than Treasury.[108]

The political context

In 1951, the transition from a political environment dominated by the government's 'counter-revolutionary' agenda to one in which it was accepted that economic management — stabilisation — was a permanent task of the state was completed. But this did not bridge the gap between the politicians and the economists. For the latter, stabilisation might go 'down' as well as 'up', Budgets could be tight as well as generous. But this was not the preferred approach of New Zealand politicians. For them, the new economics offered a way to avoid the 'down' part of the cycle. Through these years we can see the Treasury, and also the Reserve Bank, attempting to cajole their political masters into what they saw as more responsible conduct. It was the pattern that was to become familiar in the late 1970s and early 1980s — economists jousting with politicians — played out on the same stage with a different script.

The pattern was also similar in other countries. Australia's 'Horror Budget' of 1951 saw the 'first explicit use of fiscal policy for anti-cyclical purposes' in that country. This Budget was 'openly Keynesian in practice, principle and spirit, despite the fact that it was introduced to fight not unemployment but inflation … The Treasurer, Arthur Fadden, began his budget speech by explaining the inflationary process and did so by employing Keynesian "gap" analysis … increases were announced for a range of taxes'.[109] This Budget's unpopularity provided little incentive for other politicians to try the same approach.

The Conservative government (led by Holland's hero Winston Churchill) elected in Britain in October 1951 also adhered to the practice of economic management, but there too the inclination was to use that management to maintain economic activity, even if this involved inflation. In Great Britain in the 1950s, the manipulation of the bank rate 'became the classic means of exerting a credit squeeze, or applying disinflationary pressure, in a way that became thought of as Keynesian.'[110] More vigorous measures met with little support. The British banking authorities had failed to persuade their political masters to float sterling, because maintaining full employment would then have not always been the top priority.[111] And in 1957/58, faced with rising unemployment — 'albeit within a range where 2% began to look high' — Prime Minister Macmillan chose to jettison hostile ministers rather than his own Keynesian priorities: 'memories of dole queues in Stockton … became familiar to the British Treasury knights … as a code word for [the desirability of] expansionary measures, whatever the inflationary risk'.[112]

This difference in emphasis between ministers and officials was found in New Zealand too. From the mid-1950s, both the government's economic advisers and professional economists argued that while all policy instruments — fiscal, monetary, wage and price — should be utilised to ensure economic stability, the government was too ready to forego some or all of these for electoral reasons. The demands of the welfare state — in other words, the requirement of full employment — sat in an uneasy tension with the task of managing the economy. Such arguments were traversed by the papers at the 1953 IPA conference and in the report of the Royal Commission on the monetary system. The latter reported that since 1950 the economy would have benefited from 'stronger monetary and fiscal policies'.[113]

Apart from an eruption in 1953, Treasury's role in the new order does not seem to have been controversial. In that year G. J. Schmitt's paper on 'economic stability and the balance of payments' did cause a stir, but not on account of any belief that Treasury advice was too austere. Schmitt had explored the problem of trying to reconcile full employment with economic stability. The published version of his paper made it clear that he saw the control of imports as only one tool to that end, and not always the best one. But editorial commentators in two newspapers were suspicious of controls being justified by reference to internal economic stability, 'as if that were something to be desired, instead of the very negation of progress. What this Government and this country require is someone to examine the theory of full employment, not from the standpoint of local manufacture and imports, but from the standpoint of our exports.' 'Just how much', this editorial asked, can a 'free enterprise' government ... afford to listen to Treasury advice?'[114]

It was ironic too that in his final years, Ashwin fell out with Holland:

> There was a problem with the books while Holland was away in 1953, which led to the government borrowing from [the] Reserve Bank because the accounts were £10 million short. It was a great disaster for Sid Holland — he had caned Walter Nash for years about Reserve Bank borrowing. It became public when Clifton Webb announced it at a meeting up in Browns Bay — it hit like a bomb. He wasn't supposed to have said that. From then on Holland lost confidence in Ashwin.[115]

Holland still gave Ashwin a knighthood, making him the only Treasury Secretary to have been so encumbered. But the episode was a reminder that economic management remained, for the National government, a task for politicians rather than bureaucratics. It appears that no officials were present at a series of meetings Holland held with economic interest groups in April and May 1954.[116] Officials are barely mentioned in a 1955 article on Cabinet government by the Minister of Justice, Jack Marshall.[117] The economists who advised the 1955 Royal Commission could not be called 'economists', for fear of provoking the notion that 'experts' had taken over the proceedings — 'their services', the Commission blandly reported, 'were available to the Commission in a technical capacity'.[118]

Change was to be gradual rather than dramatic. In his farewell speech in 1955, Ashwin asserted that the Budget had now become an instrument of economic policy. The Budget files for this period are brief and uninformative, but Ashwin's comment can be confirmed indirectly. In a post-election briefing in January 1955, Treasury had argued that New Zealand was 'trying to achieve more ... [than] we can accomplish with our existing resources. Therefore all policies should be directed towards reducing demand for consumer goods and capital investment.'[119] The new Minister of Finance, Jack Watts, summoned officials to a meeting to 'review economic policy' with the goal of 'dealing with root causes' [of inflation, it could be assumed]. In a 'progress report' presented by the Treasury in May, the officials' committee canvassed the possibility of fundamental action on interest rates, hire purchase, and the control of capital issues and capital expenditure. Thus the emphasis in terms of indirect measures fell on monetary rather than fiscal policy (taxation was not mentioned), whilst in respect of direct controls, the emphasis was on ensuring that sufficient resources were available for public works.[120]

Treasury's submission to the 1955 Royal Commission began with a statement on the objectives of economic policy and the means available to the government to achieve those objectives.[121] It also explored the problem of reconciling those objectives, with an eye to the inherent conflict between full employment — of labour, resources, or both — and stability:

> [a] cursory examination suggests that a reduction in works expenditure would be desirable for achieving greater stability, reducing over full employment and safeguarding overseas reserves. On the other hand such a reduction would hamper a policy of sound development of natural resources.[122]

The government was not listening to these calls for restraint. In January 1957 Treasury reported to its minister that although in the 1956 Budget a surplus of

THE BUDGET POUND FOR 1957–58
CONSOLIDATED FUND AND SOCIAL SECURITY FUND

Where it comes from	PER CENT	PORTION OF £1	£ MILLION	£ MILLION	PORTION OF £1	PER CENT	Where it will go
INCOME TAX	35·87	7/2	99·0	80·0	5/9	28·99	SOCIAL SECURITY SERVICES
SOCIAL SECURITY	23·91	4/9	66·0	67·0	4/10	24·28	OTHER SOCIAL SERVICES
CUSTOMS DUTY	10·87	2/2	30·0	25·0	1/10	9·06	DEFENCE
SALES TAX	8·33	1/8	23·0	26·0	1/11	9·42	ADMINISTRATION
				13·0	11d.	4·71	STABILISATION
BEER DUTY	2·54	6d.	7·0	13·0	11d.	4·71	MAINTENANCE OF WORKS
ESTATE & RACING DUTY	5·43	1/1	15·0	17·0	1/3	6·16	DEVELOPMENT OF INDUSTRY
INTEREST	4·35	11d.	12·0	25·0	1/10	9·06	DEBT SERVICES
TRADING PROFITS	1·81	4d.	5·0	9·0	8d.	3·26	REPAYMENT OF PUBLIC DEBT
DEPARTMENTAL RECEIPTS	6·89	1/5	19·0	1·0	1d.	·35	OTHER
TOTAL REVENUE	100·00	£1.	276·0	276·0	£1.	100·00	TOTAL EXPENDITURE

How they explained it. The 1957 Budget in pictures and percentages. T1, 3/3/57, Archives New Zealand

£3.7 million had been anticipated for the 1956/57 financial year, an overall deficit of £10 million now seemed likely, following an £11 million deficit for 1955/56; 'at a time when Government finance should be supporting and not undermining, bank credit restraints, this would be a particularly serious and undesirable result.'[123]

The Treasury attitude towards and influence over stabilisation policy was powerfully tested during the 1958 balance of payments crisis. A Labour government took office after the November 1957 election to find a probable Budget deficit for 1957/58 of £24 million, even if it did not implement election promises or repay Reserve Bank advances to the dairy industry account. And it would be most unwise to finance government expenditure by borrowing overseas, because a fall in receipts for all the principal export commodities had depleted overseas reserves to about £50 million: 'after eight years of very high export prices, the overseas funds would only pay for six weeks' imports'.[124]

> It is obvious that the strain on the exchange reserves must be removed and that important decisions about reducing Government expenditure and increasing Government revenue ought to be made immediately, especially

Arnold Nordmeyer, the architect of the 1958 'Black Budget' that took fiscal restraint off the political agenda for a decade. New Zealand Free Lance Collection, Alexander Turnbull Library, C-26201-¹/₂

> when it is recalled how long a time usually passes before the full effect of changes in policy is felt. It is highly desirable that as much action as practicable be initiated before the approaching holiday season.[125]

The government did not act before Christmas, apart from reintroducing import licensing to protect the balance of payments.[126] Not many people at the time would have predicted that this would last another 30 years. At the beginning of March, Greensmith reported to the new Minister of Finance, Arnold Nordmeyer, on the scale of the government's probable financial deficit for 1958/59. At £99 million, this was *ten times* the deficit of three years earlier. Labour had no money with which to implement its election promises, such as an increase in pensions. Greensmith recommended that £55 million be raised through a variety of increased taxes, especially indirect taxation and the social security tax. He stressed that

> the measures adopted ought to be adequate and rigorous rather than lenient or chance-taking. Heavy and expensive borrowing can be justified to meet a short-term emergency but not to support a long-term living in excess of

income. The price of so doing, even if feasible, would be a lowering standard of living and probably a forced, rather than any planned, devaluation. Employment and other transitional difficulties are probable but should not be allowed to delay the requisite substantive action.[127]

Treasury folklore has it that Nordmeyer was not expected to adopt all the measures that they recommended. But the figures set out in this report left little room for choice. And at least one tabulation prepared in Treasury proposed increases in indirect taxes considerably greater than those that were introduced in the Budget. In the event, income tax, gift and estate duties were raised substantially, and duties on beer, spirits, tobacco and cars were doubled.[128] The outcome was an 18 per cent overall increase in taxation[129] — an enormous rise in one year. The historian Keith Sinclair referred to it as 'an economist's budget, a Treasury budget'. Certainly that was the tone of one press release:

> The sharp decline in volume of imports is contributing to an inflationary situation which requires corrective action. The government aims to maintain stability by avoiding both inflation and deflation. Firm monetary and fiscal measures provide the most equitable method of achieving this.[130]

'I was one of those', recalls one economist,

> who supported the 'Black Budget'. It was a fiscally responsible Budget, but framed around the policies which they had promised to deliver. They had promised a tax cut, and they had also promised significant increases in expenditure to implement their welfare policies. Nordmeyer explained that they could not do this responsibly in [the] circumstances that had emerged, so put up indirect taxes — [but] on things that were politically disastrous for Labour.[131]

Did the traditional concern for the public accounts weight advice towards fiscal restraint? Possibly, but Keynesian notions of demand management are also evident:

> In the inflationary situation now faced, fiscal policy must be designed to equate demand with the reduced volume of goods. The increased taxation will serve two purposes — provide sufficient revenue for Government needs and diminish demand.[132]

New Zealand applies to join the International Monetary Fund in 1961. Ralph Hanan, the Attorney-General (left), and Prime Minister Keith Holyoake (right) sign the documents, and Minister of Finance Harry Lake blots their signatures. Dominion Post, Alexander Turnbull Library, F-50970-1/2

The balance of payments improved markedly in the 1958/59 season. To take just one example, the London butter price in July 1959 was 344s per cwt, compared with 203s per cwt at the lowest point in 1958. And imports were 19 per cent lower in 1958/59 than in 1957/58. By the 1960 election, therefore, the economy was in much better shape than it had been three years before. However, Labour suffered from the memory of the 'Black Budget', as had the Australian Liberals from the 'Horror Budget' of 1951. National returned to office, only to be confronted by a balance of payments crisis remarkably similar to that which Labour had faced in 1958:

> I well remember Keith Holyoake coming into the caucus in February or March of 1961 and the shock that it gave a brand-new backbencher when he told us that the honeymoon was over and that we were faced with a serious situation, in repect of both the Government's accounts and our overseas transactions.[133]

'Computerisation', 1960-style. Bank of New Zealand staff gather around the bank's first electronic bookkeeping machine in 1960. Similar change took place at Treasury at about the same time. New Zealand Free Lance Collection, Alexander Turnbull Library, F-10144-¹/₂

National neither could — without laying itself open to charges of hypocrisy from the electorate — nor would — given the punishment meted out to Labour by the voters — rely on fiscal policy to tackle the crisis. Increases in electricity, postal and telephone charges, suburban rail fares and state house rents were all announced before the Budget, but these resulted more from National's long-standing attitude to government trading activity than they formed part of a macroeconomic strategy. Taxes were not raised — indeed, Treasury pointed out that this was not a year for tax concessions. Action on expenditure was persuasive, not directive:

> The Treasury cannot hope to be as fully aware as are many departmental officers of the scope for saving in departmental activities ... what is particularly important is that ... everyone should do all that he can and not 'leave it to the other fellow'. The Minister of Finance has particularly asked that this, and indeed the whole necessity for corrective action, be emphasised.[134]

Like Labour, only more immediately, National chose to borrow, both domestically and overseas, and also applied a 'credit squeeze' — relied on monetary policy to dampen demand. National also took New Zealand into the International Monetary Fund and the World Bank, a move which had been deferred for many years, despite Britain being a founder member of both, because of fears amongst both National and Labour voters that it would lead to a loss of economic sovereignty. From the Treasury's point of view, central issues in economic management had again been deferred rather than addressed.

Conclusion

During the 1950s, economic management was an important element in the political economy. National's idea of returning to the 'economic constitution' faltered in the face of the party's other goals, such as full employment. Consensus over economic management opened the way for discussion about who should be the 'economic co-ordinator' and the extent of the expertise this role would require. The Treasury was an obvious candidate, but for a variety of reasons, its activities were focused primarily on financial management. This would change in the 1960s, when Treasury, under Henry Lang's leadership, would draw many strands of economic management to itself.

Part Three
ECONOMISTS

Chapter 6

Mandarins or lemons? The Treasury, 1961–1979

The transformation of the Treasury

Carter wondered about the Commissioner of Works as he made the tea. Benjamin Kohl was all right really once you got to know him, but did anyone know him? After all, you could hardly say you know a person if you didn't know what school he went to. Come to think of it, no one even knew where he came from. Some said he was the son of a Lebanese scrap merchant, others a Peruvian; Carter didn't really believe in either version, but there was no doubt the man was a foreigner. He was olive-coloured, tricky, and wore rings. What's more, he played the fiddle and listened to the National Orchestra. No good ever came from people like that … still you had to trust someone and Kohl got things moving.[1]

Carter was wondering about a thinly-disguised Henry Lang, the Secretary to the Treasury from 1969 to 1976, in this 1973 satire by William Maughan, a Greek honours graduate whom Lang had recruited to the Treasury in 1965. While he was neither Middle Eastern nor South American, olive-coloured nor beringed, Henry Lang was indeed an unlikely appointee to the position, having arrived in New Zealand as a young refugee from Hitler's Europe speaking the central European-accented English which he retained throughout his life.[2] His subsequent career was a shining example of the benefits immigrants brought to New Zealand and New Zealand offered immigrants. He took to New Zealand life with enthusiasm, becoming particularly keen on skiing and tramping (neither unusual in Austria, of course), and marrying a New Zealander. He completed a commerce degree at Victoria University College between 1940 and 1943 — his best marks by far were in German, but he graduated in accountancy, qualified professionally as an accountant, and went on to do an arts degree, majoring in philosophy in 1946.

Lang was appointed to the Economic Stabilization Commission as an 'investigating accountant' in March 1946. In 1949–50 he took the Diploma of Public

Henry Lang, Secretary to the Treasury, 1968–77. Treasury

Administration course. While he had taken some economics courses in both degrees, it is likely that his understanding of economics deepened while he was studying for the DPA — even though as Secretary he modestly described his job as 'applied common sense spiced with a little technical know-how and above all an ability to speak the jargon of economists'.[3] It was at this time that Lang and J. V. T. Baker wrote their thesis on economic policy and national income. A year after returning to the public service, Lang transferred to the Treasury.[4]

Ashwin had carved out a personal domain in economic management. Lang was determined to create a central role in economic management for the department, just as Esson had striven for such a role in financial management. That role might be called 'giving advice', but it nonetheless implied a shift in the weight of policy formation from the political to the official sphere. We will consider Lang's success in achieving that goal in the final section of this chapter. It also involved a shift in the 'pecking order' within the Treasury. Interviewed in 1969, Lang explained that he did not 'see the Treasury as an institution, to quote Disraeli [sic], "whose job it is to save the candle ends at the end of an evening", but as the main advisory body on economic policy'.[5] It was an important shift in emphasis. We are reminded of the distinct characters of the words 'financial' and

> On my asking Lord Beaconsfield's secretary whether there was any chance of the appointment being completed, he said: 'It is difficult to say when one of my chief's mottoes is: "Depend upon it delay is the secret of success."'
>
> On August 13, I heard from Lord Beaconsfield offering me the appointment of Deputy, and Walter Northcote, Sir Stafford's eldest son, was appointed in my place. Mr. Gladstone wrote to me the following letter:
>
> > Hawarden Castle, Chester: August 15, 1877.
> >
> > 'My dear West,—I send you on the part of all here a line of hearty congratulation, and I also congratulate the public on an appointment so conducive to its interests.
> >
> > 'I have always looked on the Board of Inland Revenue as nearly approaching—so to speak—the ideal, and I am sure it will not degenerate under present circumstances.
> >
> > 'Smith must be a loss to you; and it is uncertain till he is further proved what gain he will be to the Admiralty. Stanley is clever, but can an heir to the earldom of Derby descend to the saving of candle-ends, which is very much the measure of a good Secretary to the Treasury?
> >
> > 'Pray remember us if you come northwards, and believe me, most sincerely yours,
> >
> > 'W. E. GLADSTONE.'

Gladstone on 'candle ends', 1877. Algernon West, *Recollections, 1832 to 1886*

'economic', and the long-standing predominance of the former — 'candle ends' — over the latter. To be in a position to put economic advice at the centre of Treasury activity, Lang had to earn his financial spurs. One anecdote has it that Lang and Ian Lythgoe, another high flyer, returned from the summer holiday in early 1962 to find that their jobs had been reversed: Lythgoe now headed the research division, and Lang finance. Cliff Terry recalls that

> traditionally in the Treasury, the guy with the power was the Finance Officer. He was the one responsible for the Budget, which traditionally had come

out of the finance or investigating side. Henry Lang, who had great ambitions always to be Secretary to the Treasury, saw that he had to become Finance Officer at some time, if he was ever going to get to the top. So he said that he drank a helluva lot of whisky with Cop Davis, who was Finance Officer, became pally with him, and eventually did achieve the Secretary's job.
Did he have a spell as Finance Officer?
Yes.
It wouldn't have been his particular predisposition?
No, definitely not. But that was the job, and he had to do it to get to the top.[6]

Where did Lang get his new idea of the Treasury from? As Easton has discussed, Ashwin was undoubtedly one influence. But another was 'OE', perhaps his European origins but certainly a later foray. Lang had spent the period from 1956 to 1958 as an economic adviser with the New Zealand High Commission in London, and this seems to have left him impressed with the professionalism of the British civil service:

> The Treasury of that time was a creation which in my view was very much Henry's, modelled on the British public sector. Henry had gone out of his way to choose an able bunch of people, and he made no secret that Treasury was going to comprise an elite bunch of thinkers. He believed that, in certain areas, it lacked such people or that it needed to be further strengthened.[7]

So 'mandarins', as the elite of the British civil service were often characterised, were to come to New Zealand. The parallel with Britain had two components. While most of the new recruits were economists, not all were. Lang's idea, appropriate to the 'Keynesian' age, was that able graduates from other 'non-relevant' disciplines could also make excellent Treasury officers. He was, recalls Roderick Deane, 'wonderfully encouraging of the Treasury recruiting graduates, but not just economists — he didn't want just economists. He wanted a diversity, much more the English, Oxford/Cambridge tradition. He was comfortable with the idea of taking in history graduates and English graduates as well as economics.'[8] Almost certainly Lang noticed a disparity between the 'human capital' of the department he was most closely associated with in London — External Affairs — and Treasury: 'There are all too few Moriartys (and Henry Langs) there', wrote one External Affairs officer about Treasury, 'and in fact [a new External Affairs recruit] would be rather outstanding among their junior people.'[9] John

Martin was asked to join Treasury by Lang. When he demurred that he was not qualified, Lang asked, 'But can you write?' Bob Hill, Ross Tanner and John Zohrab were three other 'non-relevant' recruits; the most memorable was Bill Maughan, whose appointment was questioned — what could a graduate in Greek offer the Treasury? — during an estimates debate in Parliament.[10]

The other wing was the recruitment of economists — the 'relevants'. In Britain, unlike New Zealand, academic economists had been prominent in advising the government during and immediately after the Second World War, but it was not until the 1960s — before New Zealand, but only just — that significant numbers of economists began to be employed in the civil service:

> One of the most unexpected features of the British case is the fact that the economists' acknowledged success in wartime and the conscious adoption of full employment as a major postwar policy objective did not automatically generate a substantial demand for professional economists in the peacetime civil service. During the first two postwar decades macroeconomic management was undertaken with the aid of only a handful (i.e. less than 20) professional economists.[11]

Some of the reasons for the delay were also found in New Zealand at the time — the relatively poor pay and a certain scepticism in the conservative party about the value of economic expertise.[12] The British situation changed dramatically after the election of a Labour government in October 1964, with the number of economists in the civil service increasing twenty-fold to 390 by 1979.[13]

In New Zealand, the universities were by the early 1960s turning out master's graduates in economics. Three professors were particularly important: Bryan Philpott at Lincoln, Bert Brownlie at Canterbury, and Frank Holmes at Victoria. This was not only because of their teaching and research work, but also because of the role they played in debating policy. After Philpott obtained a significant amount of research funding, especially from the Department of Scientific and Industrial Research, he set up the Agricultural Economic Research Unit, in which his master's students worked. Some thought that Philpott had a strategy to get his master's graduates into key organisations in Wellington.[14]

Bert Brownlie, who had worked briefly in the Treasury in the mid-1950s, reoriented the Canterbury department around the teaching of economic theory, and recruited able graduates from other disciplines. Holmes, the Macarthy Professor of Economics at Victoria, was four years Lang's junior, and remained close

Professor Frank Holmes, the first chair of the Monetary and Economic Council in 1961 and a close friend of Henry Lang. Dominion Post, Alexander Turnbull Library, F-23939-¼

to him after they were in London at the same time. At the age of 37, Holmes became the first chair of the Monetary and Economic Council at the time Lang returned from his secondment in London. The closeness of the two organisations was expressed both in the personal link between Holmes and Lang, and in the fact that although it was formally independent of the politicians, and had its own staff and premises, the Council was financed through the Treasury vote.[15]

Lang also forged close links with the Reserve Bank. At this time, economic analysis was more often associated with the Reserve Bank, and indeed with banking generally, than it was with the Treasury. Throughout the world, central banks found it easier to recruit economists than did treasuries, because they were more independent of governments. The Reserve Bank had a staff of 26, headed by Alan Low, in its Economics Department when this was formally established in 1960, albeit no economists in key positions in the Bank as a whole — banker and economist were still different professions.[16] The *Reserve Bank Bulletin* published more theoretical work than appeared in any Treasury organ. It also undertook econometric modelling before Treasury began doing so. 'They had a raft of economics graduates in the Bank at that stage [who] tended to sit in one large room, and had these endless debates about how to right the world.'[17]

Would such economists come to the Treasury? For Lang, the process of recruiting economists was neither smooth nor rapid. 'On his last day', Jas McKenzie recalled, 'Henry recounted that the first economist he got was Bernie Galvin, then David Preston, then Kees Weststrate. And that it was a long hard struggle'.[18] This partly reflected, as in the United Kingdom, the buoyancy of a labour market in which the public sector as a whole struggled to attract or retain able appointees. Moreover, the universities were keen to retain their able graduates. Compounding the problem were relativity issues between Treasury and other departments. In 1965, Lang and Cop Davis, the Deputy Secretary, met the chair of the State Services Commission, Allan Atkinson, to discuss the question. When Atkinson proved unhelpful, Treasury approached the Minister, pointing out that 'the down-grading in relation to comparable departments of Treasury staff below secretary level [Secretary, Deputy Secretary, assistant secretaries] has led to a drop in morale and has made it very difficult to recruit suitable people from other departments ... difficult to ensure the continued efficient administration of the department ... and not possible to carry out new control and planning tasks required by Government.'[19]

This was not exactly the same issue as that of recruiting economics graduates, but it seems that the two problems were linked. Treasury recruited six economics graduates in 1966, but no more until 1969.[20] However, the department did gradually begin to see itself as an economists' organisation. When the New Zealand Association of Economists began publishing *New Zealand Economics Papers* in 1966, its editorial board included representation from the university economics departments and the banks, but not from the Treasury. But in 1968 one of the 1966 recruits, Max Bradford, appeared on the masthead of *New Zealand Economics Papers*. In 1969 and again in 1971, Treasury officers presented papers to the Association's annual conference, and in 1973 and 1974 Deputy Secretary Noel Lough was its president.[21] The change was noticed. 'There has been', wrote one journalist in 1969, 'a welcome injection of youth into the Treasury. Mr Lang and his assistant are under 50, the director of one of the most important economic divisions is in his 30s, while a young, highly qualified graduate in his early 20s is at present working directly under the top men.'[22]

That 'director of one of the most important economic divisions' was Bernie Galvin, who was to be Secretary from 1980 to 1986, and has been described by his successor in that office as one out of the box — clever, competitive. He saw himself as the boy from Island Bay who had made it to the top of the system in the way that many Catholics had in the public service. He was enormously proud of the fact that he had reached that position. He had an incredible kind of Irish sparkle, quick, a fixer. He would seize on a problem, stitch something together and move on. He was Henry's professional son really, they were mates at a very deep level.[23]

By the late 1960s Galvin had added to his degree a stint on fellowship at Harvard. As head of the Internal Economics Division he drove, with Lang, the macroeconomic management of the early 1970s until 1975, when he was recruited by the new Prime Minister, Robert Muldoon, to head a new advisory group in the Prime Minister's Department. Galvin brought new analytic tools into the Treasury, especially cost–benefit analysis, which was applied to major projects such as New Zealand Steel, the Bluff aluminium smelter, and the development of Kapuni and Maui gas. The notion that new public investment should be able to generate a 10 per cent rate of return (the 'discount rate') dates from this time.[24]

The new leadership, the recruitment of high-achieving graduates, the generally non-hierarchical atmosphere fostered by Lang — all fostered a 'cultural revolution' during which it wasn't all smooth going for the 'old' Treasury. 'The policy was to bring in academics, whoever', Bill Robinson felt. 'It didn't matter whether they had economics, or scientific degrees, or what they were. Get these young fellows in there. And the show damn nearly blew up!'[25] May Atkins, the experienced head typist, was told that 'part of the job was to knock the new recruits into shape':

> the stationery room was open certain hours. But one of the new recruits decided he would go when he wanted to go. And if he couldn't have what he wanted you could hear him down the corridor. There was a lot of glass around where I was working and on one occasion he went out and slammed the door, and the whole of this glass shook. I don't recall what it was he wanted, I had just said, 'No, you can't have it', and that's what happened. Anyway, about half an hour later a sheepish face came round the door, and he said, 'I am sorry, I shouldn't have done that'.[26]

To some, economists were 'cuckoos in the nest'. Accountants 'saw the "real" work in Treasury as being done in the investigative divisions … "the dead hand of Treasury". It was a hard slog and not very popular … although a lot of those guys were very good at building relations.' Able recruits like Galvin and Jas Mackenzie went straight into one of the economics divisions, and didn't get the traditional grounding in accounts or an investigative division. A senior investigating officer in the 1960s who looked to precedent could aim to become Secretary or Deputy Secretary, but such opportunities seemed less likely to arise once Galvin had been promoted.[27]

The change was a matter of education but also — less certainly — of class. Public servants recruited from the 1930s to the 1950s — those who were now reaching senior positions in the department — were classically able school-leavers whose families had aspirations but little wealth or income. Many had joined the service straight from high school and gained professional qualifications on the job.[28] While some of the new recruits were the first generation in their family to go to university, others were not. By doing so full-time straight from school, all had a different socialisation to the public service cadets of an earlier era.

One product of the ferment was the 'Friends of the Clutha', which — facing 'death by drowning' — was duly succeeded by the Surfdale Progressive Association, which had its first meeting under patron John Chetwin in 1977. The founding members were mostly economists, and their favoured places of association allowed them to explore liquidity issues in depth — certainly to the bottom of the glass.[29] Many of the new graduates also adhered to the 'biscuit group', which, recalls Rob Laking, who had joined Treasury at the end of 1964,

> consisted of a group of people who came into Treasury a little after me — Jas, Chet, Max Bradford, Richard Carey, Irene Taylor [Lake], John Buddle, and a handful of others … who were all, as you'd expect, restless. They wanted to make their impact on the Treasury … Indeed we were all totally immersed in what were doing, convinced of its importance to the point where we were boring our spouses silly, because you'd go out to dinner with other Treasury people, and all they'd ever talk about was work.[30]

The biscuit group met late in the afternoon, partly in work hours, with tea and biscuits provided for sustenance. Members presented papers on different aspects of economic policy. An early statement about the group set out its goals as being 'to further the process of self-education in economic theory and policy, but also to foster an interchange of economic, and concomitant socio-political ideas … attendance should be confined mainly to recent university graduates in economics'. A list of suggested topics from 1969, which was probably the first year the group met, reveals its diversity and perhaps also, in terms of later developments in the discipline, the lack of what would become mainstream approaches to economic theory and policy.[31]

One official, who joined Treasury in 1969 after two years in the Ministry of Agriculture, remembers vigorous debate about issues such as the key elements determining economic performance. While there was a tendency to advocate reductions in protection and subsidies, this was not done in a doctrinaire way. Lang's open style encouraged debate. He would question staff about the reports they prepared for ministers — did they agree with them, and why?

While Lang often dealt directly with staff, his secretary and executive assistant also functioned as his 'eyes and ears'. He had a knack for spotting mistakes in papers, which he would discuss with their authors. Lang's consideration for his staff was legendary. He was, recalls one officer, thinking back to the early 1970s,

> a very kindly man. I had been working on the Maui [natural gas field] agreement, working through till 2 and 3 o'clock in the morning ... I was absolutely jiggered one afternoon. And I think there was a meeting at 5 or 6 o'clock. I spoke to Kathy Bridges [Lang's secretary]. 'Is Henry in his office?' 'No, he isn't', she replied. So I went and lay down on his couch. Then Henry came back. Now I suppose anyone would have done the same, but it was typical of Henry. He had a number of phone calls to make and he made them in a whispering voice so that he wouldn't disturb me. And when I did wake, he growled at me for working so hard.[32]

In an expansion of career development beyond the existing scheme of secondments to the DPA programme, Lang provided opportunities for young Treasury officers to follow in Galvin's footsteps through secondments to the IMF, the Organization for Economic Cooperation and Development (from 1973, when New Zealand joined), and to 'refresher' courses in public policy and economics at overseas universities, strategies that were maintained after his departure.

Planning for growth

More than any other impulse, it was the notion that the economy needed to grow faster that fostered the enthusiasm for bringing economic expertise into the Treasury and into government generally in the 1960s. Early in the decade, British anxiety about the country's relatively low rate of economic growth fostered enthusiasm there for 'indicative' planning of the kind that had been devised in France in the 1950s. This 'conversion of the conservatives' saw a National Economic Development Council established in 1962.[33]

A parallel sequence unfolded in New Zealand. The 1958 balance of payments crisis, followed by another nearly as severe in 1961, focused attention on the growth rate of the New Zealand economy. Thus at the opening of the 1960 Industrial Development Conference, Walter Nash stressed the need for New Zealand to achieve growth as well as stability if it was to avoid the 'stop–go' cycle that had characterised the economy in the 1950s.[34] The first official estimates for economic growth were provided in Treasury's 1959 economic survey.[35] A year later the new Minister of Finance, Harry Lake, reiterated that New Zealand's economic growth rate was lagging behind other countries, 'as was pointed out in last year's economic survey'.[36] In its second report, entitled 'Economic Growth in New Zealand', the Monetary and Economic Council examined the inconsistency of government monetary and fiscal policies over the preceding decade or so, and stressed the need for co-ordination.[37]

But would these initiatives lead to planning? In 1958, one commentator thought that 'the very word planning is an anathema to most New Zealanders, filling their minds with a morbid horror of bureaucracy and totalitarianism.'[38] Through the early and mid-1960s government and Opposition manoeuvred on the desirable style and extent of economic planning.[39] The Export and Agricultural Development conferences of 1963 and 1964 respectively promoted diversification of production and exports. The Minister of Finance sought Treasury advice on establishing an NEDC-style economic planning group. Treasury pointed out that New Zealand had neither the statistics nor the personnel to carry out such work, and indeed that it could not staff even a quite modest planning section. However, work had been started on planning in two key fields — agriculture and government — for which there were relatively good statistics; 'as our basic knowledge of the economy increases, it will be desirable to extend planning to other sections of the community.'[40]

Planning did not just require more economics and economists; it also involved econometrics, statistics and forecasting. Some early modelling was done on topics such as seasonal adjustments. But Treasury, always grappling with the 'tyranny of the immediate', was behind, and to a degree dependent on, work being done in the universities — by Bryan Philpott, in particular — the Statistics Department, the Institute of Economic Research, and the Reserve Bank.

Rod Deane remembers the key question as,

> 'How can we make better use of the tools?' ... econometric modelling was getting under way in those days, and computers were good enough — although they were huge — to utilise. I was sent off to work with the modelling team at the Reserve Bank of Australia, who were ahead of us in those days. I then returned to set up an econometric modelling research team which built the first macro econometric model — it was used extensively for economic forecasting and policy analysis for both the Reserve Bank and Treasury. We started publishing papers around 1971.[41]

In the meantime, the political concern with forward planning did not vanish — nor, presumably, did Treasury want it to. A 1967 World Bank report noted that 'New Zealand is presently lacking effective instruments for analysis and advice on long-term economic policy and development strategy. [It] should strengthen the existing planning unit in the Treasury and set up small units for sectoral planning in other appropriate departments.'[42] The issue took on a more powerful form with the convening of a National Development Conference (NDC) in 1968 as a political and planning response to the 1966/67 balance of payments crisis. While the initial impetus came from Jack Marshall, the Minister of Industries and Commerce and Overseas Trade, and Robert Muldoon, who was by now Minister of Finance, Lang was prepared to be an advocate:

> We had well over a 90% acceptance (around 600 top men in industry and the public service are involved in the NDC). The change in attitude toward the role of planning in most sectors was fostered by setting production targets and more than fulfilling the hopes of the country's agricultural leaders and was only upset by the slump in world market prices in the past two years ... other sectors [tourism, forestry, manufacturing and fisheries] became interested in national planning and the atmosphere was right for the NDC to come into existence.[43]

Lang was always a believer in consensus, but his enthusiasm on this occasion was a little staged — if not as much as Kohl's for the 'trade pavilion', the fictional NDC in *Good and Faithful Servants*. The strongest supporter of the NDC process was Treasury Assistant Secretary Bill Green, who believed that such a consultative mechanism could accomplish change. Lang, and especially Noel Lough, had a more instrumental view, hoping that the process would facilitate

The first meeting of the National Development Conference in March 1968. Henry Lang is standing furthest left, and Cop Davis, the Secretary to the Treasury, is standing third from the right. Seated in the front row are P. S. Plummer (left, Dominion President of Federated Farmers), Minister of Finance Robert Muldoon (middle) and Deputy Prime Minister Jack Marshall (right). How did Bill Maughan make fiction out of such unpromising material? Dominion Post, Alexander Turnbull Library, C-23157-½

the trade liberalisation which they saw as the key to economic growth.[44] By the time this possibility was dashed in 1972, the NDC process had lost momentum, not least because the Labour government's Cabinet Policy and Priorites Committee took over the role of the NDC central committee. 'I was still in the planning division at the change of government', recalled David Preston,

> and stayed there about another nine to ten months, but the government was simply ignoring the NDC. They were going ahead on great spending sprees, promising development to the West Coast and so on. They were [just] going through the motions, and we [thought we] might as well hit the NDC exercise on the head. They hummed and ha'd, and ... eventually it was wound up.[45]

When National returned to office at the end of 1975, Lang saw an opportunity to revive planning in a form more congenial to Treasury thinking. Lang asked Frank Holmes to chair a task force 'to look at what was good and what was bad about NDC and its aftermath'; the new government wanted 'to have a good hard look at this planning stuff'.[46] Under Holmes's direction, the Task Force on

Economic and Social Planning produced *New Zealand at the Turning Point*, a wide-ranging study which was innovative in its blending of social and economic policy but also focused on the need to link the planning system to the policy-making process. When a Planning Council was established, in 1977, Holmes became its full-time chair.

> The Secretary to the Treasury served on it as a member; so did the Minister of National Development. It was an attempt to get all New Zealanders — not representing particular interests, but drawn from particular interests — coming together and thinking about where we ought to be going as a country, not setting targets in the old NDC sense. In that sense it had a different brief to the NDC. It set up an economic monitoring group and a population monitoring group right from the start. We tried to get consensus among members on our documents. And we got a fair amount of consensus in one on the welfare state and on liberalisation, for example.[47]

By 1977 Noel Lough had taken over as Secretary to the Treasury. The sense of crisis about the economy led him to develop a medium-term economic planning capacity 'in-house'. This unit was to reinforce the Planning Council's increasing advocacy of a strong focus on liberalisation and reliance on price signals rather than indicative planning to allocate resources and guide growth.[48]

Economic management

Planning was one point of entry into Treasury for economists. More immediate, and arguably more compelling to Treasury — and providing as strong an argument for economic expertise — was the need for short- to medium-term economic management, the domain of Keynesian macroeconomics. Economic management was a crafting of fiscal, monetary — and increasingly, incomes — policies. It was a task for which officials with economics training were suited, as writing on the subject by a British economist and adviser to the 1964–1970 Labour government demonstrated.[49] So this was the other sphere in which Lang was determined that the Treasury should play the lead role. We saw in chapter 5 that in the early 1950s there was a flurry of discussion about the co-ordination of economic policy, but that for a variety of reasons the Treasury did not assume the central role. The department's profile 'subsided' with Ashwin's departure in 1955. Politicians remained in charge, and in the aftermath of the 1958 'Black Budget' governments became averse to using fiscal policy as a tool of economic management. It helped that the economy was not under as much pressure in the early and mid-1960s as it was before or later.

From the mid-1960s the circumstances and the relationships changed. As economic conditions worsened, Treasury had more opportunities to give advice which it was now better equipped to provide. But ironically, in the 1970s there was to be disillusionment with economic management on Keynesian lines. This was partly the result of the discrediting of Keynesian-style macroeconomics itself. But a narrative account reveals how powerfully policy was shaped by party and electoral considerations. The major turning points in the story are economic *and* political, and remain so through the 1980s and beyond.

It is useful to start in the mid-1960s, before fiscal policy was resorted to in 1967 for the first time in the decade. After some monetary measures were taken in September 1965, one economic commentator observed that 'instead of tackling these problems [through] taxation, the Government was doing it indirectly.'[50] And as one Treasury memorandum noted, 'the classical solution for the present difficulties is restraint exercised through budgetary and monetary measures [but the] Government does not seem prepared to take strong enough measures for such a policy to be regarded as a real possibility'.[51]

In October 1965 Treasury recommended, inter alia, a host of possible indirect tax increases, including a flat-rate tariff surcharge on imports, an increase in car sales tax from 33.3 to 50 per cent, and a petrol tax increase. It wanted the government to take the power to change indirect tax rates between elections by means of Order in Council (as had been recommended by the Monetary and Economic Council in 1964). If this was an instance of the Treasury recommending many fiscal measures in the hope that at least some would be adopted, the strategy failed — none were.[52]

Following that failure, and aware of a deterioration in the balance of payments, Treasury advised restraining demand. It knew that the government would not contemplate increased taxation, 'the classical remedy which has been employed in other countries to reduce excess demand.'[53] A package of reports presented on the eve of Christmas 1965 stressed the need for expenditure control (as well as *some* monetary measures). Current expenditure was estimated to be 9 per cent above the level of the previous year; the aim should be 3 per cent, exclusive of wage and salary increases. Works spending estimates were fully 24 per cent above the previous year. It was natural, if taxation was not to be increased, that

Treasury would lobby for restraint in both current and capital spending.

It is hard to tell how seriously the Cabinet took Treasury's advice. At its last pre-Christmas meeting it agreed to the 3 per cent growth target for 'revenue' (that is, current, not capital) expenditure, but in other respects the language was mild. For instance, Cabinet 'invited' ministers to 'instruct Departments to co-operate' with Treasury, and it said nothing about the 53 per cent rise in the estimates for electricity works.[54] 1966 was an election year, and it was no wonder that one columnist observed, in pre-Budget comment, that with the rise in GNP leaving room for Budget concessions, 'overall the budget may be the target of criticism from professional economists who think that fiscal methods should be used to restrict internal demand. But the government is not suddenly going to abandon the policies it has followed for the past five years. The electorate showed it liked the policies in 1963.'[55]

Accordingly, while Treasury continued to state the case for 'demand restraint' which would 'ease pressure on labour and other domestic resources and … reduce the external deficit', it concentrated on arguing for a 'very substantial tightening' of monetary policy.[56] One Treasury analyst had recognised the 'case against' a policy of demand restraint: that 'severe restraint may wreck major success elements in the present situation, namely the impressive build up in farm investment and livestock numbers — because it is from this sector that major export expansion must come.'[57] This was the government's preferred line. In a memo to Henry Lang of 17 May, the Minister of Finance referred to a Cabinet discussion of the line to be taken in the Budget: to 'emphasise the problems of growth — point out that we must accept some slowing down in the rate of expansion', but also that 'we have been most reluctant to take steps to dampen down the rate of investment'.[58]

The question of whether the government ignored Treasury advice foreshadowing the December collapse and subsequent balance of payments crisis has recently been debated. It seems that Tom Shand, whom Holyoake had made Minister of Labour because the finance portfolio would have given him too much power, argued that Cabinet should take Treasury advice and impose harsher monetary or fiscal measures (if not increased taxation). However, Holyoake persuaded his colleagues that National would lose the election if they took this course. Shand contemplated resigning, but did not act for fear that this would demoralise the National Party in an election year.[59]

While Treasury was certainly stressing the need for restraint in its pre-Budget advice to the minister, this reflected a general concern about an overheated economy rather than a specific anxiety about the balance of payments. Thus on 13 May Treasury wrote that it was essential 'to ease the pressure on labour and other domestic resources and to reduce the external deficit … more effective measures [must] be taken to check the rate of increase in domestic expenditure and thus the demand for goods and services'.[60]

In the event, expenditure for 1966/67 was to be £635.4 million, well above the 1965/66 level of £584.7 million, albeit somewhat below the first estimates for the year. But if this suggests that fiscal policy remained underutilised, events reveal a different story. The government was returned to office on 26 November. Two weeks later, wool prices collapsed. For the 1966/67 season, which was already under way, the Wool Commission had set a floor price for wool of 36d per pound. At an auction on December 14 the price fell to 35.3d, and by the end of the season the Commission had been forced to buy one-third of the clip.[61]

The government responded swiftly, probably encouraged by the fact that it would not have to face the electorate for three years. The files suggest that the

Harry Lake, Minister of Finance, 1960–67 (right), watching the first copies of the 1961 Budget come off the Government Printing Office press. His Parliamentary Under-Secretary David Seath is on the left. Dominion Post, Alexander Turnbull Library, C-26202-¹/₂

Blacker than the Black Budget? Fiscal measures, February 1967. Evening Post, 11 February 1967

process of seeking expenditure cutbacks was driven more by Holyoake than by either Harry Lake, the affable nonentity whom Holyoake had made Minister of Finance in 1961, or the Treasury, although the latter was almost certainly pleased at the response.[62] Other fiscal measures, announced by Holyoake in early February, aimed to dampen demand. They were the toughest since Nordmeyer's 1958 'Black Budget'. When asked to comment, he declined — 'I bestow on the Government the charity of my silence'.[63] Muldoon became Minister of Finance after Lake died unexpectedly of a heart attack ten days later. Odd though it may seem in retrospect, with Muldoon as with Lake, Holyoake was choosing someone who would not, unlike Tom Shand, be a rival. But presciently (or was this Holyoake at his most adept?) it is Muldoon's name, not Holyoake's, which is linked with the 'mini-Budget' of early May. The nickname was contemporary, even stylish, in the age of the Mini and the miniskirt. It suggested that while fiscal policy had returned to centre stage (although along with, not in place of, monetary policy), it would be handled more deftly — 'fine-tuned', as it were. The main Budget, presented on June 22, contained no new impositions, and direct taxes were not raised in 1967 as they had been in 1958.[64] From the files it is hard to discern the respective contributions of ministers and officials to either Budget, but the policy of demand restraint followed the advice Treasury had been providing. In one of his memoirs, Muldoon recorded that 'on this occasion the Government and officials were together on what needed to be done.'[65]

Equally significantly, two other aspects of economic management came into play in 1967/68: the exchange rate, and prices and incomes.[66] Muldoon recounted that while in Rio de Janeiro in October 1967 for a meeting of the World Bank and IMF he 'received a telephone call from the Prime Minister who told me that our advisers had recommended an immediate devaluation and that a committee of the Prime Minister [and senior ministers] were inclined to agree. The senior official in New Zealand was Henry Lang.'[67]

Muldoon recounts his discussions with the officials accompanying him, who included Cop Davis (now the Treasury Secretary), Noel Lough, and Alan Low of the Reserve Bank. He decided to oppose devaluation on the grounds that this might increase pressure on the British pound. When some weeks later, in November, the British pound was devalued, New Zealand followed suit, its 19.45 per cent devaluation bringing parity with the Australian dollar. The New Zealand currency's rate had not been altered since the sterling devaluation of 1949, which New Zealand had followed or, more significantly, the revaluation of the New Zealand pound in 1948. The 1967 debate on devaluation must have traversed the merits of following this course of action rather than the alternative strategies of restricting imports (as in 1938 and 1958) and deflation (1958, 1961). For the next seventeen years — the years in which Muldoon was either Minister of Finance or Opposition spokesperson on finance — changes to the exchange rate remained in Treasury's armoury of advice.[68]

The other main development in economic management followed the collapse of the long-established method of wage-fixing through Arbitration Court hearings. In 1968 the Judge of the Arbitration Court handed down a nil wage order, despite Muldoon indicating that the government could live with 2.5 per cent. National's caucus encouraged the Federation of Labour and the Employers' Federation to go back to the Court in an 'unholy alliance', and the Court subsequently agreed to 5 per cent, with the Judge dissenting from the decision of the employers' and workers' representatives. According to Muldoon, 'five per cent went straight into prices, together with the increased cost consequent on devaluation which had previously been absorbed, and the wage–price spiral was on again.'[69]

The files do not record how Treasury reacted to this decision, perhaps because opposing it would have meant taking on Shand, but in later years it was frequently instanced as a turning point. 'Incomes policies' as a subset of economic management were to become an important preoccupation of both Treasury and the government of the day.

Industrial relations loomed large in the later 1960s. Minister of Labour Tom Shand (centre) is flanked by an 'unholy alliance': the leaders of the employers (Mr Lumsden, left) and the workers (Tom Skinner, right). Dominion Post, Alexander Turnbull Library, C-26203-1/2

Treasury's increased involvement in providing economic advice — and also perhaps its changed leadership, with Lang having become Secretary at the beginning of 1969 — is reflected in the Budget records for 1969 being much more substantial than those for previous years.[70] It seemed that New Zealand's cost structure had been assisted by the November 1967 devaluation, and the Budget focused primarily on longer-term economic change (see the next section). But Muldoon also conceded that he was reluctant to impose more fiscal measures in an election year.[71] By 1970 Treasury was anxious about inflation, which had 'eaten up' the gains from devaluation:

> The two most disturbing aspects of the current situation are the large increases in wage rates and the possibility that government capital expenditure may start to rise at a rate approaching the excessive rate of current spending … the price-wage spiral is rapidly reaching the point where our competitive position in export markets will be undermined and demand for imports will rise to unmanageable proportions … to meet the present situation the Budget would have to have an immediate and deflationary effect on the economy; the monetary policies recommended will be helpful but are unlikely to bite for six to nine months. That means that fiscal policy now needs to be tough.[72]

It may be that Treasury thought that such advice would be more palatable in a post-election year. 'Demand management' was in this instance a matter of restraining demand, not buoying it up, a fact that drew attention to the cyclical character of economic activity, a grasp of which Keynesians believed was crucial to the successful application of monetary and fiscal policies. As the wage/price spiral continued, Treasury advice, under the aegis of Deputy Secretary Noel Lough (the new Secretary, Lang, was travelling with the Minister), became even firmer later in 1970, addressing in this instance fiscal, monetary, price and incomes policies as well as liberalisation. While incomes policies were fashionable elsewhere in the world, they had failed in Britain in 1969 — so it was unsurprising that while they were explored in New Zealand, they were treated gingerly by politicians. Treasury recommended a 'general deflationary policy' and consideration of a temporary wage/price freeze. The latter was implemented, and in March 1971 a Stabilisation of Remuneration Act introduced a new system of pay-fixing to replace the one that had collapsed with the Arbitration Court's nil wage order.[73]

The uncertainties of macroeconomic management were well demonstrated in 1972. Early in the year's Budget round, Treasury had feared that 'growth in the economy in the early part of [1972/73] could be small as investment is lagging … an increase in government expenditure in excess of the anticipated growth rate in output, which would have a stimulating effect on the economy, could therefore be contemplated.'[74]

Barely a month after this advice was proffered, the new Prime Minister, Jack Marshall, agreed with Treasury on stabilisation measures that included a six-week price freeze and pay pause, partly on the grounds that the 'monetary and fiscal policy were not in themselves enough to manage excess demand.'[75] In fact 1972/73 was to see the country's biggest boom, other than 1950/51, since the Second World War, as rising export prices fuelled a surge in consumption. Nevertheless, Labour, forming a government at the end of 1972 for the first time since 1960, moved swiftly to dismantle what it saw as some of the more draconian of its predecessor's stabilisation policies, in particular the Remuneration Authority established in March 1971 and the regulations promulgated at the end of the February/March 1972 price freeze and pay pause.[76]

Treasury adjusted its advice to the requirements of the new government. To observe that 'the recovery of economic activity had now advanced to the point [that there was no] need for the continued stimulus of a very expansionary balance between government revenue and expenditure' was an understatement that was predictably ignored.[77] A 1973 Budget report on the government's economic strategy was noticeable not for discussion of possible fiscal, monetary or incomes measures, but for the way it related Budget measures to the strategy, which centred on full employment, population growth, and 'micro-economic' policies in areas such as industry development and the labour market.[78]

When the Middle East war of October 1973 was followed by an escalation in the price of crude oil, New Zealand encountered a severe balance of payments crisis. What was to be done about this? The post-war philosophy of stabilisation, especially as it was interpreted by a Labour government, ruled out deflation, with its likely consequences of unemployment and bankruptcies. Devaluation — Muldoon's 1967 remedy — was disliked because of the price increases that would come in its train.

In any case, the collapse in the balance of payments was so severe that for a few months it was difficult to think beyond the very short term. In March 1974 Treasury (supported by the Monetary and Economic Council two months later) predicted a $400 million balance of payments deficit for the 1974/75 year. If this came about, it would be far worse than any similar downturn since the Second World War, mitigated only by the fact that New Zealand's reserves were at unprecedentedly high levels.[79] Six weeks later, Treasury stressed that economic prospects were 'deteriorating rapidly'; stagflation (a formerly unknown, and still unwelcome, combination of inflation with lack of growth) accompanied by acute balance of payments problems was expected throughout 1975/76.[80] By January 1975, the balance of payments deficit for the 1974/75 year was expected to be $800 million (in fact, it was to amount to a staggering $1.3 billion in the calendar year 1974, and over a third more than that in 1975).[81]

Treasury now recommended 'corrective measures' — that is, a contraction — but as a long- rather than a short-term strategy so as to minimise growth in unemployment in 1975/76. The best approach would be to resume overseas borrowing on a substantial scale, whilst squeezing the domestic economy.[82] What neither the officials nor anyone else were prepared for was that the deficit would be twice what they had predicted. The 1974 and 1975 deficits 'were equivalent to about $13^{1}/_{2}$ per cent of GNP ... the largest recorded among OECD Member countries in each year'.[83] 'There was a period', recalled David Preston, who had succeeded Galvin as head of Internal Economics in 1973, 'when what was happening was unbelievable. We were feeling, "There must be some mistake" ...

Bored or borrowing? Prime Minister Bill Rowling (right) and Minister of Finance Bob Tizard, 1975. Dominion Post, Alexander Turnbull Library, F-22663-¹/₄

When we produced our economic forecasts, then, after a few months, produced revised forecasts, there was horror round the table.'[84] Another official remembers the extra sheets of paper that were tacked onto the graph of overseas exchange transactions until the deficit literally hit the floor.[85]

In a novel alignment of the Labour government with its economic advisers, the Cabinet Economic Committee agreed in July 1974 that 'a policy of fiscal and monetary tightness be maintained until excess demand had been eliminated from the economy'. Within three weeks, Lang warned that 'it now looks improbable that we can get by without positive and quick action to reduce demand for imports.'[86] The press understood:

> In a year we have trimmed a $325 million surplus on the current account into a $334 million deficit. We have seen $500 million lopped off our official overseas reserves. We're not naked yet ... but by this time next year, unless some factor in the equation changes, we really shall be shivering.[87]

Devaluation was advocated by Muldoon, who had recently been elected Leader of the Opposition in place of the defeated Prime Minister, Marshall. But it was at this time that borrowing became a major element in the mix of policies. Bill

Bob Tizard, Minister of Finance, 1974–75. Dominion Post, Alexander Turnbull Library, F-22688-¹/₄

Rowling, the Minister of Finance, was reported as being prepared to borrow 'any money necessary to sustain New Zealand's standard of living'. This would be risky. With the Middle East awash in petrodollars, a variety of individuals surfaced as interlocuters between intensely private Arab nationals and borrowers such as New Zealand. Rowling, the *Auckland Star* reported, 'already has Treasury officers overseas prospecting loans'.[88] One deal was made in the course of a long-distance telephone call. Ray Alexander, John Martin, John Chetwin and other finance officials in London explored *all* possibilities, however will-o'-the-wisp. These 'confidential' dealings were inevitably leaked, whereupon City of London contacts suggested that New Zealand's credit would be damaged rather than enhanced by doing business with 'cowboys'.[89]

While measures to cut government spending garnered headlines in early August,[90] the government was near paralysis because of the serious illness of the Prime Minister, Norman Kirk, of which the public was unaware. The new Minister of Finance, Bob Tizard, who took over following Kirk's death at the end of August, faced a bleak situation. Treasury did have the advantage of good relations with Rowling, who was now Prime Minister. Treasury's reports for its new minister in September reveal that providing economic advice in such 'hard times' was a dangerous high-wire act. After discussing the amount of borrowing which had been undertaken, Lang pointed out that 'our present policies involve heavy risks. If our balance of payments looks as bad in 12 months as it does now, overseas borrowing will dry up and we might not be able to finance the imports needed to sustain a reasonable level of activity … we would be virtually powerless to prevent a general collapse of confidence which could result in widespread unemployment … restraints must be applied to reduce the general level of spending … most other countries are dealing with similar problems by conventional demand deflation measures which have resulted in … unemployment.'[91]

Lang went on to say that the risk might pay off provided incomes, fiscal and monetary policies were all maintained. Treasury was now drawn back into incomes policy for the first time since the change of government. Since the abolition of the Remuneration Authority, the government's main anti-inflationary strategy had been the Maximum Retail Price scheme which had come into effect in July 1974. Wages policy, it was believed, should be left to workers and employers. There was therefore little call for Treasury advice, and not much evidence of it.[92]

But as the situation continued to deteriorate rapidly, the reconstructed government decided there was a need for wage restraint, and thereby found common ground with Treasury. The latter recommended in October that action be taken to limit the impact of the forthcoming cost-of-living order provided for by new wage adjustment regulations, which would 'give a sizable boost to costs which at this stage in the economic cycle could only be passed on into increased prices'. Treasury recognised that cancelling the order would be politically unfeasible, but favoured either managing the process to produce a smaller than expected increase, or accomplishing the same result through tax cuts (which might be useful given the economic downturn). In the event the Prime Minister announced a different strategy: a general wage order of 4 per cent on the first $75 of weekly earnings. Treasury had not favoured a general wage order because 'the Government would lose direct control over the size of the January pay increase by transferring the decision to the Industrial Commission', but Rowling's issuing of a direction overcame that disadvantage.[93]

Treasury hoped for similar restraint in fiscal policy. At the beginning of the new year Treasury stuck to its strategy of maintaining the overall level of economic activity, but opposed government expenditure decisions which 'could generate levels of domestic activity too great to be supported by the balance of payments.'⁹⁴ Treasury's lack of leverage with the politicians was shown by the fact that in 1975 the Cabinet went on a spending spree.⁹⁵ As in 1974, it was after the Budget that Treasury sought either a devaluation or new measures designed to avoid one. The government hesitated, but eventually agreed to a 10 per cent devaluation.⁹⁶

Following another change of government in November 1975, stabilisation took a different turn. The new Prime Minister — and returned Minister of Finance — Robert Muldoon decided to deal with inflationary pressures personally by reaching an accord with the labour movement. To that end, he engaged in extensive discussions with Federation of Labour leader Tom Skinner and Combined State Service Organisations leader Ivan Reddish over incomes policy, in the hope of a return to some of the stability, if not the exact form, of the pre-1968 wage-fixing system. Direct dealing with the union movement was to characterise the Muldoon years. The Prime Minister was, for instance, personally responsible for the 1976–77 wage freeze, for its extension, and for the March 1978 government-subsidised freezing workers' settlement. For its part, Treasury remained involved by reporting on such matters to Muldoon.⁹⁷

The bargaining with the unions in 1976 was part of an anti-inflationary policy which most officials thought ineffective.⁹⁸ It was characteristic of economic behaviour worldwide that inflation remained a problem during a recession which, in New Zealand, had become the deepest and most protracted of any country in the OECD:

> Following an estimated 3 per cent fall in 1975, GDP may have declined by a further 1 per cent in 1976 … Non-farm real personal incomes declined for the second year running, business investment fell further and there was also a marked shift in fiscal policy from counter-cyclical stimulus in 1975 to significant restraint in 1976.⁹⁹

The tight fiscal policy saw the Budget deficit fall from 9 per cent of GDP in 1975/76 to 2.6 per cent in 1977/78. Later in 1977 political pressure to counter the contraction that came in the wake of these measures increased:

> The big wheels of the economy got together, made appointments with the Prime Minister: 'Make up your mind, if you go on cutting government expenditure this way, there will be 10,000 unemployed by Christmas.' It was a series of very loud signals. That was the time when he stopped trying to be

a statesman. For any outsider, it was stunning what happened at that stage. [Muldoon] genuinely believed it would have been a tragedy to have gone on down that road of retrenchment.[100]

There was also debate within the government. The quarterly economic survey revealed that economic activity remained sluggish. Whether to 'juice up' the economy or 'stand tight' was argued both within Treasury and between Treasury and the Prime Minister's Department. The argument continued even after a mildly expansionary mini-Budget.[101]

Graham Scott, a future Secretary to the Treasury, was an economic adviser in the Prime Minister's Department at the time:

> It seemed to me that the 1977 Budget was too tough and likely to drive the economy down, and that the government was not going to be able to live with that fiscal policy. Muldoon on his departure on an overseas trip said, 'I am not happy with the way things are going. I would like you to come up with some ideas.' We ran through all that with Talboys, the Acting PM, and with Treasury itself, and when Muldoon came back we put together one of those mini-Budgets, which increased the fiscal deficit a bit.[102]

A political or an economic cycle? Bob Brockie, *National Business Review*

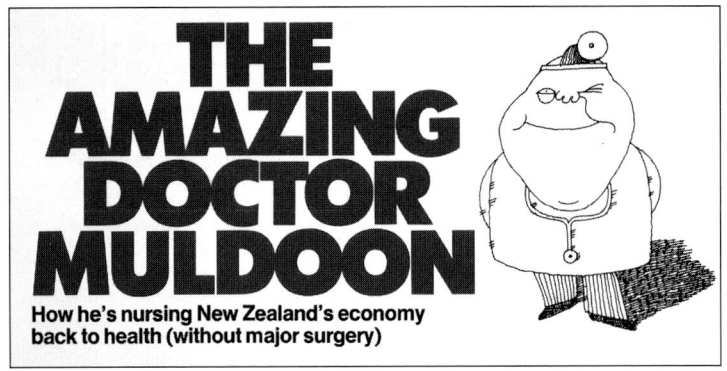

Muldoon's economic medicine, 1978. New Zealand National Party, Alexander Turnbull Library, Eph-A-NZ-NATIONAL-1978-02-front

The October 1977 mini-Budget included the payment of a special supplementary family benefit, $16 million of increased public works expenditure, the lifting of hire purchase restrictions on most goods, a reduction in trading banks' reserve assets ratios, and the introduction of a compensatory deposit scheme to offset the seasonal liquidity squeeze on trading banks during the tax payment period.[103] Further reflationary measures were introduced during 1978.[104] National won the 1978 election narrowly, receiving fewer votes but more seats than Labour. National MPs were pleased, Treasury officials less so: 'I remember the sensation of a minister making comments about how grateful the government were for us helping the government's positioning. I was pretty hypersensitive about such comments and was not amused.'[105]

This section has traced the course of macroeconomic policy during the 1960s and 1970s at considerable length. But the persistence of problems of economic management drained the energy of officials. Macroeconomic management which combined monetary, fiscal and incomes policies was to continue after the 1978 election, but the political, economic and, as will be discussed below, intellectual blows that it had taken were to influence its fate in the 1980s.

Liberalisation

Much of the longer-term advice which Treasury gave to governments during the late 1960s and 1970s advocated 'liberalisation'. This advice focused particularly on the regulated rather then the government-owned sector of the economy —

on licensing, tariffs, taxes, and wage- and price-setting. As we have noted, these activities had not historically fallen within Treasury's ambit, but the department's increasing preoccupation with economic management opened the way.

Liberalisation was rooted in economic theory. The 'neoclassical synthesis' married Keynesian macroeconomics with the study of the behaviour of the individual and firm, now subsumed under the rubric 'microeconomics'. It was from the latter body of enquiry that the notion of relying on the price mechanism to determine an efficient allocation of resources, and to promote economic growth, stemmed. It turned attention away from the 'Keynesian' preoccupation with maintaining or stabilising demand in the economy — from 'planning' — to a preoccupation with encouraging 'supply' — with the production side of the economy and the incentives it responded to. The vocabulary was different too. In the 1980s, it became common to talk about microeconomic reforms, supply-side reforms, and deregulation. While these expressions had not been heard so frequently in the 1970s, the ideas were present on the margins of economic discourse. Liberalisation had linkages forward as well as back in time. Indeed the association of the phrase with the 1980s, as in the 1987 Bollard and Buckle study, *Economic Liberalisation in New Zealand*, has unintentionally drawn attention away from the extent to which advocacy of liberalisation, and a certain number of liberalising measures, can be traced back for a decade and a half before 1984. There were several differences between this liberalising agenda and the changes of the 1980s. Firstly, the changes were far less substantial or extensive. Secondly, they were not anchored in an overarching readiness to rely on the market rather than the state as the driver of economic activity. Thirdly, they existed alongside and competed with other strategies.

For the Treasury, liberalisation fertilised the long-standing focus on guarding public spending, on 'Treasury control'. A 1967 study group argued that economic and financial management tended to coincide in areas where government expenditure was a major element in economic policy, not just at the macro-level but also at the micro-level — areas such as 'roading construction; air travel and airport construction; tourism; forest development; education; electric supply; coal mining; railways; communications; land development'.[106] Greg Whitwell noted in respect of the Australian Treasury that its 'traditional function of financial management heightened its interest in, and made it receptive to, a neoclassical viewpoint, in particular the importance of allocating resources efficiently'.[107]

I will return to issues of financial management in the next section of this chapter. The economists working in the investigating divisions that dealt with these issues had opportunities to apply economic analysis to the policies behind expenditure proposals as well as keeping an eye on the Estimates and the Treasury Instructions. Young officials familiar with microeconomic arguments in favour of the allocative efficiency of the price mechanism questioned, for example, the raison d'etre of existing forms of transport regulation which suppressed price signals. Road-user charges and the first steps towards deregulating the rail freight business were two of the results. Others challenged the system of power planning. Future demand was projected on the basis of increased supply — of both power and appliances. It was assumed that if there were more appliances there would be more demand. The notion that demand would vary with the price of the power supplied did not seem to form an underlying assumption of Electricity Department planning.[108]

Treasury advocated liberalisation most vigorously in respect of 'border' protection (the protection of domestic production from imported goods), perhaps because this was such a visible target. In long-running debates over such issues as industrial policy, frontier protection, and freer trade with Australia, there were fierce interdepartmental battles in which Treasury and Trade and Industry were the principal protagonists. The Treasury had its victories, but the influence of protectionist interests on policy was always powerful.[109] The key recommendation of a report by a World Bank team which was invited by the government to report on the New Zealand economy in 1967 was the adoption of tariffs as the main form of industry protection. Lang later told a much younger economist that he rated this as amongst the most important documents in New Zealand's economic history.[110] The Monetary and Economic Council made a similar proposal in February 1968, and so did the National Development Conference in May 1969 in its most significant recommendation — 209A. No one now remembers numbers 1 to 208, 209B, or however many further recommendations were made before the conferees collapsed from exhaustion. But 209A is still recalled more than 30 years later, and it merits quotation in full:

> The manufacturing sector should be accorded a level of protection sufficient to promote steady industrial development, increasing manufactured exports, and full employment. This level of protection however, should be such as to encourage competition, efficiency, and reasonable prices to other sectors and to consumers and should also have regard to the need to give the consumer choice and variety. It is accordingly recommended that the system of

> protection should be flexible, that import licensing should be replaced by tariffs as the main measure of protection and that this transition should be carried out in accordance with a clearly defined programme and within a reasonable time. It is recognized, however that there are cases where other protective measures including import licensing may be more appropriate than a tariff.[111]

There will be more on the fate of this resolution later. Liberalisation was also advocated in other spheres. The Ross committee on taxation, in recommending a lowering of the burden of direct taxation, took a liberalising stance in this sphere of economic life.[112] Budget reports for 1969 include lengthy discussions of exchange control, monetary policy and import licensing, each advocating greater liberalisation. Thus the purpose of the changes proposed in monetary policy was to 'foster the development and growth of the financial system and to increase the effectiveness of monetary policy.'[113] The Budget did implement new measures on monetary policy and overseas investment, such as permitting banks to compete actively for high-value deposits.[114] In 1970, Treasury tackled interest-rate policy again:

> Rates are controlled in certain areas but elsewhere natural market forces will force rates up still higher to the detriment of the Government's overall monetary control since these higher rates of interest will attract funds away from the controlled area.[115]

For its part, in 1971 the Monetary and Economic Council called for the government to 'make further progress with the changes in monetary policy which it began to institute in 1969 … to achieve a more effective and less discriminatory system of control of credit while providing competition among financial institutions to cater effectively for the requirements of savers and borrowers as the economy grew and diversified'. It quoted J. G. Phillips, the Governor of the Reserve Bank of Australia, on the increasing emphasis placed in that country and by his own institution on market-oriented policies rather than direct controls.[116]

In the same report, the Council supported the overarching idea of supply-side liberalisation: 'the Council places great emphasis on this group of policies. They are aimed at improving directly the operation of market forces, strengthening competitiveness and efficiency, and increasing the quality and quantity of the supply of resources.' However, the Council also stressed that it was 'in no way advocating a return to laissez-faire'.[117] Indeed, liberalisation can also be seen from the point of view not of a retreat from the state but of a preference for relying on indirect rather than direct controls. During the Second World War, most countries had instituted controls which capitalist economies steadily loosened during the 1950s and into the 1960s. Treasury criticised the inefficiencies of import licensing in the 1950s.[118]

Liberalisation was advocated by Treasury in one set of papers in 1970 as a means of overcoming domestic difficulties: 'the absence of effective competition for many classes of goods has erected an environment which has reduced employer resistance to attempts by unions to exploit more vigorously than in the past the shortage of labour'.[119] It was probably not accidental that it was Noel Lough, not Henry Lang, who was responsible for this advice — his commitment to liberalisation was stronger than Lang's. In this paper, Treasury argued for the replacement of import controls by tariffs, and the relaxation of exchange controls. These measures would not only 'inject an element of price competition with overseas suppliers' but provide a 'partial built-in safeguard against future bouts of cost-price inflation'. Thirty years later, a Treasury officer defined the issue in parallel terms:

> It wasn't just the unions who were involved — employers were weak bargainers because they could pass on the costs, and at the time, the financial system accommodated it. The structure of the labour market, and the structure of union bargaining via national occupational awards, meant employers would face a general wage increase, so they knew everyone was going to pass it on, so they weren't resistant. In that circumstance, if we had strangled [inflation], we would have had to strangle the economy very, very hard, and what's called the 'sacrifice ratio' — the amount of unemployment generated — would probably have been high.[120]

In a further presentation to Cabinet in May 1971, Treasury was able to say that departments were in agreement on the need to speed up the programme for liberalising imports,[121] and the 1971 Budget stated that the review of the import licensing system would be completed within five years. The Governor of the Reserve Bank saw 'the policy decision to remove import licensing as one of the most important decisions to be made in New Zealand for many a long day. It has enormous potential both for the disturbance of comfortable positions and for stimulus to productivity.'[122]

But the experts spoke too soon. While the economists and public servants might have 'got their way', the 'old' political economy was not about to lie down, as became evident at the March 1972 session of the NDC. The proposed change from quantitative protection to tariffs had created a climate of insecurity in manufacturing industries, said H. H. Saunders, President of the Manufacturers' Federation, whilst the industrialist Woolf Fisher challenged the notion that 'import licensing' was a dirty word. That session of the conference recommended by a very narrow margin that the policy of shifting to tariffs should be reviewed.[123]

This virtual reversal of the position taken by the conference in 1969 and adopted by the government in 1971 uncovered the workings of the political economy. Auckland and Christchurch manufacturers were very influential in the National Party, as were businesspeople holding import licences, who were likely to lose their privileged positions in the event of a shift to tariffs.

In his 1968 study, and in many subsequent writings, Wolfgang Rosenberg, a long-time economist at the University of Canterbury (and like Henry Lang, a refugee from Hitler), argued that an insulated economy was the best way to ensure full employment. One commentator remarked that 'there is a small but pleasing irony in the fact that the Left in New Zealand can find, in the person of Wolfgang Rosenberg, someone with enough courage to sum up its view on New Zealand's future in a book, while the Right must rely on the World Bank to put its thoughts together.'[124]

Rosenberg's approach placed reliance on the readiness of New Zealanders to support a controlled economy, behind the barriers of which all could be assured of employment. The Treasury critique focused more on profitability than on employment — a variant of its dislike a generation earlier of exchange rate changes on behalf of sectional interests. It saw the import licensing system secondarily as a job-creating system, primarily as a profit-creating system for inefficient businesses and therefore for 'rent-seeking' unions. And it was the businesses, not the workers, who had the greatest leverage with National:

> In the mid-1960s there was an outfit called the 'Cabal'. Politicians didn't admit it was there but it was, and it was quite effective. It was run by senior people in industry — there were about seven or eight of them all told, and it was very informal. Cliff Plimmer, the head of Wright Stephenson's, was one. The head of Federated Farmers was involved as well. The one I knew best was Ken Campbell, who was a friend of Doug Barker's. He was a financier and sharebroker. They met in the Wellington Club and they were key people in policy ... to do with New Zealand Steel, import licensing, Fletchers.[125]

This cluster of individuals lost some influence when Muldoon, with his strong Auckland links, became prominent, but the general pattern did not change:

> The 'three feds' which ran the country' were the Federation of Labour, the Manufacturers Federation and Federated Farmers. Others weren't in this — like the Chambers of Commerce, [which] were sometimes referred to as the Chamber of Comics because they were regarded as not having the political weight of the big three federations.[126]

So National was pragmatically rather than ideologically nationalist — it would not happily or readily torpedo the profitability of established New Zealand businesses, and on occasion acted swiftly to avert any such threat. Thus Labour's scheme for a Nelson cotton mill was cancelled in 1962, not least because of the likely effect of its production on existing producers and importers of cotton goods. The News Media Ownership Act 1965 prevented a 'hostile' takeover of the *Dominion* newspaper by an overseas investor (the Canadian press businessman Roy Thomson). In 1968 an application by Avis (like an earlier one by Hertz) to trade in New Zealand was declined on the grounds that 'overseas companies should not be given the right to operate a business … that was capable of being operated by New Zealand companies.'[127] At one point in the negotiations with Comalco to build an aluminium plant in Southland, a great deal of attention was paid to the need to assure New Zealanders the opportunity to invest in the local subsidiary.[128] And when TNT took over the Union Steam Ship Company, it acceded to government pressure that the latter remain a single unit, half owned in Australia and half in New Zealand.[129]

In 1972 National faced the unprecedented challenge of attempting to secure a fifth successive election victory. In such a context it was not surprising that both Cabinet and caucus were receptive to pressure from manufacturers and importers articulating the risks to both their profitability and their workforce. Conversely, pressure from those who might benefit from liberalisation — consumers, companies not yet in existence or domiciled outside New Zealand, workers not yet employed — was weak or non-existent. The most influential of the anti-licence lobbies — the farmers — were palliated with assistance measures.[130]

The election of the Labour government put liberalisation on the back burner, with one exception — Labour was prepared to end farm input subsidies.[131] Labour's retreat was partly ideological — it saw import licensing as an acceptable form of protection.[132] So Henry Lang's public advocacy of the benefits of trade liberalisation in an address on foreign policy was advice for the record, not the moment.[133] In any case, the scale of the collapse in the balance of payments in 1974/75 directed the government's attention elsewhere. When Muldoon became both Prime Minister and Minister of Finance after the 1975 election, monetary and trade policies moved at quite different paces. That Muldoon had shifted on monetary policy was confirmed by an early request for the economist Len Bayliss (an advocate of change) to join the new Prime Minister's advisory group. An officials' committee headed by Noel Lough

> made recommendations for what can only be described as a major leap into orthodoxy. This would be the first time in New Zealand's history that interest rates were being used to perform the function for which they were designed. A very offhand discussion with the PM makes one wonder whether in fact the Cabinet will take the jump when they come to the barrier.[134]

So for a period, Treasury was able 'persuade Muldoon … to go for more flexible interest rates. But later on, we were in an inflationary period, and he got increasingly uncomfortable about the implications of what he'd done. So then you see him in the late 1970s beginning to backtrack, to put pressure on the banks to bring the rates down.'[135]

With import licensing, not even that much change was accomplished. Treasury advocated change in its briefing to the incoming government, but National remained scarred by the business coolness when moves to liberalise import licensing had been announced in 1972: 'as a relatively junior civil servant through the 1970s I heard constant references back to that — it was seared in the minds of ministers like Talboys, Templeton and others of the Muldoon Cabinet, and it made it hard to get momentum about protection up again.'[136]

Work did continue on industry studies, in which officials analysed the situation of the industry and considered possible changes in its regulatory environment. These were joint Treasury/Trade and Industry efforts. But it was pressure from the Australians, rather than any internal dynamic in New Zealand, that produced some new momentum on trade liberalisation in 1978. After Doug Anthony, Australia's Minister of Overseas Trade, decided that Australia would abandon the New Zealand–Australia Free Trade Agreement if it were not drastically overhauled, negotiations to that effect began.

Public finance

This chapter has focused on the 'new' Treasury, the Treasury of the economists rather than the Treasury of finance and surveillance of the public accounts, yet it was the latter Treasury, the child of the 1920s, that still absorbed the time of most Treasury staff in the 1960s and 1970s. Treasury's responsibility for all the government's accounts continued to be reflected in its personnel numbers. Around 1970 the 'outer' agencies — the National Provident Fund, the Government Actuary, the Stores Board and the district Treasury officers — employed about 100 people, with about another 200 in the 'core' Treasury. All were part of a wider public service which still had centralised classification and recruiting, prescribed hours of work, and a predictable scheme of promotions:

> When I came to New Zealand, and even after I joined the public service, promotion worked very much to rule and they had those famous classification lists … you even walked into the pub after work in classification list order.[137]

The numerical weight of the department still lay in the Accounts division. 'You would move around Accounts', recalled Don Rangi,

> from the payments section to the revenue section to the imprest section. I ended up in ledgers-type, public accounts-type work. Each supervisor had a character of their own. Ron Simms in Payments was a good indoor bowling character — his influence meant that I tried that and enjoyed it. John Fitzgerald in revenue used to play bowls and cricket. Treasury had a cricket team in the mercantile league. Most of these blokes had seen war service and come back.[138]

More distant than Accounts, both organisationally and geographically, were the Stores Board and the Actuary, which were in different buildings and clearly autonomous. Public Accounts and Superannuation were both regarded as a different kind of work, even though the Director of Superannuation was usually appointed from another division of Treasury.

At the centre were the Investigating and Finance divisions. We have seen that this work had begun to be influenced by economics, for instance in the use of cost–benefit analysis, but it was a beginning rather than a transformation. Individuals like Jack Lang, Sam Parker, Ian Lythgoe and Fred Shailes, with their accounting qualifications and years of experience, were at the heart of the department's management of the public accounts, although Henry Lang and Noel Lough, both qualified in accountancy as well as economics, took a keen interest in specific financial issues, as Lang did in overseas borrowing in 1974–75.

The works programme was the responsibility of the Assistant Secretary in charge of finance, Jack Lang, for most of the 1960s, and he worked very closely with the Ministry of Works. Treasury was involved in projects of 'national importance' such as New Zealand Steel, the Comalco aluminium smelter at Bluff, and the development of Kapuni and later Maui gas. We will consider these areas of Treasury activity in chapter 7, in the context of the 'Think Big' strategy of the early 1980s. Much work was done by investigating officers looking at the programmes of particular departments, with electricity generation, roading, hospital works and defence all being of major importance. One large area of Treasury's public finance work lay with defence. It dealt with employment as well as procurement — the writ of the State Services Commission did not embrace the military — thus putting the New Zealand Treasury in this one sphere in a position analogous to that of the British Treasury, which was responsible for all staff matters.[139]

Like Treasury scrutiny of works expenditure, Treasury representation on the boards of companies in which the Crown had a financial interest had its roots in the 1920s (see chapter 3) and can be traced through the 1940s and 1950s (chapters 4 and 5). Senior officials like Sam Parker and Jack Lang were prominent in this work. Sam Parker recalled that

> when Trade and Industry got an extra deputy, Henry decided he was going to have one too. My responsibilities didn't change a great deal. We did a count at that time and found that Treasury was on at least 80 significant boards or committees. It was spread around people like me. Sometimes I was 'doing my turn'. When these things were set up, they put the enthusiasts on them, and then a Treasury man to hang on to their coat-tails. I became enthusiastic about some of them. I still meet MWD people who think of me as being relatively sympathetic to them.[140]

The change in the focus of the Treasury from managing the public accounts to managing the economy was expressed in a debate about whether such Treasury representation should continue, or whether it gave rise to a conflict of interest. When senior Treasury officers were surveyed on the practice, there were differences of emphasis between Parker and Henry Lang. Where Parker valued the ability to reconcile differences if a conflict of interest arose, Lang believed that Treasury should not have directors on companies which competed with the private sector because it had to be able to give impartial advice on 'what was best for New Zealand'. Parker stressed that if the private sector was able to do something, the government should not get involved, but Lang considered that government intervention in the private sector enabled resources to be developed that might otherwise not be.[141]

And what about expenditure control itself? A 1967 study group's report on 'financial planning and control' was fundamental in turning Treasury from an inputs to an outputs approach and initiating the process by which economic thinking became influential in financial areas. On taking up the secretaryship two years later, Lang explained that:

> Treasury was now getting away from the traditional method of simply chopping back all estimates by a certain percentage. 'Instead, we are getting alongside the departments at an early stage of their policy making ... so that when a project finally appears before the Treasury and subsequently the Government it is fully thought out and the alternatives examined.'[142]

This too reflected change in the United Kingdom, where successive enquiries in the late 1950s and early 1960s, culminating in the Plowden Report, had addressed the anxiety felt by Conservative parliamentarians and others that in the Keynesian welfare state public spending was out of control because it was no longer subject to the traditional pressure on governments to reduce spending and taxes. In New Zealand, a Public Expenditure Committee was set up by Parliament with the intention that it be more vigorous than the Public Accounts Committee it replaced. The latter had only investigated two matters between 1950 and 1962, a marked falling away from its vigour of the 1920s.[143] Plowden's main conclusion relevant to the Treasury was the 'importance of expenditure being surveyed as a whole over a period of years in relation to prospective resources.' In New Zealand, the 1962 McCarthy Royal Commission on the State Services picked up the same theme.[144]

The successive incarnations of the new expenditure order — PPBS, Sigma, COPE, CCEX, compensatory savings — were part of the same family.[145] The original tone was optimistic: 'what amounts to almost a revolution in economic techniques for New Zealand is another innovation at the Treasury', reported a journalist who interviewed Henry Lang in 1969, and is based on making the best use of resources in both the public and private sectors. Mr Lang said it started in America when Robert McNamara was Secretary of Defence and was called 'Planning, Programming and Budgeting Systems'. Simply it meant that the Treasury, instead of controlling the amount departments spent on salaries or pencils, allocated funds in terms of functions or what was achieved by the input of money. Mr Lang quoted the Ministry of Transport as an example and more particularly the function of traffic control. Salaries of traffic officers, costs of cars and other items were all grouped together around an end function — traffic control. By doing this the Government will be able to decide much more clearly where additional priorities lie.[146]

Rob Laking recalled that PPBS didn't prove to be quite that straightforward:

You can programme public spending in terms of results that you require, and you can optimise your mixes of public spending by thinking about the sort of results that you require from it — and that requires you to take a somewhat broader view of it than the traditional accounting view, or bureaucratic view really, of containing public spending by the application of … input rules of one sort or another. But we had neither the tools nor the political clout to make them happen in the mid-1960s. And probably it was just as well, because PPBS turned out to be a disastrous flop in the United States.[147]

Out of these efforts came SIGMA, a

standard input classification of public spending, with another set of numbers attached to each item, which it was supposed to identify, sort of like the output — the purpose of the spending. And given the primitive state of computing in the 1960s, this produced huge reams of detailed paper, but really no capability for analysing it. We didn't have the technology for it, really. But the new cash expenditure classification came out of what we did, as did the first primitive attempts to do multi-year programming of public expenditure we did. And by 1971 we had set up the Committee of Officials on Public Expenditure (COPE) and were starting to do the first three-year forecasts. So there was a recognition that you couldn't do the whole fully-fledged PPBS thing, but that you could introduce some rational synoptic way of making expenditure decisions, which at least looked beyond the current year.[148]

All the new systems were compromised by the generally benign view of public expenditure that held sway in the 1970s. In an area like social policy, Treasury

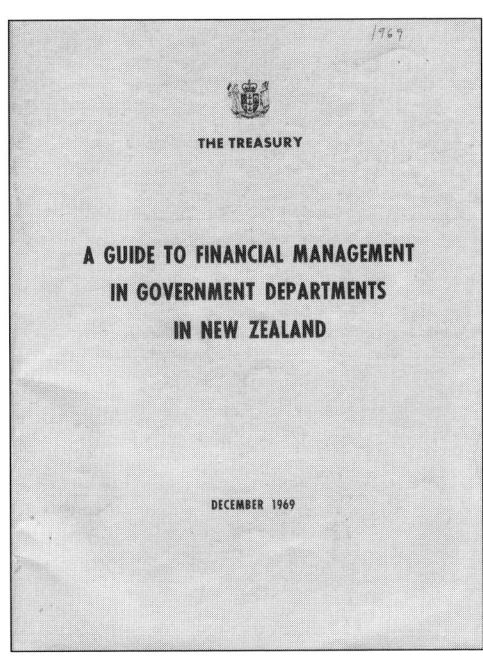

Financial management, 1969-style; on the long road to 1989. Treasury

was not in the 1970s calling into question the underlying premises of such spending. It acted to implement the recommendations of the 1972 Royal (McCarthy) Commission on Social Security and — in an era of low unemployment, and before the advent of Muldoon's national superannuation — focused on using the tax rather than the benefit system for redistributive purposes.[149] Nor, through the later 1960s and into the 1970s, did Treasury succeed in the more mundane task of meeting expenditure goals, which were regularly overwhelmed by the bidding process engaged in by ministers and permanent heads. Thus it was aimed at the beginning of the 1969/70 Budget round to hold the total increase to 6 per cent (*including* wage increases), but the result was more like 10 per cent.[150] Similarly, at a meeting of the Cabinet Committee on Government Expenditure in 1972, the three Treasury officers present (the two Langs and Shailes) explained to ministers who had considered that savings could be made from staff cuts and the simplification of administrative procedures that 'while it would be possible to make some savings, it was unlikely that they could be substantial enough to significantly affect the general level of government expenditure.'[151]

The most marked demonstration that expenditure could overshoot targets came with the third Labour government of 1972 to 1975. Recent deficits before borrowing had been of the order of the $142 million in 1969/70 (compared with $109 million in 1968/69). For 1973/74, both the Treasury and the Monetary and Economic Council recommended no more than a $200 million deficit, but a preliminary estimate in April 1973 indicated a figure of $350 million was more likely. Revenue was holding up, but expenditure was running 21 per cent over 1972/73.[152] In 1974, Treasury hoped to hold the growth in government expenditure 'well below the level of the previous two years, while maintaining existing tax rates'. In fact the Budget provided for a 14 per cent increase in real terms in the works programme. The deficit was held to $232 million in 1974/75 (thanks perhaps to the effects of fiscal drag), but looked likely to be $1.625 billion in 1975/76, twice what Treasury thought should be the *absolute* maximum.[153]

> An 18% to 20% (salary) increase per annum cannot be sustained, provision for supplementary estimates of $25 million had already been greatly exceeded, whilst substantial expenditure increases are agreed at most Cabinet meetings.[154]

Did Treasury lose ground in this area in the 1970s because the control of public expenditure was no longer its core activity? It is difficult to say. The establishment of the Cabinet Committee on Expenditure (CCEX) in 1976 reflected the new Muldoon government's determination to achieve fiscal restraint. Lang was sceptically supportive:

> I was invited to open the discussion and in essence said that officials would like to have a steer on whether they were indulging in a paper war for window dressing purposes or whether the Government in fact was willing to slaughter some sacred cows and make some real cuts in expenditure.[155]

In fact, 1976 was the one year in this era when expenditure was reduced. By April Lang was able to report that the exercise had 'been a good deal more successful than any previous attempts to cut government expenditure — the outstanding impression of [it] is the degree to which permanent heads have co-operated.'[156] But the reflation of the economy from late 1977, partly through fiscal measures, made it clear that the impulse to control expenditure had waned in the face of the political and economic realities discussed earlier. In 1977 the Committee was chaired by the Deputy Prime Minister and included the Minister of State (Holyoake) and the Minister of Justice, but by 1979 its membership was less salient. Its proceedings in the latter year demonstrate that while Treasury regularly challenged departments on particular items of expenditure, and COPE was still operating, there was no political drive to control or analyse expenditure.[157] As one of the principal Treasury officers involved at that time comments, expenditure control

> is an evolutionary thing, fundamentally based on the fact that governments themselves did not regard their own allocations as final, and ... that at the end of the year, supplementary estimates were there to fill up any holes. And ... that permanent heads, if they overspent, were subject to no particular sanctions. But if the political arm had been more rigorous, ... there would have been a greater sense of urgency in the minds of permanent heads.[158]

Ministers and officials

The relationship between ministers and officials shaped the character and activity of the Treasury. In the 1850s, the ministers *were* officials; in the late 1920s and early 1930s officials overshadowed ministers, but there was a reinvigoration of ministerial control after 1933. Would the advent of an economic advice role for Treasury alter the balance? For those providing the advice, the answer had to be 'Yes'. Otherwise, why were they providing it? But the necessity for that answer was less compelling to ministers, who in the later 1960s and 1970s mostly had the better of the argument.

The initial pattern of relations between Muldoon and Treasury officials when he took on the finance portfolio in 1967 may have been influenced by the fact that he was a junior minister feeling his way. Or perhaps the fact that he was prepared (in conjunction with Holyoake) to take firm fiscal measures made for good relations.[159] In contrast, the conjunction of minister, officials, experts and interest groups was challenged in 1972 by the newly-elected Labour government, which was suspicious of both the National Development process and the Treasury, seeing them as 'catspaws' of the long-serving outgoing government:

> A few days after the election ... Kirk called a meeting of the heads of all government departments ... He spoke to us very quietly, and you could have heard a pin drop. He told us that he and his administration expected unquestioning loyalty from the public service ... [They] were there to protect ordinary citizens from the excesses of bureaucracy.[160]

As Lang had written in 1951, 'when there is a change of government ... the advice and information given by public servants are very necessary [but] it does not follow that new governments are always willing at first to make full use of their advisers.'[161] Kirk may have been suspicious of Treasury's enthusiasm for freer trade,[162] but we have seen that incoming governments were suspicious of permanent officials in 1856, 1891, 1912, 1935 and 1949, and the break in 1973 was probably no more extreme. (The situation in 1984, when the incoming government was more attuned to the sensibilities of some officials than the outgoing one had been, was an exception to the rule.)

It seems to have been during the preparation of the 1974 Budget, with the economic situation fast deteriorating and restraints on spending became a pressing need, that Kirk initiated the procedure whereby all ministers saw Treasury reports on expenditure proposals, thus giving other ministers as well as the Minister of Finance ammunition to argue against new spending.[163] In comparison with Kirk, Rowling, himself an economist, got on well with the Treasury and with Henry Lang personally, and this relationship carried over to his tenure in office as Prime Minister. Tizard, Rowling's successor as Minister of Finance, did not have such a close working relationship with Lang. More than one Treasury officer interviewed recalled that during preparations for the August 1975 devaluation, a weekend meeting had to be rescheduled because Tizard was committed to a golf match.[164]

The relationship between Muldoon and Lang which had been interrupted in 1972 was resumed in 1975. Both men were complex individuals, fascinated with and able in the exercise of power, possessed of strong personalities, not dissimilar in their political philosophies but, in crucial ways, possessing different styles and temperaments. They had worked adequately together until 1972, but now could not. Was Muldoon or Lang more responsible? Lang clearly did not appreciate Muldoon's style, from which there was no recourse given his dual role as Prime Minister and Minister of Finance. On one occasion Lang recorded that Muldoon had made the 'usual assumption that whatever suited him had to bring joy to his slaves', on another that Muldoon had returned to his 'normal abrasive manner', and on a third that the discussion had been 'distinguished as usual by alcohol consumption rather than clarity'.[165]

Undoubtedly one trigger for the falling out was Muldoon's opposition to Labour's contributory superannuation fund and his introduction of a fully funded one. Lang had chaired the committee which devised the scheme Labour adopted, as embodied in the bill introduced in October 1973. Almost certainly he also preferred it on fiscal grounds. Even Labour politicians did not seem to grasp the fiscal impact of the National scheme, but Lang did. The way Muldoon dealt with the issue must also have been a factor. A former Treasury official gave Lang his 'absolute admiration for standing up for his sense of right' after his resignation, which was reportedly due to strong differences of opinion with his Minister, particularly over changes to the New Zealand Superannuation scheme.[166]

It was a matter of power as well as personality. Lang was more powerful than any Treasury Secretary since Ashwin, whose authority had been acquired in wartime. George Laking of Foreign Affairs has commented on Lang's 'overweening' power, whilst at least one Treasury employee, when asked to 'choose' between Lang and Muldoon, favoured the latter.[167] Lang's combination of political and bureaucratic skill became legendary. One public servant from another department sat on the Public Service Superannuation Board, which Lang chaired.

> I just loved his chairmanship. Right, 'item one' … someone would get up, 'Mr Chairman, I'd like to raise a point about …' 'Well, Mr R, didn't you read page 6, it's three lines down, it's all there … OK, next please'. There was no way people were going to bugger him around. But he was a very good chair, he wasn't ruthless, but was just *so* good.[168]

It wasn't all straightforward. Squabbles with the Department of Statistics, headed by Jack Lewin (a trade policy adversary from the early 1960s), over the latter's authority over statistical series went in favour of Statistics. Lang's diary records his intense suspicion when he learnt that Muldoon would be setting up a Prime Minister's Department. Would it corral Treasury co-ordination of economic advice or management? In this instance Lang was relieved to learn that the new agency would be an advisory group, not a whole department, and he also scored a 'coup' in getting Bernie Galvin to head it.[169]

When Lang took early retirement at the end of 1976, he did not allude publicly to his sharp differences with Muldoon, particularly over New Zealand Superannuation. The minister had prevailed over the official. Lang's long-serving deputy and contemporary Noel Lough took over. Lough's contribution will be assessed in chapter 7, but it may be that his more understated personal style, in comparison to Lang's, equipped him better to work with Muldoon.

We look back and see ebb and flow in minister–official relations, but for the officials of this decade there was also a sense of dashed expectations. The oil

Prime Minister and Minister of Finance Robert Muldoon with Bernie Galvin, Head of the Prime Minister's Department (1975–80) and subsequently Secretary to the Treasury. Dominion Post, Alexander Turnbull Library, F-31972-¹/₄

shock and its consequences were only partly responsible for this. The Auditor-General's 1978 report on financial management made it clear how little the financial reforms of the preceding decade had accomplished.[170] Expenditure control was a farce, and liberalisation had got nowhere. As for planning itself, in its NDC guise of targets this had been swept away by events, and perhaps that could not have been avoided. Even so, an audit of that endeavour by Treasury official David Preston at the 1977 economists' conference underlined that the failure had been greatest in the area for which most had been hoped — the export sector.[171]

For the thoughtful, there was more to the matter than the vagaries of politicians. Harvey Franklin's *Trade, Growth and Anxiety*, published in 1978, presciently saw that New Zealanders' ambivalence about the first two elements of his title provoked the third. In the final section of his paper, Preston analysed what he called factors inhibiting restructuring. The approach resembled that of theorists such as the American economist, Mancur Olson, who argued that change was difficult to accomplish in states and societies in which interest groups of varying kinds exercised influence in the political process — in Preston's words, 'the effects of a pressure group economy on the way allocative mechanisms are created

A Prime Minister and one in waiting. Robert Muldoon and the leader of the British Conservative Party, Margaret Thatcher, in September 1976. Dominion Post, Alexander Turnbull Library, F-76-35mm-F

and resource allocation decisions are made.'[172] For Preston, therefore, there was a political as well as an economic agenda:

> The academic economist who has the training to look at the larger picture, is inclined to retreat into an imaginary world and construct models of economic systems where lobbies do not hold sway. While he retreats to his ivory towers the lobbyists are briskly walking on their way to the Minister's office.[173]

The introduction of supplementary minimum prices for wool, meat and dairy products in the 1978 Budget provided a case in point. Farming might be restored to profitability through a devaluation, or if industry became less protected and could not pass on its costs, or if wage setting was decentralised. But a devaluation while industry remained protected would be likely to increase inflation, with increased costs passed on as increased prices, and workers seeking catch-up wage increases, and trade liberalisation would almost certainly lead in the short term to unacceptable levels of unemployment. Accordingly, National gave in

SMPs what Muldoon later called the 'equivalent of the increase [the farmer] would have had from devaluation.'[174]

There was also a challenge within economics itself. The late 1970s provides a useful stopping point for this purpose. Under the aegis of Henry Lang, the Treasury had undergone a major 'reinvention' in the 1960s and 1970s. Behind that transformation lay a belief that the government needed expert assistance in managing the economy which Treasury was best placed to provide. The reorganisation and 're-imagining' of the department, the recruitment of graduates (particularly, but not exclusively, economics graduates), Treasury's continued role in policy co-ordination and its newer role in co-ordinating planning — all these developments drew on a bank of approaches that stemmed from the revolution in the role of government and of economic expertise in the economy that had been provoked by the Great Depression.

'Stagflation' — which characterised New Zealand's as many other economies — provoked a loss of confidence among economists. George Akerloff's oft-cited 1970 article, 'The Market for "Lemons": Quality Uncertainty and the Market Mechanism', which suggested that the market for broken-down used cars survived because buyers had less information than sellers, was one expression of a focus on the behaviour of firms and individuals — microeconomics.[175] A direct challenge to 'Keynesian' macroeconomics was posed by the development of thinking about monetarism, in the forms known colloquially as 'Monetarism I' and 'Monetarism II'. Monetarism I is particularly associated with Milton Friedman, who argued in his presidential address to the American Economics Association in December 1967 that there could be no permanent trade-off between unemployment and inflation, and that policies which attempted to raise unemployment above its 'natural' rate would produce inflation but have only an ephemeral effect on employment levels. Monetarism II, also known as 'rational expectations', argued that workers and others had come to realise that any increase in the money supply would lead only to an increase in prices, not to any long-term increase in employment — in other words, that there was not even a short-term confusion.[176] These theories were to be challenged in the 1980s by 'new Keynesians', but by the later 1970s they were, in conjunction with the persistence of stagflation, devastating the confidence of officials in the possibility of managing the economy using the tools of fiscal, monetary and incomes policy in the ways that had been advocated since the 1950s.

Treasury officials always saw a cloud somewhere. Bob Brockie, *National Business Review*

No single direction seemed preferable. In 1977 Preston identified five medium-term strategies: a siege economy, 'cold-turkey' deflation, an export drive, an import replacement drive, and 'medium-term gradual adjustment' — a kind of slow-acting cocktail of the other four. In a 1978 discussion with senior Treasury officers, Lough stressed the importance of divisions collaborating on issues of medium-term development and planning, given that the country remained in recession and that there was widespread concern that new employment opportunities were not emerging in the productive sectors.[177]

Liberalisation was therefore the strongest candidate. Using resources more efficiently, said Preston, was a target on which 'the analytic fire power of economists will need to be concentrated in the next few years.'[178] But how politicians used those economists and their advice would also be an issue.

Chapter 7

Advice and dissent, 1978–1984

Introduction

Did the Treasury after 1980 fall into the hands of new right, monetarist zealots who were held at bay only by a stubborn minister in the person of Robert Muldoon?[1] This judgement is an over-simplification in two respects, one of emphasis and one of approach and analysis. Firstly, although there *was* a shift in thinking — a paradigm shift, it could be said, from trust in government to trust in markets — this had pre-1980 roots in the Treasury and parallels in changes in treasuries and finance departments elsewhere in the world.[2] Secondly, the question assimilates contests for power and contests of ideas which can usefully be separated. The conflict of the early 1980s was not only a matter of individuals with new ideas gaining influence — it was also an episode in the more than century-long history of minister–official relations, and an episode in the generation-old contest over who should guide economic management — Treasury experts or the politicians — and a visceral fight between Muldoon and those he saw as his nemeses in the Treasury and the Reserve Bank. The ideological shift sharpened the bureaucratic contest, and coloured it at that visceral level, but did not alone create it. That is why this chapter is the second in a bracket of chapters about 'economists' rather than a first in a bracket titled 'neoliberalism' or 'the triumph of the market'.

1978–1981

While the contest between Muldoon and Treasury officials was to become most acute in the three years after the 1981 election, it originated some years earlier. Immediately after the 1978 election the idea of such a contest would have seemed implausible — certainly less plausible than that government and Treasury thinking would come into alignment in the general direction of liberalisation. After National won the election despite receiving fewer votes than the Labour opposition, officials presented a 'Strategy for Growth' to the government. The title was aptly chosen. Apart from the effect of the pre-election stimulus ('the present sharp increase in consumption spending fuelled by a massive injection of liquidity from the Government deficit'), New Zealand had been in a recession for four years, a circumstance unprecedented since the 1930s. Officials now advocated liberalisation more boldly than at any time since such arguments had first been advanced in the 1960s. The policy focus should shift from demand management to 'the structure of the economy itself'. If exports were to grow, exporting must become relatively more profitable, because at present the protected domestic sector was 'able to maintain and extend its share of national income at the expense of the export sector'. Most specifically, a 20 per cent devaluation was recommended. The advice was not new, but its form was. The seven-page introduction to the 'package' was signed off by four of the country's top public servants — the Secretary to the Treasury, the Head of the Prime Minister's Department, the Governor of the Reserve Bank, and — more unexpectedly — the Secretary of Trade and Industry.[3]

This paper was submitted to the government on Treasury letterhead. The signature of Noel Lough, the Secretary to the Treasury, appeared first on the document, and was the only one to appear on all the supporting papers. Despite the officialese of its language, the package demonstrates how central liberalisation was to Treasury's conception of economic management fully six years before the 1984 election. And Muldoon was receptive — price monitoring replaced price surveillance, the forward exchange system was liberalised, a flexible exchange rate regime (the 'crawling peg'), which enabled incremental shifts in value of the currency rather than disruptive one-off devaluations was introduced, and foreign investment regulations were liberalised.[4] Over the next two years, with strong Treasury support, further important liberalising measures were either taken or initiated — the meat freezing industry was deregulated, restrictions on shop trading hours were reduced, negotiations for a new free trade agreement with Australia were begun, and reforms of the import licensing system and the deregulation of land transport were pursued.

Opinion within the re-elected National government had become more receptive to liberalisation. There was a strong 'small government' element associated with politicians such as backbencher Ian McLean and new Cabinet minister Derek Quigley. Another minister, Hugh Templeton, vigorously advocated trade liberalisation, particularly with Australia.[5] And these party political currents were in turn influenced by currents in the political economy. When National had decided in 1978 that the building of the Clyde dam should be let to private contractors, the lobbying of the latter was undoubtedly a factor:[6]

> Ron Carter and George Beca and Co. had a *big* business, had a lot of overseas work, and were very competent indeed. There was pressure from the sector, and the National government at that stage of course was sympathetic to that. And the New Zealand Contractors Federation and Association of Consulting Engineers were both bodies with a much stronger membership and much higher level of competence [than before].[7]

In 1978 the Employers' Federation rejected the European model of strong employers and union organisations working in partnership with government in favour of a deregulated, decentralised and internationally competitive labour market. Similar ideological shifts also took place within the Retailers' Federation and the Bankers' Association.[8] Ruth Richardson (who was to be Minister of Finance in a National government from 1990 to 1993), as an advocate for Federated Farmers from the mid-1970s to 1981, lobbied the government in conjunction with 'innovative new entrants, who were being denied a capacity to enter' the meat freezing industry for its deregulation.[9] Even the Manufacturers' Federation started to shift its thinking under the prodding of its executive director, Ian Douglas.

But while there were lobbies for more liberalisation and deregulation, there were also, as there had been earlier, National Party constituencies for government intervention and regulation — manufacturers who wanted protection to continue, importers who profited from import licensing, businesses which gained government contracts. A scheme to use the import licence tendering system to reduce protection was agreed to by the departments involved — Treasury, Trade and Industry, and Customs — in 1979 but only implemented in 1983. On one occasion the Cabinet Economic Committee was told that it was 'widely opposed' in the commercial community. One minister present commented that 'the list of goods covered by the scheme seemed to be excessively long and included a number of items which were produced in New Zealand'. Frustration about such a level of debate shows through even the bland official record, which noted that as 'import licensing generally applied to commodities which are produced in New Zealand the proposed list, by definition, included locally produced items.'[10]

In 1979 Federated Farmers, the New Zealand Farm Management Society and the National Party parliamentary caucus committee on agriculture pro-

Fred Turnovsky, a prominent New Zealand manufacturer. Kenneth Quinn Collection, Alexander Turnbull Library, F-89271-1/4

posed measures which included the maintenance of irrigation subsidies, upgrading of back-country roads, tax concessions on boarding school fees for pupils living in areas where no school bus was available, payment of EEC levies by the government, the indexing of loan and tax deduction rates under the livestock incentive scheme, cash advances for costs incurred because of bad weather, and tax concessions for rural employees.[11] The most significant form of assistance to agriculture was to be supplementary minimum prices, which had been introduced in 1978, in part to compensate exporters for the anti-inflationary high exchange rate:

> for three years nothing happened — prices were above the minimum — then the lamb price collapsed. I tried to talk Muldoon into lowering the threshold. I remember vividly sitting on the couch with Muldoon, with the whole agricultural establishment in the room as a Greek chorus saying not one bloody dickie bird — they didn't say a word one way or the other, they didn't bloody well support me.[12]

Muldoon was receptive to such constituencies, and remained alert to the drawbacks of any liberalisation programme — be it achieved through border protection, transport deregulation, or changes to the exchange rate — from 1979 to 1981. While the proposal to corporatise Railways was acted on in 1980, a further move was deferred:

> It is clear that a further significant removal of impediments to competition in the transport of land goods would result in a shift of substantial traffic volumes from rail to road transport. Although there would be benefits to agriculture and industry, the costs of structural adjustments would bear more heavily on the railways than the road transport industry … further studies of the implications for railways are proceeding.[13]

For similar reasons, Muldoon moved very cautiously on trade talks with Australia, and by late 1979 officials were desperate for 'some common ground to be found' before he met his Australian counterpart, Malcolm Fraser, in March 1980. Nor did the negotiations gather much momentum thereafter.[14] And in the 1979 Budget, Muldoon referred obliquely to his displeasure that a junior Treasury officer had presented a conference paper earlier in the year questioning the merits of import licensing:

> It has been suggested that New Zealand should dismantle the system of import licensing which operated for 40 years. I do not subscribe to that view. I have no intention of letting efficient industries go to the wall for the sake of a theory. Many thousands are employed in firms that would not have been started had it not been for a more secure home market.[15]

Muldoon was referring here particularly to the *employment* impact of liberalisation. But the most *vocal* defenders of protection were importers and manufacturers who benefited from the existing regime and were often long-time supporters of the National Party. This was the arena in which Muldoon had first made his way in the 1950s — the world of Auckland business, which overlapped with the world of the National Party. In his 1985 memoir, Muldoon refers to the fact that he learnt about opposition to the Nelson cotton mill in 1961 when

> a neighbour, who was a clothing manufacturer, raised it with me one Saturday morning when I was mowing my lawn. Bert Walker and Lorrie Pickering were backbenchers who were brought into the debate by the Christchurch manufacturers who were leading the attack.[16]

Twenty years later, over the proposed trade agreement with Australia, Muldoon 'was exposed to the full weight of the Auckland lobby. He knew the influential manufacturers' spokesmen, Laurie Stevenson and Earle Richardson, intimately; they in turn knew the National Party chiefs. As paymasters they felt free to make their doubts known'.[17]

The other axis was economic. The success of liberalisation depended on the abolition of import licensing, which would force production to become much more sensitive to international price signals. If there was no longer a protected sector which could pass on wage increases, wages would also have to respond. In that circumstance, a price-responsive exchange rate — as introduced in the 1979 Budget — would not add to inflationary pressures, exporters would be able to maintain profitability without subsidies, and the balance of payments would adjust automatically to changes in the supply of and demand for foreign exchange. But if import licensing was not dismantled, the whole process of adjustment would be very much slower and more complex.

The challenge to Muldoon mounted from within the parliamentary National Party after the loss of the East Coast Bays seat to Social Credit in 1980 — the 'colonels' coup' — was partly triggered by dissatisfaction with the slow pace of liberalisation. But the coup failed and Quigley, one of Muldoon's critics, did not succeed in becoming deputy leader early in 1981, Muldoon's contemporary Duncan McIntyre securing the position instead.[18] The November 1980 economic statement, which both provided short-term stimulus for the economy and explored yet another strategy for managing labour relations and wages, was what had come to be seen as classically 'Muldoonist'.[19]

Muldoon's inbuilt caution about economic liberalisation had been sharply reinforced as the impact of the second oil shock precipitated by the overthrow of the Shah of Iran at the end of 1978 unfolded during 1979.[20] Iran was New Zealand's major supplier of petroleum, and throughout the first half of 1979 the Cabinet Economic Committee was absorbed with oil supply issues. This preoccupation spilled over into an exploration of the future of New Zealand's own 'liquid fuels' which encompassed the possibility that the country could achieve self-sufficiency.[21] The latter discussion arose primarily because under the 'take or pay' contract that Labour had negotiated with the Shell/BP/Todd consortium that was developing the Maui gas field, the government would soon be paying for substantial volumes of gas regardless of whether it wanted them — gas which had a variety of possible uses, including retail supply and conversion into petroleum substitutes. The decision to build the Clyde dam also promised that a hydro-electricity surplus would be generated in the near future.[22] The Liquid Fuels Trust Board established by the government the previous year reported to the Cabinet Economic Committee in September 1979, and Cabinet duly agreed to pursue both a synthetic gasoline ('synfuel') and a methanol (another petroleum substitute) project as ways to use the gas, *and* to expand and modify the Whangarei oil refinery to allow it to use the synthetic fuel.[23] Muldoon 'came to the conclusion that a huge chunk of New Zealand's wealth had vanished for ever … that it wasn't just a matter of trying to hold the line until the economy recovered naturally, something more dramatic had to be done.'[24]

The new strategy took shape during a trip by Muldoon to Europe and the Middle East in October 1979. The Prime Minister was drawn to a policy that would restore growth to the New Zealand economy without the need for a frontal assault on the established political economy. 'Restructuring of the economy was essential … Fortuitously, the energy resources we had in coal, hydro power, geothermal steam, gas and finally oil, gave us the opportunity to create an energy-based sector.'[25] So a quite different 'growth strategy' to that advocated by the officials in December 1978 was formulated. Colloquially known as 'Think Big', it was a massive government-driven investment programme. It drew on natural gas, water to generate electric power, and ironsands from the North Island's west coast that would be used in an expansion of the steel mill near Auckland. The outbreak of war between Iran and Iraq in September 1980 ensured that the price of oil kept rising — in December 1981 it was to be triple the March 1979 figure — providing the necessary urgency.[26]

Think Big was never straightforward. There was environmental controversy about a second aluminium smelter which was to be built at Aramoana near Dunedin. The synthetic gasoline plant was experimental, and the negotiations between Mobil and the government over its construction were protracted.[27] The Treasury was hesitant about all the projects. The New Zealand Steel proposal required high levels of protection to be viable: in one report on it Treasury noted that the company had revised its original assumptions in the financial analysis, with the result that the 'national return on the project drops from something over 10% to about 7.5%. It is questionable whether a project of this size, with its considerable inherent risk, should proceed if the indicated returns are indeed so marginal.'[28] It needed import controls of almost 100 per cent, and 60 per cent of its output would have to be exported:

'Towering Inflation.' Inspired by the 1974 Irwin Allen disaster epic, The Towering Inferno, this 1981 mock movie poster attacks National's economic management. Alexander Turnbull Library, Eph-C-POLITICS-1981-01

The idea of building some more basic blast furnace capacity and using it downstream with a rolling mill — a very small rolling mill by world standards — seemed like a really crazy idea to most of us in the Treasury. And it was being promoted very strongly by the company, on the basis that the government took all the risk and protected the shareholders.[29]

But Treasury lacked leverage in the decision-making on Think Big. The Ministry of Energy, which had been established in 1977, and Bill Birch, its minister since 1978, were powerful advocates for the projects who had Muldoon's ear, particularly after Birch supported Muldoon during the 1980 'coup'. And Muldoon was now less willing to listen to Treasury advice. The September 1981 report of the officials' economic committee (which was now chaired by Bernard Galvin as Secretary to the Treasury) to Cabinet on all three projects concluded that 'the uncertainty associated with each project is substantial … in … particular … the synthetic gasoline project and the steel expansion, where the future rate of increase in oil prices and market conditions for steel dominate … the steel expansion, the aluminium smelter and the synthetic gasoline project should not all proceed at this time'. The paper included a six-page annex on the 10 per cent 'discount rate' which Cabinet had settled on in 1971. It explained that officials from all the relevant departments had reviewed the rate and concluded that it was reasonable, pointing out that the same rate was used in Australia, the United States and Canada. Yet this conclusion was qualified by a final statement that 'factors such as risk and non-quantifiable costs and benefits should also be included in the analysis'. With their discomfort palpable in every word, the officials recommended that the synthetic fuels plant should proceed 'taking full account of the risks and uncertainties associated', and that so should the aluminium smelter, as the better bet of the other two, even though 'combining the economic analysis with the risks, a good case can be made for not proceeding with either combination'.[30]

Two weeks later the Swiss company Alusuisse pulled out of the Aramoana smelter project, making it highly unlikely it would proceed. Four weeks after that, within sight of the 1981 election, and with the synfuels agreement still not finalised, Cabinet approved the New Zealand Steel project.[31]

Ideological change

If the National government had changed little, other universes had changed to a greater extent. Throughout the world the 1970s had witnessed the beginning of a seismic shift from trust in government to a trust in markets — a reflection, it could be said, of the reverse movement of the Great Depression era. That pre-Depression trust in markets was a hallmark of nineteenth-century liberalism, and the late twentieth-century variant is often labelled 'neoliberalism'. We traced some of the origins of this development in the last chapter. The combination of new economic theories and events — stagflation in particular — had a visible effect on politics and policies by the end of the decade. In the United Kingdom, the key event was the election of the Thatcher government in 1979, and its pursuit of a range of liberalising measures, questioning of 'Keynesian' macroeconomic management, in particular its strategies for dealing with inflation, and vision of a much-reduced role for government in society and the economy. But even Thatcher's election victory was the culmination of a change, not the beginning of one. Thatcher's wresting of the Conservative Party leadership in 1975, and the shift in thinking about the economy among important financial interests, were precursors to the 1979 change of government.[32]

In the United States, Ronald Reagan assumed the presidency in January 1981, forming an administration which pursued both 'supply-side' economic policies and, at least rhetorically, tight monetary policies.[33] The Bank of Canada had embraced monetarism in the mid-1970s, serving notice that its monetary policy would no longer necessarily accommodate the wishes of the Department of Finance.[34] In Australia too, change came in the 1970s. Whitwell argues that the early 1970s saw in the Australian Treasury 'the breakdown of the optimistic, meliorist (some would suggest naive) progressive view of human nature central to the Keynesian model. It saw also, though not explicitly, the disbandment by that Treasury of the notion that it was the government's responsibility to provide a safe secure environment in which the maintenance of an arbitrarily defined level of full employment was guaranteed.'[35] This revolution was most associated with John Stone, who was appointed a Deputy Secretary (Economic) in 1971. Whitwell, in testing (and ultimately qualifying) the notion that there was a 'Stone Age' in the Australian Treasury, observes that 'it was after Stone became deputy secretary ... that the department's outlook became much more obviously neo-classical'.[36]

A comparable shift in the approach of the World Bank, the International Monetary Fund and the OECD was evident from their publications. The World Bank's 1981 'Berg Report' was sharply critical of African governments for having undermined development by destroying incentives to increase output and exports, overvaluing currencies, and protecting industry.[37] In 1981, the OECD published *The Welfare State in Crisis,* the proceedings of a major conference held the year before. New thinking percolated into the OECD's country reports. The 1980 report on Denmark called for 'substantial changes in the present pattern of resource allocation and progressive elimination of the various structural rigidities hampering a smooth functioning of the economy', amongst which were instanced the transfer of resources into competing sectors and greater flexibility in the labour market. Indeed, the conservative coalition government which Danes elected in 1982 introduced a range of reforms that were very similar to those embarked on in New Zealand in 1984. And whereas a 1979 report on Finland had focused primarily on demand management, the 1981 report explored supply-side changes.[38]

New Zealand also had its own antecedents. When the former National Prime Minister Jack Marshall provoked Muldoon in 1979 by arguing that the government should revitalise private enterprise, reduce taxation and restrict spending on social welfare,[39] he was speaking in the tradition of small-state fiscal conservatism which could be traced back to before Downie Stewart, a tradition which had admittedly become less visible since the Depression, but had never vanished — Marshall himself had entered Parliament in 1946.

Another channel for neoliberalism was academia. At the University of Canterbury, 'the general style of the department for some years', explained Professor Bert Brownlie,

> had been more market-oriented, how markets worked, the different kinds of markets. I took the stance that the [main thing] in the training would be economic analysis and the two main prongs of that would be economic theory, which is effectively the theory about how markets worked — and then econometrics, the statistical empirical testing.[40]

In 1979 the Planning Council, under Frank Holmes's chairmanship, had published *The Welfare State: Social Policy in the 1980s*, which foreshadowed 1980s arguments about the fiscal burden and disincentives associated with current social policies. This was followed in 1980 by *The Stabilisation Role of Fiscal Policy*, written by two Reserve Bank economists as a challenge to that role. One of the authors was the senior economist at the Bank — soon to be its Deputy Governor — Roderick Deane, who was a strong advocate of relying on monetary policy to battle inflation.

As we have seen in chapter 6, Treasury also had its own track record. Since the late 1960s Treasury had argued that free — or freer — trade would produce greater economic dividends than would protection. Such liberalisation had become a well-established approach, to which, as the 1978 'Strategy for Growth' suggested, the senior management of the department was committed — it was not just a matter of employing 'younger advisers'.[41] Jas McKenzie recalls that Lough kept demanding that more time and effort be devoted to strategic thinking. '"Noel", I replied, "If you want a strategy you'll have to have a new division

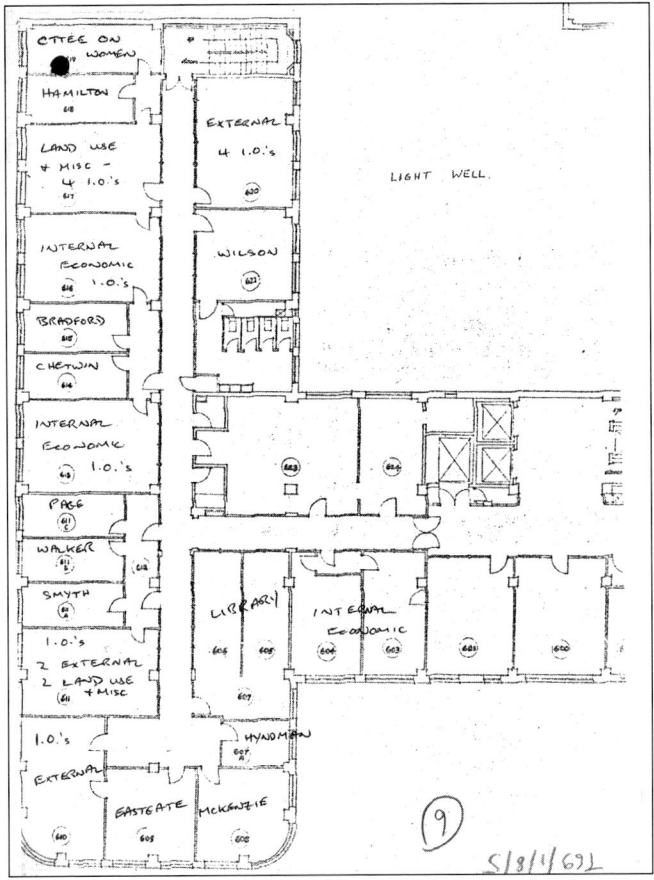

Economists on the ground: plan of part of the seventh floor, Departmental Building, Stout Street, June 1976. Treasury

to do it."'[42] 'Internal Economics II' was duly established, headed by McKenzie and with a brief to analyse 'the constraints on economic growth, the examination of alternative strategies for improving New Zealand's economic performance, the development of policies to put the preferred strategy into effect, and the promotion of a re-examination of existing policies which appear to conflict with that strategy.'[43] Lough encouraged Graham Scott to succeed McKenzie when the latter was promoted to an Assistant Secretary position on Bill Green's retirement a few months later. Scott was then working as an economic adviser in the Prime Minister's Department, and chairing the interdepartmental committee on the new trade agreement that was being negotiated with Australia.

The 'enabling' role played by McKenzie was also important. He had headed the former unified Internal Economics, the 'powerhouse' division of the Treasury in which macroeconomic analysis was undertaken by Treasury's brightest economists. In the late 1970s he had put a lot of effort into strengthening the analysis in the reports on the 'current economic situation and outlook' which Treasury provided every three months to the government:

> It had been like a Hockney, all those Polaroids put all over the bloody place and out of it you hope will emerge a picture. Jas said, 'This is nuts, where's the economics in all this?' He forced Roger Procter, Bryce, Rob Cameron — about four of them worked for six or eight months to find the ways by which these things could be assembled.[44]

McKenzie brought the intellectual energy of the old division to the new one.

> The people there were ... incredibly important, but [Jas] also cast a fatherly umbrella over it. He fostered this environment of enquiry, he was such an outstanding intellect.[45]

Treasury economists — new ideas

The phrase 'alternative strategies' in Economics II's ('internal' was rarely used) brief both suggested choosing amongst a number of possibilities and hinted at new directions. Where to go after reducing border protection was a question that McKenzie had asked. The answer — 'liberalise *everything*' — was provided by his successors.[46] A Treasury officer who went overseas to study in 1980 returned after four years to find

> the intellectual climate totally changed. The idea of macro management and a full employment economy had been discarded. The real focus was on changing structures to increase economic efficiency and reduce inflation.[47]

The importance of Economics II to this change has been identified by other writers,[48] but the change in intellectual climate has to be set in the context of the change in *approach* to policy analysis and advice that Economics II also fostered, and which will be discussed in the next section.

In terms of the intellectual changes, the two areas in which Economics II had a marked impact were in the robustness of its critique of macroeconomics and its dissemination of new thinking about government expenditure, two angles which touched directly on the respective powers of the state and the market. We can provide a biographical context for both these changes, although this was not the full story. Rob Cameron, a Victoria University economics graduate, was particularly stimulated by his experience at Harvard:

> I had started studying primarily microeconomics subjects. After I finished the first semester, I consulted one of the leading professors, Richard Zeckhauser, and said, 'I am enjoying my current studies but probably need to return to my policy background in macroeconomics.' He said, 'Rob, macroeconomics is witchcraft, continue studying markets.' It was at that point that I began to understand not that markets were always right, but their richness. When I started at Treasury, the concept of being a Treasury person was a bright elite guy who was going to make key choices which people themselves were not equipped to make. I came back with a much higher respect for the choices that people make for themselves.[49]

The impact of the new division's work was evident in the 1981 post-election briefing, 'Economic Strategy', for which it was largely responsible. Unlike later briefings prepared in the wake of the 1982 Official Information Act — and a new Minister of Finance — this was not published, and even a new National Party caucus member, Ruth Richardson, had great difficulty persuading Muldoon to let her see it.[50] It was more committed to liberalisation than the 1978 'Strategy for Growth', and explicitly challenged the current macroeconomic practices. The briefing pointed out that 'New Zealand's experience conformed with other countries in the 1970s in showing that fine-tuning has become difficult to the point of being counter-productive due to errors in economic forecasts and long and variable time lags in the response to policy changes'. The 'Strategy for Growth' had included papers on price stabilisation and demand management, albeit with sceptical comments about the existing stances on both. The closest 'Economic Strategy' came to such macroeconomic approaches was in a paper on the limitations of the balance of payments framework, the overarching message of which was that 'we have not allowed the price system to reflect sufficiently the true worth to the country of the resources employed in many areas'.[51]

The new approach was expressed in numerous Budget and other reports put up by Treasury to the Minister of Finance between 1982 and 1984. It involved a scepticism about macroeconomic approaches such as the fine-tuning of fiscal policy, incomes policy and controlled exchange rates, and a readiness to advocate microeconomic reform as the route to economic efficiency. Reports on fiscal issues focused as much on tax as on demand management. In 1983 one major Budget report analysed 'tax expenditures', which it described as 'deviations from the "generally accepted" income tax structure' that should be either modified or abolished. In common parlance, these included tax credits, deductions, exemptions and rebates, all of which reduced the taxable income of individuals or companies.[52] In contrast, in response to a request from Muldoon for a report 'outlining policies that could be employed to increase real consumption and lower unemployment and so take advantage of the cyclical improvement in the balance of payments', Treasury replied that, 'as already discussed, the ability of monetary and fiscal policy to boost real output and employment by stimulating domestic demand is severely limited, and has probably become more so'.[53]

A 1984 paper drew attention to the 'failed Mitterrand experiment' in France: 'recent events in France illustrate the weakness of expansionary policies of the Keynesian type', which had led to balance of payments difficulties and much more rapid inflation than France's trading partners were experiencing. France had to devalue, introduce a wage–price freeze, take action to cut the Budget deficit, and adopt tighter monetary policies.[54] Similarly, one of the early reports for Muldoon's never-to-be-delivered 1984 Budget, on fiscal policy, tabulated the monetary and fiscal stimuli that had been adminstered since 1972, focusing particularly on the instability of policy and the size of the fiscal deficit, which had increased not least because of the rising cost of debt servicing.[55]

Treasury papers, frequently signed off by Scott and/or prepared by Economics II officers, took related approaches to other issues. At the end of 1983, Treasury noted that one of the central conclusions of a New Zealand Planning Council Economic Monitoring Group report was that 'the balance of payments constraint operates quite restrictively on New Zealand's growth potential' because New Zealand's exports had low income elasticities of demand (that is, an increase in income would not produce a proportionate increase in demand). Treasury, in contrast, argued that 'in terms of the contribution to economic growth what matters is not the impact of export (or importable) production on the balance of payments but the national profitability of different activities within the economy. It is the ability of activities to generate income (from resources) not foreign exchange, which matters ... the major problem with the EMG's treatment of the balance of payments theory is that it fails to recognise that changes in the balance of payments position reflect changes in relative prices and costs ... which in turn affect relative rates of return to activities.'[56]

Another report for the Minister of Finance explored whether 'a "Keynesian" approach of expanding aggregate demand either by broad measures or through additional public programmes might provide an appropriate basis for reducing unemployment.' The conclusion reached was that 'further demand expansion is unlikely to reduce unemployment significantly and could indeed aggravate present difficulties beyond the short-term'.[57] Two strategies for dealing with unemployment were presented, with one of these favoured:

> The options fall into two broad categories: (a) to adopt a planning perspective so as to replace the market; (b) to improve the functioning of the market. Option (a) has several fundamental weaknesses: i the 'labour market' comprises a large number of markets for different types of occupations and skills. Co-ordinating these individual markets along with goods markets is a complex task; ii the environment is dynamic, so that events rarely validate the premises on which plans are based. Alternative (b) on the other hand suggests that a desirable direction of government policies would include: i more stable macroeconomic policies which reduce uncertainty and provide an environment conducive to investment; continued moves to improve the efficiency of resource use and overall economic growth ... iii at the micro level, policies which identify and reduce rigidities in the labour market (for example increase the ease of wage adjustment, the geographic and occupational mobility of labour and hours of work).[58]

Officials were determined to wean ministers from Keynesian thinking. A query as to whether Treasury had any method for including in cost–benefit analyses 'the true costs and benefits to the economy as a whole' of employment changes in a specific area triggered one exchange. The question had been provoked by a discussion on the relationship between efficiency and reduced staffing. A week later, a Treasury memorandum stressed that 'the most important point to get into Ministers' minds is that employment in a specific project is a cost and not a benefit. A decision to employ a person in a particular project or to fail to dismiss a person when it would be economic to do so represents a cost to the community because the community foregoes the opportunity to use that person's services elsewhere in the economy ... the basic point is that, because of the costs of information, centralised planners and bureaucrats can never determine what micro opportunities are going to be available in the market place.'[59]

These last phrases bear the hallmarks of the new thinking about institutional economics with which Rob Cameron had become familiar at Harvard, and with which others became acquainted by reading publications such as the University of Chicago's *Journal of Law and Economics* and the finely crafted arguments of Ronald Coase.[60] Through such channels microeconomics influenced not just the analysis of the best way to get growth from the economy as a whole, for instance through deregulation, but also approaches to the efficient and effective management of the government's own spending. Agency theory, for example, built on the ground traversed by public choice theory to explore the relationship between a 'principal' — such as the government — and its 'agent' — a government department, say — and assess the importance of devising incentives to ensure that the principal's goals would be realised.[61] The 1982 'three per cent cuts' exercise in reducing government spending provided an opportunity for Cameron in particular to unpack the bundle of rationales that underpinned decisions on government expenditure.[62]

In respect of one very large government agency, a Treasury memorandum of 1983 argued that with the

> further development of the Corporate Planning approach to decisions regarding the Post Office ... a distinction [between the Post Office and other departments] might become appropriate but this would, in the case of a monopoly, require the continued existence of a mechanism for ensuring that any monopoly profit is applied in accordance with the priorities of the taxpayers or shareholders who provide the organisation's capital.[63]

In other words, why treat the Post Office, with its investments and customers, as a standard government department? For instance, its existing price structure made no sense, because the prices of Post Office services were not related to the cost of providing them at specific localities. The Post Office was not persuaded by such arguments, and reckoned that Treasury saw the solution to this problem as involving various kinds of deregulation and the introduction of competition.[64] Pat Duignan, a vote analyst working on the Post Office, collaborated with Cameron to produce a 1984 paper which argued that the existing ways of running government trading activities, whether within or separated from departments, were

> a weird way to tackle this issue. We proposed thinking about things differently, about the environment they operated in, whether they faced product market

competition, what internal governance procedures they had, how their inputs were priced. We pulled this into a paper called 'Government-Owned Enterprises: Efficiency and Performance'.[65]

That the Post Office might not agree did not deeply concern the Treasury officials involved — indeed, it was further evidence of the need for reform. By 1984 the attitude of individuals like Graham Scott was that 'there was such disagreement amongst officials about the direction of economic policy [that] we would actually be better off to put in clean Treasury reports saying this was our view of the issue, without everything being homogenised back into an interdepartmental consensus'.[66]

Economics II built on rather than directly challenged existing thinking within the Treasury. McKenzie, who had been behind much of the exploration of liberalising strategies in the later 1970s, had 'no difficulty with agency theory, and very little difficulty with the basic insights of Buchanan and public choice theory'.[67] He and others came to share a scepticism about the incomes policies which were a preoccupation of Keynesian-style management. In a rare public statement on the subject by a Treasury official, McKenzie pointed out in 1983 that

> whether the consensus for a successful incomes policy can be achieved is … problematical … there may have been a time when it was possible to believe that governments could quickly reduce inflation, unilaterally and relatively painlessly, by adopting the appropriate monetary and fiscal policies. There are few grounds for such optimism now.[68]

About the utility of Keynesian macroeconomics there was more disagreement: 'I always had difficulty with the death of macroeconomics: it was under attack to the point that [one official] didn't even want us to do reviews of the current economic situation [because] the government might want to do something about it.'[69] Another official recalled that in the late 1970s and early 1980s, debate continued between those who thought that there was still a role for fiscal policy in stabilising business cycles, and those who focused on balance sheets and managing portfolios.

But most Treasury policy people were investigating officers who were not directly involved in macroeconomic policy. There was no sustained alternative position in Treasury to the neoliberal line that came from Economics II in these years. As one divisional head who was not a close associate of Scott remarked, 'Scott and the others advanced arguments forcefully and brought coherence and intellectual rigour to bear. Most of us had spent time in the international organisations where this was the common, central, thrust.'[70]

Treasury economists — new approaches

While Economics II did shift the Treasury's stance on policies, its impact on process was equally significant, and here too the role of individuals was crucial. Among those most frequently mentioned is Roger Kerr. He had joined Treasury as a 32-year-old in 1976 after graduating in French, working in Foreign Affairs, and subsequently gaining an economics degree — for Deane, he was 'the most outstanding economics student I ever had when I was teaching'. When Graham Scott was promoted to an Assistant Secretaryship in 1981, Kerr became director of Economics II. Bryce Wilkinson — another mentioned frequently — joined Economics II on his return from a Harkness Fellowship in the United States and became a section head at the beginning of 1983. Wilkinson had joined Treasury in 1970 from the University of Canterbury as one of those whom Brownlie recruited into economics from other disciplines — they were 'very, very bright people, most had got first-class degrees in science and engineering so could handle mathematical economics — which is another name for economic theory — and econometrics, and thought in an analytical way.'[71] In his first years back he, more than anyone else in Treasury, worked on the discount rate issue that had coloured Think Big.

Was the outlook of these young men — in 1980 they were all in their thirties — shaped by their backgrounds? Scott's father had worked in the newspaper business. Wilkinson's father was a research chemist (the subject in which Wilkinson himself took his first degree) with the DSIR. Kerr's parents had farmed in Nelson province.[72] The father of Rob Cameron, another active member of the division, was the manager of Gear Meat in Petone. Some economists recruited to Treasury came from more working-class backgrounds, but anecdotal evidence suggests that they were a minority. While they were not markedly different in age, background or education from their predecessor cohort of the 1960s, their style was different.

Kerr's comments — made in a very distinctive neat script with a green auditor's pen — on the draft reports that circulated daily round the department on a 'clip' were memorable. The adjectives used to describe some of them include 'vitriolic' and 'coruscating'. Kerr's annotations divert as well as inform the historian: 'I'll believe an efficient computer-based DTI resource file when I see it. God help us with (or preserve us from!) the expanded MPAG [major projects advisory group — that is, Think Big]. Has anybody given any thought to a fast track through the red tape?',[73] he asked on one occasion in 1981. Or on a letter from the Manufacturers' Association, commenting on taxation: 'this section repeats the line that Australian industry has just been given a big bagful of lollies and we want some too. It doesn't ask the prior question.'[74] Kerr headed one paper, which examined licences to import from Australia [EALS, TEALS and MEALS] under the heading SQUEALS — 'subsidiary quantity of unallocated exclusive Australian licenses.'[75] Recalls one junior officer of Kerr,

> His energy to involve himself in things across the spectrum of the department's work was enormous. And he created the culture of peer review — you were encouraged to critique other pieces of work from across the agency, very widely, encouraged to create ideas, support ginger group discussions, brainstorms, analysts writing papers — he modelled huge amounts of those sorts of behaviour, sending thoughts and pieces to Muldoon and ministers and other agencies 'for your information'. He'd be reading prodigiously.[76]

It could not be done without diplomacy, Scott reckoned:

> A think tank cannot hope to be influential in its own department, let alone across government more widely, unless it does it through networking. [If] people don't tell you the meetings are on, you never catch up with the game. Even if you've got a mandate on paper from the head of the department, everyone else ignores it unless you're being useful. We were very aware in Economics II that our success depended on persuading other people, who didn't have to be persuaded if they didn't want to [be] … They didn't lose their signing authority. They had the authority to say, 'Thank you for your advice, but I'm not planning on taking it, I'm signing the paper the way it was.'[77]

Kerr, for his part, recalled that

> 80 per cent of the reactions in the organisation were favourable and positive, 20 per cent were negative, and I would describe them as the slowcoaches, or lazy types, or not up to it, or not accepting of change. You'd give people

strokes, then you'd challenge them. That was the way these tensions were generated, and reactions came back from staff, and you learnt and they learnt.[78]

In weighing the impact of Economics II on the rest of Treasury, it needs to be remembered that it was just one of nine core divisions — two financial, three economic, four investigating (and three 'others': superannuation, stores and actuarial). The total permanent staff, exclusive of the three peripheral divisions, was 273, of whom 114 were women. Many of the women worked in the accounts section of the Financial Management Division, which remained the central accounting agency for the whole of government and was outside the ambit of any Economics II work. Among those who fell within it were the officials of the investigating divisions, who analysed the votes of other departments. Economics II's brief referred formally to it 'working closely with investigating divisions responsible for particular sections of the economy. One example is the inter-departmental industry review programme where Internal Economics II works with the Industry Division in providing Treasury input.'[79] One officer recalls

> a bit of rivalry, and tension that we had some of the so-called bright people, and a bit of freedom and resource and money to do things that other divisions got starved of. And we would come up with ideas that they would not even have the scope to think about. Didn't have time — 'we're practical, we've got to get on and do things'. For example, we might have been doing some thinking about export subsidies, say in general terms. The Land Use Division … was busy trying to make SMPs work, [and we were saying,] 'Get out of this stuff, this territory.'

There were also debates between theory and experience: 'You write this stuff and then someone says to you, you're going to overturn this whole system — this is the way we do it, and we know from experience.' Fierce arguments were triggered by the closure of small-town industries such as the Mosgiel woollen mill and the Patea freezing works — not on the basic direction, but on how to deal with the adjustment, whether there should be an impact analysis, or discussions with workers or investors; or would that just mean that the process ran out of steam? Should the approach be 'big bang' or gradual?[80]

One official described in an exit interview two of the Economics II people speaking 'most disparagingly' of those who had ideas differing from their own.[81]

Jobs for analysts and money market managers. The Evening Post *of 9 June 1984 reflected the healthy market for those with skills that were in demand.* Alexander Turnbull Library, N-P 857-23

When one long-serving officer reported in a memorandum that Treasury 'simply could not say today in individual cases whether greater efficiency (and job losses) in the public sector would result in more resources (and job gains) in the private sector', another officer minuted, 'Yes we can, analytically'; and where the memorandum writer had written, 'the markets will never be perfect', another officer annotated, 'So what? We need to hammer these simplistic perspectives. This is no argument for mismanagement'. Cameron wrote, 'I have given this a going over and Bryce will do a joint draft for our clearance. I'm worried by some of [the] perspectives'.[82]

Scott admits that 'there would have been quite senior people who would have felt, I think, that it wasn't really the right of these young people in these economic divisions to be writing critical comments on the papers they put to ministers'.[83] But Economics II could also trade on the zeal for professional expertise in economic analysis that had been at the core of the Lang 'revolution'. That expertise was changing its character in the 1980s. Until about 1980 the economics profession was dominated by academics and public servants. But at a time when the economy as a whole was grappling with unemployment, the financial liberalisations of 1969 and 1976 had increased the opportunities for economic analysts in the private sector, which usually paid better than the public sector.[84] While the single largest employer of economists, the Reserve Bank, was a government agency, it had close links with the new financial institutions as well as long-standing connections with the trading banks.

'Generally,' one student of the subject observed, professionals 'identify with the norms and values of the professional community rather than with the formal rules of the organisational hierarchy'. Scientists, engineers and doctors are characteristic examples. In the New Zealand government, the Ministry of Works and Development and the Department of Health were two examples of public agencies in which the administrative structures were 'deeply immersed in professional values and norms.'[85] And those values and norms were in turn shaped by the proportion in both professions who worked in the private sector. Public sector accountants had approached this status in the 1920s, but not cemented it; economists had never tried.

In 1979 John Martin, who was now an Assistant Secretary, wrote to the State Services Commission about the need for a new occupational class analogous to the other long-established professional occupational classes which had allowed engineers and doctors to be paid at rates approximating those in the private sector. Martin noted that 'the need for quantitative analytical skills in the State Services far outstrips the supply; pay alone is not the answer but must be part of it. In the present job market a lifting of graduate appointment salaries generally with a higher premium for good honours degrees is indicated'. He added that 'economists are professionals: and seek to share their knowledge with others of the same ilk in the Universities, the private sector and overseas.'[86]

The Commission was not responsive. But Martin's references to the 'present job market' and 'the private sector' were revealing. He touched on a possible tension between two professional roles when he observed that

> while we rightly talk about the increasing professionalism in the Treasury I would cast the net wider than the standards, for example, of the professional economist ... it is crucial that Treasury officers and the institution should maintain their professional integrity, i.e. as economists or accountants, but also as Public Servants ... I do not accept that being a 'bureaucrat' or a 'Public Servant' is in any way a demeaning occupation.[87]

One straw in the wind was the participation of Treasury officials in a one-day general strike held on 20 September 1979 to protest at the government's wage policy. Some who were PSA delegates picketed the Treasury building. In a memorandum to the other Treasury secretaries, Martin argued that he could accept that

> Industrial action related directly to officers' remuneration or conditions of service can be justified ... What I find much more difficult is action directed for instance against the Remuneration Act — a quite legitimate government measure which does not involved fundamental human values ... the act of picketing is an overt political action which is linked directly with Treasury as an institution.[88]

Martin belonged to an earlier generation than that of Mark Prebble, the PSA delegate who organised the picket outside Treasury. When asked why he did this, Prebble replied:

> Because it was my workplace. Everywhere the PSA wanted members to picket our workplaces. And I thought we were getting quite a lot of support from staff. I was pretty well known. It was a matter of keeping in touch with everybody and doing the industrial thing ... It was a glorious time around the late 1970s. Noel Lough was alleged to have said, 'Is there any member of Internal Economics who is not a card-carrying member of the Labour Party?'[89]

The appointment of Scott brought these changes in the nature of the profession into the heart of the Treasury. Normally director positions were advertised 'generically', but when that of Economics II was advertised in 1980, 'we were clear that we needed to strengthen the economic analytical capacity'. Treasury recruiters at the beginning of the 1970s had found master's degrees acceptable but seen little value in PhDs. By the late 1970s PhDs were acceptable too. John Martin, who was involved in the Economics II appointment, recalls that Scott was clearly the best candidate, and the appointment panel was able to demonstrate that, as required by the appointment procedures, he had 'clearly more merit' than any of the applicants from within the public service.

Scott was unusual not just because he was from outside the service, but because he had worked in the non-governmental sector in the United States as an economist, and as an economic consultant in Auckland. He remembers finding, when he reached the Treasury,

> this rather strange institution of the senior officers' tea room where twice a day we would all sit in a ring of chairs, eat malt biscuits and drink stewed tea. I liked the people personally, they were decent New Zealand blokes — and they were all blokes — but I disliked this whole culture, and didn't fit terribly well into it.[90]

It wasn't just the malt biscuits that fell out of favour. The circular advertising the final meeting of the 'biscuit group', which was to debate its relevance and future, alluded to a suggestion that the existence of Economics II had made an in-house forum obsolete. The convenor 'intended this as a litmus test of the tendency to control internal discussion. Ironically no one detected my irony!' For others the change was a watershed, an end to 'open access to debate among professional colleagues'.[91] The long-lived tea club lost one of its main tasks (providing tea and coffee) to the department, and also some of the active members needed to keep the surviving task (providing biscuits) going. The Staff Management Advisory Committee that had been set up by Noel Lough in 1978 to improve communication between senior management and the rest of the staff became routinised and fell into disuse.[92]

Strong professional identification as economists, including with private-sector economists, coupled with scepticism about the efficacy of government intervention, tended to engender scepticism about the politics and politicians who favoured it. In these circumstances, it was tempting not to pull your punches.

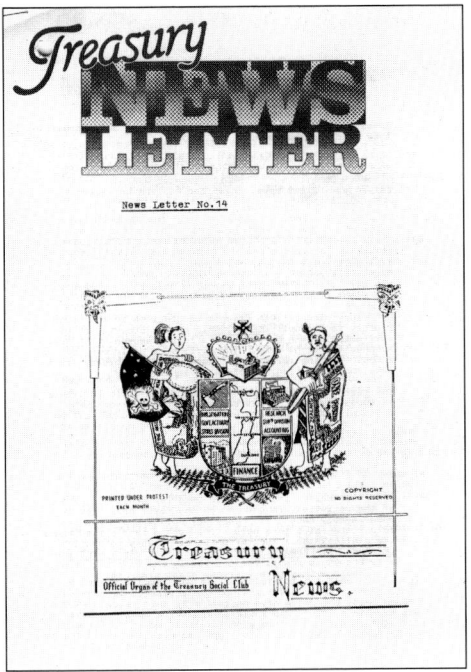

Treasury 'news', 1984. T 69/1/8/5, Treasury

Australia offered an important model. Describing John Stone's years as Deputy Secretary and Secretary from 1971 to 1984, Whitwell recounts that in

> defending preferred policy positions with intelligence, arrogance and passion … Stone resolutely refused to provide governments with alternate policy positions, believing that politicians would always choose the 'easy' option if one was available … given Treasury's command over economic advice, this left government in a difficult position: they either accepted Treasury's advice, or sought out and acted up alternative advice in the knowledge that Treasury would vehemently oppose and would be publicly known to oppose.[93]

Many New Zealand Treasury officials, including Noel Lough, had dealings with Stone, both during his time at the IMF and World Bank in Washington in the late 1960s and after his return to Canberra. Roderick Deane worked with Austin Holmes at the Reserve Bank of Australia and also in Washington with Stone:

> Because I was relatively young, if New Zealand didn't have enough seats, our delegation didn't worry if I was in the room or not. But Stone would never

allow that to happen. He would tell one of his off-siders to go and get me a seat. And they'd say, 'You're not allowed any more'. And he'd say, 'Get the seat'. And they would.[94]

If New Zealand Treasury officials did not go as far as Stone, they nonetheless forged a new professional style:

> There was a willingness to advise, regardless of what they wanted to hear. And that was so different from other agencies. You'd see it again and again and again … There were people in the Department of Trade and Industry who we would agree with. And then Harry Clark [Secretary of Trade and Industry] would change the paper and say, 'No way. This is what we are saying.' And you'd get massive battles with Roger and Graham trying to beat Harry around.[95]

In generational and cultural terms, men like Scott were not so different from the earlier middle-class economist recruits such as Jas McKenzie, Rob Laking and John Chetwin. The latter were by 1980 experienced public servants deeply familiar with the ways of government. Too familiar? The process of decision-making on the Think Big projects had roused the ire of young Treasury recruits. Thus one junior official argued to his superiors that there was 'not a strong case presented for why the government should wish to proceed [with the synfuels project] when the annexes suggest that the balance of risk does not favour the project'. After this project was duly recommended by officials in September 1981, an anonymous bureaucrat — perhaps the same one — wrote a retrospective on the negotiations 'in the hopes that readers can profit from our experience and marvel at our mistakes.'[96] The fact that Treasury reports were circulated to all ministers added another tactical dimension. If Treasury weighed the pros and cons of a decision too evenly, they would give ammunition to those who resisted reform.

The existence of a think tank such as Economics II provided the scope for officials to stand back from policy-making in a way that was less practicable for other directors, or assistant secretaries. Rob Laking had headed the Industry Division during the Think Big decisions in 1980/81, and was then involved in the 'three percent cuts' exercise in 1982:

> there was a sort of uneasy alliance between myself, as the Assistant Secretary responsible for the committee, Roger Kerr and Rob Cameron. Kerr detailed

off Rob to come up with the Treasury menu, and he was bitterly disappointed when it didn't come to anything. I always felt that he thought I wasn't pushing his ideas with enough vigour. The fact was that, being in the hot seat in that committee, next to David Thomson [the Minister of State Services], was like being in purgatory all the time.[97]

By that time, with Graham Scott having been appointed to an Assistant Secretaryship, Laking could 'see that the writing was on the wall for me — I could see that I wasn't going to be a Secretary to the Treasury.' Scott had a 'burning ambition', recalls one middle manager. 'But he had tremendous charm and great intellect.' And he organised his troops very well: 'We sent Graham in', recalled one Economics II staffer, 'hoping he would take our battle up, fight for it, and win and come back. There were times when he did win and succeed in getting senior management agreement to an approach or a strategy. Or else telling them it was happening, and the rest of them having to catch up with it afterwards.'

For McKenzie, his involvement with supplementary minimum prices was 'an albatross round my neck'.[98] Further, as Deputy Secretary, McKenzie was heavily involved through the latter part of 1982 and 1983 in the 'thankless task of chairing a committee on long-term wage-fixing with the unions and the employers. Actually, the working relations within that group were very good — Max Bradford from the Employers, Ken Douglas from the FOL (Jim Knox always came along; Ken was the thinker) — and had there been any common ground I think we would have found it, but there wasn't.'[99]

McKenzie's efficacy was also hampered by a more general malaise about the department's management. Some attributed this to its new premises. In 1979 the Treasury moved from its home for 40 years, the Departmental Building on Stout Street, to new premises in the National Provident Fund building at 1 The Terrace. The move was not without teething troubles which echoed the unsettling effect of the graduate intakes of a decade earlier:

> Treasury really fell apart when we moved to the new building. We were all so separated, instead of being one big family with all the senior officers, the investigating officers and everybody all together. I don't think people knew each other any more. And I don't think people were all that happy there either. You couldn't open windows. We were all complaining about headaches and sore eyes, but no one would listen to us. They thought we were being ridiculous.[100]

On Stout Street the Treasury had been spread over two or three floors. While the Secretary, Deputy Secretaries and Assistant Secretaries were all adjacent to each other on 'mahogany row',[101] they were not isolated from the rest of the staff. In the new premises staff were spread over a greater number of smaller floors. Possibly the retirement of Lough, Scott's 'patron', at the end of 1980 also made a difference. Bernard Galvin, his successor, had had five years in the Prime Minister's Department, working closely alongside Muldoon, by the time he returned to the Treasury. Whatever the reason, a 'schism' was now openly 'perceived to exist between the twelfth floor (the expression itself says something) and the role of Treasury. Treasury investigating officers generally do not hold the twelfth floor collectively in high regard and in some sections a unifying factor is a common critical view about Secretaries and their management abilities.' An annex to this memorandum further commented that 'Secretaries should have a very important role to play in marketing the Treasury overview. Instead the emphasis appears to be placed on serving macro policy demands, Cabinet Committees and Board functions.'[102]

A junior officer in Economics II in the early 1980s remembers that a 'generational shift [was] going on'. But the real generational shift had taken place in the later 1960s with the advent of economists. Galvin was only nine years older than Scott, McKenzie was only three years older, and Preston and Laking were his contemporaries. The Lang 'revolution', with its focus on expertise and an open style, had made further change possible. The seeming powerlessness of Treasury officials in the 1970s made it welcome. During Muldoon's last term in office, the presence in Treasury of new ideas and new people was to create many incendiary contacts between department and minister.

Collision

Muldoon and National won the 1981 election as narrowly as they had the 1978 one, with Labour again winning more votes. Labour increased its number of seats in Parliament, leaving National with an overall majority of only one seat after the election of the Speaker. Both politicians and the Treasury would be living on the edge. Muldoon retained both the prime ministership and the finance portfolio. While the neoliberal post-election briefing 'went through', recalled Jas McKenzie, 'Muldoon wouldn't even talk about it. And after that, he went bananas.' In May 1982, Muldoon startled Treasury — and other departments

'The night before budget.' Trace Hodgson, Alexander Turnbull Library, H-480-001

— by deciding on a wage–price freeze while he was attending an OECD meeting in Paris. For Bill Birch, 'it's easy to put all the responsibility on Muldoon. But when you look at the position taken by Federated Farmers, manufacturers, business people about containing inflation … a lot of pressure came from those lobby groups, which Muldoon reacted to.'[103] Treasury officials recall the event more in terms of its unsettling of lines of advice, as Muldoon responded to the emphasis on inflation at the OECD meeting, and officials analysed the implications of a freeze and attempted to dissuade him from this course of action.[104]

One of the first memorandums on the proposal could not have been more blunt: 'past experience shows that a wage and price freeze could operate only for a very short period. If it were in place for a longer period, it would require more and more complex and draconian administrative measures which would become less and less effective.'[105] Echoing the 1978 'Strategy for Growth', a recommendation against a freeze was signed off by the Secretary to the Treasury and three

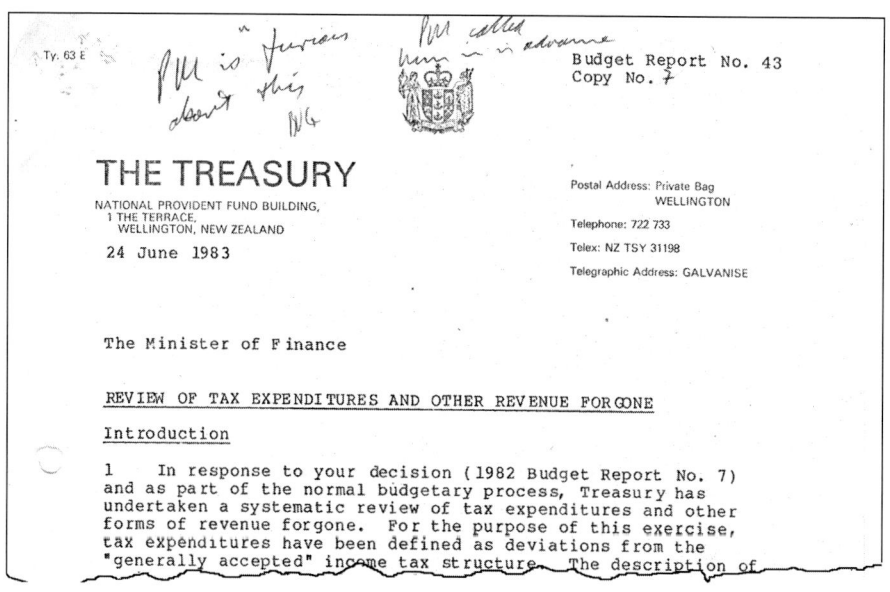

'PM is furious about this.' Muldoon's response to the Treasury report on tax expenditures. Budget Report no. 43, 24 June 1983, Treasury

other senior officials — to no avail. Muldoon eventually stopped debating the issues and told Galvin that he was going ahead with it.

The 1982 Budget round, which was under way at this time, was mostly driven by Graham Scott. Muldoon received, but did not act on, reports proposing alternatives such as an increase in indirect taxation. He saw red over a report which examined the feasibility of including capital gains, gifts and inheritance in the personal income tax base, and also advocated a tax on fringe benefits. Muldoon cabled from Paris, 're budget paper 6. Recommendation not approved. Do not waste further time on this work.'[106] During the 1983 round he became equally angry when Treasury put up the report on tax expenditures that has already been referred to. On most of the specific proposals he simply scored 'no change', but occasionally this was amplified to 'not much point in putting in a paper like this', or 'waste of time putting in a paper like this'.[107] But Galvin made an annotation that Muldoon was 'furious' about the paper, and one of those on the edge of the storm remembers it clearly:

> We were at the Beehive. Bernie and Graham and I went to give this advice to Muldoon with the paper, which would have gone up — he would already

> have seen it. We thought we were all to go in, but Muldoon summoned Bernie on his own. Muldoon swore at him — we could hear it through the closed door — 'I never want to see a paper like this again'. Bernie comes out five minutes later, white and shaking. And that was the end of that.

One divisional director recalls seeing Scott and Kerr looking 'ashen' on leaving a meeting with Muldoon in 1982 or 1983 at which he had evidently given them a 'huge bollocking' for a paper on trade liberalisation.[108] Treasury now sought alternative ways to get its views across without breaching public service procedures. David Greig recalls a final phase in the accomplishment of transport deregulation in 1983:

> Bernie Galvin said to me, 'Write a report summarising all the previous reports that you've done and I'll sign it.' Muldoon sent all the copies (one for each Cabinet member) of that back with CONFIDENTIAL stamped all over them — no one saw them. I then took one to Gair and the issue ended up in caucus, where Muldoon introduced it by saying something like, 'This is a difficult issue. Let's hear a few views on it.' Seven people spoke and said it would be terrible to deregulate transport. But when they had a vote, it was 48 to eight [in favour].[109]

Mark Prebble had been involved in the 1981 bail-out of Winstone Samsung's Karioi operation in the central North Island — David Lange called it 'social welfare for trees' — when loan legislation was passed through all its parliamentary stages in two nights. Prebble recalls that Winstone's

> so much didn't want the parlous state of their position to be revealed [that] we never managed to find out from them how parlous their position was. We did push it to the extent of Bernie Galvin going back to the Minister and saying, 'We do not think this is right', but the Minister said, 'I want you to keep going on the same basis.'[110]

Parallels could be drawn with the conduct of scientists and environmentalists, for whom respect for the findings and recommendations of their disciplines sometimes overrode their duties as public servants to the government of the day. The 1970s and 1980s was an era of environmental protest. Officials in workplaces such as the DSIR's Ecology Division found themselves at odds with government policy, in that case on native forests, and for some the claims of their employer were the lesser.

For his part, Muldoon remained formally professional. Although he twice declined to appoint Roderick Deane to the governorship of the Reserve Bank, despite his being deputy governor, he gave Deane a clear explanation on both occasions, and was also scrupulous in ensuring that issues related to Deane's superannuation were dealt with properly. On one occasion he chastised the National Party backbencher (and market liberal) Ian McLean, the chair of the Public Expenditure Committee, for having unreasonable expectations of Treasury officers.[111] Murray Horn recalls the professionalism with which Muldoon dealt with him, the Budget co-ordinator, over the Budget he was never to give. But at any meaningful level, the relationship had broken down. 'Treasury was in quarantine', as one official put it. And economists in particular were in the gun.[112]

University of Otago professor Paul van Moeseke and Victoria University lecturer Geoff Bertam were two academic economists who played key roles in the debate about the proposed second aluminium smelter. While it was fiercely opposed by environmentalists, economists questioned its economic rationality.[113] New Treasury recruits also took part in this debate: 'if someone's pet project is obviously useless and falls outside even the above vague and generous criteria, let's do it anyway ... [there is] no concept in here of budget limitations implying the need for available resources to be used as cost-effectively as possible.'[114] Such comments 'got up Muldoon's nose', recalled one Energy official:

> he didn't believe in discounted cash flow analysis — the stuff about the 10 per cent rate of return and such — he was an old-fashioned accountant, he believed in accounting rates of return, not economic rates of return. And the distinction between discounting back and compounding forward irritated him — and to be fair, it was reasonably new to a lot of people. I'm not sure that many in the Cabinet Committee really understood it.[115]

Geoff Schmitt, who was on the taxation reform task force in 1982, recalls meeting the Cabinet Economic Committee, at which Muldoon 'gave quite a strongly worded little speech which was clearly insulting to economists ... with remarks of such character as to evoke approving laughter from the other ministers'.

While economists debated vigorously over macroeconomic policy — Keynesianism versus monetarism — there was more consensus on the need for microeconomic reform, including a more price-responsive exchange rate. Thus a paper by two Victoria University economists on inflation and exchange rate policies provoked intense debate about the merits of different exchange rate regimes in combating inflation. Buckle and Pope recognised that some wage increases stemmed from internal pressures, which might be eased by, for example, 'different union and industrial structures'.[116]

In December 1983, Institute of Economic Research director Brian Easton, arguing that it was now 'widely accepted' that there was 'excessive intervention' in the New Zealand economy, advocated a 'major change in the nominal exchange rate [a euphemism for devaluation to protect against attacks from Muldoon], a wide-ranging reduction of protection and subsidies and a reform of the internal tax system' — all policies which were favoured by Treasury officials.[117]

The annual report of the State Services Commission for 1983/84 devoted a number of pages to the issue of the neutrality of the public service, commenting that

> Over the past 12 months there has been wide public debate on the relationship between the Executive and Parliament on the one hand and the Public Service on the other … the system has worked well in the past but recent signs of strain indicate that the relationship between the three parties cannot be taken for granted … individual public servants value the protection against political interference in personnel matters guaranteed them by legislation since 1912.[118]

While the Commission did not cite examples, Muldoon's criticism of the Controller and Auditor-General, former Treasury Assistant Secretary Fred Shailes, after he questioned the fiscal appropriateness of funding the current account deficit through borrowing, showed little respect for the independence of the Auditor-General's office, and his accountability to Parliament rather than the government.[119]

Muldoon's own colleagues had little leverage on economic issues. Frank Holmes, then at the Planning Council, recalled that some of Muldoon's ministers *were* exploring new directions. He told them that if they wanted a

> real strategy on national development they had to get into areas like monetary policy, exchange rate policy, fiscal policy and so on. And they said, 'Well, that's the old man's [Muldoon's] territory, we can't go into that'. I replied — 'Well you should, you know'. So they began to call in a few people from outside to talk about these things. And ultimately they produced a document which just was buried, called a 'national development strategy' … which they got Muldoon to sign. Lange had a field day, because everything in there was just about the opposite of what Muldoon was doing during the freeze period.[120]

The nadir of the relationship between Muldoon and his officials came in mid-June 1984 when, after deciding his perilous parliamentary majority was in doubt, he called an election for 14 July, four months early. The sequence of events, including the run on the New Zealand dollar in the days after the election was called, has been discussed in detail by both Gustafson and Muldoon. By this time Muldoon was uncompromising in his determination to resist the pressure on the exchange rate, a sharp fall in which would compromise the anti-inflation gains of the two-year-old wage and price freeze. He had turned down recommendations from the Reserve Bank and the Treasury for a 15 per cent devaluation in December 1982, and for a return to the crawling peg in February 1984.[121] In the week before the election, the currency outflow speeded up again. On the Monday after the election, Lange, the newly-elected leader, called on Muldoon, who would constitutionally remain Prime Minister for another two weeks, to devalue. Muldoon, convinced that a joint statement by Lange and himself would end the pressure on the exchange rate, refused to order a devaluation on the grounds that this should be a decision for the new government, which should accordingly take office immediately. When it became evident that the change of government could not be accelerated, it was therefore 'equally clear that we must act for the new Government; and that we did.' The New Zealand dollar was devalued by 20 per cent on Wednesday 18 July.[122]

A theory that the Treasury and the Reserve Bank facilitated the run on the dollar so as to precipitate the devaluation they had both long advocated was advanced shortly after the election.[123] Muldoon himself did not believe this charge. But he was viscerally angry that his anti-inflation strategy had been destroyed at a stroke. The devaluation made it impossible to negotiate a restrained exit from the wage–price freeze. In the aftermath of his crushing election defeat, Muldoon was desperate to demonstrate — to convince himself as much as anyone else, perhaps — that the devaluation had been avoidable, that his strategy would have worked if it had been supported by proper advice from Treasury and the Reserve Bank. That advice had been provided principally by or through Roderick Deane at the Reserve Bank and Graham Scott at the Treasury, and it was this pair who were in Muldoon's sights.

In late August Parliament's Public Expenditure Committee, on which Muldoon sat, established a subcommittee to investigate the circumstances surrounding the decision to devalue the dollar. Only one day of hearings was held before the government decided to close it down:

> the three people who were [to be] the principal witnesses were me, Scotty, and Peter Nichol in the Bank. We were the three who were most heavily involved in writing and overseeing a lot of the material. I was the only one to appear. When I got back to the Bank, I wrote a letter to the Prime Minister [Lange], which I informed him would be an open letter if they did not resolve matters rapidly in terms of my rights. That letter disclosed matters which, if it had been published, would not only have been very difficult for Muldoon and the previous government, but also very difficult for the present government.[124]

Devaluation had also been a sensitive issue for Labour during the election campaign. National had highlighted assumed divisions in the Labour Party on the question, and the new Labour MP Jim Anderton, also a member of the subcommittee, sympathised with Muldoon's stance.[125] But the published record of the single day of proceedings provides a sense of the raw state of this phase of minister–officials relations. When Galvin proposed to give the committee a paper 'outlining the public facts so as to get indications of what other issues the committee wanted information on', Muldoon riposted that 'this inquiry was not going to be structured by officials, and that Treasury and the Reserve Bank were not in their usual role since they were at the centre of the issue … it was inappropriate that they should act in what would be a normal advisory role.'[126]

Both Galvin and Reserve Bank Governor Spencer Russell sought to be present when officials of their departments were being questioned. 'There was nothing', Galvin said, 'any officer had done that he would not take responsibility for … the documents were official advice, with the bulk being signed by him and that if it was a question of policy advice he must take responsibility.' But Muldoon, who was not in the chair, answered, 'No, the committee had resolved that that would not be the case'; he later commented that 'the Treasury was not a monolithic body speaking with one voice.'[127] In the published record of Deane's appearance, the majority of the questions come from Muldoon. The questions are technical, but all were directed at demonstrating that the Bank and the Treasury were biased in favour of a devaluation and had bent their advice to that end. Thus Muldoon commented that 'Treasury had a figure of 15% being recommended before the question of an election had come about, and yet after a direct and positive threat, they still put in a figure of 15% and then four weeks later it had become 20%.' When a few minutes later he asked whether one measure had been advocated in order to 'put the wind up the Minister of Finance', the record reported blandly that 'there was no comment on this statement'.[128]

With the enquiry terminated, Muldoon resorted to print. *The New Zealand Economy: A Personal View*, which he finished writing in March 1985 (four months after stepping down as leader of the National Party) and published later that year, is a defence of his stewardship of the economy from 1967 to 1972 and between 1975 and 1984. In so doing it highlights both the role of the Minister of Finance — especially when the office is held by the Prime Minister — as *the* economic manager, and his resentment at the way that the 1984 devaluation had overturned his strategy:

> The whole episode brought no credit on either the Treasury or the Reserve Bank. Both have many dedicated and able public servants, some of whom have long been friends of mine and who have served me [sic] well over the years. On this occasion however the deficiencies of both were apparent.[129]

This situation was not unique to New Zealand. Whitwell quotes a senior Australian official as characterising the years from 1969 to 1984 as a period in which the Treasury was almost 'continually in conflict with politicians of both parties',[130] for much the same reason as applied to Muldoon–Treasury relations in New Zealand from 1982 to 1984: the proffering by Treasury of neoliberal policy advice which was at odds with the preferences of the Cabinet.

In 1976, Prime Minister Malcolm Fraser split the Australian Treasury between those parts of it primarily oriented to providing economic advice and those dealing with public expenditure. After the Liberals regained office, an initial spat over the immediate implementation of tax indexation (favoured by Fraser, but not by Treasury) was followed by another over devaluation (in which the roles were reversed) that provides a revealing parallel (and contrast) with the Muldoon/Treasury stand-off eight years later.[131] In the case of devaluation, the Cabinet reluctantly accepted Treasury's advice. But in a compelling demonstration of executive power, the Prime Minister announced the splitting of the department days later, a decision about which the Secretary to the Treasury was informed rather than consulted.[132]

Why didn't Muldoon follow the same course at some point between 1982 and 1984? In one sense he already had. Lang's resignation in 1976 had signalled that in a contest between a strong Secretary and a strong Minister, the latter could be expected to prevail. Whatever their private thoughts may have been, Lang's successors, Lough and Galvin, continued to follow the conventions of

Ron Simms's last ride, 21 February 1984. Inspector Ian Drew makes a presentation to Treasury's Ron Simms, who had been a Wellington bus commuter for 40 years.
Alexander Turnbull Library,
EP 1984/839, PAColl-0614

advice-giving — Stone's style was not theirs. Nor did either, as Stone did, embark on a political career after leaving office. Further, Fraser dealt with Treasury advice at one remove. He was not Minister of Finance as well as Prime Minister, and had indeed never held the finance portfolio. By contrast, the Muldoon of 1982 had presented twelve Budgets and had occupied both offices for six years. He could not admit that officials understood economic management better than he did, or had the power to get their advice accepted (as it was in Canberra in November 1976) in spite of ministerial opposition.

To Muldoon, the 'Achilles' heel' of too many of the government's advisers was a

> simplistic and theoretical approach to economic management ... Having been intimately connected with cause and effect in the New Zealand economy since I joined Harry Lake ... at the end of 1963, I have seen countless examples of simplistic departmental advice [and] criticise the time and effort that

> [officials] waste in producing and promoting proposals which they should know will not be politically acceptable ... They would respond that it is their duty ... I would tend to regard the expenditure of effort in that direction as a waste of time and public money ... economic management [is] a matter of educating the public to accept changes that are economically desirable.[133]

In February 1984, Ron Simms retired after 40 years' service in the Treasury. He'd caught the number 2 bus from Miramar every working day of those years, almost always as the first passenger. On his last day an inspector presented him, on behalf of the city bus department, with two complimentary scenic bus tour tickets and a pictorial booklet on Wellington. Simms's only regret was that he had eight rides left on his ten-trip ticket — and he would still have them that night, because he would be going home in a taxi.[134]

Ron's last bus journey invoked a Treasury that was gone or going. The developments of the early 1980s had hastened its departure. Ideology and professionalism had combined to move the Treasury on from the department that Henry Lang had left, let alone the one — Ron's department — that he had joined. Lang's professionalism remained, but within a new frame of reference. 'One is an economist first and a public servant second', thought one official of the time — and then dissented from this judgement. Others would have assented — or argued that there was no conflict. But the observation distils the essence of an important change in the Treasury of the early 1980s.[135]

Chapter 8

Managing the economy, 1984–1993

The Treasury's turn?

'During the reform years [between 1984 and 1993], the conventional relationship between elected government and bureaucratic advisors in a Westminster system was to a great extent reversed. The Treasury became the principal initiator; to know what governments would do, one read the Treasury's briefing papers, not party programmes.'[1] In the aftermath of the 1984 election, the new Minister of Finance, Roger Douglas, published that year's briefing papers in a volume entitled *Economic Management*.[2] They had been written quickly, with the snap election looming, under the direction of Graham Scott and the economics divisions: 'it was run as a project of a group of people with responsibility for the overall document. Graham was like the sponsor, it was as if we were writing for Graham — at the end of the day he was the person deciding whether it all hung together, whether this should be more pointed, that should be cut back to a suggestion.'[3] Or as one divisional head put it: 'I was in charge of doing a paper on government expenditure and revenue, but the three pages at the beginning of each chapter were written by Rob Cameron and Murray Horn.' He did not get the chance to look at it again.

The notion of economic management, that governments should — or even could — 'manage' the economy, had featured in political and economic life since the 1930s, and since the 1960s the term had been familiar to officials, ministers and economists. Two fundamental questions had been asked throughout the life of the idea: Who should do the managing — what should be the balance of power and influence between ministers and officials, politicians and professionals? And what should managing involve — what kind of management of what kind of economy?

From 1982 to 1984 the answers to both questions had been in contention, with Treasury and its minister at loggerheads. Entitling the Treasury briefing paper *Economic Management* was a call to intellectual but also political arms. And the latter call was the more fundamental. Although most discussion of *Economic Management* has focused on its economics, the politics preceded the economics in the discussion, with the first substantive chapter addressing 'the practice and organisation of economic management'. In the twilight of the Muldoon era, Treasury officials were as preoccupied with process as with outcomes.

Treasury's plan was to insulate the activity of economic management from problematic political currents within Cabinet, Parliament and the community. It attacked the influence of economic interest lobbies in the formation of policy, of spending departments and their ministers in decisions about expenditure, and the ascendancy of the short term over the medium term. It was informed both by experience and by contemporary public choice theory; it also unconsciously echoed recurrent business critiques of government from earlier in the century. Had it been fully acted on, it would have met the concerns of the 'fiscal bureaucrats' that economic management was no more than an arm of politics.[4]

Treasury officials armed with economic expertise would have guided ministers instead of doing their bidding. Or so we may assume. There is little in *Economic Management* about Treasury's own role, but what there is confirms that it would continue to be important. For example, in a discussion of the Cabinet Policy Review Committee, it was suggested that 'officials should be present although not in such numbers as to inhibit discussion. In the first instance the presence of representatives of Treasury and the Prime Minister's Department may suffice with the option to call on other officials if so desired.'[5] The gap between Treasury advice and the resulting policies would narrow, perhaps even close.

The suite of economic management policies set out in the following chapters of *Economic Management* followed the thinking that had developed in Treasury over the preceding decade and a half, and in the economics divisions over the last few years, as was discussed in chapter 7. Macroeconomic policies 'should be harmonised in a credible, understandable and readily predictable manner. The key requirements for macro policies in the immediate future are a consistently tight monetary policy in conjunction with a determined and phased programme for reducing the fiscal deficit and a more market-determined exchange rate.'[6]

The outcome would be a macroeconomic stabilisation of the economy. The use of incomes policies beyond the very short term was rejected. Conflicts between wage demands and improving the balance of payments and inflation were unlikely to be resolved through the existing 'prolonged controls on wages', which were 'almost certainly reducing employment in some areas by ... depriving employers of the ability to bid competitively for the particular type of labour they require. Rather, the solution lies in the Government ... making sure that [its objectives] are well understood ... so that employers and employees are not likely to agree to wage increases based on a mistaken view about government policy intentions.'[7]

With macroeconomics thus despatched, the focus could turn to microeconomics. The economy also needed to become more efficient through a process of adjustment which would entail placing much greater reliance on market forces:

> The question for government choice is not whether to intervene but rather to decide what set of interventions is most appropriate for a particular purpose ... With regard to choosing the most effective policy, the reason so-called market forces are the appropriate touchstone in many areas of economic activity is because most policies are to be judged in terms of how well they succeed in marshalling those forces to achieve greater welfare. Markets generally offer an efficient means for reconciling competing demands so that the government is more likely to achieve its ends effectively by harnessing and supplementing markets rather than suppressing them.[8]

Whether these markets were those for finance, products or labour, the same principle applied. Microeconomic policies implemented 'in conjunction with a regulatory environment which provides ... the appropriate incentives for production' would 'enable the economy to release its full growth potential.'[9] Treasury also aimed to broaden the tax base, which remained twice as reliant on direct taxes as the OECD average, with indirect taxes raised on only around one-third of private consumption. Treasury sought more effective control of government expenditure, and more efficient — because more accountable and responsive — public sector organisations and delivery of social services; it was 'notable that ways of promoting welfare which are consistent with better economic performance tend also to be those which take advantage of the strengths of individual incentives'.[10]

Equity was also a goal, but one seen as more difficult to specify or attain than efficiency, as this comment suggests:

> while efficiency principles are generally clear and well understood, there is no commonly agreed and well-developed set of equity criteria for marking out the approach to [tax] reform. One objective often advanced is a fair

sharing of the tax burden, but this idea is very hard to pin down. Concepts of horizontal and vertical equity are both used: horizontal equity to ensure that the system imposes the same tax burden on people in the same economic position; and vertical equity to place a greater share of the tax burden on those in a better economic position ... a starting point for approaching equity issues is to recognise the real limitations of the personal income tax system, in particular, as a vehicle for achieving an effective redistribution of resources in any broad sense.[11]

I referred at the beginning of this book to Roseveare's description of the 'tripod' of nineteenth-century British political economy: free trade, a balanced Budget and the gold standard. In a slightly different form (and with free trade at a discount), this also describes the 'economic constitution' that was favoured by Downie Stewart and the Treasury in the early 1930s. What then of the 1980s? For free trade, both external and internal, read microeconomic reform; for balanced Budget, efficiency in government and fiscal discipline; and for gold standard, an anti-inflationary, independently-administered monetary policy. Economic management would be buttressed by an economic constitution over which the professionals of the Treasury would be, if not the guardians, certainly watchful. The 'new' economics both informed and welcomed a new politics.

So what happened? Did Treasury realise both its political and its economic visions for economic management? Broadly, yes, and hindsight tempts us to assume that this outcome was inevitable. Exploring the course of events from the perspective of the time tells us more. During the first term of the fourth Labour government, both the politics and the economics of economic management proceeded generally in the direction favoured by Treasury. Cabinet was receptive to Treasury advice, monetary policy was tightened, the exchange rate was floated, and efforts were made to reduce the fiscal deficit. Finance and product markets were liberalised, the tax base was broadened, and direct tax rates were lowered. But from 1987 both the political and the economic climate were less predictable. During its second term, the Labour government was divided over whether or not to advance further in the direction it had taken since 1984. The 'compromise' it struck — which did not end the conflict — entailed keeping the welfare state and the labour market off limits, but institutionalising the new direction in monetary policy and financial management and microeconomic reform, particularly deregulation. The National government elected in 1990 was committed to the reform of the labour market, and was propelled into fiscal consolidation and the redesigning of social policy by a conjunction of circumstances and inclination — it therefore linked the social and the economic in a way that was more congenial to Treasury. Low inflation and fiscal balance were both attained, whilst in committing itself to an 'economic strategy' and 'fiscal responsibility' National also attempted to nail down the 'tripod'. But such commitments remained vulnerable to the political process, as the 1993 election, which saw the electorate shifting sharply to the left and also voting for proportional representation, underlined.

This chapter traverses the same period of years as the next. The story of economic management both sits alongside and embraces that of the management of government, which will be addressed in chapter 9. Of necessity some issues, such as the professionalisation of Treasury, will be touched on in both chapters.

Treasury, Roger Douglas and Labour

The new government that was to be so sympathetic to the 'Treasury line' was a Labour government. This was remarkable. The last time that Labour had been in government, between 1972 and 1975, had been marked by an initial chill in Treasury–government relations, with the new government being suspicious of Treasury on both bureaucratic and ideological grounds. Nor during the 1984 election campaign was it obvious that a vote for Labour would be a vote for neoliberal economic management. Neither National nor Labour advocated a liberalisation strategy of the kind that was to be followed after the election. Labour intended to control interest rates and 'plan' economic management. It was labour relations, rather than the economy per se, which featured in its electioneering on economic issues. Labour announced its determination to seek a more fruitful relationship with the trade union movement than had been achieved by Muldoon. Labour Party politicians frequently cited the compact that had been agreed to by the Hawke Labor government elected in Australia in March 1983. This was probably how New Zealanders thought a new Labour government would conduct itself. The economic summit conference that was called by Labour in early September 1984 was modelled on one that had been held in Australia. As the journalist Tony Garnier observed, the question of economic liberalisation was being debated within rather than between the two main parties. This in itself made the situation unusual, given that the character of economic management and distributive issues were traditional points of contrast between Labour and National.[12]

A first place to look for change is thus within the Labour Party. When David Lange replaced Bill Rowling as leader in 1983, Roger Douglas returned to the front bench as the spokesperson on finance, in place of Labour's last Minister of Finance, Bob Tizard. The change had added significance because Douglas had been removed from the front bench in 1980 after he released an alternative Budget without consulting Rowling.[13] In the aftermath of his demotion Douglas had published *There's Got to be a Better Way*, an eclectic 'ABC' of commentaries on a variety of economic issues. While this was not solely a market liberal tract, it did demonstrate another key Douglas attribute: 'I take the straightest possible route and get there as quickly as we can, and jump over the intervening steps'.[14] By 1984 that 'straight route' was the market (in the broadest sense of the word). Douglas's thinking had become more coherent, and he was readily identified by journalists and others as the doyen of Labour's market liberals.[15]

To what extent did discussions with Treasury officials and other economists play a role in the development of Douglas's thinking? One study argues that a 'dislike of political influence' linked his earlier interventionism and his later market liberalism, which he argued by 1983 would end the pandering to 'vested interests [and] parochial pressure groups'.[16] A Treasury official had been attached to the office of the Leader of the Opposition since 1975, and the Opposition Research Unit had hired professionally qualified economists at least since Labour's election defeat in that year.[17] One of the latter, John Whitehead, who was later to work at Treasury, recalls costing one of Douglas's tax policies using 'Treasury' methodology, and also sitting in on meetings where Douglas, Tizard and others argued about policy.[18] Douglas recollects that while 'efficiency in government had always been there in my thinking, Doug [Andrew, the Treasury official in the Leader of the Opposition's office since mid-1983] and Geoff [Swier] were able to crystallise it more'.[19] This seems fair enough. Nothing about Douglas suggested that he was anyone's disciple — Treasury officials might stimulate his thinking, but they did not instigate it.

There were other, less direct, links between Labour and the Treasury. In early 1984 former Treasury Secretary Henry Lang advised Labour on its economic policy. In March and April he had a number of lunches with Graham Scott, Bryce Wilkinson and Rob Cameron, and also met on separate occasions with Lange, Douglas, and Geoffrey Palmer. Lang's notes of the meetings record that their purpose was to discuss the possibility of an investment fund to 'pick winners' (this was to appear in Labour's election policy as an Industrial Development

Board). However, Lang's note that following his first meeting with Scott he 'talk[ed] to him, BW and RC separately at lunches and informally' suggests that a wider spectrum of issues was tackled.[20]

A number of those interviewed 'off the record' for this volume considered that other discussions between senior Treasury officials and Labour Party politicians in 1983 and 1984 tested the bounds of constitutional propriety. Treasury Secretary Galvin, when asked about such matters, responded that what officials did in their own time was their own business.[21] One confirmed contact took place after the snap election was called, and with Muldoon's foreknowledge:

> There was an intimation from the Labour Party ... that they would like to talk with us in order to tell us what they would like to have ready for [them] should they get elected ... Bernie told me that the PM said that was OK, so long as you just listen. Graham Scott and I went to Roger Douglas's apartment — I think it was in Jellicoe Towers, it was bare and we sat on apple boxes. We were with him for two to three hours. We didn't give him any information that we shouldn't have given him. We were very proper public servants. We were just *meticulous*... We did listen, and he told us what they planned to do if they were elected. It was the *whole* works ... We were *very* interested. We went back, and started to broaden our briefing papers.[22]

One interpretation of officials' actions immediately after the election is that cumulatively they added up to 'something of a coup':

> The fact that it was a snap election, and the speculation against the dollar in the weeks before it, produced an atmosphere of panic that Roger Douglas and the other finance ministers [David Caygill and Richard Prebble] were able to take advantage of ... Within Cabinet, the finance ministers ... were able to seize control ... This dominance was achieved with the support and expertise of Treasury and Reserve Bank officials ... this was the second aspect of the coup: the usurping of political power by the hardline right-wingers within the government bureaucracy.[23]

The use of 'coup' resonated with the failed 1980 'colonels' coup'. If those plotters had succeeded, undoubtedly the National government would have moved in a liberalising direction. Whether or not one accepts this sort of language, the opportunity created by the snap election, the financial crisis and the consequent devaluation was for the Treasury a second favourable influence on the Labour government's economic management. As one Treasury official put it, 'we did not create crises but we weren't above taking advantage of them'. When Douglas talked of devaluation in an early campaign speech, Lange forcefully rejected the idea that this was Labour policy.²⁴ But reform of the management of the exchange rate was an important key to the reform of the regulated economy — import licensing, farm assistance and the like — that had for so long been advocated by Treasury. And while importers and farmers would be hesitant about massive changes, financial interests would not. Revealingly, the policies most resembling the course which Labour was to follow were those of the market liberal splinter party, the New Zealand Party, led by the property entrepreneur Bob Jones. This criticised the overvalued exchange rate, the tax system which provided disincentives for work, irresponsible monetary policy, the Budget deficit, and ad hoc intervention²⁵ — all failings of economic management that were canvassed in the Treasury's briefing papers.

The financial moves taken immediately after the election — the 20 per cent devaluation and the abolition of most controls on interest rates — created much support for Labour amongst financial interests. Douglas's first major speaking engagement as Minister of Finance was at the annual general meeting of the New Zealand Finance Houses Association on 1 August. Those present 'warmly applauded' these moves and looked forward to even greater deregulation in the future.²⁶ Without the snap election and the currency crisis, this nexus between the new government and financial interests would not have been forged. 'We would not', Lange commented two years later,

> have the Government we have now if we had been elected in November 1984. We would not have had the policy. We would have celebrated through December, gone on holiday, come back and had a formal opening of Parliament and tried out our new seats … the first budget would have been drawn up in circumstances of great party orthodoxy.²⁷

A third influence is less often identified. We have seen how Treasury's public-choice thinking had developed in part against the backdrop of the business-interest politics of the 1960s and 1970s. Interest groups of primary producers and businesspeople were traditionally closer to National than to Labour. The significant subsidies that the third Labour government had attacked in its first year in office had been farming ones, and Labour fired at the same target in 1984.²⁸ Labour's criticism of Think Big was another point of conjunction with Treasury, as were its attacks on the privileges enjoyed by businesses thriving behind protective barriers: 'I remember', recalled one divisional director, 'flying on a plane … with Douglas, and we saw the New Zealand Steel Board and gave them a hard time.' Douglas himself entitled the chapter on New Zealand Steel in *Toward Prosperity*, 'Just Another Billion and We'll be Right'.[29] The establishment of the Forestry Corporation was opposed by the unions involved in forestry — the Public Service Association and the New Zealand Workers' Union — but also by sawmillers and other industry groups which saw themselves threatened by a large new competitor in the marketplace.[30] Much of the tax reform — the Goods and Services Tax (GST), which applied to all businesses, fringe benefit and other taxes — were not popular with business interests, which had succeeded in torpedoing a payroll tax proposed by Muldoon only twelve years before. In sum, the 'crony' economy was far more likely to be attacked by Labour than by National. Such scepticism also embraced government departments which were closely linked with economic interest groups. And it was fuelled by the traditional suspicion of a new administration for the officials who had served its predecessor:

> In its view they were too closely associated with the previous government which had been in power for 9 years … the top echelon of the civil service had become too inbred and closed to new ways of thinking and doing things.[31]

From this point of view, Treasury's run-ins with Muldoon became an asset, not a liability. This line of argument can be taken further. Colin James detected early that economic liberalism in New Zealand had roots in the 'Vietnam generation'. Other antecedents will be discussed in chapter 9. But unlike 'Thatcherism' and 'Reaganomics', 'Rogernomics' had no anchoring in 'strong state' nationalism or conservative ideologies of family values.[32] Like the supporters of the New Zealand Party, neither Douglas nor leading Treasury officials were social or political conservatives. They were not hand-on-heart patriots. None had conservative stances on ANZUS, relations with South Africa, or homosexual law reform (the latter became one of the most loudly debated public issues in 1985–86 after the Labour junior whip Fran Wilde introduced a private member's bill on the subject).[33] Some of those interviewed for this history commented on the number of actively Christian graduates who were recruited into the department in the 1980s. While these people believed strongly in individual responsibility, it is difficult to distinguish the influence of such thinking on policies that were already shaped by neoliberal assumptions.

With these three elements in play, Treasury's hopes for economic management got off to a good start. But the change was one of process as well as content. In these first years of the new government, the fissure between officials and ministers, economists and politicians, servants and masters, was healed. One official recalled 'a meeting very shortly after the election. We met Douglas and Lange … Lange listened and said, "Righto, you go away with Roger and work out what we're going to do." And Roger had a list. It wasn't the Treasury coming and saying, "Here's our list". Roger had a list of things which needed to be done.' The process was symbiotic. Another Treasury official remembers Douglas coming over to Treasury for discussions with a number of its officials very soon after the election: 'it was clear we were on the same wavelength, so we subsequently were "initiating" what Douglas wanted.'

The record of relations in the first weeks after the election vividly depict such a symbiosis. Douglas was fond of playing with figures and calculations — either a product or a cause of his preoccupation with taxation and benefit issues throughout his term as minister. The first progress reports for the 1984 Budget (which was finally delivered in November, the latest since 1933) show it being shaped around Douglas's wishes, but with him evidently responding to issues raised by officials. Notes on one such meeting recorded that the key requirements for the Budget were 'to deliver to the low income group; to treat the rest of the community fairly; to reduce the deficit, to move to a VAT [GST] tax, to look to areas like industry assistance and state owned enterprises for expenditure cuts and to consider some direct tax increases to fund low income assistance'.[34]

A fortnight later, Douglas expressed his desire to discuss with his associate ministers the following week 'his overall budget plan and in particular the fiscal arithmetic, including the income assistance/tax package'. Here was more symbiosis: 'in some cases reports have gone up; in other cases preparation is under way; and in some cases it will be necessary to produce preliminary reports only, especially where we have not developed our thinking sufficiently or simply cannot report fully in the time available.'[35] The first Treasury report on what became the 'flat tax' initiative of September 1987 was a statement of Douglas's ideas to the Treasury, to which the latter in turn reacted quickly — 'this paper gives preliminary and tentative reactions to the proposals listed in budget report no. 3' — and then more fully.[36]

So Douglas was crucial, as the epithet 'Rogernomics' acknowledges. But he would have been impotent without compliance from other Cabinet ministers. For Treasury, those alliances were as important to its ability to secure the kind of economic management it favoured as was the nexus with Douglas himself. The two associate finance ministers were both senior ministers holding other portfolios, thus meeting a requirement advanced by Treasury in *Economic Management*. Whether by accident or design, this emulated the Hawke government's 'troika' of finance ministers. Douglas, Caygill and Prebble were reinforced by the appointment of Trevor de Cleene, a lawyer and expert on tax avoidance, as an Under-Secretary 'with special responsibility for the Inland Revenue'. 'His appointment', wrote Douglas, 'completed the strongest team ever to manage the Finance portfolio in New Zealand history'.[37]

Also along the lines discussed by Treasury in *Economic Management*, the government established a Cabinet Policy Committee (CPC). This was not so different in character from the third Labour government's Cabinet Committee on Policy and Priorities, or, for that matter, from the Cabinet Economic Committee of the Muldoon years, but unlike these predecessors it was not supported by an Officials' Economic Committee, which would have been chaired and co-ordinated by Treasury. Scott, who was involved in advising the new government about the system, was more comfortable with this change than were others in Treasury:

> There was an argument inside the Treasury whether it was a disaster, or whether we didn't care. Some said that now Treasury has lost control of the key officials' committee, its power has gone. The other argument was: being chairman of a committee puts you in a position where you must generate the compromises and go along with them, support them when you attend the Cabinet committee meeting. And given that there is such disagreement amongst officials now about the direction of economic policy, we would actually be better off to put in clean Treasury reports saying this was our view of the issue, without everything being homogenised back into an interdepartmental consensus. Also, Geoffrey Palmer as Deputy Prime Minister was clear that he did not want homogenised advice. If there were important differences, ministers should hear about them and make up their own minds.[38]

This too was not unlike the point of view expressed in *Economic Management*. The CPC had eight members — the three finance ministers, the Prime Minister, the Deputy Prime Minister, and the senior ministers Colin Moyle, Russell Marshall and Stan Rodger.[39] However even it was not to handle most of the principal issues of economic policy. This was partly a matter of convention: fiscal questions had traditionally been considered directly by Cabinet on the initiative of the Minister of Finance, rather than going through the committee process;

and monetary policy, which had been Muldoon's exclusive domain for years, was largely handled by the Reserve Bank — and these were key areas of policy change. On other economic issues, the Minister of Finance and the two associates worked together to convince their colleagues until they were sure of a majority in Cabinet.[40] A good example came in March 1985 with the decision to float the dollar:

> In early March, when they had these meetings, Lange had gone to London and Palmer was in the meeting with us initially. We agreed to float, then Palmer left and Douglas said, 'Well, we can't have Geoffrey simply chair the meeting because we're not sure we'll get it through. So we'll have to get Lange to help orchestrate it.' So then they said, 'Well, we'll have to send somebody to London to brief him, so that he's got somebody with him when he calls up the different critical players' [the Cabinet ministers]. So it was decided that I would go. Because they didn't have a Cabinet meeting over floating. They called them in, one by one, and got them to sign.[41]

So the Douglas/Prebble/Caygill nexus was central to the policy revolution. For its part, Treasury could see opportunities to advance both the politics and the economics of economic management that would have seemed improbable just twelve months earlier.

1984 to 1987

The three years of Labour's first parliamentary term were arguably the most exciting and stimulating in the Treasury's entire history. Since the 1960s Treasury had been frustrated with Cabinets which would not take all — or sometimes any — of its advice on economic management. While the advice had changed over the years, the frustration had not — until 1984. With the perspective of nearly twenty years' hindsight, 1984 seems an irreversible turning point, but to Treasury officials at the time it looked more like an almost unbelievable window of opportunity. Indeed, Treasury was initially sometimes startled by the speed with which Douglas wanted to implement his policies, as when he wrote to it complaining that 'the time frame you envisage for the introduction of a major indirect tax will create major political problems. The entire package is put at risk if this cannot be put into effect soon.'[42] And whereas the Reserve Bank was ready to float the dollar straight after the election, Treasury held back. According to Roderick Deane, they 'were just nervous about the banks' ability to handle it

The dollar floats – but up or down? Evening Post, 2 March 1985

all … they were second-guessing the Reserve Bank, which had extensive interaction with the trading banks'. In *this* instance, Douglas did not act until Treasury advised him to, a few months later.[43]

Treasury adapted to Douglas's pace soon enough, especially in the sphere about which they and he were most passionate — liberalisation, microeconomic reform. For Douglas, tax reform 'was a fundamental part of the programme and something I enjoyed', whilst one official reckoned that 'most of the Treasury was micro-oriented — and didn't think macroeconomics was very important. Even though [it was covered] in the post-election briefings and obviously macro stabilisation was important, there was quite a period there in the 1980s where the macro side was seen as less important than the micro side … we used to have that discussion quite a lot, and there was a sort of — "those guys in forecasting, what really matters is what we're doing in reform."' For another official, microeconomics was fundamental, while macroeconomics was 'hygiene'.[44] Within the broad parameters of a commitment to liberalisation, there was enthusiastic debate on these matters amongst Treasury officials and with Douglas: 'there was almost a sense of mission in the place. Maybe we were a little naive, a little idealistic, but there was a sense that we were doing something very important in terms of shifting New Zealand onto a higher growth track, and that ultimately the reforms would lead to that.'

This bias towards microeconomics partly reflected scepticism about Keynesian macroeconomics, but also the fact that new directions in monetary and fiscal policy had been set so rapidly. A series of announcements from the Reserve Bank in the latter part of 1984 gave effect to Douglas's willingness to tighten monetary policy as the primary weapon against inflation. This speedy action had the effect of reducing the amount of attention Treasury gave to monetary policy, as did the belief that the conduct of such policy was properly the domain of the Reserve Bank. While Treasury remained involved in providing advice on monetary policy, the issues were technical rather than fundamental so long as the government's objectives in this area remained unchanged. Douglas was determined to forego tinkering with fiscal policy and to reduce the deficit. Although this goal was to prove elusive, its existence further inclined Treasury to direct its energies towards structural reform (which could be expected to facilitate disinflation and fiscal balance, insofar as it made the economy in general more efficient and tax revenues more buoyant).[45]

Thus it was in the areas of regulation, taxation, and the institutions of government that the most energy was applied between 1984 and 1987: in the reform of taxes and benefits, the winding back of assistance to industry (including import licensing and tariffs), reform of the labour market, and the introduction of a corporatist approach to the state's trading activities. The Commerce Commission was constituted to 'promote workable and effective competition', and the Economic Development Commission to (at least from a Treasury perspective) promote informed thinking about competition and regulation. The drive to establish these new institutions was part of Treasury's deep commitment to liberalisation: 'it was quite noticeable that whenever we went to an OECD meeting or whatever, people always expected that they were going to get a microeconomic foundations lecture from the New Zealand Treasury. Partly because, in a lot of those other countries, there is also an outfit called a Ministry of Commerce, or a Ministry of Economics, or something or other.'[46]

The window was open, but for how long? The political winds were boisterous. The government soon came under bitter attack from farmers and manufacturers suffering from the high exchange rate that became the norm from the middle of 1985 — indeed, the belief that Treasury was directly responsible for the rural downturn provoked the oft-cited ironic call to 'cut out the middleman, elect the Treasury'.⁴⁷ More threatening were rumblings within the Labour Party. As early as the economic summit of September 1984, one leading trade unionist expressed his belief that

> some of the statements made by the ministers responsible for economic management, trade protection, wage levels and monetary controls suggest the Treasury line of thinking was having an influence on them. He believed those ministers had been placed under an enormous amount of pressure, particularly since they came to power, by big business organisations, public service advisors, Treasury and the Reserve Bank to adopt a more market, less protectionist attitude towards economic management than the previous government.⁴⁸

Lange knew, according to a report in March 1985, 'that some of the party had expressed misgivings about aspects of the Government's economic policy ... I ask you not to use labels as a substitute for analysis ... the New Zealand economy is unique. Roger Douglas is unique ... it is clear that in some cases market forces decide the best and most efficient use of economic resources.'⁴⁹ Criticism waxed and waned over the next two years. Before the introduction of GST, Caygill remembered a series of Labour regional conferences in 1985 'to which the finance ministers were sent to debate the issues. This was an idea of Margaret Wilson's — ultimately it proved to be a very sensible idea because by the time we got to the national conference, we had won the debate about the GST at I think five out of the six regional conferences.'⁵⁰ The announcement of plans for the corporatisation of state trading activities generated comparable criticism from within the party in 1986.

Was Treasury itself at risk? In January 1985 John Stone, the long outspoken and recently resigned Secretary to the Australian Treasury, spoke at the New Zealand Treasury on 'The role of Treasury — what are the limits to a Treasury's public role?'⁵¹ Bruce Jesson questioned, as the title of his piece — 'The Hidden Persuaders' — suggests, the nature of Treasury's advice and the department's effectiveness in getting it implemented.⁵² The *Listener* editorialised that

> in the past Treasury has been expected to offer impartial professional advice to the government on options for action. The dominance of any school of thought within Treasury must diminish its ability to develop alternative strategies for consideration ... diversity in our economy offers us the best

measure of security. The same principle should be applied to the development of economic thinking within Treasury.⁵³

There was an 'eruption from within' when Bob Tizard, the Minister of Energy, who had been Labour's last Minister of Finance, publicly challenged Treasury's advice on the corporatisation of his Ministry. But after that outburst, Lange stressed that Treasury was 'a department which does not make decisions. Government makes decisions … let's stop getting silly about the Treasury. Treasury brings a report down when government asks it to bring a report down.'⁵⁴ Anyone familiar with the processes of government knew that the latter statement was correct only in form — Treasury frequently put up reports annotated, 'to note'. But Lange's loyalty was a significant factor in ensuring that Treasury retained its role as the principal provider of economic advice to the government.

The sense that there was a 'window of opportunity' also influenced relations between Treasury officials and other economists. In the 1984 issue of *New Zealand Economics Papers*, Victoria University economists co-ordinated by John Zanetti had reviewed both *Economic Management* and the Reserve Bank's post-election briefing papers. They had criticised Treasury's macroeconomics in particular, challenging its arguments about monetary policy and the exchange rate from a broadly Keynesian perspective. The Association of Economists asked its authors to make a presentation to their 1985 conference. 'The organisers of the conference', one of the participants recalled,

> had suggested that Zanetti and the rest of us who had contributed talk to the paper. To our surprise we arrived to find a room jam-packed with perhaps 100 people, some lining the walls, some from overseas, many interjecting. Treasury officials were passionate and quite emotional about the work they had done, for reasons we had not appreciated.⁵⁵

That Treasury felt it had an historic opportunity that could all too easily be forfeited was evident in the published Treasury reply, written by Graham Scott and others. This conveyed not only a sense of disagreement on macroeconomic theory, but also of a gap between academic economists focused on issues of macroeconomics, and policy-makers who were also focused on microeconomics and institutional reforms.

This meeting was often mentioned to the writer, and not only by those who were present. This may suggest that the clash was an unusual one for the economics profession. It took place only a couple of weeks before the floating of the dollar, a decision which gave a specific cast to economists' criticism of the 'Treasury line'. In the first months of the float the dollar did not move far from its post-devaluation US 44 cents. But it rose steadily during the 1985/86 year as the impact of a tight monetary policy and high interest rates attracted capital to New Zealand. By late 1987, with the New Zealand dollar hovering around US 60 cents, Brian Easton noted a 'growing demand for a change in the Government's policy stance. This call includes almost all the economists who publicly protested against the Muldoon economic policies'.[56] Numerous comments in the press and in journals during 1986 and 1987 record the debate.[57]

One argument accepted the premise of liberalising the economy, but contended that the order in which the various markets were liberalised would make a big difference to the success of an adjustment programme. Robert Buckle cited one overseas economist to the effect that the

> scope and sequencing of financial reforms must be closely linked to other trade and fiscal changes ... trade reforms — including removal of import quotas and lowering protective import tariffs — should come early in the overall reform process. The liberalisation of financial markets should also be introduced early, but gradually ... international capital controls, it is agreed, should be relaxed only at the final stage of the reform process.[58]

Brian Easton observed in mid-1986 that 'as far as can be told, fiscal and monetary policy are made without reference to the exchange rate'.[59] If the fiscal deficit were reduced the government would have to borrow less, thus reducing the pressure on interest rates. Equally, a 'tight' monetary policy would result in high interest rates and a high exchange rate.[60] For Treasury this was an unresolvable dilemma, given the government's determination to follow a tight monetary policy and its less settled stance on fiscal policy. Did this mean that Treasury should forswear the favoured monetary policy? With the benefit of five years' hindsight, Graham Scott was to concede that 'firm monetary policy had put upward pressure on the exchange rate'.[61] But at the time, it seemed best to press ahead. Deane, a proponent of the reform, had a robust view:

> The big dilemmas were round the fact that they didn't pull government expenditure back fast enough to get the fiscal deficit down fast enough. So too much weight was thrown onto some of the other policy parameters. My

Toward Prosperity: *an optimistic pre-election view from Douglas, but the political climate was souring.* Treasury

own view of all of that was that we were doing so much, so quickly, that it was better to get it done, and behind us, because the window of opportunity to get it done was going to be so short. My judgement was that you don't get many windows of opportunity, having been through that process for so long. Douglas's own view was, 'Look, we've just got to get it done. I'm just going to have to grab the opportunities when I can, I'm not going to be able to do everything at once because there's practicalities around it, there's politics around it'.

The high point of Douglas's influence was reached in 1986. In that year he was instrumental in getting Deane appointed to chair the State Services Commission, with results that will be discussed in chapter 9. And while Roger Kerr, to whom Douglas was close, left Treasury to become executive director of the New Zealand Business Roundtable, Graham Scott succeeded Bernie Galvin as Secretary to the Treasury, even though the latter was only 53. Galvin had not always been comfortable in the new environment. When Deane was asked by Douglas to go to London in March 1985 to get Lange's agreement to the floating of the dollar, Galvin said to him, Deane recalled: '"You've got to be the good public servant, Roderick, you've got to go and brief the PM, but do not try to persuade him to this view — you've got to let him reach his own judgement." He was being very proper. As usual, I told Lange what we recommended and why, in no uncertain terms.'[62] For his part, looking back, Douglas conceded that 'to be fair to Bernie, we never really got that relationship going, although I had a lot of respect for him, for what he'd done earlier. But he wasn't always a well man. And there was a *huge* pace going on.'[63]

During this period, Lange remained loyal to Douglas. In a lengthy interview he gave the *National Business Review* to mark the government's second anniversary in July 1986, Lange stressed that Douglas had been 'the economic strategist … he is not some sort of fiscal psychopath. There is a hard Labour core to him which is not often appreciated.'[64] Eight months later, Lange likened the members of a new Labour left group to 'economic neanderthals' with views bearing 'an extraordinary similarity to Muldoonism'.[65] Polls suggested that the government would become the first Labour administration to win a second term since 1938: 'New Zealanders, even in the hardest-hit provincial areas', reported one journalist in June 1987, 'may be preparing to give the Labour government a more favourable endorsement than any government has received since 1951.'[66] While unemployment had risen in provincial areas, in the principal cities it had remained lower in a reflection of the buoyancy of the financial markets. At the time of the election, 65 per cent of Labour's voters thought that the government was going in the right economic direction, while another 21 per cent liked the direction but thought the pace too fast.[67]

It is useful to remember what goals Treasury had not seen realised during this parliamentary term. Even in Douglas's heyday, it was more difficult for Treasury to make progress in some areas than in others. This was a Labour government which had strong links with the trade union movement and with public sector workers. A great deal of effort had been expended in negotiating an exit from the freeze with union leaders, and in 1985/86 wage settlements averaging 15 per cent were tolerated. The Labour Relations Act passed early in 1987 was regarded by Treasury as flawed on key points, but it had taken months of negotiations, and Treasury was unable to get its amendments enacted.[68]

Monetary policy was also not *entirely* to Treasury's liking. Looking back in 1990, Scott thought that the combination of the 1985/86 wage round with rising interest rates and other costs and the high exchange rate had 'rapidly eroded the competitiveness gains associated with the 20 per cent devaluation in July 1984'. But he also reckoned that 'monetary conditions were allowed to ease prematurely over concerns that the economy was weakening rapidly as a result of high interest rates and exchange rate pressures'. While this easing produced reductions in short-term interest rates and a fall in the exchange rate, 'the increase in inflationary pressures forced the Reserve Bank to tighten monetary policy towards the end of 1986. As a result a year was lost in the disinflationary process.'[69]

Changes in social policy were also shaped by Labour Party politics. Douglas had concentrated on tax and regulatory reform, and cleaning up the trading side of government. Government spending on health, education and to a lesser extent welfare remained largely outside his and Treasury's ambit, despite the attention that was paid to social policy in the 1984 briefing papers. Benefit reform was driven not only by Douglas but by the desire of the Minister of Social Welfare, Ann Hercus, not to see too many cuts in her area: 'there was kind of a duel going between the two of them.'[70] Social policy generally remained in the hands of Cabinet's Social Equity Committee, which was chaired by Russell Marshall, a senior Cabinet minister who had challenged Lange for the leadership in 1983. Marshall was the Minister of Education, a portfolio in which there were big increases in spending in Labour's first term.[71] A Treasury report of January 1986 noted that 'as yet we have undertaken little review work on the structure of compulsory education'.[72] Similarly, in the health area Treasury was 'not yet in a position to form a firm view on what system would be most efficient'.[73] Lange's Royal Commission on Social Policy (see chapter 9) had no input from Treasury.

Social policy proved to be the ground over which the Lange–Douglas alignment broke. In thinking about the 1987 Budget from late 1986, Douglas moved beyond tax and benefit reform into the social policy area as a whole, driven by the desire to see yet more efficiencies in public spending and thereby reduce the public debt, but also with a vision of quite different social policies: there was discussion, for instance, about the scope for commercialisation in the health and education sectors.[74] Treasury and Douglas agreed that, with savings having already been made in the departments that were to become state-owned enterprises (see chapter 9), they must now be sought in the area of social policy.[75] Douglas recalls that one paper he wrote 'had three options. A do-nothing option, a middle-of-the-road option that resulted in a Budget surplus, and a really radical option that would have taken personal and corporate tax down to $16^2/_3$ per cent; that meant a big programme of privatisation and some social changes. And that was when Lange got scared.'[76] Treasury was involved: 'He instructed us to work on a scenario along the lines of, "Let's sell the roads, let's privatise the schools and a whole swag of the rest of social services." It led to correspondence between Lange and Douglas which was one of the most tense bits of work which those of us doing it have ever had to get involved in.'[77]

In March 1987, the Prime Minister and other ministers rebelled. They were not prepared to delegate to Douglas as they had done with previous Budgets. Ministers were sceptical of a Budget strategy so preoccupied with a deficit reduction that was to be accomplished through expenditure cuts rather than tax increases. Scott reported that

> the Prime Minister raised the question with me as to what is the right ratio of Government expenditure to GNP; Mike Moore asked why we shouldn't raise taxes by other means, in particular wealth and capital taxes to fund schemes which had been postponed for the whole of this Government's period in office; Russell Marshall accused the Minister of Finance of blowing $700 million on the tax–benefit package. Phil Goff asked why does a deficit matter anyway; Stan Rodger said there would have to be asset sales.[78]

So even as the government was enjoying good political news, its commonality of purpose frayed. The immediate outcome of the standoff was a foreshadowing of asset sales rather than expenditure cuts in the 1987 Budget: 'any further large scale cuts could now only come from health, education or social welfare spending … any wholesale cuts in these areas would be socially disastrous. As a Labour government we are not prepared to contemplate that. That has left us no option but to sell some government assets and use the proceeds to pay off debt.'[79] But the longer-term impact was to distance Douglas from many of his Cabinet colleagues: 'he did, under the frustrations of arguing with those big-spending ministers in the Cabinet … become harder-edged, more definite in his beliefs'.[80]

This alienation in turn had implications for the Treasury. The three years since the 1984 election had provided a vivid demonstration of the crucial importance of politics to economic management, in this instance mostly — but not entirely — to Treasury's advantage. But success had depended on two vulnerable elements: the Lange–Douglas alliance, which was now under stress, and the state of the economy. Colin James predicted in 1986 that if the latter went sour, 'that would mean, and would for some time go on meaning, more unemployment for which Rogernomics, and so the big changes it has catalysed, would be blamed.'[81]

Troubled times: 1987 to 1990

'With the heady success of Labour's first term', one commentator has written, 'Treasury's ambition and confidence reached a high-water mark.'[82] Given the rumblings around the Cabinet table, this may be an exaggeration, but the result of the August election provided some justification for it. Labour increased its vote, and the result was widely interpreted as a victory for Lange and Douglas. It was received favourably by many — 'market euphoria greets poll', read one headline. But careful analysis of the poll suggested the fragility of Labour's position: its support from low-income and Maori voters had fallen, and National's vote had increased by more than Labour's.[83] Internal disaffection became explicit at Labour's post-election party conference in November. Activists 'clearly considered their party had been hijacked from beneath them and they were determined to wrest back a say in [its] direction. It was hard to believe, at times, that just three months ago the party had won a historic second term in power.' While Douglas was the 'chief bogeyman', Lange also needed to be protected from protesters by security people whenever he arrived or left the conference.[84]

But Lange had already staked out a different terrain to Douglas. In forming his Cabinet after the election, he gave himself a key position in social policy by assuming the Education portfolio as well as the prime ministership, and transferred Prebble and Caygill from their Associate Finance roles, replacing them with the more junior Michael Cullen and David Butcher. Prebble remained close to the Treasury as Minister for State Owned Enterprises, but Caygill shifted to Health. Cullen, who was seen as being on the left of the party, was expected to challenge Douglas on policy matters, and other ministers were also clearly at odds with the Douglas agenda. New Housing Minister Helen Clark found favour with the conference when she declared that market culture should not run rampant through social policy. Outgoing party president Margaret Wilson highlighted concerns that 'the same methods of deregulation and non-intervention of the state [applied to economic policy] will be applied to reforms in social policy'.[85] In December, Deputy Prime Minister Geoffrey Palmer, who now chaired Cabinet's Social Equity Committee, launched an initiative of his own to coordinate social policy.[86]

What did these changes signify for Treasury and its vision for economic management? Perhaps nothing? The department published its post-election briefing papers, which focused heavily on social policy, after receiving requests for some

Treasury hits the headlines. Dominion, 23 October 1987

of them under the Official Information Act. It was clearly still imbued with the sense of confidence that had flourished over the preceding three years. Release of the complete set of papers, 'by exposing our views to a wider public scrutiny would contribute to a more informed debate on policy.' But it was recognised that this exposure was 'likely to cause some public questioning of the government and its advisors'.[87]

The latter certainly occurred. Indeed, there was more criticism of Treasury at this time than at any other, with the exception of the period of benefit and expenditure cuts and high unemployment in 1991. One large-format newspaper headline read 'Treasury proposes radical reforms', with the elaboration that 'the Treasury is pressing for some extreme extensions to the Government's free-market policies', while a columnist in the same paper speculated that Treasury had 'outflanked' Douglas.[88] Liz Gordon of Palmerston North wrote to the *Dominion* that the papers, which were published with the title *Government Management*, constituted 'a failure on the part of this government department to recognise its true role in New Zealand society. Treasury staff seem to have forgotten they are policy advisors and instead they have become politicians …

Frankly it seems clear to me that Treasury is little more than a highly paid lobby group and I object to it being paid out of taxpayers' money when its work is so clearly in the interests of only some groups in society.'[89] At the annual conference of the New Zealand Sociological Association, a paper entitled 'The Treasury: A Sociological Analysis' was presented.[90] For one citizen, *Government Management* demonstrated that there was 'a need for an independent investigation into the functioning of Treasury, its neutrality, and the competence of its advice'. For another: 'the Treasury needs to be reminded that it does not set government policy ... nor for that matter does Treasury run the government.'[91] Jenny Kirk, the Labour MP for the Auckland electorate of Birkenhead, reported that she kept

> getting queries from constituents, and from Labour supporters, about who exactly are the Treasury. If you could answer the following questions I will be able to pass on this information. Who are the Treasury? What are their qualifications? How old are they? How long have they been in the department? ... Do they have experience of working in business firms outside the government departments?[92]

Had Treasury forgotten the old public service saying, 'Remember the whale — it's only when it spouts that it gets harpooned'? The publication of *Government Management*, and the reaction this elicited, raised two important questions about the place in government of Treasury and the advice it provided. In an address at the University of Canterbury in 1965, the long-time Secretary of External Affairs Alister McIntosh had argued that 'the diplomat must always remember that he is a servant, that he possesses power without substance ... The civil servant can advise; he cannot, he does not, he must not, decide. When a civil service begins to think it is the government, it is no longer a servant but a political party in embryo'.[93] 1987 was different from 1965: Treasury's advice was supported by its minister, and the Official Information Act had diluted the private character of advice to government. Nevertheless there remained, in the way *Government Management* was titled and presented, and in the inclusion of 80 pages of background material on social policy, a sense that Treasury had crossed the boundary separating the official from the political, the official from the theoretical — and certainly the digestible from the indigestible. Even given Treasury's determination to provide only what it saw as the best advice, however unpalatable, a different kind of production might well have enhanced — and would not have limited —

Treasury's ability to get policies it favoured adopted.

The second important field of debate that was opened by the publication of *Government Management* concerned the nature of 'economic management'. As we have seen, the term had arisen in the heyday of Keynesian-style macroeconomics, and the terrain to which it was applied was from the 1960s one of the two foci of the Treasury's role in government. By the 1980s it had acquired different connotations, including a much greater focus on microeconomics. As economic management acquired this progressively stronger 'micro' focus (and as this was explored by the Task Force and the Planning Council in the 1970s), it could not overlook social policy. It was one thing for the Labour Party to assent to the liberalisation of finance, trade and taxation, but what of the universalist, publicly funded welfare state? *Government Management* was released a week before the sharemarket crash, which reduced the value of leading New Zealand shares by 15 per cent on its first day, 21 October, and soon greatly intensified an economic slowdown of which there had already been some warning signs. Debate about the direction of economic management now intensified. Within months, Auckland manufacturers were reporting that 'many firms … are shedding labour in [a] desperate bid to survive the economic recession and many others are seeking advice about making employees redundant. Manufacturing was the worst hit area, job losses reflected the downturn in the economy not only because of the share-market but also the restructuring which had been going on in the economy.'[94]

An economic statement in December 1987 was partly designed to boost economic confidence in the aftermath of the crash, but it also took tax and benefit policy even further into the domain of social policy than had been the case with the 1986 reforms. The statement proposed the introduction of a guaranteed minimum family income, an increase in the GST from 10 to 12.5 per cent, and cuts in both company and income tax to a single low rate — a radical proposal that had been initiated by Douglas and worked on by Treasury and other departmental officials over the preceding three months.[95] Whilst it had been inspired by Douglas, the package was presented jointly by all the key Cabinet ministers, including Lange. However, in the eyes of Lange and the other ministers these proposals were just that, whereas Douglas saw them as settled. On 28 January Lange announced that they would not proceed. Douglas, who was out of the country at the time, learnt of Lange's statement from a journalist. On his return a few days later, he contradicted it,[96] and the relationship between the two men collapsed. Personnel changes in Lange's office probably did not assist, though one staffer recalled 'a number of times where the two of them got together for breakfast and I sat there in a note-taker position. *Just the three of you?* Yes.' But within weeks, even that informal liaison had ended.

In addresses over the next few months, Lange sketched *his* vision of the balance between economic management and social policy. In effect, it was a matter of separate spheres. On the one hand, 'in all the OECD countries it was plain by the late 1970s that a new approach to economic management was needed … Much of what has happened in economic management in the last three years can only be understood in terms of the removal of ineffective, distorting or damaging interventions.'[97] Lange had 'no problem with a programme of privatisation. In fact I believe that we should be quite honest and apparently ruthless about it and enhance the return to Government by selling control at a premium instead of the ostensibly populist process of selling to the broad spectrum and then letting them take their profit selling to the investor who is prepared to pay them for control.'[98] But on the other hand, he stressed his belief that the state must have a central role in social policy: 'I do not think that failings in the social services focussed dissatisfaction with the activities of government in the acute way that failings in economic management did', and defended the 1987 Labour Relations Act, with its limited liberalisation of the labour market.[99]

Treasury got caught in the Lange–Douglas crossfire, most seriously in the lead-up to the 1988 Budget. Douglas's recollection is that 'there was a lot of talk about Treasury making big mistakes. We'd done all this work, and we felt we were getting on top of the position, when all of a sudden we were faced with a deficit of $3.2 billion. Graham Scott gave me the papers on the plane and left me to it. But with hard work we'd got it down to $1.2 billion, which I wasn't worried about.'[100] Weeks later, however, Lange drew attention to the earlier shift in Treasury's forecast for the deficit from $1.8 to $3.2 billion. Should this have been dealt with by cutting expenditure or increasing revenue; and if the latter, should revenue have been increased through selling assets or raising taxes? The nub of Lange's intervention came when he stressed that while the government had had to restrain spending, 'we cannot find the money we need wholly on the spending side … There are some possible sources of additional non-tax revenue [and there is] tax. It would be irresponsible of me to speculate on the various options'.[101] But in the Budget, Douglas confirmed that tax reductions — a modified version of the December 1987 package — which had already been announced would proceed. Some new measures to limit tax avoidance were introduced, but the only tax increase, on tobacco, was expected to bring in a mere $110 million in a full year.[102]

If Lange did not get his way, neither did Douglas. Unable because of political constraints to pursue his social policy agenda, the Budget focused on the common ground of economic management — on financial management in the public sector, a new status for the Reserve Bank, and a swathe of privatisations, including of the Bank of New Zealand and Postbank.[103] As for Treasury itself, the 'scare' prompted Scott to initiate an internal enquiry into Treasury's work on the Budget. Following a reorganisation in 1985, responsibility for the Budget had been allocated to the Fiscal Affairs Branch and for macroeconomic policy to the Economic Affairs Branch. This separation of macroeconomic policy and forecasting from the Budget may have been intended to 'insulate' Budget-making from the temptation to use the kind of short-term fiscal measures that Muldoon had frequently resorted to, and about which Treasury had been so sceptical. Following the enquiry ordered by Scott, a Budget Management Branch was established to bring together 'those parts of the Treasury that are involved in the core work associated with the preparation of the Budget, and in providing the related economic policy and financial advice to the Minister of Finance'. Tax forecasting and modelling, macroeconomics, policy co-ordination and development, and the preparation of the Budget all came within its ambit.[104] The 'scare' of 1988 also prompted the appointment of Treasury's first communications official, Nikitin Sallee, who was recruited from the *National Business Review* and was to stay in the job until 1995.

If there was a point when the direction of 'core' economic management seemed likely to change, it came with the events that unfolded after Lange sacked Prebble in November 1988. Douglas resigned within a month, a climacteric which saw the political world 'a battlefield' above which 'political murder' was 'still hanging in the air'.[105] Some commentators predicted the 'death of Rogernomics'.[106] Graham Scott recalled that

> [the journalist] Richard Griffin had told me that the news from the ninth floor [the Prime Minister's office] was that I was to be sacked. I replied that 'if I get sacked it is by the State Services Commission, not by whoever you've been talking to on the ninth floor'. During that period I half expected to be got rid of. There were rumours flying around that that was going to happen.[107]

Scott was not sacked, but the sniping continued through the following months. The *Dominion* in particular campaigned against the 'extremist ideologues' of the newly 'orphaned' Treasury. It endorsed Opposition leader Jim Bolger's suggestion that the department be reined in through a partition: 'the Treasury should lose its role as macroeconomic advisor. A monopoly on such crucial advice is bad enough, but when it is held by the department which also holds the purse-strings, power is concentrated in too few hands. It is an added danger that a small group of ideologues are now running the monopoly.' Both the *Dominion* and Bolger advocated a division of the department along the lines of Fraser's 1976 split of the Australian Treasury (though this was not cited as a precedent), between economic advice, which would go to a new entity, and control over spending, which would stay with a Treasury which 'should in effect be retained in an accounting capacity only'.[108]

The criticism highlighted the continued adherence of the new government to the anti-inflation policy that had been pursued fairly consistently since 1984, despite the deepening recession. There were signs of an upturn in business confidence in September and October 1988, but these faded later in the year. At the end of November 156,000 people were registered as unemployed or in subsidised jobs, compared with 104,000 a year earlier and 87,000 the year before that. By March 1989 the number of full-time jobs was at its lowest level for fifteen years.[109] But both a tight monetary policy and fiscal balance — 'the deficit obsession', the *Dominion* called it — remained goals under the new Minister of Finance (Douglas's associate minister from 1984 to 1987), David Caygill. Asset sales continued, and GST was increased to recover the revenue foregone by the October 1988 personal income tax cuts (which did not entail a flat tax, but were still substantial). 'Caygill did something which always surprised me', Scott recalls. 'Without consulting the Treasury, as far as I know, he just announced, "We're going to have Rogernomics part II"; then, a little later, "We're going to have a 2 per cent inflation target". He did that on his own, as I recall it.'[110]

Yet the political environment *had* changed following Douglas's departure and the arrival of new ministers around the Cabinet table. One official remembers that 'you didn't have the situation where the Treasury minister says what he'll have, and it gets done. You had Cabinets trying to decide. Cullen's important. Clark's important. Caygill was a sort of compromiser.' Scott reported later in 1989 on comments senior Labour members made to officials when an Imprest Supply bill was going through the House: 'the only concern I have about the bill

The minister (David Caygill), the deficit and the deity. Garrick Tremain

is the perception held by some in government that the Treasury had got its figures wrong … the three instances were said in a joking manner and I hope were not criticisms of our work.'[111] And in March 1990, the Cabinet Office circulated proposed changes to the Cabinet Office Manual procedures for departmental submissions to Cabinet and Cabinet committees which appeared to circumvent the 'current policy of requiring a Treasury report on all proposals with economic and financial implications'. Treasury's memorandum to its minister pointed out that some of the problems had occurred because ministers by-passed requirements to consult, and added that although it had subsequently been told that the proposals did not imply an end to the current policy, it nevertheless wanted to 'advise you in the strongest possible terms that your ability to determine overall fiscal stance is threatened if a Treasury report is not mandatory for all spending proposals.'[112] The process of compiling the 1990 Budget tables, in which a financial surplus of $89 million was reached partly through a debatable allocation in the accounts of revenue from the sale of the Crown's commercial forests, did not help morale in Treasury.[113]

So how should we assess the impact of Labour's second term on economic management? Between late 1988 and 1990 the government went through many transmogrifications. In March 1989, Jim Anderton left the parliamentary party and set up New Labour. Lange resigned as Prime Minister in August 1989, a week after Labour's caucus invited Douglas to return to the Cabinet. Palmer became Prime Minister until — just six weeks before the election — he was dumped in favour of Mike Moore in a futile bid to prevent a heavy loss to National. But through three prime ministers and two ministers of finance, what we can call the '1988 compromise' held good. Caygill followed Lange rather than Douglas in stressing that he was not prepared to rely on the market to provide education or health.[114] Despite Treasury's efforts, social policy and labour market deregulation remained outside the ambit of economic management. But that aside, macro- and much microeconomic policy continued along the lines that had been mapped out since 1984.

We can draw two conclusions from this that are germane to the Treasury. Firstly, Treasury's advice-giving *role* survived. The professionalism of Treasury's officers, both as officials and as analysts, stood the department in good stead at this juncture. The parameters within which debates were conducted may not have been as broad as they had been in the 1970s, and

> subsequently you heard people saying, 'It's quite hard to put a contrary view.' And I think that was probably because the predominant view had *such* wide acceptance. I think the overriding thing was a feeling of … debate around the edges, but in terms of overall direction, you had a feeling of an organisation which hugely agreed with itself. But the debate was vigorous.[115]

The vigour was important, and the resulting reports were not tracts. Thus Treasury's detailed response to Douglas's tax/benefit proposals of September 1987 reiterated the objectives (improving incentives to work, earn and invest, and simplifying the tax system, which 'we strongly support'), constraints (the need for the proposals to be fiscally neutral, to safeguard — or at least not significantly worsen — the income position of low-income earners and recipients of benefits) and other desirable attributes (transparency, reduction of distortions, fairness and consistency) of any tax/benefit reform proposal. It then went on to argue that the original proposal met some but not all of these standards — notably, it was probably not fiscally neutral (that is, it would lose the government more revenue than it gained); the proposed increase in GST threatened the anti-inflation policy and blurred the net effect of the package; and effective marginal tax rates for low-income earners would remain high.[116] And the road to this careful position had been marked by intensive debate within Treasury itself about equity/efficiency trade-offs — [there was] a lot of debate about the gains you [would] get in terms of work incentives and investment incentives and what difference that would make. Some people argued quite strongly that this was going to be positive, others were concerned about equity trade-offs.[117]

In seeking independent advice on the tax/benefit proposals in January 1988, Lange implicitly questioned the objectivity of the Treasury, but this was apparently the only occasion he did so during the increasingly bitter exchanges between the two formerly close colleagues. And there seems also to have been only one occasion when Lange's team criticised the quality of Treasury's work — in relation to its failure to notice that the part-time earner rebate would cost $120 million. 'Your advisors', replied Douglas, 'have apparently emphasised [the omission] as evidence of the Treasury incompetence the Labour Party is so keen to discover'.[118]

The journalist Richard Harman said of Lange's decision to 'go public' over the forecasting issue in 1988 that it 'could only raise questions about the political future of Roger Douglas, and the political credibility of Treasury which has been linked so closely to Rogernomics'. But even at that time, Lange's reply was at least formally protective:

> REPORTER: Can I put it to you that if a manager in a private enterprise made an error in his forecasting of that scale, he'd either be down the road or in receivership so quickly you wouldn't be able to see him. Why shouldn't that apply to Mr Scott at the Treasury?
> LANGE: Oh no, that is unfair to him because you see there was an inherent difficulty. If you have your estimates being prepared at a time when you haven't even got your tax flow data, it's not surprising that you get problems.[119]

As the political commentator John Roberts wrote in 1987, 'Treasury's dominant position is not evidence of a covert bid for power by unscrupulous bureaucrats. Each step in the chain … has been an instance of deliberate political choice. Treasury is at the centre of the process because it suits politicians that it should be.'[120] Lange himself was to say later that he didn't 'blame Treasury … I have more respect for Treasury than I have for the Labour Party, in the sense that they were a consistent, cohesive … group of people that exercised strength and muscle and an all-pervasive right to go to the Prime Minister to achieve their end'.[121]

One clue to the consistency of the government's response to Treasury's advice lay in the political economy. Just as before the Depression, financial interests shaped political outcomes. In the decades between these two eras, the government's management of monetary conditions had reduced the power of these interests within New Zealand. Treasury had argued for the liberalisation of financial markets on efficiency grounds — that resources would be better used — but liberalisation also conferred power on the participants in those markets to shape the environment within which the government made monetary and fiscal policy. That this was always the case internationally had been painfully emphasised in 1939, during the oil crises, and with the downgrading of New Zealand's credit rating by an international lending agency in 1983. Now it was also true domestically:

> The shock to the economy from the stock market crash worsened a fiscal situation that was still weak, notwithstanding the improvements that had been made from 1984 to 1987. From then on, any bad news in fiscal policy, as on several occasions, was quickly translated into rises in interest rates, and the exchange rate, thus tending to slow down the economy. This was caused by the imbalance between fiscal and monetary policy made apparent because of the growing credibility of the newly independent central bank and the deregulated financial markets.[122]

In the early stages of the spat about Treasury forecasts in June 1988, a Treasury official attached to the New Zealand High Commission in London asked what he should tell financial interests in the City. When Prebble was dismissed from Cabinet on 4 November, the dollar dropped by nearly a cent against the US dollar.[123] Domestic investors too wanted tight monetary and fiscal policies, even if the short-term effects — high interest rates, unemployment — were unpalatable: 'Mr Caygill has likened the deficit to a black frost blighting the landscape … [he] assumes that once business has confidence in the Government's direction, and knows that a lower deficit will bring lower interest rates, it will invest and the economy will grow.'[124] And Caygill stuck with the Reserve Bank Bill that Douglas had introduced, shepherding it through the House in 1989. Thus were two legs of the economic constitution tripod of the 1930s — the balanced Budget and the gold standard — firmly clamped on. The liberalisation of the financial markets was thus a much more profound change in the structure of the political economy than it may have appeared to be at first sight. As one economist put it, commenting in this instance on the floating of the dollar, 'the most significant effect of Roger Douglas' policies is not their medium-term impact on the exchange rate; rather, it is the institutional changes he has made that will make it very difficult for any future governments to reverse his policies.'[125]

The arguments for giving investors this power might have centred on the gains in efficiency that would result, but the power was there irrespective of whether or not the outcomes were efficient. When Douglas returned to Cabinet (albeit for only a few months until Palmer removed all the ministers who were intending to leave Parliament at the next election), the durability of the '1988 compromise' was underlined yet again. But that also meant that Treasury's rounded vision of economic management — which, in seeking fiscal balance and efficient outcomes necessarily addressed the social area — remained off-limits. So did reform of the labour market. Indeed, with respect to the latter, both the compact and the growth agreement that were negotiated with the Combined Trade Unions (CTU) in December 1989 and October 1990 respectively attempted to realise a version of the accord which had governed relations between the labour movement and the Labor government in Australia since 1983. The compact, recalls one of those involved in the negotiations,

> was a relatively sophisticated agreement — wage increases were to be tamed to 2 per cent, and everything else had to be explicitly backed by productivity gains. The Reserve Bank wasn't formally a party to the agreement, but there was a tacit understanding that they would ease monetary policy to create some employment impetus. And the government would engage the unions on industry policy and social policy in the budgetary process.[126]

But the government had no time to implement the compact before it was swept out of office by an electoral landslide to National. As for Treasury, some of its agenda remained unfinished, so the conversion of economic management into an economic constitution had some way to go.

1990 to 1993

The Labour vote fell by more than a quarter, from 878,000 to 641,000, in the election of October 1990. While some of the lost voters went to the New Labour Party or the Greens, National's vote increased from 806,000 to 872,000 — 48 per cent of the total. Would the new government introduce or permit an economic management regime that would address what Treasury saw as the oversights of the preceding years? Throughout its six years in opposition National had continually been outflanked by Labour on policy issues, with many of National's MPs supporting the general thrust of the reforms but some, most notably former Prime Minister Muldoon, opposing them from the back benches. For Ruth Richardson, who became the party's finance spokesperson after the 1987 election defeat, 'we were at the height of our silliness when we were defeated in 1984, [and] between 1984 and 1987, it was as if we had learned nothing.'[127] Richardson's oft-voiced stance was that the new direction needed to be completed in three main areas — the labour market, fiscal balance and social policy.

But Richardson was not the National Party. In some ways she was an uncomfortable presence in a party dominated by a male leadership and habituated to pragmatic approaches to policy. While by 1990 her views were closer to those of National than Douglas's were to those of many in the Labour Party in 1984, the alignment was not complete. It was closest over the need to reform the labour market, not least because of lobbying by the Employers' Federation, which had 'concentrated on persuading National to adopt its industrial relations reform agenda — a campaign in which it has been extremely successful. National is now committed to a policy of radically decentralising the labour market.'[128]

Treasury could therefore assume that change would occur in that sphere and it did — very rapidly — under the aegis not so much of Richardson as of Labour Minister Bill Birch, who recalls that 'we finally got to the point of going back to first principles and writing just a simple, small piece of legislation, which was excellent. Ruth played the role of the critic, [and] we had some quite interesting debates — she would not have had any legislation, [but] that was going a little bit too far.'[129]

Whether National would go down the path of seeking fiscal balance and redesigning social policy was more problematic. That National's election victory was more a punishment of Labour than an endorsement of National suggested that the electorate was sceptical about much of the content, and even more the speed and some of the consequences, of the reforms, rather than calling for more. Treasury sought 'fiscal consolidation', as it was now termed. Although there had been a financial surplus of $89 million in the 1990 Budget, Treasury's accompanying three-year forecasts showed expected financial deficits of $2.2 billion in 1991/92 and $1.6 billion in 1992/93.[130]

But, as in 1984, circumstances provided opportunities. By the eve of the 1990 election, new Treasury calculations showed a substantial deficit for 1990/

91, to which would have to be added the uncertain cost of bailing out the Bank of New Zealand (see chapter 9), and even more substantial deficits for the 'out' years. Bolger was briefed by sombre Treasury officials in Wellington on the evening of the day after the election:

> Graham normally wouldn't have seen the Prime Minister-elect until the Monday, but he had to see him that night. He went in his babysitter's boyfriend's orange and black Holden ute, and parked it in an obscure part of Parliament grounds. He had to wait until some suitable time to get into the building, then he found Bolger and said to him something like, 'Congratulations on your election. By the way, the BNZ's gone under'.[131]

To which had to be added the news of the unforeseen fiscal blowout:

> Before the election, no one, it seems, knew about the fiscal crisis. Not even Treasury! In the background papers to David Caygill's last budget, Treasury estimated that the financial deficit in 1992/93 wasn't going to be $4.5 billion as they told the new government only three months later, but was only going to be a manageable $1.6b … Indeed … Treasury concluded, 'these projections show the Government continuing to progress towards its fiscal objectives', requiring only 'consolidation to achieve its medium-term targets'. Thus, sometime in the three months between July … and October 1990, Treasury 'discovered' the fiscal crisis.[132]

Dalziel's quotation marks around 'discovered' were significant. Early in 1990, Treasury had decided that fiscal consolidation and labour market reform would be two principal themes of its post-election briefing. But it was difficult to make a strong case for the former on the Budget night figures. The 1991/92 deficit was now expected to be greater than had been predicted in 1989, but while revenue was expected to fall as a percentage of GDP, so was expenditure, and overall 'the projections show a fiscal position that compares very favourably with those of the last two decades'.[133] After the election, Treasury explained to its new minister that since then,

> the largest increases have been in the projections for social welfare and debt servicing. Social welfare spending has increased as a result of changes in assumptions about beneficiary numbers and new policies (such as the GRI [Guaranteed Retirement Income, the new name for national superannuation] living alone allowance) decided too late for inclusion in budget night

projections. Debt servicing costs are higher as a result of adverse revisions to interest- and exchange-rate projections and the need to finance higher Table 2 deficits. Forecast tax revenues are around $130m lower … primarily because of downwards revisions of projected economic growth.[134]

While the recession contributed to the fiscal woes, there were also political factors. Treasury officials gathering information from departments discovered that spending decisions taken by the Cabinet since the Budget had been incorporated in the baselines for departmental allocations, which would mean higher aggregate spending in both the current and future years.[135] When Bolger saw the revised figures for 1991/92, he exclaimed:

> 'How did you let this fiscal policy get out of control?' 'How did you let this happen?' At the meeting he had this sheaf of Cabinet papers in front of him, and he turned to me and asked, 'What are these code numbers besides all these expenditure items [that had happened since the Budget]?' He had assumed, wrongly, that somehow the huge fiscal deterioration that had taken place was caught up somehow with Treasury not accounting for it or not advising the government against it. He was really surprised to learn that all these reference numbers alongside all of these expenditure items … were actually Cabinet paper references to government decisions to do each of them.[136]

Treasury, for its part, had sharpened its post-election briefing. The introduction, completed just 30 minutes before the polls closed, highlighted the fiscal crisis: 'with no change from current policy it is estimated that the Government will confront financial deficits of $3.7b, $4.5b and $5.2b over the next three years. The consequences of not correcting this situation could be very serious indeed.'[137]

Bolger was sufficiently frustrated to ask the Treasury to explain 'why the economy has not performed more impressively in recent years, despite the magnitude of the policy reforms undertaken'. This must have been a depressing task for Scott, who had been Secretary to the Treasury for the last four of those years, and arguably the department's most influential official for the two years before that. In his report, Scott conceded that 'the adjustment has taken longer and involved higher costs in terms of unemployment than many would have hoped … some [of these costs] must be attributed to problems in the policy balance mix and the reduction in policy consistency that occurred during the later parts of the period.'[138]

Richardson was receptive to this message, and not only on fiscal grounds — she also wanted to 'redesign' the welfare state:

> She saw an economy in crisis and wanted a strategic solution. She was really the only genuinely ideological Minister of Finance I worked for. She believed in small government, in deregulated labour markets, from an ideological perspective, not just from a technical one. She believed people should take more personal responsibility for themselves, that the welfare state had undermined people's self-reliance, and so on. She was against business subsidies and middle-class welfare generally.[139]

With the Minister of Social Welfare, Jenny Shipley, on her side, and Bolger resigned to expenditure cuts for fiscal reasons, Richardson had the momentum to proceed. In the December 1990 'Economic and Social Initiative' — the conjunction of the two words a fundamental challenge to Labour's separation of them — Bolger, Richardson and Birch, who was both Minister for State Services and Minister of Labour, announced a redesign of the welfare state, the review of all spending that had not been included in the Budget estimates, cuts in benefits, and the deregulation of the labour market.[140]

Some of this process will be discussed in chapter 9, which addresses the restructuring of the state sector. Fiscal consolidation was to be a rocky road — more like a catastrophe in fact, partly because the recession was deepening, but at a more mundane level, because of the intense pressure placed on officials during the preparations for Richardson's 'mother of all Budgets'. In February 1991, the Cabinet Strategy Committee requested a paper on fiscal risk which included a fascinating annex on the accuracy of tax forecasts over the preceding seventeen years: 'considerable variations between year[s] are observed … for each year significant and variable forecast errors occurred in the components of the forecasts, particularly in the other persons and company categories'.[141]

As the recession deepened in 1991, the figures got worse. Graham Wheeler, who was responsible for forecasting, had the toughest time. 'Every now and then', recalled another Treasury official, 'he would have anxiety attacks — that they had got something wrong … We would have a bit of a methodological discussion and debate and review about it.' After one inaccurate forecast, Bolger once again mused aloud about the merits of dividing the Treasury.[142] For Richardson,

> it was a lazy political argument that said, 'We find this rigour too hard to handle. We think we're pushed too hard by Treasury, so we're going to cut

them down to size — divide and rule.' For me it was a resigning issue. And you only played that card once — you don't play it unless you really mean it. I said to Bolger, 'I am not going to fly on one wing.'[143]

Treasury was uncertain about the extent to which it had the backing of its minister. Scott explained to senior managers that Richardson had 'asked to come [to the Treasury] after the Prime Minister had attacked the department and she expressed concern about our morale. I said that … Treasury staff are adults and all they know so far is that the Prime Minister attacked the department and she didn't defend it.'[144] A few weeks later, Treasury had to explain that 'overall, the positive effect of the savings announced in the December initiative and subsequent efforts by the Expenditure Control Committee have been almost off-set by a forecast deterioration in economic prospects and erosion of the tax base'.[145]

Treasury may have wondered whether it mattered that its 1990 post-election briefing to the government had been presented in a more modest form than in 1987 — and without a title. The department came under further attack over the refurbishing of the Secretary's office and the remuneration package it was offering its staff. After explaining — and defending — this offer at length, Scott informed the Finance and Expenditure Select Committee that 'owing to the subsequent media misrepresentation of the facts, he considered that proceeding with the salary package would have a negative impact on the Government's objectives, particularly the preparation of the budget. As he felt he had an overriding obligation to the Government rather than to his staff, he decided to withdraw the remuneration package. A new … package had been offered to professional staff which represents an average 3% reduction in remuneration.' He added that 'the perception was that at a time when the Treasury was urging public spending restraint it was inappropriate for [it] to [be] seen to be making these increases.'[146]

Treasury became the least favourite institution not just of superannuitants and other beneficiaries, but of many new members of National's caucus. Muldoon had turned down a ministerial position outside Cabinet and remained on the back benches, from which vantage point he attacked the government's policies both inside and outside Parliament. Other back-benchers, including 'Cam' Campion, Michael Laws, Hamish McIntyre and Gilbert Myles, were equally critical, whilst within Cabinet Wyatt Creech and Winston Peters were both sharply at odds with Richardson's approach.[147] Seven years later, Laws's vituperative judgement was that

> Treasury were a hypocritical and callous bunch who could not have forecast the conclusion to a Mills and Boon novel. At the same time as they were pushing for expenditure cuts and yet more social slashing, they gifted themselves a backdated salary increase and spent hundreds of thousands [sic] of dollars refurbishing their chief executive's quarters.[148]

Scott later described 1990/91 as 'a nail-biting period, and probably my unhappiest time in the Treasury'.[149] This was partly because of the politicians, but even more because of the recession. One Treasury manager recalls that Scott and Howard Fancy (the head of the Budget Management Branch) 'were deeply affected by the way the economy performed at this time. They would come to meetings and you could see there was a huge physical and emotional toll.'[150] Behind Fancy's March 1991 forecasts, Scott saw 'a picture of human distress in New Zealand which frankly frightens me. As support systems are pulled away from people they are becoming frightened. They are feeling helpless. There are people in business who are ... stressed to the point of not being sure of what to do next.'[151]

Economists debated the extent to which the government should loosen its fiscal policy to reduce the rise in unemployment. This was a classic debate between those who favoured boosting demand when the economy was at the bottom of a cycle, and those who argued that the underlying need was for a more adaptable labour market and a sharply reduced fiscal deficit — in other words, that the problem was structural rather than cyclical. Broadly speaking, economists of a Keynesian persuasion favoured the former explanation, and those of a neoliberal persuasion the latter.[152] Thus in 1992, the CTU's economist Peter Harris argued that 'by cutting incomes, you are reducing spending power in the domestic economy and so you are creating a domestic recession which is off-setting any benefit that might be there on the export front.'[153] In a lecture on the April 1991 benefit cuts, the economist Paul Dalziel contended that 'the monetarist experiment has simply resulted in permanently higher unemployment and a never ending cycle of fiscal cutbacks'.[154] In a substantial commentary which appeared in the *Listener* in July 1991, Dalziel, Easton and another economist, John Lepper, all argued that if the government insisted on slashing its deficit, 'demand will decline further, there will be more people on the dole, and fewer paying taxes'. 'The government should not', said Easton, 'expect to close the budget deficit at the bottom of the business cycle.' If there was proof that the structural deficit was too large, a variety of fiscal measures could be taken — but only once it had been shown how much of the deficit was structural and how much cyclical.[155]

Henry Lang wrote to Bolger in May 1991, on the eve of Richardson's first Budget, that 'in November/December the economy was clearly on a downward path. Thus it could be expected that the December measures insofar as they affected 1990–91 would reduce demand and confidence even further and make things worse. This is exactly what happened … a further downward thrust from fiscal policy is not in New Zealand's best interests … a significant deficit in 1991–92 would in my view be tolerable'.[156] Fifteen members of the University of Auckland's Economics Department wrote to the *New Zealand Herald* condemning the 'overriding priority' that was being given to reducing the Budget deficit.[157] The economist Simon Chapple argued that 'a critical factor behind rises in over-kill unemployment was the contraction in aggregate demand engineered to reduce New Zealand's inflation rate from about 18% in the mid 1980s to almost zero by 1992. Dis-inflation, resulting high real interest and exchange rates, and contractionary fiscal policies meant that aggregate demand did not expand sufficiently rapidly.'[158]

But for Scott, who reckoned that 'in macro management we can only see a few feet in front of our faces', it was necessary 'to start off on adjustment paths which look to us to be the most reliable ones'.[159] Looking back a decade later, he observed that

> we had [an] 11 per cent unemployment rate or something [like that] by then. We were obviously in very serious trouble — it was clear that the labour market was not equilibrating. And it was clear to me, although obviously not to a lot of other academic economists and others, that this was not a Keynesian problem. This unemployment wasn't coming about just because of fiscal or monetary policy — it didn't look like a cyclical problem.[160]

Revenue for 1990/91, which had been estimated at $27.181 billion in the 1990 Budget, came in $1.5 billion lower at $25.675 billion. The financial deficit for 1991/92 was 50 per cent greater than Treasury had forecast at the time of the 1991 Budget — closer indeed to its anxious forecast of October 1990 — despite all the efforts to cut expenditure.[161] When an economic upswing got under way late in 1991, explanations differed. While a commentator like Easton could believe that 'the extra expenditure injections from the government [in 1991/92] were surely a major factor in the beginning of the upswing', as was the depreciation of the exchange rate in 1991, Roger Kerr reckoned that the expansion had been sparked by

Looking for the upturn. Bob Brockie, *National Business Review*

the measures taken to reduce the deficit, and by the liberalisation of the labour market following the passage of the Employment Contracts Act in 1991.[162]

As between 1988 and 1990, the international and domestic financial markets played a crucial role in shaping the environment within which the new government responded to the unexpectedly severe economic downturn. While others counselled against making massive expenditure cuts to reduce the deficit, the markets were an important influence: 'The credit downgrade by Standards and Poor early in 1991 … brought home very clearly … the rising concerns that rating agencies and creditors were having about the growth in public and external debt'; and raising taxes 'would generate fewer gains in terms of fiscal credibility'.[163] As one scholar said during an exchange with another about the strategy, 'private sector reactions now are much more important than they were in the 1930s to 1970s'.[164]

Thus the political economy shaped the content of economic management, whilst Treasury's professional style — and temperament — shaped the advice-giving process: 'crisis management can get the adrenalin going as much as success.'[165] Even so, the expectations placed on Treasury in 1990/91 were daunting. For instance, in the six weeks leading up to the 17 December announcements, officials prepared 39 substantial 'Budget' reports that fed into them. Nor was this a matter of presenting only what the government wanted to hear. A report of early December was blunt in stating that

Economic management or social engineering? Roger Kerr of the New Zealand Business Roundtable, Graham Scott and Ruth Richardson pull the levers. Neil Bond cartoon, *Sunday Star*, 1 December 1991

the proposed distribution of benefit rates produces a very uneven pattern of effective income support. Some rates, such as GRI, provide an equivalentised level of income support that is above the highest of [the] poverty line indicators. At the other extreme, the single adult rate of sickness or unemployment benefit provides an equivalentised level that is below the lowest of these poverty line indicators ... the overall impression created by the new rate structure is that it is less equitable than the present structure and that it runs the serious risk of creating pockets of serious hardship amongst certain groups.[166]

This comment traversed the two main points of disagreement between Treasury and the government: the comparative treatment of different benefits, including the GRI; and the absolute scale of the cuts. Early in the Budget round Treasury had argued for a reduction in benefit rates of 5 per cent in real terms, and that GRI rates should 'be allowed to fall by more than this in order to close the gap between the two sets of rates'. Just two days before the announcement of the new initiatives, Howard Fancy reiterated that 'the GRI changes are particularly important in signalling our commitment to both expenditure reduction and to our longer-term intention to target social assistance to those most in need.'[167] This meant that 'if you wanted the dollars, you had to get them from half of the spending that you would otherwise have had'. Even after receiving a paper from Richardson and Shipley, Cabinet was not prepared to reduce GRI entitlements. But it then got itself into even hotter water with its older supporters by first breaching an election promise to lift a surcharge on the income of superannuitants that had been imposed by Douglas in 1984, and then imposing income testing on superannuation.[168] That the Budget night announcements were followed within three months by a retreat from the severe regime announced then compounded a less than edifying demonstration of policy-making.

Treasury analysts were divided over the benefit cuts. One 'bold' proposal put up at an early meeting with Richardson was to hold benefits in nominal terms for two years — which would be a real cut over that time. Later proposals for actual cuts opened up further debate. One official argued that the replacement rates (the proportion of income from employment that a benefit replaced) were already only about 50 per cent for some beneficiaries, which suggested that the financial incentive for beneficiaries to reject job opportunities was not strong.[169]

In a 1996 survey, ministers and officials alike singled out Treasury as a department that was not frightened to challenge received wisdom or well-entrenched views.[170] If Treasury could tussle with Richardson, it could certainly disagree with Bolger. But even the Prime Minister, who, like Lange, was not always in sympathy with Treasury advice, respected its analytical capability. Treasury for its part, conscious of the political and public focus on forecasting — particularly when forecasts changed sharply — put further effort into this sphere. The policy and forecasting team in the Budget Management Branch had tended to focus on only one of these spheres at a time. Now two distinct sections were created.

When, in the lead-up to the 1991 Budget, Treasury put together a strategy paper which looked beyond macroeconomics and 'micro' reform at 'presentation, leadership and setting realistic objectives', Bolger, who had just criticised Treasury publicly, was happy for the department to draw up an implementation plan, since his ministers were badly overloaded. Scott pointed out to Treasury managers that

> we should be very careful in the way that all of this appears. I have enough trouble, and all of you do too, with the criticisms that the Treasury is capturing the Government and one thing or another. It is simply a routine piece of public administration that I think has been badly lacking.[171]

Making a Difference. *She did.*

This project was overwhelmed by pressure of work in 1991, but Richardson asked Treasury to return to it in 1992. The resulting document, entitled *Economic Strategy*, was important for its advocacy of longer-term 'ownership' by the government of the Treasury's favoured parameters of economic management, its stress on 'stable and balanced macroeconomic strategies', and, on the micro side, on strong international linkages (partly through greater competitiveness), a more productive labour force, and the achievement of a competitive and entrepreneurial economy. Graham Scott remembered this exercise with 'a lot of pleasure'.[172]

Alongside strategy, Richardson sought fiscal certainty. In the 1993 Budget she announced

> an initiative for honest and open Government. This initiative will ensure that no Government can fool the people of New Zealand as to the true state of the nation's accounts the way the last Government did … In 1991 the Chief Ombudsman expressed strong concerns that the previous Government withheld information prior to the 1990 election … the Government has

decided that prior to each General Election there will be a public release of an economic and fiscal outlook [and] the requirement to continue this practice in the future will be built into legislation.[173]

As these comments suggested, this legislation was partly precipitated by the shock for National of finding out about the BNZ's near-collapse in 1990: 'the revelations of the losses when we came into government were quite central to the Act. It was [very much] about non-disclosure of quite fundamental information. Transparency means an early revelation of information so you don't get the big surprises.'[174]

Treasury was sympathetic, seeing the measure as complementing in the area of fiscal policy what the 1989 Reserve Bank Act had accomplished for monetary policy — a distancing of policy-making from politics. But it was also hesitant, because it seemed much harder to take fiscal than monetary policy out of politics:

> One route it could have taken was legislated limits … [That] was thought of and fairly quickly rejected. We didn't think legislative targets would hold anyway, and we were very sensitive about constitutional propriety, about any suggestion of trying to bind the government or Parliament.[175]

So 'it was more my idea than theirs', Richardson recalled, but

> having said that, I couldn't have bought that idea to fruition without their advice on how the concept might be captured. I argued for the idea because I just knew that the moment I absented myself — which was going to happen sooner or later — and was succeeded by somebody who wasn't as fiscally rigorous or focused as I was, there would just be a reversion to bad habits. And so, having pushed a lot, the Treasury helped me come up with the goods.[176]

The Fiscal Responsibility Act was introduced but not passed before the 1993 election. Graham Scott had finished his term as Secretary six months earlier. And by the time the 1993 Budget was presented, the evidence that the economy was growing was palpable, even if the strength of the expansion was still in question and unemployment was falling only slowly.[177] The conjunction of these events provides a fitting conclusion to this chapter. Via a circuitous route, Treasury had now secured most of the agenda that it had laid out in *Economic Management* in 1984. And this agenda was close to being embedded in a new 'economic constitution', with the Reserve Bank Act in place, the Fiscal Responsibility Act foreshadowed, and the government having signed up to Treasury's *Economic Strategy*, with its strong focus on the liberalisation and deregulation of microeconomic policies. For John Bradbury, who was Britain's Secretary to the Treasury from 1913 to 1919, the great merit of the gold standard was that it was 'knave-proof'. Douglas and Scott had wished to 'Muldoon-proof' monetary policy through the Reserve Bank Act; and the combination of the two acts with the economic strategy now seemed the way by which economic management in New Zealand was to be 'politics-proofed'.

But could this be done? The 1993 election was to see National's vote collapse almost as catastrophically (from 872,000 to 674,000) as Labour's had in 1990; and the electorate voted for a new proportional electoral system. This suggested that for all — or even because of all — the transformations of the preceding nine years, economic management was still embedded in the ebbs and flows of politics.

Chapter 9

Managing government, 1984–1993

Introduction

This book has explored the two principal strands of Treasury activity in the twentieth century. The first is the *financial* management of government, the important Treasury role in which dates back to the 1910s and 1920s. The second is *economic* management, in which Treasury has taken a leading role since the 1960s. Economic management initially embraced an expansive role for government, with the fiscal conservatism and preoccupation with business methods and efficiency that coloured financial management relegated to secondary importance. But the 1970s and early 1980s saw a shift to different — and more modest — notions of economic management. In such circumstances it was not surprising that 'financial management', as the term had been understood before the Depression, now returned. This involved finance itself: 'I am interested in getting back to the old money-bags role, what Treasury did in the nineteenth century — the core of the finance ministry is its old functions', said Treasury Secretary Graham Scott in the wake of the 1987 election. 'That's our knitting. I want to get on with the job of completely redeveloping how we do that knitting.'[1] And, as that statement implied, it also involved institutions: 'it is only sensible to organise economic and social activities in the form of a government department, state owned enterprise, education or health board, or whatever, if the particular form of organisation chosen enables these activities to be provided more cheaply, more effectively, or more equitably, in aggregate, than would provision through the market'.[2] So the Treasury's 1987 post-election briefing papers, which concentrated on the public sector and social policy, were published under the title *Government Management* — at the core of which was financial management and efficiency.

Commentators on these developments have stressed the departure from the dominant ways of thinking about public finance and the organisation of government since the Depression. A critical writer surveying the changes that flowed from *Government Management* saw it as being about 'commercialisation'.[3] For another, 'the constant focus on "management" rather than the older term, administration', was equally evident. '"Management" is now applied in many and varied forms.' For John Perham, the first chief executive of the National Provident Fund to be drawn from the private sector, the Fund he joined was getting 'administrative-type treatment rather than management-type treatment.'[4]

For the Treasury officials involved, the most important part of *Government Management* was its theoretical framework: 'the briefing this year is a large and complex set of papers which amount to an integrated statement of Treasury views. Though there are policy proposals included in the brief, the papers mostly provide an analytical framework against which to assess policy proposals.'[5] Some of the roots of the thinking about principals and agents, contracting, and theories of public choice which informed much of the discussion in *Government Management* were discussed in a 1989 paper by Scott and his colleague Peter Gorringe which also considered how private-sector practices could usefully inform the operations of government institutions.[6] From this perspective, the changes of the 1980s sprang from the renewed attention that had been paid to microeconomics since the 1970s.

The frequent references to theory suggest who it was who *drove* the changes. In the 1920s, businessmen and politicians had energised officials; in the 1980s, it was the officials — and economists — who energised their 'masters'. It was natural for those professionals to credit the changes to intellectual developments in economics. It was less likely that they would focus on the parallels between them and approaches to government that had been taken two generations earlier. Graham Scott commented on one occasion that 'while a theoretical perspective assisted in the development of new approaches it was scarcely necessary in order to observe the problems of traditional approaches'.[7] But as Scott's 'new' and 'traditional' in that sentence suggests, there was little awareness that the 'new' was in fact the old reborn. Scott's 'traditional' was not as old as his 'new' — which, indeed, had never disappeared. The leaning to fiscal conservatism and faith in limited government that flourished in the 1920s can be followed from that decade to the 1980s — albeit sometimes expressed in muted tones — through the rhetoric of figures such as Sid Holland and Jack Marshall. Treasury's drive to exercise financial control and management in the 1980s was fuelled — just as it had been in the 1920s — by a combination of political support for overcoming a fiscal crisis and the department's own commitment to act.

Treasury's systematic and thorough prosecution of the reform of government owed most to Graham Scott's drive and determination, and to the individuals who worked with him on it. Scott in this respect can be compared to Ashwin in the 1940s — a Secretary who was 'entrepreneurial' both in what he set out to do and in the style of his accomplishment of it. Given this bent, it was appropriate that Scott's goal (unlike Ashwin's) was to bring some of the strengths of private-sector management into the public sector.

It was Scott who gave *Government Management* its title. 'After reading the draft chapters he came back and said, "You know what this book really is, it is about government management."'[8] His approach and enthusiasms are important to understanding Treasury's reinvigorated focus on government management and public finance. Unlike most economists of his generation, he had also qualified as an accountant. And his interest in issues of management and institutions, as well as of economic policy, had even longer antecedents:

> My father was the manager of the Christchurch *Star* — he had gone from New Plymouth to turn around a bankrupt newspaper company owned by the Leys family and others. It had an effect on me. One of the reasons I got interested in management later in my career was that he was a wonderful manager himself, self-taught. So in addition to being an economist I had this interest in management, which I guess came from him.[9]

Scott took this belief that management made a difference into the public service. Murray Horn, his close associate and successor as Secretary to the Treasury, considers that Scott 'focused on managing what government did properly and professionally. There was a deep irony in that. Graham was a fan of small government because he believed so much in government. If it did things it shouldn't do, that cast doubt on the things it should be doing, on its legitimacy.'[10]

One American scholar called *Government Management* 'extraordinary', while a British academic described it as the 'manifesto' of the new public management.[11] As the latter comment suggests, New Zealand was not alone in taking a hard look at government administration. In the 1980s analogous reforms took place in many parts of Asia, in the United States, and in a variety of other countries.[12] New Zealand's 'benchmarks' — Australia, Canada and the United Kingdom — all experienced a focus on reform of the core public sector which concentrated on the quality of management and the need to give managers greater responsibility. When a Progressive Conservative government won power in Canada in 1984, Prime Minister Brian Mulroney saw 'productive management' as a top priority: 'Let managers manage'.[13] In *Government By the Market*, Peter Self notes common elements in the private-sector concepts of efficient management that were adopted in Britain, New Zealand, Australia, Canada and the United States. These included comprehensive accounting systems, performance contracts, economic incentives and decentralised management.[14]

Britain's 1988 'Next Steps' initiative, which had been devised over the preceding two years, shared the devolutionary impulse of New Zealand's State Sector Act of the same year. It argued that 'radical change in the freedom to manage is needed urgently if substantially better results are to be achieved'. The change transferred elements of the British civil service concerned with service delivery to hived-off agencies, each of which would have a chief executive, a contractual relationship with its parent department, and a plan detailing its powers and obligations. By the end of 1992 half of the civil service were employed in such agencies.[15]

An Australian commentator noted in 1994 that 'changes … during recent decades amount to nothing less than the fundamental restructuring of the very form of the welfare state', and observed later in the same discussion that 'the revival of the classic obsession with a work orientation is an international phenomenon … economic adjustment occurring in most OECD countries involved a concerted effort in the late 1980s and early 1990s "to ensure that social security systems do not unduly weaken the incentives to work, to save and to change jobs"'.[16]

But although the trends are comparable, the details are not. In Canada in the 1980s, while 'a few crown corporations' paid dividends to the government, all received budgetary funding.[17] Britain had worked to set sound pricing and investment criteria for state-owned enterprises since the early 1960s, well before any comparable New Zealand initiatives. But a 1976 report found that these rules 'had been largely ignored or violated … governments have repeatedly intervened in the day to day business of the industries, either in the furtherance of macro-economic policy or demand management or to protect politically powerful groups of employees, customers or suppliers against market forces.'[18] It was perhaps for these reasons that in both Britain and Canada (from the election of Conservative governments in 1979 and 1984 respectively) the drive was towards privatisation rather than the devising of new regimes for state enterprises.[19]

In Australia, reforms introduced by administrative direction rather than legislation were 'continually amended and extended as additional possibilities or new topics of concern emerged'. This was in sharp contrast to the situation in New Zealand, where a large number of changes were introduced simultaneously by the Public Finance Act 1989. Accrual accounting, which was applied at that time to the New Zealand public accounts, came to Australia in the late 1990s.[20] There was a difference between the more co-ordinative or 'big business' framework of the British reforms and the more purely competitive 'public choice' model of the New Zealand ones. And while Next Steps may have had parallels with the State Sector Act, it was introduced in the face of British Treasury scepticism, not with the Secretary to the Treasury driving it, as in New Zealand.[21]

State-owned enterprises

There are five Treasury 'stories within the story' of the reform of public finance and government in the 1980s and early 1990s. The first in time, the corporatisation of many government trading activities, was followed by the selling — 'privatisation' — of government assets, the first major announcement about which was made in the 1988 Budget. The other three, which proceeded more or less in parallel, were the reforms of the core public sector, of the management of Treasury itself, and of the social services provided by the state. Broadly, from Treasury's point of view, the first and second involved divesting the government of tasks it should not engage in (either directly or at all), and the third and fourth making it do what it did better, while the fifth sat between the two pairs. All required the application of elements of the corporate model, which therefore provides an explanatory framework.

The corporatisation of state trading activities was a massive exercise which cannot be fully analysed within one section of one chapter. Two aspects merit focus in a history of the Treasury. The first is the fiscal and institutional recasting involved, the second the impact on the Treasury itself. The parallels with the 1920s are particularly marked. In both decades Treasury sought both fiscal gains and to enhance its leverage within the government system by subjecting development or trading departments and activities to private-sector disciplines which included streamlined corporate structures, the preparation of commercial balance sheets, and the payment of interest on capital. And in both eras, identical or similar agencies were 'reformed': the Post Office, the Works and Lands departments, and the Railways. In the 1980s, other agencies which had come into being or significance since the 1920s — 'Think Big' entities, the Forest Service, the Electricity Department, Broadcasting and the Airways — were also targeted.

The major difference between the 1920s and the 1980s was that the process went further faster in the latter decade, reflecting both the determination of the government, once its course was set, and the waning of the ethos of state-directed development. That this would be the case was not initially apparent. While there was support inside the new Labour government elected for the application of commercial principles to the trading activities of government departments, the pressures of other business, such as tax reform, and of politics itself took their toll.

In May 1985, Finance Minister Roger Douglas sought Cabinet's agreement on a 'comprehensive approach' to state-owned enterprises (SOEs), as Treasury had named them, 'so they operated on a commercial basis, shifting responsibility for non-commercial functions elsewhere, exposing them to private sector competition, and letting their managers manage'.[22] Neither the departments affected nor — or therefore — their ministers were necessarily happy, and the friction between the other agencies and Treasury became palpable. Even before the 1984 election, one Treasury think-piece had asked 'whether the Ministry [of Energy] needs to become more commercial and whether the operating units of the Ministry need to become more autonomous and develop into decentralised profit centres'.[23] Energy slammed another paper written after the election: 'Treasury's report has some serious misconceptions … [and we] conclude that Treasury comments are largely inappropriate. They are attacking the Energy Plan when the focus of their concern should more properly be the planning environment.'[24] Treasury then criticised 'the energy planning which gave rise to surpluses, the pursuit of foreign exchange and liquid fuels self-sufficiency, the assumptions used in the economic analysis at the time of the go-ahead decisions, and finally, the general approach involved in picking winners and accepting commercial risk.'[25]

There were run-ins with the Post Office. One minor but legendary example was provoked by delays in the installation of new telephones in the Treasury building. Assistant Secretary John Chetwin wrote a blistering letter to the Director-General of the Post Office, to which the latter replied that 'the contents had made me disappointed and angry … it is not uncommon these days to hear expressions of amazement at the spectacular redevelopment of central Wellington but I doubt that many people … have paused to consider the immense strain this has place[d] on Post Office resources.' Chetwin briefed Galvin that it had taken the Post Office 'two months to respond to a request to shift some telephones. When they did arrive it took three men the best part of three days to complete the repositioning of one internal extension. That suggests to me inefficiency rather than pressure of work.'[26]

One Treasury official recalls putting up a paper on the reorganisation of state forestry on commercial lines which was opposed by both Andy Kirkland at the Forest Service and Merv Probine at the State Services Commission, and consequently did not get through the Cabinet Policy Committee. The official and a colleague then went to Richard Prebble, one of the Associate Finance Ministers, and the next Cabinet meeting agreed to the establishment of a commercial forest service.[27]

Such manoeuvring meant that guidelines for the reorganisation were not settled on until December 1985. The law changes were spelt out by Douglas in a May 1986 economic statement which Prime Minister Lange stood squarely behind: 'we should have state trading enterprises running efficiently on the basis of competitive neutrality with the private sector ... Our state corporations will be every bit as efficient as if they were privatised. There will be no government guarantee for their loans ... They will, in fact, be on their own.'[28]

Just before the May announcement, Roderick Deane took up an eighteen-month appointment at the State Services Commission at the behest of Douglas, who got it through over the objections of Minister of State Services Stan Rodger. Deane suspended — temporarily, as it seemed then — a meteoric career at the Reserve Bank — because Cabinet had offered him 'interesting and challenging' things to do. His appointment was 'absolutely critical' for the creation of the SOEs, according to Douglas.[29]

The SOE model became operational when nine corporations were created in April 1987: three Post Office spin-offs (Postbank, New Zealand Post and Telecom), two Ministry of Energy spin-offs (Coalcorp and Electricorp), corporatised elements of the Forest Service and Lands and Survey (Forestrycorp and Landcorp), the Airways Corporation, and Government Property Services. It was soon applied to any zone in which the government was, or plausibly might be, engaged in commercial or financial activity. Obvious additional targets were soon identified: the Ministry of Works, the Shipping Corporation, the Rural Bank.[30]

Other candidates were less straightforward. In respect of the Reserve Bank, 'the issue for Treasury was less one of wanting to accommodate [its] unique status … as a central bank, than of determining a set of funding and accountability arrangements that satisfied the Treasury's concern to impose a measure of commonal[i]ty on all crown agencies.' In this instance the Bank, feeling that neither this model nor that of a core ministry fitted, succeeded in having a 'central bank' model implemented instead, albeit with some accountability arrangements comparable to the SOE model inserted in the legislation.[31]

Maori development and broadcasting were two other spheres that registered on the SOE radar. In 1986 an officials' committee based in Treasury was set up to consider questions arising from the 'interim report of the committee to consider accelerating Maori economic development and the case for a Maori development bank'. This report highlighted the fact that most Maori assets were held in the agricultural sector, which had been affected adversely by the new government's economic strategy and in which profitability was low. It was partly this conclusion that led the government to support the establishment of a private Maori Resource Development Corporation in 1987.[32]

A royal commission comprising Professor Robert Chapman (as chair), Judge Mick Brown and the company directors L. A. Cameron and E. A. Nelson was set up by Broadcasting Minister Jonathan Hunt. This reported in September 1986 that it favoured the state continuing as both a commercial and a non-commercial broadcaster, with a strong regulatory role for the Broadcasting Tribunal. It 'dismissed too lightly the Treasury submission which advocated a lessening of central regulation in favour of a market-driven ethos'.[33] An eighteen-page dissenting opinion from Cameron called, in contrast to the main report, for full separation between commercial and non-commercial broadcasting, if the state continued to operate both. Two SOEs — one for public non-commercial radio, the other for public but commercial television — were legislated for in 1988.[34]

The corporatisation process put acute pressure on Treasury's own financial and accounting capability. We have seen that since the 1920s the financial side of Treasury had overseen the Crown's investments in a variety of enterprises and trading formations. Expertise in that area had become thin on the ground by the mid-1980s. A number of individuals with strong backgrounds in finance — Sam Parker, Fred Shailes, Dick Battersby, Brian Tyler — had retired or departed, Shailes and then Tyler to be Auditor-General. While John Cook had also been very active in such financial areas, sitting on many boards in the 1970s, his background was more in economics than in finance, and his years of work raising loans for Muldoon meant that he was kept at arm's length by the new leadership in Treasury. John Anderson, another senior accounting and finance expert, had retired early but later worked on a contract basis. On a more general level, the economists in the department had become convinced that there was a conflict between Treasury representation on boards like that of the Development Finance Corporation (DFC) and its role of advising the government on economic policies which would affect such enterprises. The economic advice role now overshadowed the commercial or 'shareholder' role, and it was at this time that such representation largely ended.[35]

The responsibility for corporatisation lay with Industries Branch, one of the six entities into which Treasury was reorganised in 1985. This was headed by John Chetwin, one of Treasury's most practical policy experts, with Doug Andrew in a senior role. Margaret Galt, who worked on corporatisation, found both to be 'very good. Chet would come immediately to see you if you were in difficulties, and Doug had a breadth of understanding even Treasury officers tended to miss — they tended to be looking at trees. He was certainly very instrumental in developing the SOE model, in an overview of where we should be heading — which organisations did you make into SOEs, which didn't you?'[36]

Andrew and 'Chet', like most of the analysts in the branch, were economists whose analytic focus had been on microeconomic reform — improving the operations of markets — rather than on finance. This befitted their brief, which was not only financial but also to 'develop, and facilitate the introduction of, policies to improve the efficiency of resource use'.[37] Margaret Galt was one of two contractors who were brought in to assist with the restructuring of the gas and oil sector (the Think Big projects). She had acquired relevant experience in her dealings with the Shipping Corporation as an employee of the Ministry of Transport:

> We established this model which enabled us to determine which bits of the company were making losses, and so on. We also then were able to value the company in terms of its economic worth. And tell the government, if it was to proceed with this company, 'This is how much it is valued at, this is its cash flows, and this is how much money you're going to have to put in.' Now when, subsequently, the government decided it wanted to do a similar thing to all the Think Big projects, it was a very similar exercise. And they looked around the public servants and said, 'Who has done such an operation? These two have only done it with this tinpot little shipping corporation. But at least they did it.'[38]

In November 1986 the branch estimated it needed approximately twice as many analysts as it had if it was to meet its responsibilities, which at that time included establishing the nine new corporations and several other agencies by 1 April 1987. Academics with international reputations were brought in to deal with the 'more difficult conceptual issues', whilst the branch had recruited four contractors and hoped to employ more.[39]

The shortages of numbers and expertise shaped the work environment. The analysts who negotiated with the boards of SOEs on the transfer of assets 'remember it as a hectic but stimulating time. Some question, with [the] benefit of hindsight, the adequacy of staff resources and preparation as the process gained its own momentum.' Treasury had, perhaps naively, expected that departments whose operations were to be corporatised would display a 'co-operative analytic approach to asset transfer'. Instead, it had difficulty obtaining information from them. This was partly because of deficiencies in recordkeeping, but

> was complicated by the incentives for departments to side with the Establishment Board, so that the Government had difficulty obtaining unbiased advice about the businesses it was trying to sell. This unusual situation of the purchaser having access to all the information, while the vendor [the government] had very little, weakened the Government's negotiating position.[40]

Relations with the establishment boards themselves were challenging. Valuing Forestry Corporation's assets took months of manoeuvring. Whereas Telecom's Establishment Board initially suggested $698.4 million as the valuation for the business that would be entered on its first balance sheet, a figure of $3.2 billion was eventually agreed upon. The long-running battle over the valuation of the assets which were to be assumed by Electricity Corporation of New Zealand (ECNZ) — whose CEO was none other than Roderick Deane — set accounting and economic criteria against each other, much as had happened over Think Big. Should the assets be valued with reference to the cost of creating or replacing them, offset by depreciation? Or should the valuation take into account the cost of producing additional product — electricity — over the long term, the investment required for which would be far more costly than existing investment? As during the costing of the Think Big projects in 1981, Treasury favoured economic over commercial pricing; it responded to ECNZ's offer of $3.7 billion with a figure of $8.5 billion.[41] But was the valuation up to the seller? In this environment Treasury was wearing four hats, financial and economic, and seller (the Crown allocating its assets to an SOE) and buyer (the Crown as owner of the SOE for economic as well as financial reasons).

Only after these first experiences were establishment negotiation procedures changed. In particular, the 'perverse' incentives which were believed to trigger some of these conflicts were reduced by creating separate establishment and operational boards.[42] The 'dialogue' between Treasury and ECNZ went on long after the inception of the latter, and in the end was resolved with the help of the prominent business leader Ron Trotter, who in March 1988 'arranged a secret late-night meeting … He asked Prebble and Douglas to come in while Treasury officials were "safely tucked up in bed". He and Deane rehearsed the pertinent figures outside, crouching over car headlights to read the piece of paper … and the deal was finalised next morning.'[43] At $6.3 billion, the agreed figure was much closer to ECNZ's ultimate bid of $5.5 billion than to Treasury's $8.5 billion. Business rather than economic criteria had won out, but this was in large part because a true sale of the assets — that is, privatisation — was favoured.[44]

Meanwhile, in a landmark Court of Appeal decision Justice Cook ruled that the injunction against actions inconsistent with the 'principles' of the Treaty of Waitangi in the State-Owned Enterprises Act 1986 had the effect of a constitutional guarantee within the field covered by the Act. Responses to issues raised by the court's decision included the Treaty of Waitangi (State Enterprises) Act 1988 and the establishment of a Treaty of Waitangi Policy Unit (TOWPU, later the Office of Treaty Settlements) under the ambit of the Justice Department. Treasury itself advised the government on legal and other challenges initiated by Maori groups to the corporatisation or sale of some of the Crown's assets.[45]

This discussion has considered the corporatisation of the 1980s in the context of Treasury's long-standing financial responsibilities. The political controversy provoked within the Labour Party by the strategy has been addressed in the previous chapter. Opposition from unions whose members might be affected by changes in employment conditions, notably the Public Service Association, was also very vigorous.[46] This anxiety was understandable. Within months of the establishment of the corporations, around 5000 state employees (roughly two-thirds of them rail and forestry workers) had taken voluntary redundancy. A further 2000 public service positions were lost in 1986/87 as a result of the commercialisation of various public services. The greatest impact of corporatisation was felt in the coal-mining settlements of the West Coast and the forestry

A Wellingtonian looks for a post office in the aftermath of corporatisation. Eric Heath

townships of the Volcanic Plateau, where it fell disproportionately on the Maori population.[47] In a chapter in her study of the corporatisation of New Zealand Post entitled 'Success, but at what personal cost?', Vivienne Smith records that on the day the new entity began operations as an SOE it had 12,000 employees; nine years later, there were only 6760. Some 432 of the 1200 post offices were closed early in 1988 — on one day in February, 564 people lost their jobs. The changes also upset many clients of these outlets. A further set of redundancies came in 1991/92, when the introduction of more efficient procedures reduced the number of mail-handling staff by a third.[48] Treasury officials questioned about such job losses expressed sympathy but were not dissuaded from continuing the policy. 'Labour shedding was a immediate first step in improving productivity', argued one in 1990. Another explained that

> everyone recognised that Railways had to shed staff, but it was very, very difficult for the government to get rid of staff, politically. One of the reasons that the corporate model was developed was to distance the government from those decisions so you could do things that were rational, that should have been done. One of the biggest tragedies was that we did all that restructuring in the 1980s, not in the 1960s, when, if you'd put out of work 10,000 railway workers, they would have found other work quickly.[49]

With the government committed to an anti-inflationary tight money policy, it was not surprising that in the short term new jobs in other sectors failed to materialise and unemployment figures rose. Looking back, one senior Treasury official of the time felt that while there was an awareness that much physical capital would be written off in industries that were run down, and that investment would have to go into new growth areas, there was insufficient concern about the ability of people to retrain without active assistance.[50]

Precise information about the fiscal and efficiency benefits of corporatisation is hard to come by. Duncan and Bollard note the limitations which inevitably arise from 'the absence of balance sheets in departmental structures and the paucity of revenue and expense data. Very few comparisons have been available, for instance, between Telecom and New Zealand Post and the equivalent divisions of the New Zealand Post Office'. For 1992 they identified five levels of financial performance amongst the corporations they analysed: basket case (one organisation), gradual turnaround (one), sharp turnaround (three), steady to increasing profitability (two), and profitable and expanding (three). In some instances, such as Coal Corporation and Forestry Corporation, whose predecessors had been perpetual loss-makers, the new enterprises were able to both cut staff dramatically and pass on the costs of restructuring their balance sheets to the government. Others, such as State Insurance, Government Computing Services and Petrocorp, had a history of profitability.[51]

The fiscal payback looked better if the dividend-paying history of SOEs *after* the initial balance-sheet restructuring was examined. All the SOEs paid dividends yearly, whereas in their former guises they had made no contribution to the Consolidated Fund and had often been subsidised. For Treasury, fiscal gains were also bureaucratic gains. The complete disappearance of such large and diverse departments as the Ministry of Energy and its divisions, the Post Office in its old guise, the Forest Service, Lands and Survey, and the Ministry of Works was an extraordinary bureaucratic accomplishment which surpassed what Treasury had achieved in the 1920s. Institutional as well as financial pressures on the public revenue were irrevocably removed. But this proved not to be a stopping point, as arguments for *selling* corporatised and other assets became increasingly insistent.

Selling assets[52]

While the protracted negotiations over asset valuations were one factor encouraging the government to consider privatisation — 'the solution to the asset-valuation exercise was to think about selling assets'[53] — there were others. Treasury accepted the principle that 'compared with private ownership, state ownership is likely to give directors and managers of SOEs inappropriate and inadequate incentives to act strictly commercially'.[54] From this point of view, Treasury's advocacy of privatisation needs no explanation — it was a logical outcome of its analysis. But there were two other factors grounded in Treasury's responsibilities for financial management: debt reduction and risk avoidance. For politicians of both major parties determined to reduce public debt, asset sales were a feasible solution — they were more palatable than expenditure cuts, for instance. The desire to avoid risk to the Crown's balance sheet had initiated Treasury's involvement with government trading activities in the 1920s and survived thereafter. Speaking of Petrocorp, one official commented that

> it is difficult for the government to manage an SOE if it is in a high-risk area, and oil exploration is a classic high-risk area. The government doesn't have the ability to pull out of things, and that's what you need in a high-risk area. And Petrocorp was doing most exploration in South-East Asia at that point.[55]

Treasury's responsibilities and its experience both made it far more attuned to the fiscal risk than the fiscal opportunities of owning assets. Where critics of privatisation mourned the loss of public control of a strategic resource and the income stream it had produced, Treasury saw lids placed over bottomless financial pits. As Graham Scott recalled:

> time and time again I saw Cabinets that would sweat blood and tears for months saving ten million here and fifteen million there, and then one of these enterprises would come in and say ... 'Whoopsy, we've just lost a whole lot of money', which would be two or three times the amount that they'd been saving in the Budget.[56]

Scott was thinking particularly of the financial difficulties of the DFC and the Bank of New Zealand in 1989–90, when they were still wholly or partly Crown-owned. The problems with the DFC arose after its sale. The buyers had sought a warranty that its accounts were a true reflection of the state of the business.

Treasury received legal advice that it should not make this commitment because the purchasers had as much information as the Crown, and because in previous sales the Crown had been clear that it was providing no such warranties. When the DFC subsequently collapsed, the Crown came under intense pressure to fund a bail-out of investors. Both Treasury and its ministers were opposed to doing this. Instead, Treasury helped the DFC to develop a scheme whereby more than 90 per cent of its creditors would agree to the restructuring of its debt and a gradual sale of its remaining assets that would allow them to be paid out. This endeavour took until November 1990 to finalise an agreement:

> The final stages of the negotiations involved a good deal of nail-biting. [At one point] we suddenly faced the prospect of the elaborate jigsaw we were designing being declared structurally unsound before we had even tried to put the pieces together.[57]

In late 1988 the government had received an offer from Brierleys, whose head, Ron Brierley, had recently been made chair of the BNZ, to purchase its 83 per cent shareholding in the bank. The National Australia Bank was also interested. However, because both proposals had disadvantages and there was disquiet within the Labour Party about a sale, action was deferred. Treasury and its Minister (by now David Caygill) were attacked in the press: 'will [Caygill and Treasury] finally succeed in driving [the BNZ's] price so low that they'll have to pay the Australians to take it over?' However, outsiders had little sense of how parlous the bank's finances were — it was seeking a $500 million capital injection from the government. When in June 1989, following a reconstruction of the bank's management, it sought additional capital through a rights issue, the government renounced its rights in favour of Capital Markets Ltd, which acquired a 30 per cent shareholding.[58] But by early 1990 the bank was in further difficulties because of the volume of loans on which it was losing money, in Australia in particular. The government had the apparent choice of walking away from the bank, with all the likely consequences for the financial system and the economy (not to mention for Capital Markets' owners, Fay Richwhite) should it collapse, or acting to rescue the bank and the investment of its fellow shareholder. In practice, there was no choice. As in 1894, the bank was too important to be allowed to go under, and the government had to 'swallow the bitter pill of having to commit even more taxpayer funds to a bank it didn't want to own'. Caygill decided that this was too sensitive an operation to be rushed — or divulged —

and the deal was not yet done when the 1990 election resulted in a change of government. The new Cabinet had no choice but to confirm Caygill's $420 million rescue package.[59] Agreement on the sale of the BNZ to the National Australia Bank was reached in November 1992.

For Treasury, a key theme throughout the BNZ crisis was its inability to get information from the bank's board. It explained to its minister in May 1989, for instance, that 'our understanding of the Bank's thinking on future capital and business options remains unclear because we have been unable to ascertain the extent or timing of any capital injection required'.[60] As the agent of the majority owner of the bank, Treasury thus had responsibility but not power. The information flow improved once Capital Markets was represented on the board, but it remained inadequate. While the size of the Australian loan portfolio rose from $1.3 billion on 31 March 1989 to $2.2 billion a year later, the extent to which this additional business deepened the bank's financial difficulties remained lost in the 'shifting sands of Australian loss provision'. Treasury and the minister only learnt of the full extent of this deterioration the day before the bank's annual general meeting in July 1990.[61]

Treasury faced technical as well as informational challenges. Even more than with the setting up of the SOEs, selling assets required skills which had not previously been in demand in the public sector. Officials were involved in 'putting together equity deals, debt deals, financial structures and all that was a skill which we had never had any reason to have before'.[62] In the 1990/91 year, for example, Treasury spent $108.2 million on consultants, $78.2 million of which was related to asset sales — a figure dwarfed by the $5.2 billion received from the sales (including of Telecom) made that year. During the drawn-out process of the sale of the BNZ, merchant bankers CS First Boston were contracted on at least four occasions to provide advice on issues which Treasury lacked the resources or expertise to assess.[63]

Even with the assistance of consultants and advisers, the pressure on Treasury officials was intense, because of both specific events and the sheer number of sales. Accounts of privatisations are replete with comings and goings, deals made then coming unstuck. Petrocorp was converted into a publicly listed company with 70 per cent government shareholding, then

> put out for tender, and the lead tender was [from] British Gas. It put in a relatively clean tender. But when it was announced that it had been the lead

bidder, its negotiators flew to New Zealand and put a contract on the table that had a number of onerous clauses quite different from the original tender. Basically, they wanted a tax-free status and thought the New Zealand government would not want to upset the British government by pulling out, and would never wear the egg on its political face. Treasury went and said, 'It is not worth selling, you must pull out and re-tender', and the government agreed.[64]

To Bill Falconer, a former Ministry of Energy official who had become the CEO of Petrocorp,

> the reality was that the two New Zealand bidders, Fletchers and Brierleys, were looking for a bargain. In those days there was an expectation that privatisations would deliver a bargain to the successful bidders, and in hindsight most of them got them. The offshore bidders were also looking for a bargain — they were all opportunists, nobody wanted to have a little oil company stuck down in this end of the world. Until British Gas came along, and they took it quite seriously. They were prepared to bid 81 cents a share, but then realised that the success of the thing depended on a whole range of contracts, which were with the government. So they said to government, 'Please give us some security that you'll manage these contracts in a way that we can properly value the future of the business.' Meanwhile, there's a whole lot of reaction in the paper — 'selling the Crown jewels', 'family silver', 'colonialism' rears its head again — the cartoonists were having a great time. So, I am told, someone rang Fletchers and asked, 'Can you match the British Gas price, without conditions?'[65]

The Treasury's 1989 annual report listed nineteen entities which the department was preparing for sale. The sales of Air New Zealand, Postbank and part of the BNZ were announced the day after Roger Douglas's resignation. Amongst the sales in the year to June 1990 were those of the Rural Bank, the Government Printing Office and the Tourist Hotel Corporation.[66] Selling the THC was difficult, according to the Treasury official involved, because it was a 'mediocre asset and a lot of the risk in the balance sheet wasn't clear'. The purchaser, the South Pacific Hotel Corporation, claimed an indemnity from the Crown because the weakness in the asset had not been adequately disclosed. Was the Crown or Fay Richwhite, the Crown's agents for the sale, responsible? SPHC's claim was not successful.[67]

Many of the privatisations were even more controversial than the corpora-

Selling forestry cutting rights, 1989. Peter Bromhead

tisations had been — 'next to unemployment [privatisation] was the issue about which Labour voters felt most betrayed and which still leaves a lingering resentment', argued the columnist Bruce Jesson in 1992.[68] Selling publicly owned assets provoked concerns about sovereignty and nationhood when, as with Telecom, the principal buyers were overseas investors. In other cases, there was a perception that the government was facilitating the sale of assets to its friends at favourable prices. A May 1990 television programme alleged that businessmen who had donated millions of dollars to Labour's 1987 election campaign had been paid back through favourable privatisation deals.[69] In 1992/93 the populist politician and sacked National Party Cabinet minister Winston Peters alleged that Fay Richwhite had received favourable treatment from the government in the course of the rescue of the BNZ in 1990.[70] Bolger, however, refused to initiate an enquiry; and in any case, such claims touched politicians and businesspeople more directly than the Treasury.

Another line of criticism came from scholars. One characteristic Treasury argument was that even if there were currently no competitors in a market or industry, the environment could be considered to be a competitive one if the barriers to entry were not insurmountable.[71] But the economist Brian Easton, citing one of the founders of contestability theory, William Baumol, has cautioned that this theory did not seem robust enough to apply to markets in which there were even minor costs of entry and exit.⁷² In 1996 Treasury cited a number of studies which suggested that private ownership did lead to better performance, but conceded that there had also been 'studies which have not been able to find unambiguous results relating to different modes of ownership'. Treasury's managers may not have been surprised about this caveat insofar as it applied to New Zealand. Scott on one occasion referred to a prominent executive from a consulting firm telling him 'that I would be horrified if he were to show me the results of ... intelligence tests ... of people who are in chief executive positions in a number of businesses in New Zealand. In fact a very high proportion of people in senior management positions ... are substantially below average in terms of basic competence.' Scott attributed this weakness to the 'incentives that lay with those firms for many years and the way that they made profits', but this only added to the difficulties of evaluation.⁷³ As Treasury's 1996 paper pointed out, estimating the effects of privatisation was often difficult because the process often coincided with other changes, for instance in the objectives of the business or the regulatory environment.⁷⁴

The success of privatisation could be addressed more directly: did the government get enough for its assets? Duncan and Bollard conclude that 'from hindsight, some of the agreed asset prices have turned out to be too low. The most controversial case was the Rural Bank, which delivered very large profits during its first year in private ownership. There [was also] much criticism of the sale of the Government Printing Office [but] in two other sales, surprisingly high prices were reached.'⁷⁵ Postbank had turned a $51 million loss into an after-tax profit of $32.8 million in its first year of operation as an SOE, and the ANZ Bank confirmed its strength by paying more than twice its asset backing for it.⁷⁶ Telecom was sold in June 1990 for $4.25 billion. By the time the American owners of 90 per cent of the company sold up seven years later, Telecom had paid its shareholders $5.1 billion in dividends.⁷⁷ Does this mean that the government should have demanded more for the enterprise? *Government Management* had argued that a sale price should capture anticipated future earnings.⁷⁸ But changes in the environment in which a company operated, and its own actions — such as restructurings and investments — make it difficult to evaluate an historical sale price. If buyers failed to run a new enterprise successfully, did this mean they should have paid less, or managed better? If they succeeded, had they paid too little or managed well?

The most problematic sale for Treasury was that of the government's 89 per cent share of New Zealand Steel to Equiticorp. The government was to be paid in Equiticorp shares, for which it would get a minimum of $3.52 whenever it on-sold them. The brokers Buttle Wilson agreed to either purchase the Crown's shares for $327.2 million, or find another purchaser. The sale was finalised the day before the October 1987 stock-market crash. By the time it was reported in the press, Equiticorp shares were trading at only $2.75, and two weeks later they had fallen to $1.85. Buttle Wilson made an agreement, to which the Crown was not a party, under which Equiticorp would arrange for the sale of the shares if no buyer were found. The government duly sold its shares to an Equiticorp subsidiary, Ararimu Investments Four Ltd, for $327 million in March 1988.[79]

After Equiticorp went broke, its receivers took the Crown to court on the grounds that Equiticorp had illegally arranged funding to purchase its own shares as part of the transaction — and that the Crown should have been aware that this was likely to happen. Two Treasury officials and one Trade and Industry official were subpoenaed for the case, which was not heard until 1995 — when the spouse of one recalls being served a summons at home for $267.5 million. The judge held that 'fragmented knowledge held by various officials and the Crown's selling agents, legal and financial advisors can be aggregated to establish the sum of what the Crown knew ... that Crown officials knew of documents suggesting that Equiticorp was funding the purchases and ... they therefore should have made further enquiries before going ahead with the sale.' The judge accordingly found for the receivers, and the Crown had to repay $267 million of the $327 million it had received in the transaction.[80] Many of those interviewed questioned the realism of this finding. As one (non-Treasury) official put it, 'accountability is one thing, blame is another. A lot of people sign stuff out. You do not have time, despite what Justice Smellie said in the Equiticorp case, to check everything.'

As with corporatisation, this discussion has examined privatisation from the point of view of Treasury's long-standing responsibilities for public finance. That the 1980s exercise went beyond that of the 1920s in selling assets is harder to explain, but it is possible that the Depression prevented such sales being investigated in the earlier period. Privatisation — and corporatisation — in the 1980s also highlighted the need for Treasury to familiarise itself with private-sector accounting and business practice. This was not so much for the purpose of handling what would eventually become a waning workload of corporatisation and privatisation, but in order to supervise the reorganised public sector.

The core public sector

Corporatisation was a fertile plant. The political commentator John Roberts observed in 1987 that while arguments about the need to make officials more accountable for their actions had 'been employed to justify the creation of corporate institutions for trading functions', it seemed 'unlikely that the wave of reform will stop short of the "non-tradeables"'.[81] And indeed, *Economic Management* had argued in 1984 that 'the aim of management should be the implementation of systems in the public service that can perform broadly the same role for the public service as the price system does in the private sector'.[82]

The reformers had a mandate from the Labour government. The passing of the Official Information Act in 1982 had suggested that there was bipartisan support for greater openness in government, and Labour also retained a preoccupation with securing accountability from the public sector from its last term in office. Deputy Prime Minister Geoffrey Palmer, a constitutional lawyer, had written that 'better administration will require new methods of accountability to be developed, even for the core public service … the time has come for bold innovation.'[83]

The very idea of a Treasury paper embarking on such reform was novel, and *Economic Management* implicitly called into question the existing regime and the role of the State Services Commission in managing it:

> Departments are run by Permanent Heads, whose responsibility is to the State Services Commission and to Ministers for running their departments effectively. However, Permanent Heads either face unclear objectives, or alternatively face objectives that can be hard to measure. Although some departments now have some form of management plan, most … do not.[84]

When a paper on 'efficiency and economy in the public service' was published in 1965, it was natural that it was written by a State Services Commissioner rather than a Treasury official.[85] In its 1985 annual report, the SSC referred to the need to move from a public service which was 'administered' to one which was 'managed' by managers who placed more emphasis on results.[86] The political scientist Jonathan Boston noted in 1996 that neither the SSC nor its predecessor, the Public Service Commission, had provided the leadership in the public service that had been expected of them at the time of their establishment. Neither had focused on the 'efficient and economical management of the public service', being much more absorbed in employment and particularly wage and salary issues. While the office of the Public Service Commissioner had initially played a leading role in this field, it had been overtaken by Treasury in the 1920s. In both the 1920s and the 1980s, severe fiscal pressures gave the Treasury an important point of entry into the debate.[87]

The reform of the state sector was launched in December 1987, the month after the government was heavily criticised at the Labour Party conference about the direction it was taking. It came into effect three months later against a backdrop of demonstrations and protests by public servants who were concerned about both the underlying principles of the State Sector Act and its implications for their employment conditions. The fact that wage-fixing became a matter for the chief executives of each department was one of a number of controversial provisions which provoked demonstrations against the new law before it came into effect.[88]

The aim of the reform was not to turn core departments into private firms, but to find ways of replicating the disciplines that were imposed on the latter by the possibility that they could be, for instance, taken over or bankrupted. Four key aspects of the approach were: to make chief executives more directly accountable for the performance of their agencies; to give them more discretion to make decisions; to distinguish what they were asked to produce (outputs) from the results that were desired (outcomes), so that both could be properly assessed; and to switch to an accounting system that measured inputs on an accrual basis, and could measure outputs. 'The basic thrust of all the reforms is to improve the incentives for efficiency within the sector. These four changes [are] all more towards the sorts of arrangements that are found in the private sector to help overcome agency problems.'[89] The language employed also came from the business world: 'contestability, contracting, customised services, outputs, outcomes, ownership interest, performance agreements, purchase agreements, stakeholders, strategic planning, transparency, transaction costs, agent-principal relations and so on' all entered the state sector lexicon.[90]

Driven by the same underlying principles as the organisational reform, the 1989 Public Finance Act was also triggered by the government's exasperation that expenditure continued to outrun revenue. The tax reforms of the mid-1980s had increased revenue dramatically (helped by continued inflation), yet fiscal deficits continued — so what else could be tried? Scott recalled that 'we had come to the conclusion that we had a structural fiscal policy problem that had to do with the role of government, the accountability systems in the government, incentives and information problems all over the government, that would not be addressed by … mechanical accountants' devices'.[91]

In the course of the 1985/86 expenditure review and Budget round, a Financial Management Support Service had been established in a revival of a task force set up in 1979. Its head reported to a steering committee comprising the Auditor-General, the Secretary to the Treasury, the chair of the State Services Commission, another senior public servant, and a merchant banker. The FMSS aimed to improve the state of the government accounts, a need identified by Fred Shailes in 1978, in subsequent observations by both Shailes and his successor as Auditor-General, Brian Tyler, and in a 1984 report by the Public Expenditure Committee of Parliament.[92] It was to be the financial management equivalent of Economics II, recalled one official. Ian Ball, who became director of the task force in January 1987, was to play as important a role in this sphere as had Scott and Deane in the creation of the SOEs. 'I think', he recalled, that

> there was very little of Treasury's brain applied to managing the government's own internal financial performance. People within Treasury would think about the performance of the organisation almost solely in terms of the way it managed government's impact on the wider economy.[93]

The new Acts had one particularly good outcome — or output — for historians and other curious outsiders. For the first time in its 148-year history, Treasury began to produce an annual report. The second of these explained that the Public Finance Act had introduced the financial management reforms that were necessary to make the State Sector Act a reality. The Public Finance Act required departments (and the government as a whole) to operate on an accrual accounting basis, which was standard in business. Under the existing cash accounting system, an item such as a photocopier would be recorded in the year in which it was purchased. Under accrual accounting, the cost of that purchase would be figure in a balance sheet throughout its working life. The Act made chief executives responsible for the introduction of accrual accounting in their departments. It envisaged that there would be a 'purchase' agreement between minister and chief executive for the delivery of outputs, and also an 'ownership' relationship, in that a department would have to act in a way that protected the 'owner's' — that is, the Crown's — interests.[94]

The drive for this innovation came from officials. When Parliament's Finance and Expenditure Committee received few submissions on the Public Finance Bill, it actively solicited them from institutions — including government departments, which it recognised might have thought such an action to be inappropriate. Eventually 32 submissions were received, 21 from government departments and SOEs and five from private-sector financial organisations.[95]

Government Management had linked public-sector reform to fiscal issues:

> Successive governments … have emphasised their determination to curb the growth of government expenditure. Despite strenuous efforts … the outcome has been a relentless increase in outlays … An explanation may lie not in an analysis of programme objectives and costs but in the nature of the incentives facing public sector managers and those that seek government assistance.[96]

Historically, government accounting had been cash-based and recorded inputs, be they of goods (materials) or services (labour), through a system that lent itself to surveillance by Parliament. Now departments would be required to record their spending in relation to unique outputs which were negotiated individually. While for one Treasury official it was 'amazing' that the reform was 'driven by the Treasury at all',[97] there was also a long-term benefit for the agency:

> It was a different deal that was done between them. Previously Treasury or the SSC ticked off beforehand just about everything the department did — you couldn't move without getting Treasury or SSC approval or going through the Government Stores Board, or going to the departmental motor vehicles committee, or through the Government Office Accommodation Board … All those processes constrained people and departments. I guess the way I would put it was that what happened was that Treasury and the SSC gave up a whole lot of detailed controls — procedural controls — in exchange for enhanced control, if by control you mean, 'This is the direction you are going in.'[98]

Even the now not quite so subversive 'Surfdale Progressive Association', as Treasury's social club styled itself, was drawn into the process:

> The Association clearly meets the Public Finance Bill definition of a Crown agency as a significant financial interdependence between the Crown and the Association can be demonstrated. Analysts have previously asserted (Tsy *Verbal Report* no 1348) that were the Crown to cease to exist, members' finances would fall into disarray. Association members have also asserted

(Tsy *Verbal Threat* no 1349) that this relationship is symmetrical — namely that if the Association ceased to exist, the Crown's finances would fall into disarray.[99]

The Treasury itself was now to be subjected to the vote analysis process that applied to other departments. But what would this mean for the Treasury vote analyst, who was also a Treasury employee? Two proposed guidelines were that information would be provided to the vote analyst 'without accompanying pressure … beyond normal efforts to persuade on the validity of a proposal', and that the analyst would not be 'subject to undue pressures after expressing views on a proposal.'[100] Obviously this was a dangerous new world. It was also a world which followed a different calendar. The balance date for the financial year was changed from 31 March to 30 June, thereby reversing a decision taken in 1879 to ensure that Parliament got a year's figures when it assembled, which was usually in May or June to accommodate the seasonal rhythms of rural members. The 1989 decision was taken to ensure that departments would know their budgets before the start of the year to which they applied. It thus reflected the extent to which public finance now looked forward as much as back.[101]

While the new system saw Treasury's direct financial control of other departments diminish, the new structure by which ministers purchased 'outputs' from their departments gave Cabinet and the Treasury a much more powerful tool with which to investigate expenditure. When the possibility of 'input' cuts (effectively, restraints on wages and salaries) was raised, Treasury pointed out that such a strategy was unnecessary:

> It is important to realise that the savings that might be achieved from controls on public sector wages could be largely secured through constraint on the price that the Government is prepared to pay for outputs without direct interference in pay negotiations. A low rate of price increase for outputs would influence the prices departments are prepared to pay for inputs, including wage and salary levels negotiated by them.[102]

The expenditure control round for 1991/92 is remembered by public servants as one of the most robust ever. As we have seen, the new National government had found that the fiscal deficit was much greater than had been foreshadowed in Labour's final Budget. Immediate efforts to cut expenditure had focused on health, housing, education, social welfare and defence, decisions on which were announced in the economic and financial package of December 1990. In the new year the next dozen middle-sized departments ('tier two') were reviewed. During this second phase the crucial discussions between ministers achieved less than they had during the first phase. In the final pre-Budget phase the Cabinet Expenditure Control Committee was paired with an Officials' Committee on Expenditure Control, normally chaired by Treasury official Mark Byers, which reviewed the budgets of all departments.[103] Byers chaired this committee for another two years, during which the principle of rigid baselines — agreed expenditure levels which were 'bolted down' for future ('out') years as well as the forthcoming one — was embedded as an important tool of fiscal control.[104] This ranks alongside Treasury gaining the right to report on all spending proposals in 1930 as a cornerstone of the department's place in government. The 1991 exercise — with 1992 not far behind — was the most vigorous attack on expenditure since 1976, possibly since 1932. Scott anticipated flak:

> I would prefer not to be rung up by chief executives complaining about the arrogance and ignorance of Treasury analysts. It happens very rarely, but you will have chief executives ... who will work themselves up into a lather about their Treasury analyst ... [There is] a very heavy emphasis on the people in this room who are involved in this kind of work to manage as best they can the conflict negotiation situations that they will be confronted with.[105]

But diplomacy could not oil all wheels. Thus a paper on Vote: Arts and Culture which examined the budgets for the New Zealand Symphony Orchestra, the Film Commission and the Queen Elizabeth II Arts Council, described the $19.4 million vote as 'low quality government expenditure, benefiting groups other than low income earners'. In other areas there was a characteristic focus on the balance between public and commercial activities: 'the key issue is the role of government in science, distinguishing between public good science outputs and those with commercial applications. Present funding extends beyond public good science outputs.'[106]

Political scientists such as Jonathan Boston and Robert Gregory of Victoria University have systematically critiqued aspects of the public sector reforms in a raft of articles and chapters in books. At the nub of their critique is the argument that the private business model, while providing insights into the operations of government, was also inappropriate in many ways because government is different. In most dimensions of the public service, the provision of services cannot be disciplined by market forces; and public organisations cannot be fully responsible for the policies they implement.[107]

However, Gregory has also conceded that there were huge improvements in financial management, and that accrual accounting was successful. And Boston has commented recently that both proponents and critics of the reforms may have overestimated the degree of change. Thus, despite pressure for external recruitment, the vast majority of chief executives have continued to come from within the core public service — many, indeed, from the Treasury. And on the other hand, there was no evidence that the various changes have 'imperilled the professionalism or impartiality of departmental secretaries; nor have they significantly reduced their willingness to offer "free and frank advice".'[108]

Paradoxically, it was the reformers who remained more sceptical about the success of the process. For Scott, political will was the crucial factor. The Budget process succeeded in 1991 'because the prime minister called all the chief executives together and made it very clear … what he wanted … I would go so far as to say that even a less sophisticated system could have achieved a great deal in the presence of that political will and that even a more sophisticated system would achieve very little if the will was not present.'[109] But could the right kind of political will be fostered? In a later study, Scott praised Singapore's more corporatist approach to the recruitment of politicians, which allowed expertise from outside Parliament to be brought into government. He cited a Singapore white paper which argued that 'while it is not possible or necessary for ministers' salaries to equal the highest private sector incomes, if the financial sacrifice of becoming a minister is too large, it will be another obstacle to able Singaporeans entering politics'.[110] For his part, Ian Ball has observed that the Public Finance Act

> ignores almost entirely the role and accountability of ministers. And I think that's the limiting factor now in our public management system. Ministers themselves are very little accountable under the Public Finance Act. A chief executive has to produce a set of financial statements. A minister who has control over a portfolio which may for example be one smallish department or a number of medium-size Crown entities does not have to produce a consolidated set of financial statements for those entities. It is nowhere transparent what that portfolio set of financial statements is, and it is nowhere transparent what the set of services provided by that portfolio as a whole is.[111]

'The Best Little Treasury in the World'[112]

In explaining the likely impact on the Treasury of reforms to the financial management of the core state sector, *Government Management* noted that these 'would change the focus of Treasury's role from one of central control to one akin to that of a private sector head office'.[113] The Treasury would become not just an organisation of high-performing people, but also a high-performing organisation utilising economic and financial expertise. Scott likened Treasury's dealings with a minister to the way 'a top consulting firm treats its biggest clients. It builds its reputation by assisting the client to develop a strategy, solving a lot of problems along the way, being alert to keeping the client out of difficulties, and reminding them of their long-term objectives.'[114]

In the early to mid-1980s, years of heavy workloads and very modest pay — limited both by Muldoon's wage and price freeze and by the straitjacket of the public service executive/clerical occupational class — many Treasury officials left to take up jobs in the private sector. This was hardly the way for Treasury to become the high-performing organisation that Scott envisaged. The turnover rate for investigating officers nearly doubled from the 10.6 per cent of 1983 during the first six months of 1984.[115] The State Service Commission set up a committee of inquiry into Treasury's staffing problems:

> Three wise men, they were called, came in to move around the department and talk to the troops — Robin Williams, a former Chair of the SSC, John Perham, of Francis Allison Symes, and Bill Wilson, an Auckland chartered accountant. All these truths came out, people burst into tears, and so on — [it was] the frustration of working in a place where there was suddenly a great opportunity to fix the country up, and yet there were still too many unsuitable people getting in the way and too many good staff ... leaving.[116]

The committee concluded that 'much of the problem in Treasury is unrelated to salary', instancing working conditions, management and communications issues. While it did not recommend major changes in starting salaries, it did suggest provision for promotion to a much higher point on the scale primarily on the grounds of professional expertise. This would enable good economists to be much better paid, and managerial posts to be filled by those with managerial ability, who were not necessarily the best economists.[117] Treasury lobbied for more substantial improvements, and in mid-1985 commissioned Price Waterhouse to

No normal life? Tom Scott

carry out a study to 'establish the foundation for the remuneration of a new occupational class — economic and financial analysis'. This survey found that 'the current base salaries appear to be lower than the base salaries currently found in the market place. This is most marked at the level of the assistant investigating officer, where the current salary level is 28 percent below that of the external sample. The senior investigating level is marginally lower (3%) than the external sample while the more senior grades are approximately 12% lower.'[118] The SSC duly approved the creation of a new 'economic and financial analyst' occupational class from January 1986, and a team including John Chetwin worked out which positions across the whole public service it should encompass.

The new EFA occupational class did not immediately resolve the recruitment problem, in part because starting salaries did not alter. By October 1986 the number of analysts had fallen to 70 from a staff ceiling of 129 (plus a few contractors) in July 1984, and Scott was convinced that if he could not do something by Christmas they would be down to 50 in the New Year. The SSC resisted, and Scott made representations to the Cabinet committee, then sat by the phone during Treasury's Christmas party waiting for a response. When he got good news he sent it through to the party.[119] Pay was increased by 40 per cent for those whose skills — mainly in economics, finance and related capabilities —

were in demand elsewhere. Part of the deal was a greater ability for staff to be demoted or dismissed. The change was also exemplified by the different kind of performance review — including a 'formal performance rating exercise' — that was applied to the new occupational class. There was, one official recalled,

> a famous scale of 1 to 5. If you were meeting expectations you got a 3. If you were walking on water you got a 5 — hardly anyone ever got that. If you were pretty strong you got a 4. If you got a 2, that meant you'd either just been promoted — so that was all right for the first year — or it was a sign to shape up or think about working somewhere else [two 2s in succession meant a pay cut]. 1 was 'Get out'.[120]

This recasting — or reinvigorating — of Treasury into an institution with a strong professional financial/economic focus also entailed shedding peripheral functions. The British political scientist Patrick Dunleavy has argued that control departments seek influence and power not through expansion but through enhancing their expertise, which may entail reducing personnel numbers.[121] The New Zealand Treasury graphically demonstrated this in the late 1980s, when it 'privatised or shifted to other agencies the peripheral activities of the department, in order to concentrate on functions more central to a finance ministry'.[122] Responsibility for the Government Superannuation Fund, the Government Stores Board and the coinage was removed from the Treasury.[123] The department's six regional offices were closed in 1990,[124] and the number of staff doing routine accounting fell from over 100 to just six. Total staff numbers were just under 500 in 1986, 356 in 1989 and 313 in 1991, by when around half were economic and financial analysts.[125]

Professionalism would be buttressed by improved organisation and management. In 1985 the divisional set-up had been overhauled in a major way for the first time since 1969. In the place of the large number of divisions, a smaller number of branches, each the responsibility of an Assistant Secretary, was devised, and the system that has characterised the department ever since. The initial reorganisation was into six branches: General Economics, Social Policy and Government Services ('SPAGS'), Industries, Fiscal Affairs, Corporate and Operations. Over subsequent years the reordering of these 'baronies' was to provide important clues to Treasury's orientation and outlook.

Another endeavour involved acting on the comments of the 'three wise men', who had stressed the need for improved management and communication, and

Treasury's own internal review. 'The older ones among us', mused Graham Scott in 1991, 'will remember … the watershed in 1984 when out of a sense of hope, but also possibly desperation, the entire management of the Treasury went away for a day and put in train a process of management development in this organisation, which has now been going for seven years.'[126] One of the junior officials recalled the first phase as one of 'osmosis, consensus, enquiry and debate … one [decision] was to remove two layers … of the hierarchy. The two deputy secretaries were about to leave their positions anyway, so it was easy to remove that layer. We also removed the director layer, accompanied by some staff shuffling and departures'.[127]

Treasury's shift from thinking in terms of promotion through a hierarchy to other forms of management and advancement marked a considerable departure from standard public service practice. The establishment of departmental autonomy under the State Sector Act 1988 was a key moment. Scott, who was by now Secretary to the Treasury, circularised the staff on 1 April 1988 to explain that he, not the State Services Commission, was now their employer. The public-service-wide EFA class, which had existed for just over two years, became obsolete, although the terminology survived. Treasury was now responsible for the pay and conditions of its own staff, and could take its own steps to improve the working environment.

Was there any limit to how like a business organisation Treasury could become? 'Many of the measures used in the analysis of the performance of a private sector organisation are not appropriate to a Treasury. The Treasury does not seek a surplus or a profit from its operations, nor does it borrow to fund its activities, nor is there any obvious private sector equivalent for price comparison purposes.'[128] Nor could it reward staff with a payout from profits or through share options.

Paralleling the developments in professionalisation and management, Treasury shared another kind of 'modernisation' with other government departments. The years after the end of the wage and price freeze had been rocky for the whole department. Telephonists and secretaries, for instance, had engaged in industrial action on a number of occasions, usually during pay negotiations.[129] An Employee Assistance Programme was devised in 1985 and re-established in 1990, when the Treasury's first-ever industrial chaplain was also appointed. Stress management courses were introduced in 1986, the year that the first memorandum on a smoke-free environment was circulated, although 'it was not expected that

Treasury staff: John Nichol and Alf Kaiwai, c. 1990. Averall Gibson

a completely smoke-free environment will be achieved immediately, or even in the near future'.

Graeme Martin, a senior analyst, developed Treasury's thinking on Treaty of Waitangi issues and contributed the relevant section to *Government Management* in 1987. Seminars on Maori issues were run by outside consultants, notably Donna Awatere. Scott was determined that everyone in the department, starting with the senior managers, would go on such a course. A wharenui was opened on the fourteenth floor in 1991, when the department formally adopted a Maori name. It had been known for many years 'round the traps' as 'Te Tari Putea' — the money department. The new name, 'Kaitohutohu Kaupapa Rawa', was translated as 'the people who advise on everything to do with resources'.[130]

These changes embraced the entire department, not just analysts and managers, and they were another way in which Scott took a strong lead.[131] This was not surprising; he was not a conventional corporate head. His rendition of Elvis's 'Blue Suede Shoes' at a Surfdale function is recalled by many,[132] and in one stressful year he took a beginners' ballet class and performed in the end-of-year concert. Equal Opportunities initiatives were taken, including the collection of statistics on the respective employment situations of men and women in the

Te Wharenui, fourteenth floor of the Treasury, with early Treasury officials recalled on the pou.
Treasury

department, and sexual harassment was addressed formally for the first time. In practice, working conditions for women were not congenial, particularly for mothers:

> A whole lot of things made it very hard for women. It didn't hurt me to work long hours because I didn't have children and my husband worked hard. Two of the women had young children. One of them was working part-time and had in theory set hours, but they would make a meeting outside her acknowledged hours — it was not deliberate, they didn't think about it. Shortly after my first son was born they rang and asked me to return part-time — but I had been working 80-hour weeks just before I stopped, so I asked them whether the 'part-time' was twenty hours or 40![133]

The private-sector model applied most closely to Treasury's financial activities. We have already explored the pressure that was placed on Industries Branch. Loans activity was a parallel sphere. The government's borrowing programme, which Treasury managed, had become controversial in 1984 when the snap election led to the run on the dollar and short-term difficulties in accessing funds. Roderick Deane recalled that

Treasury staff at Castlepoint on the Wairarapa coast, where the department had a bach.
Averall Gibson

the Treasury held most of the overseas reserves, much of which were invested in long-term Japanese yen bonds. I had written to them on numerous occasions the previous year pleading with them to realise these bonds. Now Treasury told me they couldn't realise them. I had all the letters in front of me — 'This is how often I have written to you!' I was just livid with them.[134]

That experience reinforced a belief in the merit of using standard corporate practices for such activities which underlay Treasury's decision to argue for a 'treasury' unit in the department that would

> manage the Government's overseas assets and liabilities in line with commercial management principles that apply to private sector institutions. Our assessment is that constraints imposed by public policy aspects of the Government's economic programme, namely monetary, exchange rate and industry policy — are not incompatible with management of the Government's overseas currency assets and liabilities within a profit maximisation/risk minimisation framework.[135]

The constraints outlined meant that such an office could not operate under an SOE regime. The introduction of the EFA occupational class meant that it could function more like a private-sector organisation by employing qualified staff on performance pay or contract. A Reserves and Debt Management Directorate was established, and on 1 July 1988 this was reconstituted as the New Zealand Debt Management Office:

> John Zohrab took that over. He was quite managerial and very ambitious for the DMO. And very thoughtful, and really turned it into something … People wanted to work there. He even changed the carpet — everyone else had the crappy carpet — he got proper security, decent equipment.[136]

The reference to carpet is suggestive. The British Treasury was famous for its 'Fabian austerity', for 'the well-known style of an intellectual aristocracy walking on linoleum floors'.[137] DMO's carpets, followed by the controversial refurbishment of the Secretary's office in 1991 at a cost of $100,000, suggest a public face more in accord with corporate norms, even given that the refurbishment was part of an upgrading of the entire building by its owners, the National Provident Fund. Answering questions about the refurbishment of his own office area from Parliament's Finance and Expenditure Committee, Scott explained that this included a boardroom for formal meetings, and that 'he often had to meet with senior executives and politicians from New Zealand and overseas in this environment'.[138]

The new occupational class was called 'economic and financial'. Would the latter area remain a Cinderella, or would the need for financial expertise thrown up by both corporatisation and privatisation, and by the reform of the core public sector, change this situation? The old professional rivalries lingered, sustained in the Treasury by the memory of the displacement of accountants by economists at the top of the pecking order.

Here again, Scott was an innovator. As has been mentioned, he was unusual amongst his generation of Treasury officials in having studied accountancy as well as economics and qualified professionally as an accountant. 'There had traditionally been', Scott recalls, 'a real stand-off between the accountants and the economists … I symbolised an effort to change all this by joining the Accountants Society in 1989. The accountants in the department were really pleased, and sent me messages — "Accountants do it with beans" — and welcomed me into the fraternity.'[139]

While Scott was a qualified accountant who had turned to economics, Ian Ball was an accountant who had done his doctoral work in economics. Looking back, Ball saw the new common ground between accountancy and economics as of crucial significance:

> In the financial reporting area, accountants had traditionally adopted the notions of historic cost, recording the actual price of the transaction, whereas economists wanted to look at the subsequent value or opportunity cost of that same asset. [But] over the past probably twenty years, the area of intersection has become larger. Some of the work in positive accounting theory has explained the reasons why accountants do things in the way that they do. That's been of interest to economists. And also, economics has taken a greater interest in information, and what gives accounting information value. I think that has led, amongst good accountants and good economists, to an understanding of the two disciplines as being very closely related, rather than being at odds.[140]

Scott and Ball also brought public-sector accountancy into line with private-sector practice. Tony Dale was a younger Treasury official who played a key role in the drafting of the Public Finance Act. After winning the CBA Young Accountant of the Year Award in 1992, he commented that 'if the award had been running five or six years earlier it is most unlikely that we would have seen public sector accountants being recognised in this way ... it is a recognition of the changes in the public sector part of the profession'.[141] Thus, whereas in the 1920s accountancy had been seen as the key professional skill, and in the era of economic management economics had assumed that role, now the two were combined. More accountants were recruited to Treasury, 'mainly from the private sector. We offered comparable remuneration. The State Sector Act allowed us to do that, and on a contract by contract basis.'[142]

Financial expertise was also central to the work of the SOE Advisory Unit. While Treasury was not prepared to be represented on the boards of SOEs, it could not be indifferent to their activities. The unit, which was administratively linked to Treasury, monitored the performance of the SOEs, its role being to provide the Minister of State Owned Enterprises with 'relevant, timely and independent advice in respect of his responsibilities' under the Act. In 1993 the Crown Company Monitoring Advisory Unit (CCMAU) assumed the tasks of the unit and two related bodies, the Crown Research Institutes Steering Committee and the Crown Health Enterprises Monitoring Unit. Like its predecessors, it was designed to 'monitor the performance of these organisations in terms of risks they might leave with the taxpayer'.[143]

From welfare state to social services?

In the 1920s and early 1930s, attention began to be paid to the efficiency in financial terms of what were then called the 'social services', as well as to that of the developmental arms of government. 'Social services' was the term habitually used at that time to describe government spending on pensions, education and hospitals. Investigators looked for ways to economise, for instance by the wholesale amalgamation of hospital boards, which was proposed in 1932. 'Not all social service states are welfare states', K. J. Scott argued in 1954. 'The liberal attitude is that social services should be provided in the interests of efficiency, usually ... of business efficiency, just as the military attitude is that the social services should be provided in the interests of military efficiency.' By contrast, the welfare state has humanitarian or egalitarian mainsprings.[144]

There is an echo of this 'social service state' in the 1980s thinking about efficiency in spending. Thus a Treasury memorandum of July 1986 pointed out that the major area yet to be tackled in expenditure reform was 'social expenditure. There seems to be considerable potential for efficiency-improving changes within health, education and social welfare, votes which comprise over 50 percent of net Government expenditure[,] through improved targeting ... and a review of the means of provision.'[145] In practice, in 1985 and 1986 the principal work on social policy was on reforming the taxation and benefit systems, which did not impinge directly on Treasury's approach to the institutions of social policy. It was recognised in any case that major reforms would have to await the next parliamentary term and the report of the Royal Commission on Social Policy, a major inquiry initiated by Lange which was intended to guide government thinking on all social policies and was seen by many in the Labour Party as a bulwark against neoliberalism. Treasury was not the main player in this exercise.[146]

However, in late 1986 Douglas suggested that Treasury begin talking to the departments of Health and Social Welfare about undertaking fundamental policy reviews, and there was discussion about the scope for commercialisation in the health and education sectors.[147] A health review was chaired by Alan Gibbs, an Auckland businessman who had become involved in the corporatisation of the Forest Service, and its analysis was predictably informed by the argument that the health sector would benefit from better management and appropriate incentives.[148]

For their part, the Education Department and its minister pre-empted Douglas and Treasury by launching their own review. A Treasury official served on the secretariat, but not as a member (although there was a Treasury representative on two other education committees, those reviewing early childhood and post-compulsory education). This may explain why Treasury devoted an entire second volume of *Government Management* to education. It argued that the government should 'reduce funding tied to major educational institutions and redirect funding to individuals, families, local groups and smaller scale institutions [but] where government interposition between customer and provider is unavoidable, the Government should seek methods of management and accountability which will counter rather than reinforce problems arising from the role of Government.'[149]

The education task force was chaired by 'a businessman with a practical social conscience', Brian Picot,[150] whose appointment had been supported by Lange. Its report of April 1988 was nonetheless much in line with Treasury thinking, certainly in its emphasis on the bulk-funding of autonomous self-managing schools.[151] In health, the new minister, David Caygill, declined to adopt the Gibbs task force's recommendation for a more corporatised system, choosing rather to focus on ways of improving the management of hospitals and the new area health boards. Nor was there significant institutional progress in social welfare. Commenting in 1990 on a call from the International Monetary Fund for a reduction in the deficit and cuts in social spending, senior Treasury official Howard Fancy observed that 'to reverse expenditure trends [in health, education and social welfare] would most likely require changes to current institutional arrangements in these areas'.[152]

Action on the institutional front followed National's election victory in October 1990. A substantial Treasury report on social policy prepared for the new government argued powerfully for short-term spending cuts followed by institutional change and the targeting of benefits. It was 'desirable that there be … improved accountability, and the use of SOE type structures in several areas'. The SOE model, argued Mark Prebble, the report's author, had shown that savings were possible, particularly if responsibility for industrial relations could be removed from the SSC — 'labour shedding was an important first step to improving productivity'. The Accident Compensation Corporation could be opened up to competition, schools fully bulk-funded, and parallel institutional changes introduced in health and social welfare. Prebble cited a 1987 study undertaken by the consultants Arthur Andersen for the Gibbs task force, which had calculated that savings of up to 32 per cent could be achieved in hospital expenditure through increased efficiency (although others disputed the study's methodology). The SOE model was also invoked in other ways. For example, placing private-sector managers on the boards of SOEs had been 'an important means of mobilising extra skills … a similar innovative approach is needed here'.[153] The inability to give precise estimates of the likely gains from institutional change was itself an argument for making the change, according to Prebble, because

> it demonstrates the paucity of useful management information in the social services, which is itself a symptom of institutions with weak accountability. At the time when it was decided to proceed with introducing SOEs into the commercial aspects of government activity there was a similar lack of data.[154]

In its Economic and Social Initiative of December 1990, the new government acted on 'the mandate it has obtained to redesign the Welfare State'.[155] Its Minister of Finance, Ruth Richardson, announced the establishment of a number of teams, to be co-ordinated by a Prime Ministerial Committee on the Reform of Social Assistance, that would investigate different aspects of the welfare state: a 'change team' on targeting social assistance (led by Prebble); a task force on the funding and provision of health services; a ministerial working party on the Accident Compensation Corporation; reviews of housing assistance and the guaranteed retirement income (superannuation). They would report in time for the consequent decisions to be announced in the 1991 Budget.[156]

Jonathan Boston later observed that 'the enormity of the reform agenda announced in the 1991 budget cannot be exaggerated. In the space of two years … the Government intended to make major changes in virtually every area of social policy.' But in practice, institutional reform in this area fell far short of the revolution in government management that had occurred in the SOEs, the core state sector, and Treasury itself. Prebble recalls that of all the task forces, 'the only one that was really important in the final analysis was the health one. Housing did lead to a certain change, but it wasn't the housing team that did it.'[157]

Nor did the changes that eventuated fully realise the corporate model or involve other institutional reforms.[158] The report of the Change Team on Targeting Social Assistance considered new means of delivering assistance, such as smart cards, but ended up recommending against these. The SOE model found favour in the health sector, where 'most large public hospitals will be established along more business-like lines as publicly owned Crown Health Enterprises'.[159] But individual choice would still be limited, because no more in health than in

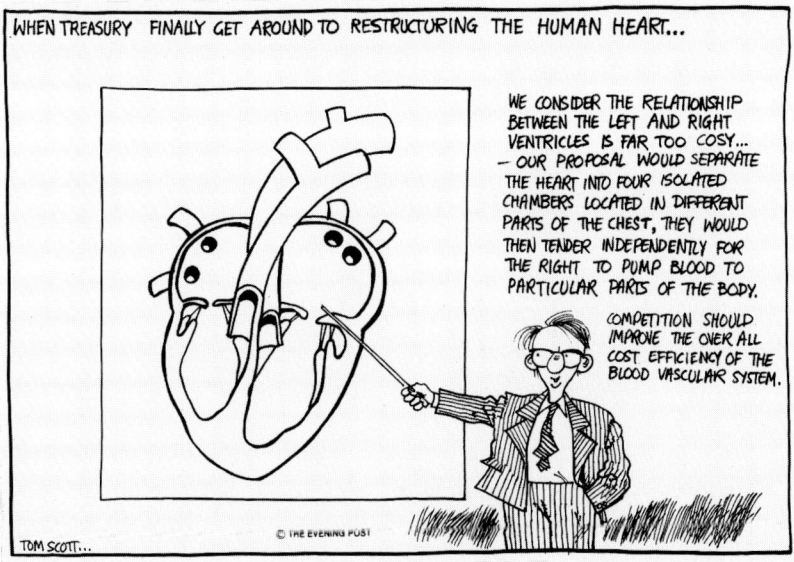

Was Treasury heartless? Tom Scott lampoons competition theory. Tom Scott, Alexander Turnbull Library, H-190-014

education could an individual 'buy' their taxpayer-funded entitlement (or that of their children). The funding of accident compensation was reformed, but not the institutional arrangements. More substantial change did take place in housing, where subsidised rents were replaced by an 'accommodation supplement' and the stock of state houses was transferred to a new state-owned enterprise.[160]

The relative failure of institutional change in the social services may have come about partly because Treasury's own concern with social policy was less intent than its attention to economic policy: 'finance ministries everywhere in the world have less focus on social policy than on economic policy. [There is] a kind of tribal, professional thing there — finance ministries are about economies, not about social policy.[161] Others concurred with this emphasis. Treasury had faced heightened hostility when it released its manifesto for social reform in *Government Management*. National's task forces and the officials' committees which supplemented them had representation from many agencies other than Treasury. The implementation of the health reforms was primarily the responsibility of the Department of the Prime Minister and Cabinet, not the Treasury or, for that matter, the Ministry of Health.[162] Scott observed in 1992 that while 'social policy has recently been an increasing concern of Governments … the breadth and intensity of the Treasury's work in these areas is unlikely to be sustained as other ministries develop their own capacities.'¹⁶³ Was this a rationalisation? Richardson felt that on some areas of social policy, her Treasury advisers were

> very, very deficient — and I'm being charitable — on execution capacity, on implementation. I didn't get the grunt out of my education advisers in Treasury that I got out of Budget advisers, for example. I didn't get grunt out of some of my social policy advisers. It wasn't [the cutting edge of the Treasury], and while at the senior Treasury levels they knew that it had to be integrated, they didn't have the high fliers, they didn't have the people with the high level of skill, and they were suffering from the 'let's gang up on Treasury' syndrome.

Richardson also conceded that there was a political dimension to the unevenness of the outcomes. 'Colleagues, when you venture out of [the finance area], tend to resent [you] poking your nose into education ... [or] health.' And although 'people like Graham Scott and Murray Horn had sat Bolger and Birch down late at night on the health reforms, and said, "Look, you either do this properly, or you don't do it at all", Bolger kept pulling the wings off the reforms.'¹⁶⁴ Beyond such aspects, it may have been that Treasury's objectives collided more violently in the social policy area than in the economic policy domain with deep-seated patterns in New Zealand's political culture. Strategies such as the health reforms were difficult to implement in a society which continued to have a predilection for exercising choice collectively rather than individually.

With respect to schools, Treasury had assumed that setting up locally controlled boards would provide a flow of information to parents, who would demand improvements in performance as they began to behave as individualist consumers of what the schools were offering — but this didn't happen.¹⁶⁵ In particular, most schools did not adopt the bulk-funding system that Picot had recommended. And also, ironically in view of Treasury's own evolution as a professional organisation, it failed to convince other professions: 'it is no coincidence that health and education have been the bête noire of government reform measures since 1987 ... By 1992, a major issue over which conflict emerges includes the actual practice, the professional attribute, of person to person conduct — teacher to pupil, medic to patient — as much as over retaining pay and conditions. The face-to-face professions feel threatened'.¹⁶⁶ And they demonstrated, through effective campaigns, their ability to keep Treasury-inspired schemes at arm's length.

The role of Treasury

The ambition to see the activities of government being 'managed', primarily in terms of corporate models drawn from the private sector, drove Treasury activity between 1984 and 1993 quite as much as did its ambition to see the economy managed differently. And while the first ambition was prompted by the contemporary focus on the desirability of microeconomic reform, of liberalisation, it was also rooted in the Treasury's traditional role as guardian of the public purse, which had become less prominent than its role in providing economic advice. Nagel has drawn attention to two approaches to the reform of government, approaches which he calls retrenching and reinventing.[167] It could be argued that the business emphasis of the 1920s was a case of retrenching and the professional emphasis of the 1980s and early 1990s one of reinventing, but in fact both impulses were found at both times.

Certainly there was less invention in the 1980s than Treasury itself thought. What little history was contained in Treasury's first annual report was erroneous; and there was nothing in, for instance, *Government Management*, to suggest that there was any historical context to Treasury's preoccupation with the state of the public finances. We therefore cannot conclude that what happened in this sphere in the 1980s and early 1990s was directly informed by past experience, although we may ask why the later episode so closely echoed the earlier.

The reinvigoration of the financial side of Treasury may have encouraged the idea that the department should be divided as the Australian Treasury had been in 1976. A commentator in 1986 expressed concern about 'the integration of the role of the government's senior economic advisors with the financial control functions of government'. This integration could result in 'inappropriate management' in two ways: financial control agencies become obsessed with deficits at the expense of economic objectives; and the combination of control and advice concentrated too much power in one department.[168]

But Treasury would not have been sympathetic to this view, and it held on to both functions. The fact that the period saw, not a shift back from economists to accountants, but a closer association between the two professions, supports that position. 'If there are problems in Treasury at the moment', wrote one official in 1992,

> I wonder if they are not most well illustrated by the phrase, 'the organisation is in transition from having a strong emphasis on policy to financial

management'. I think it is wrong to see this as what we should be aiming for in Treasury ... the trend ... should be exactly the reverse — from financial management to policy. A tremendous investment has been made in getting financial systems in place over the last few years. The result of that has been that analysts have had little time to do much else. However the time is now right to make these things work to inform policy. We should not set ourselves up as a bunch of technical experts on financial management but as an institution which can use all the information available including that from departmental financial statements to analyse policy issues. This in turn means that we need to think very carefully about our recruitment strategy. Recent experience suggests that going down the pure accounting line in terms of recruitment has not been at all successful either.[169]

Similarly, Ian Ball argued that 'accrual accounting for the whole of government will not amount to much more than an interesting accounting exercise unless the information is used for the purposes of economic management.'[170] For another commentator, renaming the institution was a possibility: '"The Ministry for Economic and Financial Policy" has a nice ring and better reflects what Treasury actually does'.[171] But the chances of this happening were no greater than those of Treasury willingly giving up either its financial or its economic responsibilities.

AFTERWORD

Chapter 10

Consolidation: The Treasury, 1993–2000

Introduction

In interviewing Treasury officials about the 1990s, I suggested that the decade, after its first years, was a far 'calmer' one for the department than the 1980s had been. This thought was always met with a vigorous rejoinder which stressed how much happened throughout the 1990s. But the contention still seems true from a number of perspectives.

Firstly, the framework of economic and financial management that had been put in place by 1993 survived the collapse of National's vote in the election of that year, the inauguration of a coalition government through a new electoral system in 1996, Bolger's departure from the prime ministership in 1997, the break-up of the coalition in 1998, and the election of a Labour-led coalition in 1999. On the political front, Bill Birch provided unanticipated continuity by remaining Minister of Finance from 1993 until late 1999. The economic environment provided more 'shocks' — the inflationary pressure of 1994–96, the Asian financial crisis which broke in mid-1997, the drought of 1998–99 — but these, too, were not as destabilising as might have been feared.[1]

Secondly, issues became less susceptible of grand solutions — an A list gave way to a B list. A Treasury retreat for middle managers in December 1994 tackled a challenge laid down by Bolger: what advice could Treasury provide on dealing with the 'problems of success'. There was general agreement, one participant recalled, 'that we faced a period of system management rather than a need to find a new paradigm.'[2]

The same mood was found within the Treasury. Early in 1997, senior managers asked whether there was now perceived to be less 'challenge' in working for the department, and instanced as a possible reason 'the change from a period of major reform to one with a greater focus on implementation'.[3] The in-house 'Buzz Report' addressed the question of what the department needed to do to

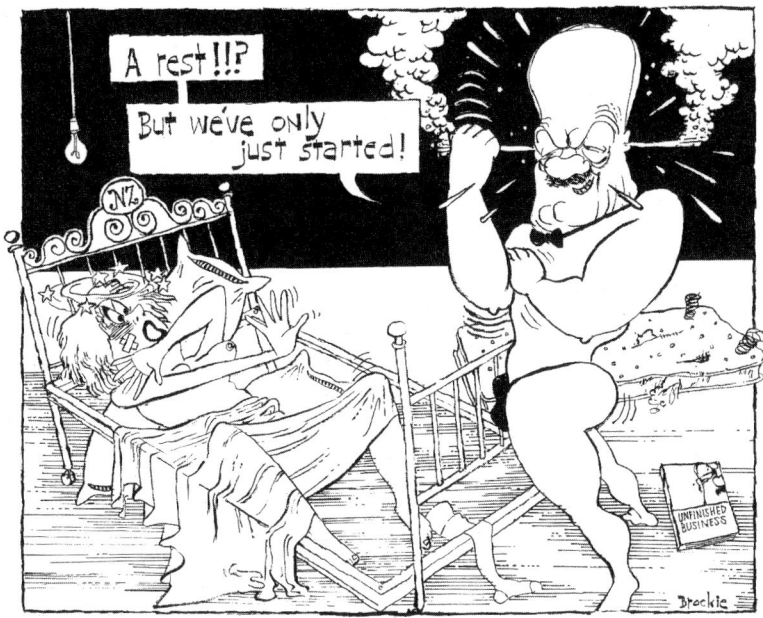

No time for a rest, let alone a cuppa. Even out of office, Roger Douglas argued that there was still much 'unfinished business'. Bob Brockie, *National Business Review*, 24 September 1993, Alexander Turnbull Library, A-296-038

maintain internal energy and enthusiasm. While arguing that it was 'difficult to see that Treasury and its staff faced a less challenging set of issues than [earlier]', it implicitly conceded the point by recognising that the challenges were less publicly visible and seemed smaller.[4]

To clinch the argument for continuity and stability, the number of articles about or referring to the Treasury dropped off markedly after 1991. Index New Zealand lists between 40 and 50 such articles for each year from 1989 to 1991, compared with 20 in 1992, 13 in 1993, and single-figure counts thereafter.[5]

Politics and economic management

The Parliament elected in 1993 was a 'hung' one, with National winning only 50 of the 100 seats and facing the certainty that a proportional representation system would be introduced in three years time. It did win more seats and votes than Labour, and retained a working majority when a Labour MP, Peter Tapsell, agreed to be Speaker. The most conspicuous change was in the respective standing of

Ruth Richardson and Bill Birch. That of Birch, a close friend of Bolger's, had risen as Richardson's had fallen at the time of her 'mother of all Budgets' in July 1991. As has been noted, National's superannuation, housing and health policies all soon faced severe problems of implementation, political flak or both, and there were a number of significant 'u-turns' in the second half of 1991. Birch had chaired the Prime Ministerial Committee on Reform of Social Assistance and the Cabinet Committee on the Implementation of Social Assistance Reform which had replaced it in October 1991. Ministers normally sat around the Cabinet table in order of seniority. At committee meetings Richardson took to sitting at the end of the table, where she was adjacent to Treasury officials, if they were in attendance.[6] An Enterprise Council was established by Bolger in part to provide a different source of economic advice, although Treasury hoped to focus this on its preferred approach to microeconomic reform.[7]

But when the columnist Bruce Jesson wrote that 'Pukekohe is having its revenge and is taking control of The Terrace and Featherston Street', he underestimated the readiness of Birch, whose home base was Pukekohe, and Bolger, who made Birch Minister of Finance in place of Richardson after the 1993 election, to stick with the main outlines of economic and financial management that had been devised since 1984.[8] The illuminating point of reference was not Birch's time as Minister of Energy and National Development (1978–84), but his chairing of the Public Expenditure Committee between 1976 and 1978. Like Coates before him, who had occupied both the Works and the Finance portfolios, Birch's outlook was shaped by office.[9] Birch and Treasury were aligned on all the major aspects of economic and financial management.

During 1994 public discussion on monetary policy focused on the extent to which the Reserve Bank's preoccupation with keeping inflation within a narrow band was hindering a reduction in unemployment.[10] In 1995, as boom conditions continued, debate focused more on what would happen should inflation exceed the 2 per cent upper limit of the target range.[11] That these debates focused in the first instance not on Treasury but on the Reserve Bank was one consequence of the 1989 legislation. For their part, both Birch and the Treasury agreed with the Reserve Bank that price stability was the appropriate goal of monetary policy, and that the Policy Targets Agreement (signed between the Minister of Finance and the Governor of the Reserve Bank and specifying the agreed inflation target) should not be substantially revisited.[12]

The benchmark for fiscal policy was the Fiscal Responsibility Act. As was

Ruth's ascent, 1994. Tom Scott

mentioned in chapter 8, the bill had been introduced by Richardson before the 1993 election; its provisions were examined by the Finance and Expenditure Committee, which she now chaired, in 1994. In its initial form the bill provided for an economic and fiscal update to be provided at the time of the Budget, six months thereafter, and before every election; in addition, a document setting out the government's long-term fiscal strategy was to be tabled with the Budget. The committee added a requirement that a Budget policy statement be published by 31 March each year, and stated what it considered to be the principles of responsible fiscal management: the reduction of total Crown debt to prudent levels; the maintenance of those levels by ensuring that the Crown's finances remained in surplus over any significant period of time; the achievement and maintenance of 'safe' levels of Crown net worth; the prudent management of fiscal risks; and the pursuit of policies that would facilitate stable tax rates and levels. If the government wished to depart from these principles, the Minister of Finance would have to specify the reasons for the departure, the approach that was to be taken, and the time that would be needed to return to the principles.[13]

Both the Labour and Alliance parties were sceptical about this approach, and the senior Labour committee member, Michael Cullen, unsuccessfully moved an amendment which defined the objectives of fiscal policy as sustainable economic growth, a more fair and equal society, full employment, and a 'triple-A' credit rating from international credit rating agencies, such as Moody's. Peter Harris of the Council of Trade Unions argued that the fiscal responsibility provisions gave legislative authority to the current policy status quo and would constrain fiscal policy too narrowly.[14] But the bill passed, which strengthened National's commitment to the approach to economic management favoured by Treasury — including the emphasis on the distinction between 'fiscal' and 'economic' — and made it more difficult for a subsequent government to change course. The Fiscal Responsibility Act also strengthened the place of Treasury in government. Along with the Public Finance Act 1989 and the State-Owned Enterprises Act 1986, it was one of the relatively few acts that the Treasury administered; along with the Public Finance Act, it was also one under which it operated. The obligation to prepare the published six-monthly economic and fiscal updates entrenched Treasury's role as the government's financial and economic adviser.

The economy began to recover from the second half of 1991. The resulting revenue gains (coupled with the 1991 expenditure cuts) facilitated the attainment of the government's fiscal goals. A small surplus in the public accounts in 1993/94 was followed by much more substantial surpluses thereafter. It was predicted that the government would have no net foreign currency debt by the end of the 1996/97 fiscal year.[15] Birch recalled that Murray Horn, who became Secretary to the Treasury in 1993, like Birch himself, 'took a keen interest in getting the debt down. The two of us made a very strong commitment to getting the public debt down. It was at an unsustainable level when we took office.'[16]

The political climate was much less conducive to an acceleration of microeconomic reform; indeed, some critics argued that the reform process stopped when its momentum should have been maintained.[17] Senior Treasury managers agreed in April 1995 with the conclusion of an in-house paper that there was 'substantial potential for catch-up' by New Zealand with other countries in areas such as reducing tariffs, education, the labour market and immigration.

The paper speculated that attitudes, aside from those of the business community, were not conducive to growth.[18] Whether or not that was the case, public-sector reform in particular proceeded neither as far nor as fast as some argued for. The welfare state was not dismantled, and the pace of privatisation slowed. This partly reflected the fact that many of the biggest potential sales had already taken place, but it was also a response to political sensitivities. When Consumer Coalition 93 opposed the sale of Electricorp, 'Bolger, always the pragmatist went cold on the proposal', although the SOE was split into two parts.[19]

A sardonic view of Bill Birch's 1996 tax cuts. Malcolm Walker, Alexander Turnbull Library, H-258-001

Public opposition to privatisation did not wane in the new parliamentary term. The sale of the Forestry Corporation provoked the Alliance party to campaign for an indicative referendum on the subject in 1996; a petition secured 242,000 signatures.[20]

Tax reform was one area in which common purpose survived. A Treasury review of the relationship between taxes and growth early in 1992 noted that 'a strategic decision had been taken in the early 1980s to move towards a broad based direct income tax and an indirect expenditure tax … Since that time, the focus had been on achieving that objective in an increasingly open and dynamic economy'. One preliminary 'key message' of the research was that 'there was little in the theoretical or empirical material' to suggest that New Zealand should 'move away from its "broad base, low rate" approach'.[21] On his side, Birch's enthusiasm for lower taxes was sufficient to make low and stable taxes a key economic strategy. Tax reductions and related social policy programmes were announced in February 1996, just nine months before the next election. The bottom tax rate was to be reduced from 24 cents to 19.5 cents, and the next from 28 cents to 21 cents, in two stages — a move which matched Douglas's reductions in the top rates between 1986 and 1988.[22]

On the core task of financial management, the control of expenditure, Birch proved to be another in a long line of fiscally conservative finance ministers. He was 'utterly reliable', recalled one Treasury official who worked with him:

> You probably always in a sense want a Finance Minister who will lean against the natural spending propensities and try and force trade-offs. And Birch did that, very vigorously. I remember the fatal mistake I made, at a Cabinet committee where he'd been arguing over what I knew was only $14,000. I got a message to Birch which said, 'I don't know that it's worth pursuing this.' The debate must have gone on for half an hour at that Cabinet committee — we probably would have easily have spent the $14,000 in ministers' and officials' time. But after the meeting I got a half hour of telling off. It was literally 'look after the pennies and the pounds will look after themselves'. There was a saying attributed to a senior Maori figure that Birch was the only person he ever knew who would reach down into a long drop to pick out 20 cents.

Fiscal restraint certainly operated in matters Maori. In its 1990 election manifesto, National had promised to settle all Treaty claims by 2000. In March 1992, Minister of Justice (and Treaty Negotiations) Doug Graham put forward proposals to the Cabinet Strategy Committee. The Crown had suffered embarrassing defeats when it had litigated Maori claims in the High Court, and it would be better to enter into direct negotiations with clients — 'chiefs meeting with chiefs'. The settlement of the fisheries claim at a national level seemed to set a precedent for land settlements, particularly with respect to the inclusion in the Deed of Settlement of a clause which recognised the 'fiscal constraints' on the Crown.[23] However, not every minister was happy with Graham's ideas. In April 1992 Richardson presented a paper to the Cabinet Strategy Committee on Treaty of Waitangi issues. Treasury took note, and Scott and Geoff Dangerfield set about enhancing the department's capability in this area. Mary Anne Thompson was recruited from Te Puni Kokiri, and recalls 'sitting in an interior windowless office, with a pad of paper and a dictionary. We looked up words like "compensation", "grievance" and "retribution".'[24]

Treasury's thinking crystallised around three elements: redress, fairness, and full and final settlement. The officials saw the settlement 'in the round', not just in fiscal terms. When the terminology changed from 'settlement' to 'fiscal envelope' it lost some of those wider dimensions, but the numbers were always going to be important. 'Back of the envelope' calculations based on possible payouts for big claims, middle claims, and to small groups resulted in a wide range of totals. Scenarios both below and substantially above $1 billion were canvassed in oral briefings to the minister. In deciding on $1 billion, therefore, Cabinet settled on a 'middle' figure.[25]

The issue was put to one side until after the 1993 election, when Birch, the new Minister of Finance, maintained Richardson's fiscal stance on settlement issues. In a draft reply to one correspondent who had sketched 'an alternative to the fiscal envelope', Birch reiterated that 'the Government can not pretend it has an open cheque-book. There are not unlimited resources to use in the settlement of Treaty claims.'[26]

In June 1994, Birch asked that further consideration be given to an accounting treatment of the settlement.[27] The publication of *Crown Proposals for the Settlement of Treaty of Waitangi Claims* in the second half of 1994 made explicit that the Crown would set aside $1 billion over about a ten-year period as 'the settlement envelope' — 'the amount in the Envelope is a political decision which cannot be open for negotiation'.[28]

There was substantial political fallout throughout 1995. The fiscal envelope was condemned as a breach of tino rangatiratanga (Maori sovereignty) at a hui of a thousand people convened by Sir Hepi Te Heu Heu at Turangi in January 1995. An envelope was symbolically burned on the steps of Parliament, and there was protest at the annual Waitangi Day celebrations. The thirteen hui held to discuss the Crown proposals with tribes were a public relations disaster to which the occupation by local Maori of Moutoa Gardens/Pakaitore in Wanganui from Waitangi Day until May provided a backdrop. The brunt of the criticism was borne by the Treaty negotiation ministers and Te Puni Kokiri, rather than by the Minister of Finance or Treasury. Treasury officials were amongst those who accompanied Graham, or occasionally the Minister for State-Owned Enterprises, Doug Kidd, to the hui, but their own minister never attended.[29] And despite the controversy, Tainui reached a settlement with the Crown in May 1995, with Ngai Tahu following suit in October 1996.

The new mixed-member proportional (MMP) electoral system which had been chosen by the voters in 1993 was duly implemented in the November 1996 election. New Zealand First, led by the former National MP and Cabinet Minister Winston Peters, got 13.3 per cent of the vote, whilst the Association of Consumers and Taxpayers, an explicitly neoliberal party that had been founded by Roger Douglas, Richard Prebble and Derek Quigley at the end of 1994 in anticipation of proportional representation, gained just over 6 per cent of vote. Perhaps because of the buoyancy of the economy, the 'left' vote slumped, with Labour down to 28 per cent (lower than in 1993) and the Alliance receiving only 10 per cent, compared with 18 per cent in 1993.

Peters, the kingmaker, was always more likely to ally himself with the party from which he had come than with a Labour Party led by Helen Clark. And unlike Labour's, National's vote was higher than in 1993. In the event, the coalition comprised National and New Zealand First. Would this marriage of convenience derail the process of economic management, a consequence of MMP which Treasury had feared? The initial negotiations provided some reassurance:

> Once it was clear that Peters would go with National, and wanted a role on the economic side, the PM said to me, 'Would you be willing to work with him on the fiscal and economic sides?' But he said he also wanted to maintain my role on fiscal management. And that became a key question in terms of dividing up responsibilities. I spent a full week continuously negotiating with Wayne Peters and developing the rules. It was my initiative, supported by the PM, to develop that agreement between us, which is really quite an historic document, but which gave responsibility to the Minister of Finance for continuing fiscal management.[30]

Winston Peters becomes Treasurer in 1996, to the concern of some of Jim Bolger's colleagues.
Alan Moir, *Sydney Morning Herald,* Alexander Turnbull Library, H-464-002

In his element: Winston Peters talks to the press. Treasury

According to Birch, Horn played a big role in settling the fiscal parameters of the coalition agreement: 'I saw him as my key adviser in making sure we got something that would work and would still leave the fiscal management with the major party.'[31] Treasury's 'output classes' — its work — had to be reconfigured to match the ministerial division.[32] The demarcation echoed the 1976 split of the Australian Treasury's functions into two departments, economic and financial, and also a kind of horizontal division between strategy and implementation, but in practice was one of form but not substance — both ministers received all Treasury reports.

Peters's reference to 'conservative and prudent fiscal management' in the first Budget he delivered as Treasurer on 26 June must have reassured Treasury, as did his readiness to divest the government of a variety of minor trading activities.[33] The terminology of the fiscal envelope was abandoned, but not the fiscal restraint which the phrase embodied. But a new political flavour was evident in a variety of ways. The coalition partners agreed to keep certain 'strategic assets' — including the Electricity Corporation (ECNZ) and its spin-offs Contact Energy and Trans Power — in public ownership, thereby cementing Bolger's 1993 pledge not to privatise the electricity industry in a formal agreement between political parties. The Crown health enterprises were to not to be profit-oriented — and were renamed 'hospitals'.[34]

In contrast, New Zealand First's impulses in social policy were conservative and close to the stream of thinking in National, of which Social Welfare Minister Jenny Shipley was an exemplar, that was unhappy about 'state dependency' — individuals receiving most of their income from government-paid benefits over a significant period — and saw beneficiaries as having obligations as well as entitlements. Treasury officials worked intensively in the first months of 1997 on New Zealand First's contributory retirement savings scheme (RSS), which was launched in July 1997 but defeated in a referendum two months later.[35] Benefits were analysed and reformed more thoroughly than they had been since 1991, and with similar motives: to increase the incentives to seek work, and to reduce the incentives to stay on benefits. Recipients of the domestic purposes benefit were required to seek part-time work once their youngest child reached the age of six, and invalids to the extent that they were able, while the level of the sickness benefit was aligned with that of the unemployment benefit.[36] Rather in contrast, the coalition partners abolished the surcharge tax on income earned by superannuitants which had been controversially reimposed by the National government in 1991.[37]

Unexpectedly, it was economic rather than political shocks which tested the coalition's skills in financial and economic management. Economic growth had already slowed when the Asian financial crisis broke in late June 1997.[38] The Treasury had no forewarning of this development: discussion amongst senior managers in May had focused on the prospect of a 'weak recovery', and the Secretary gave no inkling of the catastrophe to come when he briefed colleagues on his return from an Asian tour on 9 June.[39] In 1998, Peters explained that the government would cut $300 million of the $5 billion set aside for new policy initiatives in the coalition agreement in order to bolster operating surpluses. By the time the 1999 Budget policy statement was tabled seven months later, new fiscal forecasts signalled that there would be operating deficits and a pause in the process of reducing net Crown debt. Bill Birch, who had by now taken over the Treasurership, told his listeners that the government's main strategy was to allow the 'automatic fiscal stabilisers' to operate in the short-term, and to cut the additional policy initiatives it was committed to by a further $300 million, as well as taking other steps to bolster the medium-term fiscal position.[40] It was the public explication of these moves and the connection that was made with longer-term strategies that was novel.

Birch had become Treasurer when the coalition with New Zealand First collapsed in August 1998. The second $300 million reduction in spending commitments that was proposed only weeks after the 1998 Budget proved to be the breaking point. The return to National Party government (supported by some former New Zealand First MPs) opened the way for deregulatory initiatives. Asset sales became politically feasible, and the government sold Contact Energy and its shares in Auckland and Wellington airports.[41] And the monopoly of accident insurance held by the Accident Compensation Corporation was removed:

> the government had finally got itself to a point again of … thinking, 'Here's something we can do that's consistent with our philosophy and sort of ambitious and radical. We don't have to have this insurance delivered by state monopolies.' You can still keep bits, can still prescribe entitlements — it's actually very much like the separation of purchase and ownership we went through with core departments.[42]

As it transpired, however, this was but one initiative that would be reversed by the Labour–Alliance coalition which took office in 1999.

'No Easy Answers'

During the 1990s, economic management was conducted in a more stable environment than might have been expected early in the decade. Did this mean that it was also harder for Treasury to 'score goals' — indeed, to define the goals? For fiscal policy, the advent of surpluses moved the goalposts. In an in-house paper in 1997, Jas McKenzie, who had returned to Treasury as an adviser after a term as Secretary of Labour, observed that 'when we moved rapidly into surplus and got within cooee of achieving at least the debt target, our need for improvement became less urgent. It became more difficult to harness a political constituency for fiscal prudence.'[43] In the monetary policy field, research suggested that even more had been accomplished than had been realised. A 2002 Treasury paper found that 'in contrast to the attention they receive in public debate and the popular press, shocks from domestic interest rates and the exchange rate have been relatively unimportant contributors to New Zealand recessions and booms during the last two decades. In fact domestic interest rates shocks have tended to be countercyclical during the 1990s, thereby contributing to dampening booms and reducing the severity of recessions.'[44]

With respect to microeconomic change, one official commented that 'we all talked about the fact that it's easy to knock off the obvious things — the labour market and the fiscal part. It was harder yakker on some of the rest — social policy and even ongoing economic reform, which was quite difficult technically, in terms of utilities; there was no obvious answer like just creating an SOE.'[45] Birch agreed:

> The energy sector, in particular, was complex because you are dealing with monopoly suppliers and monopoly ownership of resources … There's been a lot of contention about the way it's been handled, the division between line and energy companies, and all that sort of thing, but the fact is that you're now getting a much more competitive energy industry, and that will have a profound impact on long-term pricing.[46]

Roading reform loomed on the horizon in the later 1990s, when it was noted that at a conservative valuation the Crown's investment in roading was roughly equivalent to ECNZ's asset base. But Treasury senior managers questioned the robustness of one analysis of the potential economic gains ($200 million to $300 million) from roading reforms: 'the basis for these figures at this stage is largely anecdotal … More work on the source of potential economic gains was requested'.[47]

Certainty on distributive issues was also elusive. Work on income distribution in the mid-1980s and late 1990s in collaboration with the Department of Labour, broke down changes into components related to changes in households (such as the rise of single-parent households), household attributes (such as age, ethnicity, and educational qualifications), and the employment status of household members. 'After accounting for these effects, a large unexplained residual remained.'[48]

The central goal of economic management since the early 1960s had been increased growth. This goal drove the development and planning conferences of the 1960s, the calls for liberalisation in the 1970s, Think Big in the early 1980s, and the substantial liberalisation of the mid- to late 1980s. The belief that microeconomic reform enhanced growth remained widely accepted in the 1990s, but Treasury discussions in late 1994, prompted by Bolger, on 'Maintaining 4% Growth to 2010', suggested that there was no simple answer to the question. Demographic factors, including 'an increase in population of around 20%, an ageing population and a change in ethnic mix', loomed as large as 'traditional' microeconomic considerations such as 'the need for New Zealand to be responsive and innovative in terms of an uncertain world trading environment.'[49]

As economic growth waned in the later 1990s, debate about the worth of the

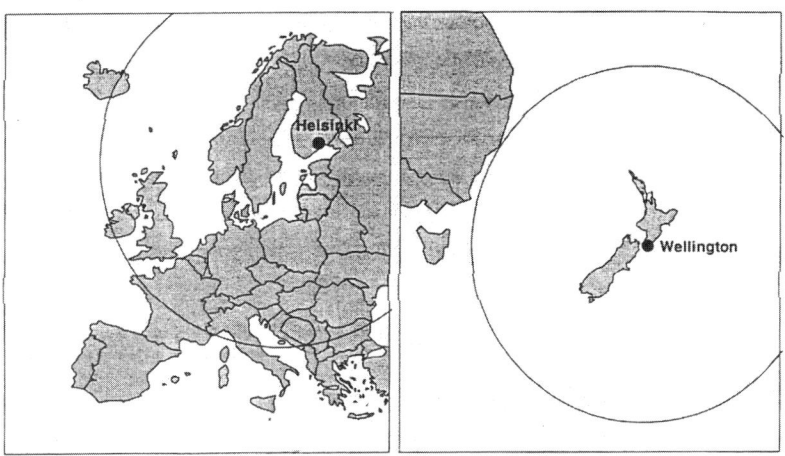

Where is everybody? Treasury's 1999 Briefing to the Incoming Government *makes a point.* Treasury

1984–1991 reforms revived. A 2001 paper by Grant Scobie demonstrated that, depending on the time periods chosen ('data mining', as economists called it), it could be concluded that compared with the pre-reform era there was either no increase in the growth rate, a little, or a lot. And while the overall growth rate *was* higher in the 1990s than in the 1980s, it was not high enough to close the gap between New Zealand and high-income OECD countries. Some analysts blamed the high exchange rates of the 1980s (in other words, revisited the sequencing argument), which by Scobie's calculation had still reduced both employment and output by 2 per cent per year between 1984 and 1996.[50] Yet research on the 1998 recession found that climatic factors — a drought — had played the major role.[51]

Many OECD statistics showed a marked convergence in growth rates amongst groupings of countries, for instance in Europe, and it was perhaps no accident that an economic geography discussion group formed in Treasury in 1999. The *Economist* picked the point up in a story on the New Zealand reforms which referred to the country's handicap in being the 'last bus stop on the planet'. The 1999 post-election briefing was the first to graphically draw attention to New Zealand's remoteness from other markets, counterposing maps in the form of circles with a radius of 2200 kilometres centred on Wellington and Helsinki respectively — the former embraced only New Zealand's 3.8 million people, the latter more than 300 million.[52] This was the first use of a map to make an argument in a Treasury publication. And the map of growth itself, it seemed, remained outlined rather than finely detailed.

Murray Horn, Secretary to the Treasury, 1993–97. Treasury

Murray Horn's Treasury

As the last paragraphs suggest, the Treasury retained its analytic capability during the 1990s. Indeed, it remained in all respects very much the institution that had been shaped by Scott and his colleagues in the late 1980s and early 1990s. Murray Horn, who succeeded Scott as Secretary in 1993, becoming at 39 the youngest man ever appointed to the position, felt that 'I suppose I was considered to be more of the same, and I was proud to continue to champion the highest standards of professional public sector management that I had inherited'.[53]

The relative calmness of the external environment within which the Treasury operated had some interesting effects. Partly as a by-product of the department's high and often controversial profile in the later 1980s and early 1990s, its senior management paid a great deal of attention to Treasury's public image. While the viability of the New Zealand economy depended on judgements made in the economic marketplace, Treasury's credibility and effectiveness was tested in the political marketplace, where it ran fewer risks than it had in the preceding half-

Five secretaries, five economists, two accountants, 1998. From left: standing, Graham Scott (1986–93), Murray Horn (1993–97), Alan Bollard (1998–2002), Noel Lough (1976–80); seated, Bernard Galvin (1980–86). Treasury

dozen years. In contrast, towards the end of the decade substantial issues arose within the department.

The furthering of initiatives taken under Scott was most evident in the organisation of Treasury. After the workload involved in corporatisation and privatisation on the one hand, and the reform of state sector finances on the other, waned, the Industries and Financial Management branches were merged in 1995 into a Commercial and Financial Branch (CFB):

> While the Industries and Financial Management Branches had been at the forefront of world-leading public sector reforms, the financial management reforms and large-scale corporatisations are now largely complete … the new Branch will focus on the opportunities that the State sector and financial management reforms have created, allowing us to give greater attention to Crown balance sheet and ownership issues, including Crown entity governance. The development of a proper Crown balance sheet creates the potential to take more of a portfolio approach to balance sheet management. The Branch will be a centre of excellence in the public sector on accounting,

management and financial economics.⁵⁴

It was in such a context that Treasury described itself as 'one of a number of institutions in the wider world of business and government'.⁵⁵ At that time it was envisaged that debt reduction, including the virtual elimination of exposure to foreign currencies, would enable the Debt Management Office to be reduced in size. In mid-1997 DMO merged with CFB to create a new 'balance sheet' Asset and Liability Management Branch, thereby bringing the total number of Treasury branches down from seven in 1990 to five, a level which Horn hoped 'would prove relatively durable'. The DMO's London office was closed, and its functions centralised in the Wellington office.⁵⁶

Many vote analysis activities of CFB were transferred to the two other vote branches, Social Policy and Regulatory and Tax. The need to improve the 'fire power' devoted to vote analysis had been flagged by Scott in 1989 and recurred frequently.⁵⁷ One of the 'fathers' of the Public Finance Act, Ian Ball, remained sceptical about this:

> The ideal vote analyst for, say, Courts or Corrections is somebody who knows something about that industry, who's probably had ten years experience in one way or another, knows their way around the balance sheet. Part of the intention was that you would get better financial performance if you had a high-level game between a well-qualified, well-experienced chief financial officer and a well-qualified, well-experienced vote analyst. And I think what we ended up with was the chief financial officers by and large being much better, while vote analysts … didn't understand a balance sheet, and in many cases, couldn't talk back.⁵⁸

But for one Treasury manager, the underlying reason for the difficulty was that while Treasury prided itself on employing the 'best and the brightest', not all vote analysis work was demanding, economists still looked down on accountants, and most senior managers came from the economics side.⁵⁹ When a senior Treasury official addressed a gathering of his colleagues, it attracted no comment that he identified himself and them as economists rather than as officials or in any other way.⁶⁰

Whether offering economic or financial advice, Treasury remained preoccupied with its public image, in a fashion inconceivable in the earlier eras of ministerial visibility and departmental invisibility. The 1982 Official Information Act, the publication of Treasury briefing papers, the regular publication of Treasury forecasts, the controversial nature of some Treasury advice, and political instability had all contributed to this new focus. The communications director had attended senior management meetings virtually from the time of his appointment in 1988, and regular communications reports, which often focused on stories about Treasury advice that had appeared in the media, were submitted from 1993.

If there was some irony in this, because Treasury had a lower profile in the media after the early 1990s, this does not mean that there were no 'alarums'. One arose when a Treasury paper costing some of Labour's 1993 election promises but also including political comment was released to the party's finance spokesperson Michael Cullen under the Official Information Act. The paper had gone to the Minister but later been withdrawn because it did not conform with Treasury policy, but both the original paper and its replacement were released to Cullen. The revised version still made some inappropriate assumptions, according to Michael Collins, a former head of the Department of Scientific and Industrial Research who reviewed Treasury's actions for the State Services Commission.[61] A furore over another draft Treasury paper exploring the feasibility of selling some of the Alexander Turnbull Library's 'non-New Zealand heritage' collections further demonstrated the risks involved in giving advice that was liable to disclosure under the provisions of the Official Information Act.[62] In comparison, the threat posed when, on a Sunday morning in mid-1995, the 'uninterruptible power supply' in the Treasury's main computer room caught fire, was dealt with so promptly that at one point the largest number of hits on Treasury's web site were coming not from economists, businesses or the public, but from fire services around the world eager to find out how the emergency had been handled.[63]

In February 1995, just when Treasury was pulling back from direct involvement in the Treaty settlement process, earlier advice it had provided was queried by Parliament's Finance and Expenditure Select Committee. Both Horn and Deputy Secretary Mark Prebble asserted that Treasury had not recommended a specific figure — 'it was a political judgement about what the rest of the community was prepared to spend on this and whether it was durable'. In *Return to Sender*, his account of the fiscal envelope story, Wira Gardner, Secretary of Te Puni Kokiri at the time, reported on the controversy that subsequently erupted about the Treasury advice. The Select Committee eventually accepted that Treasury had muddled rather than misled it.[64]

The 'wine-box' affair prompted the holding of a commission of enquiry which reported in 1997 on allegations of tax evasion by major New Zealand corporates. This scrutinised the actions of the Inland Revenue Department and the Serious Fraud Office, not Treasury. But the High Court's findings in 1996 on the sale of New Zealand Steel to Equiticorp in 1987 did throw a spotlight onto Treasury officials.[65] The following year, a team from the television programme *Assignment* acquired a copy of a Treasury report on proposed savings within the Police.[66] A major OIA request in May 1997 sought Treasury documentation on the optimal size of the conservation estate, and on the potential for disposing of land controlled by the Department of Conservation.[67]

While there were recurrent controversies over Treasury forecasts in the mid-1990s, these were less intense than those of the late 1980s and early 1990s. They were often little more than 'beat-ups', in that they paid little attention to either the inherent difficulty of the activity or the extent to which what had once been an exercise carried out 'behind closed doors' was now exposed to public scrutiny.[68]

More specific to the 1990s was controversy over Treasury's remuneration policies. In 1994 front-page headlines revealed that the department had paid staff more than $1 million in lump-sum performance payments, and in 1995 *Management* magazine reported on its performance pay system:

> A rating of one earns 85 percent of the mid-point available in the grade, a 3 rating 'meets expectations', whereas a five earns about 126 per cent. For those who rated three and above, 10 per cent of their pay comes in the form of a lump-sum performance payment ... Any staff member who is unable to maintain his or her rating is given a year to pick up performance before his or her salary is cut beyond the 10 per cent.

Horn was an enthusiast for performance pay and thought the proportion of Treasury's total personnel costs it accounted for — less than 5 per cent — was too low.[69] This desire to see more of Treasury staff's pay at risk exemplified Horn's robust general approach. While most of his Treasury peers had come from solidly middle-class backgrounds, Horn's father was a small businessman, and Horn had worked on farms before attending university. A senior manager reflecting on Horn's time as Secretary observed that

> Murray of course had a formidable brain, and you combine that with being Secretary to the Treasury, which was perceived as a very powerful position ...

Five deputies and a secretary, 1997. From left: Peter Bushnell, Mark Prebble, Murray Horn, Geoff Dangerfield, John Whitehead, Iain Rennie. Treasury

> Murray would love to get into debates, and would debate vigorously, and I think quite openly and genuinely, but you combine those two factors and some people — not only women — found it intimidating.[70]

But many women certainly did. He was an 'extrovert bright *lad*', thought one female analyst, and those qualities, which were possessed also by other senior officials, were now more noticeable than they had been during Scott's tenure as Secretary. Had the Surfdale 'boys' — now middle-aged men — with their liking for drinking songs, and for recalling the legendary 1956 Springbok rugby tour, overlooked 'the girls', who were now women? In January 1995, senior managers discussed a paper which analysed responses at exit interviews, and 'in particular, comments made about some aspects of Treasury's culture and the impacts on staff. The relatively high proportion of female staff who declined to participate in an exit interview was also noted. It was agreed that, due to the small number of interviews that have been recorded since the practice of interviewing exiting staff was reinstituted twelve months ago definite trends are still not clear.'[71] In the middle of the year, the most senior woman in the department, Deputy

Alan Bollard, Secretary to the Treasury, 1998–2002. Murray Webb, Alexander Turnbull Library, DX-001-230

Secretary Irene Taylor (Lake) parted company with Treasury, and especially with its Secretary. She had been promoted to Deputy Secretary by Graham Scott and was running Industries Branch, but found relations with Horn difficult and resigned, leaving the senior management bereft of women. Based on comments made to her by women, Lake thinks it likely that the rate of female resignations increased after her departure. And certainly an investigation was put in train which produced Margaret Hanson's report on 'Why Women Leave Treasury' early in 1997, closely followed by the in-house 'Buzz' report on the Treasury's working environment and how this might be improved. In considering the two reports, the senior management team concluded that

> clearly the retention rates for women in Treasury indicate there is an issue to be addressed. It is likely that the response will involve issues of corporate culture and Senior Managers will need to take the lead in developing and modelling any changes.[72]

One branch manager recalled that

> Murray, to his credit, allowed those investigations to go ahead … but I think there was always a worry from him, but also from others, that he didn't want to lose that challenge and debate. But increasingly the view was that we should be able to do that but also make sure people were treated well.

When Horn resigned to take up a position with the ANZ Bank in August 1997, he was still younger than most Secretaries had been when they were *appointed*. Acting Secretary Mark Prebble 'picked up and ran' with many of the initiatives that came out of the two reports.[73] The appointment of Alan Bollard as the next Secretary to the Treasury marked a further departure. Every previous Secretary had been appointed from within the department, but Bollard was an outsider who had never worked there. Birch explained that

> there was a view amongst ministers that we should encourage appointments from outside the public service. We thought that was healthy — we were encouraging officials to go out and get experience in the private sector … we thought that was good for them, and that there should be more opportunity to appoint somebody based on merit, rather than following a career path within the public service. It was consistent with the changed culture under the State Sector Act, bringing recognised private-sector management principles into the public service.[74]

In fact, there was very little movement from the private sector into management positions in government. As in the past, there was movement within the state sector, notably the migration of senior Treasury officials to other departments — Mark Byers to Corrections, Howard Fancy and Rob McIntosh to Education, Paul Carpinter (and later Geoff Dangerfield) to Commerce/Economic Development, John Chetwin to Labour, Mark Prebble to the Department of the Prime Minister and Cabinet, and Warwick Tuck to Fisheries.[75] And, in recommending the appointment of Bollard, the SSC settled on an outsider less steeped in the culture of the commercial world than some senior Treasury officials. The professionalisation of Treasury in the 1980s and 1990s paralleled rather than imitated the private sector.

1999–2000

One analysis of the 1999 election was entitled *Left Turn*.[76] Certainly the voting pattern — with Labour's vote soaring from its 1996 584,000 to over 800,000 — supported that conclusion, as did some of the new Labour–Alliance government's initiatives — most notably the renationalising of provision for accident compensation and the union-friendly Employment Relations Act.[77] What were the consequences for Treasury? Only months before the election, the new Prime

The best of times? Evening Post, 21 October 1999

Minister, Helen Clark, had asserted, in commenting on Treasury papers from earlier in the year which discussed the difficulty of explaining New Zealand's low rate of growth in productivity, that it was 'no wonder that Treasury can't find the cause of the failure of the reforms because the cause is to be found in their own headquarters where the high priests of neo-liberalism have been found for a decade and a half'.[78]

'The new government', observed former Treasury Secretary Scott, 'largely cut officials out of their deliberations in cabinet subcommittees', with the Prime Minister warning them that there was 'a fine line between giving free and frank advice and obstructing the government's policies.'[79] If this was not 1982, it did resemble 1972 or 1988. For another former Treasury official, Birch had prolonged the period during which

> nothing limited what the Treasury could or couldn't do. You had a period where ministers were fighting [among themselves] and doing everything the organisation wanted. Treasury never *really* understood how to work with other agencies and leverage change through other agencies. The way it has always done it is effectively bully it. Treasury gets a Cabinet decision, other agencies implement.

But Michael Cullen, the new Minister of Finance, 'would not do that. So you've got an institution now trying to come to terms with, "What do we do when our minister won't fight our battles for us?"' Over social policy, a sphere in which

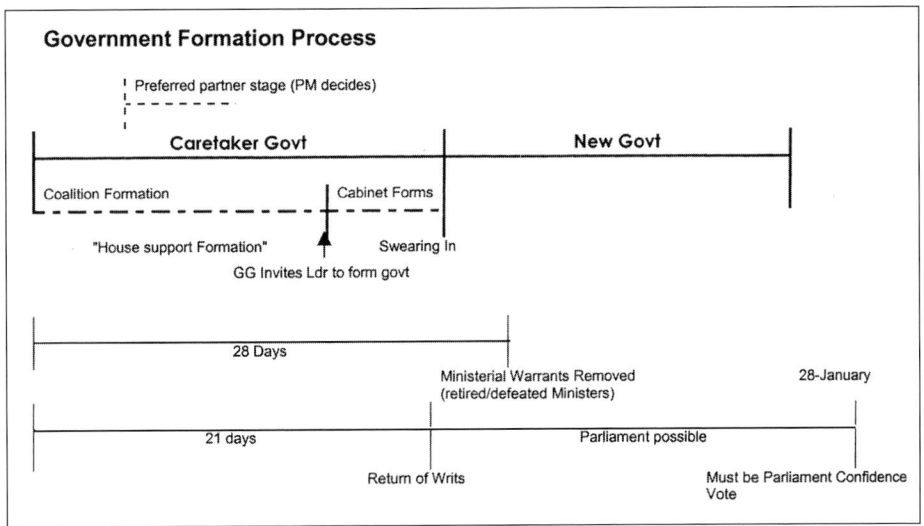

Government-making. The senior management group spells out the process in November 1999.
Treasury

both Cullen and Clark had contested Treasury advice in the late 1980s, the relationship between department and government was particularly jagged.

The reception of Treasury advice was thus far bumpier after 1999 than before, but it would be premature to conclude that in a few months Treasury had forfeited the roles in financial and economic management it had built up over 70 years. Five months before the 1999 election, the economist Brian Easton had described Cullen and Clark as 'fiscal conservatives'.[80] Three years later, in the aftermath of the 2002 election, after noting the paucity of economic debate during the election campaign, he speculated that this implicit consensus might not only be an expression of the prosperity of the preceding three years, but might embrace 'the post-war trend in economic policy … [of] opening up the New Zealand economy to the world and making greater use of the market mechanism.'[81] In sum, not only Treasury's professionalism but its politics survived: the three legs of the tripod, the Reserve Bank Act ('the gold standard'), the Fiscal Responsibility Act ('the balanced Budget') and microeconomic reform ('free trade') all remained more, not less, intact.

Appendix

Governments, Ministers, Treasury Secretaries and major events, 1890–2000

Election	Party forming government	Premier (to June 1906) Prime Minister	Colonial Treasurer (to 1907) Minister of Finance	Secretary to the Treasury	Major Events
1890	Liberal 1891	Ballance, 1891	Ballance, 1891	Heywood	
1893	"	Seddon, May 1893	Ward, May 1893	"	
1896	"	"	Seddon, Jun 1896	"	
1899	"	"	"	"	
1902	"	"	"	"	
1905	"	Seddon; Hall-Jones, Jun 1906; Ward, Aug 1906	Seddon; Hall-Jones, Jun 1906; Ward, Aug 1906	Collins, 1906	
1908	"	Ward	Ward	Poynton, 1910	
1911	Liberal; Reform, Aug 1912	Ward; Mackenzie, Mar 1912; Massey, Jul 1912	Ward; Myers, Mar 1912; Allen, Jul 1912	Campbell, 1913	
1914	Reform; National, Aug 1915	Massey	Allen; Ward, Aug 1915	"	WW1 starts Aug
1919	Reform, Aug 1919	"	Allen, Aug 1919; Massey, May 1920	"	WW1 ends Nov 1918
1922	Reform	"	Massey	Esson, 1922	

428

APPENDIX

1925	Reform	Massey; Dillon Bell, May 1925; Coates, May 1925	Massey; Nosworthy, May 1925; Stewart, May 1926	Hayes, 1925	
1928	United; Coalition, Sep 1931	Ward; Forbes, May 1930	Ward; Forbes, May 1930; Stewart, Sep 1931	Park, 1930	Wall Street crash, Oct 1929
1931	Reform/United coalition	Forbes	Stewart; Coates, Jan 1933	"	Britain off gold standard, Sep 1931
1935	Labour	Savage	Nash	Rodda	
1938	"	Savage; Fraser, Apr 1940	"	Ashwin, Feb 1939	WW2 starts Sep 1939
1943 (delayed)	"	Fraser	"	"	Economic Stabilization Commission, Dec 1942
1946	"	"	"	"	
1949	National	Holland	Holland	"	Korean War, starts Jun 1950 Waterfront dispute, Feb to Jul 1951
1951	"	"	"	"	
1954	"	Holland; Holyoake, Sep 1957	Watts	Ashwin; Greensmith, Jul 1955	
1957	Labour	Nash	Nordmeyer	Greensmith	'Black Budget', 1958
1960	National	Holyoake	Lake	"	
1963	"	"	"	Greensmith; Barker, 1965	

429

Election	Party forming government	Prime Minister	Minister of Finance	Secretary to the Treasury	Major Events
1966	"	"	Lake; Muldoon, Mar 1967	Davis	Balance of payments crisis 1966/67; NDC, 1968
1969	"	Holyoake; Marshall, Feb 1972	Muldoon	Lang	Stabilisation policies tried
1972	Labour	Kirk; Rowling, Sep 1974	Rowling; Tizard, Sep 1974	"	First oil shock, Oct 1973
1975	National	Muldoon	Muldoon	Lang; Lough, Dec 1976	
1978	"	"	"	Lough; Galvin, Dec 1980	Second oil shock, Dec 1978
1981	"	"	"	"	
1984	Labour	Lange	Douglas	Galvin; Scott, Nov 1986	Devaluation, Jul 1984
1987	"	Lange; Palmer, Aug 1989; Moore, Sep 1990	Douglas; Caygill, Dec 1988	Scott	Stock market crash, Oct 1987
1990	National	Bolger	Richardson	"	

APPENDIX

1993	"	"	Birch	Horn
1996	National/ New Zealand First	Bolger; Shipley, Dec 1997	Peters (to Aug 1998)/ Birch	Horn; Bollard (Aug 1997 to Feb 1998, Prebble, Acting Secretary)	First MMP election
1999	Labour/Alliance	Clark	Cullen	Bollard	

Notes

Abbreviations used in Notes and Select bibliography

AJHR	Appendix to the Journals of the House of Representatives
ATL	Alexander Turnbull Library
AUP	Auckland University Press
JPA	Journal of Public Administration
MF	Minister of Finance
NZIER	New Zealand Institute of Economic Research
NZJH	New Zealand Journal of History
NZJPA	New Zealand Journal of Public Administration
NZOYB	New Zealand Official Yearbook
NZPC	New Zealand Planning Council
NZPD	New Zealand Parliamentary Debates
OECD	Organisation for Economic Co-operation and Development
OUP	Oxford University Press
PNP	Port Nicholson Press
SMM	Minutes of Senior Management Group meetings, Treasury
ST	Secretary to the Treasury
VUP	Victoria University Press
VUW	Victoria University of Wellington

Introduction

1. See chapter 6.
2. Greg Whitwell, *The Treasury Line*, Allen & Unwin, Sydney, 1986, p. x.
3. Henry Roseveare, *The Treasury: The Evolution of a British Institution*, Allen Lane, London, 1969, p. 12.
4. Samuel Beer, *Treasury Control: The Co-ordination of Financial and Economic Policy in Great Britain*, Clarendon, Oxford, 1957; Samuel Brittan, *The Treasury under the Tories*, Penguin, London, 1964; *Steering the Economy: The Role of the Treasury*, Secker and Warburg, London, 1969.
5. George Peden, *The Treasury and British Public Policy, 1906–1959*, OUP, Oxford, 2000, pp. 28–9.
6. Gunther Roth and Klaus Wittich (eds), *Max Weber: Economy and Society: An Outline of Interpretive Sociology*, Bedminster Press, New York, 1968, pp. 956–1003.
7. James Buchanan, 'From Private Preferences to Public Philosophy: The Development of Public Choice', in *The Economics of Politics*, Institute of Economic Affairs, London, 1978, p. 11.
8. Buchanan, 'From Private Preference to Public Philosophy', pp. 3, 4.
9. James Q. Wilson, *Bureaucracy: What Government Agencies Do and Why They Do It*, Basic Books, New York, 1989, p. 23.
10. Macmillan, London, 1974. A more recent study is Frank R. Dobbin, 'Cultural Models of Organization: The Social Construction of Rational Organizing Principles', in Diana Crane (ed.), *The Sociology of Culture: Emerging Theoretical Perspectives*, Blackwell, Oxford, 1994.
11. M. O. Furner and B. E. Supple, 'Ideas, Institutions and the State', in M. O. Furner and B. E. Supple (eds), *The State and Economic Knowledge: The American and British Experiences*, Cambridge University Press, Cambridge, 1990, p. 28, citing Hugh Heclo, *Modern Social Politics in Britain and Sweden*, Yale University Press, New Haven, 1974, p. 305.
12. W. J. Reader, *Professional Men: The Rise of the Professional Classes in Nineteenth-Century England*, Weidenfeld and Nicholson, London, 1966, *passim*, but esp. p. 71.
13. If too much sterling was presented for settlement, interest rates would rise, commercial activity would contract, and the number of claims would decrease.
14. 1 Jun 1920, T 1, 12/287, Archives New Zealand.
15. *The Centenary of Treasury, 1901–2001: 100 Years of Public Service*, Department of Treasury, Parkes, ACT, 2001, p. 110, used of Ted Evans, Secretary to the Treasury, 1993–2001.

Chapter 1: The colonial Treasury

1. Journal of Felton Mathew, p. 14 [15], MS-1620, Alexander Turnbull Library.
2. Cooper, Anthony J. A., Family history c 1790 to 1851, MS-Papers-1886, Alexander Turnbull Library.

3 B. D. Zohrab, 'A History of the New Zealand Civil Service, 1840–1866', History Department, Victoria University College, n.d., p. 67. Cooper's salary was more than twice the £281 the government was to pay for the land on which Auckland was established.
4 Normanby's instructions to Hobson, 14 Aug 1839, in R. McNab (ed.), *Historical Records of New Zealand*, vol. 1, Government Printer, Wellington, 1908, p. 737.
5 16 Jan 1840, IA 40/11, Archives New Zealand.
6 'All the suite remained with [Captain Hobson] excepting Mr Cooper, who has resigned his office in disgust'. W. David McIntyre and Marcia McIntyre (eds), *Tour of Duty: Midshipman Comber's Journal Aboard HMS Herald on the East India Station — Australia, New Zealand and China, 1838–1842*, University of Canterbury, Christchurch, 1999, p. 121.
7 For more coruscating comment on Cooper, see Samuel Martin, *New Zealand in a Series of Letters*, London, 1845 (copy held at Alexander Turnbull Library), letter 10, 4 Apr 1844: 'it arouses a persons indignation that such vagabonds should be placed in positions of trust and responsibility'. I am indebted to Phil Parkinson for this reference.
8 A. H. McLintock, *Crown Colony Government in New Zealand*, Government Printer, Wellington, 1958, pp. 236–7.
9 Note the parallel discussion on banking liberalisation: P. L. Cottrell and Lucy Newton, 'Banking Liberalisation in England and Wales, 1826–1844', in Richard Sylla, Richard Tilly and Gabriel Tortella (eds), *The State, The Financial System and Economic Modernization*, Cambridge University Press, New York, 1999, pp. 75–117. Craufurd Goodwin, *Canadian Economic Thought: The Political Economy of a Developing Nation*, Duke University Press, Durham, NC, 1961, pp. 104–6, summarises colonial-era thinking on currency and banking issues.
10 Edward Bridges, *The Treasury*, George Allen & Unwin, London, 1964, p. 24.
11 Henry Roseveare, *The Treasury: The Evolution of a British Institution*, Allen Lane, London, 1969, p. 85.
12 The expenditures of the civil departments were gradually separated out from the civil list between 1760 and 1830; see Bridges, *Treasury*, p. 25.
13 Roseveare, *Treasury*, pp. 88–9.
14 Roseveare, *Treasury*, p. 118. David Kynaston, *The City of London: A World of its Own, 1815–1890*, Chatto & Windus, London, 1994, pp. 36–43, 126–30, indicates the slowness of much City opinion to accept the gold standard and the 1844 Bank Charter Act which constrained credit creation.
15 Roseveare, *Treasury*, pp. 136–7.
16 For detailed discussion of the changes during Gladstone's years as Chancellor of the Exchequer (1859–66), see Roseveare, *Treasury*, pp. 138–42. For an overview, see Bridges, *Treasury*, pp. 25–6.
17 Roseveare, *Treasury*, pp. 139–41 (quote p. 141).
18 Roseveare, *Treasury*, p. 118, comments that 'it seems no accident that "Conversion" and "Redemption" should be the operations most closely associated with the Debt's reduction'. The moral approach to the national debt waned between the two World Wars.
19 Roseveare, *Treasury*, pp. 186–91.
20 Roseveare, *Treasury*, pp. 166, 168–70. See also J. R. Torrance, 'Sir George Harrison and the Growth of Bureaucracy in the Early Nineteenth Century', *English Historical Review*, vol. 83, 1968, cited in Roseveare, p. 181, n. 1.
21 Roseveare, *Treasury*, p. 168.
22 Roseveare, *Treasury*, pp. 175–6; Bridges, *Treasury*, p. 109.
23 Bridges, *Treasury*, p. 110. For more, see Roy McLeod (ed.), *Government, Expertise and Specialists: Administrators and Professionals, 1860–1916*, Cambridge University Press, Cambridge, 1985; F. B. Smith (ed.), *Ireland, England and Australia: Essays in Honour of Oliver Macdonagh*, Cork University Press/Australian National University Press, Cork/Canberra, 1990, pp. 4–5.
24 M. McKinnon (ed.), *New Zealand Historical Atlas*, David Bateman, Auckland, 1997, plate 30.
25 P. Lissington, 'Early Years' [of the Treasury], ms held by Treasury, p. 16; D. McGee, *Parliamentary Practice in New Zealand*, GP Publications, Wellington, 1994, p. 302; quote is Fisher, *NZPD*, vol. 101, p. 211 (5 Jul 1898).
26 D. G. Herron, 'The Structure and Course of New Zealand Politics, 1853–1858', PhD thesis, University of New Zealand, 1959, p. 464.
27 W. D. McIntyre (ed.), *The Journal of Henry Sewell, 1853–7*, vol. 2, Whitcoulls, Christchurch, 1980, pp. 22, 37. McLintock, *Crown Colony Government*, p. 233, cites FitzGerald, another Canterbury figure, similarly.
28 *NZPD*, vol. 13, p. 194 (13 Sep 1872).
29 J. Graham, *Frederick Weld*, Auckland University Press, Auckland, 1983, p. 58, letter of 11 Jun 1854.
30 E. Bohan, *Edward Stafford, New Zealand's First Statesman*, Hazard Press, Christchurch, 1994, p. 219; see also p. 114.

31 *NZPD*, 1856–1858, p. 457 (25 May 1858); for Stafford similarly, see Bohan, *Stafford*, p. 121.
32 *AJHR*, 1864, B-1A, p. 5.
33 See T 20/3. For further on loan consolidation, see Raewyn Dalziel, *Julius Vogel, Business Politician*, Auckland University Press / Oxford University Press, Auckland, 1986, p. 86.
34 *NZPD*, vol. 6, p. 761 (26 Aug 1869). My emphasis.
35 James Froude, *Oceana, or England and Her Colonies*, 2nd edn, Longmans, London, 1892, p. 136. My emphasis. Note also the negative impact of Froude's book on New Zealand finances in 1886: Dalziel, *Vogel*, p. 265.
36 See, for instance, Dalziel, *Vogel*, pp. 99, 104–8 (p. 104: Vogel was 'working largely on his own' in devising his policy, 1870); Judith Bassett, *Sir Harry Atkinson*, Auckland University Press, Auckland, 1975, pp. 77–8, 83, 89 — 'Uncle Harry [Atkinson] is done up with his statement'; Timothy McIvor, *The Rainmaker: A Biography of John Ballance*, Heinemann Reed, Auckland, 1989, pp. 71–4, 86 — 'Grey had the Treasury Department draft estimates, prepared by Ballance, in front of him'. For Grey, see also James Rutherford, *Sir George Grey, K.C.B., 1812–1898: A Study in Colonial Government*, Cassell, London, 1961, p. 624.
37 *AJHR*, 1883, B-2, p. i (Atkinson, Financial Statement, 27 Jun 1883). In 1989 the government's financial year was shifted from March back to June. This allowed more time for taxation receipts information to be gauged, it conformed to the primary production year, and it also reflected the fact that Parliament sat for much longer than it had in the nineteenth century.
38 *AJHR*, 1883, B-2, pp. xii–xiv. The out-turn for Customs receipts was £1,397,000 (*AJHR*, 1884, Session II, B-1, p. 15). Debt servicing was still the largest single expenditure item in 1899/1900, accounting for about 28 per cent of total expenditure: *NZOYB*, 1900, p. 380.
39 Vogel to Cabinet, 24 Oct 1884, T 19/40. See pp. 45–6 for the activities of Vogel and Dillon Bell as Agents-General on financial matters. It is also possible to imagine some twentieth-century Ministers of Finance, such as Nash and Muldoon, commenting in this manner.
40 *AJHR*, 1880, H-2, p. 1. They hailed from Whangarei, New Plymouth, Masterton and Ashburton.
41 *AJHR*, 1880, H-2, p. 14. R. Hill, *The Colonial Frontier Tamed: New Zealand Policing in Transition, 1867–1886*, Historical Publications Branch, Department of Internal Affairs, and Government Printer, Wellington, 1989, p. 314, sees Cabinet deciding. See also J. E. Le Rossignol and W. Downie Stewart, *State Socialism in New Zealand*, Harrap, London, 1910, p.208.
42 *NZPD*, vol. 52, p. 31 (16 Jul 1885); see also M. Tennant, *Paupers and Providers*, Allen & Unwin and Historical Branch, Department of Internal Affairs, Wellington, 1989, pp. 25–31.
43 Although there is a record of W. Seed, the Comptroller of Customs, conducting an investigation — 'with regard to boots and shoes I learn from enquiries made of one of the largest dealers in these articles in Wellington … '; T 20/10, 1885 tariff revision, 30 Jun 1885. This was still a theme in the twentieth century: see S. G. H. Holland's strategy, for instance, discussed in chapter 6 — but it is not the only one. Note too that another element in the story of tariffs (in which Treasury was not deeply involved until the 1960s) was the shift in responsibility from Parliament to the government.
44 1885 tariff revision, T 20/10, Archives New Zealand.
45 1885 tariff revision, T 20/10.
46 1885 tariff revision, T 20/10. Dalziel, *Vogel*, pp. 260–1, explains the revision of the tariff after protests over the provisions announced in the Financial Statement. See also comment in Parliament on the lobbying process: 'Unfortunately for the labouring, agricultural, and industrial classes they were not in the position that the other classes, the professional class and the traders were in, to deputationize Ministers — as has been done lately here — in favour of a protective policy … they had not the same facilities to represent their case to the Government that the minority — the one fourth — had' (Chamberlain, 17 Jul 1885, *NZPD*, vol. 52, p. 40).
47 Agent-General to Colonial Treasurer, 26 Jul 1889, Wellington–Manawatu railway, T 20/10, explained that it would not be possible to do it without attracting attention.
48 Draft of 1886 Mortgage Debentures Act, T 20/10.
49 For more, see Bohan, *Stafford*, pp. 216–59, 268, and relevant statutes from 1866 and 1867.
50 Roseveare, *Treasury*, pp. 165–82; George Peden, 'The Treasury as the Central Department of Government, 1919–1939', *Public Administration*, vol. 61, no. 4, Winter 1983, p. 375, notes that it was from the 1860s that 'the annual estimates of all central government departments had to be submitted to the Treasury for approval, before being presented to Parliament.'

51 *AJHR*, 1866, D-7A, p. 42.
52 Le Rossignol and Stewart, *State Socialism in New Zealand*, p. 198.
53 *AJHR*, 1866, D-7A, pp. 25–6.
54 *NZPD*, vol. 6, pp. 426–7 (12 Aug 1869); pp. 526–34 (18 Aug 1869); pp. 759–62 (26 Aug 1869); vol. 7, pp. 27–8 (17 Jun 1870), pp. 206–7 (5 Jul 1870); pp. 292–3 (8 Jul 1870).
55 See comments by Sewell making his first financial statement in 1856: 'It will be remembered that according to accounts published at the beginning of the session, there was due, as Dr. Knight calculated …'; *NZPD*, 1856–1858, p. 141 (10 Jun 1856).
56 McIntyre (ed.), *Sewell Journal*, vol. 1, p. 454, n. 3; Sewell's critical comments about Knight in Feb 1854 (pp. 457–8) seem to have waned by the time he speculated about his future in May; McIntyre (ed.), *Sewell Journal*, vol. 2, pp. 20–1. For background, see McLintock, *Crown Colony Government*, pp. 233–4; R. J. Polaschek, *Government Administration in New Zealand*, New Zealand Institute of Public Administration/Oxford University Press, Wellington/London, 1958, p. 27; Edmund Bohan, *'Blest Madman': FitzGerald of Canterbury*, Canterbury University Press, Christchurch, 1998, p. 304; Knight biography, www.dnzb.govt.nz. *NZ Gazette*, 1858, p. 110 (6 Aug 1858)
57 Robert B. Bryce, *Maturing in Hard Times: Canada's Department of Finance through the Great Depression*, McGill-Queen's University Press, Kingston and Montreal, 1986, pp. 2–3.
58 *AJHR*, 1866, D-7A, p. 26.
59 1865, no. 74. This act seems to have paralleled the British act of 1834. See Chen and Palmer, 'The New Zealand Controller's Office: The Underlying Constitutional Principles', Report for the Treasury, Wellington, Mar 1998, p. 9.
60 Bohan, *Stafford*, pp. 235–6; Bohan, *'Blest Madman'*, pp. 297, 304. The FitzGeralds moved permanently to Wellington at this time, and eventually built a seventeen-room house above Oriental Bay and Clyde Quay on what later became the site of the Redemptorist Brothers monastery. Bohan, *'Blest Madman'*, p. 302.
61 Bohan, *'Blest Madman'*, p. 316. See also 'Short History of the Audit Department', Papers of W. J. Hunter, MS-Papers-1777-08, Alexander Turnbull Library.
62 G. H. Scholefield (ed.), *A Dictionary of New Zealand Biography*, Department of Internal Affairs, Wellington, 1940, vol. 1, p. 49. Batkin was probably the first to hold the title of 'Secretary', rather than 'Assistant Treasurer'.
63 *AJHR*, 1884, B-2, p. 13 (Audit); for Treasury staff salaries etc., 1881–1891, see T 20/10, Archives New Zealand.
64 *AJHR*, 1888, B-12.
65 See, for example, *Votes and Proceedings of the Victoria Legislative Assembly*, Session 1891, vol. 1, 35th annual report of the Commissioners of Audit.
66 On this section generally, see Gary Hawke, 'Law and Economic Development: The Case of New Zealand', VUW Working Papers in Economic History, 83/1, 1983; G. R. Hawke, *The Making of New Zealand: An Economic History*, Cambridge University Press, Cambridge, 1985, pp. 22–41, 103–21.
67 J. B. Condliffe, *New Zealand in the Making*, Allen & Unwin, London, pp. 110–11.
68 Herron, 'Structure and Course of New Zealand Politics', pp. 499–501; McIntyre (ed.), *Sewell Journal*, vol. 2, pp. 311–12.
69 Attorney-Gen to Col Treasurer, 5 Jan 1864, *AJHR*, 1864, B-2, no. 8.
70 Col Treasurer to Col Sec, 23 Apr 1864, and enclosure thereto, *AJHR*, 1864, B-2.
71 Col Treasurer to Col Sec, 13, 19 Jul 1864 (plus enclosures), *AJHR*, 1864, B-2 (quote from 13 Jul). The bulk of the loan in due course 'went into the hands of a large speculative Company', Julyan explained a few weeks later. Putting the best construction on the situation, he explained that this was 'no small advantage, as, of course, their aim is to run the price up'. Julyan and Sargeaunt to Col Treasurer, 26 Aug 1864. The system of Crown Agents — private businesspeople operating with the Crown's sanction — had been established by the Colonial Office in 1833 to assist colonies with finance and procurement.
72 Graham, *Weld*, p. 95. See also B. J. Dalton, *War and Politics in New Zealand, 1855–1870*, Sydney University Press, Sydney, 1967, pp. 206–7.
73 FitzGerald to Gladstone, 13 Feb 1865, fMS-074, Alexander Turnbull Library.
74 Graham, *Weld*, p. 95.
75 R. M. Dalziel, *The Origins of New Zealand Diplomacy: The Agent-General in London*, Price Milburn, Wellington, 1975, p. 54.
76 See discussion in Dalziel, *Origins*, pp. 57–60. The Crown Agents continued their association with New Zealand because their three principals continued to be appointed as New Zealand's stock agents for subsequent loan operations. See also financial exchanges with London, 1873–1880, T 20/3; *AJHR*, 1876, B-6 and attachments.
77 Dalziel, *Origins*, pp. 60–74; Dalziel, *Vogel*, pp. 214–36.

78 Dalziel, *Vogel*, pp. 235–7.
79 *NZPD*, vol. 37, p. 732 (27 Aug 1880), cited in Dalziel, *Vogel*, p. 236.
80 Dalziel, *Origins*, pp. 66, 70.
81 Julyan to Bell, 10 Sep 1884, Correspondence with Sir Penrose Julyan, T 19/40, Archives New Zealand. In this letter Julyan proposed that, taking into account all the other capacities in which he acted for the New Zealand government, a retaining fee of £800 per annum would be appropriate — 'no one knows better than yourself, how much the success of great financial operations, such as we have had to conduct, depends on the judgement and experience of your financial adviser; how great the responsibility involved, and how comparatively insignificant is the amount of the retaining fee, compared with the advantages, that sound advice in such matters is calculated to ensure.'
82 Agent-Gen to Col Treasurer, 22 Feb 1889, New Plymouth Harbour Board affairs, 1889, T 20/10. Dillon Bell himself was more sanguine, see Agent-General to Col Treasurer, 12 Jul 1889, NPHB affairs 1889, T 20/10.
83 *Otago Daily Times*, 2 Apr 1892, quoted in K. C. McDonald, *White Stone Country: The Story of North Otago*, North Otago Centennial Committee, Dunedin, 1962, p. 197.
84 Craufurd Goodwin, *The Image of Australia: British Perceptions of the Australian Economy from the Eighteenth to the Twentieth Century*, Duke University Press, Durham NC, pp. 147–9, 153.
85 Goodwin, *Image of Australia*, p. 156.
86 Miles Fairburn, *The Ideal Society and Its Enemies: The Foundations of Modern New Zealand Society, 1850–1900*, Auckland University Press, Auckland, 1989, pp. 26, 27, 240–1 (citing Siegfried, *Democracy in New Zealand*, p. 54).
87 James Belich, *Paradise Reforged*, Penguin, Auckland, 2001, especially pp. 27–31, 53–118.
88 Michael Bassett, *The Mother of All Departments: The History of the Department of Internal Affairs*, Auckland University Press in association with Historical Branch, Department of Internal Affairs, Auckland, 1997, p. 191.
89 *NZ Gazette*, 1858, p. 121 (28 Aug); A. H. McLintock (ed.), *An Encyclopaedia of New Zealand*, Government Printer, Wellington, 1966, vol. 1, p. 810.
90 Memoir by J. C. Gavin, courtesy of Donald Hay, Wellington.
91 *NZPD*, 1858–1860, p. 452 (4 Sep 1860).
92 Gavin memoir.
93 Gavin memoir.
94 Gavin memoir.
95 Gavin memoir.
96 Gavin memoir. It was not unusual for an employee to pay a sub-employee — the economist Alfred Marshall, at Cambridge, paid the young John Maynard Keynes out of his own pocket (information from Gary Hawke).
97 Register of inward correspondence, Nov to Dec 1856, T 2, Archives New Zealand. A similar pattern is revealed from the files of the actual correspondence in 1857; see, for instance, box 10, numbers 802–1199, T 1, Archives New Zealand. The role of the Union Bank of Australia is identified in Lissington, 'Early Years', p. 20.
98 Gavin memoir. For a view of a parallel Auckland world, see Russell Stone, 'An Anatomy of the Practice of Law in Nineteenth Century Auckland', in Judith Binney (ed.), *The Shaping of History: Essays from the New Zealand Journal of History*, Bridget Williams Books, Wellington, 2001, pp. 245–56.
99 Gavin memoir.
100 *NZ Gazette*, 17 Feb 1865, cited in Lissington, 'Early Years', p. 22.
101 Lissington, 'Early Years', p. 22.
102 I came up with 120, Bassett, *Mother of All Departments*, p. 31, refers to 191 in 1856; Lissington, 'Early Years', p. 22, refers to 1602 in 1866, but this must include the military.
103 Lissington, 'Early Years', p. 22.
104 *AJHR*, 1866, D-7A, p. 25.
105 *AJHR*, 1866, D-7A, p. 27.
106 For a visual grasp of the effect of the change, compare the presentation of the public accounts in *AJHR*, 1868, B-1 (for the financial year 1866/67) and *AJHR*, 1870, B-1 (for 1869/70).
107 *AJHR*, 1870, B-2, p. 4.
108 Lissington, 'Early Years', p. 19.
109 Lissington, 'Early Years', p. 22.
110 *AJHR*, 1888, B-18.
111 Treasury staff salaries, T 20/10.
112 Treasury staff salaries, T 20/10. Heywood joined Treasury in 1872, succeeded Gavin as Accountant in 1878, and was promoted to Assistant Secretary in 1885.
113 Treasury staff salaries, T 20/10.
114 Treasury staff salaries, T 20/10. By 1890 staff numbers had reached 31.
115 Treasury staff salaries, T 20/10.
116 Treasury staff salaries, T 20/10.
117 Treasury staff salaries, T 20/10.
118 Le Rossignol and Stewart, *State Socialism in New Zealand*, p. 1.
119 W. H. Oliver, *Towards a New History*, Hocken Lecture 1969, Dunedin, 1971, cited in K. R. Howe, *Singer in a Songless Land: A Life of*

Edward Tregear, 1846–1931, Auckland University Press, Auckland, 1991, pp. 88–9.
120 See especially Tennant, *Paupers and Providers*; Howe, *Singers in a Songless Land*; John E. Martin, *Holding the Balance: A History of New Zealand's Department of Labour 1891–1995*, Canterbury University Press, Christchurch, 1996.
121 Howe, *Singer in a Songless Land*, p. 92, explains that 'apart from the masses of economic statistics the Journal published articles on every conceivable subject relating to labour matters from all over the world. Early issues ranged over such subjects as the price of fruit and the numbers of telephones in London and glove making in Austria, to more substantive material on factory and labour legislation, conciliation and arbitration, trades unions, land settlement schemes, socialism, populism, communism, strikes, lockouts, women workers, unemployment and agricultural, industrial and commercial change and development generally in the US, Canada, Britain, France, Germany, India, Japan, Australia. In the first year's issue such articles were reprinted from over fifty different newspapers from these countries.'
122 I. S. Ewing, 'Public Service Reform in New Zealand, 1866–1912', MA thesis, University of Auckland, 1979, p. 15, notes that the Railways and the Post Office accounted for 72 per cent of the increase in public service staff between 1896 and 1913. Howe, *Singer in a Songless Land*, pp. 83–4, notes that large numbers of policemen carried out work for the Department of Labour.
123 Condliffe, *New Zealand in the Making*, pp. 296–7 (in the 2nd edition, pp. 180–1).
124 Bryce, *Maturing in Hard Times*, pp. 10–11, raises a parallel point for Canada: 'Did the Department of Finance, apart from the minister, take any part in preparing [the important 1879] budget? It does not look as if the personnel of the department included anyone expert in economics generally or the tariff in particular … [and] it had almost nothing directly to do with the most important and difficult financial legislation … the Canadian Pacific Railway.'
125 Treasury staff salaries, T 20/10; *AJHR*, 1896, B-7, p. 16; 1914, H-14, p. 31; Ewing, 'Public Service Reform', p. 18.
126 McIvor, *Rainmaker*, p. 193. See also Richard S. Hill, *The History of Policing in New Zealand, vol. 3: The Iron Hand in the Velvet Glove: The Modernisation of Policing in New Zealand, 1886–1917*, Dunmore Press, Palmerston North, 1995, pp. 16–17. Ward's retrenchment of 1909, when nearly 100 civil servants were laid off, was presumably similarly motivated; see D. A. Hamer, *The New Zealand Liberals: The Years of Power, 1891–1912*, Auckland University Press, Auckland, 1988, p. 327.
127 Hamer, *New Zealand Liberals*, pp. 222–3.
128 Hamer, *New Zealand Liberals*, p. 43; Le Rossignol and Stewart, *State Socialism in New Zealand*, pp. 199–200. For one example of Opposition politicking on this, see *NZPD*, vol. 109, p. 238 (13 Sep 1899). Heywood was caught in the backwash.
129 *NZPD*, vol. 91, p. 833 (1895), cited in T. W. H. Brooking, *Lands for the People? The Highland Clearances and the Colonisation of New Zealand: A Biography of John McKenzie*, Otago University Press, Dunedin, 1996, p. 167. See also Alan Henderson, *The Quest for Efficiency: The Origins of the State Services Commission*, Historical Branch, Department of Internal Affairs and State Services Commission, Wellington, 1990, p. 32.
130 *AJHR*, 1892, I-7.
131 Minutes, 22 Sep 1898, *AJHR*, 1898, I-7A, p. 37.
132 Secretary to the Treasury questioned by John Graham, MP, *AJHR*, 1898, I-7A, p. 38. Note that while Seddon, the Colonial Treasurer (and Premier), was present, he does not seem to have played a particular role. Heywood was questioned on 22 Sep. There is no evidence in either *NZPD* or *AJHR* of any further fallout or action from this inquiry.
133 *AJHR*, 1898, I-7A, p. i, 4 Nov 1898.
134 Telegram and attached minutes, 31 May 1893, Heywood papers, T 20/10.
135 Telegram, Ward to Heywood, 6 Nov 1893, Heywood papers, T 20/10. There are similar queries from Seddon in 1895 and 1896 on this file.
136 Telegram, Ward to Heywood, 27 Nov 1893, Heywood papers, T 20/10.
137 Ward to Heywood, 17 Oct 1893, Heywood papers, T 20/10.
138 Heywood to Ward, 29 Oct 1894, Heywood papers, T 20/10.
139 Heywood to Ward, 5 Dec 1894, Heywood papers, T 20/10. Wellington street directories of the 1890s do not record a Heywood living in Molesworth Street.
140 Ward to Heywood, 29 Jan 1895, Heywood papers, T 20/10. One copy would have taken the mail route through San Francisco to London, the other the route across the Indian Ocean.
141 Ward to Heywood, 26 Dec 1893, Heywood papers, T 20/10.
142 McIvor, *Rainmaker*, p. 215; Michael Bassett, *Sir Joseph Ward: A Political Biography*, Auckland

143 Financial Statement, 17 Aug 1900, *AJHR*, 1900, B-6, p. i.
144 *NZPD*, vol. 97, p. 107 (8 Apr 1897).
145 See McIvor, *Rainmaker*, p. 215.
146 Financial Statement, 12 Jul 1904, *AJHR*, 1904, B-6, pp. i–ii.
147 *NZPD*, vol. 143, p. 171 (7 Jul 1908).
148 Andre Siegfried, *Democracy in New Zealand*, Victoria University Press and Price Milburn, 1982, pp. 229–30.
149 Roseveare, *Treasury*, pp. 186–91 (quote p. 191).
150 Roseveare, *Treasury*, p. 177.
151 Roseveare, *Treasury*, p. 183. Salisbury was speaking in the House of Lords on 30 January 1900, in the immediate aftermath of a reverse in the South African War.
152 Roseveare, *Treasury*, p. 186.
153 Col Treasurer (Ward) to Agent-Gen, 7 Jul 1894, Bank of New Zealand, 1894–1895, T 16/13, Archives New Zealand. See also Bassett, *Ward*, p. 51.
154 'Papers relating to the banking legislation of 1894', Drafts of working papers relating to the banking crisis, 1893–1896, T 16/18, Archives New Zealand.
155 Agent-Gen (W. B. Perceval) to Col Treasurer, 20 Jul 1894, Bank of New Zealand 1894–1895, T 16/13. This letter was then circulated around the seven members of the Cabinet. W. P. Reeves, who was to succeed Perceval as Agent-General in 1896, minuted on this: 'I do not think the narrative of the Agent-General discloses a satisfactory state of affairs'. It was then to go to Heywood, to be kept with the Treasury records. See also Dalziel, *Origins*, pp. 149–50, 152–5.
156 Ward to Heywood, 20 Apr 1895, Heywood papers, T 20/10.
157 Siegfried, *Democracy in New Zealand*, p. 238.
158 McIvor, *Rainmaker*, p. 209.
159 Dalziel, *Origins*, p. 74. For the £5 million pound loan of 1879–80, see T 17, pts 3 and 4; *AJHR*, 1880, B-2, p. 5, B-4A.
160 Précis of events, Five million pound loan, 1910, T 17/21, Archives New Zealand. Note, however, that it was Wellington, not the High Commission, which decided to try to raise £5 million — the High Commission had originally thought in terms of refinancing £2.5 million of debentures falling due in 1911 and 1912. The name of J. W. Poynton (the Treasury Secretary) is minuted only on the cover sheet for a message of 28 Jul 1911. See also references to Perceval's abilities in McIvor, *Rainmaker*, pp. 187–8; and Keith Sinclair, *William Pember Reeves: New Zealand Fabian*, Clarendon Press, Oxford, 1965, pp. 253–4: 'Reeves became quite expert in the intricacies of London Finance.' Family connections helped. 'After a short time he was able to dispense with the services of a paid financial adviser — he was, he claimed, the only agent-general of the time to do so ... His letters to Seddon were full of detailed information about raising loans, the sale of government stock, and sticky interviews with the Governor of the Bank of England.'
161 PM to High Commissioner, 25 Aug 1911, Five million pound loan, 1910, T 17/21. The loan was controversial because most of it was taken up by the underwriters rather than the public. Associate MF Millar attacked Leader of Opposition Massey over it: *Otago Daily Times*, 10 May 1911. A file note also reveals extensive reporting of the loan in the British press.
162 I have not been able to date the inception of this practice, but it may be the late 1920s (see chapter 2) — it was established by the mid-1930s.
163 Kynaston, *World of Its Own*, p. 432. The government agreed to bear half the loss that resulted from the Bank of England taking in Barings' bills for a period of almost 24 hours.
164 Bassett, *Ward*, pp. 47–51, 54–72, is indispensable.
165 Heywood papers, T 20/10.
166 Tolhurst to Heywood, 19 Mar 1892, Heywood papers, T 20/10.
167 Heywood to Ward, 29 Oct 1894, Heywood papers, T 20/10. Gary Hawke thinks that 'Global' was the colloquial name for the BNZ Estates Company, later the Assets Realisation Board, through which the BNZ's non-performing assets were separated out.
168 Heywood to Ward, 29 Oct 1894, Heywood papers, T 20/10.
169 Heywood to Ward, 5 Nov 1894, Heywood papers, T 20/10.
170 ST to Col Treasurer, 10 Jun 1896, Heywood papers, T 20/10.
171 ST to Col Treasurer, 31 Aug 1897, Bank of New Zealand, 1897–1898, T 16/15.
172 P. Colgate, D. K. Sheppard, K. Guerin and G. R. Hawke (eds), *A History of the Bank of New Zealand 1862–1982, Part 1, 1862–1934*, Money and Finance Association, Victoria University, Wellington, 1990, pp. 11, 17.
173 ST to Col Treasurer, 31 Aug 1897, Bank of New Zealand, 1897–1898, T 16/15. Seddon minuted: 'will be considered when dealing with the Banking legislation'. N. M. Chappell, *New Zealand Banker's Hundred*, BNZ, Wellington, 1961, p. 251, indicates that Alexander McIntosh, the former General Manager of the

Royal Bank of Queensland, in fact succeeded Butt as auditor. For comment on the Assets Realisation Board, see Chappell, *New Zealand Banker's Hundred*, pp. 203–7; for its 'precursor', the Bank of New Zealand Estates Company, see pp. 192–202.
174 See reports of the general manager of the Assets Realisation Board, *AJHR*, 1898, B-15B and B-15C.
175 *NZPD*, vol. 148, p. 59 (10 Nov 1909).

Chapter 2:
Counting for something? 1910–1930

1 Esson, 1940/888, AAOM 6030, Archives New Zealand.
2 As was the post-war reinvigoration of the British Treasury by Warren Fisher (Secretary, 1919–1939); see Henry Roseveare, *The Treasury: The Evolution of a British Institution*, Allen Lane, London, 1969, pp. 252–5.
3 *AJHR*, 1914, B-6, p. xxxiv.
4 *NZPD*, vol. 228, p. 891 (30 Jul 1931).
5 *AJHR*, 1914, B-6, postscript.
6 Richard Brown, *A History of Accounting and Accountants*, Frank Cass, London, 1968 (a new impression of a 1905 publication), pp. 16, 49.
7 Brown, *History of Accounting*, p. 93.
8 Brown, *History of Accounting*, pp. 122, 125. Four hundred years later, when accountants had been professionally organised for half a century, around a quarter of all the world's 11,000 public accountants were to be found in Italy (p. 334).
9 See W. J. Reader, *Professional Men: The Rise of the Professional Classes in Nineteenth-Century England*, Weidenfeld and Nicholson, London, 1966, pp. 146–66; see also T. W. H. Brooking, *A History of Dentistry in New Zealand*, New Zealand Dental Association, Wellington, 1980, pp. 52–71.
10 Brown, *History of Accounting*, pp. 212, 235–7.
11 Brown, *History of Accounting*, p. 243.
12 Brown, *History of Accounting*, p. 245; also pp. 262, 336–7, for discussion of the problem of rival societies.
13 Brown, *History of Accounting*, 1905, pp. 259, 261, 263–4. On p. 331 it was prophesied that 'it is at least possible that at the end of another fifty years lady trustees, receivers and auditors may be as common as lady doctors are now'. No legislation was passed for either of these organisations between 1894 and 1907.
14 Alan W. Graham, *The First Fifty Years, 1909–1959*, NZ Society of Accountants, Wellington, 1959, pp. 32–3, 42. For further on the dissemination of accounting outside the United Kingdom, see R. H. Parker, 'Importing and Exporting Accounting', in R. H. Parker and B. S. Yamey (eds), *Accounting History: Some British Contributions*, Clarendon, Oxford, 1994, pp. 595–600.
15 *NZPD*, vol. 153, p. 332 (3 Nov 1910); see also Public Revenues Act 1910, esp. sec 51.
16 Cited in *AJHR*, 1910, I-11, pp. 15–16, 19. The Chairman, Romilly, was challenging none other than W. E. Gladstone, whose recommendations favoured the alternative course. This was one respect, therefore, in which the mid-Victorian fiscal revolution was not 'Gladstonian'. *NZOYB*, 1919, p. 727; 1931, p. 569, both record a number of classes of payments in respect of which pre-audit was still carried out.
17 *NZ Times*, 3 Apr 1909, cited in I. S. Ewing, 'Public Service Reform in New Zealand, 1866–1912', MA thesis, University of Auckland, 1979, p. 40.
18 J. E. Le Rossignol and W. Downie Stewart, *State Socialism in New Zealand*, Harrap, London, 1910, pp. 214–15.
19 Le Rossignol and Stewart, *State Socialism in NZ*, pp. 90–2; see also pp. 82–4.
20 Alan Henderson, *The Quest for Efficiency: The Origins of the State Services Commission*, Historical Branch, Department of Internal Affairs and State Services Commission, Wellington, 1990, pp. 38–43. See also Ewing, 'Public Service Reform', pp. 33–7, citing particularly the report of the 1912 Royal Commission on the public service, and Herdman's demand for professional management (pp. 179–85).
21 Henderson, *Quest for Efficiency*, pp. 45–6; Ewing, 'Public Service Reform', p. 35. For Barr, see also www.dnzb.govt.nz.
22 Henderson, *Quest for Efficiency*, p. 50. Other choices, such as the 'Board of Management' favoured by the Hunt Commission or control by Treasury, as in England, were not seriously considered by either government or Opposition. Note that by this time the Australian Commonwealth and four of the six states had introduced forms of board or commissioner control, with only two states retaining direct political control.
23 Inspection and reorganisation of Treasury staff, pp. 1, 13, T 1, 9/100, Archives New Zealand. This is a fuller version of the report which was published, *AJHR*, 1913, H-14.
24 *AJHR*, 1913, H-14, pp. 63, 64, 66.
25 *AJHR*, 1913, H-14, p. 68. The exact character of the 'millionaire' and the 'comptometer' is not

known, but certainly both were machines, not people. See David Green, *Statistics Count: An Illustrated History of Statistics New Zealand*, Statistics New Zealand, Wellington, 2002, p. 36.
26 *AJHR*, 1913, H-14, p. 67.
27 *AJHR*, 1913, H-14, p. 72.
28 *AJHR*, 1914, H-14, pp. 4, 92. On p. 92 there is discussion on the introduction of a scheme whereby the Post Office would pay out sums of less than £5 across the counter, so that Treasury will no longer have to mail out thousands of cheques for small amounts. There is more on the introduction of modern methods to Treasury in *AJHR*, 1914, H-14, p. 101, where the point is made that it was 'difficult to estimate the economy likely to arise during 1914–15, as most of the work in the Treasury will be entirely new, owing to the intended change in the mode of payment and the keeping of public accounts.'
29 *AJHR*, 1916, H-14, p. 2.
30 *AJHR*, H-14, 1915, p. 4; 1916, pp. 3–4.
31 *AJHR*, 1917, B-6, p. iv; T 1, 23/144: 'the vacancies in the Staff were however filled by temporary hands [of] both sexes with the result that not only has the current Treasury work been kept up to date, but the increased work consequent on the huge war expenditure and the raising of large war loans, has been most satisfactorily met.' The 1914 staff numbers are from *AJHR*, 1914, H-14, p. 39.
32 Historical Records: War, 1914–1919, T 1, 23/144, Archives New Zealand.
33 ST to Public Service Commissioner, 13 Nov 1918, T 1, 9/32/1. For the close Canadian parallel, see Robert B. Bryce, *Maturing in Hard Times: Canada's Department of Finance through the Great Depression*, McGill-Queen's University Press, Kingston/Montreal, 1986, pp. 18–21, 28–9. For the benefits of domestic borrowing to the New Zealand stockbroking, business see David Grant, *Bulls, Bears and Elephants: A History of the New Zealand Stock Exchange*, Victoria University Press, Wellington, 1997, p. 119.
34 T 1, 23/144; see also *NZOYB*, 1919, p. 764.
35 *NZOYB*, 1919, p 764. Although no totals are given with this table, the figure for the latter year (£176 million) appears to have been more than twice that for the former in nominal terms, and about 50 per cent greater in real terms — prices increased by around 50 per cent over this period (*NZOYB*, 1919, p. 787).
36 Financial Statement by Minister of Finance, Sir Joseph Ward, *NZPD*, vol. 178, p. 909 (1 Aug 1917); Finance Act 1917, sec. 40; T 1, 23/144.
37 ST to MF, 1915 loan — money raised in New Zealand, suggestions re, 25 Jun 1915, T 1, 26/2, Archives New Zealand; see also Cables re public works loan 1915, T 1, 26/1/2, Archives New Zealand.
38 T 1, 26/1/2.
39 For wartime price movements, see *NZOYB*, 1919, pp. 771–801.
40 *AJHR*, 1921, Session II, H-14, p. 6; see also Acting ST to Public Service Commissioner, 11 Jun 1920, T 1, 9/32/1, with reference to the need for additional typists to deal with correspondence over loans and pensions. The administration of pensions was transferred to the Pensions Department in 1922: *AJHR*, 1922, B-6, p. vii.
41 The first appears to have been in 1916 — see Estimates of revenue and expenditure 1916–17, T 1, 12/15/6 (and see also War expenditure, 1916–17, T 1, 12/148); from 1918 it was a series, Statement of revenue and expenditure, T 1, 12/186/year.
42 Asst ST to ST, 9 Feb 1920, T 1, 9/32/1.
43 PM to Ministers, 17 Dec 1920, T 1, 12/186/21.
44 Meeting of 12 Jan 1921, Business and government, 1920–21, T 1, 12/360, Archives New Zealand.
45 *AJHR*, 1922, B-1, Report of Controller and Auditor-General, p. 2.
46 ST to MF, 16 Aug 1922, T 1, 12/186/22.
47 ST to Acting MF, 27 Sep 1921, T 1, 12/186/21.
48 Ashwin, 27 Jan 1925, W2220, T 90, Archives New Zealand.
49 Papers on taxation, MS 985/11, Downie Stewart Papers, Hocken Library.
50 Downie Stewart to Bell, 25 Aug 1926, MS 985/1/1/22, Downie Stewart Papers, Hocken Library.
51 *AJHR*, 1918, Session II, H-14, p. 6.
52 Michael Bassett, *The State in New Zealand, 1840–1980: Socialism Without Doctrines?*, Auckland University Press, Auckland, 1998, p. 132; see also T 1, 27/13/4.
53 Minister of Agriculture to Acting MF, 26 May 1919; ST to Acting MF, 29 May 1919; Wheat subsidies and audit thereof, T 1, 27/13/4. In the event, the work was undertaken by the accountants attached to the Board of Trade; Asst ST to MF, 20 Oct 1920.
54 Controller and Auditor-General to PM, 8 Dec 1920, T 1, 27/13/4. They were not hasty; the final report was not submitted until July 1921.
55 ST to Public Service Commissioner, 14 Apr 1920, T 1, 9/32/1.
56 *AJHR*, 1922, B-5. See also letter of 24 Dec 1920, Business and government, 1920–21, T 1, 12/360, for business lobbying of government.
57 *AJHR*, 1922, B-5, p. 15.
58 John E. Martin, 'Honouring the Contract: State

Policy and Labour in New Zealand', unpublished ms, Ministry for Culture and Heritage, Wellington, ch. 3, p. 44.
59 *AJHR*, 1925, I-14, p. 2. Thanks to Ted Lundy for this reference.
60 Michael Bassett, *Coates of Kaipara*, Auckland University Press, Auckland, 1995, p. 139; R. M. Burdon, *The New Dominion*, A. H. & A. W Reed / George Allen & Unwin, Wellington, 1965, pp. 62, 119.
61 J. B. Condliffe, *New Zealand in the Making*, George Allen & Unwin, London, 1930, p. 286.
62 See Kathleen Burk, 'The Treasury: From Impotence to Power', in Kathleen Burk (ed.), *War and the State: The Transformation of British Government, 1914–1919*, George Allen & Unwin, London, 1982, pp. 84–107; S. Marriner, 'The Ministry of Munitions, 1915–1991', in R. H. Parker and B. S. Yaney (eds), *Accounting History: Some British Contributions*, Clarendon, Oxford, 1994.
63 *AJHR*, 1920, H-14, pp. 6–9; Précis of Treasury views to Statutes Revision Committee of the Legislative Council, 8 Nov 1929, Powers of Audit Office and Treasury, T 1, 40/510, Archives New Zealand. See also Downie Stewart, *NZPD*, vol. 218, p. 23 (7 Aug 1928): 'Modern methods of accountancy have been adopted throughout the Departments of State, and commercial balance-sheets are now produced annually for all State activities.' According to Henderson (*Quest for Efficiency*, p. 109), Cabinet decided on the revised form of departmental accounts on 7 November 1921.
64 *AJHR*, 1921, Session II, H-14, pp. 12–13. The Commissioner went on to quote an English Commission (sic) on business methods in the public service. The initiative foreshadowed the 1989 Public Finance Act.
65 Leicester Webb, *Government in New Zealand*, Department of Internal Affairs, Wellington, 1940, p. 119.
66 *AJHR*, 1923, Session II, B-6, p. xx (Financial Statement, 3 Jul 1923). Note that A. D. Park, a later Secretary to the Treasury, was on the committee that set up the Stores Board as an inspector in the office of the Public Service Commissioner; and that in 1925 it was agreed that Treasury, not Audit, was the proper central authority to prescribe stores procedures. Henderson, *Quest for Efficiency*, pp. 108–9. An earlier Stores Board had been established in 1913, with representation from 'purchasing' departments — the Printing Office, Mental Hospitals, Justice, Lands & Survey, Works, Post & Telegraph — but not the Treasury; *AJHR*, 1914, H-14, p. 79. Presumably that initiative had been overtaken by the war.
67 ST to MF, 31 Mar 1924, T 1, 12/186/24.
68 *AJHR*, 1925, D-2A, p. 11; Press statement, *NZ Times*, 6 Feb 1926, T 1, 12/186/25; *NZOYB*, 1932, pp. 486–7.
69 *AJHR*, 1928, F-1, p. 12. Treasury had also tackled the State Coal Department; see Bassett, *State in New Zealand*, p. 107.
70 See *AJHR*, 1927, I-14, for evidence on the changes from the Secretary of the Post and Telegraph Department.
71 In 1932 William Polson, an MP who was also chairman of the Farmers' Union, said that it was 'well known that Treasury was responsible for the super-tax on land a few years back, which had to be immediately repealed.' *Dominion*, 18 Mar 1932, on Papers of Economists' committee, Feb 1932, T 1, 52/703/[2], Archives New Zealand.
72 Brown, *History of Accounting*, p. 327; A. J. P. Taylor, *English History*, 1914–1945, Penguin, Harmondsworth, 1970, p. 229.
73 Typescript, n.d. [c. 1937], 'The Functions of Treasury', Public Revenues Act, 1926, T 1, 40/15. See also Finance Act 1929, sec. 29; and Notes on the Public Revenues Act 1926, T 40/15, which appear in fuller form in A. R. F. Mackay, 'The Treasury as a Co-ordinating Factor in Public Service Administration', *JPA*, vol. 1, no. 1 (May 1938), pp. 85–91. The full list, in 1931, included the Local Government Loans Board; Stores Control Board; Public Debt Commission; Rural Intermediate Credit Board, State Advances Board; Lands Development Board; Government Life Insurance Investment Board; State Fire Insurance Investment Board; Tongariro National Park Board; National Provident Fund Board; and the three superannuation fund boards (for the public service, the railways and teachers). Memo for Public Service Commissioner, 12 Nov 1931, T 51/95, on T 90, W2220 (Ashwin). Some of these boards were set up in the 1920s and had Treasury representation from their inception; the superannuation fund boards were established before the First World War and gained Treasury representation later.
74 Downie Stewart to Coates, 11 Oct 1926, MS 985/1/1, Hocken Library.
75 *AJHR*, 1934, G-9, p. 48.
76 27 Sep 1928, Native Land Claims, T 1, 52/587.
77 See Bassett, *State in New Zealand*, p. 142.
78 Rosslyn J. Noonan, *By Design: A Brief History of the Public Works Department / Ministry of Works, 1870–1970*, Government Printer, Wellington,

1975, p. 275. See also Local Government Loans Board Act 1926; *Local Authorities Handbook*, 1927, p. 16. 11 Aug 1932, Local government loans act 1926, policy, T 40/416, gives its personnel at that time: the Secretary to the Treasury, Commissioner of Public Works, and four local body representatives. See also Treasury official Ashwin on hospital boards, memo of Sep 1927, T 1, 52/84, cited in Bassett, *State in New Zealand*, p. 142. The first published annual report of the Local Government Loans Board appeared in 1939 (*AJHR*, 1939, B-3).

79 For a related discussion, see Margaret Arnold, 'The Market for Finance in Late Nineteenth Century New Zealand with Special Reference to Rural Mortgages', MA thesis, Victoria University of Wellington, 1981, especially pp. 97–109. Arnold identified the beginning of a change in the New Zealand finance market in the late 1890s, when the government attempted (albeit without success, the majority of shares being taken up by government departments and the Bank of New Zealand under a contingency plan) to float a loan locally (p. 109).

80 N. M. Chappell, *New Zealand Banker's Hundred*, Bank of New Zealand, Wellington, 1961, p. 188.

81 *Public Service List*, 1926, 1931/32.

82 F. W. Millar, 'Women of the Public Service', vol. 6, no. 2 (Mar 1944), p. 27; *Public Service List*, 1914/15. See also Roberta Nicholls, 'The PSC and the Equal Pay Campaign', in Henderson, *Quest for Efficiency*, pp. 252–3.

83 Acting ST to PSC, 8 Jun 1920, T 1, 9/32/1.

84 Acting ST, 18 Jun 1920, T 1, 9/32/1.

85 3 Sep, 25 Sep, 28 Sep 1920, T 1, 9/32/1.

86 *Public Service List*, 1921/22, 1926, 1931/32; Millar, 'Women of the Public Service', p. 29.

87 G. H. Scholefield, *Who's Who in New Zealand and the Western Pacific*, 2nd edn, Masterton, 1924, p. 180. Poynton was a magistrate in Invercargill from 1895 before becoming the Public Trustee in 1900.

88 'Campbell, George F. C.', Basic Information Sheet, Dictionary of New Zealand Biography.

89 *AJHR*, 1914, H-14, p. 22.

90 *New Zealand Free Lance*, 14 Dec 1912.

91 Michael Bassett, *Sir Joseph Ward*, Auckland University Press, Auckland, 1993, p. 226; information from John E. Martin.

92 ST to MF, 19 May 1916, T 1, 12/15/6.

93 *Public Service List*, 1926, 1931, 1941.

94 Henderson, *Quest for Efficiency*, pp. 133–4; *AJHR*, 1928, B-14, first report of the Board; P. V. Smith, 'The National Expenditure Commission: A Study of its Origins, Work and Effects', MA thesis, Victoria University of Wellington, 1969, p. 43. See also *AJHR*, 1927, I-16, pp. 2–5, for Esson's evidence to the Public Accounts Committee on rural intermediate credit. For more from an economist's point of view, see Grant Fleming, 'The Political Economy of Agricultural Credit in the 1920s', University of Auckland, Economics Department, work in progress paper no. 73, Aug 1990.

95 R. M. Campbell to W. B. Sutch, 30 Sep 1971, R. M. Campbell papers, MS-Papers-1900-15, ATL.

96 AAOM 6030, 1940/888 (J. J. Esson), Archives New Zealand.

97 There is an echo here of Sir Warren Fisher's propensity to speak of the 'four services' — army, navy, air force and civil. Samuel Brittan, *Steering the Economy*, Penguin, Harmondsworth, England, 1971, p. 67.

98 Campbell in 1919, Park in 1932. Esson had his by 1924. It hasn't proved possible to date the award to Hayes. David Cannadine discusses the 'renovation' of the order of St Michael and St George to honour government service in the colonies in *Ornamentalism: How the British Saw Their Empire*, Penguin, London, 2001, pp. 86–7. However, the first instance of this 'social promotion' may be Heywood, who retired in 1906 with the Imperial Service Order, instituted by Edward VII in August 1902 and granted for 'meritorious service in the clerical and administrative grades of the Civil Service throughout the British Empire'; see www.medals.org.uk.

99 *NZOYB*, 1931, pp. 578–9.

100 Downie Stewart to Siegfried, 4 Nov 1927, MS985-1/1, Hocken Library.

101 9 Dec 1927, Loan requirements 1927–29, T 1, 52/77, Archives New Zealand.

102 ST (R. E. Hayes) to Minister of Finance (W. Downie Stewart), 9 Dec 1927, Loan requirements 1927–29, T 1, 52/77.

103 10 Dec 1927, re 9 Dec memo, T1 52/77.

104 ST to MF, 13 Feb, 16 Feb 1928, T 1, 52/77.

105 In 1928/29 public works spending totalled nearly £9 million, a large proportion of which went on railway construction.

106 See biography of Furkert, www.dnzb.govt.nz.

107 ST to MF, 18 May 1928, T 1, 52/77.

108 Furkert to PM, 29 May 1928, Railways, finance and policy, T 1, 52/584, Archives New Zealand;. See also memo, Treasury, 31 May 1928: 'to continue to carry the assets and an inflated capital with a business partially dependent on other fields and then to tax those other fields and to hand the proceeds to the overcapitalised

business is certainly a new departure which may be difficult to substantiate'.
109 Burdon, *New Dominion*, p. 119.
110 Burdon, *New Dominion*, pp. 120–2, including details of the 16 Oct 1928 speech by Ward that gave rise to the misunderstanding; Bassett, *Ward*, p. 271.
111 Bassett, *Ward*, p. 271; ST to MF, 21 Jan 1929, T 1, 52/77, 1927–29. Exchanges between Ward and Downie Stewart over responsibility for the difficulties with borrowing ended with a retraction by Ward: Burdon, *New Dominion*, p. 124.
112 There were run-ins between Furkert and the Treasury. It seems that Furkert managed to get an extra £130,000 for rail construction and an additional £60,000 for irrigation. ST to Under-Secretary, PWD, 24 May 1929; US PWD to ST, 10 Jul 1929; minute by ST, 25 Jul 1929; T 1, 52/77, 1927–29.
113 ST to PM/MF, 17 May 1929, T 1, 52/584.
114 Memo for Min Railways plus related documents, 11 Mar 1930; Treasury memo, 20 Jun 1930, T 1, 52/584.
115 ST to MF, 29 Apr 1929; ST to Superintendent, State Advances, 2 May 1929, T 1, 52/77, 1927–29.
116 Assistant ST to MF, 12 Nov 1929, T 1, 52/77.
117 Bassett, *Ward*, pp. 275–82 (quote from p. 275).
118 The Scots-born William Veitch (1870–1961) had been a railway worker and union leader. He held the portfolios of Mines, Labour and Transport under Ward, and Railways under Forbes, but was not appointed to the coalition ministry. See his biography, www.dnzb.govt.nz.
119 Park minute on MPW to MF (5 Aug 1930), 8 Aug 1930, Loan requirements, 1930–31, T 1, 52/77, Archives New Zealand: 'On the basis of attached memoranda the Hon Minister of Public Works does not concur in any reduction of loan funds allocated to his Depart. This result will therefore preclude any increase as suggested in Railway Department's programme and the papers should I recommend, be referred to Hon Min for Railways accordingly.' Minister of Railways to MF, 26 Aug 1930, T 1, 52/77, 1930–31: 'So far this correspondence has resolved itself into a futile interchange of letters between myself and Treasury officials who obviously do not even to a limited extent grasp the significance of the problem.'
120 ST to MF, 16 Jul, 11 Aug 1930, T 1, 52/777, 1930–31.
121 Memos, 11 Aug, 26 Aug, 9 Sep 1930, T 1, 52/77, 1930–31; also Min Lands to MF, 23 Aug 1930: 'I can quite appreciate the Treasury's difficulty in this matter, but at the same time the Government is faced with the fact that despite its efforts in the past there is still a large number of men seeking work.'
122 ST to Acting MF; Cabinet approval; both 9 Sep 1930, T 1, 52/77, 1930–31.
123 Ministerial statement, *AJHR*, 1925, B-2, p. 1.
124 Christie to ST, 22 Sep 1928, Powers of Audit Office and Treasury, T 1, 40/510, Archives New Zealand. For example, section 22 of the Finance Act 1927 (No. 2) authorised the adjustment of public accounts in consequence of the writing-off of losses incurred in relation to the settlement of discharged soldiers. Because the wording of that section differed from that of the Repayment of the Public Debt Act, it was ruled that the amounts written off under the two acts differed, and amending legislation had to be passed in 1929.
125 ST to MF, 28 Sep 1928; Controller and Auditor-Gen to MF, 4 Oct 1928, T 1, 40/510. The 'standard authority' was A. J. V. Durell, *The Principles and Practice of the System of Control over Parliamentary Grants*, Gieves, Portsmouth, England, 1917.
126 8 Nov 1929, T 1, 40/510.
127 Finance Act 1929, T 1 40/88/29, Archives New Zealand; Law Draftsman to Forbes, 7 Nov 1929, T 1, 40/510; *NZPD*, vol. 233, pp. 1357–61 (8 Nov 1929); *Evening Post*, 9, 11 Nov 1929; *NZ Herald*, 23 Apr 1930, on T 1, 40/510.
128 Niemeyer to Park, 24 Sep 1930, Micro MS Coll 20 2945: 24 Bank of England OV9 Sir Otto Niemeyer, ATL.
129 Ransom to Niemeyer, 9 Sep 1930, Micro MS Coll 20 2945: 24 Bank of England OV9 Sir Otto Niemeyer.
130 Ransom to Niemeyer, 9 Sep 1930, attachment headed 'Powers of Treasury', Micro MS Coll 20 2945: 24 Bank of England OV9 Sir Otto Niemeyer.
131 G. F. C. Campbell to Niemeyer, 19 Sep; Niemeyer to Campbell; Niemeyer to Ransom (both 24 Sep 1930), Micro MS Coll 20 2945: 24 Bank of England OV9 Sir Otto Niemeyer. A note on the same file re a letter from an officer of the Exchequer and Audit Department, London, to Niemeyer, 21 Jan 1931, suggests that Campbell was still 'disturbed by the apprehension that the Treasury in NZ wish to obtain legislation limiting his present authority'.
132 Niemeyer to Park, 24 Sep 1930, Micro MS Coll 20 2945: 24.
133 Niemeyer to Downie Stewart, 17 Nov 1930, MS 985-1/1/75, Hocken Library.
134 *Evening Post*, 21 Oct 1930, on T 1, 40/510. Labour members were negative, but more

because of the fact of Niemeyer coming to report on the banking system than because of this report.

135 Ransom to Niemeyer, letter headed 'Powers of Treasury', 9 Sep 1930, Micro MS Coll 20 2945: 24 Bank of England OV9 Sir Otto Niemeyer. See also Burk, 'Treasury from Impotence to Power', pp. 84–107.

136 14 Feb, 13 Oct 1930, Comparative increase in departmental expenditure, explanations from departments, general instructions, T 1, 52/81. The first memorandum was prepared in the Treasury; see ST to MF, 13 Feb 1930.

137 Niemeyer to Ransom, 25 Sep 1930, proposed central bank, T 1, 52/645. Ransom wrote at the end of the letter, 'Refer to Cabinet 29/9/30'. In Britain, 'the Treasury's traditional role of guardian of the taxpayer's money was no longer sufficient, and instead its role became one of persuading spending departments and the Cabinet to establish priorities between competing claims on national resources', G. C. Peden, *The Treasury and British Public Policy*, OUP, Oxford, 2000, p. 8.

138 Memo, 13 Oct 1930, T 1, 52/81.

139 Comment by Treasury officials; see also B. Easton, 'Economy' column, *NZ Listener*, 17 May 1997.

140 Mackay, 'Treasury as a Co-ordinating Factor', p. 86.

141 For some sense of equivalent developments in Australia, see Commonwealth of Australia *Parliamentary Papers: General*: 1932–33–34 sessions, vol. 4, 'Report of the Joint Select Committee on Public Accounts, 1932'.

Chapter 3:
Treasury during the Great Depression, 1930–1935

1 Entry for 11 Jan 1933, Downie Stewart diary, 1932–33, MS 985/7/7, Hocken Library.
2 Downie Stewart diary, 1932–33, MS 985/7/7.
3 Figures from G. T. Bloomfield, *New Zealand: A Handbook of Historical Statistics*, G. K. Hall, Boston, Mass., 1984, p. 269.
4 *NZOYB*, 1932, pp. 489–90.
5 *NZOYB*, 1932, pp. 489–90.
6 Further to the 'bad blood', in December Veitch complained to the MF about a memorandum the ST had sent direct to the General Manager of the Railways — 'as I desire to keep in touch with all financial and other operations of my department … such correspondence [should] be passed through the proper channel of the offices of the Minister concerned'; Min Rlys to MF, 16 Dec 1930, Budget 1930/31, T 1, 52/663, Archives New Zealand.
7 Niemeyer to Ransom, 25 Sep 1930, Micro MS Coll 20 2945: 24 Bank of England OV9 Sir Otto Niemeyer, copy held at Alexander Turnbull Library.
8 Park to Masters, 17 Nov 1930, T 1, 12/186/30. The accounts were in due course to show that whereas the railways paid £2.13 million in interest on capital in 1929/30, only £0.685 million was received in 1930/31; *NZOYB*, 1932, p. 488.
9 ST to Acting MF, 21 Nov 1930, Railways: finance and policy, T 1, 52/584, Archives New Zealand; MF to Min Rlys, 22 Nov 1930, T 1, 52/584. Forbes was away attending the Imperial Conference in London from late August until January 1931.
10 ST to Acting MF, 8 Dec 1930, T 1, 52/663, Archives New Zealand.
11 ST to Acting MF, 22 Dec 1930, T 1, 52/663.
12 Cabinet, 18 Dec 1930, T 1, 52/663; *Dominion*, 22 Dec 1930.
13 Park to Ngata, 31 Dec 1930 ('1931' in error), T 1, 52/663.
14 R. M. Burdon, *The New Dominion*, A. H. & A. W. Reed / George Allen & Unwin, Wellington/London, 1965, pp. 129–30.
15 This applied particularly to interest payments owed overseas. The conversion to lower rates of interest of domestically held debt was practicable, and was to be carried out in 1933.
16 *Dominion*, 14 Feb 1931, T 1, 52/663.
17 Education economies, T 1, 52/622, Archives New Zealand; *NZOYB*, 1932, pp. 489–90.
18 See, inter alia, attachment to memo, PM's private secretary to ST, 27 Apr 1931, statement of revenue and expenditure 1931, T 1, 12/186/31, Archives New Zealand. Its provenance and syntax suggests that this statement was drafted in Treasury for use by the Prime Minister in the House of Representatives.
19 Burdon, *New Dominion*, pp. 132–4.
20 ST to MF, 11 Mar 1931, loan expenditure 1931/32, T 1, 52/77, Archives New Zealand. The recommendations were approved by Cabinet ten days later. Note also a discussion with Ngata on the same file, 30 Apr 1931, about the undesirability of being too open about using loan funds for unemployment relief: 'if this fact becomes known abroad it would undoubtedly react on our credit'.
21 Railways Commission, T 1, 52/641, Archives New Zealand.
22 T 1, 52/77, Archives New Zealand.
23 *NZOYB*, 1933, p. 423. In the first year, 1931/32, the Post Office contributed nearly £1 million

24 Robert B. Bryce, *Maturing in Hard Times: Canada's Department of Finance through the Great Depression*, McGill-Queen's University Press, Kingston/Montreal, 1986, pp. 73–9.
25 The 'authority' is Coates: 'for long enough I have carried this fellow — he is a heavy weight and I feel that no longer can I carry him'; Coates to Downie Stewart, 4 Dec 1935 [i.e. after the election defeat], Hocken MS 985-1/1/46.
26 Downie Stewart diary, 1931–32, MS 985/1/7/6, Hocken Library.
27 *NZPD*, vol. 229, p. 468, 21 Aug 1931. See also Burdon, *New Dominion*, pp. 135–7.
28 National economic adjustment, T 1, 52/668, Archives New Zealand; Michael Bassett, *Coates of Kaipara*, AUP, Auckland, 1995, pp. 167–8; Burdon, *New Dominion*, p. 137. No record of the proceedings of this committee was printed in AJHR.
29 Peter Clarke, *Hope and Glory: Britain 1900–1990*, Penguin, London, 1996, pp. 157–9.
30 Park to Downie Stewart, 24 Sep 1931, MS 985/13/11, Hocken Library. The letter also mentions a central bank, and the possible achievement of economies in local government through amalgamation and reorganisation, regulation, the co-ordination of transport, etc.
31 *Evening Post*, 24 Oct 1931, Powers of Treasury, T 1, 40/510, Archives New Zealand.
32 *Evening Post*, 2 Dec 1933, on B. C. Ashwin, personal file, T 90, W2220, Archives New Zealand, has the text in this form — an early version of a press release, perhaps. Provision was made in sec. 23 of the Finance Act (No. 4) to this end. See also, on the same file, Park to Public Service Commissioner, 12 Nov 1932, which lists the duties and responsibilities of the Permanent Head of Treasury; these were restated again by Park (had nothing happened?) in an urgent memo to the PSC on 18 December 1931, some two weeks after the press announcement.
33 Information from Gary Hawke.
34 Entry for 20 Nov 1931, Downie Stewart diary, 1931–32, MS 985/7/6, Hocken Library.
35 *Dominion*, 28 Jan 1932. In its editorial the *Dominion* alluded in positive terms to the precedent of the British May committee, noting that in certain respects the wording was identical. See also National Expenditure Commission, T 1, 52/702, Archives NZ; Alan Henderson, *The Quest for Efficiency: The Origins of the State Services Commission*, Historical Branch, Department of Internal Affairs and State Services Commission, Wellington, 1990, p. 124, spills the beans on Macintosh. See also Smith, 'National Expenditure Commission', pp. 39, 47.
36 'EHW' to Forbes, 13 Jan 1932, National expenditure adjustment, correspondence and suggestions, T 1, 52/702/2, Archives New Zealand. A more idiosyncratic Auckland correspondent, Maurice Tangney, made 80 economy recommendations, of which the last was that all women under 45 should wear dresses falling no more than two inches below the knee.
37 Treasury reports for the National Expenditure Commission, 1932, T 1, 52/703/[1], Archives New Zealand. The Commission was appointed on 27 Jan 1932.
38 Minutes of 23 Feb 1932; see also minutes of 17, 18 May 1932, file on and minutes of National Expenditure Adjustment Commission, T 1, 52/702, Archives New Zealand. (Note that the Treasury reports mentioned in the minutes are not attached to them, nor do they all appear to be on either 52/703 or 52/703/[1].)
39 *AJHR*, 1932, B-4A, p. 167.
40 Rosslyn Noonan, *By Design: A Brief History of the Public Works Department/Ministry of Works 1870–1970*, Government Printer, Wellington, 1975, p. 125. Furkert finished work in October 1932, about eighteen months before he was due to retire.
41 Final Report of the National Expenditure Commission, *AJHR*, 1932, B-4A, p. 171. See, for example, a statement from the Associated Chambers of Commerce quoted in Noonan, *By Design*, p. 121: Private enterprise 'has proved more competent and more economic the world over than all the splendidly extravagant schemes of money juggling a State could devise'.
42 *Dominion*, 2 Mar 1932, T 1, 52/77. Park minuted that this be placed on the capital works file on 11 May; MF to MPW, 4 May 1932, informing ministers what their departments had got. Public Works was allocated an additional £0.8 million.
43 Noonan, *By Design*, p. 124, citing *AJHR*, 1932, B-4A, p. 154.
44 Bassett, *Coates of Kaipara*, pp. 177–8.
45 ST to MF, 1 Apr 1932, T 1, 52/77.
46 Finance Act 1932, No. 11; see also minutes of 23 Feb 1932 et seq, T 1, 52/702.
47 21 Mar 1932, T 1, 52/702.
48 *AJHR*, 1932–33, B-4A, pp. 9–18; T 1, 52/703/[1].
49 Pensions, which accounted for about two-thirds

as much spending as education, were mostly for old age or war service/injury. Summary of social services spending, attachment to ST to Chair National Expenditure Commission, 11 Feb 1932, T 1, 52/703/[1].
50 *NZPD*, vol. 233, p. 244 (4 Oct 1932, Financial Statement presented by Forbes).
51 Memo, 24 Feb 1932, Civil List: Native Purposes, T 1, 1/132.
52 Final Report of the National Expenditure Commission, *AJHR*, 1932, B-4A, p. 172.
53 Bryce, *Maturing in Hard Times*, p. 31.
54 His *Indian Currency and Finance* was published in 1913.
55 Cutting from *Dominion*, 6 Jun 1930, Ashwin personal file, W2220, T 90. The full name was Economic Society of Australia and New Zealand (Wellington branch). Also Hawke to author, 5 Oct 2001; and G. R. Hawke, *Between Government and Banks: A History of the Reserve Bank of New Zealand*, Government Printer, Wellington, 1973, pp. 15–21, which clarifies the confusing usage of the time (p. 17). Treasury's submission to the Monetary Commission, presented by Ashwin, focused almost entirely on the sterling exchange system; *AJHR*, 1934, B-3, pp. 15–26.
56 Audit Officer, London, to Auditor-Gen, 17 Jun 1930, forwarded to MF, 31 Jul 1930, Reserve Bank, establishment of, T 1, 52/645.
57 General Manager, National Bank, to Prime Minister, 4 Mar 1931, T 1, 52/645.
58 Forbes to Niemeyer, 17 Jul 1930, T 1, 52/645. At this point Niemeyer was not expected to be able to visit New Zealand.
59 P. L. Cottrell, 'The Bank in its International Setting', in Richard Roberts and David Kynaston (eds), *The Bank of England: Money, Power and Influence, 1694–1994*, Clarendon, Oxford, 1995, p. 89.
60 Cottrell, 'Bank in its International Setting', pp. 105–6; Chris Stals (Governor of the South African Reserve Bank), 'Seventy-five Years of Central Banking in South Africa', address delivered 28 Jun 1996, www.resbank.co.za. The US equivalent was the Kemmerer missions to South America; Hawke to author, 5 Oct 2001.
61 23 Jan 1931, T 1, 52/645. Niemeyer was either highly attuned to 'colonial' sensibilities or lacked some himself — in a further letter to Park enclosing his report, he hoped that Park would realise that 'references to Greece, Estonia, Bulgaria etc are not intended to insinuate that New Zealand is comparable to these distant dagos.'
62 ST to MF, 23 Feb 1931, T 1, 52/645.
63 Niemeyer to Forbes, 19 Feb 1931, T 1, 52/645.
64 Hawke, *Between Government and Banks*, p. 30. At this stage the bill also specified parity between the New Zealand and British pounds.
65 Montagu Norman notes of discussion with Downie Stewart after meeting of 15 Sep 1932, Micro-MS-Coll-20-2958, Bank of England Archive — Overseas Department — Records New Zealand, ATL. While Norman recorded that this was 'only a courtesy visit' to discuss things 'affecting New Zealand and this country', it lasted one and a half hours. Downie Stewart reported in near-identical terms on this meeting; see W. Downie Stewart diary, Jun–Oct 1932, MS 985/17/1, Hocken Library, pp. 51–2. Norman, thought Downie Stewart, 'certainly does not look like a city banker. He is very tall and almost Spanish looking, with a noble shaped head and brown eyes, a pointed beard, and long artistic, tapering fingers. He was very gracious and easy to talk to and buried himself in a chair, with his characteristic attitude of joining his fingers together almost as if he were in prayer'. The hotel was the Metropole on Northumberland Ave.
66 Extract from the minutes of the committee of the Treasury, Bank of England, 2 Dec 1931, Micro-MS-Coll-20 2945, Bank of England, G14, File 282, New Zealand, ATL; 'notwithstanding ... repeated letters to the [British] Treasury on the subject certain of the Dominions and Crown Colonies continue to finance themselves by short term borrowing on the market without due consideration as to repayment. In this connection, the Government of New Zealand have heavy maturities of Treasury Bills, etc., in the near future.' The London long-term capital market had closed after sterling left the gold standard in September. Downie Stewart explained to the press in April 1932 that 'in November last year there had been a black week in London, when a perfect panic had been reached in the money market. The panic was so great that on the day of the General Election [2 Dec] the New Zealand Government received a cable saying that ... unless the New Zealand Government compelled — not asked — the banks to arrange to remit to London £1,000,000 a month for the next twelve months, the position in London would be such that it could not be coped with.' *Evening Post*, 29 Apr 1932, BNZ Archive.
67 Downie Stewart diary, Jun–Oct 1932, MS 985/17/1, p. 52, Hocken Library.
68 Niemeyer to Park, 19 Oct 1932, T 1, 52/645; the 'Regency Buck' was Sir Henry Buckleton,

General Manager of the Bank of New Zealand. For the BNZ's arguments against the central bank, see the report of the BNZ's annual proprietors' meeting in Wellington, 17 Jun 1932, in *Australasian Insurance and Banking Record*, 21 Jul 1932, p. 569. Lubbock was a director of both the Bank of England and the Bank of New Zealand (31 Jul 1930, T 1, 52/645).

69 Quoted in *Evening Post*, 9 Nov 1932, on T 1, 52/645. The bill received its first reading in December 1932.
70 Drew, New Zealand High Commission, London, to Park, 21 Nov 1932, T 1, 52/645.
71 Diary 1932, MS 985/17/1, Hocken Library.
72 See Park to Downie Stewart, 7 Sep 1931, MS 985/13/11, Hocken Library; Downie Stewart to Forbes, 14 Jan 1933, MS 985/1/1/83; Webb, *Government in New Zealand*, pp. 60–1.
73 ST to MF, 24 Sep 1931, MS 985/13/11.
74 ST to MF, 23 Feb 1931, T 1, 52/645.
75 The chair of the National Bank, Austin Harris (who had just taken over from the recently deceased William Pember Reeves), observed in reporting to shareholders that New Zealand farmers were 'hampered in many cases by the heavy burden incidental to the purchase of their farm — bought in many cases during the land boom'; *AIBR*, 21 Sep 1932, p. 775.
76 Bell to Downie Stewart, 12 Mar 1932, MS 985/1/1/24.
77 See his correspondence with Downie Stewart in 1931, 1932 and 1933; MS 985/1/1/29, Hocken Library.
78 Agatha Christie, *One, Two, Buckle My Shoe*, William Collins, London, first published 1940, 1956 edn, pp. 31, 133. With such a 'blunt' clue, the identity of the murderer was fairly obvious.
79 See comment at the time of devaluation (Jan 1933), press clippings on Ottawa conference and after, MS 985/28/35, Hocken Library.
80 Associated Chambers of Commerce to Forbes, 16 Apr 1932, T 1, 52/702/2.
81 Associated Chambers of Commerce deputation to PM, 19 Jan 1932, correspondence over the exchange rate, MS-Papers-1785-038, Alexander Turnbull Library.
82 Coates to Forbes, 23 Jan 1932, MS-Papers 1785-038.
83 Coates to Forbes, 23 Jan 1932, MS-Papers-1785-038.
84 A. C. Davidson, BNSW, to R. M. Kershaw, Bank of England, 7 Jan 1935, Micro-MS-Coll-20-2958, Bank of England Archive, Overseas Department, Records New Zealand, ATL. See also Keith Sinclair and W. F. Mandle, *Open Account: A History of the Bank of New South Wales in New Zealand, 1861–1961*, Whitcombe and Tombs, Wellington, 1961, pp. 194–203.
85 Information from Brian Easton. The Professor of Economics at Victoria University College, Bernard Murphy, was not a member of the committee.
86 *NZOYB*, 1997, p. 382.
87 Cited in Grant Fleming, 'The Role of Economists in New Zealand Policy-Making, 1912–1951: Economic Advice Structures in Development', University of Auckland, *Working Papers in Economics*, no. 59, Aug 1989, p. 10. The conference, summoned by the Reform government, brought employer and union groups together to discuss the wage arbitration system and other issues, but proved unable to reach a consensus. See Burdon, *New Dominion*, pp. 73–4.
88 *Dominion*, 6 Apr 1932, Economists committee, T 1, 52/703/[2], Archives New Zealand.
89 Bassett, *Coates of Kaipara*, pp. 167–8; Diary, 1931–32, MS 985, Hocken Library. See also comment in Sinclair and Mandle, *Open Account*, pp. 194–5.
90 Peter Clarke, *Keynesian Revolution in the Making, 1924–1936*, Clarendon, Oxford, 1988, p. 120. They had given Montagu Norman an especially hard time; see pp. 125–9.
91 The 'Premiers Plan' was largely attributed to Copland; see Sinclair and Mandle, *Open Account*, p. 194.
92 For the lack of economists in government in another dominion, see Bryce, *Maturing in Hard Times*, pp. 27, 37.
93 Brian Easton, *The Nationbuilders*, Auckland University Press, Auckland, 2001, p. 47.
94 Beauchamp to Forbes, 23 Feb 1932, T 1, 52/703/[2].
95 Wilford to Downie Stewart, 30 Nov 1932, MS 985-1/1/238.
96 The most commonly cited was T. E. Gregory, who had come to New Zealand with Niemeyer in 1930. See, for instance, J. T. Grose, General Manager, National Bank, to PM, 4 Mar 1932, T 1, 52/645.
97 Kershaw to Park, 15 Feb 1932, Micro-MS-Coll-20-2958, Bank of England Archive, Overseas Department, Records New Zealand, Alexander Turnbull Library.
98 Report of the Economic Committee, *AJHR*, 1932, B-3.
99 Grant Fleming, 'Keynes, Purchasing Power Parity and Exchange Rate Policy in New Zealand During the 1930s Depression', *New Zealand Economic Papers*, vol. 31, no. 1, 1997,

pp. 1–14. Fleming asserts that while in 1930 most economists had argued that exchange rate change should not be an integral part of an economic package, by 1932 they had changed their minds. Fleming thinks that Copland played an important role in forging this consensus. Park's dissenting opinion is in *AJHR*, 1932, B-3, p. 38; he estimated a 'total adverse effect' of £3.5 million. As it turned out, improving economic conditions meant that the effect was much less, but this would not be known for some time. See also *Timaru Herald*, 21 Jan 1932, MS 985/28/35, Hocken Library, reporting Labour leader Harry Holland citing Treasury figures on the adverse effect of the exchange rate changes on the Budget.
100 *Evening Post*, 4 Mar 1932, T 1, 52/703/[2].
101 Park to Kershaw, 30 Mar 1932, Micro-MS-Coll-20-2956, Bank of England Archive, Overseas Dept — Records New Zealand, Alexander Turnbull Library; Bassett, *Coates of Kaipara*, p. 189.
102 Diary, 1932, pp. 70–1, MS 985/17/1.
103 Cable, Wellington to SS *Rangitane*, 16 Nov 1932, Downie Stewart and Park in London, T 1, 52/717, Archives New Zealand.
104 Bassett, *Coates of Kaipara*, pp. 189–91, is informative.
105 Park to Drew, High Commission, London, 19 Dec 1932, T 1, 52/645.
106 Hislop to Park, 13 Dec 1932, T 1, 52/645.
107 Mentioned in *Truth*, c. 20 Jan 1933, clipping on MS 985/28/35, Hocken Library.
108 Entry for Friday 13 Jan 1933, Diary, 1932–33, MS 985/7/7, Hocken Library.
109 Stewart to Stephens, Canadian Minister of Trade and Commerce, 30 Sep 1933, MS 985/1/1.
110 Report 13, 20 Jan 1932, 847H.00, US State Department, National Archives, Washington DC, copy held at ATL.
111 MS 985/28/35.
112 Burdon, *New Dominion*, p. 162; *Statutes of New Zealand*, 1932–33, nos 37, 42; Park to Downie Stewart, 7 Sep, 24 Sep 1931, MS 985/13, Hocken Library. See also Memo, ST to Chair, National Expenditure Commission, 11 Feb 1932, Treasury reports for the National Expenditure Commission 1932, T 1, 52/703/[1], Archives New Zealand. The internal debt stood at £115 million; the external, mostly held in London, at £160 million.
113 Campbell to Sutch, 6 Mar 1973, MS-Papers-1900-15. For Coates's letter, see Coates to Forbes, 23 Jan 1932, MS-Papers 1785-038.
114 Easton, *Nationbuilders*, pp. 36, 40.
115 Bassett, *Coates of Kaipara*, p. 208.

116 B. H. Farland, *Coates' Tale*, B. Farland, Wellington, 1995, pp. 114–15; Michael Bassett, *The State in New Zealand 1840–1984: Socialism Without Doctrines?*, Auckland University Press, Auckland, 1998, pp. 176–7. See also Bassett, *Coates of Kaipara*, p. 204: Coates added the phrase on economic welfare to Downie Stewart's bill to make it more palatable.
117 Stewart to Kershaw, 24 Dec 1932, MS 985/1/1.
118 Diary 1932–33, MS 985/7/7.
119 J. L. Fisher to Kershaw, 25 May 1933, Micro-MS-Coll-20-2958, Bank of England Archive — Overseas Department — Records New Zealand, Alexander Turnbull Library.
120 1932–33, No. 32. The banks assumed that the demand for London funds would dry up after devaluation — in fact this didn't happen, and the Crown's indemnity obligation expired without being invoked. The Act was repealed with the establishment of the Reserve Bank in August 1934 (Finance Act 1934, sec. 12).
121 Memo, 5 Jul 1933, Micro-MS-Coll-20-2958, Bank of England Archive — Overseas Department — Records New Zealand, Alexander Turnbull Library.
122 1933, No. 11, sec. 12. For discussion, see Hawke, *Between Government and Banks*, pp. 32–3.
123 Campbell to Sutch, 16 Aug 1973, MS-Papers-1900-15, R. M. Campbell Papers, ATL.
124 Campbell to Sutch, 15 Nov 1971, MS-Papers-1900-15. The disagreement concluded when Coates's first message to Campbell the next morning was, 'put yr hat on: a day at Otaki races wd be good for us'.
125 Exchange of telegrams, Park and Coates, 5 and 6 Feb 1934, T 1, 52/645: 'Saturday's Dominion contained very helpful leading article regarding capital for reserve bank recommend you send telegram appreciation to editor'; 'Thank you I have sent a message of appreciation to Mr Earle'. Coates was at Waitangi attending the celebrations marking Lord Bledisloe's gifting of the Treaty house and grounds to the nation.
126 *NZPD*, vol. 236, pp. 624, 629 (24 Oct 1933).
127 Solicitor-Gen to MF, 28 Jul 1934, T 1, 52/645. The Bank of England had also provided the first governor for the South African Reserve Bank.
128 Solicitor-Gen to MF, 28 Jul 1934, T 1, 52/645. The opinions were proffered in a report on the government's responsibility for protecting the bank's wealth from criminal action.
129 For Park's expectation of what would happen if the exchange rate moved to 125, see *AJHR*, 1932–33, B-4, addendum by Mr Park, p. 38.
130 *AJHR*, 1932, B-3, p. 137. A. G. B. Fisher , the

Professor of Economics at Otago, took issue with many aspects of the expenditure cuts in 'The New Zealand Economic Problem: A Review', *The Economic Record*, May 1932, p. 86.
131 Noonan, *By Design*, p. 126. Airport construction was later to become significant.
132 Minutes of meeting, 21 Apr 1932, National Expenditure Commission, T 1, 52/702, Archives New Zealand.
133 For other comment by historians, see G. V. Butterworth, *Maori Affairs*, Iwi Transition Agency / GP Books, Wellington, 1990, p. 77; Ranginui Walker, *He Tipua: The Life and Times of Sir Apirana Ngata*, Penguin, Auckland, 2001, pp. 280–300, esp. pp. 289–91.
134 *AJHR*, 1934, G-11, p. 47.
135 *AJHR*, 1934, G-11, p. 48.
136 Park to Kershaw, 30 Mar 1932; Memo, 5 Jul 1933; Micro-MS-Coll-20-2958, Bank of England Archive — Overseas Department — Records New Zealand, Alexander Turnbull Library; tabulation of Budgets, 1928/29 to 1934/35, on 1935 Budget file, T 1, 52/63/35, Archives New Zealand. See also General Manager's records, 24 Feb, 18 Dec 1933, 28 Jun 1934, BNZ Archive.
137 Memo, Minister of Finance to ministers in charge of departments, 11 Jun 1933, Comparative increase in departmental expenditure, T 1, 52/81, Archives New Zealand. See chapter 2 for the background to the October 1930 instruction.
138 'JGG' to C. J. McKenzie (Under-Sec Public Works Dept), 8 Feb 1933, Loan requirements, T 1, 52/77/33.
139 Financial Statement (J. G. Coates), 9 Nov 1933, *AJHR*, 1933, B-6, pp. 19–20 (quote on p. 20).
140 Campbell to Sutch, 30 Sep 1971, MS-Papers 1900-15.
141 John Bitchener, his successor, was 69 years old.
142 Financial Statement (J. G. Coates), 9 Nov 1933, *AJHR*, 1933, B-6, p. 10. See also Bassett, *Coates of Kaipara*, p. 202.
143 Financial Statement (J. G. Coates), 9 Nov 1933, *AJHR*, 1933, B-6, p. 10. See also Downie Stewart's diary of his 1932 trip re his inquisition of Keynes.
144 T 1, 52/81. An identical circular was sent out on 11 April 1935.
145 Main estimates 1934/35, Treasury circular memorandum for permanent heads, 17 May 1934, Estimates 1934, T 1, 52/35/34, Archives New Zealand.
146 Public Works Dept to Min Public Works, 10 Mar 1934, T 1, 52/77/34, Archives New Zealand.
147 ST to MF, 29 Mar 1934, loan requirements 1934, T 1, 52/77/34.
148 Biography of G. W. Clinkard, www.dnzb.govt.nz.
149 John E. Martin, *Holding the Balance: A History of New Zealand's Department of Labour, 1891–1995*, Canterbury University Press, Christchurch, 1996, p. 172, and additional comments by John E. Martin. The Board was to be funded by an annual flat rate levy of 30s on all men aged 20 or more. It began in 1931–32 with 34 officers on secondment, including two investigating officers, and by 1936–37 had 465 officers and 450 bureau relief workers.
150 Campbell to Sutch, 6 Mar 1973, Correspondence, Sutch, MS-Papers-1900-15, Alexander Turnbull Library. Presumably the aide was Campbell.
151 Conference on unemployment and land settlement, MS-Papers-1785-021, Alexander Turnbull Library. In Canada, too, the Department of Finance seems not to have been involved in unemployment legislation. See Bryce, *Maturing in Hard Times*, p. 72.
152 Financial Statement (J. G. Coates), 9 Nov 1933, *AJHR*, 1933, B-6, p. 14. In 1932/33, £4.213 million was taken in to the Unemployment Fund and £3.789 million paid out.
153 This seems evident both from the lack of material on the subject on the Treasury files and from Downie Stewart's account on MS 985/17/1.
154 Ottawa conference, T 1, 52/708.
155 David McGill, *Guardians at the Gate*, Silver Owl Press for NZ Customs Dept, Wellington, 1991, p. 146.
156 Easton, *Nationbuilders*, p. 35.
157 Dick Campbell wrote extensively about Coates's (and his own) relations with producer boards; see Campbell to Sutch, 15 Nov 1971, 6 Mar 1973, MS-Papers-1900-15, Alexander Turnbull Library.
158 See Bassett, *Coates of Kaipara*, p. 208. Note that Belshaw served on the three-person commission which enquired into company promotion issues in 1933–34; David Grant, *Bulls, Bears and Elephants: A History of the New Zealand Stock Exchange*, Victoria University Press, Wellington, 1997, p. 149. For more on Belshaw, see Anton M. Endres, 'Economic Thought and Policy Advice in New Zealand, 1930–1935: Accommodating a Tradition of Policy Activism', Work in progress report no. 32, Economics Department, University of Auckland, 1989.
159 Campbell to Sutch, 15 Nov 1971, MS-Papers-1900-15, Alexander Turnbull Library; *Statutes of NZ*, 1934, No. 34; *NZ Gazette*, 31 Jan 1935, p. 134.

160 J 1, 1934/2/65, Archives New Zealand, cited in Barrie Macdonald and David Thomson, 'Mortgage Relief, Farm Finance, and Rural Depression in New Zealand in the 1930s', *NZJH*, vol. 21, no. 2, 1987, p. 241.

161 Memo of 1 Oct 1934, p. 5, Nash file on State Advances Corporation, T 25/7. The members of the committee were Public Service Commissioner Verschaffelt, Ashwin, Campbell, and six others.

162 For instance, the 1934 enquiry into the monetary system, and the charges of 'socialism' levelled against Coates between 1933 and 1935.

163 B. C. Ashwin, 'Practical Problems in Public Finance', lecture to Commerce Society, Victoria University College, 15 Apr 1935, Rosenberg Papers, Macmillan Brown Library, University of Canterbury, presented by Wolfgang Rosenberg, supplied to writer courtesy of Brian Easton.

164 The main aspects were the raising of the exchange rate; measures to reduce unemployment; and 'the establishment of important facilities for action', namely the Reserve Bank, the Rural Mortgagors Final Adjustment Act, and the Mortgage Corporation. Financial Statement issued by Coates, 3 Dec 1935, 1935 Budget, T 1, 52/63/35.

165 Bassett, *Coates of Kaipara*, p. 230; Financial Statement issued by Coates, 3 Dec 1935, T 1, 52/63/35.

166 4 Dec 1935, MS 985/1/1/46, Hocken Library.

Chapter 4:
A new world? 1935–1949

1 Entry for 1 March, Diary 1939, Ashwin Papers, copy made available courtesy of Barry Ashwin and Brian Easton.

2 F. B. Stephens, 'The Public Service — To-day and To-morrow', *Journal of Public Administration*, vol. 5, no. 1, Sep 1942, pp. 48–9.

3 Bob Semple, Minister of Works, quoted in Rosslyn Noonan, *By Design: A Brief History of the Public Works Department / Ministry of Works, 1870 to 1970*, Government Printer, Wellington, 1975, p. 135.

4 Jonathan Boston, 'The Treasury: Its Role, Philosophy and Influence', in H. Gold (ed.), *New Zealand Politics in Perspective*, Longman Paul, Auckland, 1992, pp. 195–6. In the 1989 edition of this article, the development was dated to the 1950s.

5 A. R. F. Mackay, 'The Treasury as a Co-ordinating Factor in Public Service Administration', *JPA*, vol. 1, no. 1, May 1938, p. 87.

6 Savage, *NZPD*, vol. 237, p. 204 (14 Nov 1933).

7 Memorandum of 27 Nov 1935, Micro-MS-Coll-20-2958, ATL.

8 Lefeaux to Norman, 10 Jan 1936, Micro-MS-Coll-2945, ATL. Note that in a letter to Forbes of 19 February 1931, Niemeyer had stressed that a central bank must be independent if it was worth establishing at all (T 1, 52/645).

9 Harvey to Lefeaux, 10 Jan 1936, Micro-MS-Coll-20-2945, Bank of England Archive, ATL. For comment on Lefeaux's limitations, see Keith Sinclair, *Walter Nash*, Auckland and Oxford University Press, Auckland, 1976, p. 191: 'a stiff Englishman too inflexible to adapt to a new or changing environment'. Lefeaux lived in a hotel for eighteen months, eventually moving to the Wellington Club.

10 Memorandum of 27 Nov 1935, Micro-MS-Coll-20-2958, Bank of England Archive, Overseas Dept — Records New Zealand, folder 1, ATL.

11 Memo by 'H. C.', 3 Dec 1935, Micro-MS-Coll-20-2958, ATL. G. R. Hawke, *Between Government and Banks: A History of the Reserve Bank of New Zealand*, Government Printer, Wellington, 1973, pp. 63–4, stresses the overlap between Coalition and Labour views on the disadvantages of not 'administering the thing from the Cabinet room'.

12 Sinclair, *Walter Nash*, pp. 124–5; *Statutes of New Zealand*, 1936, No. 1, sec. 10(1).

13 An annotated draft of the Act is on Reserve Bank of New Zealand, T 1, 52/645, Archives New Zealand. According to Lefeaux, the Secretary of the Treasury (by then this was Rodda) endorsed his views in general, so was presumably out of sympathy with the new law. Lefeaux to Harvey, 14 Jan 1936, Micro-MS-Coll-20-2945, Bank of England Archive, ATL.

14 ST to MF, 14 Feb 1936, T 1, 52/645. No credit appropriation bill was enacted in 1936.

15 Sullivan, introducing Railways Amendment Bill, *NZPD*, vol. 244, p. 96 (2 Apr 1936). See also L. C. Webb, *Government in New Zealand*, Department of Internal Affairs, Wellington, 1940, p. 69.

16 *AJHR*, 1936, H-40A. See also K. G. Reid, 'Railways Administration', *JPA*, vol. 4, no. 2, Mar 1942, pp. 32–44.

17 *Statutes of New Zealand*, 1936, Nos 2, 12.

18 *NZPD*, vol. 245, p. 441 (28 May 1936).

19 R. M. Burdon, *The New Dominion*, A. H. and A. W. Reed, Wellington, 1965, pp. 306–7.

20 Memo, assumed to be written by Copland, 6 Aug 1936, Micro-MS-Coll-20-2958, Bank of England Archive, Overseas Dept — Records

New Zealand, folder 2, ATL. With revenue of £31.14 million a surplus of £472,000 was achieved, compared with £281,000 the year before. *NZPD*, vol. 348, p. 428 (28 Sep 1937). See also (Governor-General) Galway to Prime Minister Baldwin, 26 Dec 1936, Baldwin Papers, Australasian Joint Copying Project, Alexander Turnbull Library.
21. Minute by C. A. Jeffery, Secretary, Prime Minister's office, 10 Dec 1935, Comparative increase in departmental expenditure, T 1, 52/81, Archives New Zealand.
22. Typescript, 'The Function of Treasury', n.d. but probably c. 1938, Public Revenues Act, 1926, T 1, 40/15.
23. Mackay, 'Treasury as a Co-ordinating Factor', p. 87.
24. Peter Campbell, 'Politicians, Public Servants and the People in New Zealand. II', *Political Studies*, vol. 4, no. 1, 1956, p. 19, citing *Tomorrow*, 25 Oct 1939, p. 805.
25. Webb, *Government in New Zealand*, p. 65. By comparison, 28 of the 118 ministers who served between 1912 and 1931 had degrees.
26. *NZPD*, vol. 252, p. 421 (18 Aug 1938), cited in Barry Gustafson, *From the Cradle to the Grave: A Biography of Michael Joseph Savage*, Reed Methuen, Auckland, 1986, p. 222.
27. Asst ST to MF, 4 Aug 1938, Social Security, T 1, 52/479, Archives New Zealand. The government did revise its figures in response to Treasury criticism. For the issue generally, see Brian Easton, *The Nationbuilders*, Auckland University Press, Auckland, p. 53; Sinclair, *Walter Nash*, pp. 132, 160, 164; Elizabeth Hanson, *The Politics of Social Security*, Auckland University Press / OUP, Auckland, 1980, pp. 45, 90–2, 115, which charts Treasury's opposition to the government's non-contributory scheme. See also the discussion by John E. Martin, 'Honouring the Contract: State Policy and Labour in New Zealand', unpub. ms, Ministry for Culture and Heritage, Wellington, ch 4, pp. 9–10, 13–17.
28. Ashwin to Nash, 27 Apr 1937, Ashwin Papers. Sutch also advocated the creation of new industries, and the socialisation of growing industries — the former would give the state a broader tax base, the latter more economic power. Ashwin's memo is referred to in Sinclair, *Walter Nash*, p.155. Ashwin was then an Assistant Secretary at the Treasury.
29. *NZPD*, vol. 248, p. 428 (28 Sep 1937). See also the caution about public works expressed in the Financial Statement, *AJHR*, 1938, B-6, p. 12.
30. Diary 1931–1932, p. 61, MS 985/1/7/6, Hocken Library.
31. Nor did it endear the Treasury to Labour, which opposed devaluation for very different reasons.
32. Sinclair, *Walter Nash*, pp. 79–80, 113.
33. *Tomorrow*, 25 May 1936.
34. David W. Slater, *War, Finance and Reconstruction: The Role of Canada's Department of Finance, 1939–1946*, National Library of Canada, Ottawa, 1995, p. 21.
35. Greg Whitwell, *The Treasury Line*, Allen & Unwin, Sydney, 1986, pp. 10–11, 61–5. For the United Kingdom, see A. W. Coats, 'Britain: The Rise of the Specialists', *History of Political Economy*, vol. 13, no. 3, 1981, pp. 368–9, which also discusses British use of national income statistics.
36. R. J. M. Hill, 'The Quest for Control: The New Zealand Dairy Industry and the Guaranteed Price, 1921–36', MA thesis, University of Auckland, 1974, pp. 281–4, 309; T 1, 40/648/1. No T 1, 40/648 file for 1936 or 1937 was located. Sinclair, *Walter Nash*, pp. 126–30, does not mention Treasury advice.
37. D. W. Woodward, 'Government and Economic Planning', *JPA*, vol. 1, no. 2, Dec 1938, pp. 99–107. Woodward was then the Secretary of the Bureau of Industry that had been set up by the Labour government.
38. D. K. Walker, 'New Zealand Institute of Public Administration: A Retrospect', *JPA*, vol. 10, no. 2, Mar 1948, pp. 73, 78. The Hunter committee on the recruitment of graduates into the public service had reported shortly before the war.
39. *JPA*, vol. 2, no. 2, Dec 1939, p. 7 (editorial); see also vol. 4, no. 1, Mar 1942, p. 81.
40. B. C. Ashwin, 'Practical Problems in Public Finance', paper read to Victoria University College Commerce Society, 1935, copy held at Macmillan Brown Centre, University of Canterbury.
41. *AJHR*, 1942, B-1(IV). The full series was not resumed after the war; Webb, *Government in New Zealand*, pp. 115–19; A. McGregor, 'Control of Public Expenditure in New Zealand', *JPA*, vol. 8, no. 1, Sep 1945, p. 22.
42. Information from John E. Martin.
43. Easton, *Nationbuilders*, pp. 43–57 (the chapter on Ashwin), is the indispensable starting point.
44. Ashwin, 'Practical Problems in Public Finance'.
45. Easton, *Nationbuilders*, pp. 43–4. The biographies of Nash, Savage and Fraser (Michael Bassett and Michael King, *Tomorrow Comes the Song: A Life of Peter Fraser*, Penguin, Auckland, 2000), do not analyse the relationship between Ashwin and these Labour politicians. Given that

Nash was Minister of Finance for all fourteen years of the first Labour government, the references in Sinclair, *Walter Nash*, are particularly slender — 'B. C. Ashwin of the Treasury' is re-identified on most of the occasions he is mentioned, and there is no index entry for Treasury.

46 J. V. T. Baker, *War Economy*, Historical Publications Branch, Department of Internal Affairs, Wellington, 1965, p. 275. They were resumed in 1943/44, and again in 1946/47 and subsequent years. See also Whitwell, *Treasury Line*, pp. 63–4.

47 Economic Stabilization Conference, record of proceedings, part 2, T 70/1. For more on the conference, see below. There are Scandinavian parallels — Scandinavian economists were only later seen as proto-Keynesians.

48 Sinclair, *Walter Nash*, pp. 170–1, discusses this crisis.

49 Kershaw to Governor, Bank of England, 14 Nov 1938, Micro-MS-Coll-20-2958, ATL.

50 Kershaw to Rusden, 14 Mar 1939, Micro-MS-Coll-20-2958, ATL. The New Zealand pound was then exchanged at the rate of £1 5s (£1.25) for £1 sterling — Kershaw's reference to '150' suggested that it would go to at least £1 10s (£1.5).

51 Webb, *Government in New Zealand*, p. 101.

52 ST to MF, 27 Jan 1939, Ashwin personal file, T 90, Archives New Zealand. Ashwin was appointed at an annual salary of £1650, a sum recommended by his predecessor, Rodda, on the grounds that any less would not preserve the status of the Treasury in relation to other departments. Cabinet agreed, while the related issue of whether Ashwin should be paid fees as a director of the Reserve Bank and the State Advances Corporation was to be decided by the Minister of Finance.

53 Ashwin to Kershaw, 17 Mar 1939, Micro-MS-Coll-20-2958, ATL.

54 Sinclair, *Walter Nash*, p. 172, names Good as 'Wood'.

55 Entry for 9 Feb 1939, Ashwin Diary, Ashwin Papers. Ashwin kept this journal for nine months from the time of his appointment as Secretary to the Treasury in February.

56 1 May 1939, Ashwin Diary; also 1 March comment that about half of the [parliamentary] party belonged to its left wing. See also Sinclair, *Walter Nash*, pp. 172–3.

57 1 Mar, 1 May 1939, Ashwin Diary.

58 1 Mar, 1 May, 1 Jul 1939, Ashwin Diary. The loan, issued at 4 per cent, was oversubscribed by about £250,000 without any support from either the Reserve Bank or Treasury. Lefeaux was the Governor of the Reserve Bank.

59 1 Jul 1939, Ashwin Diary.

60 1 Jul 1939, Ashwin Diary.

61 8 Oct 1939, Ashwin Diary.

62 *Dominion*, 31 Jul 1939, in Micro-MS-Coll-20-2958, ATL.

63 8 Oct 1939, Ashwin Diary.

64 *NZPD*, vol. 254, p. 881 (1 Aug 1939). Gustafson, *Cradle to Grave*, pp. 246–7, refers briefly to Savage delivering the 1939 Budget. At the beginning of his speech (p. 881), Savage observed that 'in view of the direct bearing upon the public finances, I would like to say a few words about the economic policy of the Government'.

65 8 Oct 1939, Ashwin Diary.

66 *JPA*, vol. 3, no. 1, Jun 1940, p. 51.

67 8 Oct 1939, Ashwin Diary.

68 Hon W. Perry in Legislative Council, *NZPD*, vol. 256, p. 423, cited in Baker, *War Economy*, p. 252.

69 Baker, *War Economy*, pp. 258–9.

70 Baker, *War Economy*, p. 262.

71 Sinclair, *Walter Nash*, pp. 209–10. See the tabulation of additional taxation in Baker, *War Economy*, pp. 261–3. The tax rate on individual income was raised from 1s 8d in the pound in 1938/39 to 4s in the pound by 1944/45.

72 Baker, *War Economy*, p. 264.

73 Baker, *War Economy*, p. 268 (the comment in parentheses is partly mine).

74 Baker, *War Economy*, p. 269.

75 Baker, *War Economy*, pp. 278–9. Pre-war control of food prices by the Labour government is discussed in Michael Bassett, *The State in New Zealand 1840–1984: Socialism Without Doctrines?*, Auckland University Press, Auckland, 1998, pp. 194–8.

76 Baker, *War Economy*, pp. 280–1.

77 *Report of the Economic Stabilization Conference 1940*, Government Printer, Wellington, pp. 3, 6.

78 *Evening Post*, 16 Dec 1942. For the parallel Canadian experience, and the respective roles of finance department and minister, see Robert B. Bryce, 'Prices, Wages and the Ceiling', in David W. Slater, *War, Finance and Reconstruction: The Role of Canada's Department of Finance, 1939–1946*, National Library of Canada, Ottawa, 1995, pp. 127–34.

79 Baker, *War Economy*, p. 283.

80 Baker, *War Economy*, pp. 283–5. See also Bassett, *State in New Zealand*, p. 224.

81 Ashwin to PM, 13 May 1942, T 1, 1/1, John Martin Papers. Nash had left for Washington in January.

82 Easton, *Nationbuilders*, p. 50.
83 ST to PM, 20 Oct 1942, T 1, 1/1, John Martin Papers.
84 Minutes of Economic Stabilization committee, Jul 1942 to Jan 1943, Economic Stabilization Commission minutes, T 72, 1/3, Archives New Zealand.
85 Information from Gary Hawke.
86 Reported in *Dominion*, 16 Dec 1942. Much of this is quoted by Bassett, *State in New Zealand*, p. 226.
87 M. J. Moriarty, 'Administering the Policy of Economic Stabilization', *JPA*, vol. 7, no. 2, Mar 1945, p. 30. Discussion of how this worked in the case of the Price Tribunal follows.
88 John Martin, 'Economic Policy Making in the Early Post-War Years', in Jan Whitwell and Mary Anne Thompson (eds), *Society and Culture: Economic Perspectives*, NZ Association of Economists, Wellington, 1991, p. 224; see also Moriarty, 'Economic Stabilization', pp. 29, 36.
89 Moriarty, 'Economic Stabilization', p. 36.
90 Report on officer, 31 Jan 1948, Henry Lang personal file, T 90, Archives New Zealand.
91 See, for instance, Appointment of assistant economist to ESC, 28 Jul 1948, Economic Stabilization Commission — staff, T 72, 1/6, Archives New Zealand.
92 Economic Stabilization Commission, investigation of industries, T 72/3, Archives New Zealand, *passim*.
93 Ken Durrant interview, 12 Jun 2000.
94 For the United Kingdom, see George Peden, *The Treasury and British Public Policy, 1906–1959*, Oxford University Press, Oxford, 2000, pp. 325, 359.
95 Relations between price stabilisation committee and the price tribunal, T 72, 1/4, Archives New Zealand, indicates that at least in 1941, the Price Tribunal was located with Industries and Commerce.
96 Moriarty, 'Economic Stabilization', p. 29. See also Martin, 'Economic Policy Making', pp. 222–3. The reduction in size attracted some critical comment from interest groups.
97 G. J. Schmitt to Brian Easton, 15 Feb 1997. Schmitt was Ashwin's private secretary from 1943 to 1950.
98 Bernard Greig interview, 5 Mar 2001.
99 Schmitt to Easton, 15 Feb 1997.
100 'Owing to a considerable amount of my own time being occupied with Stabilisation and other matters'; ST to Chair PSC, 9 Sep 1948, Greensmith personal file, T 90, Archives New Zealand.
101 Schmitt to Easton, 17 Feb 1997.
102 Ashwin interviewed by John Henderson, March 1970. The story from the interview is told in full in Bassett, *State in New Zealand*, p. 226.
103 Noel Lough interview, 5 May 2000. The Lang anecdote and the comment on juggling came from Gary Hawke.
104 Baker, *War Economy*, p. 302; see also p. 311.
105 Sinclair, *Walter Nash*, pp. 229–55.
106 Easton, *Nationbuilders*, p. 52.
107 Schmitt to Easton, 17 Feb 1997.
108 NZ High Commissioner, Canberra, to PM, 20 Mar 1951, MS-Papers-1624, 097/5, ATL.
109 L. C. Webb, 'The Future of Wartime Controls', *JPA*, vol. 7, no. 1, Sep 1944, p. 17.
110 A. McGregor, 'Control of Public Expenditure in New Zealand', *JPA*, vol. 8, no. 1, Sep 1945, pp. 21–35 (quote p. 30). See also the 1936 and 1937 Budget files, T 1, 52/63/36 and 52/63/37, Archives New Zealand.
111 *AJHR*, 1943, D-1, p. i, cited in Noonan, *By Design*, p. 177. Baker, *War Economy*, has only a brief reference (pp. 249–50).
112 N. Robinson, *James Fletcher: Builder*, Hodder & Stoughton, London, 1970, p. 162, cited in Noonan, *By Design*, p. 178.
113 PW 28/393, 4 Aug 1943, cited in Noonan, *By Design*, p. 178. The new Ministry was not long-lived — it was amalgamated with the Public Works Department in March 1946. See John Martin, typescript, 'Economic Policy Making', p. 18, John Martin Papers.
114 In 2003, the premises of Victoria University's Law School and an historic reserve.
115 Bernard Greig interview, 5 Mar 2001.
116 Noel Lough interview, 8 May 2000.
117 Bill Robinson interview, 15 May 2001; Bob Norman interview, 27 Jul 2001.
118 Schmitt to Easton, 17 Feb 1997.
119 Noel Lough interview, 8 May 2000.
120 Mackay, 'Treasury as a Co-ordinating Factor', p. 87.
121 McGregor, 'Control of Public Expenditure in New Zealand', p. 29.
122 Roberta Nicholls, 'The PSC and the Equal Pay Campaign', in Alan Henderson, The *Quest for Efficiency: The Origins of the State Services Commission*, Historical Branch / State Services Commission, Wellington, 1990, pp. 257–8. See also *Public Service Lists*; F. W. Millar, 'Women of the Public Service', *JPA*, vol. 6, no. 2, Mar 1944, pp. 27–32.
123 *New Zealand Gazette*, 15 Feb 1948. See also Martin, 'Economic Policy Making', p. 16.
124 Schmitt to Easton, 17 Feb 1997.
125 Ashwin personal file, T 90.
126 Schmitt to Easton, 17 Feb 1997. Note the

distinction drawn between accounting and book-keeping.
127 Bill Robinson interview, 27 Jul 2001; also G. J. Schmitt on Ashwin, Ashwin Papers.
128 G. J. Schmitt on Ashwin, Ashwin Papers; Barker, Greensmith, personal files, T 90.
129 Bill Robinson interview, 27 Jul 2001. Robinson thinks that Atkin eventually gave way.
130 11 Oct 1945, Economic Stabilization Commission: History, T 72, 1/16/1, Archives New Zealand. Note also Webb, 'The Future of Wartime Controls', p. 14, including comments on the efficiencies of monopolies compared with many small units.
131 Cited in Martin, 'Economic Policy Making in the Early Post-War Years', p. 227. Martin comments that it is hard 'to resist the conclusion that [this] was too strong for the Fraser Government and for their senior advisors. While committed to "full employment" … the Fraser Government was clearly more comfortable with pragmatic use of controls through corporatist "stabilisation" than with any ideological commitment to planning. Similarly, the Government was quick to dispel "the bogey of widespread nationalisation".'
132 Edward Bridges, *Treasury Control*, Stamp Memorial Lecture, University of London, Athlone Press, London, 1950, pp. 18–19.
133 Peden, *Treasury and British Public Policy*, pp. 318–24; Robert Skidelsky, *John Maynard Keynes: Fighting For Britain, 1937–1946*, Macmillan, London, 2000, pp. 74–90; Greg Whitwell, 'The Power of Economic Ideas? Keynesian Economic Policies in Postwar Australia', in Stephen Bell and Brian Head (eds), *State, Economy and Public Policy in Australia*, Oxford University Press, Melbourne, 1994, pp. 121–3. For New Zealand, see *NZPD*, vol. 261, p. 196 (30 Apr 1942), for Fraser, presenting the Budget: 'As in the United Kingdom and in Australia, it is proposed to turn to consumptive [sic] taxes for portion of the additional revenue required'.
134 For more on this, see Bridges, *Treasury Control*, esp. pp. 15–18; Peter A. Hall (ed.), *The Political Power of Economic Ideas: Keynesianism Across Nations*, Princeton University Press, Princeton NJ, 1989, esp. Margaret Weir, 'Ideas and Politics: The Acceptance of Keynesianism in Britain and the United States'; George Peden, 'Old Dogs and New Tricks: The British Treasury and Keynesian Economics in the 1940s and 1950s', in M. O. Furner and B. E. Supple (eds), *The State and Economic Knowledge*, Cambridge University Press, Cambridge, 1990, pp. 208–38; Peden, *Treasury and British Public Policy*, esp. pp. 351–5; Skidelsky, *Fighting for Britain*, pp. 270–2; Whitwell, *Treasury Line*, esp. pp 53–79.
135 Whitwell 'Power of Economic Ideas', p. 122. Whitwell applies Hall's model about economists, governments and coalitions of interests, arguing that all these elements were present in Australia by the end of the war. He also discusses this issue in Whitwell, *Treasury Line*, pp. 87–90.
136 Samuel Beer, *Treasury Control: The Coordination of Financial and Economic Policy Making in Great Britain*, Clarendon, Oxford, 1957, pp. 70–2.
137 Moriarty, 'Economic Stabilization', p. 37.
138 Mackay, 'Treasury as a Co-ordinating Factor', p. 87.
139 Review of H. B. G. Greaves, *The Civil Service in the Changing State*, *JPA*, vol. 10, no. 2, Mar 1948.
140 Baker, *War Economy*, p. 531, gives reasons for the failure of the OND; see also Martin, 'Economic Policy Making'.
141 Bassett and King, *Tomorrow Comes the Song*, p. 298.
142 Martin, 'Economic Policy Making', p. 20. Martin does not come up with any new suggestion as to who killed the OND, but it seems at least plausible that Ashwin had a role.
143 Whitwell, *Treasury Line*, p. 10; comment from Gary Hawke.
144 Schmitt to Easton, 17 Feb 1997. See also Bernard Galvin, *Policy Co-ordination, the Public Sector and Government*, Institute of Policy Studies, Wellington, 1991, p. 12; Martin, 'Economic Policy Making', pp. 21–3.
145 Martin, 'Economic Policy Making', pp. 224–5.
146 Gov RBNZ to MF, 19 Aug 1948, John Martin Papers. See also Sinclair, *Walter Nash*, pp. 272–3; Hawke, *Between Government and Banks*, pp. 122–3.
147 George Laking interview, 21 Nov 2000. There are other versions of this story.

Chapter 5:
Backwards or forwards? 1949–1961

1 Note the discussion in James Belich, *Paradise Reforged: A History of the New Zealanders from the 1880s to the Year 2000*, Penguin, Auckland, 2001, pp. 299, 306.
2 'Survey of National Finances' by the Prime Minister, 1 Feb 1950, Treasury Jan–Feb 1950, MS-Papers-1624-099/4, ATL.
3 Morton to Holland, 21 Jan 1950, National Party matters 1950–1951, MS-Papers-1624-113/3, ATL. Morton then went on to the point of his letter: 'would you bear me in mind when the Canberra appointment is made?'

4   Once the Board of Trade was established in December 1950 (in succession to the Import Advisory Committee established in May).
5   Memo of Assoc MF, 6 Sep 1954, Abolition of controls, MS-Papers-1624-082/5; see also Min Industries and Commerce to PM, 13 Sep 1954; MW to PM, 27 Sep 1954; Min Lands to PM, n.d.
6   *NZ Herald*, 26 Aug 1950, MS-Papers-1624-080-4, ATL; Gael Ferguson, *Building the New Zealand Dream*, Dunmore Press, Palmerston North, 1994, p. 180.
7   'Survey of National Finances', 1 Feb 1950, MS-Papers-1624-099/4, ATL.
8   'Survey of National Finances', 1 Feb 1950, MS-Papers-1624-099/4, ATL. Government expenditure for 1949/50 was £30 million higher than two years earlier.
9   Budget speech notes, 1950 Budget — topics, MS-Papers-1624-080/2, ATL.
10 'Survey of National Finances', 1 Feb 1950, MS-Papers-1624-099/4, ATL. Subsidies were expected to reach £17 million in the 1950/51 financial year.
11 4 Aug 1950, Treasury reports Aug–Sep 1950, MS-Papers-1624-101/5.
12 Peter Aimer, *Wings of the Nation: A History of the New Zealand National Airways Corporation, 1947–1978*, Bush Press, Takapuna, Auckland, 2000, p. 50. In the Budget debate, Labour's Jerry Skinner challenged the sale proposal on the grounds that during the election campaign National had said only that it would introduce private shareholding into the existing corporation. Labour, he promised, would buy back the airline if it were sold. *NZPD*, vol. 290, p. 1975 (30 Aug 1950).
13 *NZPD*, vol. 290, p. 1835 (24 Aug 1950).
14 Increased charges were announced before the 1950 Budget: *NZH*, 26 Aug 1950, on MS-Papers-1624-080-4, ATL; Michael Bassett discusses further developments in *The State in New Zealand 1840 to 1984: Socialism Without Doctrines?*, Auckland University Press, Auckland, 1998, pp. 280–1; see also *AJHR*, 1953, D-2, p. 1.
15 L. C. Webb, *Government in New Zealand*, Department of Internal Affairs, Wellington, 1940, pp. 69, 95.
16 'Survey of National Finances', 1 Feb 1950, MS-Papers-1624-099/4, ATL.
17 'Loan broadcast', n.d., Treasury, Mar–Aug 1950, MS-Papers-1624-100/1, ATL (the loan was to open on 'Monday next, May 29'). An earlier statement of 5 May addressed taxation revenue and expenditure.
18 Memo, ST to MF, 13 Jul 1950, Treasury Jun–Jul, MS-Papers 1624-101/4, ATL. Note that this would remain unusual during the 1950s — loans were often undersubscribed because interest rates were too low.
19 *NZ Herald*, 26 Aug 1950, MS-Papers 1624-080/4, ATL.
20 'Survey of National Finances', 1 Feb 1950, MS-Papers-1624-099/4. Also Frank Holmes interview, 8 Mar 2001.
21 'Survey of National Finances', 1 Feb 1950, MS-Papers-1624-099/4.
22 *NZPD*, vol. 290, p. 1266 (9 Aug 1950). See also G. R. Hawke, *Between Government and Banks: A History of the Reserve Bank of New Zealand*, Government Printer, Wellington, 1973, pp. 71–2: 'the changes introduced in 1950 were largely political in origin … the political concern originated in the belief that greater efforts were needed to combat inflationary pressures'. The PM told Parliament that both the Governor of the Reserve Bank and the Secretary to the Treasury 'entirely approved' of the amendment legislation; *NZPD*, vol. 290, 9 Aug 1950, p. 1273.
23 See the excellent discussion in Aimer, *Wings of the Nation*, pp. 4–62, esp. 53–4, 58. Bassett, *State in New Zealand*, p. 279, instances Labour's threat of repurchase as one disincentive, but Aimer, p. 61, points out that despite this there was sufficient interest within New Zealand to convince Industrial Underwriters Ltd that a new company was feasible.
24 *Evening Star*, 25 Aug 1950, 1950 Budget press comment, MS-Papers-1624-080/4.
25 *Weekly News*, 30 Aug 1950, MS-Papers-1624-080/4; ST to Assoc MF, 27 Mar 1952, Treasury Aug 1951–Apr 1952, MS-Papers-1624-101/1. Note that the programme for 1951/52 was underspent by nearly £8 million compared with the estimated £38 million, in part because of the unavailability of locomotives, cars, wagons, etc., for Railways due to rearmament pressures and shortages in the United Kingdom.
26 *AJHR*, 1951, B-6, p. 9 (S. G. Holland, Budget, 18 Oct 1951).
27 Tabulation of controls and operation, 1949–1954, Sep 1954, Abolition of controls, MS-Papers-1624-082/5; ST to MF, 21 Nov 1950, MS-Papers-1624-102/1; Bassett, *State in New Zealand*, p. 261.
28 Min Industries and Commerce to PM, 22 Jun 1951, Treasury Jun–Jul 1951, MS-Papers-1624-100/5. See also *Dominion*, 29 Oct 1954, on Gas industry, 1954–55, MS-Papers-1624-085/5: 'the government decided some time ago that the

upper limit on subsidy expenditure should be £14m'.
29 Tabulation of controls and operation, 1949–1954, Sep 1954, Abolition of controls, MS-Papers-1624-082/5.
30 L. C. Webb, 'Making of Economic Policy', in R. S. Parker (ed.), *Economic Stability in New Zealand*, New Zealand Institute of Public Administration, Wellington, 1953, p. 14.
31 Webb, 'Making of Economic Policy', p. 14.
32 McIntosh to Sir Norman Brook (UK Cabinet Office), 3 Feb 1950, McIntosh Papers, MS-Papers-6759-237, ATL. I am indebted to Gavin McLean for this reference.
33 Royal Commission on State Services, *AJHR*, 1962, H-41, pp. 61–76.
34 Draft submission to Royal Commission on State Services, Aug 1961, T 1, 50/36/20, Archives New Zealand.
35 John Anderson interview, 12 Mar 2001.
36 Cliff Terry interview, 6 Jul 2000.
37 John Anderson interview, 12 Mar 2001; Cutting on Harry Lake on the occasion of opening of new computer in the Treasury, c. Mar 1961, MS-Papers-0270, ATL. David Green, *Statistics Count: An Illustrated History of Statistics New Zealand*, Statistics New Zealand, Wellington, 2002, p. 24, records the use of Powers–Samas machines in the Census and Statistics Offices from 1926.
38 Don Rangi interview, 8 Dec 2000.
39 Don Rangi interview, 8 Dec 2000.
40 Don Rangi interview, 8 Dec 2000.
41 Bill Robinson interview, 27 Jul 2001.
42 John Anderson interview, 12 Mar 2001.
43 Cliff Terry interview, 6 Jul 2000.
44 Ken Durrant interview, 12 Jun 2000.
45 John Anderson interview, 12 Mar 2001.
46 Ken Durrant interview, 12 Jun 2000.
47 Undated memo, T 3/7/53, John Martin Papers. All but £2 million of the additional funding requested was turned down.
48 Ken Durrant interview, 12 Jun 2000.
49 Delegated authorities to ministers and permanent heads to approve expenditure were set out when the new government took office. In most cases the sum delegated to the department head was doubled if Treasury concurred. Cabinet authority for expenditure, MS-Papers-1624-099/4. *AJHR*, 1962, H-41, Appendix 6, pp. 442–6, gives the delegations as at May 1955, and later amendments to 1961.
50 *AJHR*, 1962, H-41, p. 66.
51 Notes on investigating, 1955, pp. 7–8, John Martin Papers.
52 'Functions of Treasury', [1956], pp. 6–7, John Martin Papers.
53 Comment by John Martin.
54 Cliff Terry interview, 6 Jul 2000.
55 Maori Land Settlement Account, T 1, 40/116, Archives New Zealand.
56 John Anderson interview, 12 Mar 2001; note also the Royal Commission's reference (*AJHR*, 1962, H-41, p. 67) to the junior status of some Treasury investigating officers.
57 Sam Parker interview, 12 May 2000.
58 Sam Parker interview, 12 May 2000.
59 John Anderson interview, 12 Mar 2001.
60 John Anderson interview, 12 Mar 2001. Both Barker (1965–66) and Davis (1967–68) were to become Secretary to the Treasury.
61 Bassett, *State in New Zealand*, pp. 273–8; Brian Easton, *The Nationbuilders*, Auckland University Press, Auckland, 2001, pp. 54–7; Historical notes on Tasman Pulp and Paper, George Kinnear Fraser Papers, 93-319-1/14, ATL; Geoff Schmitt, 'Exchanges with Michael Bassett, 1997–1999', pp. 63–95, esp. pp. 64–73. For more on Fletchers, see Selwyn Parker, *Made in New Zealand: The Story of James Fletcher*, Hodder & Stoughton, Auckland, 1994; Neil Robinson, *James Fletcher, Builder*, Hodder & Stoughton, Auckland and London, 1970.
62 Bassett, *State in New Zealand*, p. 273. I'm concurring here with Schmitt, 'Exchanges', p. 65.
63 Morris Guest, 'The Murupara Project: The Tasman Pulp and Paper Company Ltd and Industrial Development in New Zealand 1945–1963', MA thesis, VUW, 1997, pp. 41, 43.
64 ST to MF, 13 May 1952, Tasman Pulp & Paper, 1952, MS-Papers-1624-097-098/1, ATL.
65 Committee's recommendations to the government on Tasman Pulp and Paper company's proposals, Dec 1951, 'Forest Facts', no. 6, Tasman Pulp & Paper 1952, MS-Papers-1624-098/1.
66 Schmitt, 'Exchanges', p. 74, draws a distinction between spending on infrastructure such as rail and harbour works, and on capital works that were integral to the logging operations, such as logging equipment and housing for loggers.
67 ST to MF, 29 Oct 1953, Tasman Pulp and Paper 1953, MS-Papers-1624-098/2. See further, on raising finance in New Zealand, ST to MF, 22 Jul 1954, MS-Papers-1624-098/3.
68 ST to PM, 30 Jul 1954, Tasman Pulp and Paper 1954–55, MS-Papers-1624-098/3.
69 Comment from Gary Hawke.
70 Sam Parker interview, 12 May 2000.
71 Guest, 'Murupara', p. 42.
72 Easton, *Nationbuilders*, pp. 52–3; Acting ST to MF, 29 May 1950, MS-Papers-1624-100/1; see

also Tony Nightingale, *Mobil, Proud of Our Past, Committed to Our Future: 100 Years in New Zealand,* Mobil Oil NZ, Wellington, 1996, pp. 112–14; Noel Lough interview, 8 May 2000.
73 Gas Industry, 1950, 1952, 1953, MS-Papers-1624-085/3, ATL; IC report is dated 20 Nov 1953. The government's reluctance to let the larger gasworks go out of business reflected a wish to avoid a sudden increase in the number of electricity consumers. See also comment in *Dominion,* 24 Aug 1955, on Gas industry 1955, MS-Papers-1624-085/6, ATL.
74 ST to MF, 10 Oct 1956, Gas industry 1955–56, MS-Papers-1624-085/7.
75 ST to MF, 12 Aug 1958, Gas industry, T 1, 52/962, Archives New Zealand.
76 ST to MF, 9 Jul 1951, revision of Public Revenues Act 1926; annotation from 12 Sep 1951 (after the election); memo to Holland, 19 Jun 1952, with attachment; Public Revenues Amendment Act 1952, secs 3 and 4, T 1, 40/15/3, Archives New Zealand. Gary Hawke comments that 'authorised doctrine is still that departments are extensions of the minister (not, however of the minister's office)', but the shift in language does seem significant in this instance.
77 Peter Campbell, 'Politicians, Public Servants, and the People in New Zealand: II', *Political Studies,* vol. 4, no. 1, Feb 1956, p. 21; Local Government Loans Board Amendment Act 1954, sec. 4B.
78 Campbell, 'Politicians, Public Servants, and the People', p. 20. Republicans won back the United States presidency in the 1952 election, the party's first presidential victory since 1928.
79 Draft statement on remuneration rates supplied to Holland, 'amended along lines discussed yesterday', 4 Apr 1950, Treasury reports Mar–May 1950, MS-Papers-1624-101/3, ATL.
80 ST to PM, 29 Mar 1950, MS-Papers-1624-101/3.
81 ST to MF, 15 Sep 1950, Treasury reports Aug–Sep 1950, MS-Papers-1624-101/5.
82 Memo, Ashwin to PM, 15 Sep 1950, MS-Papers-1624-101/5. At the beginning of May 1951, Albert McGregor prepared a 'case for the defence' on the increased cost of living, arguing that 'whatever the direct causes of price increase, the Government through sound budgetary policy, the wool retention scheme and the removal of import controls has done all any Government can be expected to do to combat inflation' — all these policies had been put forward by Ashwin in Sep 1950. ST to MF, 1 May 1951, Treasury Apr–May 1951, MS-Papers-1624-100/4, ATL.

83 ST to MF, 31 Mar 1950, MS-Papers-1624-100/3, ATL.
84 Sam Parker interview, 12 May 2000. According to John Roberts, *Politicians, Public Servants and Public Enterprise,* Institute of Policy Studies, Victoria University of Wellington, Wellington, 1987, p. 32, an official first attended Cabinet meetings to record proceedings in 1948. See Foss Shanahan, 'Some Reflections on Cabinet Government in New Zealand', *NZJPA,* vol. 17, no. 1, Sep 1954; John Martin, 'Economic Policy Making in the Early Post-War Years', unpublished typescript, pp. 24–7, John Martin Papers.
85 L. C. Webb, 'Making Economic Policy', in Parker (ed.), *Economic Stability in New Zealand,* p. 27.
86 G. J. Schmitt, 'Some Administrative Problems Associated with a Vulnerable Balance of Payments', DPA paper, VUW, 1952, pp. 78–9, 99–100, copy in John Martin Papers.
87 ST to MF, 27 Mar 1951, MS-Papers-1624-100/3.
88 ST to MF (prepared by Greensmith), 23 Feb 1950, Treasury reports 1949–1950, MS-Papers-1624-101/2; memo, ST to Assoc MF (prepared by Noel Lough), 19 Apr 1950, MS-Papers-1624-101/3.
89 On the Cabinet Office, see Shanahan, 'Some Reflections', pp. 8–9.
90 Comment by John Martin.
91 L. C. Webb, 'Making of Economic Policy', pp. 29–30.
92 Webb, 'Making of Economic Policy', p. 30.
93 G. J. Schmitt to Brian Easton, 17 Feb 1997; Henry Lang transferred from the Marketing Department to Treasury on 15 May 1951 (Henry Lang, personal file, T 90, Archives New Zealand). Note that in the United Kingdom, the economic section moved to the Treasury in 1952; see A. W. Coats, 'Britain: The Rise of the Specialists', *History of Political Economy,* vol. 13, no. 3, 1981, p. 388.
94 *NZOYB,* 1950, pp. 1033–89.
95 *NZOYB,* 1950, p. 1034.
96 For a critical comment from the left, see J. P. Lewin, 'Keynes Overstressed?', *Here & Now,* Jul 1953, pp. 16–17.
97 Jack Watts, *Star-Sun,* 24 Jun 1958, T 1, 3/3/58.
98 Bert Brownlie interview, 31 Aug 2000.
99 Comment by John Martin.
100 Bert Brownlie interview, 31 Aug 2000. The first edition was published in 1948, the second in 1951.
101 Bert Brownlie interview, 31 Aug 2000.
102 Frank Holmes interview, 8 Mar 2001.

103 Bert Brownlie interview, 31 Aug 2000.
104 *AJHR*, 1956, B-3, pp. 195, 199, 220–1.
105 Brian Easton, 'Economy' column, *NZ Listener*, 4 Mar 1989, refers to BERL.
106 Alan Danks, 'The Report of the Royal Commission on Monetary, Banking and Credit Systems, 1956', *NZJPA*, vol. 19, no. 1, Sep 1956, pp. 7–8.
107 Sam Parker interview, 12 May 2000.
108 1961 Budget, T 1, 3/3/61, Archives NZ.
109 Greg Whitwell, 'The Power of Economic Ideas? Keynesian Economic Policies in Postwar Australia', in Stephen Bell and Brian Head (eds), *State, Economy and Public Policy in Australia*, Oxford University Press, Melbourne, 1994, pp. 122–3. 'Anti-cyclical' refers to using fiscal policy to counter upswings and downswings in economic activity. Note too that Australia reintroduced import licensing on 8 March 1952. NZHC Canberra to Minister of External Affairs, 7 Mar 1952, MS-Papers-1624-101/1, ATL. See also comment in Webb, 'Making of Economic Policy', p. 14.
110 Peter Clarke, *Hope and Glory: Britain 1900–1990*, Penguin, London, 1996, p. 245. Clarke argues that in fact it owed much more to techniques which the authorities had developed in the days of the gold standard.
111 Clarke, *Hope and Glory*, p. 245.
112 Clarke, *Hope and Glory*, p. 268.
113 Report of Royal Commission on Money, Banking and Credit Systems, *AJHR*, 1956, B-3, pp. 201, 203.
114 G. J. Schmitt, 'Economic Stability and the Balance of Payments', in Parker (ed.), *Economic Stability in New Zealand*, esp. pp. 109–11; *New Zealand Herald*, 14 May 1953; *Hawke's Bay Herald-Tribune*, 18 May 1953. The quotes are from *HBHT*, copy in John Martin Papers. This is also referred to in Campbell, 'Politicians, Public Servants and the People, II', p. 22.
115 Sam Parker interview, 12 May 2001; and see undated draft to MF, [T] 3/7/53, John Martin Papers, which traversed the problem that the increase in capital spending was impossible to finance from orthodox sources. This document was never submitted, as the issue had lapsed by the time it was prepared.
116 Economic talks with representatives of major groups, MS-Papers-1624-083-2, ATL. Was this because of Holland's falling out with Ashwin? In the Parliament elected at the end of 1954, half of the National Party MPs were farmers, one-sixth businessmen and a quarter lawyers or accountants. Peter Campbell, 'Politicians, Public Servants and the People in New Zealand: I', *Political Studies*, vol. 3, no. 3, Oct 1955, p. 196. There is further discussion on politicians and interest groups at pp. 204–5.
117 J. R. Marshall, 'The New Zealand Cabinet', *Political Science*, vol. 7, no. 1, 1955, p. 9.
118 *AJHR*, 1956, B-3, pp. 15–16; Frank Holmes interview, 8 Mar 2001.
119 The Treasury, 'Economic and Financial Policy, 10 Jan 1955', p. 1, John Martin Papers.
120 Minutes of meeting of MF and OCEP, 28 Jan 1955; ST to MF, 28 May 1955, T 61/1/8, John Martin Papers.
121 Reserve Bank of New Zealand, *Monetary and Fiscal Policy in New Zealand: Submissions to the Royal Commission on Money, Banking and Credit Systems by the Reserve Bank, the Associated Banks in NZ and the NZ Treasury*, Reserve Bank of New Zealand, Wellington, 1955, p. 116.
122 Reserve Bank, *Monetary and Fiscal Policy*, p. 117.
123 ST to MF (memo prepared by Albert McGregor), 22 Jan 1957, T 3/7/57, John Martin Papers.
124 Keith Sinclair, *Walter Nash*, Auckland University Press, Auckland, 1976, p. 307. Sinclair notes that the reserves had exceeded £80 million only three months earlier.
125 ST to MF, 11 Dec 1957, T 1, 3/3/57, John Martin Papers.
126 Sinclair, *Walter Nash*, pp. 309–12; Frank Holmes, 'Three Labour Leaders: Their Economic and Educational Policies', in Margaret Clark (ed.), *Three Labour Leaders: Nordmeyer, Kirk, Rowling*, Dunmore Press, Palmerston North, 2001, pp. 203–5.
127 ST to MF, 5 Mar 1958, 1958 Budget, T 1, 3/3/58, ATL.
128 Sinclair, *Walter Nash*, p. 310. However, guaranteed dairy prices to farmers were maintained, even though the London butter price in Budget week was only 62 per cent of the guaranteed price.
129 *NZ Herald*, 27 Jun 1958, T 1, 3/3/58. Revenue for 1958/59 was 34 per cent above 1957/58.
130 Press release for 1958 Budget, T 1, 3/3/58.
131 Frank Holmes interview, 8 Mar 2001; see also Holmes, 'Three Labour Leaders', pp. 203–5.
132 Press release for 1958 Budget, T 1, 3/3/58.
133 R. D. Muldoon, *The New Zealand Economy: A Personal View*, Endeavour Press, Auckland, 1985, p. 33.
134 ST to permanent heads, 14 Apr 1961, 1961 Budget, T 1, 3/3/61, Archives NZ; see also draft cable to posts, 20 Jul 1961, T 1, 3/3/61.

Chapter 6:
Mandarins or lemons? 1961–1978

1. William Maughan, *Good and Faithful Servants*, Waiata and Imperial Publishing Co., Feilding, 1974, p. 23.
2. To the pleasure of his colleagues — almost all those interviewed who had worked with him mimicked his speech, Cliff Terry most successfully.
3. Press cutting [1969], Henry Lang Papers, MS-Papers-99-032-2, ATL.
4. Lang personal file, T 90, Archives New Zealand; see further Brian Easton, *The Nationbuilders*, Auckland University Press, Auckland, 2001, pp. 255–70; J. R. Martin, 'Lang, Henry George', *Dictionary of New Zealand Biography*, vol. 5, AUP/Dept of Internal Affairs, Auckland/Wellington, 2000, pp. 278–9.
5. Press cutting [1969], MS-Papers-99-032-2, ATL. The comment was in fact Gladstone's. An important 1967 study group on Treasury financial planning and control procedures had excluded economic advice from its considerations.
6. Cliff Terry interview, 6 Jul 2001.
7. Rob Cameron interview, 29 Jun 2000.
8. Roderick Deane interview, 14 Nov 2001. Also H. Lang, 'The Role of Treasury: Control and Advice', *Canterbury Chamber of Commerce Economic Bulletin*, 610/4, 1977, p. [4].
9. Frank Corner to Alister McIntosh (Secretary of External Affairs), 14 Mar 1957, McIntosh Papers, MS-Papers-6759-253, ATL. I am indebted to Gavin McLean for this reference.
10. *Evening Post*, 15 Nov 2001; *NZPD*, vol. 347, p. 1519 (26 Jul 1966).
11. A. W. Coats, 'Britain: The Rise of the Specialists', *History of Political Economy*, vol. 13, no. 3, 1981, p. 370. See also Edward Bridges, *The Treasury*, Allen and Unwin, London, 1964, pp. 95–7, 101, on economists working in the UK Treasury.
12. Coats, 'Specialists', pp. 372, 382. Economists employed in government in the 1940s and 1950s also stressed the importance of members of their profession not 'making waves' if they were to be useful.
13. Coats, 'Specialists', p. 371.
14. Five Lincoln students — John Chetwin, Murray Horn, Jas McKenzie, Bruce Ross and Graham Scott — later headed government departments.
15. Frank Holmes interview, 8 Mar 2001.
16. G. R. Hawke, *Between Government and Banks: A History of the Reserve Bank of New Zealand*, Wellington, Government Printer, 1973, p. 220; Roderick Deane interview, 14 Nov 2001. Coats, 'Specialists', p. 387, notes that the Bank of England was, until 1960, 'positively averse to economics'. Since then 'the professionals' encroachment on the intelligent laymens's domain' in the Bank has been 'inexorable'.
17. Roderick Deane interview, 14 Nov 2001. M. J. Moriarty, 'Making Economic Policy in New Zealand', *Economic Record*, no. 32, 1956, p. 234, refers to the large economic staff of the Reserve Bank at that time, and the fact that the Bank did balance of payments estimates.
18. Jas McKenzie interview, 13 Jun 2000. Galvin graduated in mathematics but had also studied economics. He was recruited in 1955, Preston in 1961.
19. ST to MF, [1965], Treasury staff, administrative efficiency, T 50/36/1, John Martin Papers.
20. Irene Lake interview, 17 Sep 2001, and documents, Irene Lake Papers; Report on Treasury functions, etc., 1968, John Martin Papers.
21. Issues of *New Zealand Economics Papers*. See also Coats, 'Specialists', p. 379, on the cautious attitude of the Royal Economic Society to the place of economists in government.
22. Press cutting [1969], Henry Lang Papers, MS-Papers-99-032, ATL.
23. Graham Scott interview, 7 Nov 2000.
24. The origin of this rule is explained in annex to Chair OEC (Galvin) to Chair CEC, 4 Sep 1981, on Synfuels file, W4446, T 39/18/9/3/6, AALR, Archives New Zealand. The 10 per cent criterion adopted by Cabinet in 1971 was also used in Australia, the United States and Canada; David Young interview with Bernie Galvin, 26, 27 Jun 1996, ATL. See also J. T. Ward, 'Cost-Benefit Analysis', *NZJPA*, vol. 29, no. 1, 1967, pp. 18–30.
25. Bill Robinson interview, 27 Jul 2001.
26. May Atkins interview, 27 Jul 2001. In the 1950s (and probably the 1960s) the stationery room opened for 30 minutes in the morning and the afternoon. Correcting fluid was in especially hot demand, and the typing staff took to diluting the 'Snopak' supplied to investigating officers to stretch the supplies.
27. Interviews with Jas McKenzie, 13 Jun 2000; Ian Sliper, 3 Jul 2000; Cliff Terry, 6 Jul 2000.
28. Peter Campbell, 'Politicians, Public Servants, and the People in New Zealand: II', *Political Studies*, vol. 4, no. 1, Feb 1956, p. 26.
29. Secretary, Surfdale Progressive Association to ST, 5 Jul 1990; internal Treasury memorandum, Sue Lambourn to Kathleen Roach, 15 May 1998, Surfdale Progressive Association Papers, courtesy

Irene Lake, John Chetwin, give historical background — but are these trustworthy sources? The Association survived into the 1980s and 1990s (see below, chapter 9), but with a different character; its post-Budget entertainment was open to the entire department, and usually marked by a ministerial visit.
30 Rob Laking interview, 30 Jan 2001.
31 Topics included education, interest rates, aid, the Fulton report (UK), local authority finance, the National Development Conference, agricultural policy, trade negotiations, transport, and many others. See Irene Lake Papers.
32 Brian Tyler interview, 26 Jan 2001.
33 Alec Cairncross, *Managing the British Economy in the 1960s: A Treasury Perspective*, Macmillan, London, 1996, pp. 6–12 for the historical context of enthusiasm for planning; pp. 51, 63 for the NEDC.
34 *Report of Industrial Development Conference*, Government Printer, Wellington, 1960, pp. 15–16, 20–2.
35 G. R. Hawke, *The Making of New Zealand*, Cambridge University Press, Cambridge, 1985, p. 178.
36 Press cuttings on Harry Lake, 16 Mar 1961, MS-Papers-0270, ATL.
37 Monetary and Economic Council, Report no. 2, May 1962, pp. 52–69.
38 R. Polaschek, *Government Administration in New Zealand*, Institute of Public Administration, Wellington, 1958, p. 269. See also *Hawke's Bay Herald-Tribune*, 18 May 1953. The conservative press had linked planning to its criticisms of the first Labour government.
39 See, for instance, *NZPD*, vol. 342, esp. pp. 1027–9 (6 Jul 1965); J. L. Roberts, 'Return to Planning', *NZJPA*, vol. 27, no. 1, Sep 1964, pp. 47–66; J. L. Roberts, 'Power and Planning', *NZJPA*, vol. 28, no. 2, Mar 1966, pp. 76–94 — the latter refers to Treasury (pp. 80–1).
40 Memo ST to MF, 21 Sep 1965, Economic planning, T 73/1, W207, AALR, Archives New Zealand.
41 Roderick Deane interview, 14 Nov 2001. Philpott and his team at Victoria University, to which he had moved from Canterbury, were trying to develop general equilibrium models of the New Zealand economy.
42 Attachment to ST to MF, 6 Dec 1967, Summary of World Bank Report on New Zealand, p. 3, John Martin Papers.
43 Press cutting [1969], Henry Lang Papers, MS-Papers-99-032, ATL.
44 David Preston interview, 6 Jun 2001; Green's interest was in French indicative planning.
45 David Preston interview, 6 Jun 2001.
46 Frank Holmes interview, 8 Mar 2001.
47 Frank Holmes interview, 8 Mar 2001. The Minister of National Development served on it from its inception (George Gair, 1977–78, Bill Birch, 1978–84). This role was controversial: see Patsy Fischer, *The New Zealand Planning Council: A Case Study*, NZ Planning Council, Wellington, 1981, pp. 11–12; and Hawke, *Making of New Zealand*, p. 333.
48 There is an interesting discussion of the possibilities of using both planning and the price mechanism in Brian Easton, *Economics for New Zealand Social Democrats*, John McIndoe, Dunedin, 1981, pp. 59–62.
49 Alec Cairncross, *Essays in Economic Management*, George Allen & Unwin, London, 1971.
50 Digest of press comment, 1–2 Sep 1965, 1966 Budget, T 1, 3/3/66, Archives New Zealand. The measures taken at this time, not Muldoon's in May 1967, were arguably the first mini-Budget; see Brian Easton to author, 15 May 2001. Note that measures to restrain demand had been proposed in April 1964, only five months after the election. See T 1, 3/3/67.
51 Memo of 7 Dec 1965, T 1, 3/3/66.
52 Summary of various recommendations to restrain demand, 1964 to 1966, n.d., 1967 Budget, T 1, 3/3/67, Archives New Zealand.
53 Dep ST to MF, 14 Dec 1965, T 1, 3/3/66.
54 14 and 20 Dec 1965, T 1, 3/3/66. See also Easton, 'Two Economic Lieutenants', paper delivered to Stout Centre Research conference, 'Holyoake's Lieutenants 1960–1972', 27–28 Apr 2001 (publication forthcoming). The Monetary and Economic Council's 'current economic situation and outlook' of May 1966 forecast a 7.5 per cent increase in public current expenditure and a 10.8 per cent increase in public capital expenditure. Note that devaluation was not an accepted policy instrument. In respect of electricity, Treasury conceded that 'the present construction programme is the minimum the [Power Planning] Committee considers necessary to avoid power shortages … it would appear that every effort should be made to reschedule the work with a view to taking the excessive peak out of 1966/67 but without materially extending the completion dates of the major projects.' See also G. R. Hawke, 'Economic Decisions and Political Ossification', in Peter Munz (ed.), *The Feel of Truth: Essays on New Zealand and Pacific History*, A. H. & A. W. Reed for Victoria University of Wellington, Wellington, 1969.

55 *Christchurch Star*, 23 Apr 1966, T 1, 3/3/66.
56 ST to MF (copied to PM and Deputy PM), 27 May 1966, T 1, 3/3/66.
57 Memo, 7 Dec 1965, T 1, 3/3/66.
58 MF to Henry Lang, 17 May 1966, T 1, 3/3/66.
59 Discussion at 'Holyoake's Lieutenants' conference, including of letter of Tom Shand in possession of Carol Shand. Note that there was no anticipation at this time of the collapse of wool prices in December 1966.
60 ST to MF, 13 May 1966, T 1, 3/3/66. Also Easton to author, 15 May 2001.
61 Brian Easton, 'Two Economic Lieutenants', paper delivered to 'Holyoake's Lieutenants' conference, p. 4.
62 23 Dec 1966, 24, 27 Jan 1967, T 1, 3/3/67.
63 *Evening Post*, 11 Feb 1967.
64 *NZPD*, vol. 350, pp. 134–5 (4 May 1967); vol. 351, pp. 1276 (22 Jun 1967), 1329 (27 Jun 1967); Barry Gustafson, *His Way: A Biography of Robert Muldoon*, Auckland University Press, Auckland, 2000, pp. 93–4.
65 R. D. Muldoon, *The New Zealand Economy: A Personal View*, Endeavour Press, Auckland, 1985, p. 58.
66 Also significant was the changeover to decimal currency, with the new dollar worth 10s, which took place on 10 July 1967. Muldon had first come to prominence as the politician responsible for this conversion, which was managed by a Decimal Currency Board run by Treasury official Jack Searle. See R. D. Muldoon, *The Rise and Fall of a Young Turk*, A. H. and A. W. Reed, Wellington, 1974, pp. 74–80.
67 Muldoon, *New Zealand Economy*, p. 61.
68 Gustafson, *His Way*, pp. 94–5; Muldoon, *Young Turk*, pp. 92–4; Muldoon, *New Zealand Economy*, pp. 61–2; Lough comment at 'Holyoake's Lieutenants' conference, 2002.
69 Muldoon, *New Zealand Economy*, p. 64. Gustafson, *His Way*, pp. 104–5, stresses the intra-Cabinet politics of the issue.
70 The same thing is discernible, on a more modest scale, in 1962, when Lang became Chief Finance Officer and assumed responsibility for the Budget process.
71 Muldoon, *New Zealand Economy*, p. 65.
72 Budget report 12, 29 May 1970, 1970 Budget, T 3/3/70, W2412, AALR, Archives New Zealand.
73 ST to MF, 9 Oct 1970, Oct 1970 mini-Budget, T 3/3/70/1, W2412, AALR; Jonathan Boston, *Incomes Policy in New Zealand*, Victoria University Press, Wellington, 1984, pp. 94–9, 316. For Australian Treasury preoccupation with cost/wage problems and thinking about incomes policies at this time, see Greg Whitwell, *The Treasury Line*, Allen & Unwin, Sydney, 1986, pp. 181–90, 203.
74 Budget report 3, 20 Jan 1972, 1972 Budget, T 3/3/72, W2412, AALR, Archives New Zealand. In the same report, Treasury made it clear that it would prefer tax cuts.
75 Treasury memo on 'future stabilisation policy', 24 Sep 1971, stabilisation measures, Feb–Mar 1972, T 3/3/72/1, W2412, AALR, Archives New Zealand. Note also Monetary and Economic Council scepticism about the value of incomes policies outside wartime situations: Monetary and Economic Council, Report no. 18, Mar 1970, p. 38. For comparable debate over Australian Treasury advice on the 1971 Australian Budget, see Whitwell, *Treasury Line*, pp. 193–4. Holyoake retired from the prime ministership in January 1972 in favour of his deputy, Marshall.
76 Boston, *Incomes Policy*, p. 316.
77 Budget report 5, 'government expenditure and revenue, 1973/74', 13 Apr 1973, 1973 Budget, T 3/3/73, W2412, AALR, Archives New Zealand.
78 Budget report 25, 'government economic strategy', May 1973, T 3/3/73.
79 Budget report 1, 13 Mar 1974, 1974 Budget, T3/3/74, W2412, AALR, Archives New Zealand; David Preston interview, 6 Jun 2001.
80 Budget report 21, 'Economic outlook and the Budget', 27 Apr 1974, T3/3/74.
81 *OECD Economic Surveys: New Zealand*, OECD, Paris, 1976, p. 5, records $US1.6 billion (approx. $NZ1.3 billion) for calendar 1974, and $US1.45 billion (approx. $NZ1.1 billion) for calendar 1975.
82 Budget report 21, 'Economic outlook and the Budget', 27 Apr 1974, T 3/3/74. Note the shift in attitude to borrowing, which became seen as as an economic rather than a financial activity: 'The Government's power to borrow is laid down in sections 70 to 76 of the Public Finance Act 1977 … The Act could be said to embody contemporary views on the role of public borrowing in fiscal and monetary policy. This is that Government debt transactions are part of the Government's function of economic management' (David Preston, *Government Accounting in New Zealand: An Explanation of the Accounting and Financial System of the Central Government of New Zealand*, Government Printer, Wellington, 1980, p. 93).
83 *OECD Economic Surveys: New Zealand*, OECD, Paris, 1976, p. 5.
84 David Preston interview, 6 Jun 2001.

85 Roger Hurnard interview, 23 Jul 2001.
86 CEC, 3 Jul 1974; ST to MF, 22 Jul 1974, Post-Budget economic measures, 1974, T 3/3/74/2, W2412, AALR, Archives New Zealand.
87 *Auckland Star*, 30 Jul 1974, T 3/3/74/2.
88 *Auckland Star*, 30 Jul 1974, T 3/3/74/2; also John Cook interview, 24 Oct 2000.
89 Comment by John Martin.
90 *Auckland Star*, 7 Aug 1974, T 3/3/74.
91 ST to MF, 3 Sep 1974, T 3/3/74/2.
92 Boston, *Incomes Policy*, pp. 117–63, covers the third Labour government but does not directly discuss the Treasury's role. His summary of events (pp. 157–8) suggests that there was a shift at the time of the change of leadership.
93 ST to MF, 15 Oct 1974, T 3/3/74/2; also Chair OEC to Chair CCEP, 5 Nov 1974; Prime Minister announcement, 13 Dec 1974. See also Boston, *Incomes Policy*, pp. 153–5, 158, 317–18 (chronology).
94 ST to MF, 15 Jan 1975, T 3/3/74/2.
95 7 Apr 1975, T3/3/75/2. The overall figure was just under $5 billion, an increase of 18.4 per cent on 1974/75.
96 Lang record of the 1975 devaluation, Henry Lang Papers, MS-Papers-99-032-1, ATL.
97 Henry Lang journal of 1975 change of government, 1975–76, Henry Lang Papers, MS-Papers-99-032-1, ATL, pp. 11, 32, 39–40, 45–6, 48–9, 57, 64, 65, 68–78. See also Gustafson, *His Way*, pp. 250–1 on the close relationship between Muldoon and Skinner, and more generally, pp. 250–4 for Muldoon–union relations in these years; also Income Policies, Prices, Incomes and Productivity, T 61/1/2, pts 12, 13, W3158, AALR, Archives New Zealand, gives good examples of Muldoon/Skinner collaboration. For the official view of the freezes, see Boston, *Incomes Policy*, p. 182.
98 See the discussion in Boston, *Incomes Policy*, pp. 182–8.
99 *OECD Economic Surveys: New Zealand*, OECD, Paris, Jul 1977, p. 5. The OECD's January 1979 report on New Zealand, p. 5, recorded an increasingly severe downturn from mid-1977.
100 John Yeabsley interview, 25 Oct 2000.
101 See, for example, minutes, 16 Aug 1977, Cabinet Economic Committee 1977, Box 249/2, Muldoon Papers, W3694, AAXO, Archives New Zealand.
102 Graham Scott interview, 7 Nov 2000. See also Muldoon, *New Zealand Economy*, p. 106.
103 *OECD Economic Surveys: New Zealand*, OECD, Paris, Jan 1979, pp. 5, 47.
104 *OECD Economic Surveys: New Zealand*, 1979, p. 48.
105 Mark Prebble interview, 13 Feb 2001.
106 Report of the study group on Treasury procedures, 1967, p. 31, John Martin Papers.
107 Whitwell, *Treasury Line*, p. 269.
108 An outlook which should be seen in the context of the politically damaging power shortages of the later 1940s and 1950s.
109 Comment by John Martin. Thus the New Zealand Australia free trade agreement — NAFTA — of 1965 was accompanied by very detailed specification of what was included (and therefore what was not). For the Australian parallel in terms of interdepartmental politics, see Bruce Juddery, *At the Centre: The Australian Bureaucracy in the 1970s*, Cheshire, Melbourne, 1974, pp. 71–91.
110 *AJHR*, 1968, B-4, p. 14; comment by Gary Hawke.
111 Text reproduced in Monetary and Economic Council Report, no. 18, Mar 1970, 'The Current Economic Situation and Outlook', p. 33. See also Muldoon, *New Zealand Economy*, p. 68; Franklin, *Trade, Growth and Anxiety*, pp. 127–8.
112 T 1, 3/3/68, *passim* (not helpful on Treasury's stance).
113 Budget report no. 34, T 1, 3/3/69.
114 *AJHR*, 1969, B-6; see also R. S. Deane, 'Monetary Policy: The Bare Elements', *Accountants' Journal*, Jul 1970, p. 43, Irene Lake Papers. Interest rate controls remained for most deposits.
115 Dep ST to MF, 9 Oct 1970, T 3/3/70/1, W2412, AALR. For the proposal for a Treasury bill market, see Hawke, *Between Government and Banks*, pp. 165–6, 171–2.
116 Monetary and Economic Council Report, no. 21, May 1971, p. 80, refers to the promise of the introduction of Treasury bills not being fulfilled. Reports of the Monetary and Economic Council in December 1970 and June and December 1972 all recommended a shift in monetary policy from direct controls to the use of flexible interest rates and an active government debt policy. The last-mentioned report was devoted entirely to monetary policy and the financial system.
117 Monetary and Economic Council Report, no. 21, May 1971, pp. 94–102 (quote from p. 94, brief reference to public sector, pp. 101–2).
118 See, for instance, 'economic report', Jan 1955, p. 15, John Martin Papers.
119 Dep ST to MF, 9 Oct 1970, T 3/3/70/1, W2412, AALR.
120 Jas Mackenzie interview, 13 Jun 2000.
121 18 May 1971, Cabinet Economic Committee

(CEC), M6, Marshall Papers, MS-Papers 1418, box 361/5, ATL.
122 A. R. Low, Governor of the Reserve Bank, quoted in *Evening Post*, 9 Mar 1972.
123 Both reported in *Dominion*, 9 Mar 1972. See also Monetary and Economic Council, Report no. 23, Jun 1972, 'Economic Trends and Policies', p. 85.
124 *Focus*, Aug–Sep 1968, p. 24.
125 Sam Parker interview, 12 May 2000. See the discussion in Austin Mitchell, *Politics and People in New Zealand*, Whitcombe and Tombs, Christchurch, 1969, p. 41. John Martin names Francis of Francis, Allison Symes, stockbrokers, and Jim Andrews, general manager of the National Bank from 1960 to 1966, as other members of the 'Cabal'.
126 David Preston interview, 6 Jun 2001.
127 20 Dec 1967, CEC, Marshall Papers, M 34, Box 358/3, MS-Papers 1403.
128 2, 4 Feb 1970, Cabinet Committee on Overseas Investment, Invest (70) 1, Box 96/2, Marshall Papers, MS-Papers 1403.
129 8 Nov 1971, CEC, Box 396/2, Marshall Papers, MS-Papers 1403.
130 Including a wool retention scheme and fertiliser subsidies.
131 Budget reports 12, 27, 9 May 1973, 18 May 1973, T 3/3/73.
132 Budget report 25, 'government economic strategy', 18 May 1973, T 3/3/73.
133 *New Zealand Foreign Affairs Review*, Aug 1973, p. 20.
134 Henry Lang journal of 1975 change of government, 1975–76, p. 27, MS-Papers-99-032-1. Also p. 28 for Muldoon's outlook. Note that Budget report 3 on monetary policy, 1 May 1975, T 75/3/3, anticipates the 1976 changes.
135 Frank Holmes interview, 8 Mar 2001.
136 Roger Kerr interview, 16 Jun 2000; Peter Fraser, 'The Making of Economic Management: Continuity and Change at the New Zealand Treasury', MCA thesis, Victoria University of Wellington, 2000, p. 57.
137 Press cutting [1969], Henry Lang Papers, ATL.
138 Don Rangi interview, 8 Dec 2000.
139 Comments by John Martin.
140 Sam Parker interview, 12 May 2000.
141 Document tabulating responses in Irene Lake Papers, probably from 1976.
142 Press cutting [1969], Henry Lang Papers.
143 A. F. von Tunzelmann, 'The Public Expenditure Committee: The Process of Change 1962–1977', MPP paper, Victoria University of Wellington, 1977, pp. 12–15. The committee did not live up to the hopes that were held for it, save for energetic phases under the chairmanships of R. D. Muldoon (1963–66) and Bill Birch (1976–78); see pp. 39, 53, 55. See also Tom McRae, *A Parliament in Crisis: The Decline of Democracy in New Zealand*, Shieldaig Publications, Wellington, 1994, pp. 87–97.
144 Edward Bridges, *The Treasury*, Allen & Unwin, London, 1964, p. 138. See also Richard (Otto) Clarke, *Management of the Public Sector of the National Economy*, University of London, Stamp Memorial Lecture, London, 1964, pp. 12, 15, 19; Ian Johns, 'Efficiency in Government: The Changing Roles of Central Administrative Agencies', *Public Sector Research Papers*, vol. 1, no. 2, pt 1, Apr 1979, pp. 97–8.
145 Preston, *Government Accounting*, p. 79, argues that the changes placed greater emphasis on examining the outputs of the system. J. L. Roberts, *Politicians, Public Servants and Public Enterprise*, Victoria University Press, Wellington, 1987, pp. 100–8 is very helpful.
146 Press cutting, c. 1969, MS-Papers 99-0032-2, ATL.
147 Rob Laking interview, 30 Jan 2001. For an analysis of the failure of PPBS, see Aaron Wildarvsky, *Speaking Truth to Power: The Art and Craft of Policy Analysis*, Little Brown, Boston and Toronto, 1979, pp. 32–5; for its failure in Canada, see Donald C. Savoie, *The Politics of Public Spending in Canada*, University of Toronto Press, Toronto, pp. 59–61; and for the United Kingdom, Colin Thain and Maurice Wright, *Treasury and Whitehall: The Planning and Control of Public Expenditure, 1976–1993*, Clarendon, Oxford, 1995, p. 536.
148 Rob Laking interviews, 30 Jan 2001, 23 Jul 2001; also Preston, *Government Accounting*, pp. 68–72. ST to MF, 11 Dec 1969, p. 3, T 3/3/70, refers to three-year forecasts. The limitations of programme reviews, SIGMA and COPE are discussed in *AJHR*, 1978, B-1 (pt IV), pp. 15–17.
149 ST to MF, 24 May 1972, T 3/3/72: 'the proposals we have recommended here amount, with a few modifications, to acceptance in full of the corresponding Royal Commission recommendations'.
150 PM to ministers, 13 and 25 Feb 1969, T 3/3/69, pt 2; Lang to ministers, 13 Feb 1969; Government finance, 1969/70, 1970/71, 11 Dec 1969, T3/3/70, pt 1.
151 Cabinet Committee on Government Expenditure, 31 Jan 1972, T 3/3/72.
152 Budget report 5, 11 Dec 1969, T 3/3/69; 13 Apr 1973, T 3/3/73 (also report 16, 10 May 1973); Budget reports 1, 16, 13 Mar, 16 Apr

1974, T 3/3/74.
153 Budget report 3, 19 Mar 1975, T 3/3/75.
154 ST to MF, 22 Jul 1974, T 3/3/74/2.
155 Henry Lang journal of 1975 change of government, 1975–76, p. 26; see also p. 30.
156 Henry Lang journal of 1975 change of government, 1975–76, p. 52.
157 Henry Lang, 'Role of the Treasury', p. [2]; see also Cabinet Committee on Expenditure, 1979, Muldoon Papers, Box 238/4, AAXO, W3694; Henry Lang journal of 1975 change of government, 1975–76, pp. 18, 26, 30, 52, 53.
158 Brian Tyler interview, 26 Jan 2001.
159 For discussion, see Gustafson, *His Way*, pp. 96–8; Muldoon, *New Zealand Economy*, p. 58, refers not to Treasury, but to 'economic advisers', perhaps because of his attack on 'Treasury economists' of a later time on p. 62.
160 Bob Norman, *You Can't Win 'Em All: Confessions of a Public Service Engineer*, Slide Rule Press, Porirua, [1997], p.146. Muldoon, *New Zealand Economy*, pp. 88–9, discusses Kirk's suspicion of Treasury.
161 Henry Lang, 'Policy Making in New Zealand', *NZJPA*, vol. 13, no. 2, Mar 1951, p. 28.
162 Muldoon implies this in *New Zealand Economy*, p. 88.
163 David Greig interview, 9 Feb 2001.
164 Lang record of 1975 devaluation, MS-Papers-99-032-1, p. 6.
165 Henry Lang journal of 1975 change of government, 1975–76, pp. 7, 21, 73.
166 Elizabeth Hanson, *The Politics of Social Security*, Auckland University Press / Oxford University Press, Auckland, 1980, p. 146; Brian Easton, *Pragmatism and Progress: Social Security in the 1970s*, University of Canterbury, Christchurch, 1981, p. 89; Leo Downey interview, 11 Jul 2001; see also Gustafson, *His Way*, pp. 237–8.
167 George Laking interview, 21 Nov 2000.
168 Bob Norman interview, 15 May 2001.
169 Roger Procter interview, 8 Nov 2000; Henry Lang journal of 1975 change of government, 1975–76, pp. 5, 9; Lang, 'Role of Treasury', p. [4]. Note that Rowling had also planned to revamp the Prime Minister's Department if re-elected.
170 *AJHR*, 1978, B-1, pt IV, *passim*.
171 David Preston, 'Restructuring the Economy', *NZ Economic Papers*, vol. 12, 1978, pp. 98–101.
172 Preston, 'Restructuring', pp. 111–12.
173 Preston, 'Restructuring', p. 113.
174 There is a very good discussion of this issue in Gustafson, *His Way*, pp. 247–8. The quote is from a 1989 speech of Muldoon's cited by Gustafson.
175 George Akerloff, 'The Market for "Lemons": Quality Uncertainty and the Market Mechanism', *Quarterly Journal of Economics*, vol. 84, no. 3, 1970, pp. 488–500. Akerloff was awarded the Nobel Prize for Economics in 2001.
176 This discussion is taken from Whitwell, *Treasury Line*, pp. 199–201.
177 Preston, 'Restructuring', pp. 103–9; Lough, 'Notes for Discussion with Senior Officers, 14 Jul 1978', John Martin Papers.
178 Preston, 'Restructuring', pp. 111–12. A similar point is made in Easton, *Pragmatism and Progress*, p. 111.

Chapter 7:
Advice and dissent, 1978–1984

1 R. D. Muldoon, *The New Zealand Economy: A Personal View*, Endeavour Press, Auckland, 1985, pp. 129–34; Bruce Jesson, *Behind the Mirror Glass: The Growth of Wealth and Power in New Zealand in the Eighties*, Penguin, Auckland, 1987, pp. 120–6.
2 For the paradigm shift see Peter Hall, 'Policy Paradigms, Experts and the State: The Case of Macro-economic Policy Making in Britain', in S. Brooks and A. Gagnon (eds), *Social Scientists, Policy and the State*, Praeger, New York, 1990, pp. 60–1.
3 ST et al to MF, 13 Dec 1978, Economic Policy Package, Noel Lough Papers.
4 Barry Gustafson, *His Way: A Biography of Robert Muldoon*, Auckland University Press, Auckland, 2000, p. 273; Graham Scott, 'Muldoon and the Economy', talk to Muldoon conference, 3 May 2002 (publication forthcoming); report 102, 'exchange rate measures', 21 Jun 1979, Budget reports 1979, Box 159/6, Muldoon Papers, W3694, AAXO, Archives New Zealand; *AJHR*, 1979, B-6 (Budget, 21 Jun 1979), pp. 3–5, 10–11.
5 Brian Easton, *Economics for Social Democrats*, John McIndoe, Dunedin, 1981, p. 63, refers to McLean, *The Future of New Zealand Agriculture*; see also Colin James, *The Quiet Revolution: Turbulence and Transition in Contemporary New Zealand*, Allen & Unwin/Port Nicholson Press, 1986, pp. 1–3, 70; Tony Garnier, *Evening Post*, 19 Jun 1984, referred to 'the private enterprisers and libertarians and any others who have questioned the authoritarian and centralist style of leadership'; Hugh Templeton, *All Honourable Men: Inside the Muldoon Cabinet, 1975–1984*, Auckland University Press, Auckland, 1995, pp. 128–34.
6 John E. Martin (ed.), *People, Politics and Power*

7. *Stations*, Bridget Williams Books and ECNZ, Wellington, 1991, p. 282. The contract was awarded to the Zublin-Williamson consortium. Also Bob Norman interview, 15 May 2001.
7. Bob Norman interview, 15 May 2001.
8. Gustafson, *His Way*, p. 343; Brian Roper, 'From the Welfare State to the Free Market: Crisis, Class, Ideology and the State', *NZ Sociology*, vol. 6, no. 2, Nov 1991, p. 149.
9. Ruth Richardson interview, 22 Mar 2001; see also Ruth Richardson, *Making a Difference*, Shoal Bay Press, Christchurch, 1995, pp. 20–1.
10. 4 Sep 1979, Cabinet Economic Committee (CEC), Box 239/1, W3694, Muldoon Papers, AAXO. Imports which didn't compete with local products were not usually subject to licensing.
11. Budget report 44, 1979 Budget reports, Box 159/6, W3694, Muldoon Papers. Most of these proposals were not agreed to.
12. Jas McKenzie interview, 20 Jun 2000.
13. Budget, 1980 (3 Jul 1980); see *AJHR*, 1980, B-6, p. 16. The deregulation of land transport was announced in the 1983 Budget (28 Jul 1983); see *AJHR*, 1983, B-6, p. 18.
14. 24 Oct 1979, CEC, Box 239/1, W3694, Muldoon Papers; Templeton, *All Honourable Men*, pp. 134–8, 177–83, 193–9.
15. *AJHR*, 1979, B-6, p. 5. In Muldoon, *New Zealand Economy*, p. 111, it was stressed that import licensing remained National Party policy in 1984. See also Brian Easton, 'Economy' column, *New Zealand Listener*, 23 Jan 1982, for reference to the incident. Many of those interviewed for this history referred to the 'chewing' that Muldoon dealt out over the paper.
16. Muldoon, *New Zealand Economy*, p. 37. The anecdote first appeared in R. D. Muldoon, *The Rise and Fall of a Young Turk*, A. H. & A. W. Reed, Wellington, 1974, p. 56.
17. Templeton, *All Honourable Men*, pp. 135–6.
18. Gustafson, *His Way*, pp. 273, 296–308; James, *Quiet Revolution*, pp. 98–101; Templeton, *All Honourable Men*, pp. 144–50.
19. For details, see *AJHR*, 1980, B-6A, pp. 4–5; Jonathan Boston, *Incomes Policy in New Zealand*, Victoria University Press, Wellington, 1984, p. 216.
20. Templeton, *All Honourable Men*, p. 117.
21. CEC, 1979, Boxes 238/5, 238/7, 239/1, W3694, Muldoon Papers.
22. See the discussion in Gustafson, *His Way*, pp. 277–8.
23. 11 Sep 1979, CEC, Box 238/5, W3694, Muldoon Papers; Gustafson, *His Way*, pp. 280–1.
24. Graham Scott interview, 10 Nov 2001.
25. Muldoon, *New Zealand Economy*, p. 111.
26. Gustafson, *His Way*, pp. 277–8. Treasury reports refer to 'major projects', not 'Think Big'.
27. See the full discussion in Gustafson, *His Way*, pp. 282–6; also Roger Douglas and Louise Callan, *Toward Prosperity: People and Politics in the 1980s, A Personal View*, David Bateman, Auckland, 1987, pp. 152, 155–9, 168–9.
28. 2 May 1980, Treasury report 4663 of 29 Feb 1980 attached, CEC, Box 241/6, W3694, Muldoon Papers. In this context, 'national' referred to the 'overall return to New Zealand on New Zealand resources employed'. For a more qualified Treasury view, see the 2 May report itself.
29. Rob Laking interview, 30 Jan 2001. Also Douglas and Callan, *Toward Prosperity*, pp. 167–70; Gustafson, *His Way*, pp. 285–6; Brian Easton, *The Nationbuilders*, Auckland University Press, Auckland, 2001, pp. 233–4.
30. Gill to Galvin, Cook and Laking, 4 Aug 1981, Chair OEC (Galvin) to Chair CEC, 4 Sep 1981, Synfuels file, T 39/18/9/3/6, W4446, AALR, Archives New Zealand; Douglas and Callan, *Toward Prosperity*, pp. 158–9; Gustafson, *His Way*, p. 283.
31. Gustafson, *His Way*, pp. 282–5.
32. See Ross McKibbin, 'When Labour Last Ruled', *London Review of Books*, 9 Apr 1992.
33. The 'supply side' was contrasted with the demand side — 'supply-side' policies were those that would have an effect on production — 'supply' — which was the characteristic arena of microeconomic reform.
34. Donald C. Savoie, *The Politics of Public Spending in Canada*, University of Toronto Press, Toronto, 1990, p. 75.
35. Greg Whitwell, *The Treasury Line*, Allen & Unwin, Sydney, 1986, p. 203.
36. Whitwell, *Treasury Line*, p. 272; see also p. 237.
37. Cited in Giovanni Arrighi, 'The African Crisis', *New Left Review*, no. 15, May–Jun 2002, p. 7. The report's formal title was *Accelerated Development in Sub-Saharan Africa: An Agenda for Action*. Arrighi also refers to Robert Bates, *Markets and States in Tropical Africa*, University of California Press, Berkeley, 1981.
38. *OECD: Denmark*, OECD, Paris, 1980, p. 48; see also H. Schwartz, 'Public Choice Theory and Public Choices: Bureaucrats and State Reorganization', *Administration and Society*, vol. 26, no. 1, 1994, p. 62; *OECD: Finland*, OECD, Paris, 1979, p. 56; 1981, p. 5; *OECD: Germany*, Paris, 1980, p. 54; *OECD: Sweden*, Paris, 1980, p. 59.
39. Gustafson, *His Way*, p. 266.

40 Bert Brownlie interview, 31 Aug 2000. Brownlie was influenced by the writing of Gerard Debreu, a Nobel Laureate in Economics who was on three occasions a Visiting Fellow at the University of Canterbury, who in *Theory of Value: An Axiomatic Analysis of Economic Equilibrium* (John Wiley, New York, 1959) provided the first mathematical proof of equilibrium economics. This was a key text for master's-level economics students at the University of Canterbury.
41 Gustafson, *His Way*, p. 270: 'a growing group of younger advisers in Treasury and the Reserve Bank … favoured greater use of market forces and deregulation of the finance and labour markets'.
42 Jas McKenzie interview, 13 Jun 2000.
43 'An Introduction to the Treasury', Jul 1981, John Martin Papers. Discussed in Jane Kelsey, *The New Zealand Experiment: A World Model for Structural Adjustment*, Bridget Williams Books/Auckland University Press, Auckland, 1997, p. 47; Shaun Goldfinch, *Remaking Australian and New Zealand Economic Policy: Ideas, Institutions and Policy Communities*, Victoria University Press, Wellington, 2000, pp. 42–3.
44 John Yeabsley interview, 25 Oct 2000.
45 Murray Horn interview, 15 Feb 2001.
46 Jas McKenzie interview, 20 Jun 2000.
47 David Preston interview, 6 Jun 2001.
48 Peter Fraser, 'The Making of Economic Management: Continuity and Change at the New Zealand Treasury 1968–1984', MCA thesis, Victoria University of Wellington, 2000, pp. 72–3; Goldfinch, *Remaking New Zealand and Australian Economic Policy*, pp. 42–3.
49 Rob Cameron interview, 29 Jun 2000. Investigation of the antecedents of change in New Zealand has focused on the importance to New Zealand thinking of theories current in the United States, but this gives a 'bilateral' quality to the process that overlooks the world-wide character of the shift, and the many points of intersection, for both economic theory and policy, between New Zealand and the wider world. It arose partly because a 1988 Fulbright seminar examined 'The Influence of American Economics on New Zealand Thinking and Policy'. Its proceedings were published that year, and material from them has been cited by later commentators, e.g., Kelsey, *New Zealand Experiment*, pp. 54–5.
50 Ruth Richardson interview, 22 Mar 2001.
51 Fraser, 'Making of Economic Management', p. 62, citing 'Economic Strategy', p. 4.
52 Budget report 43, BM 02/9/1/1983, Treasury. For the origins of the international debate on tax expenditures, see Sven Steinmo (ed.), *Tax Policy*, Edward Elgar, Cheltenham, England/Northampton, Mass., 1998, p. xiv, and references there to research by Surrey and Bittker.
53 Budget report 46, 1983 Budget, BM 02/9/1/1983, Treasury. See also memo Treasury to MF, 8 Dec 1983, Treasury file on New Zealand Planning Council: Economic Monitoring Group, T 73/35/2/1, Treasury.
54 Regulatory framework for industrial relations: general: labour market regulation, 'Appendix 1: The evolution of views about demand management policy', pp. 4–6; n.d., but probably an attachment to memo of 13 Mar 1984, T 61/12/2/1, Treasury.
55 Budget report 9, 1984 Budget, BM 02/9/1/1984, Treasury.
56 Memo, Treasury to MF, 8 Dec 1983, pp. 1, 2, T 73/35/2/1, Treasury.
57 Summary attached to Treasury report for MF, 'Public Works as a Policy Response to Unemployment', 13 Mar 1984, T 61/12/2/1.
58 'Appendix 1', 'The evolution of views about demand management policy', n.d., but probably an attachment to memo of 13 Mar 1984, pp. 6–7, T 61/12/1/1.
59 Memo, 14 Sep 1983, T 61/12/1/1.
60 For Coase's most important papers, see *The Firm, the Market and the Law*, University of Chicago Press, Chicago, 1988.
61 See the discussion in the introduction.
62 Rob Laking interview, 30 Jan 2001.
63 ST to MF, 25 Nov 1983, Post Office, expenditure, policy, T 62/34, W4443, Archives New Zealand. Muldoon signed off on this paper.
64 Postmaster-General to Cabinet, n.d., probably early 1984, T 62/34.
65 Rob Cameron interview, 29 Jun 2000. The paper, 'Government-Owned Enterprises: Theory, Performance, Efficiency', was presented at the 1984 conference of the Association of Economists. See also 'State-Owned Enterprises: History of Policy Development and Implementation', Treasury, 1996, p. 7.
66 Graham Scott interview, 21 Dec 2000.
67 Jas McKenzie interview, 20 Jun 2000.
68 *NZ Listener*, 26 Mar 1983.
69 Jas McKenzie interview, 20 Jun 2000.
70 Ian Sliper interview, 3 Jul 2000.
71 Bert Brownlie interview, 31 Aug 2000.
72 For more on Kerr, see Anthony Hubbard, 'Crusader of the Round Table', *NZ Listener*, 4 May 1992.
73 File note, undated, but comment on a 9 Oct 1981 document, T 1, 62/55/6.

74 Kerr to Barrie Saunders, Manufacturers' Federation, 1 Nov 1982, file on NZ Manufacturers' Association, T 61/1/25.
75 Kerr to DTI, 6 Jul 1983, Trade agreement, CER policy, T 61, Australia 2/2/1, Treasury. John Whitehead recalled that 'we were very committed to tendering, for a variety of reasons. So TEALS was genuine. But when the government decided to give some [tenders] to manufacturers we suggested naming them MEALS, which also contained a kind of economic joke, as in 'there's no such thing as a free lunch.' When asked about allocating the subsidiary quantity, 'SQUEALS' seemed to follow naturally. Comment to author.
76 Geoff Bascand interview, 15 Feb 2002.
77 Graham Scott interview, 10 Nov 2000.
78 Roger Kerr interview, 16 Jun 2000.
79 'An Introduction to the Treasury', 1981.
80 Peter Rodger interview, 20 Feb 2002.
81 Exit interview, Irene Taylor, 27 Feb 1985, Staff retention and management, T 68/21/1? (file numbering obscure), Treasury.
82 Memo by Hedley Eastgate, 7 Sep 1983, T 61/12/1/1. Some of the handwritten comment is hard to read. Cameron was identified by his initials.
83 Graham Scott interview, 10 Nov 2000.
84 See, e.g., Brian Easton, 'Economy' column, *NZ Listener*, 23 Jan 1982. Easton notes that half of all New Zealand's economists were employed in government.
85 R. J. Gregory, 'Understanding Public Bureaucracy', *Public Sector*, vol. 4, nos 2–3, 1982, p. 9.
86 Martin to Probine, Commissioner, SSC, 17 Aug 1979, John Martin Papers.
87 John Martin, Notes for induction course for investigating officers, 1980, pp. 1, 6, 7, John Martin Papers.
88 Martin to Treasury secretaries, 21 Sep 1979, John Martin Papers.
89 Mark Prebble interview, 13 Feb 2001.
90 Graham Scott interview, 10 Dec 2000.
91 Peter Rodger to author, 5 Oct 2002.
92 Administration, circulars and instructions, esp. 9 Aug 1984, T 69/1/8/5, Treasury.
93 John Wanna, John Foster and Joanne Kelly, *Managing Public Expenditure in Australia*, Allen & Unwin, St Leonards, NSW, 2001, p. 97.
94 Roderick Deane interview, 14 Nov 2001.
95 Treasury official interviewed on condition of anonymity.
96 Gill to Laking, Cook and Galvin, 4 Aug, 'The Synthetic Fuel Negotiations', 18 Sep 1981, T 39/18/9/3/6.
97 Rob Laking interview, 30 Jan 2001.
98 Jas McKenzie interview, 14 Jun 2000. McKenzie's other disadvantage involved opinions that were attributed to him in respect of the wage and price freeze.
99 Jas McKenzie interview, 14 Jun 2000.
100 Averall Gibson interview, 11 Jul 2001.
101 A colloquialism not confined to the Treasury — the writer first encountered it in the Department of Internal Affairs.
102 David Greig and Peter Rodger to ST, 2 Jul 1984, T 68/21/1; see, very similarly, Rob Laking to Secretaries, 15 Aug 1983; State Services Commission, 'Committee of Enquiry into the staffing problems of Treasury', November 1984, paras 6.3, 6.4.
103 Bill Birch interview, 23 Feb 2001.
104 For Muldoon's account, see *New Zealand Economy*, pp. 120–2.
105 ST to MF, 30 May 1982, 1982 Budget, T 3/3/82, Treasury. A further memorandum from Scott of 18 Jun, 'for information only', made similar points. The freeze was introduced four days later.
106 May 1982, T 3/3/82. In a subsequent meeting Muldoon *did* concede that a report could be prepared re the possibility of tightening the criteria which allowed income to be excluded from the tax base, such as tax shelters for kiwifruit production. This led to some of the most unpopular of the 1982 tax measures, which in turn fostered the development of the New Zealand Party. See also Douglas and Callan, *Toward Prosperity*, p. 195; Muldoon, *New Zealand Economy*, p. 121.
107 Budget report 43, 24 Jun 1983, BM 02/9/1/1983, vol. 7.
108 Ian Sliper interview, 3 Jul 2000.
109 David Greig interview, 9 Feb 2001; and see Templeton, *All Honourable Men*, p. 144.
110 Mark Prebble interview, 13 Feb 2001. Also Finance Act 1981; *NZPD*, vol. 438, pp. 1088–1116 (2 Jul 1981), 1202–1331 (7 Jul 1981); Lange, pp. 1112–14).
111 MF to McLean, 26 Jul 1983, W3694, Box 309/8, AAXO, Muldoon Papers; Treasury report 929, 22 Mar 1982, Box 295/1, AAXO, Muldoon Papers; Roderick Deane interview, 14 Nov 2001.
112 Murray Horn interview, 15 Feb 2001.
113 Gustafson, *His Way*, p. 284; comment by Gary Hawke, *NZ Listener*, 11 Dec 1982, p. 49.
114 Treasury comment (author unidentified) on Energy Department energy plan draft, 22 Jun 1980, Energy Plans, T 39/29/8, W4446, AALR, Archives New Zealand.

115 Bill Falconer interview, 25 Jul 2001.
116 Mervyn Pope and Bob Buckle, 'Inflation and the Evaluation of Recent New Zealand Exchange Rate Policy', in Robert A. Buckle (ed.), *Inflation and Economic Adjustment*, Victoria University of Wellington Economics Department, Wellington, 1983, pp. 25–66 (incl. commentary by Roderick Deane), esp. p. 46.
117 *NZ Listener*, 3 Dec 1983. See also Bruce Jesson, *Metro*, Aug 1986, p. 161: 'certain features of the Treasury/Reserve Bank approach would be fairly generally accepted among economists — the removing of farming subsidies, the emphasis on market signals and greater efficiency'.
118 *AJHR*, 1984, G-3, p. 4.
119 See Gustafson, *His Way*, pp. 353–4; *Evening Post*, 22 Jun 1984.
120 Frank Holmes interview, 8 Mar 2001; also Bill Birch interview, 23 Feb 2001, and Ruth Richardson interview, 22 Mar 2001, on approaches to the economy within the National Party in the early 1980s. The *National Development Strategy* was published (although with no named authors).
121 M. P. Lissington, 'The 1984 Devaluation and Inquiry', Treasury, 1987; *Evening Post*, 3 Oct 1984; Gustafson, *His Way*, pp. 370–7, 385–6; Muldoon, *New Zealand Economy*, pp. 128–31. The crawling peg introduced in 1979 had been suspended in 1982 with the imposition of the wage–price freeze.
122 Muldoon, *New Zealand Economy*, p. 134; Gustafson, *His Way*, pp. 388–95, for this paragraph.
123 *Evening Post*, 15 Aug 1984; Tom Scott article, *Evening Post*, 11 Aug 1984; Muldoon, *New Zealand Economy*, p. 132 — here Muldoon argues that while there had been an outflow in the days before the election and reserves were extremely low, domestic liquidity was so tight that there was limited ability to speculate further and it should have been possible to ride out the pressure once again.
124 Roderick Deane interview, 14 Nov 2001.
125 *Evening Post*, 19 Jun 1984, 'Douglas admits he boobed': Douglas today 'accepted full responsibility for what he said was a mistake in a speech he delivered last night suggesting that a Labour government would devalue the New Zealand dollar … since October Labour had considered devaluation among other economic options but had rejected it.'
126 Public Expenditure Committee 1984, report on inquiry into devaluation, *AJHR*, 1984, I-12C, p. 8.
127 *AJHR*, 1984, I-12C, p. 9.
128 *AJHR*, 1984, I-12C, pp. 22, 24.
129 Muldoon, *New Zealand Economy*, p. 134. For earlier use by Muldoon of the expression 'economic management', see for instance *AJHR*, 1980, B-6A, p. 5, re the need for a 'careful approach to economic management over the next twelve months'.
130 Whitwell, *Treasury Line*, p. 273.
131 Whitwell, *Treasury Line*, p. 229.
132 For the full story, and references to more contemporary accounts, see Wanna et al, *Managing Public Expenditure in Australia*, pp. 103–15. John Whitehead commented that the outcome was the creation of *two* departments in which economists were influential.
133 Muldoon, *New Zealand Economy*, pp. 139–40.
134 'Regular Ron's last ride', *Evening Post*, 24 Feb 1984, T 69/1/8/5.
135 Irene Taylor to ST, 11 Jul 1984, Irene Lake Papers.

Chapter 8:
Managing the economy, 1984–1993

1 Jack H. Nagel, 'Social Choice in a Pluralitarian Democracy: The Politics of Market Liberalization in New Zealand, *British Journal of Political Studies*, vol. 28, 1998, p. 243. I am indebted to James Belich for this reference.
2 See Douglas's own discussion in Roger Douglas and Louise Callan, *Toward Prosperity: People and Politics in the 1980s, A Personal View*, David Bateman, Auckland, 1987, pp. 71–2, and photographs. See also Colin James, *New Territory: The Transformation of New Zealand, 1984–92*, Bridget Williams Books, Wellington, 1992, pp. 150–2.
3 Geoff Bascand interview, 15 Feb 2002.
4 The term 'fiscal bureaucrat' is used in Herman M. Schwartz, 'Public Choice Theory and Public Choices: Bureaucrats and State Reorganization in Australia, Denmark, New Zealand and Sweden in the 1980s', *Administration and Society*, vol. 26, no. 1, May 1994, p. 72, citing Emanuel Savas, *Privatization: The Key to Better Government*, Chatham House, Chatham, NJ, 1987; Jane Kelsey, *The New Zealand Experiment: A World Model for Structural Adjustment*, Auckland University Press / Bridget Williams Books, Auckland, 1997, pp. 46–50, 69, uses 'technocrat' and 'technopol'.
5 Treasury, *Economic Management*, The Treasury, Wellington, 1984, p. 126.
6 Treasury, *Economic Management*, p. 141.
7 Treasury, *Economic Management*, p. 141.
8 Treasury, *Economic Management*, p. 111.

9. Treasury, *Economic Management*, p. 115.
10. Treasury, *Economic Management*, pp. 142–4, 238–46, 249–59, 295–325, quote p. 251.
11. BM 02/9/1/1985, report 70, 19 Jul 1985, signed out by Graham Scott. The principal limitations instanced are 'heavy output losses' from people choosing not to work for taxable income; avoidance and evasion; and compensatory market adjustments to real post-tax incomes. For another discussion by a Treasury official, see Peter Gorringe, *Economics for Policy: Expanding the Boundaries*, Institute of Policy Studies, VUW, Wellington, 2001, pp. 85–8. Sven Steinmo (ed.), *Tax Policy*, Edward Elgar, Cheltenham, England / Northampton, Mass., 1998, p. xi, observes that 'twentieth century tax policy has been driven by two overarching principles — efficiency and equity'.
12. *Evening Post*, 12 Jul 1984, for comment on interest rates and planning; 26 Jun 1984, for Garnier; 19 and 20 Jun 1984, for comment on Labour industrial policy; 23 Jun 1984 (editorial), for comment on the division within Labour between those aligned with Douglas and with Jim Anderton.
13. See especially W. Hugh Oliver, 'The Labour Caucus and Economic Policy Formation, 1981–1984', in Brian Easton (ed.), *The Making of Rogernomics*, Auckland University Press, Auckland, 1989, pp. 11–52.
14. John Whitehead interview, 17 Apr 2002, citing Douglas. For a portrait of Douglas, see Colin James, *The Quiet Revolution: Turbulence and Transition in Contemporary New Zealand*, Allen & Unwin / Port Nicholson Press, Wellington, 1986, pp. 135–41.
15. See, for instance, *Evening Post* editorial, 23 Jun 1984.
16. Oliver, 'Labour Caucus and Economic Policy Formation', pp. 23–5.
17. John Whitehead interview, 17 April 2002.
18. Whitehead found it ironic, after Muldoon had attacked the proposal, to read a headline, 'Treasury can't shake Labour's figures'.
19. Roger Douglas interview, 19 Apr 2002. Geoff Swier was an economist working in the Opposition Research Unit.
20. Lang Papers, MS-Papers-99-032-1; for Labour's economic policy, see *Evening Post*, 26 Jun 1984.
21. Comment by Margaret Clark.
22. Roderick Deane interview, 14 Nov 2001.
23. Bruce Jesson, *Behind the Mirror Glass: The Growth of Wealth and Power in New Zealand in the Eighties*, Penguin, Auckland, 1987, pp. 122–3. The word 'coup' was used at the time; see, for instance, *Evening Post*, 7 Sep 1984. For later discussion, see Nagel, 'Politics of Market Liberalization', pp. 250–1.
24. *Evening Post*, 19 Jun 1984 et seq.
25. *Evening Post*, 21, 27, 29 Jun 1984.
26. See, inter alia, comment in Barry Gustafson, *His Way*, Auckland University Press, Auckland, 2000, p. 396. Nagel, 'Politics of Market Liberalization', pp. 246, 259.
27. Interview with David Lange, *National Business Review*, 11 Jul 1986.
28. Note, however, that the outgoing government had announced the abolition of supplementary minimum prices at the end of the 1983/84 season, on 27 June 1984 (cited in Lewis Evans et al, 'Economic Reform in New Zealand 1984–95', *Journal of Economic Literature*, vol. 34, Dec 1996, p. 1895.
29. Ian Sliper interview, 3 Jul 2000; Douglas and Callan, *Toward Prosperity*, pp. 167–76 (the trip is recounted on p. 174). See also Nagel, 'Politics of Market Liberalization', pp. 259–60, on the Labour Party's relations with farm and manufacturing interest groups.
30. Reg Birchfield and Ian Grant, *Out of the Woods: The Restructuring and Sale of New Zealand's State Forests*, GP Publications, Wellington, 1993, pp. 10–11.
31. Bernard Galvin, *Policy Co-ordination, Public Sector and Government*, Victoria University Press for Institute of Policy Studies, VUW, Wellington, 1991, p. 18.
32. James, *Quiet Revolution*, pp. 29–53; G. R. Hawke, 'Domestic Economic Trends: New Zealand', in G. R. Hawke and Richard B. Baker (eds), *ANZUS Economics: Economic Trends and Relations Among Australia, New Zealand and the United States*, Praeger, Westport, CT / London, 1992. See also Andrew Gamble, *The Free Economy and the Strong State: The Politics of Thatcherism*, Macmillan, Basingstoke, 1988.
33. The point is made by Bruce Jesson in 'New Zealand's Hard Labour', *New Left Review*, no. 192, Mar/Apr 1992, p. 46.
34. 16 Aug 1984, Budget administration, T 3/3/1, Treasury. For a useful overview of the tax reforms between 1984 and 1987, see Ian Dickson, 'Taxation', in Simon Walker (ed.), *Rogernomics: Reshaping New Zealand's Economy*, GP Books, Wellington, 1989, pp. 137–53.
35. 30 Aug 1984, T 3/3/1.
36. Treasury to MF, 15 Sep, 23 Sep, 20 Oct 1987, reports 3, 4 and 7, T 76/2/1 (15 Sep has MF's proposals for tax benefit reform attached).
37. John Wanna, John Foster and Joanne Kelly, *Managing Public Expenditure in Australia*, Allen & Unwin, St Leonards, NSW, 2000, pp. 154–6;

Douglas, *Towards Prosperity*, p. 66. On p. 65, Douglas refers to Treasury suggesting relatively junior ministers as Finance associates whereas Douglas himself wanted 'senior men'.
38 Graham Scott interview, 21 Dec 2001.
39 *Evening Post*, 4 Aug 1984, attributes the redesign to Palmer.
40 Galvin, *Policy Co-ordination*, pp. 18–19; James, *Quiet Revolution*, pp. 177–9.
41 Roderick Deane interview, 14 Nov 2001.
42 MF to ST, 9 Aug 1984, document supplied by Carl Bakker.
43 Roderick Deane interview, 14 Nov 2001.
44 Roger Douglas, Treasury officials, interviews. Also Alan Bollard, 'New Zealand', in John Williamson (ed.), *The Political Economy of Policy Reform*, Institute for International Economics, Washington DC, 1994, p. 97.
45 See, for instance, D. Smyth for ST to MF, report 6, 20 Oct 1987, file 'personal income taxes: general', T 76/2/1, Treasury: 'we see [reducing import assistance] as growth enhancing *as well as supporting the process of disinflation*' (my emphasis).
46 Mark Prebble interview, 7 Mar 2001. Advocacy of a 'transparency' department is found in *Economic Management*, p. 131, and Graham Scott and Peter Gorringe, 'Reform of the Core State Sector: The New Zealand Experience', *Australian Journal of Public Administration*, vol. 48, no. 1, Mar 1989, p. 88. See also Easton, 'Economy' column, *NZ Listener*, 14 Oct 1989. *Evening Post*, 19 Mar 1990: the Economic Development Commission was set up to monitor the impact of economic adjustment on jobs, but abolished in 1988.
47 The call is cited in Douglas and Callan, *Toward Prosperity*, p. 127.
48 *Evening Post*, 10 Sep 1984, reporting comments of Rob Campbell, FOL executive member. *Evening Post*, 5 Jul 1986, was to report that the 'leading trade unionist Rob Campbell aligned himself firmly with the government's economic policies against one of the union movement's most strongly held beliefs on state ownership [of the BNZ].'
49 *Evening Post*, 16 Mar 1985.
50 David Caygill interview, 16 Jan 2001; also Douglas and Callan, *Toward Prosperity*, pp. 210–14. Margaret Wilson was the President of the Labour Party.
51 Announcement of talk on T 69/1/8/5, Treasury.
52 The profile of Treasury is indicated through, for example, editorial, *NZ Listener*, 22 Jun 1985; Bruce Jesson, 'The Hidden Persuaders', *Metro*, Jul 1985; 'Gnomes of Canterbury', *Metro*, Aug 1986, p. 161.
53 'Testing Times at the Treasury', editorial, *NZ Listener*, 22 Jun 1985.
54 7 Jun 1985, T 69/1/8/5. Tizard and Douglas had disagreed on economic policy matters while Labour was in Opposition.
55 Bob Buckle comment, 25 Jun 2001. See *New Zealand Economic Papers*, vols 18 (1984), 19 (1985). See also the discussion in Geoff Bertram, 'Keynesianism, Neoclassicism and the State', in Brian Roper and Chris Rudd (eds), *State and Economy in New Zealand*, Oxford University Press, Auckland, 1993, pp. 43–5.
56 Easton, 'Economy' column, *NZ Listener*, 21 Nov 1987. In a column of 24 Jan 1987, Brian Easton cited seven unnamed economists at Victoria University, and also J. D. Gould, Bryan Philpott, David Sheppard, Conrad Blyth, Peter Read, Jan Whitwell, Gareth Morgan, Peter Harris, Wolf Rosenberg and Len Bayliss. For the critics' view after the event, see Brian Easton, *In Stormy Seas: The Post-War New Zealand Economy*, University of Otago Press, Dunedin, 1997, pp. 231–40.
57 See Brian Easton, 'The Exchange Rate Since 1981: Performance and Parity', New Zealand Institute of Economic Research, Discussion Paper no. 30, 1986. This and other macroeconomic debates are detailed and analysed in Bertram, 'Keynesianism, Neoclassicism and the State', pp. 38–47.
58 Robert A. Buckle, 'Sequencing and the Role of the Foreign Exchange Market', in Alan Bollard and Robert Buckle (eds), *Economic Liberalisation in New Zealand*, Allen & Unwin / Port Nicholson Press, Wellington, 1987, pp. 236–60. The quote is from p. 249. See also the comment by Deborah Mabbett in *Trade, Employment and Welfare: A Comparative Study of Trade and Labour Market Policies in Sweden and New Zealand*, Clarendon, Oxford, 1995, pp. 13–14.
59 *NZ Listener*, 30 Aug 1986; see also 13 Sep 1986.
60 Buckle, 'Sequencing', p. 259.
61 ST to MF, 26 Nov 1990, 1991 Budget, T 3/3/90.
62 Roderick Deane interview, 14 Nov 2001.
63 Roger Douglas interview, 19 Apr 2002.
64 Interview with David Lange, *National Business Review*, 11 Jul 1986.
65 *Evening Post*, 24 Feb 1987; see also *National Business Review*, 27 Feb 1987.
66 Simon Collins, *NZ Herald*, 27 Jun 1987. See also table in Nagel, 'Politics of Market Liberalization', p. 249, showing broad approval of the government's direction at the time of the 1987 election.
67 Nagel, 'Politics of Market Liberalization', pp.

248–9, citing data drawn from a national post-election survey designed by Jack Vowles and others.
68 Budget report 83, 18 Jul 1986, 1986 Budget, BM 02/9/1/1986; see also Pat Walsh, 'A Family Fight? Industrial Relations Reform Under the Fourth Labour Government', in Brian Easton (ed.), *The Making of Rogernomics*, AUP, Auckland, 1989, pp. 149–70.
69 ST to MF, 26 Nov 1990, 1991 Budget, T 3/3/90.
70 David Preston interview, 6 Jun 2001. Also Douglas and Callan, *Toward Prosperity*, pp. 198–9.
71 G. V. Butterworth and S. M. Butterworth, *Reforming Education: The New Zealand Experience*, Dunmore Press, Palmerston North, 1998, p. 44. Vote Education expenditure rose from $1.7 billion in 1984/85 to $3.18 billion in 1987/88 — a large increase, even taking inflation into account.
72 ST to MF (signed out by M. D. R. Irwin), 22 Jan 1986, Expenditure — Education department — policy, T 62/9, Treasury.
73 ST to MF (draft), 22 Jan 1986, 'social policy: expenditure review', T 62/9.
74 Memo, 2 Dec 1986, p. 4; annex A, meeting of 5 Dec 1986, pp. 2, 4; 18 Dec 1986, BM 02/9/1/1987. See chapter 9.
75 Meeting with MF to discuss expenditure reviews and three year forecasts, 3 Mar 1987, T 3/3/1. For more on the history of fiscal policy and expenditure control during the first term of the fourth Labour government, see Bryce Wilkinson, 'Fiscal Policy and Government Expenditure Reforms', in Walker (ed.), *Rogernomics*, pp. 92–115.
76 Roger Douglas interview, 19 Apr 2002.
77 Mark Prebble interview, 7 Mar 2001.
78 Graham Scott to Tom Berthold, 10 Mar 1987, T 3/3/1.
79 *AJHR*, 1987, B-6, p. 11 (Budget, 18 Jun 1987).
80 Graham Scott interview, 21 Dec 2001.
81 James, *Quiet Revolution*, p. 195.
82 Nagel, 'Politics of Market Liberalization', p. 243.
83 Robert Chapman, 'A Political Culture Under Pressure: The Struggle to Preserve a Progressive Tax Base for Welfare and the Positive State', *Political Science*, vol. 44, no. 1, Jul 1992, p. 1.
84 *Dominion*, 9 Nov 1987. See also James, *New Territory*, p. 245.
85 Clark and Wilson as reported in *Dominion*, 9 and 7 Nov 1987. See also Colin Hicks, 'Will a charity state replace the welfare state?', in *Evening Post*, 29 Sep 1987; Bruce Jesson, *Fragments of Labour: The Story Behind the Labour Government*, Penguin, Auckland, 1989, pp. 118–19.
86 Galvin, *Policy Co-ordination*, pp. 20–2; see also *Dominion*, 1 Nov 1989.
87 ST to MF, draft prepared by Mark Prebble, 11 Sep 1987, T 3/3/1. The papers were published in the week of 16 October.
88 Reports by Jane Clifton, *Dominion*, 23 and 26 Oct 1987.
89 *Dominion*, 6 Nov 1987. Another letter was headed, 'Treasury extremists'; 'Extreme' was also used of Treasury-favoured policies in a story by Alastair Morrison, *Dominion*, 10 Nov 1987.
90 The theme of the conference was 'Social Policy: The Struggle for Control'.
91 *Dominion*, 4 Nov 1987.
92 Jenny Kirk to Roger Douglas, 11 Nov 1987.
93 Quoted in Malcolm Templeton (ed.), *An Eye, An Ear and a Voice: 50 Years in New Zealand's External Relations, 1943–1993*, Ministry of Foreign Affairs and Trade, Wellington, 1993, p. 21.
94 *NZ Herald*, 23 Mar 1988, quoting Sutcliffe, the general manager of the Auckland Employers Association.
95 *Government Economic Statement*, 17 Dec 1987. The tax rate was not officially specified but was understood to be below 30 cents — Douglas's original proposal was for 22 cents.
96 See press coverage, also the exchange of letters between Douglas and Lange published in *NZ Herald*, 31 Dec 1988, 3, 4, 5, 7, Jan 1989; also Brian Easton, 'The Unmaking of Roger Douglas', in *Making of Rogernomics*, pp. 176–81. Easton notes that Treasury was cautious about the feasibility of a mixture of a flat tax rate and the GMFI: pp. 179, 182.
97 'The Role of the State', address at Massey University, speech notes, 17 Mar 1988, T 3/3/1.
98 Lange to Douglas, c. 1 Dec 1987, in *NZ Herald*, 31 Dec 1988.
99 'The Role of the State', speech notes.
100 Roger Douglas interview, 19 Apr 2002.
101 Lange address to the National Press Club, 29 Jun 1988, speech notes, T 3/3/1.
102 *AJHR*, 1988, B-6 (1988 Budget, 28 Jul 1988), pp. 33–8. See also James, *New Territory*, p. 248.
103 *AJHR*, 1988, B-6, pp. 7–11, 15–17.
104 *AJHR*, 1990, B-27, p. 63.
105 *Dominion*, editorial, 16 Dec 1988. See also Jesson, *Fragments of Labour*, pp. 147–8.
106 For instance W. P. Reeves, *Dominion*, 23 Mar 1989.
107 Graham Scott interview, 21 Dec 2000. For general comment on Treasury, see for instance *Dominion*, 16 Dec 1988: 'the departure of Mr

Douglas, Mr Prebble and former Revenue Minister Trevor de Cleene has left Treasury orphaned, and the future direction of policy will be less predictable as a result'.
108 *Dominion*, 14 Mar 1989; see also 16 Dec 1988.
109 *NZ Herald*, 27 Dec 1988; *Dominion*, 8 Mar 1989; Easton, 'Economy' column, *NZ Listener*, 19 Nov 1988, saw evidence of economic growth.
110 *Dominion*, 10 Feb, 8 Mar 1989; Graham Scott interview; Caygill to author, 2 Mar 2003.
111 1 Nov 1989, T 69/1/8/5.
112 ST to MF, 23 Mar 1990, T 3/3/1.
113 Was an asset or a 'crop' being sold? Nikitin Sallee interview, 9 Sep 2002. See also *AJHR*, 1990, B-6 (Budget, 24 Jul 1990), p. 5, Budget tables 2, 2A and 4, pp. 32–3, 36.
114 *Dominion*, 10 Feb 1989.
115 John Whitehead interview, 17 Apr 2002.
116 D. Smyth (on behalf of ST) to MF, 20 Oct 1987, Report 7, T 76/2/1. Douglas had proposed a guaranteed minimum family income at a relatively high level (Treasury calculated about 27 per cent above the average wage) at which many low-income earners would effectively forego any extra they earned because their GMFI would be reduced by the same amount — thus the 'effective marginal tax rate' was 100 per cent.
117 Treasury official interviewed on condition of anonymity. In 1986 the tax rate for very low incomes was set at 15 cents in the dollar. On 'uncompensated efficiency', see Brian Easton, *The Commercialisation of New Zealand*, Auckland University Press, Auckland, 1997, p. 51; see also Easton, 'The Unmaking of Roger Douglas?', in *Making of Rogernomics*, pp. 177–8.
118 *NZ Herald*, 7 Jan 1989.
119 Television news transcript, 29 Jun 1988, T 3/3/1.
120 John Roberts, *Politicians, Public Servants and Public Enterprise*, VUP for Institute of Policy Studies, Wellington, 1987, pp. 90–1.
121 Quoted in Nagel, 'Politics of Market Liberalization', p. 243.
122 Graham Scott, *Government Reform in New Zealand*, International Monetary Fund, Washington DC, 1996, p. 76.
123 Roger Douglas interview, 19 Apr 2002; Dickson, 'Taxation', p. 244.
124 *Dominion*, 22 Mar 1989.
125 Keith Rankin, *NZ Listener*, 3 Aug 1985.
126 Peter Harris interview, 27 Nov 2000; for more on the compact, and its ending up a bipartite rather than tripartite agreement, see *Dominion*, 23 Mar 1990; Owen Harvey, 'The Unions and the Government: The Rise and Fall of the Compact', in John Deeks and Nick Parry (eds), *Controlling Interests: Business, the State and Society in New Zealand*, Auckland University Press, Auckland, 1992, pp. 59–77; Kelsey, *New Zealand Experiment*, pp. 179–80. Also Gary Hawke to author, 29 Apr 2002: 'I doubt whether the Bank saw anything other than endorsement of the conclusion that if there were productivity gains, there would be no need for the Bank to respond to an increase in demand.'
127 Ruth Richardson interview, 22 Mar 2001. For more on the National Party between 1984 and 1990, see James, *New Territory*, p. 261.
128 *Dominion*, 25 Oct 1990. See also Pat Walsh and Rose Ryan, 'The Making of the Employment Contracts Act', in Raymond Harbridge (ed.), *Employment Contracts: New Zealand Experiences*, Victoria University Press, Wellington, 1993, pp. 15–18. Chris Eichbaum, 'Reshaping the Reserve: The Political Economy of Central Banking in Australasia', PhD thesis, Massey University, 1999, p. 161, notes that the National Party caucus nearly voted against supporting the Reserve Bank Bill.
129 Bill Birch interview, 23 Feb 2001.
130 *AJHR*, 1990, B-6 (Budget, 24 Jul 1990), p. 159.
131 David Greig interview, 9 Feb 2001. Bolger's account appears in his *A View from the Top: My Seven Years as Prime Minister*, Viking, Auckland, 1998, pp. 36–8.
132 Paul Dalziel, 'The April 1st Benefit Cuts', in Henry Lang Papers, MS-Papers-99-032-2, ATL. In 'The Rhetoric of Treasury: A Review of the 1990 Briefing Papers', *NZ Economic Papers*, vol. 25, no. 2, 1991, p. 263, Dalziel accepted that Treasury's revisions 'were by no means inappropriate or exaggerated'. See also Easton, 'Economy' column, *NZ Listener*, 26 Aug, 2 Dec 1991.
133 *AJHR*, 1990, B-6, pp. 159–60.
134 Budget report 1, 7 Nov 1990, T 3/3/90. Table 2 showed the government's revenue and expenditure for the year, including 'one-off' items such as income from asset sales.
135 Peter Bushnell interview, 16 May 2002.
136 Graham Scott interview, 21 Dec 2000. The *Australian*, 12 Jul 2002, reported the post-election discovery of a fiscal blowout in South Australia.
137 Treasury, *Briefing to the Incoming Government 1990*, The Treasury, Wellington, 1990, p. 2; Peter Bushnell comment. Bushnell and Graham Wheeler were responsible for the briefing.
138 Budget report 16, 20 Nov 1990, T 3/3/90. Note that in September 1990 Treasury had brought in

Sebastian Edwards, an international authority on real exchange rates, to assess New Zealand's policy settings. Edwards concluded that monetary policy had been too tight and fiscal policy too loose.
139 Graham Scott interview, 21 Dec 2000.
140 Treasury's role in the last, which space precludes examination of here, is discussed in Walsh and Ryan, 'Making of the Employment Contracts Act', pp. 21–8. According to Walsh and Ryan, who cite a number of documents from Treasury, the Labour Department and the Minister of Labour, Treasury argued against specialist labour law and institutions, but the Minister of Labour agreed with and gained Cabinet support for Labour Department advice calling for their retention.
141 Budget report 50, 19 Feb 1991, T 3/3/91.
142 See comment in *Examiner*, 21 Mar, 4 Apr 1991.
143 Ruth Richardson interview, 22 Mar 2001; also Ruth Richardson, *Making a Difference*, Shoal Bay Press, Christchurch, 1995, p. 80.
144 Graham Scott, 'Presentation to Treasury Managers', 9 Apr 1991, Treasury.
145 Budget reports 61, 19 Mar; 79, 3 May 1990, T 3/3/91.
146 *AJHR*, 1991–93, I-19A, p. 291. Scott explained that the original package would have meant Treasury staff being paid between 3 and 12 per cent less than people doing comparable jobs in the private sector.
147 Bolger, *View from the Top*, pp. 38–40, 119; Michael Laws, *The Demon Profession*, HarperCollins, Auckland, 1998, pp. 182–6, 193–8, 209–19; Gustafson, *His Way*, pp. 451–8.
148 Laws, *Demon Profession*, p. 212.
149 Graham Scott interview, 21 Dec 2000.
150 Irene Lake interview, 17 Sep 2001.
151 Scott, 'Presentation'.
152 Keynesians themselves could vary. See, for example, Easton, 'Economy' column, *NZ Listener*, 6 Aug 1990, 22 Jun 1992, in which he advocates a tighter fiscal stance and a looser monetary stance. Note that the exchange rate continued to be debated through these latter years, but as part of this wider set of concerns.
153 *PSA Journal*, Nov 1991, p. 5
154 Dalziel, 'April 1st benefit cuts'. See also Paul Dalziel, 'The Rhetoric of Treasury: A Reply', *NZ Economic Papers*, vol. 27, no. 1, 1993, pp. 91–5.
155 *NZ Listener*, 22 Jul 1991.
156 Lang to Prime Minister, 21 May 1991, Henry Lang Papers, MS-Papers-032-3, ATL.
157 Richardson, *Making a Difference*, pp. 116–17. A number of Treasury officials commented on the parallel with a letter sent by British economists to Thatcher in mid-1981, and noted that in both cases the economists were proved wrong, with an upward trend beginning at about the time of both letters.
158 Simon Chapple, *Full Employment: Whence It Came and Where It Went*, Research Monograph no. 66, New Zealand Institute of Economic Research, Wellington, 1996, p. 112. Chapple goes on to say that 'at the beginning of this project, my belief was firmly that structural shocks, initiated by the process of liberalisation, would be found to be a significant factor behind New Zealand's recent unemployment experience. After examining the data, I have been somewhat surprised to find little evidence that liberalisation played any role at an aggregate level' (p. 113). Chapple then discusses further empirical and methodological issues raised by this conclusion.
159 Scott, 'Presentation'.
160 Graham Scott interview, 21 Dec 2000.
161 *AJHR*, 1992, B-6 (part 1), Budget 2 Jul 1992, p. 87, gives a $3.162 billion deficit for fiscal 1991/92 (cf. the October 1990 forecast of $3.7 billion), compared with the Budget night 1991 prediction of $1.739 billion (*AJHR*, 1991, B-2, pp. 88–9).
162 Easton, 'Economy' column, *NZ Listener*, 27 Aug 1994. Easton refers to an exchange in the *New Zealand Herald* between Kerr on the one side and Susan St John and Keith Rankin on the other. More recently, theory and empirical research have suggested that under certain circumstances, contractionary fiscal policies can produce an expansion in output; see Robert Perotti, 'Fiscal Consolidation in Good Times and Bad', *Quarterly Journal of Economics*, vol. 114, no. 4, Nov 1999. Recent empirical research suggests that the international environment, not the anti-inflationary policy or other domestic measures, bore the primary responsibility for what they label the 1991–93 recession (a period when New Zealand's real GDP was below trend) and the recovery from it; see Robert A. Buckle, Kunhong Kim, Heather Kirkham, Nathan McLellan and Jared Sharma, 'Trade, Climate and Financial Influences on Macroeconomic Fluctuations: Analysis Using a SVAR model of the New Zealand Economy', New Zealand Treasury, draft paper, Jun 2002, esp. section 5.
163 Richardson, *Making a Difference*, pp. 94–5; Howard Fancy, 'The Role of Treasury in the Budget Process', in J. R. Nethercote et al (eds), *Decision Making in New Zealand Government*, Federalism Research Centre in association with Institute of Policy Studies, VUW, and NZ State

Services Commission, Canberra, 1993, p. 24.
164 Gary Hawke to Paul Dalziel, 20 Apr 1991, MS-Papers-99-032-2.
165 Graham Scott, interviewed in *Accountants' Journal*, Apr 1993, p. 42.
166 Budget report 26, 6 Dec 1990, 3/90. Fortunately 'equivalentised' has not passed into the English language — although 'equivalised' remains a standard technical term. The points were made in fuller form in a revised version of the report (no. 35, 11 Dec) after discussion with the Minister.
167 Budget reports 5, 9 Nov; 28, 17 Dec 1990, T 3/3/90.
168 ECC (91) 21, 19 Feb 1991, 1991 Budget, T3/3/91, Treasury; Douglas and Callan, *Toward Prosperity*, p. 89.
169 Chris Pinfield interview, 22 May 2001; comment by Roger Hurnard. For more on replacement rates, see Tim Maloney, *Benefit Reform and Labour Market Behaviour in New Zealand*, Institute of Policy Studies, VUW, Wellington, 1997, pp. 64–5.
170 Jonathan Boston, 'New Zealand: Cautionary Tale or Shining Example?', in R. A. W. Rhodes and Patrick Weller (eds), *The Changing World of Top Officials: Mandarins or Valets?*, Open University Press, Buckingham, Philadelphia, 2001, p. 201, citing Evan Voyce, 'The Provision of Free and Frank Advice to Government', MPP research paper, Victoria University of Wellington, 1996.
171 Graham Scott, 'Presentation', 9 Apr 1991. See also Scott in *Accountants' Journal*, Apr 1993, p. 39: 'I don't think it is appropriate for senior public servants to develop a political profile and I have tried hard not to.'
172 Graham Scott, quoted in *Accountants' Journal*, Apr 1993, p. 39.
173 *AJHR*, 1993, B-6 (Budget, 1 Jul 1993), p. 25.
174 Bill Birch interview, 22 Apr 2002.
175 John Whitehead interview, 9 May 2002.
176 Ruth Richardson interview, 22 Mar 2001.
177 Easton, 'Economy' column, *NZ Listener*, 7 Nov 1992.

Chapter 9:
Managing government, 1984–1993

1 *Dominion*, 10 Nov 1987. See also Tony Simpson, 'The Employment Contracts Act in the State Sector', in Raymond Harbridge (ed.), *Employment Contracts: New Zealand Experiences*, Victoria University Press, Wellington, 1993, pp. 135, 139–40; Jonathan Boston, John Martin, June Pallot and Pat Walsh, *Public Management: The New Zealand Model*, Oxford University Press, Auckland, 1996, p. 25; Alan Henderson, The *Quest for Efficiency: The Origins of the State Services Commission*, Historical Branch, Department of Internal Affairs/State Services Commission, Wellington, 1990, pp. 37–8.
2 Treasury, *Government Management*, The Treasury, Wellington, 1987, p. 3.
3 Brian Easton, *The Commercialisation of New Zealand*, Auckland University Press, Auckland, 1997, pp. 26–7, and further comment on *Government Management*, p. 94.
4 *Dominion*, 7 Jun 1989.
5 Draft, ST to MF, 11 Sep 1987, Budget, administration, T 3/3/1.
6 Graham Scott and Peter Gorringe, 'Reform of the Core State Sector: The New Zealand Experience', *Australian Journal of Public Administration*, vol. 48, no. 1, Mar 1989, pp. 81–2.
7 Graham Scott, *Government Reform in New Zealand*, International Monetary Fund, Washington DC, 1996, p. 12.
8 Mark Prebble interview, 7 Mar 2001.
9 Graham Scott interview, 7 Nov 2000.
10 Murray Horn interview, 15 Feb 2001.
11 Jack H. Nagel, 'Radically Reinventing Government', *Journal of Policy Analysis and Management*, vol. 16, no. 3, 1997, p. 351; Boston et al (citing Christopher Hood), *Public Management*, p. 3.
12 For reference to other countries, especially Malaysia, Singapore and Costa Rica, see Scott, *Government Reform in New Zealand*, pp. 85–6; for Denmark (early 1980s), see Herman M. Schwartz, 'Public Choice Theory and Public Choices: Bureaucrats and State Reorganization in Australia, Denmark, New Zealand and Sweden in the 1980s, *Administration and Society*, vol. 26, no. 1, May 1994, p. 62.
13 For Australia see, for instance, John Wanna, John Foster and Joanne Kelly, *Managing Public Expenditure in Australia*, Allen & Unwin, St Leonards, NSW, 2001, pp. 167–8, 172, 181–3; for Canada, see Donald J. Savoie, *The Politics of Public Spending in Canada*, University of Toronto Press, Toronto, 1990, p. 117.
14 Peter Self, *Government by the Market: The Politics of Public Choice*, Macmillan, Basingstoke, England, 1993, p. 176.
15 Self, *Government by the Market*, pp. 171–2; Colin Thain and Maurice Wright, *The Evolution of Public Expenditure Control in the United Kingdom*, University of Ulster, Jordanstown, Northern Ireland, 1995, pp. 79–81. Boston et al, *Public Management*, p. 116, says that the

New Zealand Treasury kept an eye on the United Kingdom's Financial Management Initiative (FMI) and Australia's Financial Management Improvement Programe (FMIP). Treasury official John Whitehead met Next Steps officials a number of times at his superiors' request while based in London from 1988 to 1992.
16 Lois Bryson, 'The Welfare State and Economic Adjustment', in Stephen Bell and Brian Head (eds), *State, Economy and Public Policy in Australia*, OUP, Melbourne, 1994, p. 297, citing D. Henderson, 'Perestroika in the West', in John Nieuwenhuysen (ed.), *Towards Freer Trade Between Nations*, OUP, Melbourne, 1989. Further, 'the government's program of economic adjustment has accorded priority to fiscal efficiency and harnessed welfare efficiency to this agenda' (p. 310).
17 Savoie, *Politics of Public Spending in Canada*, p. 250.
18 Stephen Jennings and Rob Cameron, 'State-Owned Enterprise Reform in New Zealand', in Alan Bollard and Robert Buckle (eds), *Economic Liberalisation in New Zealand*, Allen & Unwin/Port Nicholson Press, Wellington, 1987, pp. 142–3. The quote is from S. C. Littlechild, 'Ten Steps Toward Denationalisation', *Journal of Economic Affairs*, no. 2, 1981, p. 12.
19 For Canada, see Savoie, *Politics of Public Spending*, pp. 259–66; for Britain, see Daniel Yergin and Joseph Stanislaw, *The Commanding Heights: The Battle Between Government and the Marketplace that is Remaking the Modern World*, Simon & Schuster, New York, 1998, pp. 114–24, including (p. 114) a discussion of the late 1960s origin of the term 'privatisation', which was seen as preferable to the ugly 'denationalisation'.
20 Wanna et al, *Managing Public Expenditure*, pp. 184, 260.
21 Self, *Government by the Market*, pp. 172, 176.
22 Roger Douglas and Louise Callan, *Toward Prosperity: People and Politics in the 1980s, A Personal View*, David Bateman, Auckland, 1987, p. 224.
23 Unsigned draft, 12 Jun 1984, Energy Plan, general issues, T 39/29/8, Treasury.
24 Ministry of Energy to MF, 26 Nov 1984, T 39/29/8.
25 Treasury review of major projects, 22 Nov 1984, T 39/29/8.
26 Director-General Post Office to ST, 29 Oct, Chetwin to Galvin, 30 Oct 1984, Post Office expenditure — policy, T 62/34, W4446, AALR, Archives New Zealand.
27 Roger Procter interview, 25 Feb 2002; Douglas and Callan, *Toward Prosperity*, pp. 225–6; Bruce Jesson, *Metro*, Aug 1986, pp. 160–1. Kirkland nevertheless became the first CEO of Forestry Corporation; see Reg Birchfield and Ian Grant, *Out of the Woods: The Restructuring and Sale of New Zealand's State Forests*, GP Publications, Wellington, 1993, pp. 39–46, 104–6.
28 Ian Duncan and Alan Bollard, *Corporatization and Privatization: Lessons from New Zealand*, Oxford University Press, Auckland, 1992, p. 34; Douglas and Callan, *Toward Prosperity*, pp. 226–7, 232; David Lange in *National Business Review*, 11 Jul 1986.
29 *National Business Review*, 27 Feb 1987. Deane did not return to the Reserve Bank, moving to chair the SOE Electricorp in 1987, and then in 1992 becoming chief executive of the newly-privatised Telecom.
30 See Douglas and Callan, *Toward Prosperity*, p. 230, for a story about Deputy Prime Minister Geoffrey Palmer, a garden, a dog, and the Ministry of Works.
31 Chris Eichbaum, 'Reshaping the Reserve: The Political Economy of Central Banking in Australasia', PhD thesis, Massey University, 1999, pp. 146, 155–8.
32 Paul Dalziel, 'Economists' Analysis of Maori Economic Experience, 1959–1989', in Jan Whitwell and Mary Anne Thompson (eds), *Society and Culture: Economic Perspectives*, vol. 1, New Zealand Association of Economists, Wellington, 1991, pp. 205–6.
33 Patrick Day, *Voice and Vision: A History of Broadcasting in New Zealand*, Auckland University Press in association with the Broadcasting History Trust, Auckland, 2000, p. 328.
34 Day, *Voice and Vision*, pp. 324, 328–31, 388–93; Brian Easton, 'Broadcasting 1985–1990: Commercialisation vs Culture', *Landfall*, no. 175, Sep 1990, pp. 276–90. It deserves at least passing mention that sons of both Chapman and Cameron had worked as economists for Treasury; Cameron's son was one the principal devisers of the SOE model. The decision to maintain non-commercial public radio, a departure from SOE principles, is attributed to political pressure by Day, *Voice and Vision*, p. 392. An arrangement which was initially to continue until at least June 1992 survives in 2003.
35 A Senior Management Meeting of 9 Mar 1992 looked back to the early 1980s; Minutes of Senior Management Meetings, Treasury.
36 Margaret Galt interview, 16 Feb 2001.

37 ST to MF, 28 Nov 1986, 1987 Budget, BM 02/9/1/1987, Treasury.
38 Margaret Galt interview, 16 Feb 2001.
39 ST to MF, 28 Nov 1986, BM 02/9/1/1987.
40 'State-Owned Enterprises: History of Policy Development and Implementation', Treasury internal paper, Sep 1996, pp. 24, 103, 104.
41 Birchfield and Grant, *Out of the Woods*, pp. 107–42 (Forestry Corporation); 'State-Owned Enterprises History', pp. 125–8 (Telecom); John E. Martin (ed.), *People, Politics and Power Stations: Electric Power Generation in New Zealand 1880–1998*, ECNZ and Historical Branch, Department of Internal Affairs, Wellington, 1998, pp. 311–12 (ECNZ).
42 'State-Owned Enterprises History', p. 105.
43 Martin (ed.), *People, Politics and Power Stations*, p. 312; see also Peter McKinlay, *Corporatisation: The Solution for State Owned Enterprise?*, Institute of Policy Studies, Victoria University of Wellington, Wellington, 1987, pp. 53–5.
44 Quoted in *National Business Review*, 25 May 1988.
45 Ranginui Walker, 'The Genesis of Direct Negotiation, the Fiscal Envelope, and their Impact on Tribal Land Claim Settlements', *He Pukenga Korero*, vol. 3, no. 1, Raumati 1997, p. 13; *AJHR*, 1989, B-27, p. 5.
46 Birchfield and Grant, *Out of the Woods*, pp. 82–103, looks at PSA dealings with the Forestry Corporation.
47 ST to MF, attachment, 28 Nov 1986, BM 02/9/1/1987; J. Boston, 'Transforming New Zealand's Public Sector: Labour's Quest for Improved Efficiency and Accountability', *Public Administration*, no. 65, Winter 1987, p. 436; Birchfield and Grant, *Out of the Woods*, pp. 10–12.
48 Vivienne Smith, *Reining in the Dinosaur: The Remarkable Turnaround in New Zealand Post*, NZ Post, Wellington, 1997 pp. 157–74, esp. pp. 158, 163.
49 Budget report 8, 12 Nov 1990, Budgets, administration, T 3/3/90; Margaret Galt interview, 16 Feb 2001; Simon Chapple, 'Full Employment: Whence It Came and Where it Went', Research Monograph no. 66, NZ Institute for Economic Research, Wellington, 1996.
50 See Peter Gorringe, 'Does Economic Growth Lead to Growth in Welfare?', in *Economics for Policy: Expanding the Boundaries*, Institute of Policy Studies, Victoria University of Wellington, Wellington, 2001, pp. 72–94.
51 Duncan and Bollard, *Corporatization and Privatization*, pp. 44, 64–9.

52 Colin James, *New Territory: The Transformation of New Zealand 1984–92*, Bridget Williams Books, Wellington, 1992, pp. 210–13, provides a useful overview.
53 Quoted in *National Business Review*, 25 May 1988; for Forestry Corporation see Birchfield and Grant, *Out of the Woods*, pp. 159–60: 'the long-running battle to get the Corporation to accept what, to Treasury's mind, was a half-way reasonable valuation was proving too difficult and taking too long'.
54 Treasury, *Economic Management*, Treasury, Wellington, 1984, pp. 293–4; Treasury, *Government Management*, pp. 112–17 (quote p. 113). See also Stephen Jennings, 'State Owned Enterprise: Agency Issues', in Institute of Policy Studies, *Corporatisation and Privatisation: Completing the Revolution*, Institute of Policy Studies, Victoria University of Wellington, Wellington, 1987; Roderick Deane, 'Corporatisation and Privatisation: A Discussion of the Issues', address to the Napier Chamber of Commerce, 1989; Brian Easton, *The Nationbuilders*, Auckland University Press, Auckland, 2001, pp. 274–5.
55 Margaret Galt interview, 16 Feb 2001.
56 Graham Scott interviewed by Radio New Zealand, 15 Aug 2001.
57 Ivan Kwok interview, 11 Oct 2000; Richard Shallcrass, unpublished autobiographical ms. See also Ian Kennedy, *New Zealand and Japan: Adding Value*, Institute of Policy Studies, Victoria University of Wellington, Wellington, 1992, pp. 74–9.
58 *Dominion*, 13, 15 Mar, 7 Jun 1989.
59 *Dominion*, 25 Jun 1992; *Examiner*, 4, 11 Jul 1991; Shallcrass ms.
60 Cited in I. R. Millard, barrister, to R. Shallcrass, Treasury, 6 Sep 1990, attachment, 'Opinion for Solicitor-General re Capital Markets Ltd and BNZ', Annex, para 10, file BNZ sale, T 40/1/4/3, Treasury.
61 'Opinion', 6 Sep 1990, cover sheet; Annex, paras 49, 54. Millard observed that whereas in the bank's 1989 annual report provision had been made for $125 million in Australian losses, that figure had become $258 million in the 1990 annual report.
62 Graham Scott, interviewed in *Management*, Dec 1989, p. 126; see also 'Striking best possible deal at the right market moment', *National Business Review*, 23 May 1988, p. 9.
63 'Opinion', 6 Sep 1990, para 8; Shallcrass, 'Seeking Place', ch 13.
64 Margaret Galt interview, 16 Feb 2001.
65 Bill Falconer interview, 25 Jul 2001.

66 *NZ Herald*, 22 Dec 1988.
67 Richard Shallcrass interview, 6 Jun 2000.
68 *Metro*, Jun 1992, p. 78.
69 Nicola Legat, 'The New Anatomy of Power', *Metro*, Oct 1991, p. 61.
70 *Dominion*, 25 Jun 1992; Martin Hames, *Winston First*, Random House, Auckland, 1995, pp. 138–49, 177–82, discusses the political controversy of 1992–93. See also Michael Laws, *The Demon Profession*, HarperCollins, Auckland, 1998, p. 216.
71 Deane, 'Issues', p. 122: 'clear analysis of the activities of Electricorp makes it clear that other parties could readily get into the power station business'.
72 Comment by Brian Easton.
73 Graham Scott, 'Presentation to Treasury Managers', 9 Apr 1991, Treasury.
74 Treasury, *Post-Election Briefing*, Treasury, Wellington, 1996, p. 118; an appendix to Jennings and Cameron, 'State Owned Enterprise Reform', pp. 359–61, cites a variety of studies; see also B. Easton, 'Economy' column, *NZ Listener*, 3 Dec 1994, on this latter point.
75 Duncan and Bollard, *Corporatization and Privatization*, p. 42; see also *NZ Listener*, 30 Apr 1990 (satire). Note that the Government Printing Office was not an SOE when it was sold.
76 *Dominion*, 10 Jan 1989, editorial.
77 *AJHR*, B-27, 1989, pp. 1819; 1990, pp. 44–5; Bruce Jesson, *Only Their Purpose is Mad: The Money Men Take Over New Zealand*, Dunmore Press, Palmerston North, 1999, pp. 172–3.
78 Treasury, *Government Management*, p. 114.
79 *Dominion*, 21 Oct, 9 Nov 1987; Minutes, Senior Management Meeting, 15 Jul 1996.
80 Easton, *Nationbuilders*, pp. 236–7; Minutes, Senior Management Meeting, 15 Jul 1996.
81 John Roberts, *Politicians, Public Servants and Public Enterprise*, Victoria University Press for Institute of Policy Studies, Wellington, 1987, p. 80.
82 Treasury, *Economic Management*, pp. 287–8.
83 Boston et al, *Public Management*, p. 56; Geoffrey Palmer, *Unbridled Power*, 2nd edn, Oxford University Press, Auckland, 1987, pp. 81–2; Scott, interviewed in *Accountants' Journal*, Apr 1993, p. 41.
84 Treasury, *Economic Management*, p. 289.
85 J. F. Robertson, 'Efficiency and Economy in the New Zealand Public Service', *NZJPA*, vol. 28, no. 1, Sep 1965, pp. 81–104.
86 *AJHR*, 1985, G-3, p. 5.
87 Boston et al, *Public Management*, pp. 55–6.
88 ST to MF, 23 Feb 1988, T 3/3/1, Treasury; see also Jane Kelsey, *The New Zealand Experiment: A World Model for Structural Adjustment*, Auckland University Press / Bridget Williams Books, Auckland, 1997, p. 177.
89 Scott and Gorringe, 'Reform of the Core Public Sector', p. 82. For discussion of the relationship between ownership and purchase, see *AJHR*, 1989, B-27, p. 22; also Ian Ball interview, 28 Sep 2001. For more on the relationship to private-sector models, see Graham Scott, *Public Management in New Zealand: Lessons and Challenges*, NZ Business Roundtable, Wellington, 2001, pp. 37–8.
90 Boston et al, *Public Management*, p. 6.
91 Graham Scott interview, 10 Nov 2000.
92 See discussion of the antecedents in J. E. Whitcombe, 'Restructuring the New Zealand Public Service, *Public Sector*, vol. 10, no. 1, 1987. For the 'Shailes Report', see *AJHR*, 1978, B-1, Pt IV, pp. 7, 13, 27–9. The head office of the Ministry of Works and Development had only two qualified accountants directly involved in monitoring financial activities (p. 27). See also *Evening Post*, 22 Feb 1984, for the front-page story, 'Audit advice pigeon-holed since 1978'.
93 Ian Ball interview, 28 Sep 2001. The first appointee to the FMSS was David Shand, an accountant with both public service and university experience. A memo of 17 Mar 1986, Budget, administration, T 3/3/1, Treasury, records the decision to establish the FMSS.
94 *AJHR*, 1994, B-29 (94d), p. 32.
95 *AJHR*, 1989, I-4C, pp. 4–5, 31.
96 *Government Management*, p. 5.
97 Comment from John Whitehead.
98 Ian Ball interview, 28 Sep 2001.
99 29 Jun 1989, T 3/3/1. The Association organised the Treasury's annual post-Budget social function. Its secretary in 1989 was Struan Little.
100 Smyth to Senior Managers, 13 Nov 1989, T 3/3/1. Over time, more detailed protocols were established (John Whitehead).
101 *AJHR*, 1988, B-6, p. 10 (Budget, 28 Jul 1988).
102 Budget report 39, 13 Dec 1990, T 3/3/1.
103 Howard Fancy, 'The Role of Treasury in the Budget Process: Experience in 1991', in J. S. Nethercote et al, *Decision-Making in New Zealand Government*, Federalism Research Centre in association with Institute of Policy Studies, VUW, and State Services Commission, Canberra, 1993, pp. 21–32; comment by Peter Bushnell.
104 Comment by Peter Bushnell.
105 Scott, 'Presentation to Treasury Managers'.
106 Annex to Budget report 45, 23 Jan 1991, T 3/3/1. For more on science, see *AJHR*, 1992, B-27,

pp. 8–66; *Commercialisation of New Zealand*, pp. 236–8. Ten autonomous Crown Research Institutes were established to replace the Department for Scientific and Industrial Research in July 1992; *Dominion*, 2 Jul 1992.
107 Robert Gregory, 'Getting Better but Feeling Worse', paper prepared for international public mangement workshop, Wellington, Mar 2001, obtainable via Bob.Gregory@vuw.ac.nz. See also comments on Allen Shick, *The Spirit of Reform: Managing the New Zealand State Sector in a Time of Change*, SSC, Wellington, 1996, in B. Easton, 'Economy' column, *NZ Listener*, 1 Feb 1997, p. 60; and *Dominion*, 2 Apr 1997. For an overview of academic New Zealand criticism of the reforms, see Scott, *Public Management*, pp. 53–63.
108 Jonathan Boston, 'New Zealand: Cautionary Tale or Shining Example?', in R. A. W. Rhodes and Patrick Weller (eds), *The Changing World of Top Officials: Mandarins or Valets?*, Open University Press, Buckingham, Philadelphia, 2001, p. 226.
109 Graham Scott, 'Reflections about the New Zealand Budgetary Process', in Nethercote et al, *Decision-Making in New Zealand Government*, p. 120.
110 Graham Scott, *Public Management*, pp. 107–12, 114–15. See also the discussion re 'politics vs administration' in Boston et al, *Public Management*, p. 9.
111 Ian Ball interview, 28 Sep 2001.
112 Scott, 'Presentation to Treasury Managers': 'We talked a bit … over the years about trying to be the "best little Treasury in the world."' Others recall a more sardonic play on the title of the 1982 film, *The Best Little Whorehouse in Texas*.
113 *Government Management*, p. 92.
114 Graham Scott, 'Ensuring the Quality of Policy Advice', Address to AIC Conference, 'Evaluation in the Public Sector', copy held at Treasury.
115 State Services Commission, 'Report of Committee of Enquiry into the Staffing Problems at Treasury, Nov 1984', appendix 2.
116 David Greig interview, 9 Feb 2001.
117 SSC, 'Staffing Problems at Treasury', para 6.1; comment by Robin Williams.
118 Price Waterhouse Associates, *Report on a Job Evaluation and Salary Relativity Study for Economic and Financial Analysis Occupational Class of the SSC*, Oct 1985, p. 17, Treasury.
119 Comments by Graham Scott, Carl Bakker.
120 David Greig interview, 9 Feb 2001; also memo, 21 Mar 1986, T 69/1/8/5, Treasury.
121 Patrick Dunleavy, *Democracy, Bureaucracy and Public Choice*, Prentice Hall, New York, 1991,

esp. pp. 200–5; Richard Parry, Christopher Hood and Oliver James, 'Reinventing the Treasury: Economic Rationalism or an Econocrat's Fallacy of Control?', *Public Administration*, vol. 75, no. 3, 1997, pp. 395–415, includes a discussion of 'bureau-shaping' in the UK Treasury (p. 410). See also Geoff Bertram, '"Middle Class Capture": A Brief Survey', submission to Royal Commission on Social Policy, 1988, pp. 29–30, for an exploration of the argument that Treasury engaged in 'administrative capture' in the 1980s.
122 Graham Scott, 'Reflections on Managing the Treasury', 1992, Treasury, p. 9.
123 *AJHR*, 1989, B-27, p. 6. Also Graham Scott, David Greig, and John Martin interviews.
124 See Coopers & Lybrand, 'District Treasury Offices: Survey', Treasury X0479, 1987, which questioned whether Treasury was 'an appropriate parent for the operation of an accounting processing service for other government departments'; see also T 69/1/8/5.
125 *AJHR*, 1990, B-27, p. 67; *Management*, Dec 1989, p. 126; *Accountants' Journal*, Feb 1992, p. 21.
126 Scott, 'Presentation to Treasury Managers'. See also Scott, 'Reflections', p. 20: 'The gap between senior analyst and manager is huge … I want our managers to develop managerial skills to match their technical skills'.
127 David Greig interview, 9 Feb 2001.
128 *AJHR*, 1990, B-27, p. 18.
129 T 69/1/8/5, Treasury.
130 T 69/1/8/5; comment by Paul Jones; *AJHR*, 1990, B-27, p. 66. The full name was 'Nga Kaitohutohu i te Kaupapa whai rawa o Aotearoa ki te Kawanatanga' — 'The people who give advice to the government about everything to do with the resources of Aotearoa'. In 1990 the 'Surfdale Progressive Association' had canvassed its members on adopting its own Maori name; one suggestion was translated as 'the best little council of very inebriated people'; Surfdale Progressive Association, 5 Jul 1990, Irene Lake Papers.
131 See Scott, 'Reflections', pp. 34, 36.
132 Surfdale Progressive Association, 'Surfdale Strategy 1992', Irene Lake Papers.
133 Margaret Galt interview, 16 Feb 2001.
134 Roderick Deane interview, 14 Nov 2001.
135 Annex to ST to MF, 23 Nov 1986, BM 02/9/1/ 1987,
136 Murray Horn interview, 15 Feb 2001; also *AJHR*, 1989, B-27, pp. 6, 25–6.
137 Parry et al, 'Reinventing Treasury', p. 397.
138 *AJHR*, 1991–93, I-19A, p. 288.

139 Graham Scott, interviewed 21 Dec 2000.
140 Ian Ball interview, 28 Sep 2001. Accounting theory is discussed in Scott, *Government Reform*, p. 13. See also *Accountants' Journal*, Apr 1993, pp. 40–1 (comment by Graham Scott).
141 *Accountants' Journal*, May 1992, p. 25.
142 Ian Ball interview, 28 Oct 2001.
143 *AJHR*, B-27,1989, p. 26; 1994, p. 10; also Graham Scott, interviewed on *Morning Report*, Radio New Zealand, 15 Aug 2001.
144 K. J. Scott, 'The Political Theory of the Social Service State', *NZJPA*, vol. 17, no. 1, Sep 1954, pp. 10–24, esp. pp. 11–12.
145 Treasury to MF, Budget report 63, 10 Jul 1986, BM 02/9/1/1986.
146 Bruce Jesson, 'New Zealand's Hard Labour', *New Left Review*, no. 192, Mar/Apr 1992, pp. 49–50; Margaret McClure, *A Civilised Community: A History of Social Security in New Zealand, 1898–1998*, Auckland University Press, Auckland, 1998, pp. 225–8; G. V. Butterworth and S. M. Butterworth, *Reforming Education: The New Zealand Experience, 1984–1996*, Dunmore Press, Palmerston North, 1998, p. 70, n. 45.
147 Budget report 8, 18 Dec 1986, BM 02/9/1/1987; and annex A, record of a meeting of 5 Dec 1986, pp. 2, 4.
148 Robin Gauld, *Revolving Doors: New Zealand's Health Reforms*, Institute of Policy Studies, VUW, Wellington, 2001, pp. 60–4.
149 Butterworth and Butterworth, *Reforming Education*, pp. 65–6; Treasury, *Government Management*, vol. II, p. 293. See also discussion in Easton, *Commercialisation*, pp. 202–4.
150 D. Lange interview, 8 Mar 1994, cited in Butterworth and Butterworth, *Reforming Education*, p. 66.
151 For the origins of the education reforms, see Butterworth and Butterworth, *Reforming Education*, pp. 51–70, 82–7.
152 ST to MF, 4 Apr 1990, T 3/3/1.
153 Budget report 8, 1991, 12 Nov 1990, T 3/3/90. Its author, Mark Prebble, later spoke of being influenced by his colleague Peter Gorringe: 'If you are going to improve the efficiency of the delivery of social policy, you are going to find yourself getting into institutional design questions, [which is] why I was always interested in the work Peter Gorringe was doing' (interview, 7 Mar 2001). For criticism of the Arthur Andersen consultants' conclusion, see Gauld, *Revolving Doors*, p. 61.
154 Budget report 8, 12 Nov 1990, T 3/3/90.
155 'Economic and Social Initiative — December 1990', p. 18. See also Jonathan Boston, 'Grand Design and Unpleasant Realities: The Fate of the National Government's Proposal for the Integrated Targeting of Social Assistance', *Political Science*, vol. 46, no. 1, Jul 1994.
156 'Economic and Social Initiative', pp. 17–18; see also pp. 21–3. For the failure of the superannuation system, see *Evening Post*, 21 Oct 1991.
157 Mark Prebble interview, 7 Mar 2001.
158 Scott, *Public Management*, p. 71, re social policy: 'new policy and management frameworks need to be developed … the progress of these approaches in the 1990s has been largely piecemeal.'
159 *AJHR*, 1991, B-6 (Budget, 30 Jul 1991), p. 11; see also Easton, *Commercialisation*, pp. 155–8.
160 *AJHR*, 1991, B-6, pp. 14–15.
161 Graham Scott interview, 21 Dec 2000.
162 Easton, *Commercialisation*, p. 158.
163 Scott, 'Reflections', p. 10.
164 Ruth Richardson interview, 22 Mar 2001.
165 Carl Bakker interview, 5 May 2002.
166 David Bettison, 'Issues in Research: The "Exposed Hand" of Treasury', *New Zealand Sociology*, vol. 7, no. 2, Nov 1992, p. 239. For a different view, see Scott, *Public Management in New Zealand*, p. 38.
167 Nagel, 'Radically Reinventing Government', p. 354.
168 Brian Easton, 'Economy' column, *NZ Listener*, 6 Dec 1986.
169 Memo from Rob McIntosh to Peter Bushnell and Howard Fancy, 13 Oct 1992, Irene Lake Papers.
170 Cited in Richard Norman, *Accounting for Government*, Cases in Public Sector Innovation, no. 1, VUW, 1997, p. 17.
171 Gwenda Jensen, 'The New Zealand Treasury: Zen and the Art of Budget Management', School of Accounting and Commercial Law, VUW, 2001, p. 22. Cf Parry et al, 'Reinventing the Treasury', p. 397: 'where does the balance lie between the Treasury's "bureau of the budget" accounting and control functions versus what tends to be for economists the higher status "Economics Ministry" macroeconomics work?'

Chapter 10: Consolidation, 1993–2000

1 The 1991/92 recession, it was subsequently argued, had resulted from international developments rather than the tight monetary policy. See Robert Buckle, Kunhong Kim, Heather Kirkham, Nathan McLellan and Jared Sharma, 'Trade, Climate and Financial Influences on Macroeconomic Fluctuations:

NOTES TO PAGES 404–413

Analysis Using a SVAR model of the New Zealand Economy', Treasury draft paper, Jun 2002, p. 34.
2   Information from Gary Hawke.
3   Minutes, Senior Management Group meeting (hereafter SMM), 3 Feb 1997, Treasury. These, and a number of other Treasury documents, are stored electronically and have been retrieved using a keyword search.
4   Office minute 1997/B47, 26 Jun 1997, Treasury.
5   Figures taken from a word search for 'Treasury' on Index New Zealand. While some caveats apply to this method, the general conclusion seems valid.
6   Bolger and Richardson discuss in *A View from the Top: My Seven Years as Prime Minister*, Viking, Auckland, 1998, pp. 120–1, and *Making a Difference*, Shoal Bay Press, Christchurch, 1995, pp. 178–81, respectively.
7   ST to MF, 17 Jan 1992: 'the Council could be involved in the development and establishment of microeconomic policy review and reform process to ensure that the effects on business and investment are fully considered by Government before decisions are taken. Similarly business feedback on the quality and efficiency of important state agencies … could be co-ordinated through the Council.' Treasury records.
8   *Metro*, Jun 1992, p. 77.
9   For Birch's time on the Public Expenditure Committee, see A. F. von Tunzelmann, 'The Public Expenditure Committee: The Process of Change 1962–1977', MPP paper, VUW, 1977, pp. 53, 55.
10 See, for instance, Brian Easton, 'Economy' column, *NZ Listener*, 12 Feb, 26 Feb, 21 May 1994; *NZ Listener*, 16 Apr 1994 (Brash); *Dominion*, 6 Jun 1994 (Lange), 22 Jun 1994 (Brash).
11 See, for instance, Easton, 'Economy' column, *NZ Listener*, 29 Apr 1995.
12 *AJHR*, 1996, B-2, Budget (23 May 1996), p. 6; Treasury, *Briefing to the Incoming Government 1996*, Treasury, Wellington, 1996, pp. 63–74, esp. pp. 72–4. The requirement of a Policy Targets Agreement had been introduced by the Reserve Bank of New Zealand Act 1989.
13 *AJHR*, 1994–1996, I-3A, p. 28.
14 Jane Kelsey, *The New Zealand Experiment: A World Model for Structural Adjustment*, Auckland University Press / Bridget Williams Books, 1997, pp. 232–8 (reference to Cullen, p. 237).
15 W. F. Birch, *Budget and Fiscal Strategy Report 1995*, Treasury, Wellington, 1995, p. 25; W. F. Birch, *Pre-Election Economic and Fiscal Update*, New Zealand Government, Wellington, 1996, p. 3.
16 Bill Birch interview, 22 Apr 2002.
17 See, for instance, Roger Kerr, 'Myths About Economic Reform', in New Zealand Business Roundtable, *Can New Zealand Afford to Replay the Economic Past?*, NZ Business Roundtable, Wellington, 2000, p. 56.
18 SMM, 26 Apr 1995. Further discussion of long-term growth rates is found on SMM, 9 Apr 1996.
19 John E. Martin (ed.), *People, Politics and Power Stations: Electric Power Generation in New Zealand 1880 to 1998*, ECNZ and Historical Branch, Department of Internal Affairs, Wellington, 1998, p. 322; see also *AJHR*, 1997, B-2, p. 9.
20 SMM, 9 Apr 1996. SMM, 9 Dec 1996, noted that the petition was 40,000 signatures short of the number required to trigger a referendum.
21 SMM, 2/ Apr 1992.
22 W. F. Birch, *Tax Reduction and Social Policy Programme: Details* (19 Feb 1996), New Zealand Government, Wellington, 1996.
23 Ranginui Walker, 'The Genesis of Direct Negotiation, the Fiscal Envelope, and their Impact on Tribal Land Claim Settlements', *He Pukenga Korero*, vol. 3, no. 1, 1997, p. 14.
24 Mary Anne Thompson interview, 2 Jul 2002. Te Puni Kokiri, the Ministry of Maori Development, had been established on 1 January 1992, replacing Manatu Maori.
25 Richardson, *Making a Difference*, pp. 148–9, is helpful.
26 Draft, MF to J. H. Tamihere, reply to letter of 30 May 1994, Treasury.
27 SMM, 7 Mar, 27 Jun 1994.
28 *Crown Proposals for the Settlement of Treaty of Waitangi Claims: Summary*, Department of Justice, Wellington, 1994, p. 24.
29 Wira Gardner, *Return to Sender: What Really Happened at the Fiscal Envelope Hui*, Reed, Auckland, 1996; Maryanne Aynsley interview, 21 Jun 2002.
30 Bill Birch interview, 22 Apr 2002. Wayne Peters, a brother of Winston Peters, was a lawyer involved in negotiating the coalition agreement.
31 Bill Birch interview, 22 Apr 2002.
32 SMM, 3 Feb 1997; *AJHR*, 1998, B-27, pp. 33–64.
33 *AJHR*, 1997, B-2, pp. 6, 9. See also Brian Easton, *The Whimpering of the State: Policy after MMP*, Auckland University Press, Auckland, 1999, pp. 45–7, for comments on Peters' fiscal conservatism.

34 Martin (ed.), *People, Politics and Power Stations*, p. 323; *AJHR*, B-2, 1997, p. 14; 1998, pp. 10, 18; 1999, p. 19.
35 SMM, 9 Apr 1996, 7 Jul 1997; *AJHR*, 1997, B-2, pp. 14-15 (Budget speech, 26 Jun 1997).
36 *AJHR*, 1998, B-2, pp. 12–15 (Budget speech, 14 May 1998, Winston Peters).
37 *AJHR*, 1997, B-2, p. 14.
38 SMM, 25 Feb 1997.
39 SMM, 5 May, 9 Jun 1997. Lack of prescience about the Asian crisis was of course the norm worldwide.
40 *AJHR*, 1998, B-2, p. 7; 1999, B-1, Budget policy statement 1999, pp. 13, 16–19.
41 Martin (ed.), *People, Politics and Power Stations*, pp. 323–5; *AJHR*, 1999, B-1, Budget policy statement, p. 10.
42 Treasury official interviewed on condition of anonymity.
43 C. J. McKenzie to Senior Management Group, 28 Nov 1997, Treasury.
44 Buckle et al, 'Trade, Climate and Financial Influences', p. 35.
45 The reference is to the 1991 changes to labour law, and fiscal consolidation.
46 Bill Birch interview, 22 Apr 2002.
47 SMM, 24 Mar 1997.
48 SMM, 6 Sep 1999. A number of studies have explored distributive issues, including in the later 1990s: George Barker, *Income Distribution in New Zealand*, Institute of Policy Studies, VUW, Wellington, 1996; John Creedy, *Statistics and Dynamics of Income Distribution in New Zealand*, Institute of Policy Studies, VUW, Wellington, 1997; Brian Easton, *The Commercialisation of New Zealand*, Auckland University Press, 1997; Tim Maloney, *Benefit Reform and Labour Market Behaviour in New Zealand*, Institute of Policy Studies, VUW, Wellington, 1997; Tim Maloney, *Five Years After: The New Zealand Labour Market and the Employment Contracts Act*, Institute of Policy Studies, VUW, Wellington, 1998; see also Paul Dalziel, 'Did the Reforms Work? Yes and No', *New Zealand Books*, vol. 7, no. 4, Oct 1997, pp. 17–18.
49 SMM, 31 Oct, 7 Nov 1994.
50 Grant Scobie, 'So We'd Like Better Economic Growth?', Treasury in-house paper, 7 Nov 2001; Little, 'Real Exchange Rate'; SMM, 29 Mar 1999; David Skilling, 'Whither Leviathan? An Essay on the Size of Government and Economic Growth', Treasury in-house paper, 4 Apr 2002.
51 *Dominion*, 8 Dec 2000; Buckle et al, 'Trade, Climate and Financial Influences', p. 35.
52 SMM, 8 Jun 1999; *Dominion*, 8 Dec 2000, citing *Economist*, 2 Dec 2000; 'Towards Higher Living Standards for New Zealanders', 1999 Post-Election Briefing Papers, p. 8.
53 Murray Horn interview, 15 Feb 2001.
54 *AJHR*, 1995, B-27, p. 9. There is reference to a paper on the new branch in SMM, 15 May 1995.
55 Treasury poster, late 1990s.
56 ST to all staff, 8 May 1997, Treasury; *AJHR*, B-27, 1997, p. 10; 1998, p. 11. Treasury's own London office closed in 1994.
57 See interview in *Management*, Dec 1989.
58 Ian Ball interview, 28 Sep 2001.
59 Maryanne Aynsley interview, 21 Jun 2002.
60 Observation by the author.
61 M. A. Collins, 'Review of the Treasury Costings of Labour Party Policies', State Services Commission, 1994, pp. 8–10. See also State Services Commission press release, 25 Mar 1994. Subsequently it was agreed that the Minister's office, not the department, would do such costings.
62 Rachel Barrowman, *The Turnbull: A Library and Its World*, Auckland University Press in association with Historical Branch, Department of Internal Affairs, Auckland, 1995, pp. 198–9.
63 Treasury internal memorandum on the fire; Treasury had had a web site since 1993.
64 ST to Finance and Expenditure Select Committee, 14 Feb 1995, cited in Gardiner, *Return to Sender*, p. 29; and further discussion, pp. 35–7.
65 For the wine-box enquiry, see R. K. Davison, *Report of the Wine-box Inquiry*, Commission of Inquiry into Matters Relating to Taxation, Wellington, 1997; for the Equiticorp decision, see chapter 9.
66 SMM, 26 Feb 1997.
67 SMM, 5 May 1997.
68 Kelsey, *New Zealand Experiment*, p. 238; SMM, 18 Sep 1995, 7 Apr 1997, 6, 13 Jul 1998; *Evening Post*, 11 Jul 1997.
69 *Management*, Aug 1995, pp. 32–3; SMM, 7 Aug 1995. Systemic constraints ensured that few people would earn a five.
70 John Whitehead interview, 9 May 2002.
71 SMM, 30 Jan 1995. See also Irene Taylor to ST, 22 Nov 1994, Irene Lake Papers.
72 SMM, 3 Jun 1997; also 21, 28 Jul 1997. Rose Anne McLeod, listed as a full participant at the 3 June meeting, was not a deputy secretary.
73 Prebble's role was commented on favourably by interviewees Aynsley, Hurnard and Whitehead.
74 Bill Birch interview, 22 Apr 2002.
75 Discussed in Jonathan Boston, 'New Zealand: 'Cautionary Tale or Shining Example?', in R. A.

W. Rhodes and Patrick Weller (eds), *The Changing World of Top Officials: Mandarins or Valets?*, Open University Press, Buckingham, Philadelphia, 2001, p. 197.

76 Jonathan Boston, *Left Turn: The New Zealand General Election of 1999*, VUP, Wellington, 2000.

77 For comment in this vein, see *Dominion*, 4 Oct 2000 (reference to Treasury being the department 'most affected by the change of government'); *Sunday Star-Times*, 29 Jul 2001 ('Treasury Island?').

78 *Evening Post*, 21 Jun 1999.

79 Graham Scott, *Public Management in New Zealand: Lessons and Challenges*, NZ Business Roundtable, Wellington, 2001, p. 355.

80 'Economy' column, *NZ Listener*, 8 May 1999.

81 'Economy' column, *NZ Listener*, 24 Aug 2002.

Select bibliography

Archives and manuscripts

Alexander Turnbull Library, Wellington

MS-Papers-99-032, Papers of Henry Lang

Boxes 1, 2
A variety of items from Lang's period as Secretary to the Treasury (1969–76) and subsequently

MS-Papers-1403, Papers of J. R. Marshall

Minutes of Cabinet Economic Committee, 1967–1971
Minutes of Cabinet Committee on Overseas Investment, 1970

MS-Papers-1624, Papers of S. G. Holland

080/1–5	1950 Budget
082/5	Abolition of controls, survey of progress on, 1954
083/2	Economic talks with interest groups 1954
085/3–7	Gas industry, 1950s
091/1–2	Petrol 1950s
097/5–099/1	Tasman Pulp and Paper, 1951–57
099/4–102/1	Treasury reports, 1950–1952
113	National Party matters, 1950–1951

MS-Papers-1777-08, Papers of W. J. Hunter

'Short History of the Audit Department'

MS-Papers-1785, Papers of J. G. Coates

19	Special economic committee, Aug–Sep 1931
20	Special economic committee, notebook
38	Exchange rate, correspondence

MS-Papers-1886, Cooper, Anthony J. A.

Family history c. 1790 to 1851

Treasury

MS-Papers-1900, Papers of R. M. Campbell

01	Diary, 1927–29
03	Diary, 1932–1933
04	Diary, 1931 to 1934
10	Correspondence with J. G. Coates, 1933–1934
15	Correspondence with John Barr and W. B. Sutch, 1971–1973
25	Obituaries – R. M. Campbell

Australasian Joint Copying Project

Micro-MS-Coll-20-2945: 24 Bank of England: OV 9: Sir Otto Niemeyer, 1930–31
Micro-MS-Coll-20-2945: 287 Bank of England: OV 9: Sir Otto Niemeyer, 1930
Micro-MS-Coll-20-2945: Bank of England: G14, File 282, New Zealand, 1931–39
Micro-MS-Coll-20-2945: Bank of England: Governor's File: Sir Otto Niemeyer, 1938–39
Micro-MS-Coll-20-2958: Bank of England Archive: Overseas Department – Records New Zealand, 1932–39

fMS-074

Letters of James Fitzgerald to W. E. Gladstone, 1840s to 1860s

Archives New Zealand, Wellington

T (Treasury)

T 1   Inwards letters and registered files 1841–1913, 1913–

Inwards letters
1868, 1883 (sampled)

Registered subject files 1913–

1/132	Civil list: native purposes, 1913–1950
3/3/y	Budget files 1950s and 1960s
9/32/1	Treasury staff, general, 1915–1920 (listed in finding aids as 'Miss Craven's resignation')
9/100	Inspection and reorganisation of Treasury staff, 1910s and 1920s
12/15/6	Estimates of revenue and expenditure 1916–17
12/186/yr	Statement of revenue and expenditure, by year, 1918–
12/360	Business and government, 1920–21
23/144	Historical Records: War, 1914–1919
26/1/2	Cables re public works loan 1915
26/2	1915 loan – money raised in New Zealand, suggestions re

27/13/4	Wheat subsidies and audit thereof, 1919
40/15	Public Revenues Act 1926
40/88/29	Finance Act 1929
40/196	State hydro-electricity department, 1946–1951
40/416	Local Government Loans Act 1926
40/510	Powers of Audit Office and Treasury, 1928–
52/35/yr	Estimates for financial year 1949–
52/63/yr	Budgets, 1930s
52/74/6	Exchange and empire currency, 1922–25
52/77/yr	Loan requirements, 1927–29, then by financial year
52/81	Comparative increase in departmental expenditure, explanations from departments, general instructions, 1927–
52/584	Railways, finance and policy, 1928
52/587	Native Land Claims 1927–28
52/622	Education economies 1931
52/641	Railways commission, 1931
52/645	Proposed central bank, 1930–1933, Reserve Bank, 1933–
52/663	Budget 1930/31
55/668	National economic adjustment, 1931
52/702	File on and minutes of National Expenditure Adjustment Commission 1932
52/702/2	National Expenditure Commission 1932, Treasury reports for
52/703/[1]	National Expenditure Commission 1932, Treasury reports for
52/703/[2]	Papers of Economists' committee, Feb 1932
52/717	Downie Stewart and Park in London 1932
52/749	Social security 1934–1939
52/885	Economic Stabilization conference 1940
52/962	Gas industry 1950s
62/19	Expenditure, education, 1948–49

T 16 Currency and Banking

13	BNZ 1894–95
14	BNZ 1896
15	BNZ 1897–98
18	BNZ 1894

T 17 Government loans

3	Five million pound loan 1879
4	Five million pound loan 1879
21	Five million pound loan 1910

Treasury

T 18 *Correspondence from Agent-General*

35   Confidential correspondence, Agent-General and Colonial Treasurer, 1877–1887

T 19 *Miscellaneous finance and accounting papers*

40   Correspondence with Sir Penrose Julyan, 1884–96
43   Telegrams on loans and finance 1888

T 20 *Miscellaneous papers*

3   Fitzherbert accounts analysis 1867–68, audit queries 1868–74
10   1880s and 1890s, various, including papers of Jas Heywood
37   Papers presumably belonging to Mr [D. O.] Williams, 1939

T 25 *Minister of Finance Papers – Walter Nash, Minister of Finance, 1935–1949*

7   Walter Nash file on State Advances Corporation

T 66 *National Expenditure Commission 1932*

1   Questioning of public servants

T 70 *Economic Stabilization Conference 1940*

1   Conference 1940

T 71 *Economic Stabilization Committee*

1   Reports submitted to the ES Committee, 1941–1942
2   Ministerial memoranda, late 1942

T 72 *Papers of the Economic Stabilization Commission, 1942–*

1/0   Includes press coverage, 1943, 1945
1/3   Minutes of the ES Committee 1941 and of the ES Commission, 1942–43, 1949
1/ 4   Relations between price stabilization committee and the price tribunal
1/6   Economic Stabilization Commission – staff
1/16/1 ESC – history
3/–   Investigation of industries, commodities, operations, e.g. paper mills, tea, tram fares

Accession W2220

T 90 *Personal files*

B. C. Ashwin
D. W. A. Barker
N. R. Davis

H. G. Lang
S. C. Parker

AALR Treasury

Accession W207

73/1   Economic planning, 1965–1967

Accession W2412

3/3/70 et seq Budget files 1970–1975

Accession W3158

61/1/22   Incomes policies, prices, incomes and productivity, 1975–1976

Accession W4446

39/18/9/36   Synfuels 1979–1981
39/29/8   Energy plans, 1979–1986
62/34   Expenditure: Post Office: general, 1981–1986

AAOM   Estates

6029   includes wills 1931
6030   includes wills 1940
6031   includes wills 1971

Accession W3694

AAXO   Papers of R. D. Muldoon

Box 159/6   Budget reports 1979
Box 238/1   Cabinet Works Committee 1979
Box 238/4   Minutes of Cabinet Expenditure Committee, 1979
Boxes 238/6–239/2   Minutes of Cabinet Economic Committee, 1979
Boxes 239/5–6   Minutes of Cabinet, 1979
Boxes 241/5–8   Minutes of Cabinet Economic Committee, 1980
Box 249/2   Minutes of Cabinet Economic Committee, 1977

SSC (State Services Commission)

SSC 5   *Personal files*

G. F. C. Campbell
E. L. Greensmith
A. D. Park

Bank of New Zealand Archive, Wellington

Accession 4529

Confidential: Government
June 1929 to Dec 1930

General Manager's Records
Box [2]   includes material on establishment of the Reserve Bank of New Zealand, 1932–1933

Hocken Library, Dunedin

MS 985 Downie Stewart Papers

1/1	correspondence files
7	diaries, early 1930s
8	ministerial correspondence
10	exchange correspondence 1932–33
11	taxation, 1920s and early 1930s
12	Budgets and financial statements, esp. 1920s and 1930s
13	mortgagors' relief act 1931–32
17	Ottawa conference 1932
28	newspaper clippings

Brian Easton, Wellington

Papers relating to B. C. Ashwin

Irene Lake, Wellington

A variety of Treasury papers from 1969 to 1993, including papers of the Surfdale Progressive Association; papers on staff retention and management, 1983–1985

Noel Lough, Wellington

'A Strategy for Growth' – economic policy package for Prime Minister, 1978

John Martin, Wellington

A variety of Treasury papers, 1955–1980

Treasury, Wellington

T 3/3/1   Budgets, preparation and administration, 1983–1991

Select bibliography

T 3/3/82   Budget, 1982
T 3/3/90   Budget, 1990–91
T 4/2/45   New and existing policies review: Works Department, 1983
T 39/30   Industrial finance – structural adjustment assistance, 1979–1981
T 40/1/4/1/3 BNZ – sale, 1989–1991
T 61/2/5   NZ Manufacturers' Association, general, 1979–1987
T 61/11/6   Public sector borrowing requirement 1985–1986
T 61/12/2/1 Regulatory framework for industrial relations: general: labour market regulation, 1983–1984
T 62/9   Expenditure: Education department: policy: 1986
T 62/55/6   Expenditure: Works: Major Projects: Expenditure and Monitoring 1981–1987
T 69/1/8/5   Internal memoranda etc, 1976–1990
T 73/35/2/1 New Zealand Planning Council: Economic Monitoring Group, 1979–1984
T 76/2/1   Taxes on income, profits and capital gains – general, 1987

BM 02/9/1/yr   Budget reports 1983–1987

Senior management group meeting minutes, 1991–1999

Interviews

(all took place in the Wellington area unless indicated)

John Anderson	12 Mar 2001
Cathryn Ashley-Jones	2 Jul 2002
May Atkins	27 Jul 2001
Maryanne Aynsley	21 Jun 2002
Ian Ball	28 Sep 2001
Geoff Bascand	15 Feb 2002
Bill Birch (Auckland)	23 Feb 2001, 22 Apr 2002
Bert Brownlie (Christchurch)	31 Aug 2000
Rob Cameron	29 Jun 2000
David Caygill	16 Jan 2001
John Chetwin	13, 14 Jul 2000
John Cook	24 Oct 2000
Roderick Deane	14 Nov 2001
Lawrie Dennis	10, 23 Jul 2000
Roger Douglas (Auckland)	19 Apr 2002
Leo and Sheila Downey	11 Jul 2001
Ken Durrant	12 Jun 2000
Bill Falconer	25 Jul 2001

Margaret Galt   16 Feb 2001
Averall Gibson   11 Jul 2001
Bernard Greig   5 Mar 2001
David Greig   9 Feb 2001
Peter Harris   27 Nov 2000
Frank Holmes   8 Mar 2001
Murray Horn   15 Feb 2001
Roger Kerr   16 Jun 2000
Irene Lake (Taylor)   17 Sep 2001
George Laking   21 Nov 2000
Rob Laking   30 Jan 2001
Peter Lorimer   28 Jun 2000
Noel Lough   8, 16 May 2000
Jas Mackenzie   13, 20 Jun 2000
Donald McKinnon   29 Jan 2001
Bob Norman   15 May 2001
Sam Parker   12 May 2000
Mark Prebble   13 Feb, 7 Mar 2001
David Preston   6 Jun 2001
Don Rangi   8 Dec 2000
Ruth Richardson   22 Mar 2001
Bill Robinson   27 Jul 2001
Pete Rodger   20 Feb 2002
Nikitin Sallee   9 Sep 2002
Graham Scott   7, 10 Nov, 21 Dec 2000
Richard Shallcrass   1, 6 Jun 2000
Ian Sliper   3 Jul 2000
Cliff Terry   6 Jul 2000
Mary Anne Thompson   2 Jul 2002
Brian Tyler   26 Jan 2001
John Whitehead   17 Apr, 9 May 2002
Bryce Wilkinson   19 Jul 2000
Ted Woodfield   24 May 2001
John Yeabsley   25 Oct 2000

Unpublished Papers

Ashwin, B. C., 'Practical Problems in Public Finance', lecture to Commerce Society, Victoria University College, 15 Apr 1935, copy in Macmillan Brown library, University of Canterbury

Bertram, Geoff, '"Middle-Class Capture": A Brief Survey', submission to Royal Commission on Social Policy, 1988

Bordo, Michael D., and Carlos A. Vegh, 'What if Alexander Hamilton had been Argentinian? A Comparison of the Early Monetary Experiences of Argentina and the United States', NBER Working Paper W6862, Dec 1998

Buckle, Robert, Kunhong Kim, Heather Kirkham, Nathan McLellan and Jared Sharma, 'Trade, Climate and Financial Influences on Macroeconomic Fluctuations: Analysis Using a SVAR model of the New Zealand Economy', New Zealand Treasury, draft paper, Jun 2002

Cameron, R., and P. Duignan, 'Government Owned Enterprises: Theory, Performance and Efficiency', paper to NZ Association of Economists Conference, 1984

Carpinter, Paul, 'Trade, Protection and Growth: The New Zealand Experience', paper to ANZAAS conference, 1979

Collins, M. A., 'Review of the Treasury Costings of Labour Party Policies', State Services Commission, 1994

Coopers and Lybrand, 'District Treasury Offices: Survey', 1987

Dalziel, Paul, 'The April 1st Benefit Cuts', in Henry Lang Papers, MS-Papers-99-032-2, ATL

Della Paolera, Gerardo, and Alan M. Taylor, 'Finance and Development in an Emerging Market: Argentina in the Interwar Period', National Bureau of Economic Research Working Paper 6236, Oct 1997

Easton, Brian, 'Two Economic Lieutenants', paper to 'Holyoake's Lieutenants' conference, Stout Centre, VUW, 2001

Endres, Anton M, 'Economic Thought and Policy Advice in New Zealand 1927–35: Accommodating a Tradition of Policy Activism', Work in Progress, no. 32, Economics Department, University of Auckland, Mar 1987

Endres, Anton, and Grant Fleming, 'Monetary Thought and the Analysis of Price Stability in Early Twentieth Century New Zealand', Working Papers in Economics, no. 139, Economics Department, University of Auckland, 1994

Fancy, Howard, 'Budgeting in an MMP Environment', paper delivered to seminar, Institute of Policy Studies, VUW, 1995

Fleming, Grant, 'Some Neglected Questions on the "Professionalisation" of Economics', Economics Department, University of Auckland, 1988

Fleming, Grant, 'The Political Economy of Agricultural Credit in New Zealand in the 1920s', Economics Department, University of Auckland, 1990

Fleming, Grant, 'The Role of Economists in New Zealand Policy Making, 1912–1951: Economic Advice Structures in Development', Economics Department, University of Auckland, 1989

Fougere, G., 'The Last Fifty Years: Paradoxes of Import-substituting Industrialisation', Department of Sociology, University of Canterbury, 1981

Gavin, J. C., 'Memoir', courtesy of Donald Hay, Karori, Wellington

Gregory, R. J., 'Getting Better but Feeling Worse? Public Sector Reform in New Zealand', paper to International Public Management Workshop, Wellington, March 2000

Hazledine, Tim, 'Agency Theory Meets Social Capital: The Failure of the 1984–91 New Zealand Economic Revolution', Economics Department, University of Auckland, Jun 2000

Hazledine, Tim, 'The New Zealand Economic Revolution After Ten Years', Working Paper no. 161, Economics Department, University of Auckland, Nov 1996

Jensen, Gwenda, 'The New Zealand Treasury: Zen and the Art of Budget Management', School of Accounting and Commercial Law, VUW, 2001

Lissington, M. P., 'Early Years', Treasury, Wellington, 1987

Lissington, M. P., 'The 1984 Devaluation and Inquiry', Treasury, Wellington, 1987

Martin, John E., 'Honouring the Contract: State Policy and Labour in New Zealand', Ministry for Culture and Heritage, Wellington

Novitz, R., 'Treasury: A Sociological Analysis', paper to NZ Sociological Association, Palmerston North, 1987

Philpott, Bryan, 'Productivity Growth by Type of Farming, 1972–93', Research Project on Economic Planning Paper no. 259, VUW, 1994

Price Waterhouse Associates, 'Report on a Job Evaluation and Salary Relativity Study for Economic and Financial Analysis Occupational Class of the SSC', Wellington, 1985

Savage, John, 'What Do We Know About the Economic Impact of the ECA?', NZIER Working Paper 96/9, May 1996

Savage, John, and David Cooling, 'A Preliminary Report on the Results of a Survey of the ECA', NZIER Working Paper 96/7, Mar 1996

Scobie, Grant, 'So We'd Like Better Economic Growth?', Treasury in-house paper, 7 Nov 2001

Scott, Graham, 'Ensuring the Quality of Policy Advice', Address to AIC Conference, 'Evaluation in the Public Sector', Jul 1992

Scott, Graham, 'Presentation to Treasury Managers', Treasury, 9 Apr 1991

Scott, Graham, 'Reflections on Managing the Treasury', Treasury, 1992

Shallcrass, Richard, autobiographical manuscript

Skilling, David, 'Whither Leviathan? An Essay on the Size of Government and Economic Growth', Treasury in-house paper, 4 Apr 2002

State Services Commission, 'Report of the Committee of Inquiry into the Staffing Problems of Treasury', Nov 1984

Stout Research Centre, VUW/Former Parliamentarians' Association, 'Holyoake's Lieutenants' Parliamentary Conference, 27–28 Apr 2001, notes from

Stout Research Centre, VUW/Former Parliamentarians' Association, 'Revisiting Muldoon' Parliamentary Conference, 3–4 May 2002, notes and papers from

Treasury, 'State-Owned Enterprise: A History of Policy Development and Implementation', Treasury internal working paper, Sep 1996

Wallis, J. L., and B. E. Dollery, 'A Comparative Examination of Cultural Change within the Australian and New Zealand Treasuries', paper accepted for publication in *International Review of Public Administration*, vol. 8, no. 1, 2003

Select bibliography

Webster, M., 'A Study of the Evolution of the New Zealand Public Service since 1935', unpublished paper, VUW, 1989

Official publications

Appendix to the Journals of the House of Representatives (*AJHR*), especially B series (public finance)
Audit Office, *Report of the Controller and Auditor-General on Financial Management and Control in Administrative Government Departments*, Wellington, 1978
Audit Office, *Report of the Controller and Auditor-General: First Report of 1988 Covering Companies, Corporations and Statutory Boards and Other Matters*, Wellington, 1988
Audit Office, *Financial Management Reforms*, Wellington, 1994
Birch, W. F., *Budget and Fiscal Strategy Report 1995*, Treasury, Wellington, 1995
Birch, W. F., *Pre-Election Economic and Fiscal Update*, New Zealand Government, Wellington, 1996
Coates, J. G., *The Reserve Bank of New Zealand and the Gold Question*, Government Printer, Wellington, 1933
Commonwealth of Australia, *Parliamentary Papers: General*
Crown Proposals for the Settlement of Treaty of Waitangi Claims: Summary, Department of Justice, Wellington, 1994
Douglas, Roger, *Statement on Government Expenditure Reform*, May 1986
Douglas, Roger, *Statement on Taxation and Benefit Reform*, Aug 1985
Report of the Economic Stabilization Conference, Government Printer, Wellington, 1940
Finance and Expenditure Committee, *Report on the Public Finance Bill, 1989*, House of Representatives, Wellington, 1989
Finance and Expenditure Committee, *Report of the Finance and Expenditure Committee on the Fiscal Responsibility Bill*, House of Representatives, Wellington, 1994
New Zealand Monetary and Economic Council, *Reports*, 1961–1977
New Zealand Official Yearbook
New Zealand Parliamentary Debates
Oliver, W. H., 'Social Policy in New Zealand: An Historical Overview', *AJHR*, 1988, H-2, pp. 89–92
Organisation for Economic Co-operation and Development (OECD), *Reports*
Public Expenditure Committee, 'Report on Inquiry into Devaluation', *AJHR*, 1984, I-12C
Report of the Royal Commission on Money, Banking, and Credit Systems, *AJHR*, 1956, B-3
Report of Royal Commission on State Services, *AJHR*, 1962, H-41
Reserve Bank of New Zealand, Annual report, *AJHR*, B-16, –1989
Treasury, Annual report, *AJHR*, B-27, 1988–
Treasury, *Financial Planning and Control: Report of the Study Group on Treasury Procedures*, Government Printer, Wellington, 1967
Williams, Robin, et al, *Report of the Committee of Enquiry into the Staffing Problems of Treasury*, State Services Commission, Wellington, 1984

Books, articles and theses

Abramovitz, M., *Thinking About Growth, and Other Essays on Economic Growth and Welfare*, Cambridge University Press, Cambridge, 1989

Aimer, Peter, *Wings of the Nation: A History of the New Zealand National Airways Corporation*, Bush Press, Takapuna, Auckland, 2000

Aitken, Judith, 'Public Expenditure Planning in New Zealand', PhD thesis, VUW, 1983

Akerlof, George, 'The Market for "Lemons": Quality, Uncertainty and the Market Mechanism', *Quarterly Journal of Economics*, vol. 48, no. 3, 1970, pp. 488–500

Armstrong, Mark, Simon Cowan and John Vickers, *Regulatory Reform: Economic Analysis and British Experience*, MIT Press, Cambridge, Mass., 1994

Armstrong, Sir William, *Some Practical Problems in Demand Management*, Athlone Press, London, 1969

Arnold, Margaret, 'The Market for Finance in Late Nineteenth Century New Zealand with Special Reference to Rural Mortgages', MA thesis, VUW, 1981

Baker, J. V. T., *War Economy*, Historical Publications Branch, Department of Internal Affairs, Wellington, 1965

Baker, J. V. T., and H. G. Lang, 'Economic Policy and National Income', *NZOYB*, 1950, pp. 1033–89

Ball, Ian, *Measuring the Cost of Government Services*, Planning Paper no. 1, NZ Planning Council, Wellington, 1981

Ball, Ian, 'Reinventing Government: Lessons Learned from the New Zealand Treasury', *Government Accountants Journal*, Fall 1994, pp. 19–28

Ball, Ian, 'The New Approach: Financial Management Reform', *Accountants' Journal*, vol. 71, no. 5, 1992, pp. 17–21

Bassett, Judith, *Sir Harry Atkinson, 1831–1892*, AUP/OUP, Auckland, 1975

Bassett, Michael, *Coates of Kaipara*, AUP, Auckland, 1995

Bassett, Michael, *Sir Joseph Ward: A Political Biography*, AUP, Auckland, 1993

Bassett, Michael, *The Mother of All Departments: The History of the Department of Internal Affairs*, AUP, Auckland, 1997

Bassett, Michael, *The State in New Zealand, 1840–1984: Socialism Without Doctrines?*, AUP, Auckland, 1998

Bassett, Michael, with Michael King, *Tomorrow Comes the Song: A Life of Peter Fraser*, Penguin, Auckland, 2000

Bayliss, Len, *Prosperity Mislaid: Economic Failure in New Zealand and What Should Be Done About It*, GP Publications, Wellington, 1994

Beer, Samuel, *Treasury Control: The Co-ordination of Financial and Economic Policy in Great Britain*, Clarendon, Oxford, 1957

Bell, Stephen, and Brian Head (eds), *State, Economy and Public Policy in Australia*, OUP, Melbourne, 1994

Belich, James, *Paradise Reforged: A History of the New Zealanders from the 1880s to the Year 2000*, Penguin, Auckland, 2001

Belshaw, Horace, *Immigration: Problems and Policies*, Wright and Carman, Wellington, 1952

Benda, Harry, 'Bureaucrats and Politicians', *NZJPA*, vol. 13, no. 1, Sep 1950, pp. 72–9

Bettison, David, 'Issues in Research: The "Exposed Hand" of Treasury', *New Zealand Sociology*, vol. 7, no. 2, Nov 1992, pp. 232–42

Birchfield, Reg, and Ian Grant, *Out of the Woods: The Restructuring and Sale of New Zealand's State Forests*, GP Publications, Wellington, 1993

Blanchard, Olivier, 'What Do We Know About Economics that Fisher and Wicksell Did Not?', *Quarterly Journal of Economics*, Nov 2000

Bloomfield, G. T., *New Zealand: A Handbook of Historical Statistics*, G. K. Hall, Boston, Mass., 1984

Bohan, Edmund, *'Blest Madman': FitzGerald of Canterbury*, Canterbury University Press, Christchurch, 1998

Bohan, Edmund, *Edward Stafford: New Zealand's First Statesman*, Hazard Press, Christchurch, 1994

Bohan, Edmund, *To Be a Hero: Sir George Grey, 1812–1898*, HarperCollins, Auckland, 1998

Boivin, V. G., 'The Professional Division: Its Composition and Needs', *NZJPA*, vol. 13, no. 2, Mar 1951, pp. 33–41

Bolger, James, *Bolger: A View from the Top: My Seven Years as Prime Minister*, Viking, Auckland, 1998

Bollard, Alan, and Robert Buckle (eds), *Economic Liberalisation in New Zealand*, Wellington, Allen and Unwin/PNP, 1987

Booth, Alan, 'The "Keynesian Revolution" in Economic Policy Making', *Economic History Review*, 2nd series, vol. 36, 1983, pp. 115–16

Boston, J., 'The Cabinet and Policymaking Under the Fourth Labour Government', in M. Holland and J. Boston (eds), *The Fourth Labour Government: Politics and Policy in New Zealand*, OUP, Auckland, 1990

Boston, J., 'Grand Designs and Unpleasant Realities: The Fate of the National Government's Proposals for the Integrated Targeting of Social Assistance', *Political Science*, vol. 46, no. 1, 1994, pp. 1–21

Boston, J., *Incomes Policy in New Zealand, 1968–1984*, VUP for Institute of Policy Studies, Wellington, 1984

Boston, J., 'New Zealand: "Cautionary Tale or Shining Example?"', in R. A. W. Rhodes and Patrick Weller (eds), *The Changing World of Top Officials: Mandarins or Valets?*, Open University Press, Buckingham/Philadelphia, 2001

Boston, J., 'Origins and Destinations: New Zealand's Model of Public Management and the International Transfer of Ideas', in G. Davis and P. Weller (eds), *New Ideas, Better Government*, Allen and Unwin, Sydney, 1995

Boston, J., 'Politicians and Public Servants: New Zealand Developments Since 1984', in M. Clark (ed.), *Constitutional Transformations, Intended and Unintended*, Social Science Research Fund Committee, Wellington, 1988

Boston, J., 'The Problems of Policy Coordination: The New Zealand Experience',

Governance, vol. 5, no. 1, 1992, pp. 88–103

Boston, J., 'Transforming New Zealand's Public Sector: Labour's Quest for Improved Accessibility and Accountability', *Public Administration*, vol. 65, 1987, pp. 423–42

Boston, J. (ed.), *The State Under Contract*, Bridget Williams Books, Wellington, 1995

Boston, J., Paul Dalziel and Susan St John, *Redesigning the Welfare State in New Zealand: Problems, Policies, Prospects*, OUP, Auckland, 1999

Boston, J., S. Levine, E. McLeay and N. Roberts (eds), *From Campaign to Coalition: New Zealand's First General Election Under Proportional Representation*, Dunmore Press, Palmerston North, 1997

Boston, J., S. Levine, E. McLeay and N. Roberts (eds), *New Zealand Under MMP: A New Politics?*, AUP/Bridget Williams Books, Auckland, 1996

Boston, J., J. Martin, J. Pallot and P. Walsh, *Public Management: The New Zealand Model*, OUP, Auckland, 1996

Boston, J., J. Martin, J. Pallot and P. Walsh, *Reshaping the State: New Zealand's Bureaucratic Revolution*, OUP, Auckland, 1991

Boyce, Simon, 'Imperial Bonds and Public Debt Management in New Zealand Between the Wars: An Analytic Study of Public Policy Subject Files', MA thesis, Massey University, 2002

Boyce, Simon, 'Nation-building Public Servants or Anglophile Bureaucrats?', *New Zealand Political Review*, vol. 10, no. 3, 2001, pp. 44–7

Bremner, E. R., and W. J. Wills, 'Organisation and Methods in New Zealand', *NZJPA*, vol. 16, no. 1, Sep 1953, pp. 15–23

Bridges, Edward, *The Treasury*, George Allen and Unwin, London, 1964

Bridges, Edward, *Treasury Control*, Athlone Press, London, 1950

Brittan, Samuel, *The Role and Limits of Government: Essays in Political Economy*, Temple Smith, Hounslow, England, 1983

Brittan, Samuel, *Steering the Economy*, Penguin, Harmondsworth, England, 1971

Brittan, Samuel, *The Treasury Under the Tories*, Penguin, Harmondsworth, England, 1964

Brooking, T. W. H., *A History of Dentistry in New Zealand*, New Zealand Dental Association, [Wellington], 1980

Brooking, T. W. H., *Lands for the People? The Highland Clearances and the Colonisation of New Zealand: A Biography of John McKenzie*, University of Otago Press, Dunedin, 1996

Brown, Ian, *The Creation of the Modern Ministry of Finance in Siam, 1885–1910*, Macmillan, London, 1992

Brown, J. Robert, Jr, *The Ministry of Finance: Bureaucratic Practices and the Transformation of the Japanese Economy*, Quorum Books, Westport, Conn., 1999

Brown, Richard, *A History of Accounting and Accountants*, Frank Cass, London, 1968 (a new impression of a 1905 publication)

Browning, Peter, *The Treasury and Economic Policy, 1964–1985*, Longman, London/New York, 1986

Brownlee, W. Elliot (ed.), *Funding the Modern American State, 1941–1995: The Rise and Fall of the Era of Easy Finance*, Woodrow Wilson Center Press, Washington DC;

Cambridge University Press, New York, 1996

Bryce, Robert B., *Maturing in Hard Times: Canada's Department of Finance through the Great Depression*, McGill-Queen's University Press, Kingston and Montreal, 1986

Buchanan, J., 'The Constitution of Economic Policy', *American Economic Review*, vol. 77, no. 3, 1987, pp. 243–50

Buchanan, J., 'From Private Preferences to Public Philosophy: The Development of Public Choice' in *The Economics of Politics*, seminar papers, Institute of Economic Affairs, London, 1978

Buchanan, James, and Richard E. Wagner, *Democracy in Deficit: The Political Legacy of Lord Keynes*, Academic Press, New York, 1977

Buckle, Robert A. (ed.), *Inflation and Economic Adjustment: Proceedings of a Seminar, 28 April 1993*, Department of Economics, VUW, Wellington, 1983

Burdon, R. M., *The New Dominion: A Social and Political History of New Zealand, 1918–39*, Allen and Unwin, London, 1965

Burk, Kathleen, 'The Treasury: From Impotence to Power', in Kathleen Burk (ed.), *War and the State: The Transformation of British Government 1914–1919*, George Allen and Unwin, London, 1982

Burk, Kathleen, and Alec Cairncross, *'Goodbye, Great Britain': The 1976 IMF Crisis*, Yale University Press, New Haven, Conn., 1992

Burkhead, Jesse, and Jerry Miner, *Public Expenditure*, Aldine and Atherton, Chicago, 1971

Bushnell, Peter, 'Policy Advice – Planning for Performance', *Public Sector*, vol. 14, 1991, pp. 14–16

Bushnell, Peter, 'Specifying Outputs', in *Managing Resources in the New Public Sector*, New Zealand Society of Accountants, Wellington, 1989

Bushnell, Peter, and Graham Scott, 'An Economic Perspective', in J. Martin and J. Harper (eds), *Devolution and Accountability*, Studies in Public Administration no. 34, NZ Institute of Public Administration, Wellington, 1988

Butlin, N. G., 'Trends in Public/Private Relations, 1901–75', in Stephen Bell and Brian Head (eds), *State and Economy in Australia*, OUP, Oxford, 1983

Butterworth, G. V., *Maori Affairs*, Iwi Transition Agency / GP Books, Wellington, 1990

Butterworth, G. V., and S. M. Butterworth, *Reforming Education: The New Zealand Experience, 1984–1996*, Dunmore Press, Palmerston North, 1998

Caiden, G. E. 'The State Services in New Zealand: Report of the Royal Commission of Inquiry 1962: A Critique', *NZJPA*, vol. 25, no. 2, Mar 1963, pp. 11–21

Cairncross, Alec (ed.), *Public Expenditure Management and Control*, Macmillan, London, 1978

Campbell, Peter, 'Politicians, Public Servants, and the People in New Zealand: I', *Political Studies*, vol. 3, no. 3, Oct 1955, pp. 193–210

Campbell, Peter, 'Politicians, Public Servants, and the People in New Zealand: II', *Political Studies*, vol. 4, no. 1, Feb 1956, pp. 18–29

Campbell, R., and A. Kirk, *After the Freeze: New Zealand Unions in the Economy*, PNP, Wellington, 1983

Campbell, R. M., *The Public Service Commission in Operation*, NZ Institute of Public Administration, Wellington, 1950

Cannadine, David, *Ornamentalism: How the British Saw Their Empire*, Penguin, London, 2001

Carey R. H. (ed.), *Foreign Investment Policy in New Zealand*, NZ Institute of Public Administration, Wellington, 1975

Castles, F., and S. Dowrick, 'The Impact of Government Spending Levels on Medium-Term Economic Growth in the OECD, 1960–1985', *Journal of Theoretical Politics*, vol. 2, no. 2, pp. 173–204

Castles, Francis G., Rolf Gerritsen and Jack Vowles (eds), *The Great Experiment: Labour Parties and Public Policy Transformation in Australia and New Zealand*, AUP, Auckland, 1996

Catt, Helena, 'The New Zealand Election of 1990', *Parliamentary Affairs: A Journal of Comparative Politics*, vol. 44, no. 3, Jul 1991

Chapman, H. S., 'On the Political Economy of Railways', *Transactions and Proceedings of the New Zealand Institute*, vol. 3, 1870, pp. 337–51

Chapman, Robert, 'A Political Culture Under Pressure: The Struggle to Preserve a Progressive Tax Base for Welfare and the Positive State', *Political Science*, vol. 44, no. 1, Jul 1992, pp. 1–27

Chappell, N. M., *New Zealand Banker's Hundred: A History of the Bank of New Zealand, 1861–1991*, Bank of New Zealand, Wellington, 1961

Chapple, Simon, *Full Employment: Whence It Came and Where It Went*, NZIER, Wellington, 1996

Clarida, Richard, J. Gali and M. Gertler, 'The Science of Monetary Policy: A New Keynesian Perspective', *Journal of Economic Literature*, vol. 37, Dec 1999

Clarke, Peter, *Hope and Glory: Britain, 1900–1990*, Penguin, London, 1996

Clarke, Peter, *The Keynesian Revolution in the Making, 1924–1936*, Clarendon, Oxford, 1988

Clarke, Sir R., *The Management of the Public Sector of the National Economy*, Athlone Press, London, 1964

Clarke, Sir R., *New Trends in Government*, HMSO, London, 1971

Clinkard, G. W., 'Wages and Working-Hours in New Zealand, 1897–1919', *NZOYB*, 1919, pp. 860–935

Coase, Ronald, *The Firm, the Market and the Law*, University of Chicago Press, Chicago, 1988

Coats, A. W., 'Britain: The Rise of the Specialists', *History of Political Economy*, vol. 13, no. 3, 1981, pp. 365–404

Coleman, Peter J., *Debtors and Creditors in America: Insolvency, Imprisonment for Debt and Bankruptcy, 1607–1900*, State Historical Society of Wisconsin, Madison, Wisc., 1974

Colgate, P., D. K. Sheppard, K. Guerin and G. R. Hawke (eds), *A History of the Bank of New Zealand 1862–1982, Part 1, 1862–1934*, Discussion Paper no. 7, Money and Finance Association, VUW, Wellington, 1990

Coller, Frank H., *A State Trading Adventure*, OUP, Oxford, 1925
Collins, Simon, *Rogernomics: Is There a Better Way?*, Pitman, Wellington, 1987
Condliffe, J. B., 'The External Trade of New Zealand', *NZOYB*, 1915, pp. 858–962
Condliffe, J. B., *New Zealand in the Making*, George Allen and Unwin, London, 1930
Cornwell, J. E. M., 'Some Notes on the Higher Public Service in New Zealand', *NZJPA*, vol. 23, no. 1, Sep 1960
Crisp, L. F., 'The Commonwealth Treasury's Changed Role and its Organisational Consequences', *Public Administration*, vol. 20, no. 4, Dec 1961, pp. 315–30
Dalton, B. J., *War and Politics in New Zealand, 1855–1870*, Sydney University Press, Sydney, 1967
Dalziel, Paul, 'The Rhetoric of Treasury: A Review of the 1990 Briefing Papers', *NZ Economic Papers*, vol. 25, no. 2, 1991, pp. 259–74
Dalziel, Paul, 'The Rhetoric of Treasury: Reply', *NZ Economic Papers*, vol. 27, no. 1, 1993, pp. 91–9
Dalziel, Raewyn, *Julius Vogel: Business Politician*, AUP, Auckland, 1986
Dalziel, R. M., *The Origins of New Zealand Diplomacy: The Agent-General in London, 1870–1905*, Price Milburn for VUP, Wellington, 1975
Danks, A. J., 'The Report of the Royal Commission on Monetary, Banking, and Credit Systems, 1956', *NZJPA*, vol. 19, no. 1, Sep 1956, pp. 3–8
David, Paul, 'Why Are Institutions the "Carriers" of History? Path Dependence and the Evolution of Conventions, Organizations and Institutions?', *Structural Change and Economic Dynamics*, vol. 5, no. 2, 1994, pp. 205–20
Davies, Gavyn, *Governments Can Affect Unemployment*, Employment Institute, London, 1985
Day, Patrick, *Voice and Vision: A History of Broadcasting in New Zealand*, vol. 2, AUP in association with the Broadcasting History Trust, Auckland, 2000
Deane, R. S., *Corporatisation and Privatisation: A Discussion of the Issues*, Electricity Corporation of New Zealand, Wellington, 1989
Deane, R. S., 'Monetary Policy: The Bare Elements', *Accountants' Journal*, Jul 1970
Deane, R. S., 'Reflections on Fiscal Policy', *New Zealand Economic Papers*, vol. 15, 1981, pp. 28–49
Deane, R. S., and R. G. Smith, *The Stabilisation Role of Fiscal Policy*, Planning Paper no. 5, NZ Planning Council, Wellington, 1980
Deeks, John, and Nick Perry (eds), *Controlling Interests: Business, the State and Society in New Zealand*, AUP, Auckland, 1992
Dell, Edmund, *The Chancellors: A History of the Chancellors of the Exchequer, 1945–90*, HarperCollins, London, 1996
Della Paolera, Gerardo, and Alan M. Taylor, 'Economic Recovery from the Argentine Great Depression: Institutions, Expectations and the Change of Macroeconomic Regime', *Journal of Economic History*, vol. 59, no. 3, Sep 1999, pp. 567–99
Demsetz, H., 'Toward a Theory of Property Rights', *American Economic Review*, May 1966, pp. 347–59

Dick, I. D., 'A Note on Graduates in Administration in the Public Service', *NZJPA*, vol. 20, no. 1, Sep 1957, pp. 87–91

Dobb, Maurice, *Theories of Value and Distribution Since Adam Smith: Ideology and Economic Theory*, Cambridge University Press, Cambridge, 1973

Dobb, Maurice, *Welfare Economics and the Economics of Socialism: Towards a Commonsense Critique*, Cambridge University Press, London, 1969

Doern, G. Bruce, and Peter Aucoin, *The Structures of Policy-Making in Canada*, Macmillan, Toronto, 1971

Douglas, Roger, 'The Politics of Successful Structural Reform', *Policy*, vol. 6, no. 1, 1990, pp. 2–6

Douglas, Roger, *There's Got to Be a Better Way! A Practical ABC to Solving New Zealand's Major Problems*, Fourth Estate Books, Wellington, 1980

Douglas, Roger, and Louise Callan, *Toward Prosperity: People and Politics in the 1980s, A Personal View*, David Bateman, Auckland, 1987

Downs, Anthony, *An Economic Theory of Democracy*, Harper and Row, New York, 1957

Duncan, Ian, and Alan Bollard, *Corporatization and Privatization: Lessons from New Zealand*, OUP, Auckland, 1992

Dunleavy, Patrick, *Democracy, Bureaucracy and Public Choice: Economic Explanations in Political Science*, Prentice Hall, New York, 1991

Dunsire, Andrew, and Christopher Hood, *Cutback Management in Public Bureaucracies: Popular Theories and Observed Outcomes in Whitehall*, Cambridge University Press, Cambridge, 1989

Easton, Brian, 'Bernard Ashwin: Secretary to the Nation Building State', *New Zealand Studies*, Nov 1997, pp. 13–21

Easton, Brian, *The Commercialisation of New Zealand*, AUP, Auckland, 1997

Easton, Brian, *Economics for New Zealand Social Democrats*, John McIndoe, Dunedin, 1981

Easton, Brian, *The Exchange Rate Since 1981: Performance and Policy*, Discussion Paper no. 30, NZIER, Wellington, 1986

Easton, Brian, 'From Reagonomics to Rogernomics', in Alan Bollard (ed.), *The Influence of United States Economics on New Zealand*, NZ–US Educational Foundation/NZIER, Wellington, 1989

Easton, Brian, 'How Did the Health Reforms Blitzkrieg Fail?', *Political Science*, vol. 46, no. 2, Dec 1994, pp. 215–33

Easton, Brian, *In Stormy Seas: The Post-War New Zealand Economy*, University of Otago Press, Dunedin, 1997

Easton, Brian, *The Nationbuilders*, AUP, Auckland, 2001

Easton, Brian, *Pragmatism and Progress: Social Security in the Seventies*, University of Canterbury, Christchurch, 1981

Easton, Brian, *The Whimpering of the State: Policy after MMP*, AUP, Auckland, 1999

Easton, Brian (ed.), *The Making of Rogernomics*, AUP, Auckland, 1989

Edwards, John, 'The Economy Game: Treasury and Its Rivals', *Current Affairs Bulletin* (Australia), vol. 51, no. 12, May 1975

Eichbaum, Chris, 'Reshaping the Reserve: The Political Economy of Central Banking in Australasia', PhD thesis, Massey University, 1999

Eichengreen, Barry, 'History of the International Monetary System: Implications for Research in International Macroeconomics and Finance', in Frederick van der Ploeg (ed.), *Handbook of International Macroeconomics*, Blackwell, Oxford, 1994

Eichengreen, B. J., 'The Origins and Nature of the Great Slump Revisited', *Economic History Review*, 2nd series, vol. 45, May 1992, pp. 212–39

Elbaum, B., and W. Lazonick (eds), *The Decline of the British Economy*, Clarendon, Oxford, 1986

Eldred-Grigg, Stevan, *The Rich: A New Zealand History*, Penguin, Auckland, 1996

Elkan, P. G., *Industrial Protection in New Zealand, 1952 to 1967*, Technical Memorandum no. 15, NZIER, Wellington, 1972

Elkan, P. G., *The Meaning of Protection*, Research Paper no. 21, NZIER, Wellington, 1977

Else, Anne, 'Doing the Dirty Washing: Women as Scapegoats of the New Right', *New Zealand Studies*, vol. 7, no. 2, Jul 1997, pp. 17–22

Else, Anne, *False Economy: New Zealanders Face the Conflict Between Paid and Unpaid Work*, Tandem Press, North Shore City, 1996

Endres, Anton M., 'The Political Economy of W. B. Sutch: Toward a Critical Appreciation', *New Zealand Economic Papers*, vol. 22, 1986, pp. 17–39

Engel, J. A. E., 'Cost and Result in the Public Service', *NZJPA*, vol. 13, no. 1, Sep 1950, pp. 24–35

Evans, Lewis, Arthur Grimes and Bryce Wilkinson, 'Economic Reform in New Zealand 1984–95: The Pursuit of Efficiency', *Journal of Economic Literature*, vol. 34, Dec 1996, pp. 1856–1902

Evans, Peter, Dietrich Rueschemeyer and Theda Skocpol (eds), *Bringing the State Back In*, Cambridge University Press, Cambridge, 1985

Ewing, I. S., 'Public Service Reform in New Zealand 1866–1912', MA thesis, University of Auckland, 1979

Fairburn, Miles, *The Ideal Society and Its Enemies: The Foundations of Modern New Zealand Society, 1850–1900*, AUP, Auckland, 1989

Fairburn, Miles, *Social History: Problems, Strategies and Methods*, St Martin's Press, New York, 1999

Farland, B. H., *Coates' Tale: War Hero, Politician, Statesman...*, B. Farland, Wellington, 1995

Farquhar, Ian, *Jack of All Trades, Master of None: The Shipping Corporation of New Zealand Limited, 1973–1989*, New Zealand Ship and Marine Society, Wellington, 1996

Ferguson, Gael, *Building the New Zealand Dream*, Dunmore Press, Palmerston North, 1994

Fischer, Patsy, *The New Zealand Planning Council: A Case Study*, Planning Paper no. 12, NZPC, Wellington, 1981

Fisher, A. G. B., 'The New Zealand Economic Problem: A Review', *The Economic Record*, May 1932, pp. 74–87

Fleming, Grant, 'Economic Thought and Policy Advice in New Zealand: Economists and the Agricultural Sector circa 1918–1939', PhD thesis, University of Auckland, 1993

Fleming, Grant, 'Keynes, Purchasing Power Parity and Exchange Rate Policy in New Zealand During the 1930s Depression', *NZ Economic Papers*, vol. 31, no. 1, 1997, pp. 1–14

Franklin, Harvey, *Cul de Sac: The Question of New Zealand's Future*, Allen and Unwin/PNP, Sydney/Wellington, 1985

Franklin, S. Harvey, *Trade, Growth, and Anxiety: New Zealand Beyond the Welfare State*, Methuen NZ, Wellington, 1978

Fraser, Peter, 'The Making of Economic Management: Continuity and Change at the New Zealand Treasury, 1968–1984', MCA thesis, VUW, 2000

Froude, James, *Oceana, or, England and Her Colonies*, Longmans, London, 1892

Furner, M. O., and B. E. Supple (eds), *The State and Economic Knowledge: The American and British Experiences*, Cambridge University Press, Cambridge, 1990

Galvin, B., *Policy Co-ordination, the Public Sector and Government*, Victoria University Press for Institute of Policy Studies, VUW, Wellington, 1991

Gamble, Andrew, *The Free Economy and the Strong State: The Politics of Thatcherism*, Macmillan Education, Basingstoke, England, 1988

Gardner, Wira, *Return to Sender: What Really Happened at the Fiscal Envelope Hui*, Reed, Auckland, 1996

Gauld, Robin, *Revolving Doors: New Zealand's Health Reforms*, Institute of Policy Studies, VUW, Wellington, 2001

Gold, Hyam (ed.), *New Zealand Politics in Perspective*, Longman Paul, Auckland, 1985 (2nd edn 1989, 3rd edn 1992)

Goldfinch, Shaun, 'Paradigms, Economic Ideas and Institutions in Economic Policy Change: The Case of New Zealand', *Political Science*, vol. 52, no. 1, Jun 2000, pp. 1–21

Goldfinch, Shaun, *Remaking New Zealand and Australian Economic Policy: Ideas, Institutions and Policy Communities*, VUP, Wellington, 2000

Goodwin, Craufurd, *Canadian Economic Thought: The Political Economy of a Developing Nation, 1814–1914*, Duke University Press, Durham, NC, 1961

Goodwin, Craufurd, *Economic Enquiry in Australia*, Duke University Press, Durham, NC, 1961

Goodwin, Craufurd, *The Image of Australia: British Perception of the Australian Economy from the Eighteenth to the Twentieth Century*, Duke University Press, Durham, NC, 1974

Gorringe, Peter, *Economics for Policy: Expanding the Boundaries*, Institute of Policy Studies, VUW, Wellington, 2001

Gould, John, *The Muldoon Years: An Essay on New Zealand's Recent Economic Growth*, Hodder and Stoughton, Auckland, 1985

Graham, Alan W., *The First Fifty Years, 1909–1959*, New Zealand Society of Accountants, Wellington, 1960

Graham, J., *Frederick Weld*, AUP/OUP, Auckland, 1983

Grant, David, *Bulls, Bears and Elephants: A History of the New Zealand Stock Exchange*, VUP, Wellington, 1997

Green, David, *Statistics Count: An Illustrated History of Statistics New Zealand*, Statistics New Zealand, Wellington, 2002

Gregory, R. G., *Labour Market Outcomes in the UK, NZ, Australia and the US: Observations on the Impact of Labour Market and Economic Reforms*, Australian National University, Canberra, 1999

Gregory, R. J., 'Post-Reform Attitudes of New Zealand's Senior Public Servants: A Follow-Up Study', *Political Science*, vol. 47, no. 2, Dec 1995, pp. 161–90

Gregory, R. J., *Reserve Bank Independence, Political Responsibility, and the Goals of Anti-Democratic Policy*, VUW, Wellington, 1996

Gregory, R. J., 'Understanding Public Bureaucracy', *Public Sector*, vol. 4, nos 2–3, 1982, pp. 3–12

Guest, Morris, 'The Murupara Project: The Tasman Pulp and Paper Company Ltd and Industrial Development in New Zealand 1945–1963', MA thesis, VUW, 1997

Gustafson, Barry, *From the Cradle to the Grave: A Biography of Michael Joseph Savage*, Reed Methuen, Auckland, 1986

Gustafson, Barry, *His Way: A Biography of Robert Muldoon*, AUP, Auckland, 2000

Haidar, A., 'Weber, Westminster and Wellington', *Public Sector*, vol. 9, nos 3/4, Mar 1987, pp. 23–8

Hall, Peter A., *Governing the Economy: The Politics of State Intervention in Britain and France*, Polity Press, Cambridge, 1986

Hall, Peter A., 'Policy Paradigms, Experts, and the State: The Case of Macroeconomic Policy-Making in Britain', in S. Brooks and A. Gagnon (eds), *Social Scientists, Policy, and the State*, Praeger, New York, 1990

Hall, Peter A. (ed.), *The Political Power of Economic Ideas: Keynesianism Across Nations*, Princeton University Press, Princeton, 1989

Hall, Peter A., 'The Role of Interests, Institutions, and Ideas in the Comparative Political Economy of the Industrialized Nations', in Mark Irving Lichbach and Alan S. Zuckerman (eds), *Comparative Politics: Rationality, Culture, and Structure*, Cambridge University Press, Cambridge, 1997

Hall, Peter A., and Rosemary Taylor, 'Political Science and Three New Institutionalisms', *Political Studies*, vol. 44, 1996, pp. 936–57

Ham, Adrian, *Treasury Rules: Recurrent Themes in British Economic Policy*, Quartet Books, London, 1981

Hamer, D. A., *The New Zealand Liberals: The Years of Power, 1891–1912*, AUP, Auckland, 1988

Hames, Martin, *Winston First: The Unauthorised Account of Winston Peters' Career*, Random House, Auckland, 1995

Hanson, Elizabeth, *The Politics of Social Security: The 1938 Act and Some Later Developments*, AUP, Auckland, 1980

Harris, Peter, 'Rogernomics, the "Washington Consensus" and New Zealand Economic Policy', in Srikanta Chatterjee et al, *The New Politics: A Third Way for New Zealand*, Dunmore Press, Palmerston North, 1999

Hart, Oliver, 'An Economist's Perspective on the Theory of Firm', *Columbia Law Review*, vol. 89, 1989, pp. 157–74

Hawke, G. R., *Between Governments and Banks: A History of the Reserve Bank of New Zealand*, Government Printer, Wellington, 1973

Hawke, G. R., 'Economic Decisions and Political Ossification', in Peter Munz (ed.), *The Feel of Truth*, Price Milburn for Victoria University, Wellington, 1969

Hawke, G. R., *Law and Economic Development: The Case of New Zealand*, Working Paper in Economic History no. 83/1, VUW, Mar 1983

Hawke, G. R., *The Making of New Zealand: An Economic History*, Cambridge University Press, Cambridge, 1985

Hawke, G. R., and Richard B. Baker (eds), *ANZUS Economics: Economic Trends and Relations Among Australia, New Zealand, and the United States*, Praeger, Westport, Conn., 1992

Hayek, F. A. von, 'Scientism and the Study of Society', *Economica*, Aug 1942, Feb 1943, Feb 1944

Heclo, Hugh, and Aaron Wildavsky, *The Private Government of Public Money: Community and Government inside British Politics*, Macmillan, London, 1974

Henderson, Alan, *The Quest for Efficiency: The Origins of the State Services Commission*, Historical Branch, Dept of Internal Affairs/State Services Commission, Wellington, 1990

Hennessy, Peter, *Whitehall*, Secker and Warburg, London, 1989

Herron, David, 'The Structure and Course of New Zealand Politics, 1853–1858', PhD thesis, University of New Zealand, 1959

Hill, R. J. M., 'The Quest for Control: The New Zealand Dairy Industry and the Guaranteed Price, 1921–36', MA thesis, University of Auckland, 1974

Hill, Richard S., *The History of Policing in New Zealand, vol. 2: The Colonial Frontier Tamed: New Zealand Policing in Transition, 1867–1886*, Historical Publications Branch, Department of Internal Affairs and Government Printer, Wellington, 1989

Hill, Richard S., *The History of Policing in New Zealand, vol. 3: The Iron Hand in the Velvet Glove: The Modernisation of Policing in New Zealand, 1886–1917*, Dunmore Press, Palmerston North, 1995

Hirschman, A. O., *The Passions and the Interests: Political Arguments for Capitalism Before Its Triumph*, Princeton University Press, Princeton, 1977

Hirschman, A. O., *Shifting Involvements: Private Interest and Public Action*, Princeton University Press, Princeton, 1982

Holmes, Frank, 'Three Labour Leaders: Their Economic and Educational Policies', in Margaret Clark (ed.), *Three Labour Leaders: Nordmeyer, Kirk, Rowling*, Dunmore Press, Palmerston North, 2001, pp. 201–13

Holt, L., 'Public Finance and Control of Investment in New Zealand', *Economic Record*, supplement to vol. 15, 1939, pp. 58–68

Holt, Richard, *Second Amongst Equals: Chancellors of the Exchequer and the British Economy*, Profile Books, London, 2001

Horn, Murray, *The Political Economy of Public Administration*, Cambridge University Press, Cambridge/New York, 1995

Howe, K. R., *Singer in a Songless Land: A Life of Edward Tregear, 1846–1931*, AUP, Auckland, 1991

Select Bibliography

Immergut, Ellen, 'The Theoretical Core of the New Institutionalism', *Politics and Society*, vol. 26, no. 1, 1998, pp. 5–34

James, Colin, *New Territory: The Transformation of New Zealand 1984–92*, Bridget Williams Books, Wellington, 1992

James, Colin, *The Quiet Revolution: Turbulence and Transition in Contemporary New Zealand*, Allen and Unwin/PNP, Wellington, 1986

Jesson, Bruce, *Behind the Mirror Glass: The Growth of Wealth and Power in New Zealand in the Eighties*, Penguin, Auckland, 1987

Jesson, Bruce, *Fragments of Labour: The Story Behind the Labour Government*, Penguin, Auckland, 1989

Jesson, Bruce, 'New Zealand's Hard Labour', *New Left Review*, no. 192, Mar/Apr 1992

Jesson, Bruce, *Only Their Purpose is Mad: The Money Men Take Over New Zealand*, Dunmore Press, Palmerston North, 1999

Johns, Ian, 'Efficiency in Government: The Changing Role of the Central Administrative Agencies, 1962–1978', *Public Sector Research Papers*, vol. 1, no. 2, parts I, II, 1979

Johnson, A. W., 'The Treasury Board of Canada and the Machinery of Government of the 1970s', *Canadian Journal of Political Science*, vol. 4, no. 3, Sep 1971, pp. 346–66

Johnson, Harry, and Elizabeth Johnson (eds), *In the Shadow of Keynes*, Basil Blackwell, Oxford, 1978

Johnston, Jeanette, and Adrienne von Tunzelmann, *The State in Business: Public Enterprise in New Zealand*, Planning Paper no. 15, New Zealand Planning Council and State Services Commission, Wellington, Sep 1982

Juddery, Bruce, *At the Centre: The Australian Bureaucracy in the 1970s*, Cheshire, Melbourne, 1974

Kagel, J. H., R. C. Battalio, H. Rachlin and L. Green, 'Demand Curves for Animal Consumers', *Quarterly Journal of Economics*, vol. 96, no. 1, Feb 1981, pp. 1–15

Kelsey, Jane, *The New Zealand Experiment: A World Model for Structural Adjustment?*, Bridget Williams Books/AUP, Auckland, 1997

Kelsey, Jane, '"Selling off New Zealand" … and Claiming it Back', *New Zealand Studies*, vol. 7, no. 2, Jul 1997, pp. 3–8

Keohane, Robert, and Helen Milner (eds), *Internationalization and Domestic Politics*, Cambridge University Press, Cambridge, 1996

Kerr, Roger, 'Myths About Economic Reform', in New Zealand Business Roundtable, *Can New Zealand Afford to Replay the Economic Past?*, New Zealand Business Roundtable, Wellington, 2000

Klamer, A., D. N. McCloskey and R. M. Solow (eds), *The Consequences of Economic Rhetoric*, Cambridge University Press, Cambridge, 1988

Klein, Herbert S., *The American Finances of the Spanish Empire: Royal Income and Expenditures in Colonial Mexico, Peru, and Bolivia, 1680–1809*, University of New Mexico Press, Albuquerque, 1998

Krasner, Steven, 'Approaches to the State: Alternative Conceptions and Historical Dynamics', *Comparative Politics*, vol. 16, no. 2, Jan 1984, pp. 223–46

Kuttner, Robert, *'Everything for Sale': The Virtues and Limits of Markets*, Knopf, New York, 1997

Kynaston, David, *The City of London: A World of its Own, 1815–1890*, Chatto and Windus, London, 1994

Kynaston, David, *The City of London: Golden Years, 1890–1914*, Chatto and Windus, London, 1995

Kynaston, David, *The City of London: Illusions of Gold, 1914–1945*, Chatto and Windus, London, 1999

Kynaston, David, *The City of London: A Club No More, 1945–2000*, Chatto and Windus, London, 2001

Laking, Rob, *A New Approach to Financial Management*, NZ Institute of Public Administration, Wellington, 1969

Laking, Rob, 'Social Policy and the Future of Bureaucracy', in A. von Tunzelmann and J. Johnston (eds), *Responding to the Revolution: Careers, Culture and Casualties*, GPO Publishing, Wellington, 1987

Lang, H. G., 'Policy Making in New Zealand', *NZJPA*, vol. 13, no. 2, Mar 1951, pp. 25–32

Lang, H. G., 'The Relationship Between Economic and Foreign Policy', *New Zealand Foreign Affairs Review*, vol. 23, no. 8, Aug 1973, pp. 16–25

Lang, H. G., 'The Role of Treasury: Control and Advice', *Canterbury Chamber of Commerce Economic Bulletin*, no. 610, 1977

Lang, K., 'Trade Liberalisation and the New Zealand Labour Market', Research Monograph no. 53, NZIER, Wellington, 1989

Laws, Michael, *The Demon Profession*, HarperCollins, Auckland, 1998

Legat, Nicola, 'The New Anatomy of Power', *Metro*, Oct 1991

Le Rossignol, J. E., and W. Downie Stewart, *State Socialism in New Zealand*, Harrap, London, 1910

Lindblom, C., *Politics and Markets: The World's Political-Economic Systems*, Basic Books, New York, 1977

Lipsey, David, *The Secret Treasury*, Viking, London, 2000

Lipsey, R. G., 'The Understanding and Control of Inflation: Is There a Crisis in Macro-Economics?', *Canadian Journal of Economics*, vol. 14, no. 4, Nov 1981, pp. 545–76

McCloskey, Donald, *The Rhetoric of Economics*, University of Wisconsin Press, Madison, 1985

McClure, Margaret, *A Civilised Community: A History of Social Security in New Zealand, 1898–1998*, AUP, Auckland, 1998

McCulloch, B., and I. Ball, 'Accounting in the Context of Financial Management Reform', *Financial Accountability and Management*, vol. 8, no. 1, 1992, pp. 7–12

Macdonagh, Oliver, 'The Nineteenth Century Revolution in Government: A Reappraisal', *Historical Journal*, vol. 1, no. 1, 1958, pp. 52–67

Macdonald, Barrie, and David Thomson, 'Mortgage Relief, Farm Finance, and Rural Depression in New Zealand in the 1930s', *NZJH*, vol. 21, no. 2, Oct 1987, pp. 228–50

McGee, David, *Parliamentary Practice in New Zealand*, GP Publications, Wellington, 1994

McGill, David, *The Guardians at the Gate: The History of the New Zealand Customs Department*, Silver Owl Press for NZ Customs Department, Wellington, 1991

McGregor, A., 'Control of Public Expenditure in New Zealand', *JPA*, vol. 8, no. 1, Sep 1945, pp. 21–35

McGregor, A., 'The Government Financial Year', *NZJPA*, vol. 15, no. 2, Mar 1953

McIntyre, W. D. (ed.), *The Journal of Henry Sewell, 1853–7*, vol. 2, Whitcoulls, Christchurch, 1980

McIntyre, W. D., and Marcia McIntyre (eds), *Tour of Duty: Midshipman Comber's Journal Aboard HMS Herald on the East India Station – Australia, New Zealand and China, 1838–42*, University of Canterbury, Christchurch, 1999

McIvor, Tim, *The Rainmaker: A Biography of John Ballance*, Heinemann Reed, Auckland, 1989

Mackay, A. R. F., 'New Zealand Public Finance', PhD thesis, University of London, 1935 (copy in Treasury library)

Mackay, A. R. F., 'The Treasury as a Co-ordinating Factor in Public Service Administration', *JPA*, vol. 1, no. 1, May 1938, pp. 85–91

McKinlay, Peter, *Corporatisation: The Solution for State Owned Enterprise?*, VUP for Institute of Policy Studies, VUW, Wellington, 1987

McLeod, Roy (ed.), *Government, Expertise and Specialists: Administrators and Professionals, 1860–1916*, Cambridge University Press, Cambridge, 1985

McLintock, A. H., *Crown Colony Government in New Zealand*, Government Printer, Wellington, 1958

McRae, Tom, *A Parliament in Crisis: The Decline of Democracy in New Zealand*, Shieldaig Publications, Wellington, 1994

Mabbett, Deborah, 'Reassessing Protectionism', *Victoria Economic Commentaries*, vol. 17, no. 1, Mar 2000, pp. 11–16

Mabbett, Deborah, *Trade, Employment, and Welfare: A Comparative Study of Trade and Labour Market Policies in Sweden and New Zealand, 1880–1980*, Clarendon, Oxford, 1995

Maier, Charles (ed.), *Changing Boundaries of the Political: Essays on the Evolving Balance Between the State and Society, Public and Private in Europe*, Cambridge University Press, Cambridge, 1987

Maloney, Tim, *Benefit Reforms and Labour Market Behaviour in New Zealand*, Institute of Policy Studies, VUW, Wellington, 1997

Mankiw, N. Gregory, and David Romer (eds), *New Keynesian Economics*, MIT Press, Cambridge, Mass., 1991

Mannheim, Karl, *Ideology and Utopia: An Introduction to the Sociology of Knowledge*, Routledge and Kegan Paul, London, 1960

Martin, John, *A Profession of Statecraft? Three Essays on Some Current Issues in the New Zealand Public Service*, VUP for Institute of Policy Studies, Wellington, 1988

Martin, John E., *Holding the Balance: A History of New Zealand's Department of Labour, 1891–1995*, Canterbury University Press, Christchurch, 1996

Martin, John E. (ed.), *People, Politics and Power Stations: Electric Power Generation in New Zealand, 1880–1998*, Electricity Corporation of New Zealand and Historical Branch, Department of Internal Affairs, Wellington, 1998

Martin, Samuel, *New Zealand in a Series of Letters*, Simmonds and Ward, London, 1845 (copy held at ATL)

Mascarenhas, R. C., *Public Enterprise in New Zealand*, NZ Institute of Public Administration, Wellington, 1982

Massey, Patrick, *New Zealand: Market Liberalization in a Developed Economy*, St Martin's Press, New York, 1995

Maughan, William, *Good and Faithful Servants*, Waiata and Imperial Publishing Co., Feilding, 1974

Middleton, Roger, *Government versus the Market: The Growth of the Public Sector, Economic Management, and British Economic Performance, c. 1890–1979*, Edward Elgar, Cheltenham, England / Brookfield, VT, 1996

Middleton, Roger, *Towards the Managed Economy: Keynes, the Treasury and the Fiscal Policy Debate of the 1930s*, Methuen, London, 1985

Millar, F. W., 'Women of the Public Service: Their Background and Future', *JPA*, vol. 6, no. 2, Mar 1944, pp. 27–32

Miller, Gary, and Thomas Hammond, 'Why Politics is More Fundamental than Economics: Incentive-Compatible Mechanisms are not Credible', *Journal of Theoretical Politics*, vol. 6, no. 1, 1994, pp. 5–26

Miller, R. (ed.), *New Zealand Politics in Transition*, OUP, Auckland, 1997

Millward, R., 'The Comparative Performance of the Public and Private Ownership', in E. Roll (ed.), *The Mixed Economy*, Macmillan, London, 1982

Mitchell, Austin, *Politics and People in New Zealand: Studies*, Whitcombe and Tombs, Christchurch, 1969

Moe, Terry, 'Political Institutions: The Neglected Side of the Story', *Journal of Law, Economics and Organization*, vol. 6, 1990, pp. 213–53

Moe, Terry, 'The Politics of Structural Choice: Toward a Theory of Public Bureaucracy', in O. E. Williamson (ed.), *Organization Theory: From Chester Barnard to the Present and Beyond*, OUP, New York, 1990

Mommsen, W. J. (ed.), *The Emergence of the Welfare State in Britain and Germany, 1850–1950*, Croom Helm, London, 1981

Monetary and Economic Council, *Economic Growth in New Zealand*, Monetary and Economic Council, Wellington, 1962

Moriarty, M. J., 'Administering the Policy of Economic Stabilization', *JPA*, vol. 7, no. 2, 1945, pp. 27–37

Moriarty, M. J., 'Making Economic Policy in New Zealand', *Economic Record*, vol. 32, 1956, pp. 224–38

Moriarty, M. J., 'Pressure Groups', *NZJPA*, vol. 13, no. 2, Mar 1951, pp. 16–24

Mueller, Dennis C. (ed.), *The Political Economy of Growth*, Yale University Press, New Haven, 1983

Select bibliography

Muldoon, R. D., *The New Zealand Economy: A Personal View*, Endeavour Press, Auckland, 1985

Muldoon, R. D., *The Rise and Fall of a Young Turk*, A. H. and A.W. Reed, Wellington, 1974

Murray, Georgina, 'New Zealand Corporate Capitalism', PhD thesis, University of Auckland, 1989

Musgrave, R. A., *Fiscal Systems*, Yale University Press, New Haven, 1969

Musgrave, R. A., *The Theory of Public Finance: A Study in Public Economy*, McGraw Hill Kogakusha, Tokyo, 1959

Nagel, Jack H., Editor's Introduction, *Journal of Policy Analysis and Management*, vol. 16, no. 3, 1997, pp. 349–56

Nethercote, J. R., B. Galligan and C. Walsh (eds), *Decision-Making in New Zealand Government*, Federalism Research Centre, Australian National University/Institute of Policy Studies, VUW, and State Services Commission, Canberra, 1993

New Zealand Institute of Public Administration, 'The Public Service as a Profession', *NZJPA*, vol. 15, no. 1, Sep 1952

New Zealand Planning Council, Report no. 22, *The Public Sector: An Overview*, Wellington, New Zealand Planning Council, Sep 1982

New Zealand Planning Council, Economic Monitoring Group, *The Government Deficit and the Economy*, New Zealand Planning Council, Wellington, 1984

Nicholl, Peter, 'Opening the Books: A Response', *New Zealand Economic Papers*, vol. 19, 1985, pp. 117–22

Nightingale, Tony, *Mobil, Proud of Our Past, Committed to the Future: 100 Years in New Zealand*, Mobil Oil NZ, Wellington, 1996

Noonan, Rosslyn J., *By Design: A Brief History of the Public Works Department/Ministry of Works 1870–1970*, Government Printer, Wellington, 1975

Norman, Bob, *You Can't Win 'Em All: Confessions of a Public Works Engineer*, Slide Rule Press, Porirua, 1997

Norman, Richard, *Accounting for Government*, Cases in Public Sector Innovation, no. 1, VUW, 1997

North, Douglass C., *Institutions, Institutional Change and Economic Performance*, Cambridge University Press, New York, 1990

O'Brien, P. K., 'Britain's Economy Between the Wars: A Survey of a Counter-Revolution in Economic History', *Past and Present*, no. 115, May 1988, pp. 107–30

O'Connor, James, *The Fiscal Crisis of the State*, St Martin's Press, New York, 1973

Offe, C., *Contradictions of the Welfare State*, Hutchinson, London, 1984

Oliver, Michael J., *Whatever Happened to Monetarism? Economic Policy-Making and Social Learning in the United Kingdom Since 1979*, Ashgate, Aldershot, Hants/Brookfield, VT, 1997

Oliver, W. H., 'Social Policy in the Liberal Period', *NZJH*, vol. 13, no. 1, Apr 1979, pp. 25–33

Oliver, W. H., *Towards a New History?*, Hocken Library, University of Otago, Dunedin, 1971

Oliver, W. Hugh, 'The New Zealand Labour Party and the Rise of "Rogernomics", 1981–1984', MA thesis, Massey University, 1987

Olson, Mancur, *The Logic of Collective Action: Public Goods and the Theory of Groups*, Harvard University Press, Cambridge, Mass., 1965

Olson, Mancur, *Power and Prosperity: Outgrowing Communist and Capitalist Dictatorships*, Basic Books, New York, 2000

Olson, Mancur, *The Rise and Decline of Nations: Economic Growth, Stagflation, and Social Rigidities*, Yale University Press, New Haven, 1982

Palmer, Geoffrey, *Unbridled Power: An Interpretation of New Zealand's Constitution and Government*, OUP, Auckland, 1987

Park, A. D., 'The Administration of the State Advances Corporation', *JPA*, vol. 3, no. 2, Dec 1940, pp. 26–37

Parker, R. H., and B. S. Yamey (eds), *Accounting History: Some British Contributions*, Clarendon, Oxford, 1994

Parker, R. S. (ed.), *Economic Stability in New Zealand*, New Zealand Institute of Public Administration, Wellington, 1953

Parry, Richard, Christopher Hood and Oliver James, 'Reinventing the Treasury: Economic Rationalism or an Econocrat's Fallacy of Control?', *Public Administration*, vol. 75, no. 3, 1997, pp. 395–415

Peacock, Alan T., and Jack Wiseman, *The Growth of Public Expenditure in the United Kingdom*, Princeton University Press, Princeton, 1961

Peden, George, *British Rearmament and the Treasury, 1932–1939*, Scottish Academic Press, Edinburgh, 1979

Peden, George, 'Sir Richard Hopkins and the "Keynesian Revolution" in Employment Policy', *Economic History Review*, 2nd series, vol. 36, 1983, pp. 281–96

Peden, George, *The Treasury and British Public Policy, 1906–1959*, OUP, Oxford, 2000

Peden, George, 'The Treasury as the Central Department of Government, 1919–1939', *Public Administration*, vol. 61, no. 4, 1983, pp. 371–85

Pen, J., *Modern Economics*, Penguin, Harmondsworth, England, 1965 (translated from Dutch edn, c. 1958)

Perotti, Robert, 'Fiscal Consolidation in Good Times and Bad', *Quarterly Journal of Economics*, vol. 114, no. 4, Nov 1999

Pliatzky, Leo, *The Treasury Under Mrs Thatcher*, Blackwell, Oxford, 1989

Polaschek, R. J., *Government Administration in New Zealand*, New Zealand Institute of Public Administration/OUP, Wellington/London, 1958

Pollard, Sidney, *The Wasting of the British Economy: British Economic Policy, 1945 to the Present*, Croom Helm, London/Canberra, 1982

Pouquet, Andre, 'The French Civil Service', *JPA*, vol. 1, no. 2, Dec 1938

Preston, David, 'Restructuring the Economy', *NZ Economic Papers*, vol. 12, 1978, pp. 96–115

Preston, David A., *Government Accounting in New Zealand: An Explanation of the Accounting and Financial System of the Central Government of New Zealand*, Government Printer,

Wellington, 1980

Pugh, Michael, 'Doctrinaires on the Right: The Democrats and Anti-Socialism, 1933–36', *NZJH*, vol. 17, no. 2, Oct 1983, pp. 103–19

Pusey, Michael, *Economic Rationalism in Canberra: A Nation-Building State Changes its Mind*, Cambridge University Press, Cambridge, 1991

Quigley, Neil, 'The Mortgage Market in New Zealand, and the Origins of the Government Advances to Settlers Act, 1894', *NZ Economic Papers*, vol. 23, 1989, pp. 51–79

Reid, K. G., 'Overhead Administration in the New Zealand Government Railways', *JPA*, vol. 4, no. 2, Mar 1942, pp. 32–44

Reserve Bank of New Zealand, Associated Banks in New Zealand and New Zealand Treasury, *Monetary and Fiscal Policy in New Zealand: Submissions to the Royal Commission on Monetary, Banking and Credit Systems 1955*, Reserve Bank of New Zealand, Wellington, 1955

Rhodes, R. A. W. (ed.), *Transforming British Government*, Macmillan, London, 2000

Richardson, Ruth, *Making a Difference*, Shoal Bay Press, Christchurch, 1995

Rigby, T. H., 'Bureaucratic Politics: An Introduction', *Public Administration* (Sydney), vol. 32, no. 1, Mar 1973, pp. 1–20

Riker, William H., *Theory of Political Coalitions*, Yale University Press, New Haven, 1962

Robbins, Lionel, *The Theory of Economic Policy in English Classical Political Economy*, 2nd edn, Macmillan, London, 1978

Roberts, John, *Politicians, Public Servants and Private Enterprise: Restructuring the New Zealand Government Executive*, VUP for Institute of Policy Studies, Wellington, 1987

Roberts, Richard, and David Kynaston (eds), *The Bank of England: Money, Power and Influence, 1694–1994*, Clarendon Press, Oxford, 1995

Robertson, J. F., 'Efficiency and Economy in the New Zealand Public Service', *NZJPA*, vol. 28, no. 1, Sep 1965

Robertson, R. T., 'Government Responses to Unemployment in New Zealand, 1929–35', *NZJH*, vol. 16, no. 1, Apr 1982, pp. 21–38

Robinson, C., 'Prospects for Women in the Public Service', *JPA*, vol. 6, no. 2, Mar 1944, pp. 3–8

Rock, David, *Argentina 1516–1982: From Spanish Colonization to the Falklands War*, University of California Press, Berkeley, 1985

Roll, Eric, *Where Did We Go Wrong? From the Gold Standard to Europe*, Faber and Faber, London, 1995

Rollings, N., 'British Budgetary Policy 1945–1954: A "Keynesian Revolution"?', *Economic History Review*, 2nd series, vol. 41, 1988, pp. 283–98

Rollings, N., 'The "Keynesian Revolution" and Economic Policy-Making: A Comment', *Economic History Review*, 2nd series, vol. 38, 1985, pp. 95–100

Romer, Elizabeth, and Howard Rosenthal, 'Modern Political Economy and the Study of Regulation', in Elizabeth Bailey (ed.), *Public Regulation: New Perspectives on Institutions and Policies*, MIT Press, Cambridge, Mass., 1987

Roper, Brian, 'Business Political Activism and the Emergence of the New Right in New Zealand, 1975 to 1987', *Political Science*, vol. 44, no. 2, Dec 1992, pp. 1–23

Roper, Brian, 'The Dynamics of Capital in Crisis: The Political Economy of New Zealand, 1974–1987', PhD thesis, Griffith University, Brisbane, 1990

Roper, Brian, 'From the Welfare State to the Free Market: Explaining the Transition. Part 1: The Existing Accounts', *NZ Sociology*, vol. 6, no. 1, 1991, pp. 38–63

Roper, Brian, 'From the Welfare State to the Free Market: Explaining the Transition. Part 2: Crisis, Class, Ideology and the State', *NZ Sociology*, vol. 6, no. 2, 1991, pp. 135–76

Roper, Brian, and Chris Rudd (eds), *State and Economy in New Zealand*, OUP, Auckland, 1993

Rosenberg, W., *The Magic Square: What Every New Zealander Should Know About Rogernomics and the Alternatives*, NZ Monthly Review Society, Christchurch, 1986

Roseveare, Henry, *The Treasury: The Evolution of a British Institution*, Allen Lane, London, 1969

Rowe, J. W., 'Import Reliance 1950–1965', *NZ Economic Papers*, vol. 1, no. 1, 1967

Rubinstein, W. D., *Capitalism, Culture, and Decline in Britain, 1750–1990*, Routledge, London, 1993

Rudd, Chris, and Brian Roper (eds), *The Political Economy of New Zealand*, OUP, Auckland, 1997

Rutherford, James, *Sir George Grey, K.C.B., 1812–1898: A Study in Colonial Government*, Cassell, London, 1961

Savas, E. S., *Privatization: The Key to Better Government*, Chatham House, Chatham, NJ, 1987

Savoie, Donald C., *The Politics of Public Spending in Canada*, University of Toronto Press, Toronto, 1990

Schmitt, G. J., 'Staff and Line', *NZJPA*, vol. 15, no. 2, Mar 1953, pp. 30–5

Schumpeter, Joseph, *History of Economic Analysis*, OUP, New York, 1954

Schwartz, H., 'Public Choice Theory and Public Choices: Bureaucrats and State Reorganization in Australia, Denmark, New Zealand, and Sweden in the 1980s', *Administration and Society*, vol. 26, no. 1, 1994, pp. 48–77

Scott, Graham, *Government Reform in New Zealand*, International Monetary Fund, Washington DC, 1995

Scott, Graham, *Public Management in New Zealand: Lessons and Challenges*, NZ Business Roundtable, Wellington, 2001

Scott, Graham, et al, 'Opening "The Books": A Reply', *NZ Economic Papers*, vol. 19, 1985, pp. 95–115

Scott, Graham, and Peter Gorringe, 'Reform of the Core Public Sector: The New Zealand Experience', *Australian Journal of Public Administration*, vol. 48, no. 1, 1989, pp. 81–92

Scott, K. J., 'The Political Theory of the Social Service State', *NZJPA*, vol. 17, no. 1, Sep 1954, pp. 10–24

Self, Peter, *Econocrats and the Policy Process: The Politics and Philosophy of Cost-Benefit Analysis*, Macmillan, London, 1975

Self, Peter, *Government by the Market? The Politics of Public Choice*, Macmillan, Basingstoke, England, 1993

Shanahan, Foss, 'Some Reflections on Cabinet Government in New Zealand', *NZJPA*, vol. 17, no. 1, Sep 1954, pp. 1–9
Sharp, Andrew, *The New Zealand Colonial Secretary's Office and the Department of Internal Affairs: A Short History*, Government Printer, Wellington, 1966
Sharp, A. (ed.), *Leap into the Dark: The Changing Role of the State in New Zealand Since 1984*, AUP, Auckland, 1994
Shepsle, Kenneth A., 'Studying Institutions: Some Lessons from the Rational Choice Approach', *Journal of Theoretical Politics*, vol. 1, no. 2, 1989, pp. 131–47
Siegfried, Andre, *Democracy in New Zealand*, VUP/Price Milburn, Wellington, 1982
Silverstone, Brian, Alan Bollard and Ralph Lattimore (eds), *A Study of Economic Reforms: The Case of New Zealand*, Elsevier, Amsterdam, 1996
Simpson, Tony, 'Public Sector Structural Reforms: A Failed Counter Revolution?', *New Zealand Studies*, vol. 7, no. 2, Jul 1997, pp. 9–16
Sinclair, Keith, *Walter Nash*, AUP/OUP, Auckland, 1976
Sinclair, Keith, *William Pember Reeves: New Zealand Fabian*, Clarendon Press, Oxford, 1965
Sinclair, Keith, and W. F. Mandle, *Open Account: A History of the Bank of New South Wales in New Zealand, 1861–1961*, Whitcombe and Tombs, Wellington, 1961
Sinclair, Timothy J., 'Relative Autonomy: An Empirical Critique', MA thesis, University of Canterbury, 1988
Skidelsky, Robert, 'The Decline of Keynesian Politics', in Colin Crouch (ed.), *State and Economy in Contemporary Capitalism*, Croom Helm, London, 1979
Skidelsky, Robert, *John Maynard Keynes: A Biography, vol. 3, Fighting for Britain, 1937–1946*, Macmillan, London, 2000
Skidelsky, Robert, *Keynes*, OUP, Oxford, 1996
Skocpol, Theda, *Protecting Soldiers and Mothers: The Political Origins of Social Policy in the United States*, Harvard University Press, Cambridge, Mass., 1992
Slater, David W., *War, Finance and Reconstruction: The Role of Canada's Department of Finance, 1939–1946*, National Library of Canada, Ottawa, 1995
Smith, F. B. (ed.), *Ireland, England and Australia: Essays in Honour of Oliver Macdonagh*, Cork University Press / Australian National University Press, Cork/Canberra, 1990
Smith, P. V., 'The National Expenditure Commission: A Study of Its Origins, Work and Effects', MA thesis, VUW, 1969
Smith, T. R., 'An Administrative Class for New Zealand?', *NZJPA*, vol. 14, no. 2, Mar 1952, pp. 32–41
Smith, T. R., 'Thoughts on State Trading Organisations', *NZJPA*, vol. 11, no. 2, Mar 1949, pp. 58–65
Smith, Vivienne, *Reining in the Dinosaur: The Remarkable Turnaround at New Zealand Post*, New Zealand Post, Wellington, 1997
Snowdon, Brian, Howard Vane and Peter Wynarczyk, *A Modern Guide to Macroeconomics: An Introduction to Competing Schools of Thought*, Edward Elgar, Aldershot, England, 1994
Sowell, Thomas, *Knowledge in Economics*, Basic Books, New York, 1980
Stein, Herbert, *The Fiscal Revolution in America*, University of Chicago Press, Chicago, 1969

Steinmo, Sven (ed.), *Tax Policy*, Edward Elgar, Cheltenham, England/Northampton, Mass., 1998

Steinmo, Sven, Kathleen Thelen and Frank Longstreth (eds), *Structuring Politics: Historical Institutionalism in Comparative Analysis*, Cambridge University Press, Cambridge, 1992

Stephens, F. B., 'The Public Service – To-day and To-morrow', *JPA*, vol. 5, no. 1, Sep 1942

Stewart, Michael, *Keynes and After*, 2nd edn, Penguin, Harmondsworth, England, 1972

Sylla, Richard, Richard Tilly and Gabriel Tortella (eds), *The State, the Financial System and Economic Modernization*, Cambridge University Press, New York, 1999

Taylor, John B., 'Reassessing Discretionary Fiscal Policy', *Journal of Economic Perspectives*, vol. 14, no. 3, Summer 2000

Templeton, Hugh, *All Honourable Men: Inside the Muldoon Cabinet, 1975–1984*, AUP, Auckland, 1995

Tennant, M., *Paupers and Providers: Charitable Aid in New Zealand*, Allen and Unwin/Historical Branch, Wellington, 1989

Thain, Colin, *The Evolution of Public Expenditure Control in the UK*, University of Ulster, Jordanstown, Northern Ireland, 1995

Thain, Colin, and Maurice Wright, *The Treasury and Whitehall: The Planning and Control of Public Expenditure, 1976–1993*, Clarendon, Oxford, 1995

Thorp, Rosemary (ed.), *Latin America in the 1930s: The Role of the Periphery in World Crisis*, St Martin's Press, New York, 1984

Timberlake, Richard, *Monetary Policy in the United States: An Intellectual and Institutional History*, University of Chicago Press, Chicago, 1993

Tobin, J., 'The Monetarist Counter-Revolution Today: An Appraisal', *Economic Journal*, vol. 91, Mar 1981, pp. 29–42

Tomlinson, Jim, *Employment Policy: The Crucial Years, 1939–1955*, Clarendon, Oxford, 1987

Tomlinson, Jim, *Problems of British Economic Policy, 1870–1945*, Methuen, London, 1981

Traue, Jim, 'The Commodification of Information', *New Zealand Studies*, vol. 7, no. 2, Jul 1997, pp. 23–9

Treasury, *Briefing to the Incoming Government 1990*, Treasury, Wellington, 1990

Treasury, *Briefing to the Incoming Government 1993*, Treasury, Wellington, 1993

Treasury, *Briefing to the Incoming Government 1996*, Treasury, Wellington, 1996

Treasury, *Economic Management*, Treasury, Wellington, 1984

Treasury, *Government Management: Brief to the Incoming Government*, 2 vols, Treasury, Wellington, 1987

Treasury, *Towards Higher Living Standards for New Zealanders: Briefing to the Incoming Government 1999*, Treasury, Wellington, 1999

Treasury, *The Treasury: A Profile*, Treasury, Wellington, c. 1992

Tullock, Gordon, 'Problems of Majority Voting', *Journal of Political Economy*, vol. 67, Dec 1959, pp. 571–9

Vogel, Steven K., *Freer Markets, More Rules: Regulatory Reform in Advanced Industrial Countries*, Cornell University Press, Ithaca, New York, 1996

Von Tunzelmann, A., 'The Public Expenditure Committee: The Process of Change, 1962–1977', MPP paper, VUW, 1977

Vowles, Jack, 'Waiting for Realignment? The New Zealand Party System, 1972–93', *Political Science*, vol. 48, no. 2, Jan 1997, pp. 184–209

Walker, D. K., 'New Zealand Institute of Public Administration: A Retrospect', *JPA*, vol. 10, no. 2, Mar 1948, pp. 67–86

Walker, Ranginui, 'The Genesis of Direct Negotiation, the Fiscal Envelope, and their Impact on Tribal Land Claim Settlements', *He Pukenga Korero*, vol. 3, no. 1, 1997, pp. 11–18

Walker, Ranginui, *He Tipua: The Life and Times of Sir Apirana Ngata*, Penguin, Auckland, 2001

Walker, Simon (ed.), *Rogernomics: Reshaping New Zealand's Economy*, GP Books, Wellington, 1989

Wallis, J. L., and B. E. Dollery, 'Understanding Cultural Changes within an Economic Control Agency: The Case of the New Zealand Treasury', *Journal of Public Policy*, vol. 21, no. 2, 2001, pp. 191–212

Walsh, Pat, 'An "Unholy Alliance": The 1968 Nil Wage Order', *NZJH*, vol. 28, no. 2, Oct 1994, pp. 178–93

Walsh, Pat, and G. Fougere, 'Fiscal Policy, Public Sector Management and the 1989 Health Sector Strike', *NZ Journal of Industrial Relations*, vol. 14, no. 3, 1989, pp. 219–29

Walsh, Pat, and Rose Ryan, 'The Making of the Employment Contracts Act', in Raymond Harbridge (ed.), *Employment Contracts: New Zealand Experiences*, VUP, Wellington, 1993

Wanna, John, Joanne Kelly and John Forster, *Managing Public Expenditure in Australia*, Allen and Unwin, St Leonards, NSW, 2001

Watts, M. D., 'Price Control', *JPA*, vol. 9, no. 2, Mar 1947, pp. 49–55

Weaver, R. Kent, and Bert A. Rockman (eds), *Do Institutions Matter? Government Capabilities in the United States and Abroad*, Brookings Institution, Washington DC, 1993

Webb, L. C., *Government in New Zealand*, Department of Internal Affairs, Wellington, 1940

Webb, L. C., 'A Note on Mill's "Liberty"', *NZJPA*, vol. 11, no. 2, Mar 1949, pp. 6–18

Webber, C., and A. Wildavsky, *A History of Taxation and Expenditure in the Western World*, Simon and Schuster, New York, 1986

Weber, Max, *Economy and Society: An Outline of Interpretive Sociology*, Bedminster Press, New York, 1968

Weller, Patrick, *The Treasury and the Politics of Advice*, Department of Political Science, University of Tasmania, Hobart, 1977

Weller, Patrick, and James Cutt, *Treasury Control in Australia: A Study in Bureaucratic Politics*, I. Novak, Sydney, 1976

West, Algernon, *Recollections: 1832 to 1886*, Smith, Elder and Co., London, 1899

Whitcombe, J. E., 'Restructuring the New Zealand Public Service', *Public Sector*, vol. 10, no. 1, 1987, pp. 3–9

Whitwell, Greg, *The Treasury Line*, Allen and Unwin, Sydney, 1986

Whitwell, J., and M. A. Thompson (eds), *Society and Culture: Economic Perspectives*, NZ

Association of Economists, Wellington, 1991

Wildavsky, A., *The New Politics of the Budgetary Process*, Harper and Collins, New York, 1988

Wilenski, P., *Public Power and Public Administration*, Hale and Iremonger, Sydney, 1986

Williams, J. W., *The New Zealand Economy in War and Reconstruction*, Institute of Pacific Relations, New York, 1948

Williamson, John (ed.), *The Political Economy of Policy Reform*, Institute for International Economics, Washington DC, 1994

Williamson, Oliver, *The Economic Institutions of Capitalism: Firms, Markets, Relational Contracting*, Free Press, New York, 1985

Williamson, Oliver, and Sidney Winter, *The Nature of the Firm: Origins, Evolution, and Development*, OUP, New York, 1991

Wilson, James Q., *Bureaucracy: What Government Agencies Do and Why They Do It*, Basic Books, New York, 1989

Winch, Donald, *Classical Political Economy and Colonies*, Bell, London, 1965

Winch, Donald, *Economics and Policy: A Historical Study*, Fontana, London, 1969

Wise, H. L., *War-time Price Control in New Zealand*, Whitcombe and Tombs, Christchurch, 1943

Woodward, D. W., 'Government and Economic Planning', *JPA*, vol. 1, no. 2, Dec 1938, pp. 99–107

Wright, Maurice, 'Treasury Control 1854–1914', in Gillian Sutherland (ed.), *Studies in the Growth of Nineteenth-Century Government*, Routledge and Kegan Paul, London, 1972

Wright, Maurice, *Treasury Control of the Civil Service, 1854–1874*, Clarendon, Oxford, 1969

Wright, Maurice (ed.), *Public Spending Decisions: Growth and Restraint in the 1970s*, Allen and Unwin, London, 1980

Wright, R. W., and R. L. Mansell, 'Myopic Project Evaluation: New Zealand's Second Smelter', *New Zealand Economic Papers*, vol. 15, 1981, pp. 50–63

Yergin, Daniel, and J. Stanislaw, *The Commanding Heights: The Battle between Government and the Marketplace that is Remaking the Modern World*, Simon and Schuster, New York, 1998

Yonay, Yuval P., *The Struggle Over the Soul of Economics: Institutionalist and Neoclassical Economists in America Between the Wars*, Princeton University Press, Princeton, NJ, 1998

Young, David, *Values as Law: The History and Efficacy of the Resource Management Act*, Institute of Policy Studies, Wellington, 2001

Zanetti, G., et al, 'Opening the Books: A Review Article', *New Zealand Economic Papers*, vol. 18, 1984, pp. 13–30

Zohrab, B. D., 'A History of the New Zealand Civil Service, 1840–1866', Honours thesis, History Department, Victoria University College, 1936

Index

Note: Page numbers in *italic* refer to illustrations.

accident compensation, 396, 397, 398, 415, 425
accountants and accountancy
    history of profession, 77–8
    training, 77–8, 179–81, 197–8
    in Treasury, 78–83, 91–2, 106–11, 160, 393–4, 420
ACT party, 411–12
agency theory, 15, 290–1
Agent-General (in London), 38, 45–7, 61–2, 65–8
agriculture, 143, 148, 155, 159, 230, 242, 271–2, 326–7
Agriculture Department, 59, 60, 147
Air New Zealand, 375
Alexander, Ray, 249
Alexander Turnbull Library, 421
Allen, James, 75–6, 108
Alliance party, 407, 409
aluminium smelters, 259, 262, 280, 282
Anderson, D. F., 95
Anderson, John, 195, 197, 201, 367
Anderton, Jim, 309, 341–2
Andrew, Doug, 318, 367
ANZ Bank, 377
Arbitration Court, 169, 170, 175, 244
Ashwin, Bernard, *161*
    and Keynesian economics, 162
    and Tasman Pulp and Paper, 203
    focus on public finance, 135, 148
    inspector, 88
    on first Labour government, 151
    promotions, 120
    qualifications, 95
    relations with Fraser, 172
    relations with Holland, 216
    relations with Nash, 166, 167, 172, 175, 187
    relations with Savage, 157, 165, 166
    Secretary to the Treasury, 17, 156–7, 160–87, 193, 205–6, 209–10, 213
Asian financial crisis (1997), 414
asset sales, 333, 339, 340, 372–8, 408–9, 415
asset valuations, 368–9

Assets Realisation Board, 70
Atkin, C. R. J., 182, 203
Atkin, Tom, 183
Atkins, May, 233
Atkinson, Harry, 36, 47
Auckland, 52
Auditor-General/Audit Department, 37, 39–42, 51, 78, 79, 82, 87, 99, 106–9, 122, 143–4, 270, 307, 366, 381
Australian Treasury. *See* Treasury (Australia)
aviation, 190, 192–3, 344, 365, 375
Awatere, Donna, 390

Baker, J. V. T., 211, 227
balance of payments issues, 163–4, 187, 218–19, 221–3, 236, 241–2, 247–8, 288–9
Ball, Ian, 381, 385, 393–4, 401, 420
Ballance, John, 36, 61, 64, 67
Bank of England, 19, 142, 153, 163, 164. *See also* Niemeyer, Sir Otto
Bank of New Zealand, 66, 68–70, 94–5, 339, 347, 357, 372–5
Bankers' Association, 276
Barker, D. W., 95, 183, 201, 203, 258
Barr, Peter, 80, *81*
Barr and Hercus (Dunedin auditors), 89
Batkin, Charles, 41, 49
Battersby, Dick, 366
Baumol, William, 376–7
Bayliss, Len, 260
Beauchamp, Sir Harold, 128–9, 132, 135
Beer, Samuel, 13, 185
Begg, James, 121
Bell, Francis Dillon, 38, 45–6, 49, 67, 131
Belshaw, Horace, 134, 139, 158, 166, 212
benefit cuts (1991), 353–5
Bertram, Geoff, 306
Beveridge, W. H., 184
Birch, Bill, 281, 303, 346, 349, 404, 406, 408–15, 425
Board of Trade, 89

Bolger, Jim, 347, 348, 349, 350, 355, 376, 399, 416
Bollard, Alan, 371, 377, 425
borrowing. *See* loan financing
Boston, Jonathan, 379, 380, 384, 385, 397
BP (New Zealand) Ltd, 204
Bradford, Max, 232, 234, 301
Brierley Investments, 373, 375
British Treasury. *See* Treasury (UK)
Brittan, Sam, 13
broadcasting, 155, 364, 366
Brown, Judge Mick, 366
Brownlie, Bert, 212, 213, 230, 284, 292
Buchanan, James, 15
Buckle, Robert, 329
Buddle, John, 234
Budget preparation, 34–8, 64, 88, 144–6, 177–8, 243, 304–5, 333, 339, 349, 355, 397, 413–15
Bushnell, Peter, *423*
Business and Economic Research Ltd (BERL), 213
'business methods' in government (1910s/20s), 80, 89–94
Butcher, David, 334
Byers, Mark, 384, 425

Cabinet committees, 208, 212, 248, 265–7, 302, 306, 314, 323, 332, 334, 349, 365, 384, 410
Cameron, L. A., 366
Cameron, Rob, 287, 290, 292, 300, 313, 318, 319
Campbell, G. F. C. (George), 85, 88, 89, 96–9, *100*, 100–1, 106–9
Campbell, Richard M., 100, 137, 139, 142, 144
Campion, 'Cam', 350
Canadian Treasury. *See* Treasury (Canada)
Capital Markets Ltd, 373–4
Carey, Richard, 234
Carpinter, Paul, 425
Carroll, Ross, 199
Caygill, David, 319, 323–4, 327, 334, 340–2, 344, 373–4, 396
central bank. *See* Reserve Bank
Chapman, Robert, 366
Chapple, Simon, 352
Chetwin, John, 234, 249, 300, 364–5, 367, 386, 425
City of London, and New Zealand borrowing, 43–9, 201, 249, 344
Civil Service Commissioners (1866): 39–40, 54
Civil Service Reform Act 1886: 59

Clark, D. G., 78, 87
Clark, Helen, 334, 426–7
Clinkard, G. W., 147
Clyde dam, 276, 280
Coal Corporation, 365, 371
Coalition government (1931–35), 112–14, 119–50
Coase, Ronald, 290
Coates, Gordon, 90, 103, *113*, 118–19, 122, 132–4, 137–50, 151
coinage, 388
Collins, Michael, 421
Collins, R. J., 96, 99, 100, 101
Colonial Bank, 68–9
Comalco, 259, 262
Commerce Commission, 326
Comptroller of Public Accounts, 38, 40–2. *See also* Auditor-General
Condliffe, J. B., 58, 153, 158
Contact Energy, 413, 415
contestability theory, 376–7
Cook, John, 366–7
Cooper, Emily, 25, 26
Cooper, George, 24–6, 33
Copland, Douglas, *133*, 133–5, 155, 158
core public sector, 379–85
corporatisation. *See* state-owned enterprises
credit downgrade (1991), 353
Creech, Wyatt, 350
Crown Agents (in UK), 44, 45, 46–7
Crown Company Monitoring Advisory Unit, 394
Crown Law Office, 38
CS First Boston, 374
Cullen, Michael, 334, 407, 421, 426–7
culture, expenditure on, 384
currency. *See* exchange
Customs Department/duties/revenue, 24, 25, 37, 50, 51, 52, 59, 64, 71, 90, 116, 119, 131, 138, 147, 148, 159, 164, 165, 170, 187, 276

Dale, Tony, 394
Dalziel, Paul, 347, 351
Dangerfield, Geoff, 410, *423*
Danks, Alan, 213
Davidson, A. C., 133–4
Davis, N. R. ('Cop'), 201, 229, 232, *238*, 244
Deane, Roderick
  CEO of Electricorp, 368–9
  chair of SSC, 330, 365, 369, 391–2
  economist/deputy governor at Reserve Bank, 237, 284, 306, 308–9, 324–5, 329–30

Index

on Kerr, 292
on Lang, 229
overseas, 237, 299–30
debentures, 26, 27, *68*
de Cleene, Trevor, 323
Defence Department, 57
Depression (1929–35), 112–50
deregulation. *See* microeconomic reforms
Development Finance Corporation (DFC), 367, 372–3
Diploma of Public Administration, 159–60, 208
Dobell, Marjorie, 175
Douglas, Ken, 301
Douglas, Roger, 313, 317–33, 337, 339, 342–4, 364–5, 369, 411
DSIR. *See* Scientific and Industrial Research, Department of
Duignan, Pat, 291
Duncan, Ian, 371, 377
Durbin, Lou, 211
Durrant, Ken, 198, 212

Easton, Brian, 307, 329, 351, 352, 376–7
economic advice, 14, 156–60, 186–7, 206–14, 227–8. *See also* economic management; liberalisation; ministers and officials, relations between
'economic constitution' (pre-1935), 130–9, 152, 162, 316
Economic Development Commission, 326
economic liberalisation. *See* liberalisation
economic management, 206–14, 239–53, 337–45, 353–8, 400–1, 415–17
Economic Management (1984 post-election briefing), 313–16, 323, 328, 379
economic planning and co-ordination, 185–7, 206–14, 272
  for growth, 235–9, 416–17
economic stabilisation measures (1940s), 162, 167–76, 181, 183, 186–7, 195
  staff transfer to Treasury, 211, 212
'Economic Strategy' (1981 post-election briefing), 298
Economic Strategy (Treasury document, 1992), 355–6, 358
Economics II (Treasury think tank), 285–302
economists
  and Labour politicians, 157–9
  in private sector, 296
  in public discussion of policy, 114, 134–6
  in Treasury, 230–5, 286–302, 393–4, 420

Economy Committees (1931), 117–19
education, 123, 395–6, 399
efficiency in government, 79, 316, 318
electricity sector, 255, 364, 365, 368, 369, 408, 413, 415, 416
Employers' Federation, 276, 346
Employment Contracts Act 1991: 353
Employment Relations Act 2000: 425
Energy, Ministry of, 281, 328, 364, 365, 371
Entrican, Pat, 202, 203
Equiticorp, 378, 422
Esson, James Jacob, *75*
  focus on public finance, 135
  'indispensable' on commissions and boards, 99–100, 102, 118, 121, 124
  Park's mentor, 131
  social prominence, 100–1
  Treasury career, 81–2, 87, 92–3, 96
exchange control, 164, 256, 257
exchange crisis (1938-39), 163–4
exchange rate
  devaluations: (1933), 112–16, 130–9; (1949), 244; (1967), 244; (1984), 306–10
  dollar floated, 324–5, 329, 330–1
  revaluation (1948), 187
expenditure control, 101–5, 110, 116–24, 143–9, 154–6, 206, 240–1, 262–7, 270, 341, 383–4, 410
External Affairs Department, 229

Falconer, Bill, 375
Fancy, Howard, 351, 354, 396, 425
Fay Richwhite, 373, 375, 376
Featherston, Isaac, 45
Federated Farmers, 259, 276, 303
Federation of Labour, 259
Finance Acts: (1929), 107–8
Finance and Expenditure Committee, 381–2, 393, 407, 421
financial management, 13–14, 78–89, 177–8, 195–7, 261–7, 270, 359–401, 419–20
  professionalisation of, 78–83, 106–11
  repatriation of, 83–9
fiscal policy, 193, 250–2, 291, 316, 329, 340, 346–9, 352
  See also expenditure control; taxation
Fiscal Responsibility Act 1994: 356–8, 406–8, 427
Fisher, A. G. B., 158
Fisher, Woolf, 258
FitzGerald, James Edward, 40–1, *41*, 45, 78
Fitzherbert, William, 34–5, *35*, 45

FitzRoy, Robert, 26, 27
Fletcher Holdings, 203, 375
Forbes, George, 76, *105*, 105–6, 118–20, 125–6, 135, 137
forestry, 202, 203, *321*, 364, 365, 368, 371, 409
Fox, William, 36
Franklin, Harvey (*Trade, Growth and Anxiety*), 270
Fraser, Malcolm, 278, 310–11
Fraser, Peter, 158, *168*, 172, *184*
Froude, James, 36
full employment, 184–5, 192, 194
Furkert, F. W., 103, 121, 122
Fussell, E. C., 214

Galt, Margaret, 367
Galvin, Bernard, 214, 232–4, 269, *270*, 302, 304–5, 309, 310–11, 319, 330–1
Gardner, Wira, 421
gas industry, 204–5, 279–80, 282, 371, 374–5
Gavin, J. C., 41, 50–2, *51*, 56, 57, 61
Gibbs, Alan, 395, 396
Gisborne, William, 37, 49
Gladstone, William Ewart, 29–30, *30*
Goff, Phil, 333
Goodfellow, William, 148
Goods and Services Tax (GST), 321, 322, 327, 337, 340, 342
Goosman, Stan, 190
Gordon, Liz, 335
Gorringe, Peter, 360
Government Actuary, 261
Government Computing Services, 371
Government Management (1987 post-election briefing), 334–7, 359–63, 377, 382, 386, 390, 396, 398, 400
Government Printing Office, 375, 377
Government Property Services, 365
Government Stores Board, 91–2, 197, 261, 294, 388
Government Superannuation Fund, 388
Graham, Doug, 410–11
Green, Bill, 237, 285
Greenberg, Sol, 199
Greensmith, E. L., 182, 183, 213–14, 219
Gregory, Robert, 384, 385
Greig, Bernard, 178–9
Greig, David, 305
Grey, Sir George, 26, 27, 33
Griffin, J. L., 121
Griffin, Richard, 339
Grose, A. T., 125, 132

growth, planning for, 235–9, 274–82, 416–17

Hall, John, 46
Hampton, R. G., 172
Hanan, Ralph, *221*
Hanson, Margaret, 424
Harbutt, Thomas, 38
Harman, Richard, 343
Harris, Peter, 351
Hayes, R. E., 93, 94, 96, 100, 101, 102, 103, 107
Health Department/Ministry, 296, 395, 397–8, 413
Hercus, Ann, 332
Herdman, Alexander, 80
Heywood, James, 56, 57, 60–4, 69, 70
High Commission (of NZ, in London), 67–8, 74, 344
Hight, Dr James, 134, 158
Hill, Bob, 230
Hobson, William, 24, *26*
Hogben, George, 58
Holland, Harry, 119
Holland, Sidney, 188–94, 216, 360
Holmes, Frank, 230–1, *231*, 238–9, 284, 307
Holyoake, Keith, 208, *221*, 241, 266
Horn, Murray, 306, 313, 361, 399, 408, *418*, 418–25, *423*
hospitals, 413
housing, 397, 398
Hunt, Ernest W., 90
Hunt, Jonathan, 366
Hunt, W. D., 80

import licensing, 164, 219, 256–60, 276, 278, 293, 320–1
income distribution, 416
incomes policy. *See* prices and incomes policies
Industrial Development Conference, 236
Industries and Commerce Department, 147, 169–70, 174, 214
Inland Revenue Department, 214, 323
Institute of Economic Research, 236, 307
Institute of Public Administration, 159, 167, 210, 211
interest rates. *See* monetary policy
Internal Economics II (Treasury think tank), 285–302
International Monetary Fund (IMF), 176, 223, 235, 283, 396

Jesson, Bruce, 327, 376

Johnson, Pete, 187
Jones, David, 119, 148
Julyan, Sir Penrose, 46–7
Julyan and Sargeaunt, 45, 46–7

Kerr, Roger, 292–4, 300, 305, 330, 352–3, *354*
Kershaw, R. M., 164
Keynes, J. M., 20, 125, 135, 137, 158–9, 184
Keynesian policies. *See* macroeconomic management
Kidd, Doug, 411
Kirk, Jenny, 336
Kirk, Norman, 249, 267–8
Kirkland, Andy, 365
Knight, Charles, 37, 41
Knox, Jim, 301
Korean War, 192, 193, 194

Labour Department, 58, 59, 64, 147, 416
Labour (or Labour-led) governments
    (1935–49), 151–87
    (1957–60), 218–21
    (1972–75), 246–51, 259, 265–6, 267–8
    (1984–90), 308–10, 317–24
    (1999–), 425–7
labour market deregulation, 342, 346, 353
Labour Party, 119–20, 152–3, 156, 165, 192, 297, 309, 317–21, 327, 332, 341–2, 343, 380, 407, 412, 421
Labour Relations Act 1987: 331, 338
Lake, Harry, *221*, 236, *242*, 243
Lake, Irene (Taylor), 234, 423–4
Laking, George, 269
Laking, Rob, 300–1, 302
Land and Income Tax Department, 87, 88, 147, 182
Landcorp, 365
Lands (and Survey) Department, 59, 64, 106, 363, 365, 371
Lang, Henry, *227*, *238*
    advises Bolger, 352
    advises Labour Opposition, 318–19
    background, 226–7
    early years in Treasury, 211, 213, 227
    in Economic Stabilization Commission, 175–6
    qualifications, 262
    research work, 211, 213, 227
    Secretary to the Treasury, 227–35, 245, 248, 250, 255, 259–60, 268–9, 310
    senior officer, 201, 244, 265
Lang, Jack, 261, 262, 265
Lange, David, 305, 308, 318, 320, 323, 327, 333, 337, 338, 342

Langton, John, 40
Larkworthy, Falconer, 45
Law Drafting Office, 107
Laws, Michael, 350–1
Leathwick, Ralph, 199
Lee, John A., 165
Lefeaux, Leslie, 153, 163, 165
Lepper, John, 351
Le Rossignol, James Edward, 79–80
Lewin, Jack, 269
Liberal government (1891–1912), 57–70
liberalisation, 253–60, 270, 273, 275–6, 325
loan financing, 35, 38–9, 43–9, 67, 83–5, 104, 117, 122, 146, 169, 191–2, 223
lobbying, 276–9
Local Government Loans Board, 94, 178, 205–6
Lough, Noel
    cadet, 179, 180, 181
    committed to liberalisation, 237–8, 257, 260
    Deputy Secretary, 246
    in Economic Stabilization Commission, 212
    in research division, 212–13
    president, Association of Economists, 232
    Scott's 'patron', 302
    Secretary to the Treasury, 269, 273, 275, 284–5, 297, 302, 310–11
    training and qualifications, 179, 181, 262
Low, Alan, 231, 244
Lythgoe, Ian, 228, 261

Macbeth, Norman, 213
Macintosh, A., 121
Macintosh, James, 80
Mackay, Athol, 111, 182, 183, 186
macroeconomic management, 239–53, 272, 286–92, 306, 314–15, 325, 326
macroeconomics, 272
manufacturing sector, 38, 255–6, 257–9, 276, 279, 303
Maori Affairs Department, 200. *See also* Native Department; Te Puni Kokiri
Maori issues, 56, 123, 143, 200, 366, 390, *391*, 410–11
Marketing Department, 155
Marshall, Alfred, 48
Marshall, J. R. (Jack), 217, 237, *238*, 246, 284, 360
Marshall, P. B., 210
Marshall, Russell, 323, 332, 333
Martin, Graeme, 390
Martin, John, 199, 212, 229–30, 249, 296–7, 298
Massey, William Ferguson, 86, *87*, 87–8, *91*

Masters, Robert, 117
Mathew, Felton, 24
Maughan, William (Bill), 226, 230
McCarthy, T. G., 95
McCombs, James, 119
McGregor, Albert, 95, 211, 212–13
McGregor, Duncan, 58, 60, 61, 63
McIntosh, A. D., 195
McIntosh, Miss L. M., 96
McIntosh, Rob, 425
McIntyre, Duncan, 279
McIntyre, Hamish, 350
McKenzie, Jas, 232, 234, 284–6, 291, 300, 301, 302, 415
McKenzie, Jock, 60
McKillop, E. R., 175, 178, 203
McLean, Ian, 275, 306
microeconomic reforms, 254, 272, 287–90, 306–7, 315, 325–6, 337, 408–9, 415–16, 427
microeconomics, 134, 254, 290
mini-Budgets, 243, 252, 253
ministers and officials, relations between
    (1840–1910), 31–9, 60, 61–4
    (1949–61), 206–14, 215–17
    (1967–77), 267–73
    (1978–84), 274–84, 302–12
    (1984–90), 317–33, 360
    (1999–2000), 426–7
MMP (mixed-member proportional electoral system), 411–12
Moeseke, Paul van, 306
monetarism, 272
Monetary and Economic Council, 213, 230, 231, 255, 256, 266
monetary policy, 152–4, 240–1, 243, 250, 256, 260, 316, 324, 326, 329, 331–2, 340, 406
Moore, Mike, 333, 342
Morgan, Phil, 197
Moriarty, Jim, 173, 175, 211
Mortgage Corporation, 143, 148–9, 154
mortgage debentures, 38
Moyle, Colin, 323
Muir, Ron, 199
Muldoon, Robert, *238*, *270*
    Leader of the Opposition, 248
    Minister of Finance, 237, 243, 244
    Opposition backbencher, 346, 350
    Prime Minister and Minister of Finance, 251–3, 260, 274–312 *passim*
    relations with officials, 268–9, 302–12
'Murupara project', 201–4

Myles, Gilbert, 350

Nash, Walter, 153–4, 157–9, 165–9, *171*, 171–2, 187, 216
National Airways Corporation, 190, 192–3, 364, 365
National Australia Bank, 373–4
National Development Conference (NDC), 237–9, 255–6, 258
National Efficiency Board, 89
National Expenditure Commission, 114, 121–4, 143
National (or National-led) governments
    (1949–57), 188–218
    (1960–72), 221–3, 237–8, 241–6, 258–9
    (1975–78), 238, 251–3, 268–73
    (1978–81), 274–82
    (1981–84), 302–12
    (1990–93), 316–17, 345–58, 383–5, 396–9
    (1993–96), 404–11
    (1996–99), 411–15
National Industrial Conference (1928), 134
National Party, 278–9, 305, 317, 346
National Provident Fund, 182, 261, 360
Native Affairs Commission, 143–4
Native Department, 94, 143–4. *See also* Maori Affairs Department; Te Puni Kokiri
Nelson, E. A., 366
neoliberalism, 282–6
New Plymouth Harbour Board, 47
News Media Ownership Act 1965: 259
New Zealand–Australia Free Trade Agreement, 260
New Zealand Contractors Federation, 276
New Zealand Business Roundtable, 330
New Zealand Economic Papers, 232
New Zealand First party, 411, 412, 414
New Zealand Institute of Economic Research, 213
New Zealand Planning Council, 239, 284, 288–9, 307, 337
New Zealand Post, 365, 370, 371
New Zealand Sociological Association, 336
New Zealand Steel, 262, 280–2, 321, 378, 422
New Zealand Wars, 43–5
Ngata, Sir Apirana, 103, *105*, 117, 119, 144
Nichol, John, *390*
Niemeyer, Sir Otto, 108–10, 116, 118, 126–7, 130, 142
Nordmeyer, Arnold, *219*, 219–21
Norman, Montagu, 126, 127, 127–8, 130, 153, 166

INDEX

Oamaru borough and harbour board, 47
Official Information Act 1982: 335, 336, 379, 421, 422
officials and ministers. *See* ministers and officials, relations between
oil shocks, 279
Olson, Mancur, 270
Organisation for National Development, 186
Organization for Economic Cooperation and Development (OECD), 235, 283, 315, 326, 417

Palmer, Geoffrey, 318, 323, 334, 342, 379
Park, A. D., *129*
    at Mortgage Corporation, 139
    at State Advances Corporation, 154
    background, 97
    executor of Esson's will, 100
    'Financial Adviser' to government, 92
    focus on public finance, 135
    ill-health, 138, 139
    Secretary to the Treasury, 93, 96, 109–10, 116–20, 126–31, 136–40, 144, 148
    senior official, 106, 108
    social prominence, 101
Parker, Sam, 201, 203, 261, 262, 366
Peden, George, 13
Perceval, W. B., 67
Perham, John, 386
Peters, Winston, 350, 376, 411, 413
Petrocorp, 371, 372, 374–5
Phillips, Alec, 197
Philpott, Bryan, 213, 230, 236
Picot, Brian, 396
political economy
    (19th cent. Gladstonian), 18–19, 130, 316, 427
    (pre-1935), 89–94, 130–46, 152, 316
    (post-1935), 152–6
    (1949–51), 188–94
    (pre-1984), 258–9, 276–9
    (post-1984), 316, 427
Porter, R. F., 49, 50, 53
Postbank, 339, 365, 375, 377
post-election briefings
    (1978), 274–5, 287, 303
    (1981), 287, 302
    (1984), 313–14, 379
    (1987), 334–7, 359–63, 377, 382, 386, 390, 396, 398, 400
    (1990), 350, 396

    (1999), 417
Post Office, 58, 61, 92, 102, 106, 118, 166, 191, 290–1, 363, 364–5, 365, 371
Pound, J. P. G. ('Jacko'), 198
Poynton, J. W., 96, 97
Prebble, Mark, 297, 305, 396, 397, 421, *423*, 425
Prebble, Richard, 319, 323, 324, 334, 339, 344, 365, 369, 411
Preston, David, 232, 238, 247–8, 270, 271, 273, 302
prices and incomes policies, 169, 170, 172, 174, 194, 246, 250, 251, 302–4
Prime Minister and Cabinet, Department of, 398
Prime Minister's Department, 252, 269, 275, 314
privatisation. *See* asset sales
Probine, Merv, 365
Public Accounts Committee, 39, 61, 75, 90, 108, 160
public choice theory, 15, 290, 291
Public Expenditure Committee, 263, 305, 308–10, 381, 406
public finance. *See* financial management; fiscal policy
Public Finance Act 1989: 363, 380–2, 385, 394, 408, 420
Public Revenues Acts: (1867), 54; (1926), 92
public sector reform, 39, 80, 379–85
Public Service Act 1912: 80
Public Service Association, 297, 321, 369
Public Service Commission, 181, 211, 379
Public Service Commissioner, 80–3, 89, 91, 96, 97, 98, 117, 143–4, 380
Public Works Department, 57, 64, 94, 97, 102, 106, 121–2, 143, 144. *See also* Works, Ministry of

Quigley, Derek, 275, 279, 411

radio broadcasting, 155, 364, 366
Railways, 38, 57, 92, 102, 103, 104, 106, 116, 118, 154, 191, 255, 278, 363, 370
Rangi, Don, 196
Ransom, Ethelbert Alfred, *105*, 108, 109, 116, 118, 119, 122
Reagan administration, 283
Reddish, Ivan, 251
Reeves, William Pember, 67
Reform government (1912–28), 80, 83–94, 103
Reid, J. S., 172
Remuneration Authority, 246, 250
Rennie, Iain, *423*

523

Reserve Bank
  beginnings of, 124–30, 140–3
  inflation target, 406
  influence of, 214, 275, 308, 365–6
  largest employer of economists, 231–2, 296
  'nationalisation' of, 152–4
  Treasury links with, 178, 231–2, 236, 324–5, 326, 406
  See also exchange rate; monetary policy
Reserve Bank Act 1989: 344, 357–8, 365–6, 427
Retailers' Federation, 276
Richardson, Earle, 279
Richardson, Ruth, 276, 287, 346, 349–50, *354*, 355, 397, 399, 406, 410
Richmond, Christopher William, 34, 49–51
roading reform, 255, 416
Roberts, John, 343, 379
Robertson, Donald, 80, 98
Robinson, Bill, 197, 233
Rodda, G. C., 95, 147, 161, 163
Rodger, Stan, 323, 333, 365
'Rogernomics', 321, 322. *See also* Douglas, Roger
Rose, G. G., 182
Rose, John, 40
Rosenberg, Wolfgang, 258
Roseveare, Henry, 12–13
Ross, Alex, 187
Rowling, Bill, *248*, 249, 268
Royal Commissions
  Broadcasting (1986), 366
  Cost of Living (1912), 134
  Monetary, Banking and Credit Systems (1955), 212–13, 216, 217
  Public Service (1912), 80
  Social Policy (1988), 332, 395
  Social Security (1972), 265
  State Services (1962), 195, 198–9, 263
Rural Bank, 365, 375, 377
Russell, Spencer, 309

Sallee, Nikitin, 339
Saunders, H. H., 258
Savage, Michael Joseph, 119, 153, 158, 165, 166–7
Scientific and Industrial Research, Department of, 201, 230, 305, 421
Schmitt, G. J. (Geoff), 187, 208–9, 211, 216, 306
Schmitt, L., 174
Scobie, Grant, 417
Scott, Graham, *354*, *419*
  age, 300, 302
  and Muldoon, 305, 308
  Assistant Secretary, 292, 301, 304, 313, 318–19, 328, 329
  director of Economics II, 285, 288, 291, 292–3, 298
  economic adviser in Prime Minister's Department, 252, 285
  on 'biscuit group', 298
  on new (1999) government, 426
  qualifications, 361, 393–4
  Secretary to the Treasury, 330, 338–40, 347–8, 351–2, 356, 357, 359–61, 380–1, 384–7, 389–90, 393–4, 398–9, 410, 424
Seath, David, *242*
Seddon, Richard John, 61, 62, 64, 70
Semple, Robert, 166
Sewell, Henry, 33, 43
Shailes, Fred, 261, 265, 307, 366, 381
Shanahan, Foss, 207–8, *208*
Shand, Tom, 241, *245*
Shepherd, Alexander, 26, 33, 40
Shipley, Jenny, 349, 355, 414
Shipping Corporation, 365, 367
Shirtcliffe, George, 121, 123
Shortland, Willoughby, 26
Simms, Ron, *311*, 312
Sinclair, Andrew, 33
Skinner, Tom, *245*, 251
Smith, S. Percy, 58
social policy, 332–3, 334–9, 342, 346, 349, 353–5, 395–9, 420, 426–7
'social services', 123, 395
Social Welfare Department, 395
South Pacific Hotel Corporation, 375
Special Economy Committee, 119, 135
Stafford, Edward, 34, 40
stagflation, 247, 272
State Advances Corporation, 104, 106, 154, 178
State Insurance, 93, 371
state-owned enterprises, 363–71, 394
State-Owned Enterprises Act 1986: 369, 408
State Sector Act 1988: 362, 380, 381, 389, 394
State Services Commission, 232, 262, 296–7, 307, 339, 365, 379, 382, 386–7, 389, 421
Statistics Department, 236, 269
Stevenson, Laurie, 279
Stewart, William Downie, *113*, *128*
  in Opposition, 118, 119
  Minister of Customs, 148
  Minister of Finance, 88, 93–4, 102–4, 107,

110, 118–21, 127–8, 130–3, 135, 139
   on Labour politicians, 157
   on 'state socialism in New Zealand', 79–80
   opposes devaluation, 112–13, 130–2, 137–41
   relations with Coates, 112–13, 132, 150
   resignation, 113, 138
Stone, John, 299, 311, 327
Stores Control Board, 182
Stout, Sir Robert, 64, 108
Strakosch, Henry, 126, 127, 130
'Strategy for Growth' (1978 post-election briefing), 274–5, 287, 303
Stubbs, Rodney, 197
Sullivan, Dan, 166, *184*
Sunley, R. M., 182
superannuation, 123, 182, 261, 269, 294, 347, 354–5, 388, 414
supplementary minimum prices (SMPs), 271–2, 277
supply-side reforms. *See* microeconomic reforms
Sutch, W. B., 139, 140, 157, *158*, 159, 214
Swier, Geoff, 318

Talboys, Brian, 260
Tanner, Ross, 230
Tapsell, Peter, 405
tariffs, 38, 255, 257
Task Force on Economic and Social Planning, 238–9, 337
Tasman Pulp and Paper, 201–4
taxation, 88, 90, 256, 395, 409
Taylor, A. B. ('Johnny'), 95, 183, 203, 204
Taylor, Irene, 234, 423–4
Telecom, 365, 368, 371, 376, 377
television broadcasting, 364, 366
Templeton, Hugh, 260, 275
Te Puni Kokiri, 411, 421
Terry, Cliff, 196, 197–8, 228–9
Thatcher government, 282–3
'Think Big' strategy, 279–82, 292, 293, 300–1, 320–1, 367, 368
Thompson, Mary Anne, 410
Thomson, David, 300
Tizard, Bob, *248*, *249*, 268, 318, 328
Tocker, A. H., 125, 134
Tourist Hotel Corporation, 375
Trade and Industry Department, 255, 260, 275, 276, 378
trade policies. *See* import licensing; liberalisation; tariffs
Treasury (Australia), 159, 283, 310–11, 413

Treasury (Canada), 39, 40, 118, 124, 159, 283, 362
Treasury (NZ)
   accommodation, 52, 53–4, 55, 178–9, 301–2, 393
   actuarial branch/division, 181, 261, 294
   annual report, 381, 400
   articles published about, 405
   'biscuit group', 234, 298
   Economics II (think tank), 285–302
   forecasting, 343–4, 349, 422
   histories of, 11–13
   Industries Branch/Industry Division, 300–1, 367–8, 419, 424
   Maori staff, 182, 197
   organisational structure, 198, 211–12, 285, 294, 339, 367, 388, 392–3, 419–20
   possible division of, 349–50, 400
   professionalism, 14–18, 388–9, 425, 427
   public relations, 420–2
   reform of, 386–94
   research division, 211–12
   reserves and debt management, 391–3, 420
   role of, 49–57, 108–11, 120, 195–206, 400–1
   salaries, 56–7, 85, 96, 350, 386–8, 422
   social clubs, 197, 234, 382–3
   staff numbers, 13–14, 56–7, 59, 85, 95, 195, 261, 294, 386–8
   staff qualifications, 179–81, 182
   vote analysts, 384, 420
   women staff, 95–6, 181, 197, 294, 390–1, 423–4
Treasury (UK), 28–30, 65–6, 363, 393
Treaty of Waitangi issues, 369, 410–11, 421
Tregear, Edward, 57–8, 60, 61, 63
Trevelyan, Charles, 30
'tripod' of laissez-faire capitalism. *See* political economy
Trotter, Ron, 369
Tuck, Warwick, 425
Turnovsky, Fred, *277*
Tyler, Brian, 366, 381

unemployment, 116, 119–20, 147–8, 369–71
Union Steam Ship Company, 259
United government (1928–31), 103–11
United–Reform coalition government (1931–35), 112–14, 119–50

Veitch, William, *105*, 106, 116, 117, 118
Verschaffelt, Paul, 117
Vogel, Julius, 33, 36, 37, 38, 45–6, *46*, 55, 67

wage and price freezes. *See* prices and incomes policies
Walls, Hew, 213
Walsh, Fintan Patrick, 175, 176, 186
War Assets Realisation Board, 182
War Emergency Account, 193–4
Warburton, J. K., 79
Ward, J. N., 49
Ward, Joseph, *58*, 61–71, *62*, 79, *87*, 87–8, 97, 99, 103, *105*
waterfront dispute (1951), 193, 194
Watts, Jack, 194, 217
Webb, Clifton, 216
Webb, Leicester, 173, 175, 210
Webb, Paddy, 166
Weber, Max, 14–15
Weld, Frederick Aloysius, 33, 34
Wellington, 53–4, 94–5
Weststrate, Kees, 232
Wheeler, Graham, 349
Whitaker, Frederick, 43
White, Jack, 187
Whitehead, John, 318, *423*
Whitwell, Greg, 12, 254
Wilde, Fran, 321

Wilford, Thomas, 103, 135
Wilkinson, Bryce, 292, 318, 319
Wilkinson, Phil, 197
Williams, K. S., 146
Williams, Les, 201
Williams, Robin, 386
Wilson, Alan, 199
Wilson, Bill, 386
Wilson, Margaret, 327, 334
Winstone Samsung, 305
Wise, H. L., 172
Wood, George, 187
Wood, Reader, 43–5
Woodward, Jonas, 53
Wool Commission, 242
wool retention scheme, 194
Works (and Development), Ministry of, 94, 178, 203, 210–11, 262, 296, 363, 365, 371. *See also* Public Works Department
World Bank, 176, 223, 283
World War I, 83–9, 115
World War II, 167–76

Zanetti, John, 328
Zohrab, John, 230